THE NATURE OF POLITICAL THEORY

The Nature of Political Theory

ANDREW VINCENT

UNIVERSITY PRESS

OXFORD

UNIVERSITY PRESS

Great Clarendon Street, Oxford OX2 6DP

Oxford University Press is a department of the University of Oxford.
It furthers the University's objective of excellence in research, scholarship,
and education by publishing worldwide in

Oxford New York

Auckland Bangkok Buenos Aires Cape Town Chennai
Dar es Salaam Delhi Hong Kong Istanbul Karachi Kolkata
Kuala Lumpur Madrid Melbourne Mexico City Mumbai Nairobi
São Paulo Shanghai Taipei Tokyo Toronto

Oxford is a registered trade mark of Oxford University Press
in the UK and in certain other countries

Published in the United States
by Oxford University Press Inc., New York

British Library Cataloguing in Publication Data
Data available

Library of Congress Cataloging in Publication Data
Data available

ISBN 0-19-927125-9

Typeset by Newgen Imaging Systems (P) Ltd., Chennai, India
Printed in Great Britain
on acid-free paper by
Biddles Ltd., King's Lynn, Norfolk

Preface

The original idea for this book started life some ten years ago. At the outset, it was envisaged as a short text, but subsequently it appeared virtually to take on a life of its own. The initial serious research began during a two year fellowship in the Research School of the Social Sciences at the Australian National University, between 1994 and 1996. My thanks go to the Research School, and particularly to Barry Hindess, who then headed the politics section. I am sure Barry's perspective will differ markedly from my own; nonetheless, his independent critical thinking and open, friendly support were great stimuli to my initial reflections on this whole issue. Whilst in the Research School I ran a seminar series over a year, on the theme 'Whither Political Theory?' Many of the papers were later published in an edited volume entitled *Political Theory: Tradition and Diversity* (1997): however, the seminars themselves were an additional impetus to thinking more deeply about the whole issue of theory. In many ways the series was, in part, a preface to the present study. My thanks go to all the participants in that seminar programme.

After my research period in Australia, I found myself involved in a process of detailed administrative work at Cardiff University which slowed my research momentum. I sought solace in some easier writing projects. But the ideas for the present work kept up their own peculiar underlying intellectual momentum. Between 2000 and 2001, I was fortunate to be offered a sabbatical research fellowship in the Humanities Research Centre in the Australian National University, Canberra. My thanks also go here to my old University in Cardiff for this period of research leave, which allowed me time not only to finish another project on nationalism, but also to return to the present topic under the excellent writing conditions provided by the Centre—I was thus able to complete a large proportion of the present book. It also enabled me to meet up again with old friends and colleagues in Canberra. I am especially grateful to the then Director of the Humanities Research Centre, Iain McCalman and Caroline Turner (Deputy Director) for providing such first class friendly and supportive conditions.

In 2001, I joined the politics department at Sheffield University and have managed over my first couple of years to complete the present book in the midst of new teaching and administrative responsibilities. My thanks go to the political theory group in the department—that is, Mike Kenny, Matthew Festenstein, Andrew Gamble, James Meadowcroft, and Duncan Kelly—for enjoyable political theory conversation and encouragement. Over the last decade, and more, during which I have thought intensively about political theory, I have incurred innumerable intellectual debts. There have been so many interesting conversations from which I have learnt to see political theory issues in a new light. My thanks go to (to name but a few) Ed Andrew, David Boucher, Bob Brown, Maria Dimova-Cookson, Michael Freeden, Maurice Goldsmith, Knud

Haakonssen, Duncan Ivison, Barry Jones, Roy Jones, Rex Martin, Peter Nicholson, Raymond Plant, Andrew Sharp, Vicki Spencer, Peter Sutch, and David West. I have also been very fortunate, in the final stages of completing the manuscript, to have had such a good editor in Dominic Byatt at Oxford University Press.

My family have provided vital companionship during this whole period. My wife Mary, my children Lisa, Sara, Jason, and Rachael, and their respective spouses Stephane, Steve, and Rebekah, my amazing grandchildren Josie, Carla, Laura, and Chloe and my valued friend Diana, have all sustained and nourished me in their own unique ways.

Andrew Vincent
Sheffield University

Contents

1   **An Eclectic Subject**   1

    Foundations   3
    Theory and Politics   7
    Pattern of the Book   10

PART ONE   17

2   **We Have a Firm Foundation**   19

    Classical Normative Political Theory   19
    Institutional Political Theory   28
    Historical Political Theory   37
    Empirical Political Theory   51
    Ideological Political Theory   65
    Conclusion   73

PART TWO   81

3   **Foundations Shaken but Not Stirred**   83

    Logical Positivism   84
    Ordinary Language   88
    A Digression on Death and Putrefaction   91
    Wittgenstein and Essential Contestability   95
    A Reckoning with Essential Contestability   100
    Conclusion   104

4   **Bleached Foundations**   108

    The Concept of Justice   109
    Conceptions of Justice   111
    Procedural Theories   113
    Social Justice: Desert and Non-Desert   115
    Justice and Mutual Advantage   118
    Justice and Utility   120
    Justice as Impartiality   124
    Sexual Justice   127
    Spheres of Justice   130
    Conclusion   132

PART THREE   139

5 Shoring Up Foundations   141

Conventions   143
Oakeshott and Conventionalism   145
Communitarianism   154
Political Liberalism   162
Conclusion   167

6 New Conventions for Old   171

Nationalism   171
Neo-Aristotelianism   177
Republicanism   187
Conclusion   200

PART FOUR   205

7 Segmented Foundations and Pluralism   207

A Word about Pluralism   209
Liberal Pluralism   211
Multicultural Pluralism   215
Difference Pluralism   219
Conclusion   226

8 Standing Problems   232

Nietzsche and the Twilight of the Idols   233
Heidegger and Humanism   239
Derrida and Foucault   242
Rorty and Connolly   250
Lyotard and the Differend   253
Conclusion   257

PART FIVE   269

9 Dialogic Foundations   271

The Philosophical Context   272
Critical Theory   275
Critical Theory Fulfilled   278
Positivism and Knowledge Spheres   280
The Critique of Foundationalism and the Subject   282
Universal Pragmatics and Fallibilism   285
Discourse Ethics and Deliberative Democracy   288
Conclusion   290

10 Circular Foundations 294

The Hermeneutic Context 296
Language, History, and Prejudice 297
Enlightenment and Positivism 301
Dialogue and Fusion 303
Ethics and Politics 306
A Dialogic Conflict 310
Conclusion 315

Conclusion 319

Bibliography 327
Index 345

1

An Eclectic Subject

The basic question underpinning this book is—what do we think we are doing when we practise political theory? The subject matter of this present book is usually touched upon lightly in the first chapter of most political theory texts, namely the discipline itself as a practice. It is often considered unproblematic and something to clear out of the way as quickly as possible. The main body of the standard texts is then commonly devoted to the substantive normative analysis and promotion of a concept or series of political concepts, such as rights, justice, equality, and democracy. Theory, in this mould, is commonly seen as a form of practical philosophy, orientated to, for example, certain kinds of substantive conceptual, normative, and evaluative forms of analysis. In this context, the majority of introductory books on political theory are not so much introductions to political theory, as introductions to a *particular* conception of political theory.

Any claim that theory should be discussed or introduced in any other way is usually met with the following kind of responses: no one really wants to spend time mulling over the subject of theory, apart from the fact that it might be considered to be intrinsically tedious. Theory is, so the argument goes, by nature an 'active' or 'engaged' discipline. A great deal of time can therefore be wasted looking over comparative methods of political theory. The important point about theory is to 'do it', not stand back from it and wonder what it is one is doing whilst prosecuting it. The task of theory, in this reading, might therefore be defined as the application of forms of constrained, rigorous, and stringent value analysis to political issues in order to produce substantive policy recommendations and forms of institutional design.

The above points have some cogency—however, there are a number of immediate responses: primarily, the nature of theory itself can be intrinsically interesting, since it blends in unexpected ways with the more substantive analyses. In fact, a closer examination of twentieth-century theory reveals how varied its approaches and readings of politics actually are. Another formulation of this point is that the 'nature of theory' can itself be a substantive question for political theory. The *way* one theorizes can affect quite radically the nature of the subject matter, or the way the political world or public policy actually looks. A theory will configure what is the appropriate object, area, and method of study. In consequence, the theory cannot be divorced from its object. For some thinkers, indeed, political theory actually constitutes the political object. This latter view is clearly contentious—however, it is nonetheless a viable and philosophically-defendable conception of theory. Therefore, to carry on reflection in political theory as if the divorce between on the one hand, theory, and on the other hand, the objective or practical world of politics, was set in some kind of foundational stone—is simply unhelpful dogmatism.

Another response relates to the 'political' and 'historical' dimensions of theory. The study of politics is always tied to human interests and conceptions of value. There is no disinterested apolitical interest in political theory. In political theory, such immediate interests are just taken to a higher level of theoretical sophistication and abstraction, but they are not abandoned or bypassed. Furthermore, human reason can itself be viewed as historically (as well as politically) contingent. Reason does not stand with a 'god's eye view' surveying the historical and political landscape. It is always tied to certain contingent values or traditions. This historical perspective does not imply that we become lost in some form of relativism, or even that we lose any sense of objectivity. However, it does mean that we become more aware of our finitude and historical situation, and that consequently we will have a much more constrained or fallibilist sense of knowledge.

Finally, there is one function that any and all political theory regularly performs: namely, to think as a political theorist is always to raise critical and perplexing questions. Systematic self-critical reflection is crucial to the health of the discipline. My only claim here is that this critical reflection should be that much more thorough-going and comprehensive, not just about substantive arguments, values, and concepts in immediate political and moral theory, but also about the 'process of theorizing' itself. Again, the status of the theorist and the nature of theory are as puzzling as the substantive problems of the political world and the two elements interweave and play upon one another. This is not an issue of 'meta-theory'; conversely, it is a deep substantive issue of theory itself.

In summary, the manner in which the discipline has been practised (theoretically) relates closely to its internal substantive character. Further, one should be careful of the idea, often fostered within conceptually-orientated analytical political theory, that there is just 'one' abstract method or subject *called* political theory, and then there is another thing—the object that is explained or accounted for *by* theory. Dividing *theory* and its *object* in this way—the *theory* as neutral method and the *object* as the substantive problem to be accounted for—is an epistemological position. It is not an objective reality. In fact, it is a philosophically-contentious view of theory. In addition, historically, the above conceptualist view is a limited perspective in terms of the way theory has actually been practised during the twentieth century. To do theory in this way alone could give the student of political theory the wholly-false impression that a very particular, if hegemonic, philosophical method, is the *only* or the *true* way that theory can or should be done. Many theorists have, nonetheless, still contended that some form of rigorous conceptualist approach, tied loosely to public policy, is the only viable defence of the utility of the discipline. Consequently, any other way of approaching theory could be categorized as academic self-indulgence, or as simply false. In the minds of such critics, political theory needs to earn its supper with clear substantive guidance for policy-making and institutional design. However, there are many ways of earning a supper, and whether 'the utility of theory for public policy' or 'utility itself' should be the only or key measure of the value of work, should also be a subject for theory to investigate and reflect on. In other words, this book is an appeal to a more thorough critical reflection on the nature of political theory itself.

FOUNDATIONS

In trying to give some shape to political theory in the twentieth century, a formal theme has to be adopted to make the narrative comprehensible. The conceptual theme focused on here is relatively straightforward—namely, the concept of a foundation. The term 'foundation' is used in a very broad sense. It is taken to imply some class of statements or propositions, which are favoured absolutely over others. To be foundational, this class of statements is regarded as 'fundamental'—'fundamental' implying that its possessors cannot avoid deferring or referring back to it. This class of statements is, in other words, always presupposed by a diversity of other statements. Insofar as this class of statements is fundamental, it can be considered near inescapable or near unavoidable in any theorizing. Foundational statements also allow inferences and systematic deductions to be made, which explain and account for a range of other statements. Foundational statements, therefore, have an encompassing capacity. They ensure the overall 'coherence' of a range of other statements. This coherent set of interlinked statements constitutes a theory. My use of the term 'foundation' has close parallels with other terms such as 'metaphysics', 'first principles', or 'absolute presuppositions'.

Foundations—particularly in the sense of metaphysical foundations—have been central to the Western tradition. Rather than move into a detailed account of the origin of metaphysical or foundationalist analysis, three uses of foundationalism in twentieth century political theory are indicated. This is purely an indicative list and there may be considerable overlap between these 'ideal types'. The first use implies a rich, substantive, or comprehensive foundation; the second is a thinned down, translucent, or bleached foundation; the third focuses more closely on the logic of presuppositions. I call these the comprehensive, immanent, and logical senses of foundation.

The richer foundation implies a comprehensive, perfectionist, and transcendental theory, which entails some form of objective standard of moral judgement. In terms of twentieth-century political theory, this conception is most characteristic of the impact of philosophical idealism on political theory in Britain, Europe, and North America (see Boucher and Vincent 2001). 'Comprehensive' implies that a foundational conception is identifiable in terms of its ability to explain—its encompassing power. It is therefore the reach of the explanation that is crucial. The term 'foundational' here is virtually synonymous with classical understandings of metaphysics. The attempt to examine reality as a whole can be seen, for example, in Spinoza's monism, Leibniz's monadology, or Hegel's absolute idealism. The perfectionist element imports a 'value' into the total view. This is where foundations can become virtually-religious principles. Metaphysical foundations can thus be perceived as the highest and most perfect form of human knowledge—accounting for God, freedom, and immortality. This form of metaphysical foundation not only speaks of the reality behind appearances, but also offers the initiate the very essence of reality through which some form of perfection of knowledge and practice can be attained. Another way of putting this would be that there are degrees of truth and reality, and to rise in the grasp of that scale of forms and degrees of truth requires a certain type of character and virtue.[1] The grasp of metaphysical foundations thus moves apace with the development of human virtue and character.

Finally, there is also a transcendent element to this comprehensive understanding of foundations. The sense of transcendence, which most antagonizes anti-metaphysical writing, is the idea that foundational metaphysical resources lie outside the empirical, factual, or experiential realm altogether, namely in some form of luminous transcendent reality. The sole concern is therefore to identify certain rich suprasensible or transcendental foundations. Thus, the transcendent non-empirical foundation helps us to account for the world being one way rather than another. The divine craftsman of Plato's *Timaeus*, the unmoved mover of Aristotle, the neo-Platonic demiurge, the Augustinian God, or the Hegelian *Geist*. This is the view from a transcendental nowhere—a god's eye view, *sub specie aeternitatis*, from the rim of the world, spectating on human doing. It explains 'how' the world is (as it is), rather than the 'that' of the world. It is worth noting, however, that this notion of foundation does not necessarily imply any religious principle—it can be a wholly-secularized concept.

The second sense of foundationalism is the immanent conception. The basic idea is that one can gain access to a universal foundation without recourse to any comprehensive rich metaphysical claims. The essential claim is that there are certain concepts, which are absolutely self-justifying. In other words, the concept itself contains the resources for its own universal justification and presence. The task is to reconstruct and show these deep internal or immanent justifications. The argument can therefore drag itself up by its own foundational bootlaces—autopoietically. A virtuous circle of reasoning therefore takes place that studiously avoids using the terminology of metaphysics or foundationalism: in fact, it often claims to be anti-metaphysical. This idea is most prevalent in the various forms of twentieth century neo-Kantian constructivism. More recent forms of the immanent argument concentrate on what is implicit in reason, action, discourse, or communication.

For Jürgen Habermas, for example, genuine philosophical thought 'originates in reflection on the reason embodied in cognition, speech, and action' (Habermas 1984: 1). Habermas has been concerned to reconstruct the universal conditions, which are presupposed in all reasonable communicative action. Habermas is trying essentially to develop a universalistic foundation from what is *immanent* in human rationality and dialogue. However, this is not a foundational structure in the sense of a 'first philosophy'—it no longer claims to be the final arbiter. It cannot therefore assign the various positions of the sciences as an overall adjudicator. Philosophy is more fallibilist, interacting with the various natural and human sciences. However, immanent within all communicative action there is a type of interaction that is orientated to reaching understanding. Habermas keeps this distinct from what he calls 'nonsocial instrumental action' and 'social strategic action'. This fundamental interactive discourse consists of the type of elucidation and argumentation in which we suspend immediate action and in which participants, as Habermas puts it, seek to redeem the validity of claims that have been challenged. Habermas wants essentially to redeem the universalistic conditions of possible understanding. Thus, implicit within the pluralism of forms of communication we can detect a general but stubborn claim to reason that points to the possibility of the argumentative emancipation through mutual dialogue. There is, in other words, an immanent universal and foundational telos in our communicative actions that is orientated to mutual understanding. It transcends all systematically-distorting communication. It can potentially therefore orientate our collective political practices.

In a slightly different but resonant enterprise—which still focuses on the theme of foundational immanence—Alan Gewirth advances an ethical (and political) system as a body of hierarchically-structured descriptive and prescriptive claims, each logically dependent on one another. For Gewirth, 'the most important and difficult problem of philosophical ethics is whether a substantial moral principle can be justified'. The novelty of Gewirth's justification is the attempt to derive, logically, normative principles from what is *immanent* in the concept of human action. The main thesis is, therefore, 'that every agent, by the fact of engaging in action, is logically committed to the acceptance of certain evaluative and deontic judgments and ultimately of a supreme moral principle'. This is 'The Principle of Generic Consistency', which requires that he respect his recipients' necessary conditions of action'. To prove the thesis, Gewirth maintains that 'the very possibility of rational interpersonal action depends upon adherence to the morality that is grounded in this principle. Because every agent must accept the principle, on pain of self-contradiction, it has a stringent rational justification that is at the same time practical because its required locus is the context of action' (Gewirth 1978: ix–x). Every agent, when acting in the world, is consequently committed to a determinate normative content. Action, to Gewirth, has two categorical features—voluntariness and purposiveness. Forced choices are *not* actions. The agent necessarily regards his purpose as good, in order to act on it, even in the most minimal sense, and hence there is an implicit value judgement. Thus, 'one cannot refrain . . . from action except voluntarily or purposively' (Gewirth 1978: 90–1). Therefore, for action to be action it must be both *purposive* and *voluntary*. Action for a purpose is trying to realize a *good* or end that constitutes a *reason* for acting. Thus, 'action as the voluntary pursuit of purposes commits the agent to accept certain normative judgments on pain of self-contradiction'. This entails, for Gewirth, that the 'very possibility of purposive action is dependent on its having a certain normative structure. And it is from the judgments that are necessarily constitutive of this structure that the supreme principle of morality is logically derived' (Gewirth 1978: 48). The upshot of Gewirth's scheme is that one finds immanent universal foundational justificatory grounds for moral (and political) principles implicit within all human action.

Neither Habermas nor Gewirth would describe their arguments as metaphysical or overtly foundationalist. In fact, they would probably be worried by such an assessment. However, in my reading, this is simply because they focus on the older classical sense of foundational metaphysics (as comprehensive and perfectionist). Neo-Kantian types of constructivism are still universally foundational—however, it is an immanent foundation. It still encompasses morality and politics at a fundamental level. Thus, for neo-Kantians, one cannot contradict reason unless one has absolutely- and immanently-presupposed reason. Of course, neo-Kantians (like twentieth-century phenomenologists) would tend to eschew the title 'metaphysical' or 'foundational'. Yet the possessors of reason still defer to the foundations immanent in reason, dialogue, or action. The inferences from these foundations are regarded as inescapable. Such immanent foundations also allow systematic inferences and deductions to be made, which explain and account for a vast range of other statements. However, it is still a thinned down, more abstemious and bleached foundation, compared to its comprehensive cousin.

The third sense of foundationalism is the logical use. Rational argument needs a formal structure; part of that structure requires some class of statements, which are fundamental *to* that structure. All rational argument and thought therefore involves fundamental presuppositions. Logical foundationalism implies therefore just this: that all human thought begins somewhere and foundational analysis is the examination and comparison of these 'starting points'. Logical priority, in order of assumptions, is therefore the mark of this concept of foundationalism. This is one reading of Collingwood's notion of metaphysics as the historical science of absolute presuppositions. For Collingwood, every statement we make, even the most mundane, is an answer to a question and every question is premised on a presupposition. Relative presuppositions involve answers to particular questions and involve further presuppositions, relative to other questions. Such relative presuppositions can be verified or tested. Absolute presuppositions, however, cannot be verified and they are always absolutely prior to any question to which they are related. Absolute presuppositions are neither true nor false, since they are absolutely presupposed. Some assumptions are absolutely fundamental or absolutely foundational, in the sense that they are relative 'to all questions to which it is related as a presupposition, never as an answer' (Collingwood 1969: 31). Foundational statements or propositions therefore convey what is absolutely presupposed in any discourse. Metaphysics is therefore the science of absolute presuppositions. Without entering into the complex minutiae of Collingwood's thought, this might be described as a *logical* rendering of metaphysics, namely to say anything significant you must make background assumptions.

The third sense therefore suggests that logically we must begin our thinking with some form of foundation. In this sense, all political theory is rooted in some form of foundation and to study theory is to be made aware of these foundations. It therefore indicates where we begin our thinking. Critics might still argue that analysing any such foundation is just too abstract and waste of time. However, as C. S. Peirce noted, the complaint that the study of metaphysical foundations is too abstract, is in itself ridiculous, since all the natural sciences (and many social sciences for that matter) are far *more* abstract and remote than metaphysics. Equally, it is nonsensical to say that the objects of foundational metaphysics are not observable or easily studied. Most objects in the sciences (and social sciences) cannot be directly or easily observed.

Energy, gravitation, or supply and demand curves, for example, cannot actually be seen. Peirce comments that metaphysics, as the observation and study of foundational claims, is also based on observation and 'the only reason that this is not universally recognized is that it rests upon kinds of phenomena with which every man's experience is so saturated that he usually pays no particular attention to them'. In this sense, foundational beliefs are part of our everyday activity. Peirce continues: 'The data of metaphysics are not less open to observation, but immeasurably more so, than the data, say, of the very highly developed science of astronomy'. What metaphysics is therefore is the study of the 'general features of reality and real objects'.[2] Thus it should form an integral part of political theory.

In summary, this book works with the various senses of foundation. The term 'foundationalism' is used to anchor the various discussions as parts of a coherent enterprise. Much (although not all) of the very early twentieth-century rendering of political theory rests upon a more comprehensive and transcendental sense of foundationalism. This latter sense of foundation also forms the wholly-negative backdrop to much mid-twentieth century criticism of metaphysical foundationalism and even the rejection of the practice of political theory. Various readings of the immanent understanding of foundationalism underpin the recovery of much normative theory in the final decades of the twentieth century. Both the comprehensive and immanent forms of foundationalism also impact upon the disparate attempts to find alternative justificatory foundational grounds for political theory within domains such as communitarianism, nationalism, and the like. The theme of foundationalism in general also forms the negative backdrop to the postmodern, anti- and post-foundationalist and post-conventional critiques which developed in the last two decades of the twentieth century. My employment of the third sense of logical foundationalism indicates that, in the final analysis, I regard foundationalism as far broader than just early classical and normative political theory uses. Metaphysical foundationalism (understood either comprehensively, immanently, or logically) figures, wittingly or unwittingly, in virtually all political theories, including empiricist-orientated theories throughout the century.

THEORY AND POLITICS

It is important to offer some brief clarification of the compound term 'political theory' and some of its cognates. I do not draw any rigid distinction between political theory and political philosophy. They are considered, on most occasions, as synonymous. Is this legitimate? The question here is broader than just theory and philosophy; other domains are also implicated. Thus, is political theory the same as political thought (treated more historically) or political ideology? In fact, political ideology and political thought are often taken as more immediate cognates, although many political theorists find this unacceptable. Would political theorists or philosophers be content, for example, to be described as political ideologists? Is there some crucial difference here? Political theory also has multifaceted relations with other secondary cognates, such as moral philosophy or philosophical anthropology. In fact, it is arguable that moral philosophy became inextricably entwined with political philosophy in the work of the Rawlsian generation of theorists.[3] Should we be concerned about this apparent synonymity of the above terms? Some might have no worries at all, except possibly with the concept ideology. Others might wish to separate out philosophy from the rest or just dismiss dogmatically the whole question as just too intellectually uncomfortable. Again, political philosophy can be seen as narrower, political thought as too broad and political ideology as too action-orientated, and thus all need to be kept distinct. However, regardless of these various views, there is still a continuous overlap and symbiosis of these terms in the European political vocabulary.

The compound term 'political theory', itself is of comparatively-recent vintage, certainly in the manner that we now employ it. It is a product of the nineteenth and twentieth centuries. In the nineteenth century, the word 'theory' often had pejorative connotations, being seen as equivalent to 'mere speculation' or 'untested facts'. This is reflected in some of the senses indicated in the OED (namely, where a theory can denote a 'mere hypothesis or conjecture'). Despite this, the word 'theory' itself, from its earliest use in European vocabularies, has been imbricated with 'reflective thought' in general and philosophy in particular. Theory does clearly follow the changing contours of philosophical traditions. In ancient Greek culture, theory was characteristically associated with observation. A *thea* was a spectacle; the one who observed the spectacle was a *theoros*. *Theoria* meant beholding a spectacle. Theory was thus envisaged as the intermediary between the event and the observer. It accounted for the event or practice. Theory was not separate from event. Knowledge was, in a sense, the unmediated event itself. In addition, theory was connected, from its earliest inception, with philosophy and knowledge, by the view that philosophy was a contemplative 'seeing' or 'observing'. In Plato, for example, *theoria* implied (as above) the observation of a spectacle. In Aristotle, *theoria* took on a more obviously-recognizable format of intellectual observation and contemplation in accordance with *sophia*. The friend or lover (*philia*) of wisdom (*sophia*) had the ability to see or behold (*theoria*) through the eye of the mind. *Theoria* therefore virtually became the act of knowing itself. Although *theoria* appears detached, it still mediated between the observer and the world. It was also regarded as the best 'walk of life'. However the more modern understanding of theory, particularly since the development of modern natural science, is viewed as something we build and apply. It enables us, for example, to link experiential data together, hypothesize and then instrumentally manipulate the world. Greek classical theory, however, did not have such a problem (at least in its own terms) with the world which theory observes or describes. In Aristotle, theory was closely linked with events in the world. In more modern usage, though, theory is seen to be disengaged from the world, and, certainly since the advent of Cartesianism, is subject to self-doubt concerning its own status and its claims to knowledge. Theory therefore needs confirmation and testing.[4]

The association of theory with the contours of philosophical traditions has meant that theory has been of necessity linked to the present day, to the changing fortunes and character of philosophical thought. Whether the conceptions of philosophy be

Aristotelianism, Platonism, Cartesianism, Kantianism, Hegelianism, phenomeno-logy, Marxism, pragmatism, poststructuralism, or analytic philosophy, all can attract, unselfconsciously, the designation 'theory'. Thus, political theory, whatever detractors or critics may say, tracks the fragmented terrain of philosophical thought. In this sense, there is a direct and obvious overlap in the usage of both theory and philo-sophy. Yet the issue is not quite as clear-cut as one might hope. Whereas all philosophy implies theory, not all political theory necessarily implies philosophy. This is borne out in the general pattern of political theorizing. If, for example, one considers the work of thinkers such as Bodin, Machiavelli, or Burke, then this point is more obvious. None appear to write in what might be considered a philosophical manner, although their ideas are undoubtedly both political and theoretical. Even in their own terms, it would be odd to class, say, Burke and Machiavelli, *simpliciter*, as political philo-sophers. In addition, much political theorizing during the twentieth century, would not be classed conventionally as philosophy—this would especially be the case with empirical or institutional political theory, and much of what goes under the rubric of political ideology. One additional problem is that the notion of what philosophy is also continues to mutate. Philosophy itself is not a stable or consistent practice. Consequently, political theory is not clearly distinguishable from political philosophy in *all* circumstances. At most, one could conclude that political philosophy is a con-testable species within an even broader and even more contestable genus of political theory. In summary, the term 'theory' is not a straightforward concept.[5] It has a continuing multifaceted relation with philosophy—however, on occasion it can also be considered to be broader than the term 'philosophy'.

Finally, how does theory relate to the term 'politics'? My own supposition is that politics is not an independent 'thing' which we theorize *about*. This judgement is more the *pathology* of one modern conception of theory. The self-consciousness of politics is not written into the nature of the world; it is rather the outcome of a com-plex series of reflective critical vocabularies, which have become intertwined with and constitutive of practices. In this sense, politics is a rich 'world of experience', which already embodies the solidified forms of past conceptual artifice. Thus, when thinking about politics, we do not come to an unmediated natural entity or social object, which needs external explanation. Conversely, politics is itself a richly-textured artefact of reflective languages. The modernist separation of the 'fact-orientation' of politics from 'abstracted' theory is itself tied in this case to the growth of forms of philosophical materialism, naturalism, empiricism, and positivism in the late nine-teenth and early twentieth centuries, and its consequent seepage into common sense. The 'factual-orientation' view of politics is thus the product of certain comparat-ively recent historical developments in the understanding of political theory and philosophy.

In summary, politics is not one simple thing to which we refer. It is the site of a multiplicity of vocabularies. Theory is therefore more ambiguously linked to practice. We are often in a double-bind here. In a premodern sense, we still expect to see polit-ical theory as intimately linked, almost mimetically, with a consensual conception of politics. Yet, in a modernist and postmodernist frame, theories often constitute, contest, and skate over the surface of politics. Politics becomes a much more elusive quarry. Politics is therefore neither an unmediated *tabula rasa*, nor a way of being that can be studied on an unproblematic empirical level and then simply be addressed by theory. The nature of political theory is therefore taken to be both internally complex and deeply contested. This contestation over what it is about and what it ought to do, relates to certain foundational debates. Finally, the way political theory has largely been articulated in the twentieth century has been standardly within a particular academic frame. Unlike political ideology, its main practitioners can be located within this unique academic professional setting. Thus, in analysing twentieth-century theory, I understand it predominantly as a *self-conscious disciplinary practice*.

PATTERN OF THE BOOK

The present book can be read on two distinct levels. There are systematic concise expositions of distinct movements and arguments that have characterized the various phases of political theory during the twentieth century. These can be read independently by students of politics as individual studies. However, there is also a deeper argument, which moves through the whole text, focusing on the theme of foundationalism. This theme is closely linked to the contention that we should rethink the way in which we configure, examine, and teach political theory. Thus, the deeper argument aims, through a close examination of political theory in the twentieth century, to challenge the current ways in which we practise and think about political theory.

Consequently, the book should not be read as a history of political theory in the twentieth century. This would involve a much more detailed and bulky text with a great deal more scholarly apparatus. More importantly, it would also invoke a particular *view* of the way political theory should be considered, analyzed, and studied. In this sense, a history of political theory would not actually perform the task that I have set myself. The present discussion is rather about the *ways* theory has been conceived and practised in the twentieth century; it is not an overtly historical or even methodological enterprise—although it has historical and methodological components. There is a chronological dimension to the way the discussion is laid out. However, this is incidental rather than substantively significant. Further, it is also important to realize that in examining the way theory has been practised, I am offering a selective interpretation. Consequently, there is a lot that is missed out. Most readers will have a favourite theorist who does not appear in the discussion. Any attempt at such a broad interpretive sweep will inevitably miss aspects of the theoretical landscape. The study is not therefore intended to focus on the micro-level of theoretical output, but, rather to offer a broad-brush interpretation of key dimensions of the way theory has been conceived. It should therefore be seen as an *interpretation* of the nature of political theory in the twentieth century.

In terms of the actual substance of the text, the most significant omission is the bulk of twentieth-century political ideology. Ideology is discussed at times—however, for various reasons, I do not include substantive discussion of political ideologies in the text. The reasons are that, first, and quite minimally, I have already covered this area fairly comprehensively in another book (Vincent 1995). Second, and far more importantly, there is something immediately theoretically problematic in raising the issue of political theory as synonymous with political ideology. Undoubtedly, political ideology is a dimension of political theory, considered at the broadest, most generic level. However, their relationship remains both deeply complex and philosophically unresolved. Many political theorists would, admittedly, be completely untroubled by the use of political ideology, as either closely tied to or conceptually synonymous with political theory. However, for many other twentieth-century political theorists—as I will argue—this synonymity or conceptual tie remains profoundly troubling, if not irksome. This deep unease with the label 'ideology' can be seen quite starkly in their judgements of ideology as *opposed* to political theory. Thus, although ideology will appear at points, and will be discussed as a facet of political theory, substantive discussion of ideology is largely avoided. I should emphasize, though, that this omission is not because I personally consider that ideology should not be discussed under the rubric theory, but rather that, in critically reconstructing the broad contours of political theory in the twentieth century, ideology remains problematic.

Further, the present book does not deny the importance, interest, and pedagogic value of more standard conceptualist, historical, or 'grand theoretical' introductions to theory. However, it does make a plea for a more ecumenical, reflective, tolerant, or open demeanour, namely that there just may be different, but still quite legitimate answers to the question 'what is political theory?' Acceptance of this view would involve a supplementation of standard analytical conceptualist (or historical) approaches with some reflection on the more general nature of theory itself. Thus, the student being introduced to political theory should minimally be made aware of the contestable internal dimensions of the discipline and to its complex genealogy during the twentieth century. This latter point needs to be underscored. This is not a book simply about political theory in general. Conversely, it is about political theory, predominantly in the twentieth century, in the Anglo-American and European contexts. The book, uniquely, aims to chart and analyse this very peculiar practice. The underlying motif is to work with the grain of theories and to map out their internal structures. The focus of the book is therefore limited, for pedagogic reasons, mainly to political theory in the twentieth century. It is also written from the standpoint of someone educated in predominantly-occidental modes of political theory; that is, within a distinctly-Anglo-American perspective. This is not a 'politically correct' apologia—rather, it just indicates the range of ideas to be dealt with. The ideas dealt with relate to a complex political and intellectual tradition and this book largely shares the preoccupations of that tradition. However, it is also important to emphasize that this tradition is still polyvocal.

The way the book is constructed follows, as mentioned, a rough chronology, although it should not be thought of as progressive. There are continuous overlaps and interweavings between phases. As indicated, the structure of the book is built around the idea of foundations. Foundations are taken to be deeply contested, not only in terms of substantive normative foundations, but also in terms of the different epistemologies and ontologies embodied in the discipline. Thus, there is a play between these various understandings of foundations. Virtually all the elements discussed in this volume coexisted at the close of the twentieth century. In addition, when I use the term 'political theory', understood as a self-conscious disciplinary practice, it is considered to be a comparatively recent enterprise. Although this may sound odd, political theory is understood, in this book, to be a creature of the late nineteenth and twentieth centuries, although carrying a long tail of antecedents and ancestors. This is not to undermine the practice in any way, or to diminish its role, it is rather to be critically aware of its genealogy and not to overdo talk of its antiquity.

The pattern of the book adopts the following sequence. Part One explores the *prima facie* generic foundations of political theory in the twentieth century. This is an attempt to sort and analyse the overarching perceptions of political theory, at a broad level of generality, during the bulk of the century. The five positions outlined are: classical normative theory, institutional theory, historical political theory, empirical political theory, and ideological theory. Some of these components—particularly the classical normative, institutional, and aspects of historical and empirical theory— have a far stronger contextual resonance; that is to say, they are more closely tied to a historical periodization, approximately from 1900 to the 1940s. Other components contain a much more currently recognizable patina. The way this discussion is initially formulated may appear idiosyncratic: however, it is my contention that the idea of political theory, despite being open to wide-ranging debate during the twentieth century, was nonetheless in a state of internal flux until, in effect, the early 1970s. Part One summarizes and provides a systematic overview of this state of flux. It is also important to underline the point that the categories outlined (those used as organizing pedagogic devices) are not necessarily-self-enclosed or discrete fields of theorizing; conversely, there are complex overlaps between them. There is, as such, no pristine essence to political theory. Political theory is and always has been rather an uneasy combination of different modes of thought.

Part Two focuses on a dominant Anglo-American perception of political theory, whose halcyon days were from the 1940s until the early 1990s. There are two chapters in Part Two. The first, 'Foundations Shaken but Not Stirred', covers the advent of logical positivism, the development of conceptual analysis, the so-called death of political theory, linguistic philosophy, and the impact of Wittgenstein's thought, and particularly the idea of 'essential contestability'. The second, 'Bleached Foundations', focuses on the development of justice-based theory, predominantly after the publication of John Rawls' *Theory of Justice* in 1971. Part Two, in general terms, alludes to the point that political theory at this stage actually did begin with an overt and systematic challenge to the more comprehensive metaphysical foundationalism of particularly-classical normative theory. In fact, at one point, the challenge involved a denial that political theory even existed, or a claim that what had existed had just expired. However, its challenge to comprehensive foundationalism was deeply evasive and still embodied a veiled and somewhat unstructured commitment to certain core foundations. In addition, early justice-inspired theory, although also anti-foundational (in that it also opposed comprehensive metaphysical foundationalism), actually went out of its way to develop a new universal but immanent foundationalism, even if in some cases it was a very thin or bleached version. The whole of early justice-based theory was consequently seen, by some, as a resurgence of classical normative theory or 'grand theory'.

Part Three deals with, first, the initial critique of Rawls and justice-based theory. This movement was not so much a resistance to the idea of foundationalism as to its universalist pretensions. However, since the immanent foundational claims in early Rawlsian and related theories were so closely linked to the universalist aspiration, the critical resistance to Rawls et al. looked as if it was opposing all forms of foundational argument. However, what was really taking place was, on the one hand, a qualified rejection of universalism and, on the other hand, an attempt to find a much more secure, realistic, and sociologically or historically meaningful foundation. In effect, this was a response to what was perceived to be the immanent danger of the *loss* of foundations present within the overly optimistic arguments of early justice theories in the 1970s. The critical response to justice theory, in my terminology, was the attempt to root political theory in a form of conventionalism. This was, therefore, an effort to 'shore up' the more comprehensive foundations of political theory by locating them in communal or social conventions. The concept of 'convention' is used here, therefore, as a linking device to establish coherence between a number of quite disparate theories. Convention roughly denotes a continuous, established, social, or historical practice or rule. This is one of the richest and most complex developments in political theory, which has preoccupied a great deal of the discipline through the last two decades of the twentieth century. Part Three is divided into two chapters. The first, 'Shoring Up Foundations', examines the sophisticated origins of a conventionalist argument in the writings of Michael Oakeshott, the better known writings of communitarianism and the reactions of the later Rawls, in terms of his ideas on political liberalism. The second, 'New Conventions for Old', analyses the conventionalist writings of nationalism, neo-Aristotelianism, and republicanism.

Part Four has two chapters. Overall, it deals with the potential implosion of foundational argument implicit within conventionalist logic. The first chapter, entitled 'Segmented Foundations', examines the processes of internal fragmentation implicit within the logic of the conventionalist arguments, using the generic conceptual theme of *pluralism* to analyse liberal pluralism, multicultural pluralism, and difference-based pluralism. The basic argument made in this chapter is that conventionalism does not cease to work at the level of the nation, ethnos, or community. Every traditional community, nation or ethnos is constituted by multiple sub-communities, sub-ethnie, and sub-cultures. Thus, the argument about conventions and meanings is pushed several steps backwards and the foundational claims consequently segment further. The second chapter is entitled 'Standing Problems'. The core argument in this chapter is that conventionalist argument, if pursued, is still profoundly reductionist, although there are several more *degrees* of reductionism. In this sense, radical conventionalism can mutate into the thesis of perspectivism, and consequently Friedrich Nietzsche becomes the central figure. In this scenario, conventionalism therefore links up with the intellectual movements of postmodernism and poststructuralism. However, there is an odd and at times deeply-self-contradictory logic within this radical postmodern setting, which will be explored. The committed postmodern or poststructural critic aims to search out foundationalism in all the remote and hidden corners of political theory. However, their own use of critical theorizing becomes continually suspect through their own arguments.

Part Five again has two chapters. Overall, this Part deals with an alternative to the postmodern movement, which appeared in the mid-twentieth century and developed in parallel with it to the end of the century. The alternative is focused on later forms of critical theory and hermeneutics, dating originally from the 1960s and 1970s. Both see themselves as post-conventional and post-foundational. Both encompass a wide range of thinkers—however, for the sake of brevity, the focus of the chapters is on the work of Jürgen Habermas and Hans-Georg Gadamer, and their mutually critical relationship. The linking element underpinning these discussions is the focus on language and dialogue as the central facets of political theory. Both thinkers, in my view, successfully utilize the notions of language and dialogue to develop a viable perspective on political theory that does not succumb to postmodern or conventionalist claims and yet still employs foundationalism as an immanent format. The first chapter, entitled 'Dialogic Foundations', deals briefly with the intellectual context of both Habermas and Gadamer, and then examines Habermas's theory in detail. The second chapter, entitled 'Circular Foundations', deals with Gadamer's hermeneutical contribution to political theory and the critical debate between Gadamer and Habermas. It also indicates that Gadamer's approach offers some profound insights into how we might conceive of political theory in the future. The conclusion to the book gives a brief restatement of the arguments and suggests a shift in the manner in which we think about and practise political theory towards a more hermeneutic perspective.

Notes

1. There may be very deep reasons for this in terms of the way philosophy has been conceived in the Western tradition (see Hadot 1995). Philosophy, for Hadot, was conceived originally in Greek and Roman periods as a 'spiritual exercise' initiating the person into a higher reality.
2. For Peirce, the reason for the negative view of metaphysics is that it has been historically too dominated by theologians, who are unfit for the more rigorous task of metaphysics. He remarks that you might as well get 'Wall Street Brokers to write metaphysics' (Peirce 1940: 311, 314).
3. As Chantal Mouffe notes, the so-called revival of political theory in Rawls et al. 'is in fact a mere extension of moral philosophy; it is moral reasoning applied to the treatment of political institutions. This is manifest in the absence in current liberal theorizing of a proper distinction between moral discourse and political discourse' (Mouffe 1993: 147).
4. As Hans Georg Gadamer comments, 'We are [now] said to "construct" a theory. This already implies that one theory succeeds another, and each commands, from the outset, only conditional validity, namely insofar as further experience does not make us change

our mind. Ancient *theoria* is not a means in the same sense, but the end itself' (Gadamer 1979: 412).

5. *Theory* is a contested concept. It can claim to represent, correspond to, or reflect political objects or events in the world. Further, it can also claim to embody the inner direction, essence or telos of the world, which it then represents. Alternatively, *theory* can actually constitute what we understand by the world; the key question is then whether *theory* provides an internally-coherent account. This is not an exhaustive list by any means, but it brings to our attention the fact that *theory* is an open-textured concept. Its use cannot be easily tied down to one stipulative meaning within the domain of politics.

PART ONE

2

We Have a Firm Foundation

Part One deals with five conceptions of political theory that have marked out the terrain of the discipline during the twentieth century and still penetrate the general perception of its nature. Each conception embodies a foundational component— a definite ground on which the discipline can build and find sustenance. The five elements of theory are classical normative, institutional, historical, empirical, and ideological political theory. It is important to realize these are somewhat arbitrarily demarcated. There are considerable overlaps and crossovers between these elements, thus one should not see them as wholly discrete ideas. However, they are distinct enough, in their various formats and aims, to be considered independently. The discussion of each will, however, draw attention to crossovers. These conceptions of theory have also tended to mark out different dimensions of the profession of theory as it developed during the twentieth century. As indicated in the introduction, there is a weak sense of chronology underlying this analysis—weak in the sense that there is a sequence of sorts, but, at the same time, all nonetheless coexist simultaneously within the discipline of politics by the second half of the twentieth century.

CLASSICAL NORMATIVE POLITICAL THEORY

The present discussion of classical normative theory will only provide a perfunctory overview. The idea of classical normative political theory is the intellectual template for later twentieth century conceptions of normative theory, in particular from the 1970s. The latter concern forms the bulk of the discussion of the book.[1] In examining late twentieth century forms of normative theory I will, though, draw further distinctions between thicker and thinner normative forms, as well as between self-consciously universalist and more conventionalist variants of normative theory. Many of these distinctions have antecedents in mid- to late-twentieth century perceptions of the older variants of classical normative theory. Further, classical normative political theory—in the older sense—may also be described as *partly* the creation of nineteenth and twentieth century theory. This latter point will also be briefly touched upon at the end of this section and further explored in the sections on historical and institutional political theory. However, initially, a working distinction is drawn between the older structures of classical normative political theory and the late twentieth century renditions of it. It is the former which will be the focus of this section. However, it is still important to realize that exponents of normative political theory (in the most general and inclusive sense), often see their own discipline as the very acme of the study of politics. Some doubts will, however, be registered on this point.

I will first offer a brief, very formal sketch of certain common regulative themes and traditions of classical normative political theory and indicate how many twentieth century theories perceive that tradition. Second, some doubts will also be registered as to how far we can successfully utilize this older structure of thought.

In terms of the first point: there is usually an open and explicit avowal by many (but not all), in the late nineteenth and twentieth-century academic politics profession, that there are a series of perennial or universal concerns, which go back to ancient Greek civilization, which can be focused under the rubric of normative political theory. Political theory, literally and etymologically, therefore, appears to be the science of the *Polis* (city state). Consequently, there is a conventional canon of theorists, from Plato to the present day, who are seen to be part of a common and enduring normative enterprise, focused on the Polis (often translated as a state in nineteenth and early twentieth century theory). Political philosophy can thus be considered, for some, as a universal or timeless enterprise. It exists, in a formal sense, when reflection reaches a certain level of systematic sophistication and self-criticism. It focuses on the coherence, internal and external relations, and ends of social or communal existence, usually with a view to prescribing how we ought to live in future. Standardly, these systematic reflections will be generated from within contingent political circumstances, however, they are usually seen to have repercussions and implications well beyond those circumstances. Political theory therefore describes our situation and prescribes what ends or purposes should be sought in political life and how we might attain them.

On a purely regulative level, a number of common themes characterize the enterprise of classical normative political theory. Primarily, there are concerns focusing on our present social condition, its origin and what precisely we should value in our present situation. Thus, there is a general interest in the nature and role of public institutions—particularly with regard to the state, state surrogates or the governing structures—and the public rules and primary values (such as justice or freedom), which have a powerful effect on the lives of all citizens within the boundaries of the community. There is a strong sense of the ontological, moral, and practical significance of political or communal life over any other form of human existence. Non-political pursuits are, in essence, seen to be enabled, protected, controlled, and nurtured within an adequate political sphere.[2] Political life is, though, commonly seen as the key condition for the realization of a 'good life'—a life where the human being can attain well-being and flourish. In consequence, classical normative political theory involves the systematic search for the best structures and means to achieve this good life and flourishing. In turn, this conception of the good invokes and utilizes forceful suppositions about human nature and establishes how these suppositions can be developed or fulfilled in political structures. Thus, the choice of a particular political form of life and a conception of human nature frequently go together. Overall, there is an underlying preoccupation with the nature of human beings and what we might expect, or not expect, from them. The structure and nature of political institutions will therefore depend heavily on the reading of human capabilities and powers. In addition, there is usually a common anxiety over any difference, disson-ance, or conflict within civic existence, and a more general preference for some form of consensus or common good, to avoid the possibility of factionalism, division, and civil unrest. In sum, the classical normative view embodies the belief that there are common aims, purposes, or goods which can be, or are, embodied in political life. These can be minimal thin conditional rule-bound goods or maximal thick cultural goods. This latter point links in closely with conceptions of the importance of order, security of existence, and the maintenance of common values in politics and the related critical examination of the preconditions of both order and disorder.

The above themes are admittedly extremely general and open-ended. The most cursory reading of the history of political thought will give rise to the conclusion that classical theories do vary very widely over above themes. Commentators on norm-ative political theory have, in fact, commonly drawn further distinctions between 'traditions' of theory, in order to try to pin down and make sense of the diversity. There are, though, many ways in which older forms of classical political theory have been classified. No classification has been definitive. A classification though is more of a tool of analysis, a way of thinking though the material. Such traditions are largely *ex post facto* 'invented' phenomena. History, in this sense, is always present history.

The way in which the past of theory is classified tends to metamorphose between the various interpretations of political theory. Historians of political thought often favour fairly complex contextual classifications, which focus on larger or more sub-stantial periodizations. These cover such things as classical Greek, early, middle and late medieval, early modern and modern, and so forth. Each stage then usually becomes a micro-focus for further more detailed classifications. These have become the 'stock-in-trade' of the large number of histories of political thought. This more unwieldy structure can also be simplified into the diverse languages of political the-ory, such as natural law, classical or civic republican, classical political economy, and the science of politics (see Pagden 1987). Those more engaged with twentieth century developments in moral and political philosophy favour much simpler, less contextually-sensitive classifications, than historians of political ideas. Thus, categor-ies such as consequentialism and deontology are taken to encompass a whole range of material. More dramatic cosmic classifications of normative political theory can be found in the likes of Leo Strauss. Strauss focused on the theme of cultural crisis. He saw, for example, three consecutive 'waves of modernity', which gave rise to a dynamic distinction between classical and modern political philosophy. Thus, for Strauss, the first wave was initiated by Machiavelli—who is regarded as the founder of modern political philosophy. Machiavelli is seen to have basically subordinated all morality and religion to politics. The second wave is associated with Rousseau, where moral standards are sought from the contingent values of history. For Strauss, the latter stage laid the philosophical groundwork for later German Idealism and historicism. The third wave was initiated decisively by Nietzsche and Heidegger. It retained the insights of Rousseau's and German Idealism's historicism, but denied the rationality of the process and introduced the theme of nihilism. Heidegger is taken by Strauss as the most radical expression of the self-consciousness of the modernity of the third wave. Strauss was therefore clear in his own mind, that a distinction had to be drawn between classical and modern political philosophy.[3] In like manner, Dante Germino, in another archetypal history of political thought, saw three cosmic phases or traditions in political theory: theocentric humanism (where God is the measure and centre of all things), anthropocentric humanism (where humanity is the measure of all things), and finally, messianic humanism (which seeks a qualitative transformation of human existence and is the groundwork for twentieth century totalitarian movements) (Germino 1967). This also has some loose parallels to W. H. Greenleaf's distinctive classification of traditions in political theory in terms of order, empiricism, and rationalism (see Greenleaf 1964).

The above types of classification—from the more mundane contextualist historical position to the cosmically dramatic—could be the subject of a separate detailed study. However, the classification adopted (more pragmatically) here focuses on certain broad intellectual tendencies, which are taken as very general indicative signposts.[4] There is no sense here that they should be taken as anything other than 'ideal types'. The first category focuses on order and nature. The basic theme is that there is a complex pre-established, unchanging, usually divine, order, which provides the rules and structures for all human willing, reasoning, and judgement. These rules and structures are the ground for all legitimacy, authority, duty, and obligation. Law and justice are also embedded in this universal prestructured nature. The function of theory is to identify that order, explicate it and show how it fits the world, or, how the world of political and legal institutions can be modulated and adapted to reflect this inner purpose or natural teleology. This tradition can be associated with broad philosophical movements of Aristotelianism, Platonism, and medieval Christianity. It also has strong associations with the long-established tradition of natural law. Ethics, in this context, is associated with universal pre-existent reasonable rules. The modern adaptation of this tradition appears more tenuously, and usually without overt teleology and metaphysics, in forms of cosmopolitanism and some human rights theory.

The second tradition is empiricism. This raises the spectre of human will and artifice. This is the tradition which, although having roots in classical Greek thought, develops systematically from the sixteenth and seventeenth centuries. Faith is separated from the use of reason. Reason is more focused on the theme of individual autonomy, artifice, and will. It concentrates on the crucial role of human interests, preferences, wants, desire, and interests. Furthermore, it tends to be sceptical of any overarching knowledge claims (particularly large scale metaphysical claims) and relies more upon the collation of empirical information, data and facts about human behaviour, so that generalizations can be corroborated or tested. Improvements will gradually arise as human knowledge grows. Politics, in this reading, can be seen as a function of the correct technical means or administration of the world. One of the foremost seventeenth century spokesmen of this tradition is Thomas Hobbes, although Machiavelli is also often taken to be another key figure. Ethics, in this tradition, is relative to human desires and passions. In consequence, moral rules are vulnerable to mutable human wants and passions and their contingent settings.

Further, because of this potential vulnerability and contingency, it makes moral and political behaviour potentially more suspect, unreliable, and particular. Morality can simply become prudence and expediency. Contractarian arguments flourish in this setting. Reason of state, sovereignty, and political order also become important. Order needs to be guaranteed in the context of diverse individual interests. Further, the way individual preferences and wants can be coordinated also becomes significant. Force or coercion is one path. However, doctrines, such as liberalism, have usually favoured—in the twentieth century—education, self-regulating markets, welfare and the encouragement to consent, contract, and public reasoning as more acceptable ways of coordinating differences.

The third tradition is historical reason. This concentrates on the contention that all human life is subject to the contingency of sociological and historical circumstance. In many ways this is also integral to the sociological and historical perspectives (qua Marx, Weber, Tönnies, Durkheim, or Duguit). Every human being is thus seen as a child of their own time. They cannot escape from this destiny. Human nature is therefore contingent, mutable, and with no fixed essence. Humans do not have universal interests. Ethics are dependent upon the communal circumstances of individuals. Moral rules can be rich and determinative, but often at the cost of any universality. Many modern day conventionalists, communitarians, multiculturalists, and nationalists appear to have their roots in this general perspective. However, a great deal depends in this tradition as to whether a teleology of emancipation, or the like, is attached to historical contingency. In writers such as Burke, Hegel, or Marx an underlying teleology can make overall sense of historical changes in terms of a sequence of events with an underlying purpose. However, if one abstracts the teleology, then history becomes more a matter of random chance, with no aim, purpose, or sense. This is largely the position of many postmodern writers. Genealogy, in Foucault for example, can be considered as a form of analysis utilizing strong accounts of historical mutation and sociological reduction without any teleology.

The above three traditions should be seen as largely-contemporary artifice. Certain political thinkers overlap a number of these traditions. Thus, they should be taken as indicative cartographical references, which will be referred back to during the course of the mapping of political theory—they are a way of orientating understanding. They do not indicate a past reality.

Turning briefly now to the perception of classical normative political theory in the twentieth century, there is a pervasive assumption of a long, continuous, and coherent dialogue (or series of dialogues between and within traditions) about politics, going back to the Greeks. Normative theory is envisaged as a generic category, which covers all theories whose primary focus has been concerned with setting standards, prescribing forms of conduct and recommending certain forms of life and institutional structures. Therefore, normative theory covers—as a general category—the *whole* of the classical conception of political theory. This tradition was, for some, lost in part of the twentieth century, and then recovered from the 1970s. It therefore embodies what some modern commentators have called 'the return of grand theory'. The significance of the idea of 'return' is due to the fact that (in one important interpretation), it had been resisted or downgraded by other significant sectors of twentieth century political theory. These 'other' sectors will be discussed in detail in Part Two. Yet these other sectors of political theory became, in turn, less influential in the last two decades of the twentieth century. In fact, in some scenarios—for example, in the debate over the death of political theory—such accounts have come to be regarded, with hindsight, as just peculiar. Thus, in this more inclusive reading, normative theory (or grand theory) was able, apparently, to return in all its full glory by the end of the twentieth century. Much of the significant normative work in political theory, in the last three decades of the twentieth century, has self-consciously placed itself in this traditional location.

It would also be true to say that many of the notable figures of early- to mid-twentieth century political theory, such as Leo Strauss, Bertrand de Jouvenal, Hannah Arendt, Eric Voegelin, Michael Oakeshott, Yves Simon, Simone Weil, Friedrich Hayek, and many others, clearly perceived themselves to be part of this ongoing grand normative tradition. In this case, it was not a broken tradition (as perceived by many Anglophone analytic theorists), but rather a continuing and vigorous one. In addition, the early- to mid-twentieth century period was also the era of the academic institutionalization of the standard history of political thought textbooks. This, again, buttressed the self-perception of an unbroken normative tradition. How indeed could one possibly doubt the existence of this long tradition: it was there, vouchsafed by a large number of scholarly texts! In the late twentieth century theory, this self-perception of a continuous normative tradition has continued unabated.

Apart from the above mainstream theorists, ironically, most of the widely used political theory textbooks, in the 1940s to 1970s (and even until comparatively recently), took a slightly more reserved or even conservative line on normative theory. The reasons for this reluctance rests on the point made above, for example, that Anglophone conceptualist analytic theory was the more dominant perspective, for a time, and it tended to downgrade direct normativism. Thus, conceptual understanding, rigorous analysis, and impartial evaluation took clear priority over normative or prescriptive recommendation. The closest one comes to normativism is in the elusive concept of 'conceptual evaluation', which is usually a shorthand for a more duplicitous normativism. Thus, conventionally, within the analytic conceptualist position, a political concept, after rigorous analysis—the adjective 'rigour' bestowing a furtive symbolic imprimatur—'evaluation' takes place and then, magically, ones interpretation of the concept becomes the favoured reading.

There are a number of examples of these types of textbooks, which range from a minimal restrained analytic conservatism to a more confident evaluative position. The general theme is a rigorous conceptual analysis conjoined with an evaluation—although sometimes just one aspect is emphasized. Andrew Hacker, for example, saw the key goal of political theory as simply to enhance conceptual understanding and clarity. John Plamenatz, in a more famous definition in 1960, defined political theory as 'systematic thinking about the purposes of government' (Plamenatz 1960: 37; Hacker 1961: 20). Alan Gewirth defined political theory as 'the moral evaluation of power' (Gewirth 1965: 1); David Raphael, in another well-known text of the 1970s and 1980s, defined theory as the clarification of concepts and the critical evaluation of beliefs (Raphael 1976: 3; see also Kateb 1968: 15; and Blackstone 1973: 25). Even after this period, the same rough themes still keep on reccurring. Thus, David Miller directly echoes Plamenatz in defining political theory as 'systematic reflection on the nature and purposes of government' (David Miller et al. 1987: 383). Philip Pettit considered political theory as 'the project of evaluating the different social structures that political activity enables us to contemplate as alternatives'. He describes this as a normative enterprise, which is designed to 'evaluate rather than explain' (Pettit 1993b: 217; and 284–5).[5] Will Kymlicka or Jean Hampton's introductions are also more openly focused on rigorous normativism, although, again, still from a more distanced conceptualist and evaluative viewpoint (Kymlicka 1990; Hampton 1998).

In most of the above theorists (with some exceptions) there is not a great deal of recognition of the complex 'traditions', which inform the classical normative perspective. Complex traditions are often seen to be the preserve of historians of political thought. Thus, the usual standpoint, on what many take to be the classical normative political theory tradition, is oddly thin and selective. The point of political theory for many is 'presentism'. It is not to mull over the past, but rather to deal with the present and its manifold political problems. Consequently, only certain dimensions of contemporary normative theory appear to be aware or interested in the complex antecedents of many of their own ideas in, for example, the empiricist tradition. They also appear oblivious to the historical tradition, which is premised on the idea that virtues cannot be universal, but are rather an expression of their own time and place—moral, political, philosophical, and religious ideas all reflecting a contingent sense of place. In some ways, one of the most recent and popular faces of this historical contingency and mutability argument appears in Thomas Kuhn's writings on paradigms in natural science, which, after its publication, spread like wildfire in the social science and humanities vocabularies (Kuhn 1962). However, this still did not prevent many able political theorists, well into the late twentieth century, offering universalistic theories, and being seemingly untroubled by the complex and deeply researched claims of the historical reason tradition. However, again, many others in the twentieth century have clearly been concerned by the import of such historical arguments. In fact, part of the deep anxiety of political theory at the close of the twentieth century—particularly over issues such as universal human rights, international justice, and the future of nationalism—is focused on forms of historicist argumentation. Certainly, the arguments presented to us in writers such as Wilhelm Dilthey, Benedetto Croce, R. G. Collingwood, Michael Oakeshott, or Hans-Georg Gadamer, and many others, are still far from being adequately assessed.

One further point also needs to be made here, which registers doubts about the whole idea of traditions of classical normative political theory. This is an argument, which will be returned to again. The basic point of the normative argument is the claim that there is a pattern of theorizing from the ancient Greeks, which can be said to have continued through the twentieth century. Despite my brief discussion of the three traditions of theory, it is still wise to remind ourselves that all history is still present history. There is also a question mark over the idea of a 'continuous practice' linking past and present normative political philosophy. Indeed, in thinking seriously about the present state of political philosophy, and its future, it is worth considering whether political theory has a clearly-identifiable past.

The term 'political theory', and the practice of being a political theorist, are relatively commonplace now. However, they became commonplace only in the middle of the twentieth century in particular professional academic settings. We can now self-define ourselves as 'political theorists' or 'political philosophers' without too much trouble in being understood. We also commonly assume that there always have been such creatures, from the Greeks to the present. It appears, *prima facie*, to be a reasonable assumption to make. Yet, if we pause for a moment, and ask the question: did Aristotle, Augustine, Aquinas, Montesquieu, Machiavelli, Burke, Adam Smith, Hume, Kant, Herder, Hegel, or T. H. Green have any conception of *themselves* as, distinctively, political theorists? Did they clearly separate out, or demarcate, the separate realms of moral philosophy, political economy, history, psychology, and metaphysics, as distinct from political theory? Did they have the same understanding of politics? The rapid answer to the above questions is an emphatic no. Neither Hume, Burke, Kant, Hegel, J. S. Mill, nor T. H. Green, saw themselves as political theorists, or even primarily, as political philosophers. They were rather philosophers (or, conversely, they might not in some cases even have seen themselves as philosophers), who addressed, as part of their theorizing, an area called politics—which might not, in fact, be our understanding of the term. Politics was often—but not always—intimately connected with morality, political economy, and psychology. There was, thus, little sense of a wholly-discrete or exclusive area called political philosophy or political theory, which could be clearly demarcated in the manner that we now do.

The exclusive sense of political theory as a discrete discipline, which had a canon of esteemed thinkers and clear curricula, is largely an invention of the twentieth century. The idea of the canon of 'great theorists' began to be articulated in the mid-to-late nineteenth century and developed in the twentieth century. It was not until the mid-twentieth century that it became more academically established, and not until the 1970s did political theory acquire its first independent journals and wider institutional recognition. Thus, the vision of an articulate consistent enterprise that was temporarily lost or died and then was refound or resurrected is not convincing (see Bourdieu 2000: 30). It is more of a present imposition. Political philosophy, as it arose in the 1970s, as a wholly discrete academic activity and profession, was very much a unique enterprise.

This whole process of gradual consolidation of the subject was strengthened by the academicization and professionalization of political studies in universities in the late nineteenth and early twentieth centuries. The 'action orientation' of political theory was often sloughed off in the academic setting. Thus, the general relation between political studies and actual politics has remained a perennial worry to the present. There is consequently a difference between, on the one hand, the aggregation of concerns, loosely grouped under the heading political philosophy or political theory in the ancient, pre- and early-modern eras, and, on the other hand, the twentieth century wholly university-based academic profession and specialism called political theory. Political theorists now largely address other political theorists. Not many think, except in rare or apologetic moments, of addressing themselves to a readership outside of this setting. What might unselfconsciously be called political theory, before this institutionalization and professionalization process, often addressed itself, if not directly to the populous, then often to more immediate perceptions of political urgency. This is by no means a hard and fast distinction, however; it is clear that political theory now is not so crucially motivated by any sense of external political urgency, as by the endemic problems of highly-specialized languages and the intrinsic pressures of an institutionalized profession in the modern, highly competitive, university profession measured by research output. The problems of political theory now are often the problems of artifice, internal to the discipline. The world is filtered through highly-specialized languages. In fact, the way in which we usually provide a balm to this potential irritant is by assuming that the actual world is really a problem of adequate theory. We do politics as a practice through theory. Politics is what goes on in the distillations of books and academic journals. Theorists occasionally imagine themselves as philosopher kings or advisers to politicians, but it is usually illusion.

In summary, what perpetuates political theory now is not the sense of social or political malaise or crisis (except as ritually recreated in rhetoric) so much as the immensely powerful institutional, career, and professional interests of the academic discipline in universities, coupled with another important factor. Political theory still attracts interest and generates excitement, because it still glows with the dubious patina of political engagement. Political theory can still fascinate by allowing politics to appear in the form of masque. Those who are repelled by this masque or shadow-boxing have also oddly given their imprimatur to the disengagement of political theory from practical politics, which only adds to the lustre of the discipline for votaries of a different intellectual persuasion. Followers of Michael Oakeshott, Leo Strauss, and even Michel Foucault have often made this claim. If politics is affected, it is usually by chance.

Political theory, however, does still admittedly occasionally allow itself to be carried directly into the political arena—kicking and screaming for the sake of the audience—by political ideology. Yet, the relation between political theory and political ideology still remains deeply ambiguous and unsettled. There is a Mannheimian point here (see Mannheim 1966). Political theory was originally in a similar position to that of ideology, qua Mannheim. Political theory was thus not far off political preaching at times. Saint Simon, Fourier, Proudhon, de Tocqueville, Bentham, Comte, or Fichte saw little distinction between social science, political theory, and political action. Ideas were seen to have influence and power in the world. A revolutionary idea could potentially revolutionize society. However, by the end of the nineteenth century, social science and political theory were progressively being absorbed into the burgeoning universities. In the same manner that Mannheim saw ideology becoming progressively transformed *from* an active revolutionary practice *into* a new academic discipline—the sociology of knowledge—so political theory was also transformed within a sanitized academic disciplinary frame. As ideology was in a sense deideologized, so political theory was depoliticized. As some have seen the end of ideology, it is not surprising that others saw the end of political philosophy—although this is definitely not the orthodox reading of the death of political philosophy.

It might be contended against the above arguments that a sociology of professions or disciplines does not necessarily affect the *content* of the disciplines. A sociology of science neither affects the content of science, nor the importance of scientific discoveries. In addition, if one allows the sociology thesis too much sway, then it could be said to trivialize the whole discussion of theory. It could even, self-reflexively, be said to destroy or undermine itself. There is some truth to these points. However, in emphasizing the way a discipline has formed, trains its members, establishes its criteria for publishing and teaching, we must be minimally aware of a 'social dynamic'. To deny it is simply naïve or myopic. It should neither be over-emphasized, nor should it be avoided. It is not a sociological speculation, but a simple matter of historical detail that political theory, as a specialized profession and academic discipline, is a product largely of the twentieth century. It is also understandable that it should try to create a past for itself. This gives it intellectual weight and gravitas, but we should always view such claims with a critical eye. When academic political theory rests contentedly on its institutional laurels and appeals to its own intrinsic academic authority we should be sceptical.

INSTITUTIONAL POLITICAL THEORY

The institutional approach, in its most direct sense, identifies the function of political theory as articulating the meaning and practice of the state—that is both the philosophical idea and constitutional legal practice of the state. The word that most adequately describes this is the German term *Staatslehre*. The origin of this idea can be found in philosophers such as G. W. F. Hegel and J. G. Fichte, within their various *Rechtsphilosophien*.[6]

Staatslehre, in its most direct sense, means that to learn about politics one has to learn about the state, and to learn about the state means not only to account for its various empirical and constitutional forms, but also to study the normative ideals embodied within it. This form of study encompasses, by default, historical, legal, and philosophical issues. In continental European, and some American contexts, the juristic concept of the constitution was also connected closely with the state idea. The German tradition of *Staatslehre* consequently fully accommodated the study of constitutions as part of the more general study of the state. Thus, constitutional study was seen as integral to the state idea. In fact, well into the twentieth century, French, German, and Italian political studies have been closely linked with both legal and historical studies. Thus, *Staatslehre* (in various shapes), quite simply, was the first serious form in which the idea of political theory was practised in Europe, Britain, and North America, as a sophisticated academic enterprise. However, one should be very careful here not to distinguish too firmly between historical studies, law, and political theory. In a similar way, it would also be mistaken, before 1900, to make clear distinctions between highly autonomous disciplines of history, law, philosophy, sociology, and politics. The distinctions did exist, but *only* to a very limited degree. In many ways, *Staatslehre* itself was at the confluence of a series of forms of study: the history and nature of the moral sciences, the development of history, the historical and comparative study of law and institutions, and the history of philosophy. It was therefore an opportune 'linking concept'. Political theory, at this point, was conceptually linked with a number of other perspectives, which we would now tend to keep separate.

It is hardly surprising, in this context, that this form of study has important historical, legal, and philosophical dimensions. The state, as an organizing or framework-making concept, is ideal for such synoptic or inclusive studies. In fact, when the first academic studies of the state arose in the mid-nineteenth century—carrying through well into the twentieth century—they were commonly composed by historians, legal, and constitutional theorists as well as philosophers. In the early twentieth century many early sociologists, such as L. T. Hobhouse, Max Weber, Leon Duguit, Émile Durkheim, R. M. MacIver, and Ferdinand Tönnies, also carried on this broad tradition of writing about the state as the central concept.

One major problem with the state focus, though, is the open quality of both the concepts of the 'state' and 'institutions'. Thus, in terms of the concept state, minimally, on a juridical level, one can say that it is a unique form of public power, which is idiosyncratically distinct from other renditions of political power. However, on an institutional level, this public power can mean the actual or fictive sovereign body, or persons; the legal or constitutional structure of rules; the legal personality of the ruler(s), offices, or institutions. It can also denote the government, an element within a government, such as the executive, judiciary, or legislature, or a compound of these. In addition, it can imply the collective or popular will of all the people (qua general will). It can also indicate something even more embracing, like the 'entire hierarchy of institutions by which life is determined, from the family to the trade, and from the trade to the Church and University' (see Bosanquet 1899: 150). The list could go on here. If one reviews the history of the state, there has been an enormously wide range of theories and practices, each with their own unique interpretation. Such state theories usually embody long complex and overlapping traditions of analysis (see Dyson 1979 or Vincent 1987).[7]

Where does this focus on institutionalism and the state derive from? In the early- to mid-nineteenth century, psychology, economics, anthropology, sociology, and political science simply did not exist as independent disciplines in universities. Despite their recognition, to some degree, as traditions of thought, they were not researched or taught independently as autonomous subjects. It was not until the 1860s and 1870s that they began to take on institutional form. In the United States, economics was the first to form a professional organization, in 1885, followed by psychology in 1892, and sociology 1905. Political Science formed its own professional association in North America—the American Political Science Association—in 1903 (see Dorothy Ross in Farr and Seidelman (eds.) 1993: 83). Political studies developed gradually in the United States during the 1870s and 1880s and was firmly established by the early 1900s. In Germany and France, the state idea had already taken a firm shape in academic terms during the early nineteenth century and it was to these traditions, particularly the German, that early American scholars of politics commonly turned for intellectual sustenance. In Britain, however, it was only in the early- to mid-twentieth century that discipline began to develop.[8] The period of dominance of the 'state perspective' was approximately between 1870 and 1920. This did not mean that the state idea disappeared, rather, it lost its dominant place within the discipline. However, as James Farr comments, in North America, well into the New Deal era, 'political scientists cast their work on government, parties, and policies in terms of the state' (Farr in Farr and Seidelman (eds.) 1993: 64).

Some commentators have seen the interests in political science, qua the state, stretching back to eighteenth century enlightenment debates concerning the constitution and republicanism (see James Farr in Farr and Seidelman (eds.) 1993: 66 *ff*.). However, in North America, the first academic figure to actually introduce political studies to universities was Francis Lieber, a German exile, whose first politics courses were wholly premised on *Staatslehre* principles. Lieber was appointed to a Chair of History and Political Science in Columbia in 1857. In 1880, the autonomous School of Political Science was founded in Columbia University under John Burgess, again, another committed *Staatslehre* exponent. Subsequently, in the United States, between 1880 and the early 1900s, many of the early influential teachers and writers on political science sought postgraduate training in German universities, and developed even broader interests in the historical development of institutions, as part of a comprehensive science of humanity (*Geisteswissenshaft*). In fact, virtually all the key figures in American political science up to the 1920s, such as John Burgess, W. A. Dunning, W. W. Willoughby, Charles Merriam, Woodrow Wilson, and T. D. Woolsey held to the major facets of the *Staatslehre* approach. However, it is also important to grasp that to adhere to the state as a way of speaking about politics does not imply anything about the substantive theoretical content. The state concept was open both ideologically and empirically.

In Britain, the situation was slightly different. For some scholars, Britain qua the state, was even an 'aberrant case' (see Dyson 1979, ch. 7). From the 1870s, the influence of German thought was overwhelmingly present in many philosophers, theologians, historians, and historians of law and political institutions. However, it was still a mixed reception. Some, such as the dominant school of British philosophers between 1870 and 1920, the British Idealists (e.g. T. H. Green, Bernard Bosanquet, Henry Jones, Edward Caird, and David G. Ritchie), were open and receptive to the German ideas, although not without very severe reservations on certain philosophical issues (see Vincent and Plant 1984; Boucher and Vincent 2001). Equally, historians of law and institutions, such as F. W. Maitland, William Stubbs, and Henry Maine, also responded with great interest to German scholarship in law and history. Others, such as Henry Sidgwick, James Bryce, and A. V. Dicey were more uneasy and sceptical—although the significance of the 'state' and the importance of the 'historical comparative method' for studying it, were usually not in contention. There was also awareness that British intellectual tradition, and particularly the state tradition, were dissimilar to continental Europe. Thus, the structure of Parliamentary government, the manner in which subordinate agencies were subject to parliamentary scrutiny, the long-standing tradition of common law, and the peculiarities of the unwritten constitution, made legal and political theorists and historians less willing to speak so self-consciously of the British state. Odd elusive terms like 'crown' were often preferred. The canon of Whig historians, from Burke onwards, contributed towards this more elusive perspective. The British experience was considered different, if not unique. This was an idea that punctuated political studies in Britain well into the twentieth century. However, substantial *Staatslehre* texts, such as Bluntschli's *Theory of the State*, were still translated into English during this period and obviously had a receptive audience.

Why was the state focus so central to political studies and political theory? The answer to this is complex. There are both external and internal reasons. The external reasons refer to the broader social, political, and historical context of political study. First, there was a symbiosis between, on the one hand, the growth of states and nationalism in the nineteenth and early twentieth centuries, and, on the other hand, the concentration on the concept of the state within political studies. Thus, in historical terms, for example, Italy was only unified as a state in 1861 and Germany in 1871. The United States was itself searching for a secure sense of identity and unity throughout the nineteenth century, especially after the enormous upheaval of the civil war in the 1860s. Overall, the nineteenth and twentieth centuries encompassed a period of accelerated *state-making*, the enthusiastic formation and promulgation of nationalisms often through developing public education systems, and the widespread creation and application of state constitutions. The language of the nation state was also embodied in calls for sovereignty and self-determination—a call which increased throughout the twentieth century, especially in the period of post-1945 decolonization. The fact that the discipline of politics grew within the universities of most modern states during the late nineteenth and twentieth centuries and that the primary focus of the initial political studies was the concept of the state is not therefore fortuitous. In fact, within current international relations the state is *still* largely the central academic focus.

Some scholars have also argued that political studies, as they developed in the late nineteenth and twentieth centuries, were remarkable for being so closely linked to the character of their own nation state traditions (see Castiglione and Hampsher-Monk (eds.) 2001). Certainly this would be true of Britain, France, and Germany. This linkage was made explicit by Lieber in America, as early as 1858, when arguing for the need for political science in North American universities. He remarked to his American audience that 'we stand in need of a national university, the highest apparatus of the highest modern civilization. We stand in need of it, not only that we may appear clear with equal dignity among our sister nations . . . but on grounds peculiar to ourselves' (Lieber in Farr and Seidelman (eds.) 1993: 21). The same point was also noted by later twentieth century commentators on North American political studies. Thus, in the Presidential address to the American Political Science Association in 1991, Theodore Lowi noted that 'American political science is itself a political phenomenon and, as such, is a product of the American state'. Lowi continued, 'every regime tends to produce a political science consonant with itself'. Consequently, there is not one political science, rather each form adapts to the tradition it studies. Thus, for Lowi, the 'consonance' between the state and the discipline of political science is a subject worthy of study in itself (see Theodore Lowi in Farr and Seidelman (eds.) 1993: 383).

The 'state focus' was also closely tied to educational imperatives. To concentrate on the state was not only to learn about the history of institutions, but was *also*, and more importantly for some scholars, to be inculcated with national sentiment. This was essentially embodied in the idea of civic education (civics), or citizen education, and the various arcane celebrations and ceremonies of citizenship—a perennial theme in many states during the twentieth century. Citizenship education was a way of encouraging both civic awareness and consensual civic virtue.[9] Further, with the massive growth of the state sector in the nineteenth and twentieth century, there was a strong perception of the need for trained personnel to fulfil the growing requirements of the specialized public services and bureaucracies within states. In addition, many of those who entered into the early stages of teaching and promulgation of political studies in universities, were themselves often committed to the idea of state-based reform. To train and teach the new recruits for state bureaucracies, to carry out specialized research for governments and to be able to affect subtly the direction of governmental thinking, through institutional design, were seen as desirable aims by many in the politics discipline. As John Gunnell comments, 'This search for a science of politics was never disjoined from the practical concerns of political education and political reform'. Thus, through the establishment of politics in universities, it was hoped that, through civic education and scientific expertise, the discipline itself could 'command the attention of government' (see Gunnell in Monroe (ed.) 1997: 49). It was in this context that Theodore Lowi viewed the setting up of the American Political Science Association, in 1903, as simply part of a 'progressive reform movement' in American politics (see Lowi in Farr and Seidelman (eds.) 1993: 384).

In many ways, this practical reform strategy was born from the initial contact of North American and some British intellectuals with German and French universities. There was a perception of a close and productive relation, in these latter countries, between the state and academic elites. In France, this was manifest in the *Grand École* tradition, and, in terms of the discipline of politics, in the original *École Libre des Sciences Politiques de France*.[10] The same idea developed in Britain, in the early 1900s, particularly through the work of the Fabian Sidney Webb, amongst others, in setting up the London School of Economics and Political Science, which was also initially committed to ideas of educating future public servants and administrators, providing skilled specialized social scientific research and permeating governmental thinking with social science. What the American and British reformers failed to take into account were the subtle but definite differences between British and American state traditions and those of mainland Europe. In Britain and America, particularly, there was often an underlying deep-rooted estrangement of universities and intellectuals from the realm of the state.

However, there were also a number of internal reasons for this 'state focus', which relate closely to the discipline of politics itself. These, again, can be subdivided in terms of the *strategic* demands for disciplinary consolidation, and the *creative* potential of the state concept. In terms of *strategic* demands, the state idea provided the academic discipline of politics with a ready-made and deeply-significant curriculum and subject matter. If a discipline proposes establishing its own distinctive status, with its own unique curricula, 'it will try also to assume a subject matter and techniques of study that are *sui generis*. And what subject matter can be regarded as purely political? . . . If there is any subject matter at all which political scientists can claim exclusively for their own, a subject matter that does not require acquisition of the analytical tools of sister-fields . . . it is, of course, formal-legal political structure' (Eckstein and Apter 1963: 10–11). In other words, in terms of the contest of the faculties, politics could not come to the academic bargaining table empty-handed or reliant upon the vocabulary of law, history, sociology, or philosophy—despite the fact that it was frequently a refuge for historical-minded philosophers and theoretically-minded historians or lawyers. Thus, where economics had become progressively more technical, law validated a powerful public profession, history had become more specialized, and philosophy more technically focused on logic and epistemology, then, 'in such company, politics, too, had to make its bid for a place at the table by posing as the sovereign of a small but technically advanced and entirely independent territory' (Collini et al. 1983: 374). The sovereign territory which politics claimed to be able to interpret, and which marked out the unique and singularly important field of political study, was of course 'the state'. This provided the fundamental academic *raison d'être*.

The *creative* potential of the state concept was singularly important in terms of its relation to classical normative political theory—discussed in the previous section. It is also a key to understanding the background to the next section on the historical political theory. The state, in effect, became the linchpin of the narrative sequence underpinning classical normative political theory. This was also partly facilitated by the classical background of many scholars, well into the early stages of the twentieth century. It was comparatively easy for such writers to immediately translate the Greek term *Polis* into 'city-state', or just 'state'. Many late nineteenth and early twentieth century books were written, therefore, on the 'Greek state' or 'Roman state'. The *suprema potestatis* of Roman law became the modern concept of sovereignty, which was seen to characterize the Roman 'state'. Political science, qua Aristotle, was therefore configured as the 'science of the state'. This assimilation of classical normative political theory into state language was crucial in establishing a unified logical sequence or narrative from the ancient Greeks to the present. In effect, the whole history of political theory could then be read through the concept of the state. The problems of politics were therefore the problems of the state. The problems of the Greek, Roman, medieval, sixteenth, or seventeenth century worlds became familiar problems, because they were *all* focused on the state. The state established a supervenient narrative over the ancient and modern political worlds.

Thus, classical normative political theory found a unifying theme in the state. Political science, *in toto*, was 'summed up' in the science of the state. The term 'science' was synonymous with 'systematic knowledge'. The science of the state could therefore be summed up in the attempt to both describe, on a comparative level, the empirical details of forms of state, and, further to indicate how the good life could be attained. In this sense, the preoccupation with the institution of the state was generated by an interest in both the actual comparative historical detail of institutional arrangements, through which humans have tried to organize their social existence (as Aristotle had done with his well-known typology of constitutions), combined with normative and ethical theories about the 'best institutional arrangement'. Political studies, focused on the state, therefore wove together descriptive and comparative historical detail with normative ideals. The normative ideals were regarded initially as being as significant as the empirical components. In summary, the state focus not only allowed the sequence of classical theory to be unified, combined comparative historical detail with normative ideal, but also provided a creative intellectual framework for contemporary research.[11]

It would be true to say that the state concept, as a way of studying politics and political theory, fell into marked decline from the 1920s. This point will also be examined again in the later section on empirical political theory. However, one should be careful of simply equating (as is commonly done) the decline of the state, and the historical comparative method, with the rise of more scientific, positivist, or behavioural methods. Undoubtedly, in the social sciences in certain countries, North America being a key example, there was a marked shift towards a more positivistic agenda. The empirical methods of political study became of much greater interest. Yet, the idea of the state remained important to American political science, well into the 1940s. If anything it was the 1950s that saw a more decisive change. In addition, the state theme never fell into quite the same decline in Britain and Europe, as in North America. Descriptions of state institutions, woven with theoretical and normative ideas, were still the stock in trade of a great deal of political studies in Britain up until the close of the twentieth century. Further, the partial decline of the state theme coincided with a number of significant events and movements in ideas. There was a growing interest in forms of ethical and political pluralism, in both Europe and North America, and a partial shift away from the state. Philosophical Idealism, in Britain and Europe, also declined rapidly in influence, not least because both it, and the 'theory of the state', were associated obliquely with the horrific events of the First and later Second World Wars. It is worth reminding ourselves of the fact that the dominant strains of sophisticated state theory and *Staatslehre* had strong links to German thought and this alone was enough to make them suspect in the 1920s (and again in the 1940s). In America, this academic suspicion of state theory continued into the 1950s, ironically through the large number of German academic émigrés, who had fled from the Nazi 'total state', who entered American academic life and developed their own unique brand of state scepticism.

As suggested, it would still be far from true that the 'state idea' simply disappeared in the 1920s. The situation did, however, become much more complicated. On one level, the institutional or state focus divided into two broad tendencies, which can be seen implicitly in the various nineteenth-century accounts of the state. In the classical normative theory reading, the 'is' of the state could not be separated from the 'ought'. The normative was integral to the descriptive. However, increasingly, in the decades after the 1920s, a second tendency developed, namely, the empirical and normative were separated out. There was an intrinsic tendency for the historical arguments and comparative method to be relatively self-sufficient, even during the nineteenth century. This was already present within the framework of *Staatslehre*. The study of public law, and the description of institutions, were also separate strands within *Staatslehre*. Important dimensions of the discipline were therefore already *implicitly* recognized as empirical and descriptive forms of study. In addition, from the early 1900s, the stress on positivistic or empiricist forms of study (over the normative) was becoming much more commonplace in disciplines, such as political economy and sociology. This inevitably impacted on the study of politics. This led, in turn, to a widening gulf between the 'is' and the 'ought' of the state. Further, there was a rush of studies in the early twentieth century, associated with writers such as Graham Wallas, George Sorel, and Gustav le Bon, amongst many others, which began to undermine any sense of the normative rationality of the state or citizens. In this context, an empirical method such as social psychology would provide greater insight into politics.[12]

We can therefore observe a subtle mitosis within institutional *Staatslehre*. On the one hand, the 'ought' dimension of the state withered. The normative treatment of the state, namely, the 'philosophical theories of the state', fell seriously out of favour by the 1920s, and remained so until the 1980s. This demise was also partly reinforced by philosophical currents in this same mid-century period, which will be examined in Part Two. On the other hand, one crucial reason for this demise was due to the rise of empiricism in the social sciences and philosophy. It was felt within political science that anything that could be said meaningfully about the state could be said more adequately by empirical studies. In this reading, all classical political theory had to offer was the vague possibility of some testable hypotheses. Admittedly, this tendency to dismiss normative political theory—as embodied in the state idea—was more acceptable in the United States than in Europe.[13]

As a consequence of the withering of the normative component, the 'empirical' dimension of state theory expanded massively and diversified into a range of empirically-orientated studies, with little or no consciousness of their origins. This empirical dimension constituted the underlying substance to comparative politics, comparative constitutional studies, political sociology, political anthropology and, from the 1920s, the new discipline of international relations (see Boucher in Vincent (ed.) 1997c). It also constituted the underlying genealogy of public administration and public policy studies. By the 1950s and 1960s, for example, the 'historical comparative method' of *Staatslehre* had mutated into the comparative politics. Some older classical normative political theory components were still present, but in a semi-dormant form. Thus, most of the reputable comparative politics texts, well into the 1970s, still felt the need to make earnest and respectful nods in the direction of honorary comparative politics forbears, such as Aristotle or Montesquieu. Yet, more recently again, comparative politics itself has also fallen on harder times within political studies, mainly, one suspects, because it carries the dormant virus of state theory.

The continuing cognitive shift of many political scientists away from institutions towards behaviour or informal politics, also partly accounts for this unease with comparative politics. Thus, many would now contend that interests in institutionalism and even comparative politics (qua comparative institutions), have now faded beyond redemption. Underpinning this latter judgement is the view that institutional-based study is virtually useless for understanding politics. It is the informal political behaviour, in such things as policy networks, policy communities, and political parties, which provide far greater insights into political processes.

However, the latter judgement is still somewhat premature, since many of the themes of the older *Staatslehre*, and thus institutional study, have been partly, if unwittingly, revived in the recent manifestation of 'the new institutionalism' during the 1980s. Further, some normative theory, in the 1990s, tried to revive the empirical and institutional dimension in terms of the heavy emphasis on 'institutional design' (see Goodin (ed.) 1998). The differences between the more 'traditional institutionalism' and the 'new institutionalism' arise largely from the fact that the new institutionalism derived primarily *from* a critical reaction to empirical political science, particularly neo-pluralism. The new institutionalism also bears the marks of a long exposure to positivism and the need to appear 'empirically rigorous'. The basic gist of the new institutionalism is that political study, as opposed to being 'society-centred', should now be 'state-centred'. Certain writers have thus spoken of 'bringing the state back into political science', which they think had been abandoned within pluralism and neo-pluralism (see Krasner 1978; Nordlinger 1981; Evans et al. 1985). State officials and processes are taken seriously as partly autonomous from societal preferences and interests. The state must therefore be examined at the macropolitical level. It is the organization of political life, which makes the key difference. Political scientists, for example, March and Olson, see this as equivalent to a 'paradigm change' in political study (March and Olsen 1984; Olsen 1991). Hardly surprisingly, the 'informalist' and 'neo-pluralist' critics of this view have suggested, among other things, that this new paradigm has become *too* state-centric and that, contrary to the new institutionalists, the state always acts in some societal interest (see Jordan 1990). In the latter critics, we therefore see the time-honoured reassertion of the value of informal empirical studies, in an almost direct replay of earlier debates in the 1920s and 1950s.

In sum, for institutional theory, political theory comprises the systematic study of the concept of the state. This is clearly the *first* and initially most important type of political theorizing to develop in the nineteenth and early twentieth century. Certainly, if we are discussing the first attempts at setting up the teaching and scholarship in universities, then it is this area which is most significant. This conception of theory, as well as being state-centric, also blends empirical, historical, legal, and philosophical themes. This conception was largely abandoned by the 1920s and 1930s, although, as suggested, elements of state theory mutated into other components of political studies, such as comparative politics, public administration, and policy studies. Despite early and mid-twentieth century criticism of institutionalism, the state idea has been partly resurrected in the 'new institutionalism', although usually anointed with a little empirical oil. In addition, interests in state theory have also been partly reclaimed, during the 1990s, within some recent normative political theory, in the context of 'institutional design'.[14]

HISTORICAL POLITICAL THEORY

This third section focuses on historical political theory. The gist of this approach is that the study of political theory is unavoidably historical. *Prima facie*, theory is viewed as a sequence of related theoretical contributions. Theory might thus be described as an extended dialogue or conversation over what is important in politics. Therefore, to be aware and educated, one needs to be conscious of the canon of theorists, from the Greeks to the present day, and be prepared to engage in that ongoing critical dialogue or multilogue. Although the history of political theory is a familiar idea to many generations of students, nonetheless, this particular conception of theory is one of the more complex ideas within the whole foundational scenario outlined in Part One.

The reasons for this complexity are not hard to find: first, the concept of 'history' itself is as contested as the concept politics. We often take the existence of disciplines and areas of intellectual expertise for granted, but this can often blind us to certain important issues concerning the genealogy of such ideas. The formation of disciplines and sub-disciplines, although creating more manageable bodies of knowledge, nonetheless can create the appearance of overly coherent autonomous bodies of thought, where none actually exists. Like most disciplines, the origin of history outside the university environment is hard to pin down. As Michael Oakeshott commented, 'activities emerge naively, like games that children invent themselves. Each appears, first, not in response to a premeditated achievement, but as a direction of attention pursued without premonition of what it will lead to. How should our artless ancestor have known what (as it has turned out) it is to be an astronomer, an accountant, or an historian' (Oakeshott 1991: 151). History, in its broadest sense, is concerned with our beliefs and attitudes to the past, however, there are a number of different ways in which the past can be conceived. There are also many methods through which this past can be understood or recovered—which are essentially the domain of historiography.[15] There are also diverse domains in which history is written—church history, war, economics, science, philosophy, or social history, and so forth. In fact, the notion of history, as in most disciplines, has been subject to extremes of mitosis in the nineteenth and twentieth centuries.[16]

Second, certain forms of political theory are, intrinsically, historically orientated. History, in other words, is part of their *substantive* structure. The most obvious examples of this are Hegel and Marx. History can also be related to theory as an essential academic 'method' of study or mode of human understanding. The problem is that these two dimensions often overlap in intricate and confusing ways. Thus, the method can, for example, become a norm of research and even of political thought, and the norm can be perceived as academic method, as, for example, in Marxist history. A historical study of theory can also be perceived as a way of revealing 'great universal normative themes' about human conduct. Alternatively, some historical-minded theorists would claim that the history of political ideas has no normative function whatsoever. History is just history and normative theory is just normative theory. This presupposes a categorical distinction between history and theory, also echoed in the writings of many normative and analytical theorists during the twentieth century. In fact, many analytical philosophers—particularly admirers of the American philosopher W. O. Quine—would see the distinction between history and philosophy as absolutely categorical (on philosophical grounds).

The appeal of the history of political theory, as the key way of doing theory, is the outcome of a range of preoccupations. These can be roughly subdivided into those which are *internal* to the practice of political theory itself, and, secondly, those which form the *external* context of the practice of the history of political theory.

In terms of the internal reasons: first, the history of political theory is closely related to the two previously outlined conceptions of theory. Primarily, the history of political theory is largely the medium through which the ideas of classical normative political theory have been transmitted to readers.[17] Second, as stressed in the previous section on institutional political theory, the state idea can also be seen as the linchpin of the narrative sequence(s) underpinning classical normative political theory. The assimilation of classical normative political theory into a 'statist' language actually establishes the sequence. The whole history of political theory can then be read through the concept of the state. In sum, the history of political theory links symbiotically with both the perceptions of classical and institutional political theory.

A second internal reason relates to political vocabulary. A number of theorists, over the late nineteenth and early twentieth centuries, commonly used such terms as political theory, the history of political thought, and political science, synonymously. Thus, the legal historian Frederick Pollock, in his 1890 politics textbook, *Introduction to the History of the Science of Politics*, defined the history of political theory as simply the 'history of the science of politics' (Pollock 1890). This was a common perspective taken by most commentators up to the 1930s in Britain, and even the United States. Ernest Barker, in his 1929 inaugural Cambridge lecture for one of the first politics chairs, also made this same terminological point. Political science, for Barker, was simply *equivalent* to political theory, understood as 'a method or form of inquiry, concerned with the moral phenomena of human behaviour in political studies', which could then be studied historically (Barker 1978: 18). Herbert Laski also noted in his inaugural lecture, in the London School of Economics, 'nothing in our field of investigation is capable of being rightly understood save as it is illustrated by the process of its development . . . A true politics, in other words, is above all a philosophy of history' (Laski in King (ed.) 1978: 4).[18] For Laski, therefore, 'The past is never dead, because it is capable of recreation at each moment of time' (Laski in King (ed.) 1978: 6). John Gunnell has also commented, with regard to contemporaneous American politics academics, that 'nearly everyone agreed that the role of political theory was to develop the concepts and principles of a scientific political science and the history of political theory was a central part of this project' (Gunnell 1987: 16). The intrinsically historical character of politics was, therefore, for a short time, the accepted currency. Thus, the fundamental point is that the distinction between political theory and history, which became central to later self-conceptions of political theory in the century, did not really exist in the political vocabulary of the earlier part of the twentieth century.

The more stark separation between the history of political theory and political science was not made, at the earliest, until the late 1920s, and even then not very decisively until the 1950s. It is also important to be clear here that this separation between political science and the history of political theory was *also* a separation from normative political theory. Political science, by the 1950s, categorized normative political philosophy as blandly synonymous with the historical dimension. The subsequent internal distinctions between the history of political theory, normative and analytical political philosophy was a later phenomenon again. This latter phenomenon only began, in a somewhat half-hearted form, with the hegemony of the early analytic conceptualist movement in Anglophone philosophy, which had a characteristically ahistorical ontology.[19] The inaptly named 'return to grand normative theory' was not, in fact, a 'return' at all, but rather something *de novo*. There were definitely traces of a past manner of theoretical activity, but this form of political theory was indelibly marked by its time and intellectual circumstances.

A third internal reason for the relation of history to theory, relates to one important philosophical current of the early twentieth century, manifest in the underlying influence of both Idealism and hermeneutics. In the early twentieth century, the work of writers such as Dilthey, Collingwood, and Croce was deeply significant. In these philosophers, history was viewed as the *history of thought*. Although there were variations, within the Idealist and hermeneutic framework, as to exactly how history was regarded, one very general point was common to them all, namely, that the history of theory was profoundly important. For some thinkers, such as Hegel, the history of philosophy was viewed as speculative teleological development of ideas focused on ideas such as freedom. History embodied a rational teleology. For others, such as Collingwood, the speculative dimension was rejected. History was, however, still the history of thought, but it was regarded as an independent mode of understanding with its own unique requirements and perspective. Thus, the history of political theory— as either the teleology of reason or an independent mode of understanding—was seen as crucial. The Idealists and hermeneuticists therefore gave an implicit philosophical imprimatur to the role of history within the human and social sciences.

In terms of *external* contextual reasons for the development of the history of political theory, it is worth noting briefly why academic history itself developed. It grew, as a self-conscious discipline, during the nineteenth century.[20] What united the discipline of history, from the 1860s, and in fact well into the 1930s, was the view that it was focused on national civic education and the grooming of individual moral character (see Soffer 1994: 33). A similar process took place in North American and European universities.[21] There is therefore a more than fortuitous relation between, on the one hand, the rise of universities and the development of historical, literary, legal, and political curricula, and, on the other hand, the rise and consolidation of nation states during the late nineteenth and early twentieth centuries.[22] History was made by national historians for national ends.[23] History was neither focused on modern debate nor social criticism. Contemporary history was avoided. Events and texts were 'frozen with meanings for national ends' (Soffer 1994: 36).[24] Training for students was largely concerned with character formation and good citizenship. The employers of many of these graduates in Britain, in the late nineteenth and early twentieth century, were the India and Colonial Services, diplomatic core and general civil service. Employers wanted graduates with a strong sense of communal ideals and national rectitude. Universities consequently 'successfully transformed a set of values encoded in the concept of "liberal education" into a licensing system for a national elite' (Soffer 1994: 6; see also Condren 1985: 36, n.5).

The same individuals who constructed the history curriculum also promoted the history of political theory. In other words, history set the *tone* of histories of political theory. Consequently, the history of political theory did have a definite role and function, from its inception, and, in fact, well into the twentieth century. This role is something that has been praised, vilified, submerged, and often resurrected. Loosely described, first, it would inform students about an ongoing tradition of 'great' individual thinkers, identified with their 'classic texts'. The concept tradition is deployed, often coupled with a progressive teleology, to hold the whole enterprise together. The great classic texts are marked out for their originality, their systematic coherence, intellectual and moral influence, and the manner in which they dealt with the great *perennial* problems of political existence; second, to instruct students—through the texts—in the great questions and universal moral virtues; third, to educate (overtly or covertly) readers, in national ideals and culture; fourth, to inform them about the way the state has developed (usually in a teleological progressive manner leading up to the twentieth-century liberal democratic state). The genealogy of this whole academic enterprise is comparatively short, a fact that frequently goes unnoticed.

The first text, with secure claims on this approach, was Robert Blakey's two-volume work *A History of Political Literature from the Earliest Times* (1855). No doubt background models for this approach were histories of philosophy and literature. In fact, Blakey viewed the history of political theory as a sub-category of the more general notion of 'literature'. In British universities, the history of political theory emerged falteringly in curricula from the 1870s, usually under the rubric of the moral sciences, history or jurisprudence, and usually from the prompting of historians with comparativist interests, such as Seeley, Pollock, Maitland, and Acton. However, it did not develop vigorously in Britain until the twentieth century.[25] The idea was, however, initially, more self-consciously prosecuted in North America, where politics departments had a more autonomous self-conscious existence from the 1880s. From this period, texts of history of political thought expanded in number in both Britain and America, for a growing market of courses. As one scholar has remarked, on the growth in such texts between 1880 and 1940, that what has now become the traditional objective canon of texts seems to have been itself partly the product of 'the demand for undergraduate textbooks' (Boucher 1989b: 224). In Britain, though, most were still produced initially in history departments well into the 1950s.

In the early twentieth century, the most famous of these early texts was G. H. Sabine's *History of Political Theory*, originally published in 1937 in North America, but then reprinted widely up to the end of the twentieth century (see Easton 1953: 249; Gunnell 1987: 19–20). The timing of its publication is significant. Sabine's commitment to the moral importance of learning about the development of the democratic tradition of the West, in the face of 1930's totalitarianism in both Russia and Germany, embodies the deep underlying ethical and civic educational purpose of the historical perspective. Despite the brief methodological fulminations of the 1970s and 1980s, the same idea has lurked as a subtext in histories of political thought throughout the twentieth century. In fact, those who fulminated most on the method question have ironically performed a similar normative role in differing historical circumstances.[26]

Before moving onto an account of the 'two waves' of debate about the history of political theory in the twentieth century, it is important to note that the debate also relates to wider discussions over the history of philosophy. As mentioned, many twentieth century philosophers have often made a rigid distinction between history and philosophy. In this latter perspective, past philosophers are dealt with in the context of how far they relate, or come up to the requirements of contemporary philosophy. The usual assumption is that the present form of philosophy is the most rigorous, therefore other philosophies must be measured against contemporary strictures. This has largely been the position of the analytic style of philosophy to the present day. Such philosophers have a ready answer to the question as to whether philosophy is closely related to history and that would be a resounding no. History is history and *not* philosophy. However, there are alternative strong philosophical traditions—which overlap with the history of political theory—namely, the Idealist and hermeneutic perspectives. Thus, Dilthey, Collingwood, Oakeshott, and Croce provide a very different reading of the relation of history and philosophy. As Collingwood put it, 'the right way of investigating mind is by the methods of history' (Collingwood 1993: 209). The present discussion will not dwell on this larger debate, although the general character of the analytic response to political theory will be discussed in Part Two.

Turning now to the two waves: the *first* wave developed with theorists such as Leo Strauss, Eric Voegelin, and Hannah Arendt. Their ideas have in fact gone on echoing—in a peculiarly decontextualized manner—up to the close of the twentieth century. The issue that worried these theorists was the decline of politics and political theory. The context of their reflections was usually the critique of political theory by mainstream empirical political science (which will also be explored in the next section), as well as by their deeply personal reactions to German politics and philosophy during the decades leading up to the Second World War (see Gunnell in Farr and Seidelman (eds.) 1993: 182). Arendt and Strauss had both been Martin Heidegger's students in Germany in the 1920s and agonized over his involvement with National Socialism. These theorists also intensely admired classical Greek thought. In Strauss and Arendt, this led to a sense of the critical and moral importance of the great tradition of political philosophy. However, this conception of tradition was commonly underpinned by a distinction between classical and modern political philosophy (or the ancients and the moderns) and a fear of the effects of modern political philosophy, political science, and modern liberalism on the ancient tradition. This change from the ancient to the modern was perceived as a crisis.[27]

The notion of a crisis of the West appeared as a continuous motif in particularly Strauss's writings. The crisis of the West is, in fact, the crisis of political philosophy. The crisis is that the West no longer knows where it is going; it has lost, or is in doubt about its own fundamental values. Modern philosophy contributes to this crisis, by adhering blindly to the relativizing beliefs in both natural science and modern historicism. For Strauss, however, every society needs universal values to remain 'healthy' (Strauss 1977: 3; Bloom 1980: 113). The central motif of classical political philosophy was therefore universal moral values. It focused on the search for the best life and an objective knowledge of the good, both facets denied by historicism and positivism. These classical moral solutions will not though provide any contemporary recipes. For Strauss, only we can find solutions to our problems. But classical theory can be the starting point for the serious consideration of our problems. As Strauss's disciple, Allan Bloom, put it, 'men live more truly and fully in reading Plato and Shakespeare . . . because then they are participating in essential being and are forgetting their accidental lives' (Bloom 1987: 380). Political philosophy therefore aspires to 'build on the foundation laid by classical political philosophy, a society superior in truth and justice' (Strauss 1977: 9). It aspires to a kind of ahistorical foundational wisdom.

However, for Strauss, political philosophy is *not* directly the history of political philosophy. There are two readings of the history of political philosophy in Strauss. The first, corrupting version, is 'historicism', which contends that political philosophy and history cannot ever be separated. Historicism, in alliance with modern political science, undermines genuine political philosophy and turns it into ideology. Thus, for Strauss, 'the decay of political philosophy into ideology reveals itself most obviously in the fact that in both research and teaching, political philosophy has been replaced by the history of political philosophy. This substitution can be excused as a well-meaning attempt to prevent, or at least to delay, the burial of a great tradition' (Strauss 1977: 7–8). When historicism dominates the history of political philosophy, then, for Strauss, the great tradition will inevitably become a series of foolish antiquarian footnotes. The uncorrupted, second version of the history of political philosophy is auxiliary to classical political philosophy. Political philosophy cannot be wholly historically contingent. For Strauss, even if related to historical circumstances, it can still embody a truth, which transcends those circumstances. Every political situation 'contains elements which are essential to all political situations: how else could one intelligibly call these different political situations "political situations" ' (Strauss 1959: 64). The function of the uncorrupted *history* of political philosophy is, therefore, first, to understand the political philosophers as they understood themselves in terms of their original intentions (Strauss 1959: 68; Bloom 1980: 128). As Bloom comments, 'we must put our questions aside and try to find out about what were their questions' (Bloom 1980: 123). Pre-eminently, we need the careful systematic study of texts—'that and not much else' (Bloom 1980: 115). Second, regardless of historical contingency, we must presume that their doctrines may be true and that there is a tradition of such writers with similar aims. As Bloom comments, 'philosophy has, at its peaks, largely been a dialogue between the greats, no matter how far separated in time' (Bloom 1980: 118). For Straussians, texts should therefore move their readers morally. They should be read in the mode of direct address. Such a reading combats the 'impoverishment of the world of experience' (Bloom 1980: 129).

In summary, the first wave of the history of political theory saw a crisis of relativism and nihilism generated by modern philosophy, historicism, and natural science. Genuine history is a moral enterprise, committed to the text and recovering its original intentions, as a source for potential ahistorical universal and foundational truths about the 'human condition', which can act as a groundwork for addressing the sense of crisis. This first wave rose in the 1950s and submerged in the 1960s. Apart from the believers, not many could really take Strauss' conception of apocalyptic crisis very seriously, although some adherents have continued with its central themes till the close of the twentieth century.

The *second* wave developed in the 1970s and declined slowly in the 1990s—although still retaining powerful institutional allegiances to the present day.[28] This second wave, if anything, was committed to something like Strauss's detested historicism. It is often termed 'revisionist history' or the 'new history'. Its main proponents were Quentin Skinner and J. G. A. Pocock, with a very large number of camp followers. Skinner has been probably the more consistently influential of the two. The background influences were R. G. Collingwood, Wilhelm Dilthey, J. L. Austin, H. P. Grice, and John Searle, in other words, an interweaving of Idealism, hermeneutics, and linguistic philosophy. In Pocock's case, Oakeshott and Kuhn were also significant influences, although in subsequent years, the Kuhnian notion of paradigms waned (see Pocock in Pagden (ed.) 1987: 21). Pocock and Skinner also differed on the basic detail of their methodological ideas. However, the underlying unity of the second wave was focused on an outright rejection of the 'purported' history of political theory tradition up to the 1970s. Authors such as John Plamenatz, C. B. Macpherson, and George Sabine, who furnished popular texts on the history of political theory up to the 1970s, were rejected by the new history writings as both theoretically wrong and obsolete.[29] There was also a dismissal of the Namierite idea that all political theory, *per se*, was cant. Political theory *was* important to the new history writers, although it was never quite clear why.

What characterizes this second wave? In the case of Skinner, there are a number of key concerns, which can be divided up in terms of positive appraisals of what should be done, and negative judgements of what had been wrong in previous histories. The first focuses on the necessity of recovering authorial intentions, the second on the criticism of perennial problems. On the positive side, the goal is to understand the meaning of texts as they were understood in their time. On the negative side, an attempt is made to characterize the discipline of the history of theory more narrowly in order to obliterate superfluous purposes. Basically, a historian of political theory cannot argue for something, which the participants themselves could not have understood or uttered. Thinking and communicating are regarded as socially specific activities. Thus, linguistic conventions, traditions, and paradigms are fundamentally constitutive of a reality.

On the positive dimension, the first thing is to recover authorial intentions. Thus, the question is—what was an author doing or intending in writing a text. The interpreter needs to understand both what an author was saying in a particular context and something of the audience to whom it was addressed. Further, this implies knowing what particular linguistic conventions are implied in that context. As Skinner remarks, 'To understand what any given writer may have been *doing in* using some particular concept or argument, we need first of all to grasp the nature and range of things that could recognizably have been done by using that particular concept' (Skinner in Tully (ed.) 1988: 77). Speaking and writing are both viewed as linguistic contextual activities. Following J. L. Austin's work, Skinner argues that one needs to grasp both the locutionary meaning of utterances, and what the speaker was doing with that speech act, namely, what Austin called the illocutionary meaning (see Skinner in Tully (ed.) 1988: 94).

It is worth briefly noting here that intentions are not so central to Pocock's work. Rather, he sees the need to piece together the complex languages or discourses in which texts are articulated. Actions and texts are more open-ended in Pocock than in Skinner's view. Texts have a multitude of possible meanings. Pocock therefore comments that the text may be an 'actor in an indefinite series of linguistic processes' (Pocock in Pagden (ed.) 1987: 30–1). Historians are thus asked to identify the diverse languages *through* which an author operated. Each language game or discourse has its own idioms and idiosyncratic vocabulary. As Pocock comments, 'The historian is in considerable measure an archaeologist; he is engaged in uncovering the presence of various language contents in which discourse has from time to time been conducted' (Pocock in Pagden (ed.) 1987: 23). It is the writer's discourses (earlier Pocock had called them paradigms), which are of primary interest, not just the authorial intentions. However, Pocock adds the qualification here that 'we do not say that the language context is the only context, which gives the speech act meaning and history, though we shall infallibly be accused of having said that; we say only that it is a promising context with which to begin'. He situates his own project as mid-way between Saussure's *langue* and *parole* (Pocock in Pagden (ed.) 1987: 20 and 29). For Pocock, discourse is not an intentional creation and it is considered as prior to speakers and texts. Pocock thus uses specific aspects of texts to illustrate discourses. In this he is more like Oakeshott in seeing philosophy as separate from genuine history (see Boucher 1985: 152). Pocock, in fact, appears to view himself now more as a historian, although not many historians would probably recognize this self-description.

For Skinner, conventions enable the historian to elicit authorial intentions. Conventions, texts, and intentions are therefore equally important. He comments that one needs to 'focus not just on the text to be interpreted but on the prevailing conventions governing the treatment of the issues or themes with which the text is concerned' (Skinner in Tully (ed.) 1988: 77). All utterances are made in a context, which includes linguistic conventions, and a wider range of social and intellectual conventions. This body of conventions makes up what Skinner calls, on a number of occasions, the ideological context. Tully defines Skinners' use of ideology as a 'language of politics defined by its conventions and employed by a number of writers' (Tully 1988: 9). This conventional context, of necessity, incorporates secondary and tertiary literature of a period, to reveal the full structure of conventions. It follows, as Skinner comments, 'if we are interested in . . . the process of ideological formation and change, we cannot avoid involving ourselves in extensive historical inquiries' (Skinner in Tully (ed.) 1988: 101). Consequently, Tully describes Skinner's *Foundations of Modern Political Thought* as 'not only a map of the great political ideologies of early modern Europe, it is also a guide to the location and the ideological and political explanation of the incremental manipulations and grand transformations of them' (Tully 1988: 12). This comment alone, however, seems to undermine many of the methodological points made earlier by Skinner. 'Incremental manipulation' and 'grand transformations' do not quite to fit arguments, which insist on stringent contextualism and the denial of perennial beliefs.

The relation between political ideology and political action, and what forms of political thought and action are involved in disseminating ideological change, are also of key importance to second wave writers. As conventions and ideological contexts change, so do political actions. Theories can vindicate or subvert an order of conventions. As Tully put it, 'Since a political ideology represents a political action . . . to change some of the conventions of the ideology is to change the way in which some of that political action is represented. The manipulated conventions redescribe and so recharacterize the political action' (Tully (ed.) 1988: 11).

The other main dimension of this second wave is the *negative* critique of other modes of doing the history of political thought. This is not only a critique of first wave theories, but also of histories of political thought throughout the twentieth century. It convicts its predecessors of a number serious lapses, particularly that of promoting the idea of perennial truths. They are also accused of a 'mythology of doctrines', that is, writing 'mythologies' not genuine history (Skinner 1969: 7). Second, they are convicted of promoting a 'mythology of coherence', namely, assuming that an author of a classic text must have had a coherent theory. Coherence will thus be supplied by the historian of thought, if it is missing (Skinner 1969: 12 *ff*.). Third, there is 'mythology of prolepsis' (Skinner 1969: 22), that is, focusing on the implications of a text as against its authorial meaning. Fourthly, they are seen to be guilty of the 'mythology of parochialism' (Skinner 1969: 24), that is the familiarity of a particular idea leads the historian to link it teleologically with one in his or her own day. It appears, therefore, that the bulk of the history of political theory has failed miserably during the twentieth century.

There have been many criticisms made of the general character of this second wave, which are difficult to summarize in a short compass. However, on the positive side of his work: the idea of recovering authorial intentions is by no means unique. The bulk of the first wave was committed to it as an approach. Strauss, Arendt, Sabine, and Bloom were quite explicit in using this theme to counter excessive historicism. Both Skinner and Strauss, in fact, see the conventional linguistic context and authorial intentions as crucial. However, for Skinner, it *appears* to be impossible to move beyond the context, whereas, for Strauss, the context and intentions are themselves the *source* of moral universals. Thus, on the same body of basic arguments, Skinner denies and Strauss affirms perennial problems. Yet, the denial of perennial problems raises difficult issues.

The first concerns how we identify a linguistic context? There is little agreement on what is meant by context in the various new histories and how precisely it relates to texts. Thus, how long does a context have to exist before it becomes a context? How does a context hold together? How does one know a context, as opposed to a series of texts? How would one know if something was alien or integral to a context? A context looks more like an arbitrary composite, derived from multiple sources, which is given an honorific unifying title. However, one might still argue that a context is constituted by secondary and tertiary literature. However, by the same revisionist logic, this literature needs a context to be understood; yet, each bit of further literature needs a context, thus, we have a *reductio ad absurdum*. To deny this logic would be self-contradictory. The term context, as such, has no reality and is more of a convenient sociological abstraction. Further, can a full account be given of *any* historical context? How one would know when it was complete, or when it was deficient? If we paused for a moment and reflected on the question—what is the context of European or American thought at this present moment? Surely, the issue of identifying a satisfactory context is just very weird, except on the most impressionistic level?

A second range of problems with the second wave relate to the problem of self-reference. By the logic of their own arguments, second wave texts *must* themselves be historically contingent—unless they have attained an ahistorical *sub specie aeternitatis* position, which they also contend is logically impossible. To grasp the meaning of this second wave of theory we would therefore need to reconstruct the conventions and linguistic context of their own contexualizing histories, before we could trust their judgements about how to do history. Furthermore, their own historical judgements would have no reference beyond their own linguistic context, wherever that begins or ends. One would need to ask what were they trying to say in terms of linguistic conventions, who were their intended audience, and what was the secondary and tertiary literature in their era? The full context of second wave argument is, of course, virtually impossible to identify, thus, things do not look very hopeful in this direction. If it is said that it is too soon to identify their context, then, we should, by their logic, believe nothing that they say, since we have *no* possibility of understanding it or validating it. Further, by their own definitions, their textual work could not provide any insight into the past or future. We could not expect *any* universal methodological truths about how to do the history of political theory. Each piece of methodological writing is only understandable within a particular set of contingent conventions.

If one reversed the reflexive logic here and argued, in effect, that we can actually make philosophical judgements, which have an atemporal reference, qua perennial problems, then certain consequences flow. We might speak, for example, about literature in the past, even in a different context to our own. Yet, this is done in *our* language. What else could it be? Even trying to share the linguistic context of a past is 'sharing' something common. We do not *become* the past or talk to the dead in the language of the dead. We remain in the present. Further, we appear to be able to understand a past, but still not agree with it regardless. Thus, if we can understand, interpret, and articulate a past idea, we can also disagree or agree with it. We can dismiss it or employ it as valuable. We can therefore use present standards to make judgements about past concepts or values. We have, in other words, a perennial concept, which the new wave theories standardly deny. The alternative to this is the contextual logic of the second wave arguments: to insist on past linguistic contexts (which can only be understood within those past linguistic contexts, and never in terms of our present terms). This means that the past is always impossible to understand or judge. By definition, we would have no linguistic access to it. We have, in fact, a battery of arguments, deployed by second wave theories, to convince us of the irrelevance of past thought for present political theory. This was the root of Skinner's critique of Plamenatz and Sabine. As John Dunn put it, 'I simply cannot conceive of constructing an analysis of any issue in contemporary political theory around the affirmation or negation of anything which Locke says about political matters' (quoted in Tuck 1985: 82). John Locke's thoughts on property or natural rights are therefore irrelevant to the present. Dunn has now performed a *volte-face* on this issue; however, his earlier strange views are still not without support.[30]

However, Skinner's erstwhile admirers, James Tully and Richard Tuck, in their writings have also forced some distance from him on this issue, Tuck remarking in his *Philosophy and Government* (1993) book that 'the better our historical sense of what those [seventeenth century] conflicts were, the more often they seem to resemble modern ones' (Tuck 1993: xii). Surrounding such debates are also a series of problems concerning the role of history. The core issue is focused on the question: can political theorists really disentangle themselves from the complex histories and structures of their own political cultures and would they even want to disentangle themselves? It is clear, for example, that the bulk of what may be termed normative political theory in the twentieth century, to the present moment, is prepared to plunder mercilessly past texts for arguments or values, without the slightest blush for methodological rectitude. John Rawls associated himself with Kant, Nozick with Locke, and Hayek with Adam Smith and David Hume. This is a well-tried strategy. What can the methodologically purist historian of political theory say to this strategy? The usual response is to say that history and normative political theory are different activities and neither the twain shall meet. Ironically, this more or less agrees with the judgement of many conceptualist analytic philosophers. However, the cost of denying any possibility of perennial problems can be high.[31]

However, should one be concerned about the truth of what one studies? In one sense, those 'impurists' (those who plunder past thinkers for present arguments) are concerned about truth. The 'purist' historian of political theory does not seem so concerned with this question. However, why are certain thinkers or texts chosen in the first place by the purist? What is it about these texts or thinkers, which should focus our attention? Furthermore, what is the present status of *our* arguments, even our methodological arguments? What truth-status do they have? Every argument becomes historian's fodder once spoken or written. In one sense, in judging the past and what is relevant in the past, we are taking a stand about what is true. However, this is something that we apparently want to deny to our forbears, that is, their views may also have some truth content.

One final puzzling aspect of the arguments concerning the study of the history of political theory, in the original Skinnerian sense, is exactly *why* one does it? What can be learnt from studying it? The older practitioners of the history of political theory had a ready answer, which the second wave would have found deeply disagreeable, that is, studying the past is a form of civic or national education, or, a way of gaining access to perennial debates about universal virtues. However, the second wave answers to this question are unusually sparse. One answer is that studying the history of political theory, although having no substantive reference to the present, can make us more rounded or more perceptive individuals. In other words, the function of studying the history is to advance self-understanding in the present—although presumably once *this* has been written or spoken, it also becomes a historical remark, which needs contextualizing. It is also not exactly clear how studying the past in this manner advances our present self-understanding, or makes us more rounded persons, or why we ought to be concerned about it.

When one approaches the negative judgements of the second wave (on previous histories of political thought), then the whole theory begins to look deeply shaky. Basically the second wave theories created a straw man. As many critics have pointed out, even the most cursory reading of the majority of historians of political thought in the twentieth century, simply does not fit the procrustean picture drawn in the new history. Virtually all historians of political theory have been concerned about intentions, within, possibly looser, conceptions of context. Further, any close reader of Skinner will immediately notice that his own 'historical writings demonstrate, . . . that he is prepared to ignore many of his negative conclusions in order to facilitate historical practice' (Boucher 1984: 296). His *Foundations of Modern Political Thought* illustrates this point time and again. All of his negative myths of coherence, mythical writing, prolepsis, and parochialism, the use perennial ideas and the concept of influence, are *all* on show in his substantive political thought writings.[32] This is absolutely undeniable. For example, the above two-volume work, is committed to the theme of the 'process by which the modern concept of the State [capitalized by Skinner] came to be formed'. This concept of the state is conceptualized 'in distinctively modern terms—as the sole source of law and legitimate force within a territory' (Skinner 1978: vol 1, x). It is this perennial, coherent, 'evolving' concept which underpins his political thought books. This 'state' contention makes Skinner look both very much of a traditionalist, in terms of twentieth century histories of political thought, and also, ironically, very much of a modern contributor to the *Staatslehre* tradition. Essentially, he views the evolution of premodern and modern political theory through the concept of the state. There is nothing intrinsically wrong here, except that it bears no relation to his methodological claims.

In sum, the second wave is now a faltering wave—in fact in some ways it has already collapsed in all but name. As others have commented, what purports to be a new method is really just another contestable 'philosophical argument about interpretation' (Gunnell 1987: 102 and Hollis in Tully (ed.) 1988: 181). This second wave, because of its highly significant publishing success and institutional recognition, still has a powerful presence in the academy. However, the dangers of this are apparent in the self-congratulatory writings of some disciples. Consequently, when a historian of political thought comments that the contributors to an edited book 'are committed to the view, which this series is interested to advance, that ideas can only be studied in what the series editors [that is Skinner et al.] call "their concrete contexts" ', and that 'this is an explicit, and now familiar rejection of those older modes of intellectual history which studied texts in terms of sources and influences' (Pagden (ed.) 1987: 1–2), then, one senses that many are in need of a 'wake-up' call. When a highly-contested philosophical approach concerning interpretation has become so institutionalized that it produces such statements of orthodoxy, it is time for a disruptive reformation.

There is one further, more tangential, aspect to the second wave, namely another movement, which links in indirectly with certain dimensions of the second wave. This is the, mainly German, *Begriffsgeschichte* movement. The key theoretician here is Rheinhardt Kosellek (Kosellek 1985). The *Begriffsgeschichte* method sees concepts as reflective of external events and practices. It argues that there are internal features of language and meaning that shape the ways in which we gain access to the social world. The method consequently involves an immensely sophisticated treatment of concepts at both the analytical and historical levels. The *Geschichtliche Grundbegriff* task is thus to map concepts over a specified period. As yet, the focus has largely been on the German-speaking world during a specific period—1750–1850—which the *Begriffsgeschichte* group calls the *Sattelzeit* period (see Koselleck 1985). Some contemporary popularisers of *Begriffsgeschichte*, such as Melvin Richter, have tried, with commendable zeal, to invoke or stimulate a dialogue between the second wave theorists and the German writers (Richter 1995; Richter Symposium 1999). Despite Richter's efforts and some half-hearted attempts at exploring the links, the debate has never really taken off in Britain and North America (Ball, Farr, and Hanson (eds.) 1989; and more significantly Ball 1988). As yet, it seems only to have had a very marginal impact on the Anglophone academic world. For Skinner, and second wave writers, however, there are *no* histories of concepts, as such, only the uses of concepts in contingent arguments or discourses, in specific contextualized moments. Given that the focus of the *Begriffsgeschichte* is seldom contextual and tends to rely on source materials, such as philosophical or theoretical texts, dictionaries, and encyclopaedias, which are regarded with suspicion by the new wave theorists, the prospects for fruitful cross-fertilization between these accounts does not look hopeful.[33]

In conclusion, the history of political philosophy has served a number of different roles and functions during the twentieth century. Some of those bear upon the status of history itself as a discipline, in the late nineteenth and twentieth centuries, others are internal to the discipline itself. Initially, in terms of the external cultural and political setting in which it developed, the history of political theory was viewed as part of the education of the citizen, particularly the professional citizen, teaching virtue and leadership qualities through the great classic books and providing sustenance for character development. It was also, by the early twentieth century, perceived to be an important aspect of training in civic awareness and national consciousness. The history of political theory thus embodied the narrative of the nation.

Internally, the value of the history of political philosophy was seen to be its embodiment of the fundamental ideas of political science from the Greeks to the present day. This was also integral to the metier of *Staatslehre*. The conceptual separation between institutional state theory, classical normative political theory, and the history of political theory was not significant in the early decades of the twentieth century. The importance of history, qua the history of thought, was also reinforced by philosophical Idealist thinkers. For many such thinkers, the history of theory either embodied a teleological concern with the realization of certain ideas like freedom or human self-realization, or, alternatively, an exemplification of the importance of the historical mode of understanding in itself. Thus, the history of theory had a form of philosophical imprimatur. The crises of the 1930s and 1940s focused historians of political theory on the values implicit in the apparent embattled Western liberal 'tradition'. The practice of the discipline was seen to enable intelligent citizens to understand the deep operative ideas implicit within liberal democratic institutions and thus confront the menace of totalitarianism. This was particularly the case in much of the political thought literature produced during this period. By the 1950s, the discipline moved into what I have called, the 'first wave' of anxiety. Partly as a result of internal criticism from empirical science, and partly as a result of anxieties over a perceived crisis of confidence in the West, the history of political theory emphasized the theme that it was concerned with a search for the ultimate knowledge of the right order. The history of theory was thus seen experiencing a process of decline through modernity. For Arendtians and Straussians, particularly, the need was to rediscover the universal virtues of the classics by careful attention to texts, contexts, and authorial intentions, but avoiding, at the same time, the trap of historicism. This entailed opening old questions like that between the ancients and the moderns.

By the 1960s and early 1970s, the discipline settled for a short period. However, potential divisions and problems were only under the surface. There were roughly three perceptions of its role during this period, which continued until the end of the century. The first, retained ideas from earlier periods, and saw the history of political theory as a continuous canonical tradition, which addressed the 'great questions', and could even therapeutically diagnose and address the modern ills. Straussians and Arendtians have maintained their own views on this issue. Analytic-minded philosophers enunciated a second response (which was also largely the view of many political scientists during the 1950s and 1960s), that is, the history of political theory could be viewed as a useful resource of testable hypotheses and conceptual conundrums. We could therefore pick up Machiavelli or Hobbes and debate with them and consider whether they were offering sound arguments. In this sense, the historical side was largely sloughed off and the analytic aspect moved to the fore. Hobbes became a proto-rational choice theorist, Machiavelli a proto-realist on power, Kant became the godfather of human rights or the friendly uncle of cosmopolitan ethics, and so forth. This was lineage characteristic of more analytic-inclined histories of political theory in the twentieth century. The third view was largely a continuation of an earlier Idealist theme, by other means, namely Marxist history. History was seen to have teleological significance (in this case a materialist teleology), which linked the whole historical enterprise. The history of political theory was thus significant as part of an underlying historical pattern of human emancipation. Work, such as C. B. Macpherson's *The Political Theory of Possessive Individualism* (1962), exemplified this mode of argumentation.

By the later 1970s, however, the second wave developed. This was primarily concerned with historical method, in terms of a focus on authorial intentions and a rigorous contextualism. The effect of this movement was to heighten sensitivity to the methods through which we study texts and contexts. This was the positive contribution of the second wave. However, some scholars have also seen this as the 'real transformation' of the history of political theory during the twentieth century, although transformation from *what* remains inchoate. As mentioned earlier, if one examines the substantive work of this second wave it is not really so different from the preoccupations of earlier histories. As one scholar has remarked on this movement, 'new histories of political thought can be viewed, not as radical departures from, but as defences of the last bastions of the traditional approaches to the study of the history of political thought against the encroachment of social science upon the sphere of historical understanding' (Boucher 1985: 258).

EMPIRICAL POLITICAL THEORY

The gist of empirical political theory is concerned with making generalizations about political phenomena and constructing testable hypotheses from which predictions can be made. It embodies three linked claims: the first is the more general one, that politics is about informal day to day activity, mundane decision-making, power and the allocations of resources. The corollary of this is that politics, at root, is neither overtly institutional nor theoretical. The second claim is that such activity can be explained in a manner which has parallels with the explanatory nature of the natural sciences. Third, such explanatory social scientific accounts can not only take over many, if not all, of the functions or roles previously performed by classical, historical, and institutional political theory. It could test the claims of such earlier theories either by falsifying or corroborating them. It could also offer valid recommendations, on the basis of established corroborated empirical evidence, as to where policy might proceed in future. In other words, empirical theory takes over (on a firmer ground) the role of institutional and political design. This even supersedes normativism. At its peak of confidence, empirical political theory imagined that it could literally *become* the whole of political theory. Empirical theory is therefore the *telos* of political theory itself. Although many recognized this at the time as a 'pipe dream', it is nonetheless important to realize the strength of this contention for its votaries.

This section will first briefly indicate the relation of empirical theory with the previous accounts of theory. Second, given that empirical theory developed under the rubric of 'political science', this latter term will also be briefly clarified. Third, the discussion will shift to an examination of the behavioural movement, which contains the most optimistic formulation of empirical political theory. This will also entail a cursory discussion of the idea of positivism. Fourth, the decline of the empirical approach, or, at least, the decline of its imperial ambitions, will be considered in the light of critical responses and the development of 'post-behaviouralism'. In this context, there will be a succinct discussion of the after shocks of empirical theory on political theory. The main after shock is rational choice theory.

The shape of empirical theory in the 1950s was premised largely on a rejection of both institutional state theory, historical and traditional normative theory—except where they could be shown to contain an empirically-verifiable content. Institutional state theory was seen to be hidebound by its formal attachment to institutions and the historical comparative method. The task was to consider informal behaviour. The state also was seen, by many empirical theorists, as too vague and imprecise a concept. Further, the bulk of classical political theory was considered a body of highly questionable unverifiable assumptions. The only viable substance to classical theory was a very limited range of testable hypotheses. The history of this body of questionable assumptions was therefore considered as innocuous antiquarianism. At this point, as mentioned, there was a strong suggestion that political science *was* political theory, in the sense that all the traditional senses of the term 'political theory' had been vacated. This perspective on political theory, particularly in America, had a strong grip until the late 1960s, when it came under criticism. However, one should not imagine by any means that the issues were resolved. They merely faded from discussion and could well arise again.

Second, given the close correlation between empirical theory and political science, it is important to get some purchase on the development of the idea of 'political science' itself. There are three uses of the term 'political science', which were all prevalent during the late nineteenth century. The first, and original use dates back to late eighteenth century thinkers, such as Montesquieu, Condorcet, Adam Smith, Adam Ferguson, and David Hume, where it was usually understood as the 'science of the legislator'. The Scottish Enlightenment thinkers were particularly significant here. In fact, other areas, like political economy, were frequently viewed as a subset of political science. Adam Smith, for example, in his *Wealth of Nations*, described 'political economy' as a 'branch of the science of a statesman or legislator' (Smith 1979: 428). There was therefore little or no demarcation of what might now be regarded as separate disciplines. Smith's *Wealth of Nations* blends political economy, moral philosophy, political theory, and history as part of a unified enterprise. The term 'political science' was picked up by North American commentators, from the vocabulary of the Scottish Enlightenment, and used in debates over the new Constitution and Republic.[34]

Political science was also linked to a more general demand for 'social science'. One major intellectual input into this process was the Enlightenment itself. It is problematic to generalize about the Enlightenment, given its very differing manifestations across Europe and North America (see Haakonssen 1995; Schmidt 2000). Minimally, though, many Enlightenment thinkers were making an effort to grasp human affairs through the open use of reason, in order to perceive identifiable and verifiable causal patterns. There was, in other words, a greater appetite for empirical facts concerning nature, human nature, and society. Theorists were often inspired by success of Newtonian physics, and the new 'experimental philosophy', in searching for these patterns. There were, for these diverse writers, therefore parallels between the science of nature and the science of politics. For Hume, for example, 'It is universally acknowledged that there is a great uniformity among the actions of men, in all nations and ages, and that human nature remains the same, in its principles and operations. The same motives always produced the same actions: The same events follow from the same causes' (Hume 1975: 83). Inconstancy of human action was 'no more than what happens in the operation of the body, nor can we conclude anything from the one irregularity, which will not follow equally from the other' (Hume 1981, Book II, Part III, Section 1: 403–4). Thus, theorists, such as Hume, Turgot, and Montesquieu, believed in the possibility of causal social laws. Political science was also viewed as an 'applied science', which could spawn social projects for social and political improvement. It could potentially show how to increase the happiness of state populations. Thus, as many theorists of the period urged, every government concerned to maximize the pleasure and minimize the pain of its citizens, should take serious note of political science. This early conception of political science was though still inclusive of—what we would now regard as—separate disciplines. Sound moral precepts were regarded as both morally obligatory and empirically correct, that is, for human nature to achieve its political ends. Political science was consequently regarded as a subtle blending of moral and empirical generalizations. Only political economy came nearer to what we might now regard as 'empirical science', namely, creating empirical generalizations, which did not have to be necessarily linked with moral precepts.[35]

The second view of political science reflects the development of the idea of political studies in the late nineteenth century. This use of political science traded on a perception of the classical Greek view, where political science was, quite literally, the 'science of the polis'. Political science was therefore a basic synonym for both classical political theory and institutional theory. There was, though, a growing awareness of the significance of political science as a more uniquely empirical approach, but it was still regarded with scepticism. Ernest Barker (the first professor of political science in Britain) noted, in his inaugural lecture, that 'I am not altogether happy about the term "science". It has been vindicated so largely, and almost exclusively, for exact and experimental study of natural phenomena . . . I shall use it, as Aristotle . . . to signify a method or form of inquiry by the name of Political Theory' (Barker in King (ed.) 1978: 18). In this sense, theorizing about politics meant the systematic linkage of ideas about politics. Barker, and many others, considered that this is what Plato's and Aristotle's work on politics had been concerned with. Such a science blended empirical and more abstract normative considerations. This use of political science also characterized the *Staatslehre* tradition up to the 1920s, in Europe and North America. Political science therefore *meant* systematic institutional political theory. However, *Staatslehre* itself also began to be regarded as suspect during this later period. Given that it tended to unify legal, political, historical, and philosophical ideas, it also suffered from the increasing emphasis on the segmentation of disciplinary areas in the early twentieth century. In general, therefore, despite Ernest Barker's nostalgic appeal, this more inclusive notion of political science, qua *Staatslehre*—as closely linked to classical political theory—was fading fast.

The third use of political science developed from the 1920s. It is here that we find the groundwork for both the apparent separation of political theory and political science and subsequent attempts at the reabsorption of political theory *into* the imperium of empirical theory. This third use also forms the backdrop in the 1950s to the sense of spiritual crisis in political theory that pervaded the writings of Strauss, Arendt, and Voegelin.[36] This third conception was an open attempt, in tandem with other social sciences such as sociology and anthropology, to emulate the methods and achievements of the natural sciences. It not only separated out normative and historical political theory from political science, but also led, in some cases, to the attempt to colonize the whole concept of political theory. For some, therefore, political theory *became* political science. This latter notion still pervades some American conceptions of political theory, particularly in its rational choice mode—often now called 'positive political theory'.

This third sense of political science became, for a time during the twentieth century, the dominant use. During the late 1920s a loose sense of identity began to develop in the social sciences in America.[37] This third sense developed in North America in two stages.[38] The first stage, from the 1920s up to 1940s, has been seen as a prelude to behaviouralism. Largely under the leadership of Charles Merriam in Chicago University, the politics-profession in North America began to turn its attention away from institutional and historical study towards more empirical and quantitative techniques.[39] Large political science conferences were held in Chicago between 1923 and 1925 devoted to the new empirical 'science of politics', which, in the words of one commentator, converted 'virtually every leader of the profession to the behavioural persuasion' (Jensen in Lipset (ed.) 1969: 5). Chicago, under Merriam, subsequently became a centre of this new scientific approach to politics. Under Merriam's academic leadership graduate students such as Leonard White, V. O. Key, Gabriel Almond, Harold Lasswell, Herbert Simon, and David Truman, amongst many others, devoted their talents to this new empirical discipline. This earlier period was, on one level, reacting to the legalism, institutionalism, and comparativism of the earlier phase. However, an interest also developed in a more strict approach to informal behaviour, focused on public opinion surveys, voting patterns, and socialization processes. This still entailed a blend of empirical political science with continuing concerns about the normative importance of democracy.

The second stage focused on behavioural political science, which had a powerful impact in the 1950s and 1960s period. This had a far more immediate and longer term effect in America than in Britain or Europe. Disciplines like politics, sociology, and anthropology, all became enthralled with the prospect of attaining greater scientific empirical rigour.[40] For proponents of behaviouralism one should distinguish *behaviourism* and *behaviouralism*. Both shared the belief that the approach of the natural sciences was most fitting for the study of humans. However, for

David Easton, for example, political science 'has never been behaviouristic' (Easton in Farr and Seidelman (eds.) 1993: 294; see also Farr in Farr, Dryzek, and Leonard (eds.) 1995: 202). For Easton, *behaviourism* 'refers to a theory in psychology about human behaviour', as embodied in the work of psychologists such as J. B. Watson and B. F. Skinner, the founder of operant conditioning. There is a form of physiological reductionism in behaviourism, which behaviouralists found uncongenial. Politics in terms of attitudes, meanings, and beliefs could not be reduced in this manner. However, political theory critics of behaviouralism, such as Dante Germino, were quite clear that there was little to choose between the two empiricisms and the distinction was merely rhetorical (see Germino 1967: 193–5).

David Easton, in a retrospective article, saw seven main themes within *behaviouralism*: a concern with discoverable uniformities in political behaviour; to be able to test and verify empirical generalizations; to focus on techniques for acquiring and interpreting empirical data (i.e. questionnaires, interviews, sampling, regression analysis, factor analysis, and rational modelling); the precise quantification and measurement of empirical data; the analytical separation of values or evaluative concerns from factual data[41]; the concern to systematize the relation between research and theory; and, finally, the aim to engage, as far as possible, in pure science, but with an eventual eye to 'utilize political knowledge in the solution of practical problems of society' (see also David Easton in Monroe (ed.) 1997: 14). The central preoccupations thus became the recording and quantifying of political behaviour. Political systems with input and output functions replaced the study of states; the study of democracy became electoral behaviour and public opinion quantification and surveys; pressure or interest group behaviour replaced the study of societies.

The behavioural movement of the 1950s coincided with other important developments. There was, first, the coincidence with the end-of-ideology movement, which repudiated both normative political theory and political ideology (in some cases the two terms were regarded as synonymous). This involved some degree of self-satisfaction with the role and achievements of liberal democracy in practice. Ideology and normative theory had thus both become redundant (see Vincent 1995, ch. 1). There was, in addition, a clear belief in the 1950s, amongst a generation that had lived through the 1930s and 1940s, with the wars, Gulags, show trials, Nazism, Jewish pogroms, and Stalinism, that ideological or normative-based politics embodied dangerous delusions. Ideologies might serve a function in developing immature societies, yet in industrialized democratic societies they no longer served anything more than a decorative role. Consensus and convergence on basic aims had been achieved in liberal democracies. Most of the major parties in industrialized societies had achieved, in the welfare mixed economy structure, the majority of their reformist aims. The left had accepted the dangers of excessive state power and the right had accepted the necessity of the welfare state and the rights of working people. As Seymour Martin Lipset remarked, 'This very triumph of the democratic social revolution of the West ends domestic politics for those intellectuals who must have ideologies or utopias to motivate them to political action' (Lipset 1969*a*: 406; see also Bell 1965). With basic agreement on political values achieved, politics became focused on more peripheral pragmatic adjustment, GNP, prices, wages, the public-sector borrowing requirement. All else was gesture and froth. As Lipset commented 'The democratic struggle will continue, but it will be a fight without ideologies' (Lipset 1969a: 408).

The 'end of ideology' also coincided with the heroic age of sociology—a science free from all superstition and yet embodying commitments to freedom and liberal democracy. In the social sciences of the 1950s, ideology *was* the foremost superstition, which needed unravelling. The development of empirical social science therefore demanded a value-free rigour, scepticism, empirical verification, or falsification, unsullied by the emotional appeals of ideological or normative political theory. A positivistic separation of facts and values lurked beneath all these judgements. In addition, the end of ideology coincided with the 'death of political philosophy' movement (which will be discussed in Part Two), consensus politics in Britain, and finally with the more disturbing phenomenon McCarthyite anti-communist purges in North America.

Apart from some extreme adherents of behaviourism, positivistic political science did not always demand the complete elimination of normative theory and ideology. There were those who would have liked to see this elimination, or, at least, transmutation into rigorous empirical political theory. However many political scientists, such as David Easton, Robert Lasswell, Robert Dahl, Karl Deutsch, and Heinz Eulau, had been trained initially as more traditional political theorists. They did not therefore construe political theory as a total waste of time. The historical and normative vision could offer hypotheses for empirical testing. In this sense, the hard contrast, which occasionally appears between political theorists and political scientists can be misleading.[42]

For John Gunnell, the crucial factor defining the stance of behavioural theory, was tied to the political theory writings of the 1920s and 1930s émigré generation, including figures such as Strauss, Arendt, Brecht, Adorno, and many others, who adopted a deeply-critical stance to political science, associating it with individualistic liberalism, relativism, potential nihilism, and social crisis. In this critical context, political scientists, for Gunnell, 'eventually felt constrained to make a choice' (Gunnell 1993b: 220). In the end, this was not so much a debate about method, as about the culture of liberalism and democracy. Gunnell thus notes that by 'the early 1960s, the conflict was not simply one between individuals such as Easton and Strauss. It had been passed to a new generation of scholars who had been trained in the new ways of political theory, denied by the émigrés and by the founders of the behavioural movement, and who had already begun to lose sight of the roots of the conflict between the paradigms into which they had been initiated' (Gunnell 1993b: 250).[43]

The intellectual background to behavioural political science lay in the popularity of what might loosely be termed positivism in the twentieth century. One of the leading philosophers of Viennese positivism, Carnap, was teaching in Chicago during the 1950s. A new generation of political scientists became familiar with this philosophical position. Positivism gelled with the idea of a genuine 'empirical political theory'. Positivism was essentially though a broader programme tied up with a more general conception of science. Theories in the natural sciences were viewed as unified systems of explanation, incorporating laws, which were 'controllable by factual evidence'

(Nagel 1961: 4). The basic contention was that scientific theories could grasp an objective reality through a neutral observation language. Reality was definitely *not* structured or constituted by natural science theory. Theories tell us, in a moderately detached way, *about* a reality.[44] Explanations in the natural sciences, utilizing a neutral observation language, could thus be defined as systematically related propositions about an external reality, propositions which may, in certain contexts, be described as laws supported by empirical evidence. The general framework within which this kind of theory functions is usually called positivism. Political science, from the 1950s particularly, stressed this approach.

The concept positivism is, however, complex. It denotes two broad ideas. First, it indicates those who accept the designation positivist, such as Auguste Comte or the Viennese logical positivism movement—although the latter are occasionally cited as neo-positivist. Comte's legacy—especially via positivist sociology—formed a background set of beliefs, which resonate with later positivist sympathizers in the twentieth century. Comte's idea that positive science (or philosophy) would triumph ultimately over metaphysics and religion (both the latter being viewed as prior, more primitive, stages of human development); his insistence on a clear boundary between empirically-tested facts and imaginary theoretical constructions; his strong belief in progress through science; and, his assertion of the linkage between moral and material progress (i.e. the knowledge that science provides would allow all manner of technological control in both the natural and the social and political fields), all impacted on early twentieth century positivist theory.

The second sense of positivism, which reasserts many of the Comteian ideals, embodies a more general adherence to certain epistemological theses, for example: the unity of the sciences; the belief that the only valid standard of knowledge we have lies either in the empirical sciences or logic and mathematics; the assumption of the reality of sense impressions; the conception of a scientific theorist as a dispassionate observer who never asserts anything which has not been empirically proved; an intense dislike and mistrust of metaphysical thought; adherence to a notion of philosophy as analysis, and its being parasitic upon science; the acceptance of the clear distinction between fact and value; more specifically, the belief that the natural and social sciences share a certain common methodology; also the belief in a growing body of empirically-tested positive knowledge.

There have been *two* broad manifestations of this latter positivist tendency this century. The first relates to the neo-Kantian distinction between theoretical and practical reason, a distinction that is supposed to make room for autonomy and moral judgement. Increasingly neo-Kantianism, in the twentieth century, became sceptical of the moral autonomy that Kant had postulated. Values became increasingly suspect. Facts though were certain. This distinction became a crucial plank in the neo-Kantianism behind Max Weber's sociology work and his distinctions between value free social science and moral discourse. Weber was no simple-minded positivist. Moral and religious values were of importance to individuals, but he still adhered to the idea that there was a clear heterogeneity between facts and values and that science had no answers to the question how we ought to live. Under Nietzsche's tutelage,

Weber raised the question: could there be any rational foundation for our basic values? For Weber the fact that he could not answer this question was a matter of anxiety. The other positivist manifestation—which we are most familiar with—is what might be termed the Anglo-Saxon 'liberal social science perspective', which adopts the positivist position, often on consequentialist grounds. There is something more Comtian and utilitarian, than neo-Kantian, in this latter approach. However, it still contains all the expected positivist components. The separation between facts and values, particularly, is foundational. David Easton's contemporaneous comment here is quite typically positivist, 'The factual aspect of a proposition refers to a part of reality; hence it can be tested by reference to the facts. In this way we check its truth. The moral aspect of a proposition, however, expresses only the emotional response of an individual . . . Although we can say that the aspect of a proposition referring to a fact can be true of false, it is meaningless to characterize the value aspect of a proposition in this way' (Easton 1953: 221).

In summary, the concept of political theory aimed at by behaviouralists was seen to be value free and objective. The overt aim was to emulate the natural sciences, namely, to collect empirical data, discover correlations, draw up generalizations, and formulate testable theories, which allowed prediction. As one exponent, George Homans, put it, 'As we have come to accept . . . the standards of natural science for testing the truth of propositions, so we should take more seriously [in the social sciences] the standards of natural science in explanation. In that we have been laggard' (Homans 1967: 28). It is no surprise in this context that political behaviour could take on the alluring shape of the natural world—embodying empirical facts, which could be described and studied.

The general conception of the theorist here was that of a neutral observer who carefully describes and explains the objective world. The function of the theorist was not to interpret the world, but rather to explain it through rigorously-tested categories. In general, empirical theory resisted any historical, normative, metaphysical, or ethical presence. Values were seen in the context of emotive responses. Facts were regarded as preconstituted givens—that is, prior to theory and representation. Empirical theories observe, explain, generalize, and establish causal relations. Theories, in effect, order the empirical facts in a comprehensible manner. The substance of such empirical theories was often initially drawn from behavioural psychology, neo-classical economics, systems theory, mathematical modelling, and the like. Such theories explain political behaviour outside the framework of political ideas, ideologies, or institutional frameworks. This tendency became the more dominant method of the discipline up until the late 1960s, although, as stressed, it has always had a much stronger following in North American political studies.

Yet, it is also important to emphasize here that, in the understanding of empirical theory, everything that was of importance in normative classical and historical notions of political theory, namely, a clear perception of the reality of politics, an understanding and explanation of its processes and a unambiguous set of prescriptions for how society should be organized, were *all* present in the aspirations of empirical theory. Social change and reform were an integral part of the vision of empirical theory.

Science was viewed as a social instrument. Thus, normative and historical theory in this context, were literally superfluous.

Consequently, David Easton and a number of North American political scientists were clear that political theory had, in future, to be much more empirically rigorous in order to even survive academically. Easton, in his famous article, 'The Decline of Political Theory', saw the majority of classical normative political theorists as simply academic parasites, feeding on past ideas and retailing antiquarian useless information about past values. Herbert Simon, at the same time, bewailed that 'there will be no progress in political philosophy if we continue to think and write in the loose, literary, metaphysical style... The standard of rigour that is tolerated in political theory would not receive a passing grade in an elementary course in logic' (Simon 1952: 494–6). Political theory needed to mutate into empirical political theory. This is the complete reversal of Ernest Barker's lament, in his 1928 inaugural lecture, where political science *becomes* normative and institutional theory. In Easton's vision, a purified normative and historical political theory *becomes* empirical political theory. As William C. Mitchell signalled optimistically in 1969, political theory in future 'will become increasingly logical, deductive, and mathematical. In terms of its content we will make increasing use of economic theory, game theory, decision theory, welfare economics, and public finance' (Mitchell in Lipset (ed.) 1968: 129).[45]

Oddly, Mitchell's comment is not too distant from the conclusions of Brian Barry's 1990s essay, 'The Strange Death of Political Philosophy', where he identifies, anachronistically, the hopeful lines of future political theory as studies of voting behaviour, game theory, welfare economics, and value analysis (Barry 1991). However, in Barry's case, this is more of a general alliance with economic analysis. The oddity is that this latter judgement is written by a normatively inclined political theorist who worked through part of the earlier behavioural phase. In Barry's case, though, it is more of a reaction to the impoverished nature of Oxford analytical political theory, in the 1960s period, and the woeful shortcomings (as he perceived it) of the history of political theory as an approach. However, Barry's odd assessment of future developments in theory is neither the kind of suggestion that gets the pulse racing, nor does it actually represent what really took place in the last two decades of the twentieth century.

Since the 1970s, and the so-called 'post-behavioural revolution', there has been more circumspection about the 'scientific' position. Most empirical theorists in this period became more hesitant. In fact, Easton, the doyenne of the earlier behavioural persuasion, recategorized himself as 'post-behavioural' (see Easton 1953, 2nd edition 1971, Epilogue, Part A). For Easton, the reasons for this post-behavioural development lie within the criticisms of the counter culture movements of the late 1960s, the utter inability of the behavioural movement to deal with the complex normative issues arising out of the Vietnam war and the detailed civil rights debates, all of which gripped the minds of most students studying politics.[46] Behavioural political science had no way of addressing the deep social, moral, and legal debates concerning gender, war, race, rights, and social justice that dominated the late 1960s and 1970s moral and political arguments. Political science seemed to be completely mute on such issues.

Contrary to the basic premises of behavioural theory, ideology, and normative theory did seem to be more effective in addressing such issues.

However, it was also argued by a number of political theorists, during the 1970s, that empiricism was both a challengeable epistemological and ontological thesis. In fact, the epistemology revealed the character of the ontology. Empirical political theory was a clear example of a deeply-embedded ontology. It revealed not so much any foundational truths about politics, as certain embedded and unchallenged ways of understanding our 'political being'. Thus, empirical political theory had to be considered as just another epistemology. It was a philosophically-contestable epistemology, amongst other epistemologies. The basic foundational distinctions between, for example, explanation and interpretation, or facts and values, made within the epistemology of empirical theory, were not therefore categorically true. They were, conversely, philosophically-challengeable assumptions. In this context, empirical political theory began to lose its privileged and hegemonic status.

The above point was further underscored by critical developments in the philosophy of science. Reflection on the methods of natural science did not cease with the claims of hypothetico-deductive methods or logical positivism. The collective phenomenon of 'post-empiricist science', developed in writers such as Thomas Kuhn, Michael Polanyi, Peter Winch, Paul Feyerabend, and Mary Hesse, which grew over the 1970s and 1980s, raised a new series of detailed questions about the way in which we view natural science explanation and by default all empirical theories. Western science, as envisaged within this post-empiricist programme, was not the high point of civilization and human knowledge, conversely, it was an epistemological moment.[47] As such, we do, in fact, have a great deal to learn from careful and sensitive examination of different cultures and distinct knowledge structures. We also need to pay more careful attention to self-reflexive critique within our own systems of knowledge, that is to say, purportedly objective empirical data is not, in reality, so easily detachable from theoretical models. Interpretations can have a constitutive effect. Theories can be seen, ironically, as the facts of natural science. This post-empiricist view of science throws considerable doubt on the projects of verification, covering law theory and hypothetico-deductive methods—all pervasive in behavioural and empiricist investigations.

Although the post-empiricist programme did not deny the separate role of natural science language, a number of points were made which linked, fortuitously, with ideas in both interpretive and normative theorizing. First, theory is neither *about* reality, nor an adjustment to reality, rather it has some role to play in *constituting* reality. Assumptions implicit in certain theories confer meanings and shape the world. There are no brute facts, which are not permeated with interpretative assumptions. There is thus no unmediated or uninterpreted reality. Valid knowledge is not the putative representation of something external.[48] In consequence, it is more difficult to speak of the clear truth or falsity of beliefs or their measurement against some external empirical standard. Theories can be more or less persuasive or fruitful in the way in which they constitute realities. Truth or falsity would be premised on alternative ideological or theoretical schemes. Such schemes would also be subject to historical change.

For many exponents of empirical political theory, there are deep problems with such a view. For example, how could one gain any reliable or testable empirical data from such elusive ideas? Further, it is not possible to quantify interpretations. If theory is constitutive in this way, then the whole empirical project looks suspect. The debate between empirical theory and political theory has not been resolved at all in political science. There have been some modifications within political science. There is now an awareness of the bewildering variety of approaches occasioned by the post-behavioural phase. Thus, some more recent political scientists have tried to accommodate themselves to what is called 'methodological pluralism'. For others, though, this variety generates dismay and anxiety. Felix Oppenheim suggested that this post-empiricist perspective does inevitably lead to the rejection of the older forms of positivism and behaviouralism. But, he contends that political scientists should now avoid both the Scylla of old-fashioned behaviouralism and the Charybdis of simple-minded relativism. He also notes that 'to reject . . . behaviouralism is not to abandon empiricism' (Oppenheim 1981: 194). For Oppenheim, constructing good explicative definitions and explanations in political science still has loose parallels with good natural science, in demanding accuracy and simplicity. Yet, he admits that this would not, in political science, produce fully fledged empirical covering laws, in the older sense of positivism.

One after shock of empiricism, which might be said to be now carrying the torch of empirical political theory to the present day, is rational choice theory (see Easton in Farr and Seidelman (eds.) 1993: 302 ff.).[49] The origins of rational choice lie within the discipline of neo-classical economics as well as offshoots of utilitarianism.[50] In terms of the actual serious development of rational choice, it appeared precisely at the point of the decline of behavioural theory during the 1950s and 1960s— although, initially, it was a very marginal and rather occult specialism, out on a limb as it were from mainstream economics. Despite its economic base, it is still regarded as somewhat quaint by mainstream economists. The seminal books, which constitute the cornerstones of the perspective, are Kenneth Arrow's *Social Choice and Individual Values* (1951), Anthony Downs *An Economic Theory of Democracy* (1957), and Mancur Olson's *The Logic of Collective Action* (1965). Another significant text, which also had an important impact was James Buchanan and Gordon Tullock's work *The Calculus of Consent* (1962), which drew the analogy between voters and market-based consumers. However, rational choice did not make overtly optimistic claims for itself until the 1980s. Yet, in the last two decades of the twentieth century it became, in North America, the fastest growing element of political studies, and has even been blessed with a distinctive title (to indicate its special status), namely, 'positive political theory'—which presumably makes the rest of political theory look a trifle negative.[51] It would now be true to say that in North America it has taken over the empirical mantle from institutional theory, behaviouralism, and pluralism. It has also moved confidently into related disciplines, such as International Relations. As one synoptic study concludes, 'scarcely an area of political science has remained untouched by its influence' (Green and Schapiro 1994: 2). Some keen exponents of rational choice consequently see this as a great triumph for the perspective (William Riker 1990: 177–8).

Although there are a number of variants of rational choice theory (including Marxist rational choice), the gist of the perspective is 'the application of the analytic method and techniques of modern economics to the study of political processes' (Brennan 1997: 89; see also Roemer 1986; Carver and Thomas (eds.) 1995). A basic definition of rational choice is therefore 'the economic study of non-market decision-making, or simply the application of economics to political science. The subject matter of public choice is the same as that of political science: the theory of the state, voting rules, voting behaviour, party politics, the bureaucracy, and so on. The methodology of public choice is that of economics, however. The basic behavioural postulate of public choice, as for economics, is that man is an egoistic, rational utility maximizer' (Mueller 1989: 1–2). In other words, it is concerned with government or politics viewed through the market. As always happens in such theories, it has divided fairly quickly between various schools, for example, the Virginia School of Public Choice (associated with Buchanan and Tullock) and the Chicago school (associated with George Stigler and Olson), sometimes referred to as the 'private interest regulation' school.

The key assumptions of rational choice are fairly rigorous and parsimonious. They are: first, the centrality of individuals for all forms of social explanation, including groups. Thus, rational choice is methodologically individualist. Second, each individual is assumed to be rational. Third, rationality denotes agents choosing the 'option which they believe best fulfils their purposes' (Brennan 1997: 98); or, as Riker puts it, 'that, within certain limits of available information . . . actors choose so as to maximize their satisfaction' (Riker 1990: 173). This notion of rationality is wholly instrumental and says nothing about the contents of options or preferences.[52] A clear analysis of basic incentives will go a long way towards explaining human behaviour. Fourth, the individual is self-interested. This does not entail either complete egoism or the impossibility of collective action. Far from it, for rational choice exponents, it provides a more logically satisfying way of explaining public choice and collective action.[53] Fifth, the actual process of rational choice is a form of decontextualized utility maximization. Each agent is trying (rationally) to maximize their utilities and minimize their losses. Faced with a number of options, the agent will pick one which best serves or maximizes efficiently her objectives. Essentially we are looking at the integuments of, what is often referred to as, *homo economicus*. Rational choice also assumes that there will be a consistency in choices and options; preferences will be ranked according to their utility for us. This constitutes a basic equilibrium. Thus, from any collection of preferences, the agent is able to calculate a choice from which she can expect the greatest utility payoff. This particular line of reasoning has led many rational choice theories into 'game theory' and various forms of mathematical modelling. Finally, all rational choice analysis shows 'a predilection for formal deductive method, deriving 'interesting' (i.e. non-obvious, often counter intuitive) propositions via sometimes long and complex chains of logical reasoning from a minimal set of plausible axioms' (Brennan 1997: 96). These assumptions of rational choice are considered to be universal, empirical (in the sense that they form the basis for testable research programmes), and scientifically orientated. Indeed, even some of its more rigorous critics still applaud its empirical and scientific aspirations as its most valuable asset (see Green and Schapiro 1994: 10).

Rational choice in many ways ideally fills the more optimistic self-perception of empirical political theory. It embodies a purportedly rigorously empirically testable and scientifically-based research programme and yet, at the same time, it can fulfil all the requirements (for its proponents) of a normative political theory, once one has accepted the above foundational assumptions.

The problem on the empirical front is that it is far from clear that it has had much empirical success. The central contention of a recent synoptic study of rational choice therefore notes, 'curiously . . . the stature of rational choice scholarship does not rest on a readily identifiable set of empirical successes'. The authors comment that most critics do not in fact focus on the empirical or operationalized aspect of the doctrine. They note that this aspect of rational choice work (which they examine exhaustively) is generally 'marred by unscientifically chosen samples, poorly conducted tests, and tendentious interpretations of results. As a consequence, despite its enormous and growing prestige in the discipline, rational choice theory has yet to deliver on its promise to advance the empirical study of politics' (Green and Schapiro 1994: 5 and 7). Part of the problem here, for the authors, is that this empirical weakness is rooted in the desire to establish a universal empirical theory of politics, which has resulted in rational choice being 'method driven' rather than 'problem driven' (Green and Schapiro 1994: 202–3; see also Schapiro 2002).

The bulk of the criticism on the normative front focuses on a number of well-trodden paths. Rational choice is clearly premised on an unquestioned empiricist metaphysics. However, its basic foundational elements neither seem very plausible, nor ultimately very reasonable to its critics. Basically—apart from the fact that they are not really empirically verified—the above set of assumptions are regarded frequently as simply false and misleading. The assumption of the isolated or atomized individual is highly questionable and sociologically and historically contentious. It embodies an excessively narrow and slightly weird perspective on human beings. Minimally, it simply cannot account for the complexity and idiosyncrasies of human individuals, when they act morally or politically. To reduce all individual action and choice to instrumental personal preference rankings, utility maximization and self-interests does little or no justice to human nature or human action. The same point holds for more orthodox utilitarianism. It might give us some very partial insight into some collective actions, but that it is about it. It also employs an excessively narrow and deeply-arbitrary conception of human rationality.

Apart from certain more random and idiosyncratic offshoots in, for example, Marxist rational choice, critics see not so much a universal foundational empirical political theory, as a somewhat pessimistic ideological doctrine, driven by a parochial North American conception of neo-classical liberal market economics and utilitarian calculus (which even orthodox economists would feel uneasy with). Its importance reflects more on the power and influence of North America, rather than any theoretical depth or long term intellectual significance. Intrinsic to this model are a number of deeply-questionable foundational assumptions. It is essentially inclined ideologically to be pessimistic about all government-led initiatives—simply because they are not generated through market choice. It is deeply cynical of all human motivations, seeing self-interest and personal utility maximization at the root of all morality and politics. Essentially its view of human beings is profoundly sterile. It has close connections with a range of public policies concerning the slimming down of government (rolling back to the state), the reduction of public expenditure, the movement from progressive to proportionate taxation regimes, the market-based privatization of government, the wholesale introduction of competitive market processes into all areas of government, administration, and public service. It provides ideological succour for ideas such as cost–benefit analysis, private finance initiatives, value for money policies, cost-effectiveness measurement, market testing, introducing competition in the delivery of all public service, and the like, many of which have permeated public policy debate in Britain and North America (see Peter Self 1993, 2000). As the original 1960s rational choice theorists wanted to model the democratic voter on the market-based consumer, so rational choice in the 1990s and 2000s has wanted to model government bureaucracies, health care, education, and the like, on the private firm. This movement in public policy is not only due to rational choice theory. However, rational choice is still complicit in a more general ideological shift.

In terms of the general perception of political theory, there are some odd sociolo-gical parallels with behaviouralism. Like behavioural political theory, rational choice has mainly been a North American phenomenon, taking up a powerful niche in the contemporary politics academy. It also shares a basic positivist fideism. However, there is a key difference to behavioural theory. Behavioural theory, in the 1950s and 1960s, faced a comparatively weak and demoralized profession of political theory. Apart from the European contingent of émigrés theorists, such as Arendt or Strauss, the bulk of theory (outside empirical theory) was constituted by forms of logical positivism and linguistic philosophy (to be examined in Part Two). These forms of philosophy were rooted (unwittingly in many cases) in an empiricist foundationalism, which gave immediate credence to empirical claims as genuine first-order knowledge. Thus, behaviouralism was able, fairly easily, to roll over the opposition, for a time. However, rational choice—despite its success in the academy—developed during the 1980s. This coincided with the so-called rediscovery of normative political theory, the early confident halcyon days of the methodological debates around Skinner's work, Rawls justice-based argument, postpositivist and many other diverse critiques. In this sense, it encountered a wide-ranging diverse opposition from within other domains of political theory. This has considerably (and thankfully) limited its scope.

In conclusion, the dominant aims of political science still remain tied to the informal and empirical, rather than the formal, institutional, historical, or normative. Although some of the more extravagant mid-twentieth century claims of empirical political theory to 'colonize' completely the whole of political theory have now con-tracted, political science is still the far more dominant partner within North American and European political studies. Empirical political theory, despite the post-empiricist and post-positivist arguments, still remains committed to the measurable, quanti-fiable, and testable. However, the aspiration for empirical theory (particularly in offshoots such as rational choice) to absorb political theory, *in toto*, is not absent, but rather dormant.

IDEOLOGICAL POLITICAL THEORY

Ideology is one of the most contested conceptions of political theory. The gist of this perspective is that political theory is and always has been (unless obscured by historical or abstruse philosophical theories) a deeply practical mode of thought, which is connected directly with the sphere of political action. Ideology, in other words, is the *truth* about political theory. In this perspective, when the political philosophers of the past were writing and thinking about politics—Machiavelli, Hobbes, and Locke—they were actually writing as ideologists. Thus, ideology, as a practical political engagement trying to navigate the political realm, change perceptions, and construct public policy, is the *reality* of political theory. Thus, ideology draws our attention, minimally, to one important dimension of theory—the practical, engaged dimension—which can occasionally and unexpectedly get ignored in the sheer welter of abstract theorizing. However, in claiming this kind of role for itself, ideology not only conflicts quite directly with some dominant perceptions of normative political theory, but also with dimensions of historical and empirical theories.

The relation with normative theory is the most difficult and sensitive. After a brief introduction concerning the concept ideology, the debate over the relation between ideology and political theory will be analysed in terms of, first, attempts to fully integrate ideology and political theory, in other words, to make them indistinguishable; second, in terms of efforts to completely demarcate them. Both of these categories—integration and segregation—have positive and negative poles, which therefore gives rise to two further sub-categories for each response. Some of the arguments have already have been touched upon in previous sections of Part One, thus the expositions will be brief.

The concept of ideology is a comparatively new political word dating from the early 1800s, and not in any recognizable form until the 1840s, and again not in any popularized form till the late nineteenth and early twentieth century (see Vincent 1995, ch. 1). Its first use, in the writings of Destutt de Tracy, focused on the Enlightenment orientated idea of an 'empirical science of ideas'. It had no immediate political connotations. In Marx and Engels' use, in the mid-nineteenth century, it took on a definite political and critical sense. However, it was not until the twentieth century that it really came into its own within popular political discussion. However, given that political theory was also, etymologically, a novel term, dating from the mid- to late-nineteenth century, neither concept can really claim great longevity, except rhetorically. In many ways, despite its commonplace use in academic and ordinary speech, it still remains the poor and often vilified cousin of political theory.

Thus, beginning first with the *negative integration* thesis. One of the first to imply that political theory and political ideology could be fully integrated was Marx. However, Marx, and the subsequent Marxist tradition, present a complex picture.

Primarily, political theory and ideology are reduced to the same category, although *both* denote an illusion. The material conditions of economic life form the real basis to social existence. Cultural and political structures can only be understood via these material conditions and the ensuing class struggles. Since the material basis is primary, all ideas have to be explained via their connection to the material base. They cannot be explained in themselves. They constitute the ideology of a society. Marx, in one of his synoptic semi-autobiographical pieces of writing, the *Preface to the Critique of Political Economy*, called the above idea the 'leading thread' of his studies (Marx and Engels 1968: 182). It is understandable, in this reading, that Engels, and others, should thus have referred to all ideology (including political theory) as the 'false-consciousness'. Its chief delusion is its inability to see its own class basis. The history of ideology is therefore subsumable under a history of class interests. Political philosophers are quite literally professional ideologists or professional purveyors of illusions. The social and economic sciences therefore need to explain the eruptions of ideology and political theory.

Ideology and political theory thus become *social objects* to be explained within a broader empirical social theory. Much twentieth century sociology—both structuralism and functionalism—continued to view political ideas as aspects of a broader science of society. Social science, in general, has often seen both political theories and ideologies as *social objects* for study. In fact, for Durkheim and Talcott Parsons, sociology *per se*, contained a complete social epistemology, which provided clear answers to all the older philosophical problems of knowledge. Humans (and their cognitive existence) have no distinctive attributes outside of society. A science of society thus explains political theory and ideology.

We have already encountered the above basic argument within empirical political theory. With the rise of empirical theory in the mid-twentieth century, the 'illusory' dimension of normative political theory came to the fore. This view was encapsulated in the perspective of behavioural political science. The general frame of the 'end of ideology' perspective also caught the same drift of argument. Social science, in effect, offered a science of society. The development of empirical theory demanded a value free rigour and clear verification processes, unsullied by appeals to normative political theory or ideology. As Edward Shils commented, 'science is not and never has been part of an ideological culture. Indeed the spirit in which science works is alien to ideology' (Shils 1968: 74). The only salvation for political theory or ideology was to mutate into empirical political theory.

This was the general view of the behavioural movement. Classical normative theory, the history of political theory and ideologies persisted with a use of *theory* 'that lingered from an earlier period in the discipline's history'; and as James Farr noted 'In being empirical and explanatory, however, theory in behavioural research was to be value-free and objective. There was, it was argued, a logical gulf between fact and value, between "is" and "ought", which in no way could be spanned. Normative topics like freedom, justice, or authority—the staples of a prescientific study of politics— were best understood in terms of one's subjective emotions or expressive states. They were also laced with a "strong dose of metaphysical discourse" '. Farr continues that, for behaviouralists, 'endlessly reinterpreting the great books of dead men and tirelessly disputing the meaning of the good life had nothing to do with science' (see Farr in Farr, Dryzek and Leonard (eds.) 1995: 204; also Heinz Eulau 1963: 8–10). Ideologies and political theories, in the older sense, could serve cohesive functions (as social objects to be studied) in developing societies, however, in large industrialized democratic societies they were largely redundant or decorative. Consensus on basic social and political aims had been agreed. All the rest was froth.[54]

Moving to the second thesis of *positive integration*. In this context, the integration of political theory and political ideology should not be a matter of concern. There are, again, however, different perspectives. Many adhere, unwittingly, to the integration of the terms, that is, where ideology becomes an unwitting synonym for political theory. Thus, one often encounters quite unselfconscious references to 'liberal ideology', and the like, in discussions, which otherwise appear to be exclusively focused on the category political philosophy.

Even more ironically, this unwitting use appears within the 'second wave' of history of political theory writings (outlined earlier). This is, in fact, doubly ironic given the overtly close attention to language, and the avoidance of anachronism, characteristic of the second wave theories (see Leslie 1970). If we bear in mind that the term 'ideology' is a neologism from the nineteenth century, carrying a baggage of uses, it is, to say the least, strange to find Quentin Skinner, in a number of writings, referring to, for example, 'History and Ideology in the English Revolution' or 'The Ideological Context of Hobbes' Political Thought' (see Skinner 1965, 1966). James Tully, explicating Skinner's method, also reflects this usage. Thus, for Tully, the new method demands we place all texts in an 'ideological context'. Tully continues, that an ideology for Skinner, 'is a language of politics defined by its conventions and employed by a number of writers. Thus, scholasticism, humanism, Lutheranism, and Calvinism are ideologies and both scholasticism and humanism comprise the general ideological context of the Italian city-states during the Renaissance' (Tully 1988: 9). Luther and Calvin thus become political ideologists![55] Placing an idea or text in context—the sacred mantra of second wave theory—makes 'political theory, . . . a part of politics, and the questions it treats are the effects of political action'. Tully continues, that 'since a political ideology represents a political action . . . to change some of the conventions of the ideology is to change the way in which some of that political action is represented' (Tully 1988: 10–11). Consequently, Tully describes Skinner's whole substantive two-volume opus, *The Foundations of Modern Political Thought* (1976), as 'a map of the great political ideologies of early modern Europe' (Tully 1988: 12). Thus, political theory and ideology become *one*. One searches in vain, in such contextualist writings, for a glimmering of recognition that the concept of ideology itself, is a deeply troubled, comparatively quite new, idea containing deep unresolved tensions.

Another semi-conscious response on this same issue is provided by the communitarian movement of the 1980s and 1990s (who will be examined in more detail in Part Three). One of the hallmarks of their arguments is the association of theory with situated communal practices. Thus, ideas cannot be defined independently of the human relationships, which constitute them. Communitarianism argues, therefore, that political and moral goods cannot be determined by abstract reasoning. All human 'goods' arise from particular historical communities. There is no concept which stands apart from a social context. Morality is neither invented nor discovered, but interpreted as already existent (see, for example, Walzer 1987: 21). We 'read off' an existing tradition of discourse. The community becomes the locus of the good. Unwittingly, again, this appears to tie all political theory closely to political ideology, *neither* has any distinguishing marks. They are simply different names for the same communal discourse.

Not all in the historical domain, however, are as unaware in the 'use' of the concept ideology. In an open and explicit use of ideology to denote both political activism and political theory, Richard Ashcraft comments that, 'only an ideologically grounded approach with respect to current political problems can provide a bridge between the traditions of political philosophy and the perception of what counts as "political" phenomena' (Ashcraft 1975: 20). Political philosophers are, or should be, considered unequivocal ideologists. In response to the idea that philosophy is something higher or more saintly than ideology, Ashcraft asks, 'how is it even possible for . . . epistemological presuppositions to stand apart from the very conflict they propose to "study" and are assumed to transcend' (Ashcraft 1975: 26). Ashcraft, appears to be directing his fire at both historians of political theory and analytical philosophers, arguing that 'some of the responsibility for the divorce of traditional political theory from present concerns of political life rests squarely with those teachers of political theory who have encapsulated the meaning of politics within the frozen worlds of "analysis" or "history"' (Ashcraft 1975: 19). As Ashcraft continues, for many political philosophers, the title ideologist is though 'the original sin' (see Ashcraft 1980: 695). Ideology appears to relinquish all claims for universality. For Ashcraft, however, this universality is well worth losing. He suggests that most theorists in the past *were* actually concerned about problems in society and were actually, what we now think of as, ideologists. To make them just philosophers is a modern self-indulgence.

Further, it is worth noting that more contemporary neo-Marxism does not always take a negative view of ideology (as contrasted to genuine science). It can also take an immensely positive view of the integration of political theory and ideology. Thus, the most noted twentieth-century Marxist, Antonio Gramsci, saw proletarian ideology as an effective tool of political struggle against bourgeois ideology. The hegemony of political ideas was thus considered of immense importance. Ideas take on a partial autonomy from the material base. There can, in other words, be an authentic and useful Marxist ideology, qua political theory. Aspects of this 'partial autonomy' view are reflected in some later twentieth century Marxist writers such as Gramsci. It is also the predominant view of twentieth century critical theory.

In a more general, late twentieth century scenario, language overall—in both theory and ideology—has not always been viewed as a transparent conveyor of meaning. Languages, even the sophisticated languages in political philosophy, cannot gain any real distance or neutrality from the subject of politics. Ideology and political theory are both focused on language and language is focused on social action. Speaking can therefore be considered a way of acting. The study of ideologies and political theories can therefore be seen as the study of the social world itself. The medium of language itself is embedded within an historical and political inheritance. Thus, language cannot stand back from social conflict, it is the medium of expression and experience of such conflict. In other words, ideology and political theory neither reflect neutrally on, nor simply represent the world, but rather partly constitute it. Ideology and political theory are enmeshed in complex relations and struggles of power. To analyse this process is the self-appointed task of, for example, discourse analysis, forms of structuralist Marxism, psychoanalysis, semiotics, and much postmodern genealogy. All reject the 'neutralist' thesis concerning ideology and theory, stressing conversely, the constitutive and expressive role of language.

This critique of the language of political theory and ideology has been especially characteristic of Michel Foucault's writings (which will be examined in Part Four). Foucault even suggested abandoning the concepts of ideology and political theory altogether. They would be replaced by painstaking genealogical explanation, which examines *how* certain discourses and regimes of truth (*epistemes*) come about. For Foucault, all knowledge related to power and domination. As he stated, 'what one seeks then is not to know what is true or false, justified or not justified, real or illusory . . . One seeks to know what are the ties, what are the connections that can be marked between mechanisms of coercion and elements of knowledge, what games of dismissal and support are developed from the one to the others, what it is that enables some element of knowledge to take up effects of power assigned in a similar system to a true or probable or uncertain or false element, and what it is that enables some process of coercion to acquire the form and the justification proper to a rational, calculated, technically efficient, and so forth, element' (Foucault in Schmidt (ed.) 1996: 393). Knowledge always conforms to restraints and rules and power also needs something approximating to knowledge.[56] Thus, for postmodern-inclined writers, neither political theory nor ideology represent any external objective reality. Ideology and political philosophy, for Foucault, are both subjects for genealogy. We are always encultered beings who express, contingently, our diverse communal narratives through theory or ideology. There is no external reality, which we can represent.

A related dimension to this attack on representation theory concerns the broad tradition of twentieth century purported nonfoundationalism. Although not directly focused on this integration thesis, there are a number of the arguments within this tradition (taken as broad category), which facilitate the conceptual linkage between political theory and ideology. For example, for nonfoundationalists there are no givens and no raw data in the world. The idea of an empirical given is a 'myth'. Further, there is nothing external to our symbolic systems. We live and think in several worlds with distinct, often incommensurable systems of symbols. In addition, there is an abandonment of correspondence accounts and a focus on coherence. Statements therefore become true, not by referring to an external given world, but rather in terms of whether they cohere with distinct systems of symbols (see Goodman and Elgin 1988: 8). In a similar vein, for Richard Rorty, poetic creativity must now replace representations of reality; irony and gaming are set over against knowledge claims. Rorty summarizes this drift of argument by completely identifying political philosophy with ideology. He suggests the utter uselessness of 'the distinction between "ideology" and a form of thought . . . which escapes being "ideology" ' (Rorty 1989: 59). In this context, there are no clear criteria to differentiate them. If political philosophy still claims a special insight into the world, as distinct from other forms of thought like ideology, then it is simply mistaken. For the nonfoundationalist the representational perspective of some philosophers is better understood as pathology rather than philosophy.

Moving now to the *negative segregation* thesis: this dimension forms the standard response of much twentieth century Anglo-American political theory, although a great deal depends here on exactly how one perceives political theory or philosophy—particularly philosophy. A common and quite pervasive view of philosophy during the twentieth century is to see it as a higher, more critical or purer calling. No matter what the philosophy espoused, it is seen as distinct from ideology. The most characteristic conception of ideology is that of a tainted or debased product, which lacks the virtues of political philosophy. In this interpretation, political philosophy is generally marked out by a reflective openness, critical distance, a focus on following the argument regardless, and an awareness of human experience, which transcends political struggles. Ideology, on the other hand, would be viewed as the opposite. It closes reflection, throws itself into partisan struggle, its ideas are designed instrumentally to manipulate actors, close argument, and ultimately to achieve political power. It has no concern with truth.

A large number of twentieth-century political theorists have held variations of this thesis, for example, Germino, Arendt, Oakeshott, Voegelin, and Strauss. Strauss is quite typical here. Philosophy is seen as an ancient quest for wisdom and universal knowledge, that is, 'the knowledge of God, the world and man' (Strauss 1959: 11). Political ideology, however, is indifferent to the distinction between knowledge and opinion, is wholly tied to historical contingencies and is concerned with the uncritical espousal of myths. Ideology denotes both modernity and nihilism. The broader theme, which underpins this idea, in Strauss, is the debate between the ancients and moderns, discussed earlier. For Strauss, the modern era has seen a decline of political philosophy into ideology (see also Oakeshott 1991). This negative appraisal is reflected, in different terminology, in the twentieth century analytic style of philosophy. In logical positivism, for example, philosophy is viewed as a second-order activity. It did not contribute any first-order knowledge, as in natural science.[57] Propositions, which might loosely be grouped under the label 'normative' or 'metaphysical', do not tell us about the world, rather they reveal the emotional or psychological state of individuals. In this sense, ideology, with most other evaluative domains of thought, becomes subjective emotional meaningless gush. Further, in early ordinary language philosophy, the task of philosophy is perceived to be the close attention to the ordinary use of words and concepts. However, ordinary language is still in agreement with logical positivism that philosophy does *not* include justification or prescription. The same point would hold for the philosophy of the later Wittgenstein. Political philosophy has a more substantive role to play, but it is still a second-order activity distinct from direct normative claims as might be found in ideology.

One important facet of these portrayals of political philosophy is again the separation from both political practice and ideology. Ideology, in this case, looked, in all these scenarios, deeply suspect. It was this kind of analysis, which basically formed the wholly dogmatic backdrop to the bulk of Anglo-American political philosophy. Thus, David Raphael, in a popular text book of 1976, noted that ideology is simply 'a prescriptive doctrine that is not supported by argument'. This was a widely accepted credo till the last decade of the twentieth century (Raphael 1976: 17; for similar judgements: Hacker 1961: 6; Corbett 1965: 139–40; Kateb 1968: 8; Gewirth 1965: 2; Quinton 1967: 1; Germino 1967: 42 *ff*.; Copleston 1983: 23; Minogue 1985: 32; Gaus 2000: 36–42). This might be described as the standard liturgy of conceptual introductions to political theory throughout the second half of the twentieth century. In the majority of these introductory works, despite the ritualized claims to analytical rigour, the judgement of ideology is usually always simply asserted and never argued.

Even for significant recent normative thinkers, such as John Rawls, a similar background creed holds. In his *Political Liberalism* book, Rawls argued, for example, that philosophical abstraction was required when social divisions were deep. He commented that in 'political philosophy the work of abstraction is set in motion by deep conflict. [and] Only ideologues and visionaries fail to experience deep conflicts . . . profound and long-lasting controversies set the stage for the idea of reasonable justification' (Rawls 1993: 44). Again, Rawls offered no evidence or argument concerning the point that ideology (qua ideologues) never deals with either conflict or abstraction. Ideology appears as simple-minded and unreflective. In fact, ideology is abstract through and through from beginning to end and 'liberal ideology' (in its various formats) has always, in fact, suggested the same kind of things that Rawls advocates. Further, the fact, for example, that Rawls's writings were often appealed to in 1980s ideological debates in Britain and America, over social policy and social justice, might make one pause for a moment's reflection as to precisely where political philosophy ends and where ideology begins. Despite what its promoters say, the above negative segregation of political philosophy and ideology is not a time-honoured position, but simply an artifice of a certain type of mid-twentieth-century political theory.

The final most neglected thesis focuses on the *positive segregation* of political philosophy and ideology, namely, where each is seen to make a valuable, if distinct, contribution. There are not many examples of this strategy. One recent and sophisticated attempt has been by Michael Freeden. For Freeden, ideologies are manifestly not the poor relation of political philosophy. Conversely, they provide equally valid insights. They both reflect and produce social and political realities. They are also far more subtle and pervasive than commonly understood. To neglect the study of ideology is therefore to 'weaken our comprehension of political thought' (Freeden 1996: 2).

Freeden terms his approach towards ideology 'conceptual morphology'. The morphological approach is semantically based, focusing on the question, 'what are the implications and insights of a particular set of political views, in terms of the conceptual connections it forms?'. For Freeden, this approach grasps 'internal ideational arrangements'. Meaning is always dependent on *frameworks* of interpretation. An ideology is therefore viewed as human 'thought-behaviour' embodied in ordinary spoken and written language. Consequently, ideologies are defined as 'those systems of political thinking, loose or rigid, deliberate or unintended, through which individuals and groups construct an understanding of the political world they, or those who preoccupy their thoughts, inhabit, and then act on that understanding' (Freeden 1996: 3 and 125). They are political maps for navigation in the political realm containing core, adjacent, and peripheral conceptual elements.

For Freeden this 'thought-behaviour invariably includes, but is not identical with the reflections and conjectures of political philosophers' (Freeden 1996: 2). What then is the relation of political philosophy and ideology? Freeden essentially sees political theory as a capacious category containing political philosophy and ideology as subcategories. He is basically trying to recapture the importance of ideological analysis for political theory. He thus separates out the history of political theory, political philosophy, and ideology. The easiest way of looking at the relation of these terms is to articulate, briefly, Freeden's view of the advantages of morphological study of ideology. It combines a *diachronic* approach (which traces in effect the historical development of language and records the various changes), with a *synchronic* approach (which examines language as it actually is at a point in time with no reference to historical argument). Morphology balances both dimensions, superimposing a 'diachronic on synchronic analysis and multiple synchrony on the examination of a single system'. (Freeden 1996: 5). This provides a handle for understanding his view of political philosophy and the history of political theory. Political philosophy has tended (to date) to be overly focused on the synchronic dimension, whereas the history of political theory has been predominantly diachronic. Ideology, among other things, balances both dimensions.

One major problem for Freeden is that Anglo-American political philosophy, in the twentieth century, has quite definitely tried to open up a chasm between itself and political ideology. This is the *negative segregation* issue discussed above. Philosophy is characterized as wholly synchronic, reflective, self-critical, whereas ideology is caricatured as crude, unreflective, and irrational. Freeden takes the primary functions of political philosophy as justifying, clarifying the consistency, truth and logicality of political theories, and evaluating ethical prescriptions. However, this role should not be performed to the exclusion of ideological study. Political philosophy and ideology are *not* mutually exclusive. Both are forms of political thinking shaped from political concepts and their interrelationships. But they are not synonymous and should be segregated positively (see Freeden 1996: 42). The claim that the only function of political theory is correct or truthful conceptual usage, *qua* synchronic analysis, is seen by Freeden as simply wrong headed. He is also keen to stress the historical and sociological realities within which political ideas are constructed. Yet, he also moves away from a great thinker's approach. The real world of political action and 'thought behaviour' does not often bear much relation to the canon of great thinkers, except at several removes. Overall, Freeden puts in a balanced plea for theoretical ecumenism. No dimension of political theory should claim dominance. There should be 'mutual fertilization' and tolerance (Freeden 1996: 110).

For Freeden, ideologies do contain an odd mixture of emotion and reason and occasionally some flawed rationality. However, he adds that even the most rationalistic political philosophical philosophies contain non- or un-rationalized components (Freeden 1996: 30–1). This is not only a problem for ideology. Further, an over-emphasis on synchronic abstracted reason and logic can lead to a virtually semi-private professional academic language, which bears little or no relation to politics, as perceived and used by the mass of ordinary citizens. In addition, ideologies are neither strictly true nor false. In what sense, for example, would liberalism or socialism be true? This conclusion obviously leads to a degree of relativism, which Freeden considers inevitable. Yet, as he adds, 'the decline of the status of "truth" in the social sciences has combined with the realization that the older abstractions and model-building of political theory cannot satisfy the critical exploration of concrete idea-phenomena. The more political philosophers attempt to engage in their perfectionist enterprise, the more remote from the sphere of politics, . . . do their findings become' (Freeden 1996: 131). Finally, one also has to acknowledge that despite the more dominant Anglo-American role of analytic philosophy, that philosophy itself during the twentieth century has also been polysemic and contested. This adds a new dimension of complexity to the relation to ideology.

Freeden's general conclusion is therefore that we should not treat political philosophy and ideology as 'entirely discrete categories', but they are also *not* synonymous. Each has distinct roles. However, political theory (as a general overarching concept) should not *just* be limited to clarification of meaning. Ideology is not though imperfect political theory. Political theory, in effect, needs a new ecumenical approach, which incorporates ideology as an equally valid process with political philosophy.

CONCLUSION

Despite the above arguments, the more dominant position in political theory throughout the second half of the twentieth century has clearly been the *negative segregation* thesis. The basic contention of this latter thesis is that a belief in liberalism, rights, freedom or justice, and the like, is not just a matter of allegiance or having a cognitive ideological map. It is rather something we believe in with *good justificatory reason*. A justification, qua normative or analytical theory, therefore involves citing good arguments and valid reasons. It is not simply about being persuaded or converted. Justifying is not like becoming a fan of a football team. Justifying is tied to critical reasoning about what is fundamental to us. It follows that there can be good and bad, or true and false reasons. To suggest the contrary (qua ideology) that there cannot be true or false reasons or beliefs, would be asserting an absolute truth, which is a performative contradiction in, for example, Freeden's argument. Proponents of the *negative segregation* thesis thus suggest that ideologies are always irrational, cultural, and emotive assertions, which should always be kept distinct from genuine justificatory normative political theory.

However, given the totality of the discussion in Part One, it is difficult to know precisely what *genuine* political theory really is. Further, the justificatory-based argument equally cannot assert that reasons can be good or bad or true or false. The claim is that good reasons must be asserted to justify a belief; yet what would be the 'good reason' for asserting that there must be good reasons for asserting beliefs— *ad nauseam*? In other words the justificatory reason argument is, itself, logically premised on a questionable metaphysical supposition. The critic is trying, in one sense, to 'convert' her audience to a 'justificatory reasons' position. However, what would be the *independent* true reason for affirming the belief that there are true and false reasons? What counts as a good reason for many religious believers, or multiple other human practices, is clearly *not* a good reason for non-believers. What some consider to be good critical philosophy, others consider to be uncritical nonsense. In other words, there is an underlying hubris, simple-mindedness and dogmatism in the justificatory reason argument, which makes it incapable of any philosophical self-reflexivity. In addition, there is little or no awareness concerning exactly how political philosophy has been practised in the twentieth century. It certainly has not—even with the Anglo-American fold—been solely focused on the 'normative justificatory reasons' perspective. To think otherwise takes intellectual myopia to a high art form.

This negative appraisal could be pursued much farther; however, what is surely a much more reasonable path is that we should consider seriously something like the *positive segregation* thesis. This is not an argument which denies the distinctive roles of normative justification, ideology, or history. However, ideology is seen to be as serious and equally valid a mode of study as (what is very loosely called) political philosophy. This theoretical ecumenism looks a much more hopeful way forward. This latter thesis also gels with the far broader ecumenical thesis, concerning the nature of political theory, outlined within Part One, which has, in effect, analysed certain dominant perceptions of the political theory during the twentieth century, at a broad level of generality. The five positions outlined were: classical normative, institutional, historical, empirical, and ideological political theory. As suggested, some of these components have more obvious contextual references. It is, for example, a matter of fact that the first real attempts to do political theory, as a disciplinary practice, figured in the institutional and historical state-based theory context. This latter theme has now largely dropped into the background. Other components discussed have a much more current status. It is important though to underscore the point, again, that the categories discussed are not self-enclosed forms of theorizing; conversely, there are complex overlaps between them. The conclusion is that there is *no* pristine essence to political theory. Political theory is and always has been an uneasy combination of different modes of thought.

Notes

1. The systematic account of normative political theory will be postponed until Part Two and later chapters.

2. The nature of the non-political (e.g. the realm of the family or the economy) tends to mutate between various classical theories.

3. As Strauss (with Joseph Cropsey) remarked in an introduction to a standard textbook 'The kind of political philosophy, which was originated by Socrates is called classical political philosophy until the emergence of modern political philosophy in the sixteenth and seventeenth centuries. Modern political philosophy came into being through the conscious break with principles established by Socrates', (Cropsey and Strauss (ed.) 1987: 2). For Strauss, classical political philosophy included the teaching of the Stoics and medieval scholastics.

4. This classification is adapted from the much more detailed work of Oakeshott (1991), Greenleaf (1964), and Boucher (1998).

5. He also distinguishes between three sub-forms of political theory. These are contractarian thinking, concerned with 'what arrangements are eligible, what arrangements would properly be chosen if people were contracting into society'; value centred analysis, which asks 'what arrangements are valuable, what arrangements best answer the currently recognised political values'; and the institutional-centred approach, which 'explores the matter of what political values can be reliably institutionalised by government, what values are feasibly values', see Pettit (1993b).

6. However, it reached its academic zenith in nineteenth century juristically inclined writers, particularly in Germany, such as Lorenz von Stein, Carl von Gerber, Paul Laband, Otto von Gierke, Georg Jellinek, and Johann Caspar Bluntschli.

7. The term institution can imply something, which is wholly legalistic, structural, and formalized, as against something, which is informal and more dynamic, in terms of political behaviour. This point is the backdrop to a standard criticism of state or institutionally orientated theory in the twentieth century. For many, it was also one reason to give up the state-based focus.

8. The first politics chair in Britain was created in the 1920s in Cambridge University. The first sociology chair in Britain was created in the University of London in 1907. However, no more chairs in sociology were created until 1945.

9. This theme of citizenship education has, for example, been resurrected once again and legislated on by the New Labour administration in Britain in 2002.

10. Gunnell remarks on this theme that Charles Merriam, amongst others, inspired by the German example 'remained constant in his belief that social control exercised through general civic education and intercourse between academic and political elites was the solution to the problem of how to bring knowledge to bear upon politics', Gunnell in Monroe (ed.) 1997: 52.

11. For Gunnell, the state 'defined the domain of political science as an autonomous field, and, as a supervenient vision of political reality, it served to underwrite the legitimacy and authority of political science vis-á-vis politics. It was, for many, a secular substitute for the mystery and social bond of religion. It offered a way for political science to talk about its subject matter' (Gunnell 1993: 58)

12. In addition, severe doubts about the role of the normative theory of the state were rife, especially after the First World War. L. T. Hobhouse's violent polemic in 1918 on *The Metaphysical Theory of the State*, was not untypical of this negative assessment. Hobhouse's preface links the German Gothas bombing London with Hegel's *Philosophy of Right*, which he was annotating in his back garden during the raid, see Hobhouse (1918: 5–6).

13. In the British political studies, the state focus was much more equivocal. Constitutions and institutions were still seen to embody a range of important theoretical ideas. This would particularly be the case in British writers such as W. H. Greenleaf or

A. H. Birch. However, this particular view was also resisted vigorously by both Marxist and realist-inclined theorists, who saw empirical institutional factors and economic power as the key determinants of politics.

14. It would also be true that certain forms of thought such as environmentalism and feminism have also refocused attention on the state, however, the upshot of these are slightly less clear.

15. That is the study of the principles, theories, and methodology of scholarly historical research and presentation.

16. Thus, as one scholar has remarked, 'To speak of the history of political thought as if it were a distinct and easily identifiable discipline with sets of procedures and definite aim would be to misunderstand the business of studying past political thinkers. Just as there is no agreement among historians in other fields about the exact nature of their specializations, there is very little consensus on the nature and purposes of studying the history of political thought', (Boucher 1985: 74).

17. On one hand, history can be viewed as parasitic upon classical theory itself. The history *needs* classical theory to subsist. Thus, classical theory might be viewed, in one sense, as a kind of first-order activity. The history is a second-order activity. However, this makes the relation too one-sided. On the other hand, the history of political theory is that which makes classical normative political theory possible. Wittingly or not, the historical dimension can be said to bring classical theories together as sequences, united by abstract themes or traditions. In this sense, the very existence of classical normative political theory is parasitic upon the history of theory. The history of political theory can thus be said to make the conception of classical normative political theory possible.

18. Laski adds, a few pages later, 'Political philosophy is never separable from the general body of ideas in a generation . . . We need, in a word, so to write the history of political ideas that they fall naturally into their place as the expression of one aspect of a process of thought that is not neatly divisible into two separate categories. We must seek to project our narrative on to a plane where the relation of a whole to its parts is capable of being seized in its full significance', Laski in King (ed.) (1978: 6).

19. However even this phrasing is ambiguous, given the predisposition of the analytic movement (specifically in its logical positivism format) to despise 'normative' theory. It would be more correct to say that the analytic style (and positivism in general) led to a virtual dismissal of both the history of political thought and normative theory.

20. It first became an honours degree in Britain in Oxford in 1872 and Cambridge in 1873. The first chair of history—although set up in 1724, was first filled by a committed historian in 1866. The Chichele Chair of Modern History in Oxford was created in 1862.

21. 'The satisfaction of national pride and culture, and the rendezvous with destiny that it often implied, whether in England, Germany, or America, reflected the distinctive meaning of government education, and history in each country', Soffer 1994: 6. For German historiography, university history and the nation state, see Georg Iggers, 'Nationalism and Historiography 1789–1996: The German example in historical perspective' in Berger, Donovan, and Passmore (eds.) 1999: 15–29. This edited book includes other examples of such practices across Europe.

22. See S. Berger, M. Donovan, and K. Passmore (eds.) 1999. The final concluding chapter of this book, entitled 'Historians and the nation-state: some conclusions' is a good survey of this issue.

23. As Soffer comments on the development of the discipline in Britain: 'The acceptance or rejection of new disciplines was part of a larger debate about the relative merits of continuity and change within an expanding society . . . Among these contending fields,

history provided the most consistent moral panorama able to satisfy a variety of intellectual, emotional, and aesthetic needs' see Soffer 1994: 3. The development of history in Britain naturally coincided with the creation of the Dictionary of National Biography, the English Historical Review, Historical Association, and the Public Records Office.

24. The only exception was the adoption of a Whiggish evolutionary teleology which fitted well with the idea of the gradual growth of the British constitution and national life. The study of history thus 'remained a national narrative about high politics and the constitution', (Soffer 1994: 42).

25. As one scholar has remarked 'the history of political thought arose at a time when history itself as a discipline in England had not firmly become an established identity. Indeed academic history which freed itself from classical studies was very weak in English universities until late in the nineteenth century', Boucher (1991: 29).

26. Quentin Skinner, despite all the earnest methodological arguments, has shown a clear willingness to use historical resources for present doctrinal disputes. His attachment to civic republicanism is a clear example.

27. As Strauss commented, 'The kind of political philosophy, which was originated by Socrates is called classical political philosophy, until the emergence of modern political philosophy in the sixteenth and seventeenth centuries. Modern political philosophy came into being through the conscious break with principles established by Socrates', see Cropsey and Strauss (1987: 2).

28. The initial feverish character of the method debates in the 1980s have dampened down and now become much more institutionalized in weighty book series.

29. There are distinct approaches in Sabine, Macpherson, and Plamenatz. Sabine is more overtly committed to perennial issues, which have an ultimate moral dimension. Plamenatz wanted to analyse the perennial arguments and concepts of various 'philosophies of man', Plamenatz (1963: xiv–xv). Macpherson was committed to a Marxist form of analysis.

30. Another writer in the same methodological school—David Wootton—has observed, approvingly, that 'many contextualizing studies serve in effect to distance us from the past', see Wootton (1993: 9).

31. Another dimension of denying perennial problems and over-committing oneself to contextual history is creating a developed incapacity to theorize. As Richard Ashcraft comments 'some of the responsibility for the divorce of tradition political theory from the present concerns of political life rest squarely with those teachers of political theory who have encapsulated the meaning of politics within the frozen worlds of "analysis" or "history"', Ashcraft (1975: 19).

32. As Boucher comments 'Skinner's predilection for searching for origins disposes him to employ many of the historical devices associated with the mythology of doctrines, but the same preoccupation also has a tendency to generate the mythology of prolepsis', Boucher (1984: 298).

33. The *Begriffgeschichte* argument is discussed again in Chapter 3.

34. As James Farr comments, 'Like the Scots, the American founders explicitly and repeatedly used the very terms to pick out this nascent science. Thereafter, these terms—*science of politics, political science, science of government, science of legislation*, and their kin—would help reshape American political discourse and indeed the very institutions and practice of American political life'. During the revolution period of the 1780s and 1790s, the rhetoric of 'political science' was utilized by all participants, although its precise 'identity' was never

really established. It also later figured in debates about the nature of republicanism, see James Farr in Farr and Seidelman (eds.) (1993: 66–8).

35. Political economy was developed in the writings of François Quesnay and A. R. J. Turgot. Yet, even within political economy, science was still equated with practical reform and social utility. Further, many eighteenth century theorists commonly associated 'social rules' and 'sociological generalizations'. Social rule-following was linked in such writers with a loose idea of empirical causal laws. Whereas, in the twentieth century, the two domains would be commonly demarcated, in these earlier writers, maxims of government always hovered *between* social rules and empirical laws. 'Is' and 'ought' were therefore linked in these early views of political science. It is worth reminding ourselves immediately that, at this stage, political theory was indistinguishable from political science.

36. Discussed under the 'first wave' of the history and theory section. Strauss, for example, accused behavioural political science of fiddling 'while Rome burns', Strauss in Storing (ed.) (1962: 327).

37. In 1923 the North American Social Science Research Council was formed as a loose umbrella organization, see Ross in Farr and Seidelman (eds.) (1993: 82). Political science was part of this more general 'scientific aspiration'.

38. David Easton saw four stages: first, a formal legal stage, followed second, by a combination of traditional and informal approaches, then, third, the full-blown behavioural phase, and finally, the postbehavioural, see David Easton in Monroe (ed.) (1997: 12).

39. As David Ricci remarked 'The 1920s and 1930s came to be marked . . . by a steady flow of empirical research and descriptive studies, designed to enlighten first political scientists, and then their students and the public, as to the condition of American politics', see David Ricci in Farr and Seidelman (eds.) 166. See also the programme for politics study laid down by Charles Merriam 'Recent Advances in Political Methods' (1923), in Farr and Seidelman (eds.) (1993: 131 *ff*.).

40. Not all are so complementary here. One North American commentator noted that 'At one extreme, the use of "empirical" is almost more of a benediction than a denotation. To be "empirical" is to be virtuous in procedure and realistic in outlook, and not to be empirical is to stray from the narrow and true path', (see Spragens 1973: 19).

41. As Easton puts it in another article 'behaviouralism adopted the original positivist assumption (as developed by the Vienna Circle of the positivism early in this century) that value-free or value-neutral research was possible', Easton 'Political Science in the United States: Past and Present' in Farr and Seidelman (eds.) (1993: 295).

42. As Gunnell comments 'Few of the behaviouralists understood themselves as antitheoretical, and probably few initially understood their concern with scientific political theory as a rejection of their earlier education [in political theory]'. It was only later that they 'eventually felt constrained to make a choice between scientist and theorist as a primary identity', Gunnell (1993: p. 220).

43. For Gunnell, Strauss, Arendt, Morgenthau, Adorno, Voegelin, Neumann, Brecht, Horkheimer, Marcuse, and others 'reshaped the discourse of political theory'. He continues that 'they all propagated the thesis that liberalism, either inherently or because of its degenerate condition, was at the core of a modern crisis and implicated in the rise of totalitarianism' (see Gunnell in Farr and Seidelman (eds.) 1993: 182).

44. As Ernest Nagel comments: 'the sciences seek to discover and to formulate in general terms the conditions under which events of various sorts occur, the statements of such determining conditions being the explanations of the corresponding happenings. The goal

can be achieved only by distinguishing or isolating certain properties in the subject matter studied and by ascertaining the repeatable patterns of dependence in which these properties stand to one another. In consequence, when the inquiry is successful, propositions that hitherto appeared to be quite unrelated are exhibited as linked to each other in determinate ways by virtue of their place in a system of explanations' (see Nagel 1961: 4).

45. It is worth noting the fuller quotation. Mitchell looked forward to the rosy prospect of a political theory in which 'Models of political systems analogous to types of economies and markets will proliferate . . . Statistical testing of models involving election results and governmental budgets, will become the major enterprise . . . For sometime we shall be able to make do with verbal, geometric and algebraic models, but eventually the economist will overwhelm with higher level mathematical statements', Mitchell in Lipset (ed.) (1968: 129–30).

46. The postbehavioural movement had 'its birth in efforts to cope with some of the unresolved problems generated by behaviouralism: the indifference to moral judgements; the excessive commitment to formal mathematicized statements flowing from the use of scientific methods; the focus on theoretical criteria to the neglect of social issues; the preoccupation with social forces as determinants of behaviour, overlooking, in the process, important cognitive (rational) elements; and a profound forgetfulness about the history of political systems that helps to shape their present', Easton in Farr and Seidelman (eds.) (1993: 306).

47. The assertions made in the general programme are well summarized by Mary Hesse as follows: 1. In natural science data [are] not detachable from theory, for what count as data are determined in the light of some theoretical interpretation, and the facts are determined in the light of some theoretical interpretations, and the facts themselves have to be reconstructed in the light of interpretations. 2. In natural science theories are not models externally compared with nature in a hypothetico-deductive schema, they are the way the facts themselves are seen. 3. In natural science the law-like relations asserted of experience are internal, because what counts as facts are constituted by what the theory says about their inter-relations with one another. 4. The language of natural science is irreducibly metaphorical and inexact, and formalizable only at the cost of distortion of the historical dynamics of scientific development and of the imaginative constructions in terms of which nature is interpreted by science. 5. Meanings in natural science are determined by theory; they are understood by theoretical coherence, see Hesse (1981: 171–2).

48. This body of argument has been explored by a number of thinkers. For many Anglophone philosophers Davidson's article 'On the Very Idea of a Conceptual Scheme' has been deeply influential. Davidson speaks of the 'myth of the given' in much theorizing, and that we should abandon the basically Cartesian and Kantian distinction between a conceptual scheme *and* reality. The term 'myth of the given' appears, however, to have been first coined by the American philosopher Wilfred Sellars. As Davidson argues, 'In giving up the dependence on the concept of an uninterpreted reality, something outside all schemes and science, we do not relinquish the notion of objective truth . . . Given the dogma of dualism of scheme and reality, we get conceptual relativity, and truth relative to a scheme. Without the dogma, this kind of relativity goes by the board. Of course truth of sentences remains relative to language, but that is as objective as can be', see Davidson (1973–4: 20).

49. This is a fairly short exposition of rational choice. However, a slightly longer analysis of a sophisticated 'political theory' rendition of rational choice can be found in Part Two Chapter 4 in a discussion of David Gauthier's work.

50. Thus, rational choice writers will often see their roots in the classical eighteenth century economic perspective of, for example, Adam Smith. Others, such as David Gauthier or

Geoffrey Brennan, view Thomas Hobbes as a more viable predecessor, see Gauthier (1986: 186) and Brennan (1997: 92).

51. The APSR personnel newsletter incorporates adverts for rational choice posts in Universities in North America *within* the political theory section, under the title 'positive political theory'.

52. 'rational choice theorists generally agree on an instrumental conception of individual rationality, by reference to which people are thought to maximize their expected utilities in formally predictable ways. In empirical applications, the further assumption is generally shared that rationality is homogeneous across the individuals under study', Green and Schapiro (1994: 17).

53. As has been noted, 'In their efforts to explain political outcomes, rational choice theorists appeal to deductive accounts of incentives, constraints, and calculations that confront individuals. Systematic analytic inquiry into the strategic behaviour of individuals has led rational choice theorists to approach traditional questions of political science in novel ways', Green and Schapiro (1994: 3).

54. In the 1990s, Francis Fukuyama, on a different theoretical basis, anticipated a new end of ideology (or end of history in his case), with the triumph of global liberalism, see Fukuyama (1992).

55. This might be described as one of the better examples of conceptual anachronism.

56. 'the path from the empirical observability for us of an ensemble to its historical acceptability, to the very epoch when it is effectively observable, passes through an analysis of the knowledge-power nexus that supports it, see Foucault in Schmidt (ed.) (1996: 394).

57. As T. D. Weldon remarked 'It is not the job of philosophy to provide new information about politics . . . or any other matters of fact. Philosophical problems are entirely second order problems. They are problems, that is, which are generated by the language in which facts are described and explained by those whose function it is to construct and defend scientific, historical, or other types of theory', Weldon (1957: 22).

PART TWO

PART TWO

3

Foundations Shaken but Not Stirred

Part One outlined the basic foundational components of the discipline of political theory during the twentieth century. There have been considerable overlaps and cross-fertilizations between these ways of conceiving theory. All, with the exception of institutional political theory, have remained important foundational elements, even if coming under assault and being subject to quite radical internal modification. One looks in vain for any overarching coherence. Many of these foundational components remain mutually hostile, often claiming for themselves the 'true title' of political theory—a process that continues throughout the century. However, one theme is common to them all and that is that there is a perception of a more or less distinct core or settled foundation to the discipline in practice. There is, in other words, a fundamental importance to the discipline of theory and a foundational core to the approach can be formally identified, whether it is in the roots of human nature, reason or the search for the good life, the teleological development of the state, the ground of historical understanding, empirically-tested assumptions, or the ideological platforms of political action.

In Part Two the discussion focuses on a sequence of changes in the perception of political theory dating largely from the 1940s and culminating in the late 1970s.[1] Given that a lot of the discussion so far has been involved with the first four decades of the twentieth century, it could look as though there is some kind of underlying narrative sequence at work in the discussion. There is a minor chronological element here, although it is not very significant. As mentioned, all of the previous components in Part One, continued to underpin conceptions of theory throughout the twentieth century. In some areas, such as the empirical, historical, and ideological, the discussion scans across the whole century.

The present chapter is entitled 'Foundations Shaken but Not Stirred' because each of the ways of conceiving the theory to be discussed, retained a sense of a core foundation, even if, in some cases, it was a remarkably thin foundation. The foundations were so thin at times that there was serious speculation, in some quarters, that the whole enterprise of political theory appeared to have expired. This present chapter will thus cover the advent of logical positivism, the development of conceptual analysis, linguistic philosophy, and the impact of Wittgenstein's thought, particularly on the idea of 'essential contestability'. The second chapter of Part Two concentrates on the 1970s developments focused originally on John Rawls' *Theory of Justice*.

However, there are three important qualifications to be made here. The first is that there was still never any doubt in any of these developments, about the foundational importance of certain philosophical methods and the universality of their application to issues such as politics or morality. Thus, although, in the early stages, the philosophical structures led to a thinned down (virtually skeletal at times) perception of political theory, nonetheless, there was still an unwavering sense of the universality of philosophical theory, with little or no initial self-doubt about its own method. In fact, one might hazard the judgement that, if anything, it suffered from intellectual hubris, an almost overweening sense of its own rightness and appropriateness as the only universally-applicable philosophical approach. The second qualification is that many of the formulations of this notion of theory also blended well, at times fortuitously, with other conceptions of theory already discussed in Part One. This was particularly the case with empirical political theory. There was therefore a foundational blending of concerns here (particularly with logical positivism), where some of these newer conceptions of theory appeared to give philosophical and foundational support to the empirical enterprise. The third qualification relates to the new developments of theory in the 1970s. The advent of this was the publication of Rawls' *Theory of Justice*, in 1971, which initiated a veritable industry of commentary, as well as a new found confidence in the whole enterprise of political theory. A number of commentators have even postulated the beginnings of political theory in this period. At first glance, this appeared either to be a break again from what had already been taking place in theory (qua logical positivism or linguistic philosophy), or, for others, it was a return to a grand, older tradition of normative theory. There is some sense to both of these judgements, however the stress in this discussion will be laid on the continuity of certain philosophical or theoretical concerns and the manner in which there was internal sequence to be observed within the Rawlsian setting. This point underpins the overall assessment of theory, in this context, namely that universal foundations were shaken by critique but never really stirred.

LOGICAL POSITIVISM

The 1930s and 1940s saw radical changes in the philosophical climate in the English-speaking world. Initially, the most significant of these was the advent of logical positivism, a concentration on conceptual analysis and a more general interest in Wittgensteinian-inspired linguistic philosophy. The general ambience was one of analysing and clarifying political concepts. Philosophy was seen increasingly as a 'second order activity' concerned with 'tidying up' the logic and sense of political speech. A loose description of this general style would be 'analytic philosophy'. The style of analytic philosophy was born largely out of a reaction to earlier philosophical styles, particularly philosophical idealism, which had largely dominated philosophical discussion in the 1870–1920s period (see Vincent and Plant 1984; Boucher and Vincent 2001). Analytic philosophy was, on one level, very different to idealism. It was a much more pared down and sparse form of philosophical thinking which paid inordinately close attention to the logic, semantics, syntactics, and pragmatics of both concepts and speech. This close, finely honed attention to concepts made it less overtly ambitious. In fact some would say it made it distinctly conservative. Treatises could be and were written on single concepts. There was no room for broad-ranging metaphysical speculation, philosophical systems, or creative linkages between diverse areas of human experience. The whole enterprise of philosophical analysis had become infinitely more concentrated or focused.

However, the negative reaction to idealism was part of a more general reaction to *any* foreign philosophical import. Philosophical refugees or asylum seekers were treated harshly. This became particularly persistent during and immediately after both the First and Second World Wars. One irony here is that the major impetus to both logical positivism and linguistic philosophy also came from Germany and Austria particularly, although many would add, of course, that these movements nonetheless allowed a rediscovery of a latent British empiricist tradition going back to Hobbes, Locke, Hume, and Mill. This negative reaction to foreign imports marked out the general attitude of British, and much American philosophy, largely up to the late 1980s. Initially, in the 1930s period, the negativity was to idealism and Hegelianism in particular. The ghosts of this negative reaction to Hegel carried over for several decades. The negativity then moved, almost imperceptibly, in the 1950s and 1960s, to a disquiet with the claims of Marxism, existentialism, phenomenology, and Freudianism. The major figure to be standardly vilified by analytic philosophy from the 1950s up to the 1980s was Martin Heidegger; the intellectual fastidiousness concerning his relation with Nazism being a major undercurrent. However, by the 1980s and 1990s, analytical philosophy had a new *bête-noir* to surpass the rest—postmodernism and poststructuralism, the names Jacques Derrida and Michel Foucault becoming, in some cases, virtually demonized. Thus analytic philosophy has largely flourished not so much by what it has produced as by what it has opposed.

The heyday of this movement in analytic political philosophy was largely between the 1940s and early 1980s. In many ways analytical theory *was* an inheritor of an empiricist tendency. Some of the basic distinctions between, for example, logical or analytic and empirical propositions can be found, in a slightly cruder format, in David Hume's writings, amongst others. In general, for those educated in political theory in the English-speaking world during this period, analytical political theory was the most significant aspect of political theory—usually subsisting in an uneasy collegiality with the history of political thought. Analytic theorists took a similar attitude to the history of political theory as behaviouralists, namely, that the canon was a potential source of not so much testable hypotheses as certain interesting arguments and concepts, which could be critically engaged with. The growth of this analytical perspective initially coincided directly with the triumphant rise of empirical political theory, behavioural political science, and the end of ideology debates of the 1950s and 1960s. The relation between these was not fortuitous. There was some mutual massaging taking place. Empirical political science could pose as the 'first order' provider of genuine empirical political knowledge, for which analytical political philosophy could function as a 'second order' handmaid, clarifying speech and logic, and acting as a philosophical gatekeeper for genuine social science.

The earliest and most vociferous expression of this new found confidence of analytic philosophy was logical positivism. It was *the* most characteristic expression of this early period. Logical positivism developed initially in 1920s and 1930s Vienna amongst a group of mathematicians, scientists, and some philosophers. Its most notable philosophical voices were Moritz Schlick, Rudolf Carnap, Friedrich Waismann, Otto von Neurath, Herbert Feigl, and Victor Kraft. In Britain, the most well-known exponent was Alfred Ayer. Many of the initial Viennese group, like Carnap and Feigl, became émigrés to North America during the 1930s and had some impact on the burgeoning behavioural perspective.[2] The basic premises of the movement were first, a strong empiricism—namely that all knowledge was founded on testable experience, and second that mathematics and logic were independent of direct experience. The conception they had of mathematics (and logic) was largely dependent upon the work of Bertrand Russell, Alfred North Whitehead, Gottlob Frege, and the early Ludwig Wittgenstein. Complete negativity was expressed towards metaphysics—as being distinct from both experience and logical truth. Consequently, philosophical idealism—which was committed to metaphysics—was ruled out of court in the premises of logical positivism.

Logical positivism had a vision of a unified scientific enterprise. The *only* valid knowledge was scientific. Consequently there were only two types of meaningful propositions that could be made about the world. The first were those which embodied in the sphere of mathematics, logic, or lexicography, which largely embodied tautologies and were thus trivial, if significant. These were often given the title 'analytic' propositions. The second form of proposition was found in the substance of the empirical sciences. These have been variously called 'synthetic' or 'empirical' propositions. The crucial point about the latter propositions was that their truth could be empirically confirmed. In fact, this was the very *raison d'être* of the sciences in general. The term identifying this process of empirical confirmation was the 'verification principle'. Meaningful universal empirical or factual statements were those that could be empirically verified by rigorous scientific method. Such statements, quite literally made 'sense'. Verification enabled a lucid distinction to be made between true and false statements or theories. It provided a clear criterion of meaningful discourse. However, there was a third class of statement which embodied quite literally the whole range of the humanities and many social sciences. Classically, these were statements appearing in metaphysics, ethics, theology, much political philosophy, aesthetics, and the like. The worst offender for logical positivists was metaphysics. In effect, the verification principle was the method for eradicating metaphysics. Metaphysics did not figure in any account of meaningful propositions. Metaphysical statements were neither tautologous nor empirically verifiable. If they did not equate with these they were quite literally nonsense. The metaphysician 'produces sentences which fail to conform to the conditions under which alone a sentence can be literally significant' (Ayer 1952: 35). Metaphysicians, like ethicists, aestheticians, or theologians, professed to tell us something about the world, but nothing could be verified. One upshot of this in moral philosophy was the doctrine of emotivism that saw morality having no descriptive or logical sense. It was simply the expression of laudatory emotions.

In summary, therefore, for logical positivism, analytic propositions were *a priori* claims to be found in mathematical, logical, and lexical statements. Synthetic empirical propositions were those characteristically found in the sciences, which could be empirically verified. Philosophy was seen as a universal 'second order' activity. It did not offer or contribute any first order knowledge to the world. First order knowledge was the domain of the sciences. The world of the philosopher was thus taken as a given one, which the philosopher examined and used as the material of argument. In many ways this was a congenial vision of the role of philosophical theory for behavioural political scientists.

The early Wittgenstein is often taken as an inspiration for the logical positivists. Undoubtedly, his *Tractatus Logico Philosophicus* (1921) was read and admired by the Vienna group.[3] The basic doctrines of the *Tractatus* were of considerable interest to the group. Wittgenstein arguments, at this point, were close to Bertrand Russell's doctrine of logical atomism.[4] The core theory underpinning Wittgenstein's work is often called the 'picture theory', which asserts that our language pictures the world. Words stand for the facts or configurations of objects that they represent. As Wittgenstein put it in the opening sequence of the *Tractatus*: 'The world is everything that is the case' and 'The world is the totality of facts' (Wittgenstein 1922: sections 1 and 1.1). Meaningful sentences must correspond to the reality of facts, in Russell's case, logical atoms. Wittgenstein also postulated that there were ultimately irreducible simple facts or states of affairs in the world to which sentences refer. These atoms are pictured by elementary propositions. Elementary propositions or sentences consist of the names of the elements arranged in ways that reflect the structure of facts. As Wittgenstein notes, 'We make to ourselves pictures of facts' (Wittgenstein 1922: section 2.1). This constitutes the truth or falsity of sentences.[5] Language is therefore words arranged in sentences that mirror those facts. Complex propositions or sentences are held to be 'truth functional' compounds of elementary sentences or propositions.

For the early Wittgenstein, logic is essentially a set of rules for constructing propositions out of fact-picturing propositions. All statements referring to the rules of propositional logic are tautologies. Mathematics and logic are again tautologous. They do not picture the world in any way. Tautologies are true by definition. This point was admired particularly by the logical positivists, if not by Russell. There is also an implicit adherence to the verificationist principle. For Wittgenstein, sentences that are not verifiable are without sense. However, unlike the logical positivists, Wittgenstein was not keen to dismiss them as utter nonsense or emotion. Even if we cannot discuss such things as ethics, aesthetics, and metaphysics, they still appear as more mystical to Wittgenstein, rather than nonsensical. Unlike the logical positivists, Wittgenstein clearly felt the pull of metaphysics, aesthetics, and ethics, even if he denied their epistemological role, whereas virtually none of the Vienna group felt this impulsion. Even Wittgenstein's friend and admirer, F. P. Ramsay, sensed reprovingly this impulse in him, remarking famously that some things cannot be said, but neither can they be whistled. In the final analysis, however, the status of the *Tractatus* arguments came under suspicion (as Wittgenstein was aware), since they also were neither tautologous nor verifiable. In this context, Wittgenstein refers to his own philosophy as not so much a philosophical doctrine, as a ladder, which once one has ascended and realized what has been argued, can be cast aside as no longer useful or meaningful. In other words, it is the end of philosophy.

There were though certain implications from this whole logical positivist perspective for political theory. First, it gave far more credence to the role of empirical political theory and behavioural claims. Verification, in the 1950s, became a significant term for political science and empirical political theory. The second important implication was that logical positivism established an altogether more constrained second order role for political theory. Third, it raised very serious doubts about normative, historical, and ideological conceptions of theory. In one reading it could be said to have *completely* bankrupted them.

ORDINARY LANGUAGE

There is one further development which in many ways blends with aspects of logical positivism—namely, ordinary language philosophy. We should not imagine that ordinary language philosophy simply supplanted logical positivism. Conversely, there was an integration of sorts, particularly in political theory writers like T. D. Weldon. This idiosyncratic combination of ideas formed much of the standard fare of political theory textbooks up to the 1970s.

Language became a general foundational preoccupation of philosophers in the twentieth century. Heidegger, Ryle, Austin, Foucault, Derrida, Wittgenstein, and Rorty all focused on it. Many of these approaches to language will be touched upon in this book. In the early phase, in the 1940s and 1950s, two dominant Anglophone approaches to language can be identified in terms of political theory: first, there was the demand to correct and tidy careless and misleading ordinary language. The second approach adopts a more descriptive attitude to ordinary language, accepting the different and frequently messy nature of conceptual usage. The first figures more in the domain of logical positivism, although it still underpins some ordinary language theory. Essentially it sought to correct language through the verification principle. The second dimension is most closely associated with the work of the later Wittgenstein and Austin. Wittgenstein's later influence stems from the publication of his *Philosophical Investigations*. The discussion of the latter book will be postponed for a moment in order to render its fuller impact.

The second reading saw a range of philosophical problems endemic to logical positivism, not least the difficulties of making out an acceptable argument for the verification principle.[6] Further, the hard-nosed logical positivist distinction between analytic and empirical propositions was also seen as unhelpful with regard to ordinary speech. Conversely, the task of philosophy was perceived to be the close attention to the *ordinary* uses of words and concepts. 'Ordinary language' became a phrase to conjure with. The analyst was seen to be engaged in the neutral description and elucidation of concepts. Philosophical problems were seen to be a combination of syntactics and semantics. Whereas logical positivism saw meaning as dependent upon the rigid categories of the analytic and synthetic—combined with verification—ordinary language philosophy viewed meaning in terms of common linguistic usage. The diverse varieties of usage of words could not be simply swept aside with the category of verification (although it is clear that *not* all logical positivists wanted this). The emphasis therefore shifted from the precise meaningful definition of words (and their contextualization as empirical or analytic) towards elucidating concepts in their diverse rich uses.

Underpinning the above conception is a particular view of language. Language is seen as an activity. Words are deeds and tools. Typical of this approach is J. L. Austin's speech act theory (Austin 1962, 1971). Speech acts are what Austin termed 'performatives'. Thus, in many everyday utterances, we perform an act *in* speaking. For example, the performative, 'I promise', is not reporting or describing the practice of promising. Rather, it is itself invoking the conventional practice of promising. It is doing by saying.[7] People perform acts with words all the time in ordinary language and yet the same sequence of words can perform different acts. The full sense of one sequence of words can mean different things in different conventional contexts. Even non-verbal acts depend on conventions. The speech act thus depends crucially on conventions in ordinary language usage.[8] A successful speech act takes place when conventions subsist which standardize the use of words and listeners are fully conscious of them. The gist of what Austin is claiming is that we are, first, always in the midst of language, and second, that meaning relates to conventional use within ordinary language. Third, there is an enormous variety of meanings contained within ordinary usage. Therefore, the philosophical emphasis moves away from defining and tidying up concepts, to the complex task of elucidating conventions and uses of words in particular linguistic contexts. This did not mean, for Austin, that ordinary language provided all the possible answers. As Austin noted, 'ordinary language is *not* the last word; in principle, it can everywhere be supplemented and improved upon and superseded. Only remember, it is the *first* word' (Austin 1971: 185).

However, one should not overdo the distinction between ordinary language philosophy and logical positivism. Although ordinary language theory did concede, unlike logical positivism, that normative questions about justice were legitimate to ask, it was still at one with logical positivism in resisting the idea that philosophy could provide any solutions to such normative issues. Ordinary language was still in agreement with logical positivism that philosophy did not include any *modus operandi* for justification or prescription. All that Austin might have suggested is that if we wanted to understand justice, we should look at the conventions. Political concepts could not, *per se*, be recommended. Political theory was still a second-order activity, distinct from direct normative claims. Thus, both schools of thought acknowledged the 'second' and 'first-order' distinction. Philosophy did not generate any knowledge. In addition, both philosophies were suspicious of metaphysics.[9] Ordinary language theory had an almost conservatively proprietorial sense of the subtle conventions embedded in ordinary language. Logical positivism was simply hostile. Some analytic philosophers, like Strawson, in the 1970s, did try to modify the understanding of metaphysics, but the basic enmity has remained an undercurrent, even to the present day (see Strawson 1974; also Walsh 1966: 194–5).

One of the most oft-cited expositors of this period on political theory is T. D. Weldon, particularly his book *The Vocabulary of Politics* and his article 'Political Principles' (see Weldon 1953, 1956). Weldon offers an idiosyncratic toothy self-confident blend of logical positivism and ordinary language philosophy.[10] There is both the observation of meaning in use and the demand to tidy up language and dismiss certain uses.

For Weldon the whole of normative political philosophy rests on a mistake. It is a mistake about language. Mistakes, as Weldon notes, arise from 'carelessness over the implication of language ... from the primitive and generally unquestioned belief that words, and especially the words which normally occur in discussion about politics ... have intrinsic and essential meanings which it is the aim of political philosophers to elucidate'. The search for 'word essences' is 'a wild goose chase' (Weldon 1953: 11–12, 28). Words can be relatively stable in a society over time, but that is simply because the objects and situations confronted remain stable. But there is nothing behind or beyond institutions which they express or realize. There is no essential justice or rights. Words do not have essences to Weldon, they have uses, qua Austin and Wittgenstein. Unfortunately, many of the great political thinkers of the past had been searching, in vain, for stable essences. Echoing the mantra that philosophy does not offer any first order knowledge, Weldon remarked that 'it is not the job of philosophy to provide new information about politics ... or any other matters of fact. Philosophical problems are entirely second order problems. They are problems, that is, which are generated by the language in which facts are described and explained by those whose function it is to construct and defend scientific, historical, or other types of theory' (Weldon 1953: 22). In this conclusion, we have the undiluted ordinary language stress.

However, there is also logical positivist side to Weldon. He assures his readers that generations of intelligent political philosophers were performing some kind of role, although it remains obscure. It appears to be a combination of empirical description and the recommendation of reasonably obvious prejudices, which have no cognitive status. Personal prejudices though do not have to be dishonest or misplaced. Weldon admits that his own prejudices are basically those of J. S. Mill (Weldon 1953: 16). However, there are no ultimately reasonable foundations to be discovered. He continues, that the bulk of political philosophy does look, in these circumstances, delusional (Weldon 1953: 177). This is particularly the case with normative argument. Such arguments are neither logical nor empirical. Conversely, they evince strong emotions and only tell us about the psychological states of individual theorists, not about the world. This is the classic doctrine of emotivism. In this sense, the large bulk of normative political theory and political ideology moves directly into the obfuscatory realm of subjective laudatory 'hurrahs' and emotive ejaculations.[11] As Weldon notes, unequivocally, normative political theory has 'formulated questions of a type to which no empirically testable answers could be given, and such questions are nonsensical' (Weldon 1953: 14–15). There are no verifiable aspects to democracy, rights, or justice. Without a hint of hubris, he articulates the main thesis of his book: 'To show that the questions put by the traditional political philosophers are wrongly posed... In the light of these discussions to show that the theoretical foundations of political thinking... are all equally worthless... To show that this conclusion is in no way devastating or even alarming... All that is discarded is some metaphysical lumber' (Weldon 1953: 14–15).

The logical positivist demeanour in Weldon comes out strongly under the rubric of facts and values. Here we see logical positivism and ordinary language theory falling in line with an open positivist mentality. Weldon solves the fact/value issue with verve. He conjures an imaginary party, remarking, 'suppose we are looking at the dog of our hostess. I say "Fluffy is a Peke", and you reply "No, he is an Aberdeen". We know what we are disagreeing about and how to settle the issue. If [however] I say "The Athens of Pericles was a democracy", and you reply "No, it was an oligarchy" the matter is rather more complicated because of the vague and conflicting uses of "democracy" and "oligarchy"' (Weldon 1953: 85). For Weldon, the answer to this party conundrum focuses on the distinction between facts and values. The issue of 'Fluffy: Peke or Aberdeen' can be sorted out empirically with unassailable and testable facts. The fact that Fluffy is a Peke is thus empirically verifiable (unless of course someone had renamed the Peke 'Pericles'). However, the proposition concerning Periclean democracy (as in any metaphysical or ethical statements) involves values, which are not verifiable. For Weldon, therefore, the whole problem is solved!

A DIGRESSION ON DEATH AND PUTREFACTION

I wish to pause the argument here for a moment to reflect on one moment in political theory, which connects up with Weldon's views. This is the oft-noted 'death of political theory'. Many assume that the corpse of political theory was discovered by Peter Laslett. Famously, in an introduction in 1956, to the first volume of the *Philosophy Politics and Society* series, Laslett commented,

It is one of the assumptions of intellectual life... that there should be amongst us men whom we think of as political philosophers. Philosophers themselves are sensitive to philosophic change, they are to concern themselves with political and social relationships at the widest possible level of generality... For three hundred years... there have been such men writing in English, from the early 17th century to the 20th century, from Hobbes to Bosanquet. Today, it would seem we have them no longer. The tradition has been broken and our assumption is misplaced... For the moment, anyway, political philosophy is dead. (Laslett introduction, series 1, 1956: vii)

Why did it happen for Laslett? The gulf, between thinkers such as Bosanquet and the 1950s generation of political philosophers, was caused, in large part, by the manner in which logical positivism called into question 'the logical status of all ethical statements, and set up rigorous criteria of intelligibility which at one time threatened to reduce the traditional systems to assemblages of nonsense' (Laslett introduction, series 1, 1956: ix). Laslett thus blamed the logical positivists for the demise of political philosophy, although he did lump a somewhat disparate group under its label, who should not be there—including Ryle, Russell, and Wittgenstein. Ordinary language philosophy (of which Weldon was also a part) did not really advance the case much beyond commenting, on a second order level, that moral and political discourse does actually exist, although it was not the function of political philosophers to recommend it.

The sense of the mortification was more widespread though, and not all blamed it on logical positivism. Whereas Laslett thought the corpse fairly fresh, Leo Strauss, smelt advanced putrefaction in a late 1950s jeremiad. The death of political theory, in fact, had been a protracted one, over the three waves of modernity (discussed in Part One). Yet, political philosophy had given up the ghost well before the twentieth century. The last rites had however been said by modernism in the twentieth century. Political philosophy had become fatally divorced from political science. For Strauss 'science' was now seen as the highest form of knowledge—an idea also later pursued by Habermas and Gadamer. In this sense, for Strauss, it is hardly surprising that 'political philosophy is in a state of decay and perhaps putrefaction, if it has not vanished altogether' (Strauss 1959: 17). The only function that political philosophy now performs is as an adjunct to political science. It is a kind of antiquated performing bear, which lumbers its way through well-worn routines under the guise of the history of political theory. For Strauss all this putrefaction figures against the dramatic backdrop of the cosmic clash between the ancients and moderns. Thus, the cause of death was a compound of the rise of modernism, the hegemony of natural science positivism, the splitting of disciplines like political science from political philosophy, and the nihilistic scepticism over the role of values in human life. For Strauss, many other elements have already left the political philosophy fold—economics, sociology, and psychology. Political philosophy had even muttered a soulful *et tu Brute* to history (although whether Strauss would have been happy with the renewed partnership in the last few decades of the century remains an open question).

The modern behavioural movement, which Strauss bewailed, also predicted the death of the older political theory. However they considered this positively. Many were clear that political theory had in future to be more empirically rigorous in order to survive. David Easton thus saw traditional political theorists as academic parasites. The cause of the decline of political theory in this scenario, has more indirect links with logical positivism. In fact, as Gunnell notes, 'One of the ironies . . . is the behaviouralists, in distancing themselves [from political theory] . . . and in their search for an articulate and defensible notion of science and theoretical identity, ultimately attached themselves to another body of [European] émigré literature—the philosophy of logical positivism and empiricism' (Gunnell 1993b: 7). In this same period, another cognate movement also clearly gave succour to the 'death thesis', namely, the 'end of ideology' (as discussed in Part One). The 'end of ideology' was, again, a temporary phase, although it is worth noting that the 'underlying premises' of the movement would still be upheld today by many who regard themselves as genuine political scientists.

One might think that the 'death of political theory' idea would have passed gently into the collective unconscious of the political studies, however theorists well into the 1990s have still gone on feeling the impulsion to reflect upon it. Brian Barry in the retrospective introduction to the second edition of his well-known *Political Argument*

(1990), commenting on political philosophy in 1956, notes that Laslett and others who coined the phrase 'death of political theory' were probably right, 'If this (*Politics Philosophy and Society*) was the best work that could be found in 1956 (and it probably was), then political philosophy was perhaps not dead but at the least moribund' (Barry 1990: xxxii). The central question that arises here is what conception of political theory is Barry working with here? Certainly, for Barry, nothing happens in political philosophy—apart from his own *Political Argument* published in 1965—until the publication of Rawls' *Theory of Justice* (1971), a book which basically discredited, for Barry, the whole logical positivist and ordinary language perspective once and for all (Barry 1991: vol. 1, 19).

Equally strange is the issue of the timing of the death, for recent commentators. Obviously, for Barry, the discipline was moribund during the twentieth century up to 1971. He mentions writing his doctoral thesis in the early 1960s and having to 'make the stuff up as one went along' (Barry 1991: vol. 1, 18). When Laslett noted in 1950 that no one was writing political philosophy like Bosanquet or Laski, it should be recalled that the former died in 1928 and the latter in 1950. Thus, Laslett can have only meant that political philosophy had died for a decade at the most. It is also interesting that he considered Bosanquet as a political philosopher on par with Hobbes. However, in a later *Companion to Contemporary Political Philosophy* (1993) volume, one of the editors, Philip Pettit, comments that 'from late in the [nineteenth] century to about the 1950s political philosophy ceased to be an area of active exploration. There was lots done on the history of the subject . . . But there was little or nothing of significance published in political philosophy itself' (Goodin and Pettit (eds.) 1993: 8). This locates the demise from the 1870s until the 1950s. An even firmer dating can be found in Richard Tuck's essay in the same *Companion* volume (and it should be noted that Tuck is drawn into this volume as an apparent specialist on the historical approach to the discipline). Tuck comments that,

The period from 1870 to 1970 was a very strange one in the history of thinking about politics in the Anglo-American world (and, to a lesser extent, on the Continent also). There are a number of alternative ways of characterizing its strangeness. One is to point to the absence of major works on political philosophy . . . Another is to remind ourselves that serious commentators in the 1950s could believe that 'for the moment . . . political philosophy is dead'. (Tuck in Goodin and Pettit (eds.) 1993: 72)

This general drift of judgement is also partly reflected in the rather ambiguous idea of the 'return of grand theory' in the 1970s. Thus, for Tuck, like Barry, Rawls' *Theory of Justice* publication date appears again as *the* decisive point.

These general remarks—by no mean academic figures in the discipline of theory—are none the less deeply perplexing. To characterize the 1920 to 1950s period as bereft of political philosophy (qua Laslett) is far-fetched and odd. This period covers, to name but a few, the work of J. P. Sartre, Carl Schmitt, Hannah Arendt, Leo Strauss, Simone Weil, Simone de Beauvoir, Bertrand Russell, Hans Kelsen, Bertrand de Jouvenal, Yves Simon, Dante Germino, Giovanni Gentile, Benedetto Croce, L. T. Hobhouse, G. D. H. Cole, Leon Duguit, Herbert Laski, John Dewey,

R. G. Collingwood, Jacques Maritain, Antonio Gramsci, Georg Lukacs, Karl Popper, Herbert Marcuse, Theodore Adorno, Michael Oakeshott, Eric Voegelin, and Friedrich Hayek. However, to consider that the longer period from 1870 to the 1970s as bereft of theory is utterly cranky. The much longer perspective, going back to the 1870s, also encompasses diverse brands of utilitarianism, the extensive flowering of neo-Kantianism across Europe, the spectacular rise and dominance of forms of neo-Hegelian idealism (which dominated British and much American philosophy up to the 1920s), the colossal impact of evolutionary and biologically-influenced theories (Herbert Spencer et al.), legal and ethical pluralism, and so forth. The list could go on. Alternatively, in the same period, we can see a massive amount of material written on Marxism, Leninism, reformist and pluralistic socialisms, conservative and corporatist theories, diverse forms of anarchy, syndicalism and anarcho-syndicalism, different forms of liberalism, conservatism, early feminism, fascism, nationalism, or indeed the enormous volume of material on state theory (*Staatslehre*) in Europe and America from 1870 to 1930. One should also be aware that this apparently moribund period covers the Russian and Chinese Revolutions, two World Wars, the rise of fascism and communism, decolonization, the creation of the United Nations and human rights documentations, and massive changes in conceptions of statehood, citizenship and sovereignty, and so forth. But, apparently, for perceptive theorists such as Brian Barry, Philip Pettit, and Richard Tuck, nothing happened for the whole of the twentieth century in political philosophy until Rawls published his *Theory of Justice* in 1971.

In this context, one can sympathize with John Gray's judgements, commenting on the above *Companion* volume, although it is equally applicable to Brian Barry's views. Gray locates it as 'belonging to a sub-genre in fantastic literature', redolent of the Jorges Luis Borges imaginary world of Thön. He also notes the total absence of any discussion of fascism, nationalism, monarchism, or theism. Further, there seems to be no awareness of the significance of what was, at the time of its publication, taking place in the Soviet Union, the Middle East, and most other societies in the world. He comments that the editorial methodology appears to accord political reality only to those theories which are of interest in a limited area of mainly North American academic discourse. The *Companion* should therefore be read as a 'mirror of the subject as we find it today and not of the world in which we live' (Gray 1995: 15). It is a distorting mirror, expressing the hegemony 'of an unhistorical and culturally parochial species of liberal theory [which] disables the understanding when it is confronted by the most powerful political forces of our age'. One could come away from the book in complete ignorance of 'every world-historical transformation of our age' (Gray 1995: 16–17).

Leaving Gray's criticism to one side, what it also disturbing in the above reflections on the 'death of political theory', is, first, the level of ignorance and myopia in the various commentaries; and yet the same vague bogus claims go on being repeated up to the end of the century. The most accessible reason for this kind of total weirdness is that there are those who still believe that their own immensely parochial and historically contingent understanding of philosophy is the only possible and correct understanding of the subject. This contains again all the hubris of Weldon, without some of the cultural excuses that make us smile at his eccentricity. Second, the thinking that gave rise to the debate about the death of theory, is largely rooted in forms of analytic philosophy and social science-based positivism. This form of thinking is still present in the political theory discipline. Thus, the roots of this kind of judgement are all still very much intact, if partly submerged.

It is clear though that certainly by the 1960s a number of theorists, within the generic analytic-based ordinary language domain, felt that something had gone wrong. As Condren comments, 'despite earlier rumours of death, political theory is a modish activity heavily populated at its centre by a relatively unreflexive corpus, a rump which is apparently happy to wriggle from one set of priorities to another' (Condren 1985: 37). There were though a number of articles, which encouraged the wriggle and indicated that political theory might, after all, have a role. One of the most often cited of these is Isaiah Berlin's 'Does Political Theory Still Exist?' The basic argument is, though, hardly startling, except in the historical context in which it was written. The gist of the piece is that in addition to the standard logical positivist fare of analytic and empirical propositions there is a third type, which, of course, had been relegated to the sphere of emotion or nonsense by logical positivism. This third sphere should however be recovered as uniquely meaningful in its own right. It involves normative or genuinely practical philosophical questions. Thus, when we speak about concepts like the state, liberty, or authority we are examining what is 'normative' in such notions. Further, there is usually little agreement on the meaning of such concepts. However this is not unexpected or necessarily worrying. These questions invoke human self-interpretations and self-conceptions. As Berlin comments 'men's beliefs in a sphere of conduct are part of their conception of themselves and others as human beings' (Berlin 1962: 13). We are, as Charles Taylor has often reminded us, self-interpreting creatures. We need to examine the 'manner' and 'form' in which we seek to constitute ourselves. Thus, against the earlier dismissal of normative propositions, Berlin comments 'to suppose . . . that there have been or could be ages without political philosophy, is like supposing that as there are ages of faith, so there could be ages of total disbelief' (Berlin 1962: 17). Normative issues thus lurch into view again in the later 1960s, this time with a hesitant analytic benediction.

WITTGENSTEIN AND ESSENTIAL CONTESTABILITY

The recovery of interest in normative argument within the analytic style is due to a complexity of factors, which can only be glossed briefly. First, the social and political circumstances of the 1960s and early 1970s were requisite for this development. This was a period which saw an upsurge of counter-culture movements, wide scale social radicalism, a tremendous swelling of concern for civil rights legislation, on issues of race, sexuality, gender, poverty, and reproductive rights. Much of the legislation, which allowed greater freedoms and rights over issues such as abortion, homosexuality, educational rights, and so forth, was initiated in this period. Further, for a whole generation of young Americans and Australians (and many others across the world)

this domestic radicalism was set against the backdrop of the Vietnam War. This gal-
vanized a significant grouping of younger people. Issues such as just war theory,
imperialism, colonialism, the rights of individuals, moral and civil obligations, rights
to freedom, justice, and the like, took on a very personal urgency for a generation.
Coupled with this, in the academic politics discipline, behaviouralism was beginning
to falter. It had no resources to address the deep moral and social anxieties of this
period, its repudiation of moral discourse being well established by now. Its normative cupboard was bare and uninviting. A number of the then newer generation of
political theorist, such as Alasdair MacIntyre, Charles Taylor, and Peter Winch, were
also vigorous critics of positivist social science. Despite still being largely rooted, at
this stage, in the analytic and ordinary language tradition these theorists took up the
moral and normative dimension, signalled by Berlin, with great vigour. There were
two theoretical aspects to this recovery of the normative dimension. The first fits
more neatly with the ordinary language tradition discussed so far. This is the impact
of the later Wittgenstein and the 'essential contestability argument'. The second is the
Rawlsian contractarian arguments of the 1970s. The latter development will be taken
up in Chapter 4.

The crucial figure in the transition from ordinary language philosophy towards
the recognition of the importance of normativism was Wittgenstein, particularly his
late work the *Philosophical Investigations*. This, and other works, were profoundly
influential on a whole range of philosophical positions. For the moment the focus
will remain on the impact on ordinary language philosophy and particularly on the
idea of essential contestability.

The central theme again is language. Language is seen as the carrier of human
culture. To master a language is to take on a culture. It is only in language—and
therefore in a culture—that we can mean something (Wittgenstein 1963: part 1,
section 38). Meaning neither (as in the *Tractatus*) tries to picture the world, nor
does it lie within ideas or concepts. Meaning is not independent of language, it is
embedded within it. Words are seen to embody a rich profusion of meanings in
different linguistic contexts. Philosophical problems will often grow out of the rich
profusion and vagaries of language itself. However, words in themselves have no
essence, rather as Austin and others argued, they have diverse ways of being used.
Using a concept implies nothing in addition to its use. The meaning lies *in* the use,
namely in what speakers actually do with it in different contexts. Concepts thus do
not necessarily refer to palpable things in the world at all. There is nothing *outside*
language. Words do inhere in objects in the world. This might be considered a form
of linguistic idealism (see Pitkin 1972: 120), although it is doubtful that Wittgenstein
would have been happy with this label.

Insofar as language has a use function, it has a social dimension. We do not invent
purely private uses of words; otherwise there would be no communication. This is a
much debated argument in Wittgenstein—he denies that there could ever be such a
thing as a private language. What enables us to identify a meaning in use is that there
are public (not private) rules governing the use of concepts. Public rules function like
conventions in Austin. Words have a meaning because they relate to certain shared

rules of usage. At one point, Wittgenstein refers to these rules as equivalent to a kind of grammar, not a surface grammar, but rather a deep grammar, which embodies the variety of possible uses of a word. These rules (or depth grammar) are embedded in what he refers to as 'language games' or 'forms of life'. Language games are simply ways of operating in the world. There must be shared rules, conventions, and language games for there to be any common or shared meanings. However language games are prodigiously diverse and cannot be reduced to other language games. There is no master form of life. As one writer comments, 'meaning is determined by the word's "distribution" in language, the "linguistic environment" in which it occurs' (Pitkin 1972: 11). The same concept will often come under different language games. Wittgenstein is insistent here that there is no essence to words. However, the different uses of the word may well have what he calls 'family resemblances'. A word like game, for example, may have a number of uses—from Olympic games to board games—however Wittgenstein insists that we should not just assert that 'There must be something common, or they would not be called "games"—but look and see whether there is anything common at all.' Wittgenstein contends that if you look 'you will not see something that is common at all, but similarities, relationships' (Wittgenstein 1951: section 66).

We often take language games for granted. They are not hidden, but they can be overlooked, partly because they are so familiar. Yet to grasp any language game or form of life is always equivalent to mastering the rules of a game and its complex techniques. To know the techniques and rules of a game is to be able to perform the requisite actions. All human action, for Wittgenstein, is, in fact, linked directly to language. To follow a rule is distinct from habit or behaviour. One *must* intend to follow rules. Thus rule-following, is by definition, purposive or intentional. Meaning, as embodied in rules, is thus intrinsically tied to intentional activity. Thus, discourse or language is tied intimately to action. This is the root to Austin and Searle's conception of 'speech acts'—although both the latter thinkers produce a much more differentiated and complex analysis of types of action. Words are forms of action. When we mean something it arises from the rules and intentions embedded in forms of life or language games. Language is viewed as integral to all our actions in the world. Thus, in Wittgenstein, there is not only a sophisticated epistemology and philosophy of mind, but also a philosophy of action intimately tied to the philosophy of mind. Both are rooted in a linguistic conventionalism. This also forms the root to Peter Winch's well-known study, *The Idea of Social Science*, and the basis for his central distinctions between natural and social science (Winch 1958).

In this sense, the role of philosophy—parallel to other ordinary language philosophers—is largely analytical and descriptive. It might be described (as mentioned above) either as a linguistic idealism, or, alternatively, as a linguistic phenomenology. It does not *solve* philosophical problems, as such; conversely, through a careful attention to the way words are used, it can *dissolve* philosophical problems. As Weldon argued, many difficulties arise with concepts since the speaker will often try to fix upon one particular use as some kind of essence. In this context, Wittgensteinian analysis issues clear reminders to speakers. Some philosophers will still attempt to gain greater clarity and will thus fixate upon one particular use of a concept. However, in this context, as Wittgenstein remarked, language tends to 'go on holiday'. Philosophy, in drawing attention to the diversity of usage, performs what Wittgenstein refers to as a therapeutic function. It helps to emancipate individuals from conceptual muddles resulting from inattention to the diversity implicit in language and the way it functions in human affairs. In this sense, it is not recommending, but reminding us of what we already know.

If we turn now directly to political concepts: as with ordinary language theory, analysis has a function—to analyse and clarify the complex internal structure of concepts, such as justice, rights, obligations, and so forth. As with Hegelian idealism, descriptive phenomenology, *Verstehen* based hermeneutics, or the Oakeshottian conception of philosophy, all that can be done is to analyse what *is* already the case, namely, to understand the existing conceptual structures and to assemble reminders of what is the case. Political theory cannot move (in theory) into the sphere of direct normative recommendation, although it still does take normative argument seriously.

It is in the above context that ordinary language theory, qua Wittgenstein and Austin, is particularly opposed to essentialism in conceptual usage. The function of political theory should be the registering and elucidation of the diverse uses of political concepts. The term 'essential contestability' is thus set up in direct opposition to essentialism. Essentialism in simple format, is a doctrine, which can be identified with, for example, Plato's philosophy of ideas, where the function of political philosophy is seen to be the attempt to identify the 'essential' meaning of ideas such as justice. The crucial philosophical question for essentialism is therefore what is the *core* or essential element of justice. Once the essence has been identified and defined, then it can be used to correct and explain the nature of justice in general. Any reference to justice, by definition, must refer to its essence. The same argument would hold for all political concepts. If it makes sense, we should be able to give some definition of its essence. If a word makes sense and can be defined, then it has some kind of reality. However, essential contestability directly adopts the Wittgensteinian mantle in denying that concepts and words have essences.

For W. B. Gallie, who coined the term 'essential contestability' in a lecture in 1956, it implied that many disputes about concepts are intractable. Although the *same* concept is at issue, there are different uses and criteria of application of the concept that are in direct conflict. To link this directly with Wittgenstein, each particular use is embedded in a language game or form of life. For Gallie, therefore, certain concepts have 'no clearly definable general use which can be set up as a correct or standard use' (Gallie 1955–6: 168). Different criteria for concepts embody standards of excellence, but these are diverse and in dispute. Each party discussing, say, art, democracy, or a religious doctrine will claim, with reasonable arguments, to have the correct usage. This endless disputation is neither due to what he calls, 'metaphysical afflictions', nor some deep psychological cause. There is something else at the root. There are, in other words, perfectly genuine disputes about concepts with respectable argument and evidence on all sides. The proper use *itself* 'involves endless disputes about their proper uses' (Gallie 1955–6: 169). Another resonant term, employed by a later theorist, is that of 'cluster concepts' (see Connolly 1983; Freeden 1996).

Gallie postulates four major initial characteristics of such concepts. They must be appraisive 'in the sense that it signifies or accredit some kind of valued achievement'; second, the achievement 'must be of an internally complex character'; third, it follows that any description of the concept, of necessity, involves a number of rival accounts; fourth, that parties who are interested in the concept recognized that the concept can be modified. In other words, there is a recognition of the 'open' character of the concept. In addition to these four 'more important' characteristics to essentially contested concepts, Gallie postulates further aspects. Thus, he contends, fifth, that all parties 'recognize the fact that its own use of it is contested by those of other parties'. The concept can be used against other uses both defensively or aggressively (Gallie 1955–6: 171–2). He also contends that there must be some form of original 'examplar' or prototype, whose authority is recognized in some way by all the contestants. Thus, 'to follow an examplar is to exert oneself to revive its (or his) way of doing things' (Gallie 1955–6: 177). Although, he adds, there is no way of ascertaining who actually does have the most correct revival. In other words, there is no way of absolutely attaining a 'best use'. Finally, he contends that the concept and its achievements could not have developed in the way they have 'except by the kind of continuous competition' (Gallie 1955–6: 178).

Some critics would say that reason demands 'universal assent' and essential contestability appears to undermine this. Gallie replies that this may be necessary in the natural sciences, 'but it fails completely as a description of those elements of reason that make possible *discussions* of religious, political and artistic problems' (Gallie 1955–6: 196). This is emphatically not an argument concerning irrationality. Further, for Gallie, the critic might say that he is confusing logical use or proper use of the concept now and its historical conditions. He contends that the two can be linked at any time. Any appraisal of a concept must include 'not simply consideration of different uses . . . *as we use it to-day*, but consideration of such instances as display its growth and development' (Gallie 1955–6: 197–8). For Gallie, even if this is a 'form' of historicism, it is not fallacious, but, is a necessary component of the analysis of any concept.

It is important to note here that essential contestability is distinct from simple contestedness, in terms of historically or sociologically different meanings. Thus, Gallie's thesis, as he asserts it above, is *not* simply about historicism, sociological relativism, or meaning variance and shift. Further, it is also distinct from the thesis that the criteria of the application of a concept may be in dispute, but the protagonists do not deny that some form of resolution is possible or desirable, and that it would be definite progress if it could be resolved. Essential contestability is a far stronger philosophical perspective, which asserts that disputes about certain concepts are actually endless. There will always be good reasons to continue disputation and there is no definite way to resolve these disputes. This invokes a strong incommensurability thesis and a deeply-sceptical demeanour. In this sense, it appears to be most faithful to its Wittgensteinian roots.

A number of theorists have applied essential contestability as the favoured method for political theory with variable success.[12] It remained (with variations of ordinary language theory), an undercurrent on many courses on Anglophone conceptual political theory throughout the second half of the twentieth century. It also ties in closely into doctrines of epistemological pluralism and particularism, moral pluralism and fortuitously a Millian form of liberalism, or what John Gray calls, 'the chronic character of normative and epistemic dissensus' (see Gallie 1955–6; Gray 1977: 335–6; Flathman 1989: 4). It also supports, as Gray puts it, 'a conception of political philosophy' (Gray 1977: 345). In fact, Gray takes the noteworthy step of identifying essential contestability as a 'definite metaphysical' position, in addition to being committed to a pluralist liberal vision (Gray 1978: 395). Interestingly, the metaphysical dimensions of this vision do not often get a mention; this would be largely due to the more general allergic reaction to metaphysics during the twentieth century.

A RECKONING WITH ESSENTIAL CONTESTABILITY

Despite the fact that Wittgenstein and the essential contestability thesis have had a powerful role in underpinning the general pedagogical approach to political theory, there have also been a series of challenges and attempts at modification, some more successful than others. The legacy of Wittgenstein has moved in different directions. Orthodox earnest philosophical scholarship on the 'master' has gone on regardless— this philosophical hagiography (which unfortunately always happens to interesting thinkers), will no doubt keep publishers busy well into the future. The present account considers four reactions to Wittgenstein and the essential contestability thesis, some of these will be taken up again later in the book, since they are still very much part of contemporary discussion of difference theory and postmodernism. Many of the criticisms revolve around positive and negative reactions to the same elements of the essential contestability (basically Wittgensteinian) arguments. There is clearly a great adaptability in the Wittgensteinian argument.[13]

One of the core areas of debate over the essential contestability argument relates to the potentially deep—what some would regard as disabling—relativism and incommensurability of the argument. The *positive* view of this can be identified loosely with two responses. The first can be called the deconstructive reception, both to this argument and to Wittgenstein's later thought. In this reading, the essential contestability argument does not push far enough. The second response focuses on Gallie's potential historicism and emphasizes that essential contestability should move progressively and naturally into more conceptually-orientated history (*Begriffsgeschichte*). The *negative* response also has two faces. The first reacts critically to the collapse of agreed definitions of concepts, and demands a reconstruction of concepts to make them clearly operational within political debate. The second negative response focuses, again, on the disabling relativism, but wends around this by drawing a distinction between a strong and weak essential contestability theses.[14]

The first positive response can almost be observed evolving over the various editions of William Connolly's *The Terms of Political Discourse*, since its publication in 1974, as he moves from the more conventional late Wittgensteinian position, via Foucault, into a genealogical position. This is by no means an unusual process. There is an immanent danger of an extreme Pyrrhonism within Wittgensteinianism and essential contestability, which is clearly adaptable to postmodern and poststructural analysis. It can, of course, for some, simply remain as fruitless scepticism.[15] Essential contestability basically lets the genii of linguistic and ontological multiplicity out the philosophical bottle. It does not show *a* way out of the fly bottle, but rather it shows *multiple* routes out, which is enough to confuse any good-hearted fly. Multiple language games, ontological incommensurability, and linguistic idealism (without teleology) provide a scenario for multiple constructed realities. Thus, if language is our only access to reality (either as a *tertium quid* between speaker and something vaguely 'raw', but unknown, outside, or, as simply a self-sufficient thing in itself), then there are potentially multiple realities, which we can address. To take the slightly harder edged non-foundational approach (which gives up the 'raw things' to which languages might correspond), there is nothing that can be appealed to resolve questions. To try to impose a monoglot answer is to engage in, what Jean François Lyotard has neatly called, a form of linguistic terrorism. Language games are all we have and there is nothing to adjudicate between them. There is nothing over, above, or outside. As both Lyotard and Richard Rorty—both who claim Wittgenstein as a philosophical mentor—argue, we have to give up *any* possibility of a master vocabulary. There are therefore no metanarratives. Rorty and Lyotard contest at the edges here—since Rorty (unlike Lyotard) thinks that language games overlap and can debate (Rorty 1989; Lyotard 1991*a*). However, the basic gist of their Wittgensteinianism, moves in roughly the same postmodern direction. One use for this argument is in the sphere of social multiplicity. The recent more fashionable postcolonial, multicultural, and difference theories have given rise to protracted debates over issues such as difference. Thus, James Tully's work, *Strange Multiplicity*, quite self-consciously uses Wittgensteinian argument to uphold postcolonial and indigenous claims on constitutionality, law and justice (see Tully 1995).

The second positive reading picks up the historical aspect of the essential contestability argument. Thus, Terence Ball is critical of essential contestability for its analytic tendency to adopt an ahistorical attitude, which he thinks is mistaken (Ball 1988: 14).[16] He sees analytical philosophy as notable for its dismal non-appreciation of the historical dimension of concepts, which he considers odd, given their linguistic emphasis. He argues for the need to move beyond conceptual analysis into 'critical conceptual history'. Gallie hints at this potential in his original article, but never takes it any further. For Ball, politics is always a conceptually constituted activity. The language we use is never neutral, in fact, our political discourses can transform us—or constrain us. Thus, for Ball, 'as we speak, so we are. We live in a world or words. We are tied to words. It is who and what we are'. How we classify and act 'is deeply delimited by the conceptual, argumentative and rhetorical resources of our language. The limits of my moral and political language, we might say, mark the limits of my moral and political world' (Ball 1988: 4). As the concepts constitutive of our speech change, 'so too do we'. Concepts use and meanings are always linked to predicaments in which individuals find themselves, although they may often be invisible to those who use a discourse (Ball 1988: ix–x).

The important point here is that these concepts that constitute our political lives are both contestable *and* historically mutable. Language games thus have histories that are deeply relevant for their current usage. As Ball notes, 'Every concept is the repository of earlier associations and uses' (Ball 1988: 5). They trail 'clouds of etymology'. Language is also the medium of memory and shared experiences. Ball comments that 'To remember our language . . . may enable us to gain a degree of critical purchase on the present. By the same token, of course, our language serves to distance us from the past by enabling us to appreciate the vast differences between past people's conceptually constituted practices and our own. To encounter and attempt to understand them in all their strangeness requires the stretching of our own concepts and categories' (Ball 1988: 3). Discourse is not though autonomous from speakers. Practical action cannot be separated from the intentionality of the concepts we use. We do not have discourses, in one sense they have us. Yet, Ball is quick to remind his readers that we can get tangled in misleading metaphors here—such as the idea that language speaks us (qua Foucault), which for Ball is a deceptive 'caricature' (Ball 1988: 11).

For Ball, it is the critical conceptual historian who charts these complex conceptual changes. He is keying directly here into the work of the *Begriffsgeschichte* historians (briefly mentioned in Part One under historical political theory). He uses their ideas to emphasize the historical dimension to essential contestability and tries to make it mutate it into conceptual history (Ball 1988: 14–15, see also the introduction to Ball, Farr, and Hanson (eds.) 1989). In fact, Ball takes one of the key themes of the *Begriffsgeschichte* group, particularly from the writings of Rheinhart Koselleck, that concepts can experience, what he calls, a dramatic *Sattelzeit* period (Kosellek 1985). This is a time of unprecedented conceptual change or mutation. The period that Koselleck focused on was 1750–1850. This period saw, for example, the rise of the major political ideology-based 'isms', which, as Ball remarks, 'by supplying speakers with a new means of locating themselves in social and political space, actually reconstituted that very space. Political conflict accordingly became overtly ideological' (Ball 1988: 9–10). Ball suspected that the closing decades of the twentieth century might be part of another significant *Sattelzeit* period. Consequently, a historically informed essential contestability argument takes on an immensely important function for Ball.

The first *negative* reading of essential contestability can be found in the *reconstructive thesis* of Felix Oppenheim (Oppenheim 1981). In general, Oppenheim regards language in a very particular manner. There may well be ordinary language, but there are also specialized technical languages. The former type of language is far too blunt and crude a tool. It embodies diverse and often contradictory usage, but this invites linguistic correction. As Oppenheim comments 'It is necessary to construct language as free as possible of the imperfections of ordinary usage' (Oppenheim 1981: 177). In other words, the theorists needs to 'reconstruct basic concepts' to avoid ambiguity and confusion. Essential contestability, however, wallows in the confusion of ordinary language. It encourages, as Oppenheim notes, 'vagueness, open-endedness and ambiguity' (Oppenheim 1981: 194). These are not assets for political theory to cultivate, but obstacles to be overcome. Real political theory sees the confusion of ordinary concepts as an open invitation for 'tidying up'. Unlike the 'reportive' and 'stipulative' approaches of essential contestability, reconstruction favours explicative definitions, which 'can be appraised as good and bad in terms of their suitability for scientific communication' (Oppenheim 1981: 179). Constructing such explicative accounts parallels constructing good scientific theories for Oppenheim, in terms of accuracy, simplicity, and fruitfulness. A good explicative account reveals the inner structure of concepts and facilitates generalizations. Although this sounds something like a qualified return to a positivist perspective, Oppenheim is insistent that he rejects the older forms of positivism and behaviouralism. Yet, to reject the old fashioned positivism is not to abandon empirical theory. Oppenheim however does want to separate the realms of values and facts (qua value non-cognitivism, as opposed to the value cognitivism of essential contestability). Justification *is* distinct from description. Moral beliefs are not descriptive. This does not mean that political study is value free, rather that the theorist has to be conscious of values as distinct elements which are not subject to truth or falsity claims.

Thus Oppenheim sees endless conceptual analysis of ordinary language in all its general confusion and vagueness, and commitment to value cognitivism, as a false and damaging pathway.[17] He also tries to return the whole argument back to a much more positivistically inclined theory which actually sees language as something to control, tidy up, and use with greater technical precision. Relativism should be avoided and objectivity sought. There is, though, a lurking sense in Oppenheim of a neutral metatheory—a form of subtle technocratic ideal that is to be imposed on political language. All, or most of the old problems of logical positivism and behaviouralism rise again here.

The final negative reading, like Oppenheim, sees essential contestability again as far too much inclined to extreme relativism and incommensurability. However, in this case, the alternative sought is not value non-cognitivism, but a variation of rigorous value cognitivism, which returns the discussion to the perceived older tasks of normative classical political theory. In this case, the argument modifies essential contestability. John Gray, for example, sought, for a moment in his diverse theoretical career, to revise essential contestability in order to distance it from 'sceptical, relativist, historicist and conventionalist traditions'. This would facilitate the possibility of future 'conclusive rational resolution' to political theory conceptual debates. Essential contestability allowed for the possibility that, although certain concepts were deeply contested, this did not mean that there could not be 'good reasons' and some kind of reasonable resolution to philosophical problems. This weakens the whole classical Wittgensteinian essential contestability account. It does, however, leave open the possibility, once again, as Gray is keen to urge, for 'perennial political problems'. He comments that, 'the revised essential contestability thesis endorses a classical conception of political philosophy as an intellectual activity capable of yielding determinate results, and, so, of assisting reflective agents in their search for a good society' (Gray 1977: 346; see also Gray 1978: 394–5). This allows the theorist, such as Gray, to endorse much of the analytical philosophical dimension, and then to put it to work to defend a singular account of concepts such as justice and liberty. It also still preserves the autonomy of the discipline of political theory. This latter perspective begins to provide some insight into the Rawlsian generation, which will be pursued in Chapter 4.

CONCLUSION

What was the general upshot of these logical positivist, ordinary language, and essential contestability perspectives? One of the major effects was to give political theory a predominantly 'conceptualist focus' in the second half of the twentieth century. The general requirement was for a phenomenological description of each political concept.[18] This constituted what one commentator has perceptively called an 'issue orthodoxy', namely, 'a general belief that politics can be defined in terms of a finite range of distinct universal or "basic" issues, encapsulated by such terms as *power, justice, obligation, state*' (Condren 1985: 44).

Further, the historical situation of these concepts was of little interest. Moral seriousness and argumentative rigour were more significant measures of good theory. Theory texts (or theorists) from the past appeared selectively, in so far as they made a critical contribution to the phenomenology of the concept.[19] Concepts, although debatable and variable in meaning, were not assumed to change too much over time. The interests were therefore wholly synchronic. The thought that we might not be dealing with the same concept, or that our own mental world might be alien to the past, seems not to have been of any concern. Yet the fact that linguistically sensitive thinkers had little or no appreciation of the problem of history, has struck a number of commentators as odd. The bland conceptualist synchronic assumption seemed to be: 'if we shout loudly enough Plato will reply in English' (Condren 1985: 50).[20]

In addition, this conceptual approach, or issue orthodoxy, spawned a number of political concepts texts, such as the early Macmillan publications, begun in the 1960s and recovered again in the 1980s. Not everyone moved in unison on the theme of conceptual analysis, but the crucial point of the enterprise was clear. For several generations of political theory or political philosophy academics and postgraduates—outside of the history of political theory domain—conceptual theory and issue orthodoxy passed as mainstream technical or professional political theory. Theorists developed intellectually, reading and teaching within the issue orthodoxy conceptual approach. The idea was presumably that the reader was actually getting unsullied 'pristine political theory', when what they were really getting was a very focused and occasionally somewhat parochial angle on theory. This is not to demean the work itself, which was and is often insightful and pedagogically immensely useful, but the assumptions behind it have *never* been seriously addressed. Theorists oddly seem to favour historical and conceptual blinkers to a more open perspective. The energy underpinning this issue orthodoxy enterprise appeared to diminish slightly in the last decade of the century, although it remains very much *the* established form.

Further, this 'issue orthodoxy' trend underpinned many introductory texts in political theory, particularly from the 1950s onwards. Stanley Benn's and Richard Peters' *Social Principles and the Democratic State* started this trend and it carried on till the end of the century. The key dilemma for such texts—which have usually standardly been ahistorical alphabetic lists of 'key' concepts—is whether concepts should either be subjected to a neutral phenomenological description or a critical tidying up. This is the old difference between logical positivism and ordinary language theory. Most texts incorporate a confused blend of both. David Raphael, for example, in a popular textbook, *The Problems of Political Philosophy*, used to introduce many generations of students to political theory, commented that the discipline was, unsurprisingly, focused on clarifying concepts. This involved three elements: analysis of the concept (which specifies its basic elements), synthesis (which shows the logical relationships between concepts), and finally, improvement of the concept. The first two were standard ordinary language fare. The latter entailed 'recommending a definition or use that will assist clarity or coherence' (Raphael 1976: 13). It also involved a selective and dismissive attitude to what previously went under the rubric of theory. As Raphael commented, for example, 'The history of political philosophy since the sixteenth century contains a great deal of tedious-looking discussion . . . Much of it is indeed tedious' (Raphael 1976: 15–16). Here we experience again the Weldonian and logical positivist hubris.

Raphael was aware that many ordinary language thinkers believed that we should reject any normative improvement for political philosophy. He commented that 'A philosopher may think that his task is simply to chart the old and new meanings, but it seems to me that the process of clarification must often inevitably carry with it a sharpening and so a slight change of the meaning of the concept' (Raphael 1976: 14). However, for Raphael, the ahistorical analysis of concepts does have a beneficial dimension. He comments that 'The clarification of concepts is like cleaning the house. When you have cleaned the house, there is not much to be seen from your work. You have not acquired any new possessions, though you will have thrown out some things that are not wanted and are just a nuisance. What you have at the end of it is a tidier house, in which you can move around more easily' (Raphael 1976: 16). This is not a once and for all job and it needs to be done regularly by each generation. The rubbish clearance, or conceptual cleanliness, view of political theory is again reminiscent of Weldon et al., where removal of 'mental lumber' is seen as central. Raphael's hesitant argument that concepts can be sharpened or improved is still *not* a contention that political theory constructs or offers any definite normative answers. Political theory is *not* about normative argument, it is about clear thought—a form of continuous intellectual hand-washing—on the important concepts constituting the issue orthodoxy. This encourages the belief that the theorist is still engaged in an academically reputable, universally important, and yet socially accountable activity.

Notes

1. In many ways much of the discussion of logical positivism and early linguistic philosophy could have fitted in Part One with ease. There would have been some sense to have had an

extra category in Part One. However, my reason for separating this latter discussion out into Part Two is because I wish to establish the sequence of arguments which leads through from logical positivist debates to Rawlsian justice-based theory.

2. In Carnap's case, for example, at Chicago University, his courses were also of great interest to the new generation of political scientists.

3. The English translation appeared in 1922 with a preface by Bertrand Russell.

4. Which was largely an attempt to say what reality would be like if it were describable in language derived from Russell's and Whitehead's *Principia Mathematica*.

5. Words like 'if' 'for', and 'not' do not picture the world.

6. Alfred Ayer in his retrospective interview in the 1970s, with Bryan Magee, on being asked about the defects of logical positivism, remarked, 'Well, I suppose that the most serious of the defects of positivism was that nearly all of it was false', see Magee (1978: 131).

7. The tense is important here. Thus 'I promised' is no longer performative.

8. Further, Austin argued that we should also take note of what he called the locutionary force of utterances—namely, the grammatical and literal meaning; the illocutionary force of what is performed in uttering something; and, finally, the perlocutionary force which embodies the effect of uttering something. Locutionary and illocutionary acts depend upon appropriate conventions, which enable the utterance to do what the speaker wants it to do. Conventions need to be known. Speech acts have to be faithful to conventions to be successful.

9. As G. J. Warnock commented in 1969 'there are no doubt in "our climate of thought" many factors . . . that are in some way unfriendly to the metaphysical temperament'. For Warnock, one key reason for this unfriendliness is that 'metaphysical speculation has often arisen from, and often too been a substitute for, religious or theological doctrine', see Warnock (1969: 96).

10. 'Weldon is at least as much of a positivist as he is a Wittgensteinian analyst, that is, one who is committed to the thesis that "meaning is use"', see Blackstone (1973: 24).

11. The term 'ejaculation' was Alfred Ayer's whimsical addition.

12. The most well known would be Steven Lukes' *Power: A Radical View* (1975) and W. E. Connolly's *Terms of Political Discourse* (1983).

13. He has been adapted to the conservative thought by some writers, although this has always been vigorously denied by others (Wertheimer 1976: 19). Others have adapted essential contestability argument with an emphasis on its philosophical neutrality in relation to forms of life. The neutrality is so strongly stressed that it miraculously reappears as a species of neutralist liberalism. The 'standing over language games' becomes 'the standing over theories of the good'. A philosophy of language thus becomes theory of formal liberal equality.

14. The latter view is adaptable to the more traditional concerns of perennial problems and some recent normative political theory.

15. 'It seems hard to draw limits to the capacity of essential contestability to infect moral concepts'. Thus, for the authors, every debate would be subject to fruitless reduction. Thus, they continue 'Exactly how political arguments are to be conducted . . . in the face of nagging essential contestability is a problem that Gallie does not explore', Lesser, Plant, and Taylor-Gooby (1980: 9–10).

16. Further, he maintains that not all concepts have or could be contested at all times.

17. There are direct parallels here with Karl Popper's response to ordinary language philosophy, see Popper (1976).

18. In Richard Flathman's work, in the 1970s and 1980s, it appeared to be reaching its apotheosis, a conceptual analysis potentially of every political concept which moved. By the late 1990s there appeared to be a more 'Nietzschean' anxiety lurking in the wings and a possible weariness.

19. The general sentiment being that 'dealing in some way with the "basics" is the least we can expect from a great political theorist', Condren (1985: 45).

20. Another related problem to this demeanour is that 'A sort of conceptual inflation will thus be encouraged, resulting in an ever expanding syndrome of "basic" or "fundamental" or "enduring" issues, which by its existence robs such predicates of their meaning'. However, as Condren adds, for most conceptual theories 'a little historical, linguistic, logical, and metaphysical dubiety may be thought a tolerable one to pay', Condren (1985: 48, 55).

4

Bleached Foundations

The upshot of Chapter Three is that logical positivism, ordinary language philosophy, and the essential contestability thesis had an important impact on political theory. Although there are dimensions of this general approach which have been abandoned, others have been retained. Essential contestability, for example, has not so much been rejected or refuted as subsumed into the subconscious of political studies. It now simply 'crops up' as a relative background commonplace of vocabulary that students of politics are expected to know something about. A second point is that despite all the above theories' rejection of metaphysics (with varying degrees of intensity), nonetheless, all saw the philosophical method, implicit in conceptual and analytical political theory, as both foundational and universal. Although scepticism prevailed on most other issues, there was little reflexivity or doubt about its own validity. The foundations were thin but firm. Thus, the approach to political theory, although critical and sceptical, remained secure.

Political theory was supported in the 1950s and early 1960s by twin pillars: first, the secure 'second-order' activity of rigorous and morally serious conceptual analysis (or what I referred to as linguistic phenomenology), and second, the 'first-order' knowledge of empirical social science, namely political theory in empirical practice. The foundations that were shaken were those of traditional or classical normative and the history of political theory. Political theory survived and flourished in a new shape. It had wriggled hard and shifted focus. This 'twin pillar' approach rested very securely with logical positivism, but became discomforted with ordinary language and essential contestability theory. The discomfort was however alleviated by the fact that ordinary language theory retained (latently) the underlying empiricist and realist foundationalist standpoint. It also repudiated comprehensive metaphysics, which was still seen as either utterly innocuous or noxious empty speculation. If one blinked hard, both ordinary language and essential contestability theory (in one form) could survive harmoniously with the empirical social science perspective.

However, there were major problems with the essential contestability thesis. The reactions to essential contestability, canvassed in Chapter Three, often focused on the more problematic issue of the potentially deep relativism and incommensurability implicit in such argument. Some theorists, of a postmodern persuasion, later found this relativism totally congenial, others wanted to pacify the relativism within a historical framework, others again sought to abandon it altogether. However, for a generation of political theorists educated in ordinary language, conceptual analysis, and analytical theory, such movements of ideas could not simply be put to one side. What was needed was a modified analytical emphasis—a tempered essential contestability—which recovered, in a more fulsome manner, what Berlin and others referred to as the normative and justificatory sphere. The question is what would such a recovery entail?

There were two subtle moves in this normative direction. The first signalled that normative concepts were crucial to humans as self-interpreting creatures, and that these concepts could be evaluated, improved, and sharpened by political theorists. This also had some loose connections to the idea of 'tidying up' concepts. This path had been recognized within ordinary language and essential contestability theory. There had even been a number of hesitant moves to 'improve' political concepts. The fertile words here were *sharpening, clarifying,* and *improving*. As emphasized, they were distinct from an explicit *construction* of a justificatory theory, which purports to show why we should adopt one structure of norms or values rather than another. This latter point, however, constituted the second subtle move. If the theorist could show that the original form of essential contestability is hopelessly caught in a relativist loop, and that it did not adequately account for the manner in which normative arguments were deployed, then it was a very short step to modify or adjust the essential contestability argument. This modification suggested that rigorous conceptual analysis was needed, to a degree, since political concepts often embodied deep internal divisions that required elucidation. However, once the analysis was completed, an aspect of the concept could be shown to be more in accord with our everyday intuitions than other forms. This aspect was more in accord with an 'essential use' by humanity. A normative theory could then show us—at a very abstract, sophisticated, and systematic level—the skeletal structure of the deep intuitive values held by all humans. An aspect of the concept could be shown to approximate to this deep structure. A normative political theory therefore showed the basic concrete human values stripped down to their basic form. This, in essence, provided the basis for a reasoned normative and justificatory theory, which in effect, supplied a final resolution for the essentially contestable concepts. Essential contestability was thus the *hors d'oeuvres* to the substantial main course of the concept, which although initially internally contested, could be finally resolved within a normative theory. Thus, classical normative theory *returned* again anointed with analytical oil. For others, nothing actually returned, but, conversely, a new conception of political theory developed, which contained some familiar resonances with a past structure. It is in this general scenario that we see the growth of normative theory in the 1970s and 1980s, focusing particularly on justice.

THE CONCEPT OF JUSTICE

Normative-based justice theory was one of the main preoccupations of the last three decades of the twentieth century, although the movement began to falter in the 1990s. The key work was Rawls' *Theory of Justice*, published originally in 1971. The reason why justice was singled out for normative theory was simply because it was seen, quite literally, as the basic or most central concept of politics. It became a form of arch-concept. Some also saw it as the major preoccupation of the history of political theory from the Greeks to the present. In this sense, it replaced the concept of the state, qua *Staatslehre*, which performed the same linking function earlier in the twentieth century.[1] Another way of putting this is that, in the same way as theorists earlier in the century saw the state as the crucial supposition for politics, so post 1970s normative theory saw some minimal sense of justice as the logical presupposition to politics. The argument was that unless there was some conception of justice, society could not exist. This point was though contentious in itself and not all subscribed to it. For some, justice was one virtue amongst others (Campbell 1988). It was also clearly *not* one thing. There were a range of contested meanings. There was another important reason as to why justice was focused on. Justice was seen to be synonymous with reason, in a formal sense. Put simply, to be reasonable was to grasp the centrality of justice. This was an enormously important contention, which reveals much about the conception of justice at the close of the twentieth century. There are, though, several issues to analyze here.

If one asks the question what is meant by justice?, the first answer would be that, like equality, one has to distinguish the *formal* and *substantive* senses of the concept. This distinction relates back to Aristotle, who distinguishes between the generic sense of justice, as proportion and balance, and the various substantive species of justice. In Aristotle, this notion of balance is the central plank of both ethics and justice. Justice is regarded as the most perfect of all the virtues and injustice the whole of vice. Justice is a mean or measure at the centre of *all* virtues. Correct proportion or measure between two extremes constitutes the doctrine of the mean. All virtues exemplify this balance between extremes, therefore, it follows that justice is at the heart of all the virtues.[2] In its most perfect form it is the ideal disposition of the soul. For Plato, also, justice is a balance and proportion between the soul (or internal faculties) and state.[3] Justice and perfect reason are achieved when there is a precise balance between the ordering of an individual's faculties and their place in society. This is the soul-state analogy in Plato's *Republic*.

The generic or formal sense of both justice and reason is concerned therefore with correct weighting and proportion in judgement. Another way of putting this is that reason and justice are concerned with treating equal cases equally and unequal cases unequally. Both justice and reason can be therefore defined as treating like cases alike, which is equivalent to the universalizability rule. Thus, reason and formal justice are conceptually coordinate. This idea is given a strong reading in Chaim Perelman's book *The Idea of Justice and the Problem of Argument* (1963). For Perelman, the injunction 'like cases should be treated as alike' is the core element of justice; it is also a principle of formal logic. Formal justice is thus 'a principle of action in accordance with which beings of one and the same category must be treated in the same way' (Perelman 1963: 16). Thus, it is illogical to treat differently those cases, which are alike in relevant respects. In effect, this might be considered as a rule of logical impartiality. Cognitively, impartiality is essential to our experience of the world. Without it we cannot re-explain, re-identify, or act self-consistently. For Perelman, therefore, the fundamental rule that governs theory and practice, and respect for which manifests the rationality of both thought and his action, is 'the rule of justice', which implies treating like beings and situations alike (see Perelman 1963: 132).

In sum, the core of justice is equivalent to the *formal* factor in all rational activity. This formal factor also has close relation to equality. The rule of justice, 'treat like cases alike' is the same as 'equality of treatment' or 'equal consideration of interest'. However, both formal justice and equality are distinct from *substantive* species of equality and justice. This formal substantive distinction is also directly echoed in H. L. A. Hart's *Concept of Law*, where he notes that 'justice is traditionally thought of as maintaining or restoring a balance or proportion, and its leading precept is often formulated as "Treat like cases alike"; though we need to add to the latter "and treat different cases differently"' (Hart 1961: 155–9). It is also implicit in Rawls' early distinction between the 'conception of justice' as opposed to 'concepts' or principles of justice. As Rawls notes: 'Men disagree about which principles of justice should define the basic terms of their association, yet we may still say, despite this disagreement, that they each have a conception of justice' (Rawls 1971: 5). For Rawls, every person 'may be supposed' to have this conception of justice and 'societies will differ from one another not in having or in failing to have this notion but in the range of cases to which they apply it and in the emphasis which they give to it' (Rawls 1997: 198).

The distinction between a concept and conceptions also harks back to the modified essential contestability thesis, mentioned earlier. Rawls (and most other like-minded theorists) is suggesting that, despite wide-ranging disagreement about justice, a key aspect of the concept can still be identified and developed, which corresponds with our deep intuitions. This point builds upon the connection between 'reason' and 'justice'. In effect, it purports to resolve the issue of justice—although it moves indiscernibly between the formal and substantive accounts. Reason is concerned with abstract conclusions drawn from premises that everyone accepts. The same point can be observed, for example, in Brian Barry's work. For Barry, principles of justice capture a notion of equality, which is equivalent to 'reason as universalizability'. Thus, he comments that 'The criterion of reasonable acceptability of principles gives some substance to the idea of fundamental equality while at the same time flowing from it. This is, if you like, a circle—but not a vicious one'. They are both 'expressions of the same moral idea' (Barry 1995: 8). Reason, justice, and a notion of equality are equivalent to impartiality and universalizability.[4]

CONCEPTIONS OF JUSTICE

However, this more general sense of justice and reason is characteristically subdivided, in twentieth-century discussion, between various species of justice. Rawls' work is one important detail in a much larger canvas. Aristotle originally distinguished distributive from commutative and corrective justice.[5] However, Aristotle's (and Plato's) view of the connection between just states of affairs and a balanced human character, is of little interest to the bulk of twentieth-century justice discussion, with the exception of certain contemporary neo-Aristotelians (who will be examined in

Part Three). All these species of justice are nonetheless tied to proportion and balance, in reward or punishments, or exchanges of goods. They correspond with the equality principle (and reason), namely, to treat 'equals equally and unequals unequally, but in proportion to their relevant differences'. The most significant *species* of justice to appear in the twentieth-century literature are procedural and distributive (or social justice) notions, although retributive justice, remains a juridical subtext to some justice discussion.[6] Another way of formulating this distinction is between patterned and unpatterned distribution. Procedural or unpatterned notions can overlap with the patterned or distributive in a number of areas. However, they will be kept distinct here for heuristic purposes.

It is important to indicate briefly some of the general underpinning assumptions of conceptions of justice. In sum, theories of justice presuppose they are dealing with human agents in terms of their political, social, and economic arrangements. Human agents are the central locus of value—both as the focus of value and of the process of valuing. Second, all persons are, by degrees, regarded as rational and moderately self-interested creatures.[7] Humans may be socialized, in some formats, but their altruism or concern for others is still limited.[8] The notion of rationality here remains slightly vague. The crucial questions here are—how does one deal with scarce resources, and competition for those resources, amongst a groups of relatively self-interested human beings? How does one attain a moderate degree of fairness in this situation? Third, scarcity of resources implies some competition between individuals, which needs to be regulated. This latter assumption could entail either minimal background rules (Robert Nozick, David Gauthier, James Buchanan, or Friedrich Hayek), or a much wider-scale redistribution of resources (John Rawls, Thomas Scanlon, or Brian Barry). We can shorten these assumptions to: the centrality of human agency, the inevitability of moderate self-interest, and competitiveness for scarce resources.

Each of the two major branches of justice theory mentioned above—proceduralism and distributive justice—needs to be subdivided again, to grasp the diverse usage of the concept in practice. The forms of proceduralism, which will be briefly discussed are Friedrich Hayek's commutative account of justice and Nozick's slightly more awkwardly placed entitlement theory.[9] Under the rubric of distributive or social justice, there is a great deal more complexity. Twentieth-century discussion of distributive (or social) justice has been concerned largely with the slightly more abstract distributive principle(s) 'to each according to his or her due', or, more simply, the fair allocation of burdens and benefits in society.[10] The fine-tuning of this idea arises with the interpretation of what *is* the more substantive principle that determines *due*. There are a wide range of such principles. However, each principle can be formulated in a similar way, for example: 'to each according to his or her rights, deserts, needs, services, work, moral worth, ability, skill or status', and so forth. These diverse principles can be made greater sense of if we subdivide them again between *desert* and *non-desert* orientated distributive principles. One other small point here is that different principles will often link in with different ideals or visions of a good society.[11]

Desert theory contends that if someone has performed a merit-worthy activity or possesses a valuable quality, then they should be rewarded in relation to that activity or quality. In the last few decades, the bulk of attention has fallen to non-desert orientated principles, with some recent exceptions in the literature (see Sadurski 1985; Sher 1987). In the main, desert has been bypassed by the bulk of justice theorists. Non-desert principles cover the larger bulk of contemporary justice theorizing. The formal claim of non-desert theories—usually premised upon an initial rejection of desert argument—is that distribution is justified via a wide-ranging agreement or consensus on a rational procedure, empirical assumption or moral principle, or a pluralistic combination of these, which forms the basis for distributing burdens and benefits. Non-desert principles vary widely. One convenient way of typologizing them is to distinguish between *two* forms of non-desert orientated distributive principles, namely, the rationalist (basically contractarian claims) and the more empiricist claims (such as need). The latter is concerned to establish an uncontested empirical ground for distribution—characteristic of minimums in welfare states.[12] The former is concerned with the ideal rational conditions in which individuals come to a contractual decision about the manner of distribution in society, in specified rational circumstances. This latter theme particularly has dominated justice-based literature over the last three decades.

The contractarian claims have been usually subdivided again between, what Brian Barry has usefully typologized as 'justice as mutual advantage' and 'justice as impartiality' arguments (see Barry 1989). In the former theory, justice is seen as the outcome of a mutual bargaining process among individuals in an initial position (Buchanan 1975 and Gauthier 1986). Essentially, this theory is a sophisticated form of rational choice argument. In the latter, justice is seen to be the outcome of a rational agreement between discrete individuals in a hypothetical situation or original position where constraints are placed upon the context and character of reasoning that can be used (Rawls 1971, Barry 1995*b*, and Scanlon 1998). The contract device, in Rawls particularly, aims to represent a choice situation and show why individuals have good reasons to adopt justice as fairness. It is not (especially in his more recent work) seen as a bargaining position *per se*, as in Gauthier. One other dimension that appears in the literature is an attempt to establish a plural concept of justice, which is premised on the diverse principles that can be deployed in different contingent contexts (Michael Walzer 1983 and David Miller 1999).

PROCEDURAL THEORIES

Procedural theories of justice argue that justice is concerned with rule-following or rule-consistency. The most characteristic form of this is the idea of justice as upholding the 'rule of law'—although there are again considerable variations on this theme. Within the proceduralist positions there is strong anti-constructivism. Both Hayek and Nozick reject desert as both interventionist and potentially entailing the diminishment of liberty. For Hayek, justice is concerned with the formal consistency between a set of social rules. He thus drew a distinction between teleocratic and catallactic orders. The teleocratic order is directed at a specific purpose, whereas a catallactic order (which for Hayek corresponds to a free liberal society), is a spontaneous order, which arises from the diverse activities of individuals. Justice is concerned with facilitating the maximum freedom of individuals to pursue their own personal interests or goods. Justice, in this context, is concerned with maintaining procedural rules to provide the conditions for individual freedom. It is not concerned with fair outcomes. Consequently, there is a direct antagonism with distributive justice. Injustice is concerned, conversely, with intentional acts of restraint, interference, or coercion. The outcomes of a market order are neither just nor unjust, since they are not the result of intentional actions. As Hayek notes,

> It has of course to be admitted that the manner in which the benefits and burdens are apportioned by the market mechanism would in many instances have to be regarded as very unjust *if* it were the result of a deliberate allocation to particular people. But this is not the case. Those shares are the outcome of a process the effect of which on particular people was neither intended nor foreseen ... To demand justice from such a process is clearly absurd, and to single out some people in such a society as entitled to a particular share evidently unjust. (Hayek 1976: vol 2, 65)

The Hayekian scheme implies beliefs about the importance of individualism, the liberty and rights of individuals, the significance of the free market economy, and a more limited conception of the constitutional state.

The principles that generally govern the frameworks of distributive justice are morally arbitrary to Hayek and reflect largely the personal interests and goals of the individuals who frame them. Even if such deep principles could be found, they could not be put into practice in a society 'whose productivity rests on individuals being free to use their knowledge and abilities for their own purposes' (Hayek 1978: 140). Distribution implies a plan and planners who will attempt to impose their principles coercively upon others. Such processes inevitably create injustices by their very arbitrariness, which is incompatible with a plural society. This was the major theme of Hayek's *The Road to Serfdom* (1944). Distributive justice thus tends to move societies, under the mirage of social justice, toward totalitarianism. Conversely, a genuinely just society should allow individuals maximum freedom to pursue their own interests without interference. If individuals were to receive benefits or burdens on the basis of needs or merits then this would also undermine the efficiency of the market order. Hayek does though acknowledge some role for the state to alleviate extreme hardship. Apart from the manner in which justice is generated, proceduralists, such as Hayek, repudiate all forms of contractual theory—although the outcome and subsequent account of the proceduralist view is markedly similar to the 'justice by mutual advantage' argument.

In Nozick, justice is concerned with a historical entitlement theory, which embodies principles that govern legitimate acquisition and transfer of goods. His theory is essentially showing that anarchistic principles are compatible with a minimal state. In *Anarchy State and Utopia* (1974) individuals are envisaged (without any philosophical argument) as possessing certain basic rights to life, liberty, and property. He takes it wholly for granted that such atomized individuals exist. Thus, the whole argument appears as just an elaborate fictional game. The book in fact opens with the unambiguous assertion that 'Individuals have rights and they are things no person or group may do to them (without violating their rights)' (Nozick 1974: xi). These rights are indefeasible and act as negative side-constraints upon all individuals. They also act as procedural devices that pre-exist any notion of the good. Rights create no duties other than those that are freely consented to. In fact, for Nozick, consent is crucial at every stage of the argument and the whole process of politics. The rights themselves are thus foundational. The non-interference with rights is what Nozick calls the Kantian principle of inviolability. Persons are to be respected as ends in themselves. For Nozick, there is also clearly no value whatsoever in the world outside of individuals. As Nozick notes, 'there is no social entity with a good that undergoes some sacrifices for its own good. There are only individual people, different individual people with their own individual lives' (Nozick 1974: 32–3). Each individual has their own interests and shapes the meaning and value to their own life.

The above theory forms the basis to Nozick's notion of justice. His theory is essentially concerned to establish that each person is protected or guaranteed their entitlements. Nozick distinguishes between end-state principles and historical principles. It is the latter that is compatible with justice. This distinction parallels another he makes between patterned and unpatterned principles. Most distributive and social justice theories draw upon patterned distribution under principles like need and the like. Nozick claims alternatively that unpatterned distribution entails respect for the inviolability of individuals rights, particularly life, liberty, and property. Each individual owns themselves—their own body and its labour. If the individual acquired property through labour, legitimate acquisition, or just transfer then he or she is absolutely entitled to it. Justice exists where everyone has their entitlements. In this sense, there can be no compulsory redistribution and no interference with individual property (unless a good was unjustly acquired as in fraud or theft and then rectification can take place). Justice is, in the end, a matter simply of how a distribution comes about. Again here, there is no theory of the good being articulated by Nozick. A society, if it has a central framework of laws and a dominant protection agency (a minimal state) will only be concerned with maintaining procedural justice. In this sense, Nozick's conception of unpatterned distributive justice closely resembles, in outcome, many of the major themes of proceduralism, qua Hayek.

SOCIAL JUSTICE: DESERT AND NON-DESERT

On the distributive or social justice dimension, desert theories, as mentioned, are less common in the twentieth century. Desert arguments also vary greatly in content and approach. Notions of merit, worth, services or work, have very different characters for different cultures. Further, there is no clear social or political form that arises with any of these desert theories. Thus, if one took, say, a desert based reading of a 'moral worth' principle, to each according to their moral worth, two possible uses of the argument can be immediately observed, each with very different social visions.

The first argument would proceed as follows: only human persons are intrinsically valuable; objects are valuable insofar as they are given value or they contribute to human personhood. Thus, only persons or agents are subjects of worth and respect. To be a person requires a certain level of well-being. There are, in other words, certain necessary conditions for being a person. If we respect persons, we are logically committed to fulfil the necessary conditions for personhood. It follows that we are committed to all persons having these necessary conditions fulfilled. Fulfilling these necessary conditions may well require wide-scale social and economic distribution. Distribution of goods would therefore be premised upon the equal moral worth of individuals, each person being equally morally deserving of the distribution of goods necessary for personhood to be realized. This use of moral worth could imply a radically distributive conception of the state.

However, a second rendition of the argument starts from the same premise— that only persons are of intrinsic value and only persons can be respected—but produces very different policy outcomes. To be a person requires a certain level of well-being. But what constitutes a person? One answer could be that a person is a self-maintaining agency, having a will or capacity for self-determination. Yet, the capacity for self-determination is dependent upon the purposes or aims adopted by the agent. If someone has rounded or rich purposes, then this will be reflected in their character, surroundings, and circumstances. In other words, one can ascertain, to a certain degree, whether someone has capacities for personhood by observing their circumstances, that is, their social, economic, and personal conditions of life. Consequently, circumstances are created by human actions, all actions are structured by will, which is dependent upon the richness and comprehensiveness of one's purposes; therefore, conditions and circumstances are often the product of human persons. To change conditions means to change the purposes and aims of individuals. To change conditions needs, however, an assessment of the nature of the person. To simply give, say, financial resources to certain people, would not address their problems, the problem being psychological and moral. They might have very limited purposes or aims. This whole argument may all sound rather abstract, but it formed one crucial plank underpinning anti-statist voluntary charity claims in the late nineteenth century (and in fact well into the twentieth century). Moral worth is premised on personhood, but personhood is measured or determined by the nature of purpose.[13] Distribution (social justice) would be determined by the capacity for self-determination. Thus, certain persons are viewed as more 'deserving' than others. There are, in other words, deserving and the undeserving persons. The deserving person requires assistance. The deserving have simply been subject to unforseen circumstances and should be assisted. The undeserving do not. This implies a very different form of social vision of society (see Vincent 1984; Vincent and Plant 1984: ch. 6).

However, the larger bulk of twentieth-century justice theorizing has been premised on anti-desert arguments. The formal claim of non-desert theories is that distribution is justified through a wide-ranging agreement or consensus on a rational procedure(s) (contract), empirical assumption(s) (need), or some plural combination of these, which forms the basis for distributing burdens and benefits. As mentioned earlier, non-desert principles vary widely. One convenient way of typologizing them is to distinguish between *two* dominant forms of non-desert orientated distributive principles: rationalist and empiricist claims. The latter is concerned to establish an uncontested empirical ground for distribution—characteristic of social needs-based minimums within welfare states. The former is concerned with the ideal rational conditions in which individuals come to a decision about the manner of distribution in society, in specified rational circumstances. These themes, particularly the latter, have dominated theoretical justice literature over the last three decades of the twentieth century.

The empiricist claim argues, in effect, that human need is the crucial ground for distribution of burdens and benefits. Therefore, in the eyes of some of its proponents, it has no desert status. Needs *require* responses. Agents do not *deserve* them. Once a need is discovered it automatically generates an obligation. There is therefore no ambiguous or contestable moral or desert basis to the welfare state. To determine a need does not require (in this view) ascertaining any moral or psychological status of the agent. Needs are independent of the avowals of individuals. If you need something, then you need it, whatever you might or might not say. Needs are empirically identifiable by independent agents. They can therefore be ascribed to people whether they are aware of them or not. They are not just expression of wants or interests. They are, further, not just indicative of psychological states, interests, or individual preferences. A cruder way of putting this is that wants are more psychological, whereas needs are physiological. This is an important point for need proponents, partly because market activity is concerned with satisfaction of individual preferences, wants, and psychological preferences. Welfare, qua distributive justice, is however addressed to common basic human physiological needs. The upshot of this distinction being that the welfare state, if linked with distributive justice and focused on an empirical needs principle, *cannot*, by definition, be subject to market forces or market testing. Thus, for its proponents, needs, unlike moral desert or interests are clear, determinate and objective entities. This makes them intrinsically more authoritative.

Historically, much welfare state literature is dominated, implicitly or explicitly, by the concept of human need. Social services and social minimums are seen as meeting such needs. For critics of need-based claims, there remain a number of unanswered questions. Are there for example any absolute human needs? Needs, when actually specified, always appear to be subject to social, geographical, historical, and many other such contingencies. There are clearly different dimensions of need. Karl Marx, for example, in his early writings differentiated a number of different human needs that would be met under communism. Thus, there are needs of the body (food, drink, shelter), needs of the mind (to understanding and knowledge), and needs for social life (communication, work, and so forth). In consequence, there is an implicit distinction here between absolute and relative needs. Once the distinction between relative and absolute needs is accepted, it then becomes more difficult to make a clear distinction between wants or preferences and needs. The line between these becomes more difficult to negotiate. Further, there is a problem as to whether needs are purely empirical. For example, X usually needs Y *for* some Z. If you do not know what it is needed for, then the need becomes unintelligible. Thus, a car needs petrol to move and function. However, once one says what it is needed for (a Z), then Z becomes a *mode of justification*, which needs to be assessed. Thus, needs are not self-sufficient for generating obligations. Needs are conversely relative to end-states—certain Zs. Thus, need moves from the empirical to the normative sphere, which, of course, undermines the initial thrust of the empirical argument. These, and other criticisms, have undermined some of the force of the needs-based distributive argument.

JUSTICE AND MUTUAL ADVANTAGE

The second dimension of the anti-desert position is the rationalist position. As indicated, there are two forms of this contractarian argument that have dominated the literature. These are justice as mutual advantage and justice as impartiality. Both repudiate each other's views on justice.

David Gauthier's work is a typical formulation of justice as mutual advantage, which is, as mentioned, also a sophisticated form of rational choice argument. The central aim of Gauthier's *Morals by Agreement* (1986) is to derive principles of morality and justice from the non-moral, more empirically orientated, premise of the rational self-interested agent. The above book can thus be read as an attempt to defend Western liberal market society by 'representing its ideal nature in relation to reason' (Gauthier 1986: 353), although it is a very particular empirical, economic, and highly instrumental view of reason. It is not reason in itself. Subjective interests and preferences are regarded as primary. Conventions, which do exist, are the outcome of bargaining process between individuals trying to maximize their interests. There is a strong—if deeply suspect—assumption here of relatively equal bargaining powers between all individuals. Gauthier thus sees his account of justice as mid-way 'between the simple individualism of Robert Nozick and the implicit collectivism of John Rawls' (Gauthier 1986: 268).

The assumptions behind his work are focused on isolated rational individuals, each embodying a capacity for practical reason. Gauthier openly admits that his work, *Moral by Agreement*, is underpinned by a foundational metaphysics of the self. This is essentially a form of methodological and moral individualism (Gauthier 1988: 220–1).[14] It is an account premised largely upon neo-classical economic theory. Each person thus seeks the maximum satisfaction of their interests. This maximizing strategy 'lies at the core of economic theory, and is generalized in decision theory and game theory'. (Gauthier 1986: 8). As Gauthier comments on rationality, 'We order our desires, in relation to decision and action, so that we may choose to maximize our expectation of desire-fulfilment. And in so doing, we show ourselves to be rational agents. I shall not question this maximizing view . . . agreeing with economists and others that there is simply nothing else for practical rationality to be' (Gauthier 1988: 174). Morality and rationality are thus all relative to 'economic man', who, according to Gauthier, is 'the natural man of our time'. Each person is viewed as 'a Robinson Crusoe' in the market society (Gauthier 1986: 91). Markets and morals share the same non-coercive capacity for 'reconciliation of individual interests with mutual benefit' (Gauthier 1986: 14), which is essentially Adam Smith's 'invisible hand' argument. Every human being has the desire for 'indefinite appropriation, seeking to subdue more and more of the world to his power'. This fact, for Gauthier, 'runs deeper than our disavowals' (Gauthier 1986: 316). Yet, Western civil societies have discovered the secret of how to harness the 'efforts of the individual working for his own good, in the cause of ever increasing benefit' (Gauthier 1986: 17).

Gauthier's view of justice is therefore essentially a hypothetical social contract account, reliant upon the foundational assumptions of methodological individualism and instrumental economic rationality. Justice provides devices to enable egoists to get along. Principles of justice are the result of instrumentally rational self-constraint. Justice and instrumental reason essentially coincide in cooperative interaction with each pursuing their own interests. Voluntary compliance, in fact, eliminates much of the need for social institutions and their costs. Basically, individual self-interested agents mutually agree to cooperate, since it is to their *mutual* advantage. All individuals are viewed equally as maximizers of their own interests. Gauthier's starting point for bargaining here is regarded as pure. The prisoner's dilemma lies behind the theory, namely, participants can either cooperate or defect, yet, it is better for all, if all cooperate, rather than if all defect. As Gauthier comments 'in Dilemma-structured situations, each maximizer will confront the uncomfortable truth that the outcome of the apparently rational, maximizing behaviour of herself and every other person, leaves her, and indeed each person, worse off than need be, given where it leaves the others' (Gauthier 1986: 176). In consequence, individuals are constrained to facilitate mutually-advantageous outcomes. The rational self-interested agent grasps the force of moral claims in overcoming the problems of the prisoner's dilemma. However, individuals, when they bargain, are, as Gauthier puts it, 'non-tuist'. Non-tuist means, taking no interest in those with whom they interact and exchange. Tuism implies a concern or interest in others. Gauthier notes that 'The demand for justice is . . . prior to any particular tuistic concerns' (Gauthier 1986: 220). Motivation is always purely individual and egoistic.

Yet only bargains which derive from a relatively fair initial position—in accordance with what Gauthier calls 'minimax relative concession'—will be acceptable to all agents. Minimax relative concession reflects the practice of bargaining itself. Rational egoists basically always try to minimize concessions to other bargainers. Equal concessions are rational, assuming both agents are equally rational. Mimimax relative concession is therefore both a ground for rational individual bargaining and an impartial constraint on each person's behaviour. As Gauthier comments, 'The just person is disposed to comply with the requirement of the principle of minimax relative concession in interacting with those of his fellows whom he believes to be similarly disposed. The just person is fit for society because he has internalized the idea of mutual benefit' (Gauthier 1986: 157). Thus, individual attempts to maximize interests will always be a form of constrained maximization. Whereas Hobbes' solution to the prisoner's dilemma is the terror of the sovereign, Gauthier's is constrained maximization, a constraint that is internal to will and rational choice. Gauthier (in a completely ahistorical manner), tries essentially to make Hobbes compatible for twentieth-century game theoretic language. For Gauthier, the appeal to rationality is not though a concealed moral premise. He admits that if 'I became convinced that an appeal to equal rationality was . . . a concealed moral appeal . . . then I should abandon the core argument of *Morals by Agreement*' (Gauthier 1986: 186).

Gauthier sees a further constraint on rational choice, namely a proviso that prohibits bettering one's own position by worsening another's. The proviso basically affirms 'enough and as good for others'. For Gauthier, it is rational and just 'for each individual to accept a certain constraint on natural interaction . . . as a condition of being voluntarily acceptable to his fellows as a party to cooperative and market arrangements' (Gauthier 1986: 192). In sum, morals by agreement expresses 'the real concern each of us has in maintaining the conditions in which society can be a co-operative venture' (Gauthier 1986: 18).

Justice as mutual advantage arguments usually tend to end up with the same or very similar basic rule of law structure and social vision as proceduralists (discussed earlier). Proponents of both sets of arguments also share overlapping foundational beliefs about the importance of individualism, the negative liberty and rights of individuals, the importance of the free market economy, and a more minimalist conception of the constitutional state. Apart from the manner in which justice is generated—proceduralists such as Hayek, for example, repudiate the contractual idea—the outcome and subsequent account of the scope of justice would tend to be markedly similar, in both justice by mutual advantage proceduralist arguments.

JUSTICE AND UTILITY

Before moving to impartialist arguments, it is worth discussing another cognate theory to rational choice and mutual advantage, which has never really shown its clear conceptual relation with justice or rights—that is utilitarianism. On one level the attractions of utilitarianism are obvious. It is only concerned with equal happiness and welfare, in some cases of all sentient life. Its basic question is always: does the consequence of an action, or policy X, produce an increase in happiness or welfare for Y. In this sense, it looks like a theory that readily solves moral or political problems on a very basic level. Yet for utilitarians one would never want to inquire what a just act is, in itself. The only point to ascertain is whether its 'consequence' produces happiness or greater welfare. This is, though, one point to immediately underscore with all forms of utilitarianism. Utilitarian arguments do *not* standardly try to argue for a substantive account or concept of justice; conversely, a situation—which some might regard as a case of justice—is morally and politically acceptable (and justified), in utility terms, if and only if, it can be shown to have the consequence of maximizing interests, preferences, welfare, or happiness. This also means that justice is *not* significant or meaningful, in itself, but *only* insofar as it corresponds with something 'I' or 'we' might 'want'. In this sense, it is a misnomer to think of utilitarianism offering a theory of justice, except indirectly. It is a wholly second order theory. It offers no first order substantive principles of justice or rights. It has therefore no substantive or rich moral content. It works with an essentially simple principle of utility maximization and it claims that, as long as one can measure or calculate neutrally and impartially good or bad consequences from actions, then the principle is efficacious. All this second order argumentation assumes though that some generally acceptable meaning can be given to 'utility'.

Even if utilitarianism is an intuitively attractive second order principle, still, one quite crucial problem is that it contains *no* agreement on the concept of utility. Basically, utility itself has never been agreed upon amongst utilitarians. It usually, vaguely, equates with welfare, well-being, or quality of life. However, the substance of this basic welfare varies enormously, since it depends upon what someone, or group, wants, desires, or prefers. The oldest version equates it with pleasure, or the balance of pleasure over pain. No utilitarian would now, however, use the hedonic or pleasure criterion alone. It just carries too many deep problems, for example, is there any way of effectively calculating interpersonal comparisons, on the basis of such an inchoate 'state of mind' as pleasure? In consequence of this weakness, the preferred term then became 'preferences', or the maximization of 'preference satisfaction' (or desires), particularly for economistically inclined utilitarians. Preferences refer not just to a state of mind, but to *actual* preferences and *actual* experiences. However, it still remains far from clear that one really can make precise interpersonal comparisons even between actual preferences or experiences.

One can, however, see here the close links between utilitarianism and rational choice. Both doctrines only give a small focused snapshot of one meagre aspect of human thought and action. Both commonly ignore the complexity of individual persons, for the sake of aggregating preferences or preference satisfactions. Both also try to apply a neutral decision-making procedure for social, moral, and public choice. The 'reason' they employ is largely instrumental. All moral and political dilemmas are resolved, in this scenario, by the rational calculation of utilities. Some utilitarians have noted that conscious preferences may not always provide full insight into an agent's interests. They have, therefore, moved the utility goal posts, once again, to notions such as 'rational preferences', or, more significantly, 'interests'. Interests, in this sense, usually refer to resources, which will prove useful for the long-term welfare of the agent, but, which may not be immediately articulated as conscious preferences. This latter point has subtle links to the older distinction, initially and fatefully introduced by J. S. Mill, between higher and lower pleasures. The basic point is that there are certain 'resources', 'utilities', or 'actions', which are valuable regardless or not as to whether they correspond with our immediate desires, preferences, or conscious interests. This idea, though, is deeply problematic for all utilitarians, since it negates the logic of the consequential position and speaks rather of things being 'intrinsically good'. It is questionable as to whether this is really utilitarian at all, although some have had the temerity to call it 'ideal utilitarianism'.

The relation between these various senses of utility remains unresolved and problematic. However, one can overdue the differences between some of these readings. Thus, although preference utilitarians reject pleasure-based arguments and welfare or interest-based utilitarian theories are sceptical of preference readings, nonetheless, all such positions conceptually overlap. Welfare or interests assume, in the final analysis, that agents would prefer, or gain some pleasure from, such policies. Thus, many of the problems that dog hedonic accounts still lie just below the surface of welfarist or preference utilitarianisms.

Utilitarians, when considering utility, have also differed on the pertinent object for any utility calculus. This raises the additional crucial distinction between act and rule utilitarianism. Rule utilitarianism suggests that we should calculate according to specific rules or norms to ascertain the greatest utility. Act utilitarianism suggests that we should focus on which action produces the greatest utility. It is therefore the act itself, not the following of a rule, which is crucial. In point, act utilitarians usually see the following of a rule as likely to undermine maximum utility in certain situations. Act maximization is seen as more flexible for policy making. However, the range of possible actions (qua act utility) could be enormous. If there were no rules on which to base calculation, then act utilitarianism could well be impossible to practise, for even the most assiduous policy-maker. In this sense, for some, rule-based utility calculus (even if cruder) is far easier to work with and inculcate in a bureaucratic domain.

It is also worth noting here that there has been a definite subtle shift in utilitarian concerns from an initial focus on utility, as a way of discussing *personal* moral conduct (in the early to mid-twentieth century), towards a concern (in the late twentieth century) with utility as a more public philosophy, namely, as a way of collectively managing or reforming public policy.[15] Many current utilitarians, although prepared to admit that utility is intuitively striking on the level of personal morality, still see it as much more defensible on the public level, as a form of government house utilitarianism (see Goodin 1995, 1997).

Many critics of utilitarianism have argued that utility, nonetheless, ignores the complexity and communal rootedness of human agents. Utility criteria try to evade any contexts for ethics or politics, and tend to speak with an impersonal, universal, neutral, and calculating voice. In this sense, utilitarianism shares some of the early Rawlsian and neo-Kantian need to be universally foundational, neutral, and separate from historical or communal concerns. For critics, however, this instrumentally rational way of viewing values is worlds apart from what happens in most moral or political situations. However, current utilitarians, who feel philosophically queasy about its rigorous application to personal morality, are, nonetheless, fairly certain that utility calculation is probably necessary and quite desirable in areas such as public policy and economic decision-making. Interpersonal utility calculation is seen to be quite feasible in this latter domain. In fact, some would argue that it is the basis for all sensible public policy-making. The criticism often made against utility—at this point, usually by neo-Kantians that it undermines the separateness of persons—can in fact, be partly met by the contention that public policy *does* actually aim to aggregate persons' concerns. In the process of policy aggregation, many aspects of the 'distinctiveness of persons' will inevitably drop out. However, that by definition, almost always has to happen for any policy objective to be achieved. Yet each person's interests will, ideally, still have been considered equally. In this sense, utilitarianism might be seen, on one reading, as an ideal way of thinking about issues of justice; since it works impartially and universally, it does not fixate on the content of justice, or the intrinsic good involved, but rather focuses on the much more mundane and manageable task of seeing whether a practical consequence will maximize welfare. It thus enables clear determinate policy. The public sphere inevitably places a wide range of constraints upon what is possible, and utility provides a functional and rational 'road map' through these diverse constraints. In this sense, utilitarian argument would have a vital role to play in arguments about justice.

However, the above still does not overcome certain crucial problems. Dominant public policy outcomes can be deeply despotic. In the final analysis, utility is simply what the majority of agents 'want', or, what satisfies them. There can be no qualitative assessment of preferences, desires, or wants. Wants have no content. Further, it is not clear why the simple fact of a desire entails that it *ought* to be maximized. Yet, the fear of what this quantitative view might entail—namely, anything that the majority *want* becomes a good to be maximized, for example, attacks on minorities of asylum seekers—has led to attempts, by other utilitarians, to smuggle in selective qualitative criteria. We then see notions such as 'rational interests', 'rational preferences', 'long-term welfare', or 'ideal higher utilities', being deployed in arguments. Yet, the latter undermine all the impersonality, neutrality, and calculative advantages of the quantitative versions of the argument. Many utilitarians, fearing the consequences of qualitative assessment, usually immediately shift ground again back to the quantitative view, which is indifferent to moral content and agnostic over moral ends (except in relation to their consequences). However, even here there is nothing, as indicated, to prevent a large majority being deeply delighted and immensely happy about gross inequalities or injustices.

Utilitarianism is a highly promiscuous second order doctrine. It has, quite literally, appeared in many different ideological formats and there is no necessary link at all to ideas of welfare state policy, caring for the poor or being concerned with social justice. Many extreme anti-statists and anti-welfare liberal theorists, such as Herbert Spencer, in late nineteenth-century Britain, employed a form of utilitarianism to make their extreme libertarian case (see M. W. Taylor 1992). If we recall the point, made above, that utilitarianism, as such, actually contains *no* theory of justice or rights, at all, then we should hardly be surprised to see that second order utilitarian argument can appear virtually anywhere. It can defend *or* totally undermine social justice. Utility trumps all comers. As long as a value, doctrine, or policy can be shown to have the consequence of maximizing the preferences, wants, interests, of the greatest number, then it is acceptable. This may be convenient, on one level, for simple-minded immediate public policy-making, and government house utilitarianism, on a managerial level, but, it is, at the same time, morally and politically bankrupt. An efficient public policy programme for racially based pogrom could quite simply be justified on consequentialist utilitarian calculus. The important point missed by utilitarianism is that no wants or preferences appear in a political or moral vacuum. It is the context in which a utility claim arises which is all important.

If one adds these critical points together, then it is hard so see what utilitarianism has to offer political theory except permanent conceptual poverty and confusion. No one agrees on what utility means. There is no substantive utilitarian theory of justice or rights. Utility can justify *any* policy or ideological doctrine, once the theorist has blindly accepted the inexplicable foundational utility premise. Utilitarians themselves desperately refine and wriggle around the qualitative domain, but are continually undermined by their own consequentialist logic. The notion that inexplicable preferences or interests can be aggregated or compared is never explained, except by *ad hominem* appeals to what might 'appear to be' happening in actual public policy. No clear evidence though is adduced for this claim. Thus, maximum happiness or welfare remains a remote metaphysical or magical abstraction. It is a fiction which keeps utilitarians happy (and obviously maximizes their welfare in universities), but is useless for the mass of humanity. Finally, there is no clear relation between anyone having a desire, interest, or preference and having something they 'ought' to pursue. It is not explained therefore why having a preference entails that 'I ought to prefer it'. In sum, utility despite its lurking presence in many debates about justice and rights, is virtually useless, except on a very simple level in bureaucratic activity.

JUSTICE AS IMPARTIALITY

The other major dimension of rationalist contractual argument is justice as impartiality. Whereas justice as mutual advantage (qua Gauthier or Buchanan) is more Hobbesian in character, justice as impartiality is more neo-Kantian. The latter has been the most written about component of justice argument and its most well-known exponent is John Rawls. The primary motive of this theory is not self-interest, rather the belief is that what happens to other people matters in and of itself. Thus, individuals should *not* look at the world solely from their own point of view, but rather should seek a wider rational and more consensual basis of agreement. Justice as impartiality is thus interested in the content of agreements. This draws justice distinct from bargaining power. Justice is not necessarily to one's advantage, it is rather concerned with deliberation by those who share rational beliefs in impartiality and universalizability. In sum, it implies that justice is the outcome of a rational agreement between discrete individuals in a hypothetical situation, or original position, where constraints are placed upon the character of reasoning that can be used.

The basic idea in Rawls is startlingly simple, namely, to identify a fair arrangement in society for all parties to agree to without knowing how it will affect them. The idea is to cut out the possibility of arbitrariness in decisions about justice. This is the basis of Rawls' objection to desert accounts. It might, for example, be claimed that ability is a natural endowment which should be a basis for desert. But natural endowments are not things the agent is personally responsible for. If the agent is not responsible for them, then they cannot be a basis for desert. Endowments are genetically arbitrary, therefore they are irrelevant for distribution. Further, any assessment of desert, premised on moral worth or services performed, would inevitably reflect the interests of agents. Justice, for Rawls, should not reflect or reinforce arbitrary chance or interests, but rather should aim to nullify them for the sake of basic fairness (Rawls 1971: 101–2).

The device by which this nullification is achieved in *The Theory of Justice* is the 'original position'. This allows individuals to choose principles for the organization of justice in society behind a 'veil of ignorance'—a form of rational disinterestedness equivalent, in function, to the old idea of the social contract and state of nature. As Rawls notes, 'My aim is to present a conception of justice which generalizes and carries to a higher level of abstraction the familiar theory of the social contract as found, say, in Locke, Rousseau, and Kant. In order to do this we are not to think of the original contract as one to enter a particular society or to set up a particular form of government. Rather, the guiding idea is that the principles of justice for the basic structure of society are the object of the original agreement' (Rawls 1971: 11). This view directly echoes Kant who remarked that 'The original contract is not a principle explaining the origin of society; rather it is a principle explaining how it ought to be . . . It is not the principle establishing the state; rather it is the principle of political government and contains the ideal of legislation, administration, and public legal justice' (quoted in introduction to Kant 1965: xxx). Rawls has, in his first book, a strong belief in underlying rules or norms of rationality. There are parallels here with depth grammar and the Wittgensteinian essential contestability argument. We use language, but do not often consider the grammar that underpins it. Analogously with rational, moral, and political thought, we function morally but do not think about the underlying grammar of rules and assumptions of ethics. These norms and rules, Rawls suggests, can be teased out by rational inquiry.[16] Careful analysis can reveal this deep structure of rules.

How is it possible to show these basic deep rules? One needs a procedure to reveal them, which remains impartial and neutral, namely, an agreed procedure. The basic question underlying this agreed procedure is, what principles of justice would rational individuals choose in a situation of agreed equality? Or, to put it another way, how ought society to be organized if it is to conform to principles chosen by rational individuals—uninfluenced by knowledge of their vested interests, social situation, natural endowments, life plans, or how such principles would affect them personally. The veil of ignorance allows this 'teasing out' process to take place. This 'veil' device conceals personal or particular abilities and powers from choosers, but allows general information, provided by the social scientific disciplines. The individual is considered in an asocial and ahistorical setting, but is nonetheless rational and has knowledge of societies and history. This is essentially a hypothetical thought experiment to Rawls. To try and gain some degree of fairness and neutrality, it is abstracted from personal interest.

In this original position, the individual is assumed (and this is apparently shown by the various disciplines) to be a self-interested rational chooser, with definite conceptions of a plan of life, who will try to minimize losses and maximize benefits in any choice situation. Humans are also depoliticized. Benevolence and altruism are ruled out. Further, each individual is assumed to desire certain primary goods, that is, social primary goods like self-respect, rights, liberties, opportunities, powers, income, and natural primary good health and intelligence. Parties would try, as far as possible, to maximize their primary goods as part of a rational plan. These thin goods are assumed to be desired by everyone and are distinct from any 'thick' substantial goods, which every person has, but which are more or less incommensurable in a pluralistic society. Rawls suggests that agreement can however be gained, even in a pluralistic setting, on a thin conception of goods. The goods that all individuals require can be derived from a model (which despite being premised on self-interest), nonetheless is supposed to model ideal moral choice.[17] This initial position thus attempts to account for our basic deep underlying sense of justice.

Rawls suggests that there would be certain constraints on our choices in this original situation (see Rawls 1971: 122–6, 131–6). Any principles chosen would have to be general (embodying no particular interests embodied), universal in application (thus holding for all moral persons), public (i.e. known by all and embodying no private administrative rules). They must also have a standard of ordering for conflicting claims between individuals. They must also be the final court of appeal in any practical reasoning. The precise choice procedure that Rawls adopts is the 'maximin principle' or maximum minimorum, namely, 'we rank alternatives by their worst possible outcomes: we adopt the alternative the worst outcome of which is superior to the worst outcomes of the others' (Rawls 1971: 152–3). Individuals in Rawls' view would naturally tend to be risk averse.

Rawls suggests that a general sense of justice derives from the maximin principle, namely that liberty, income and wealth, and the bases of self-respect would be distributed equally unless an unequal distribution of any or all of these goods is to the advantage of the least favoured. This general notion can be broken down into two basic principles, which affirm equal rights to equal basic liberties for all and second, the difference principle, which affirms (in a more complex format) that social and economic inequalities will be to the greatest benefit of the least advantaged and attached to offices and positions open to all under conditions of fair equality of opportunity. Both principles of justice apparently match our intuitive sense of what justice is. There is also a lexical ordering of these principles (Rawls 1971: 243). The first principle is rationally and intuitively prior. Liberty can only be restricted for the sake of liberty. Thus, Rawls comments, 'the desire for liberty is the chief regulative interest that the parties must suppose they all will have in common in due course. The veil of ignorance forces them to abstract from the particulars of their plans of life thereby leading to this conclusion' (Rawls 1971: 543). Distribution, in this context, for Rawls would be neutral with regard to the good. Individuals would contract to a society and principles of distributive justice by their own reason and judgement. The actual basic goods to be distributed would also be agreed by all. Overall, Rawls' argument is the most sophisticated defence of a social liberal polity during the twentieth century.

The most committed supporter of Rawls' earlier theory has undoubtedly been Brian Barry. For Barry, apart from a few articles after the publication of Rawls' *Theory of Justice*, 'everything [from Rawls] since then has tended to weaken the theory' (Barry 1995: xii).[18] Barry thus continues to believe in the 'possibility of putting forward a universally valid case in favour of liberal egalitarian principles', which he also considers to be what Rawls' *Theory of Justice* was really about (Barry 1995: xi, 3, 5). For Barry, justice must go beyond single societies. He consequently disapproves of Rawls' later work *Political Liberalism* (1993), a disapproval that becomes much more marked when he considers communitarian notions of justice. For Barry, *contra* the later Rawls and communitarians, mass political culture is 'labile' and there is 'no such thing as a set of underlying values waiting to be discovered' in any culture. Deriving any conclusions from a bogus notion such as political culture is, as he puts it, wholly 'tendentious'.

Principles of justice, to Barry, are impartial because they capture a kind of equality, which is also embodied in reason. Reasonable agreement to Barry (without all the trappings of Rawls' original position) can suffice for the theory. Impartial reason does not evaluate outcomes. It is a second order impartiality which acts as a test to be applied to moral and legal rules (Barry 1995: 194). But as Barry remarks, 'It is . . . a great mistake . . . to suppose that justice as impartiality is intended to constitute a complete, self-sufficient moral system'. Justice as impartiality is *not* designed to tell us how to live. Rather, it addresses how we are to live together with different ideas on how to live (Barry 1995: 77). Despite being a second order hypothetical contractarian theory, justice as impartiality is not a view from nowhere. It is drawn (for Barry) from the most earthy ethics imaginable (Barry 1995: 255). Justice as impartiality 'entails that people should not look at things from their point of view alone, but seek to find a basis of agreement that is acceptable from all points of view', namely putting oneself in another's shoes. Impartiality is, though, a bounded notion to Barry. In fact, 'there is always some concept available that would carry the moral burden equally well if not better' (Barry, Brian 1989: 19). Thus, unlike Gauthier, but like Rawls, Barry places constraints upon reason in order to control self-interest and make the outcomes ethically appealing. Justice becomes a rational process of negotiation over private interests, but under implicit moral constraints.

SEXUAL JUSTICE

Before moving on from Rawls' theory it is worth mentioning that a number of political theorists have tried to both modify and extend the Rawlsian early argument on justice. One example of this has been in the feminist critique of Rawls by Susan Moller Okin, particularly her *Justice, Gender and the Family* (1989).[19] Political theory, in general, for Okin (amongst the majority of feminists) has not taken gender with due seriousness. She still sees Rawls' conception of justice as universal, but inadequately adjusted to the issue of gender. Given her adherence to Rawls' thin universalism, convention or culture are also considered utterly inappropriate for making judgements about justice.

Liberalism has provided a number of possible openings for feminist criticism and argument, particularly in its social contract and natural right format. The social contract perspective in, for example, Hobbes begins by stripping humans down to their basic motivations, in order to build a picture of the commonwealth. The image

of deconstructed humans could be seen as intrinsically 'sexless' or 'genderless'—
although there are strong views to the contrary (see Pateman 1988). The later addition
by Hobbes of families—fatherly authority and male rulers—is for some feminist
commentators, an unjustified addition to the contract argument. Social contract
theory, unless customs are imported into the argument, provides a medium for talking
about human equality. Social contract writers, such as Locke, also attacked divine right
and patriarchal theory. A feasible logical extension from criticizing patriarchalism in
political sovereignty, is criticizing patriarchal authority in the family (see Okin 1979:
200). This step was never made by Locke, although it is a *potential* implication of
his argument. The arguments for social contract turn on the idea of separate free,
consenting, and equal individuals, *not* males or females. Finally, politics for contract
theory is built upon foundations of reason, not custom or tradition. Again, this
represents a *potential* challenge to the supposed 'natural order' of patriarchy. With
some exceptions, most liberal theorists, up to and including Rawls, did not initially
take these potentialities very seriously.

However, some feminists have been deeply critical of what is implicit in the whole
contract perspective. For example, the background to Okin's conception of liberal
justice theory lies in Carole Pateman's seminal work *The Sexual Contract* (1988). This
latter book argued that the sexual difference and subordination of women are integral
to the fabric of liberal political theory. Seventeenth-century contract theories are seen
as working within a particular conception of the public and private—a distinction that
Pateman considers central to the whole critical feminist project. What we see on the
surface as a contract of equals, in these liberal theorists, is, in reality, a sexual contract
that excludes women (see Pateman 1988: 77 *ff*.). Basically the conception of the public
(and political) and the private are both constructions of patriarchy. Women, qua the
family or domestic realm, are confined to the non-political. Since contracts (qua
contractarianism) are made at the political or public level, women are by definition
ruled out. Further, since freedom, justice and rights, and similar vocabularies, tend to
figure in the public or political realm, women are further excluded. In consequence,
to define the political in this contractarian mode, is an overtly gendered political
act. This is a central theme that feminism wants to address. This, for Pateman, *still*
remains a subtext in the late twentieth-century justice theories. The whole discipline
of political theory, to the present moment, therefore unwittingly ostracized women.

Okin basically agrees with Pateman's argument that liberalism's past is patriarchal.
Women in western thought have been confined by nature to the family, as defined
by patriarchy (Okin 1979). She is also aware that theorists, such as Rawls, embody
similar motifs. However, she does not see Rawls's liberalism as inherently flawed.
Feminists, for Okin, must still 'acknowledge the vast debts of feminism to liberalism.
They know that without the liberal tradition, feminism would have had a much
more difficult time emerging' (Okin 1989: 61). The gist of Okin's claim is that the
arguments concerning justice and the difference principle can be extended into the
sphere of the family and the domestic realm. Okin regards this as a logical extension
of Rawls' work. Justice *per se* is not a masculine or gendered concept. She thus tries
to develop a conception of liberalism and social justice which is sensitized to gender

differentiation. For Okin, Rawls' theory of justice can potentially encompass women. The autonomous individual—beloved of liberal theory—actually does develop and mature within the family. Children morally learn a great deal in the family. If relations are implicitly just in the family, this will be internalized within the growing adult. The family, in this sense, is an area that can be seen as intrinsically political. The autonomy of women and children should be subject to the same form of impartiality as in the public sphere. For Okin, if liberalism claims to address itself to all human beings, it has to take on board the feminist claim that the 'the personal is the political'. Thus, the nurture of children, domestic work, and the like, must therefore be included in any discussion of justice.

Okin admits though that this proposed change would require a deep cultural shift in the way the family, child care provision, and work in general are viewed. Okin argues therefore that Rawlsian rational contractors would address gender in the veil of ignorance. Any contractor (not knowing their gender) would want to address issues of the domestic division of labour and sexual roles (Okin 1987: 67–8). There is nothing forced, for Okin, in this extension of the argument. A genuine modern humanist liberalism has to address itself to the realm of private attachments (see Okin 1989: ch. 8). Therefore, the task facing feminists is to adapt liberal theory—which was initially premised on the separation of the public and private realms—into a theory usable for all women both in their private and public capacities. The state should be used to expand basic justice to gender issues and the institution of the family. For Okin, liberal justice theory, in future, will see the family as a basic political institution. It will also see the necessity of extending justice to processes within the family.

In summary, the primary objective of liberal feminists is to bring women into the full rights of democratic citizenship. They envisage a future where legal, political, social, and economic rights will have been achieved for all women. They will be on an equal footing with men in all spheres. This will be achieved by reason, persuasion, and constitutional reform. The reformed family will still remain, but men will have an equal role in the domestic duties, and womens' careers and lives will in no way be hampered artificially by the rearing of children. The institution of the family is thus seen to have a continuing and important role, but it will be supported financially and socially in order to prevent inequalities occurring. Liberal feminism thus anticipates a future of sexual justice.

There are three unresolved problems with the liberal feminist position to mention in passing. First, there are clearly different schools of liberalism, and it is important to note that there have been significant variations within the liberal feminist argument. The most important variation is between a classical and social expression of liberalism. It is possible to make a case for a classical liberal feminism. For example, if one focuses on the idea of a free market economy, it is clear, on one reading, that *all* (regardless of gender) should have equal access to compete in the market. Markets, so the argument goes, are impersonal and gender neutral. Monopolies, whether private, public, or gendered, are intrinsically suspect. Unjustified male monopoly, like any economic cartel, is implicitly frowned upon by the logic of market theory. Free markets therefore imply free individuals, including women, who can compete on equal terms. The theme of an overt feminist liberal capitalism has not really been developed within feminism, although it is clear that it would be overtly hostile to Okin's Rawlsian stance and more at home with a Gauthier or Hayek.[20] However, even with the classical liberal fold there are markedly different justificatory stances and little sign of unanimity. For example, the natural right based liberalism of, say, Mary Wollstonecraft, is clearly antagonistic to the utility-based liberal arguments of J. S. Mill. The arguments are virtually irreconcilable in some formats. Both the latter arguments are also very different again (and opposed to) the Rawlsian inspired social liberalism of Okin. This more recent social liberal feminist argument (regardless of its extension of the Rawlsian impartiality) is potentially as much at odds with both the natural rights and utilitarian liberalisms of Wollstonecraft and J. S. Mill as it is with the classical liberalism of Friedrich Hayek. Second, in terms of the literature on twentieth-century feminism, socialist, radical, and postmodern feminist writers have all been hostile to the future of *any* form of liberal feminism.

Finally, in terms of feminist arguments in the last two decades of the twentieth century, justice-based arguments have been subject to deep criticism from another strand of feminism associated with the 'ethic of care'. The psychoanalytic work of Nancy Chodorow, and more particularly Carol Gilligan in the early 1980s, on the distinctive qualities of the female personality, gave rise to the supposition that women have a very different moral view on the world. For Gilligan, particularly, women have a 'caring' approach. They are more altruistic, nurturing, and self-sacrificing. Gilligan links this disposition with an 'ethic of care', which she contrasts to a more male-orientated 'ethic of justice' (see Chodorow 1978; Gilligan 1982). Morality for women is therefore more concerned with a moral imagination, a caring disposition, attending to responsibilities and relationships, rather than finding the right or best principle, following rules and attending to rights and fairness, which are characteristic of the 'ethic of justice'. In many ways, the conflict between the ethic of care and the ethic of justice has marked out a great deal of feminist debate in the closing decades of the twentieth century (see Squires 1999: 141 *ff*.). Other writers, such as Sara Ruddick and Jean Beth Elshtain, also argued that women are primarily involved in the preserving the lives of children and nurturing. Women are thus different to men in certain fundamentally important ways. This has given rise to the development of 'maternalist theory' within feminism. However, unlike Gilligan, Elshtain and Ruddick think that such an idea could have an immense impact on restructuring the public sphere.[21]

SPHERES OF JUSTICE

Moving away from the Rawlsian argument, one final justice-based theory to mention here, briefly, focuses on a more pluralistic stance. Michael Walzer's theory of justice identifies different distributive criteria applying within different social spheres. Distributions, in one sphere, may therefore not be appropriate in another. Thus, there is no one clear principle (qua Barry or Rawls) that can adjudicate for all spheres. Walzer is clear that spheres should not intermix or try to dominate other spheres. He draws a parallel distinction between simple and complex equality. Simple equality is where there is one dominant good which all spheres should acclimatize to. Complex equality implies a multiplicity or plurality of goods in different spheres. Yet, to maintain this pluralism requires that the barriers between spheres are patrolled, in order to prevent conversions between distinct goods.[22] These spheres underpin Walzer's account of justice.

The core idea is relatively simple. Basically different social goods should be distributed, for different reasons, in accordance with different procedures, by different agents. Each social good therefore prescribes its own norms of distribution. No person or good should be dominant in all spheres. Ironically, both Rawls and Barry, in one sense, are after something similar, but they want to abstract from the diverse particulars to find their *modus operandi*, whereas Walzer wants to enter *into* the diverse particulars. Walzer is seeking a society free of domination and committed to complex egalitarianism, not unlike forms of pluralistic guild socialism or syndicalism earlier in the twentieth century. This implies, for Walzer, that there can be no one overarching universal account of justice. The main spheres in contemporary liberal societies are security and welfare, money and commodities, office (employment), work, free time, education, kinship and love, divine grace, recognition (public honours), and political power.[23] Walzer thinks these all have analogues in most societies. Each sphere should have relative autonomy in the criteria and manner of its distribution. Justice is therefore plural and differentiated. The meaning of the good and its criterion of just distribution are also often tightly interlocked. The criterion for the distribution of public honours is not therefore the same as that for medical care. Attaining an honoured status does not mean you gain the same status in, say, medical care. One cannot cross spheres. Money, for example, cannot be converted into religious or educational advantage. Walzer seems particularly concerned that money should not be a dominant good, namely one that tyrannizes over other goods. However, writing this book in prosperous, but deeply unequal, North America, Walzer appears peculiarly out of touch and distant from his own society (let alone other societies), namely, where money continuously crosses spheres and buys all manner of privileges and honours as a matter of basic social convention. The North American university system is a living testament to monied privilege in education. However, distributive justice, for Walzer, is still seen to be open-ended, in terms of what is distributed and the manner in which it is distributed.[24]

Thus, in sum, within the rationalist contractarian position there are two distinct stresses on justice. For Rawls and Barry, the function of justice is to supply a reasonable basis for agreement, for taking account of diverse or plural interests and conceptions of the good. In Gauthier, justice is seen as the outcome of a bargaining process among individuals, showing why individuals, reasoning from non-moral premises, can still nonetheless accept the constraint of morality. Voluntary self-constraint is central. To pursue personal advantage, rational individuals need to cooperate. Thus, Gauthier claims to show the devices which enable egoists to get along. Both the above 'rationalist' accounts of justice are constructivist and contractualist. Neither are reliant upon intuitive or naturalistic moral beliefs. For Walzer's (or David Miller's) pluralist account, Rawls' idea of primary goods does not fit with the idea of different spheres. Both Rawls and Barry, for Walzer, are insufficiently aware and sensitive to the diversity of particularistic goods. Walzer clearly sees no universal external rational foundations for ethics or the good life. John Rawls' 'original position', Ronald Dworkin's 'insurance game' or Bruce Ackerman's 'perfect technology of justice', and the like, cannot redeem the world by abstract theory, since they are all suspect procedures from the start. We do not need external theoretical foundations for a practical life, rather we draw upon the complex and diverse interpretations within spheres or form of life.[25] However, for Walzer's critics, there is altogether too much relativity of meanings within his spheres. There also seems no clear way of criticizing or objecting to certain social structures, such as a caste system. Although Walzer denies it, he seems to undermine the possibility for social criticism. His theory also seems to be in immanent danger of becoming a descriptive sociology of spheres.

CONCLUSION

The bulk of the justice debate (outlined in this chapter) has been situated within a broad analytical frame of argument, whose roots lie within earlier ordinary language and essential contestability argument. Virtually all the above arguments would claim to be rigorously philosophical, in a self-conscious analytical mode (understood as rigorous and finely-honed attention to language, logic, and concepts, combined with moral seriousness). However, from the 1970s, the essential contestability and ordinary language forms of argument were subtly remodulated within broader normative justificatory accounts. With the normative restored to pre-eminence, essential contestability theory and conceptual analysis became the background 'philosophical rigour' component within justificatory arguments. Linguistically-based essential contestability argument already contained the belief that there must be, within political and moral concepts, some core element, some commonly accepted 'exemplar' or family resemblance, which allows debates to become intelligible and meaningful. Without this core, arguments would collapse into relativism and incommensurability. If this latter dimension of the concept is emphasized, then, it follows that one key element of any conceptual analysis *must* entail finding and detailing the contents of this core component. Consequently, what one finds in most theories of justice (or equality) is the distinction between the conception of justice or equality and concepts of justice or equality. Further, one also stumbles on the claim that that there are deep consensual universalist, if very thin, intuitions about morality and justice, to which theories of justice refer or approximate. In addition, there is the contention that reason (or reasonableness) itself contains potentially deep normative resources and implicit logical entailments. 'Reasonable' essentially entails 'followable by all'. Justice can thus be defined as treating like cases alike, which is seen as synonymous with reason and universalizability. Justice is therefore seen to be premised upon the reasonable, widely shared intuitions and values, which can be developed and tested in a theoretical construction. The task of political philosophy, for neo-Kantian rationalism, is consequently to 'examine whether some underlying basis of agreement can be uncovered and a mutually acceptable way of resolving these questions publicly established' (Rawls in Strong (ed.) 1992: 97).

For justice proponents, the deep normative resources provided by the idea of 'reasonableness' cannot be undermined by showing that cultures or communities have different traditions or customs.[26] In other words, it is possible to engage in rigorous analysis of the internal diversity of concepts, such as justice, but once the core intuitions and elements have been fully grasped, and the theory has carefully abstracted and synthesized these intuitions into clear rules, then the concepts can begin to take on an essential shape. The theorist can then make careful inferences and justify a reading of justice which will have public policy implications. In the most general terms, political philosophy, therefore, examines rigorously the basic principles that underpin or regulate reasonable cooperation. Justice is premised upon widely shared values, which can be tested in a theoretical construction. This embodies the underlying logic of desert-based, rationalist contractarian (i.e. both justice as impartiality and justice as mutual advantage), and the various proceduralist accounts of justice. It does not, however, encompass the needs-based argument, which claims to rest on empirical rather than normative foundations.

Justice-based theory still upholds, indirectly, what was referred to in Chapter Three, as the 'issue orthodoxy' approach. Within this approach, the major task of the political theorist is still seen as the analysis of a finite range of concepts, which are taken to 'sum up' politics. The difference in the justice arguments (and much recent justificatory-based arguments) is that a core component has been identified, which allows the theorist to move confidently beyond the realm of linguistic phenomenology into the broad justification of a particular conceptual issue (such as justice), and ultimately, into the policy sphere. Furthermore, like ordinary language and essential contestability, the justificatory normative approach is stalwartly ahistorical. This ahistorical stance is not so much a self-conscious philosophical position or intended policy, as a default reaction to an annoying irrelevance. Normative theory, qua justice, thus remains firmly and inflexibly synchronic in character.

A similar mode of argument characterizes the relationship of justice theory with the more diachronic ideological understanding of politics. Political philosophy, trying to maintain its professionalism, universal patina, and moral gravitas, usually denies its relation with the grubby world of ideology. This again is never really argued, rather, just asserted. The oddity of this point is that the dominant branches of justice discussion (particularly the contractarian arguments) have all been resolutely ideologically liberal in character. In the case of proceduralists (such as Hayek), justice as mutual advantage theorists (such as Buchanan and Gauthier), and impartiality theorists (such as Rawls, Scanlon, or Barry), and even justice as a plural mix (such as Walzer and Miller); *all* have been keen to express their political (one might hesitate to say ideological) credentials and the majority are stalwartly liberal. All have stressed the practical policy implications of their work.

If, however, one asks a basic question, 'what is liberalism?', then issues become less clear. There have been many typologies of liberalism. As indicated earlier, a simpler distinction would be between classical and social liberalism. The classical view, which is a predominantly procedural view in its modern guise, insists that individual rights must always come first and must take precedence over collective goals.[27] This perspective also covers the 'justice as mutual advantage' arguments. Michael Walzer characterizes this procedural liberalism as 'committed in the strongest possible way to individual rights and, almost as a deduction from this, to a rigorously neutral state, that is, a state without cultural or religious projects or, indeed, any sorts of collective goals beyond personal freedom and physical security' (Walzer in Gutman (ed.) 1994: 99). Yet, this is also a view that one finds, according to Charles Taylor, in writers such as John Rawls, Ronald Dworkin, and Bruce Ackerman.[28] This conception of liberal society has no substantive view about the ends of human life. Society is rather united behind an idea of formally equal respect for individuals. For Taylor, the roots to this procedural view are culturally very deep. He sees Kant as probably the single most important figure articulating this perspective. Human dignity focuses on autonomy and the ability of the individual to determine their own notion of the good life. Thus, procedural liberalism enshrines a politics of equal respect which is hostile or indifferent to difference, because it insists on the uniform application of rights and is thus suspicious of any collective goals. Taylor has his own thoughts on the problems that this notion of liberalism has caused in the Canadian situation, vis á vis Quebec.

Social liberal thought, on the other hand, was more committed to collective welfare goals, pursued through the state. Essentially social liberals reacted to certain themes present within classical liberalism, notions like atomized individualism, the negative conception of liberty, the radically free market economy, and minimal constitutional state theory. They wished to replace these with a socialized and developmental understanding of the individual; a 'positively inclined' conception of liberty, linked to notions like self-realization and self-development; a conception of a mixed economy; and a more responsive, collectivized, and ethical conception of the state. State intervention was generally premised upon the idea of the common good and the realization of human personalities.[29] The social liberals were, in effect, developing the embryonic form of the welfare state theory. Their arguments were rooted in forms of evolutionary theory, social utilitarianism, and philosophical idealism.

One problem here is knowing where to place rationalist contractarians such as Rawls and Barry? Barry (possibly Rawls also) would not be comfortable being classed as a classical liberal ideologist. Yet, despite Taylor's' classification, the distributive policy implications of the impartiality argument makes it more appropriate for the social liberal category. The key point to draw out from this distinction between classical and social liberalism is that, such arguments move quite directly into the ideological sphere and become subject to a great deal more of political play and contingency. Once one observes theories of justice squabbling over public policy (as happened during the 1980s and 1990s), then the vigorously asserted philosophical patina begins to look flakier and less convincing. What seems to be taking place is an ideological dispute. In fact, given that there is no clear resolution in sight concerning the nature of liberalism, the argument about justice looks in immanent danger, once again, of collapsing into an essential contestability debate.

Like ordinary language and essential contestability, the foundations of justice theory are still vehemently anti-metaphysical, although, in my reading, they simply replace a comprehensive with an immanent metaphysics. There is also an implicit and resonant acknowledgement of the importance of empirical political science, although the justificatory arguments have moved well beyond the 'second order' position of earlier conceptualist theory. For Rawls, 'justice should be so far as possible, independent of controversial philosophical and religious doctrines' (Rawls in Strong (ed.) 1992: 95). Justice is *not* metaphysical, although it is, nonetheless, deeply and immanently founded. There is also an underlying confidence in the universality of reason and philosophical method. The term 'constructivism' often arises here, especially in neo-Kantian thinkers. In essence, it is a form of foundational self-recovery kit. Constructivism implies, in the words of one recent neo-Kantian writer, that one reasons 'with all possible solidity from *available* beginnings, using available and followable methods to reach attainable and sustainable conclusions for relevant audiences' (O'Neill 1996: 63). Constructivism does not simply invent, it rather builds—virtually hermeneutically—upon what is present in reason. Reason coordinates in the sense of providing a negative internal authority. It must allow for a variety of agents—all human agents in fact—and be able to guide action and discriminate between categories. In other words, reason must be truly universal—implying 'holding for all cases'. This notion of reason is neither purely formalistic nor idealized. It apparently neither assumes any metaphysical conceptions of persons, reason or action, nor roots itself in any particular communities. Yet, for its proponents, although abstract, this conception of reason still begins with the 'gritty realities of human life' (O'Neill 1996: 61). It tries to draw out, from the principles embodied in the ordinary processes of reasoning, a normative pattern. The end result may be abstract, but it is not an idealized view of what ought to be. It is rather based on an existing practical reason attainable by all.

In conclusion, for its votaries, the foundations of twentieth-century justice theory remain both secure and of universal import. However, as most proponents would admit, they are also minimalist or bleached foundations, usually premised on a very abstracted notion of reason. Thus, in a number of thinkers we find rationality, reason, or reasonableness taking on an extra heavy immanent foundational load, as in the writings of Rawls, Gauthier, O'Neill, Barry, Okin, Scanlon, or Gewirth, amongst many others. In fact, some variation of immanent foundational universal reason, or instrumental rationality, standardly fills the void left by the apparent demise of comprehensive metaphysics. However, it is worth noting here that the notion of reason is itself deeply contested, even between, for example, Gauthier's 'instrumentalist' rational choice conception, the utilitarian consequentialist and neo-Kantian impartialist conceptions. In sum, one can describe the bulk of the theories of justice developed in the last three decades of the twentieth century as embodying a bleached immanent foundational minimalism. It is this position which generated a wave of renewed criticism from the 1980s.

Notes

1. Interestingly it may well be that the concept of deliberative democracy is now becoming the modish concept taking over the baton from justice.
2. As Aristotle noted 'Justice is perfect virtue because it practices perfect virtue', Aristotle (1966: 141).
3. This can be seen within his definition of justice: 'everyone ought to perform the one function in the community for which his nature suited him', Plato (1948: 127).
4. Barry, in putting forward this idea, claims to 'draw upon ordinary beliefs critically and selectively, employing a general theory of justice as a touchstone' (Barry 1995: 10).
5. For Aristotle, distributive justice concerns the sharing or apportioning of honours and goods. It aims to give to each member of a community a share proportionate to their merit. If a person is not equal (with regard to 'merit') they should not receive equal shares. One cannot distribute equally to the unequal (treat like cases alike)—flutes can only be given to those who can play the flute. Aristotle calls this 'geometric proportion'. The other species is corrective justice. This applies to regulating loss or gain; subdivided between commutative and judicial justice. Commutative determines the relations of economic or contractual exchanges according to some standard. Judicial seeks to make a standard prevail in legal disputes proportioning punishments to crimes.
6. Another way in which distributive and proceduralist theories of justice might be typologized is in terms of 'conditions' and 'outcomes' orientations. Although the fit is not perfect; many distributive theories have traditionally argued that justice is concerned with fairness of outcomes. Proceduralists, on the other hand, have been concerned with fair conditions (like the general application of the rule of law or equality of opportunity) for individuals. Characteristically, though, proceduralists have not regarded unequal outcomes of human exchange and interaction as evidence for injustice.
7. Rationality can be understood as the most efficient manner of achieving satisfaction of interests or preferences, weighing up costs and benefits; alternatively, it could imply the capacity to universalize one's judgements (universalizability), thus to be neutral and impartial; or, it could imply that one acts for the highest good of all human beings.
8. For David Hume, for example, individuals realize that rules of justice which secure stability and property are ultimately in their own self-interest. He remarked 'To the imposition . . . and observance of these rules, both in general, and in particular, they [human beings] are first induced only by a regard to interest . . . Thus self-interest is the original motive to the establishment of justice', see David Hume (1981: 499).
9. Robert Nozick describes his own theory as distributive, but it is an 'unpatterned' distribution with no direct or intentional human intervention.
10. As David Miller puts it: 'A just state of affairs is that in which each individual has exactly those benefits and burdens which are due to him', see Miller (1979: 20).
11. As John Rawls notes 'A social ideal . . . is connected with a conception of society, a vision of the way in which the aims and purposes of social cooperation are to be understood. The various conceptions of justice are the outgrowth of different notions of society, against the background of opposing views of natural necessities and opportunities of human life', Rawls (1971: 9).
12. I am not suggesting that need *is* definitely an empirical claim, but rather that part of its initial appeal and force in argument has been its empirical 'tag', see Chapter Five, 'The Claim of Need and Politics' in Raymond Plant (1991).

13. The capacity for controlling one's life through such purposes, in this argument, is 'character'. See Vincent and Plant (1984: ch. 6).
14. James Buchanan adopts a similar view. He sees his approach as individualistic in, what he calls, 'an ontological-methodological sense'. In this sense, 'Each man counts for one, and that is that'. What any such individualistic society needs to establish for Buchanan is therefore 'orderly anarchy' (see Buchanan 1975, 1 and 4).
15. The concentration on collective choice, welfare, and preferences again shows the close links with current rational choice argument.
16. As Rawls comments: 'A correct account of moral capacities will . . . involve principles and theoretical constructions which go much beyond the norms and standards cited in every-day life', Rawls (1971: 47).
17. Gauthier has pointed out here that Rawls is therefore quite clearly not a rational choice theorist—something that Rawls in his later work has reinforced.
18. Rawls' later work will be examined in Part Three.
19. See also Okin (1979, 1981, and 1987). Martha Nussbaum has also developed her own comparative analysis of social justice, by what she calls the 'capabilities approach'. The capabilities in question are considered as universal, see Nussbaum and Glover (eds.) 1995. Nussbaum's more general perspective is discussed in Part Three, Chapter Six. In terms of other forms of extension of Rawlsian argument (which I do not have the space to develop), there have been a number of attempts to extend the whole debate on justice into an international setting by Charles Beitz, amongst others, see for example, Beitz (1979).
20. One problem is that many feminists have associated the market qualities of competition, individualism, and self-interest with masculinity.
21. Ruddick and Elshtain particularly think that 'maternal thinkers who make responsibility to children and families their central commitment could radically reform public values, could even create an "ethical polity" devoted to a politics of compassion', see Boling (1991: 608).
22. Spheres could look like language games or forms of life.
23. Walzer spheres are much more constrained and finite by comparison with Wittgenstein's language games.
24. David Miller has adapted Walzer's thesis to his own pluralistic account of social justice. Instead of premising it on spheres and social goods, he speaks of 'modes of human relationships' (Miller 1999: 25 *ff*.). He suggests that human beings stand in many and different types of particular relationships to each other and we need to focus on these to make sense of justice. Despite the complexity of these particulars, he isolates three basic modes—solidaristic community, instrumental association, and citizenship. He takes his task to examine 'the underlying principles of justice that spring directly from the various modes of relationships' (Miller 1999: 26). Each mode calls forth different or contrasting principles of justice and needs to be contextualized. This notion enables individuals to see where at times they might be crossing modes and thus misunderstanding their relationships.
25. We cannot totally step back to assess communities, morality, or justice with a view from nowhere, although we can criticize them from within using internal standards of rationality.
26. As Brian Barry comments 'justice has certain formal characteristics . . . [and he adds that] the universal validity of this proposition cannot be challenged by showing that a lot of people in some benighted society think otherwise.' (Barry in Miller and Walzer (eds.) 1995: 7).

27. This is close to Michael Sandel's use of the term 'procedural republic' for this liberalism, see Michael Sandel, 'The Procedural Republic and the Unencumbered Self' in T. B. Strong (ed.) (1992).
28. For Taylor the *procedural* view is best encapsulated in Ronald Dworkin's paper on 'Liberalism' in Hampshire (ed.) 1980, 113–43; see Taylor in Gutman (ed.) (1994: 56).
29. The term 'new liberal' or 'social liberal' is immensely complex and contested. I have not attempted to examine the term, but have largely taken it for granted in this chapter that we can speak of its ideology and social theory. This is by no means an uncontested position. My own attempt to assess the new liberalism can be found in Andrew Vincent (1990, 1995: ch. 5), Vincent and Plant (1984: ch. 5), and most recently Andrew Vincent in Simhony and Weinstein (eds.) 2001. See also Michael Freeden (1978) and Simhony and Weinstein (eds.) (2001).

PART THREE

5

Shoring Up Foundations

The conclusion to Part Two was that political theory, despite arguments about its demise, had in fact maintained a strong presence and concern with foundationalism. The foundations were temporarily shaken, but nothing very significant stirred. The only area to be discomforted was the perception of what an older normative (partly fictional) conception of theory was focused on. We are though still speaking here in incomplete terms. All the domains of theory, outlined in Part One, were still active during this period of the 1970s and 1980s. Further, in normative theory, there were still continuing significant contributions from a number of theorists outside the analytic tradition, some of which will be touched upon in this and later chapters. However, within the domain of ordinary language and essential contestability theory, there remained a strong universalist synchronic commitment to a conceptually-orientated philosophical method. Essential contestability, in effect, refocused attention on the normative and interpretative dimension of language.

Ordinary language thought wobbled though on the issue as to what could be done with such normative concepts. The more sceptical response argued that nothing much could be done, in the final analysis, except engage in a form of descriptive linguistic phenomenology. Recommendations or improvements were initially ruled out. Others advocated a form of mental hygiene—a tidying and sharpening process. Yet another response was to modify and remodulate the appeal of such political concepts. Analysis was therefore retained as a necessary preliminary, but this was viewed as a prolegomena to a future justificatory political theory. The future theory became focused on the hyper concept of justice. Once the core component of justice, as the key political virtue, had been identified and shown to be a reflection of foundational intuitions about morality and reason, then a full blown justificatory theory could be constructed. This became one of the main preoccupations of many political theorists during the late 1970s and 1980s.[1] The major issue that arises in all justice-focused arguments is the identification of the immanent universal grounds of justice, which apply regardless of any particular time or place. This was, as discussed, a thin or bleached foundationalism, as opposed to a metaphysically rich or substantive one. However, the main pressure point on this thin universalism arose from another dimension of the essential contestability argument that concentrates on an epistemological anxiety and incommensurability of language games or forms of life. This epistemology led in turn to a stress on more contingent, conventional and particularist factors.

To briefly rehearse the late Wittgensteinian case again in order to show the precise conceptual links to the present chapter: the basic argument is that language does not provide *any* clear or unambiguous universal foundations. Words do not refer to elementary objects in the world. Conversely, meaning is resident in linguistic conventions. Propositions about the world therefore must be grasped in the context of language games, linguistic contexts, social practices, social conventions or forms of life. Each of these variegated contexts embodies a series of particular rules governing the range of uses of concepts. Concepts become meaningful within these rule-governed settings. There is, therefore, no unmediated reality outside of language. Nothing is independent of linguistic convention. The conventions in Wittgenstein also remain somewhat hermetic and deterministic in their effect. Overall, this entails, as discussed in Part Two, a rejection of all conceptual essentialism—thus the derivation of the term 'essential contestability'. Metaphysics and thick foundationalism characteristically, for Wittgenstein, ignore the multi-dimensional character of language and try to focus on the essences of key concepts. This leads in turn, to claims about the objectivity of certain readings of concepts. For Wittgenstein, this latter approach is philosophically flawed.

To emphasize linguistic context is not necessarily to collapse, as some critics argue, into an unstructured relativism. Social conventions overlap and often have complex family resemblance. Further, a language game can embody a whole way of life and thought. In one sense, the language game or convention can also become a micro-foundation—although Wittgenstein would more than likely reject the whole vocabulary of foundationalism. To become a Buddhist, for example, is to root one's life and thought in a body of linked rules or conventions. These rules or conventions provide a contextual foundation for a whole way of life—which is by no means arbitrary—although it is still relative to the social practice of Buddhism. But Buddhism, in itself, is not, from this perspective, a universal foundation independent of language, which can be used for rational deductions. It is rather a *commitment* to a particular form of life, which then forms a basis of reasoning. The overlaps, resemblances, and complex relations between concepts, used in different language games, inevitably make 'fixing' the meaning and boundaries of concepts that much more difficult.

In this context, when applied to political theory, concepts can only be elucidated within the forms of life within which they occur. We should not therefore think that some essential meaning can be identified outside of socio-linguistic contexts. Reason, meaning, and action are, in this theory, always internal to practices and forms of life. There is no outside or independent body of values, interests, or reasons, which can assess the practices in which humans engage. A meaningful concept presupposes a form of life. Thus, the human self is embedded and identified within a complexity of practices. The nature of the human beings is only revealed in this multi-faceted context. Consequently there is, for example, no one overarching account of human nature or the human self. Human nature is inevitably diversified and read differently across differing forms of life. Human nature would thus be essentially contestable. Alternatively one might argue that humans, as such, have no nature whatsoever, there are *only* conventions. This latter position would be the more extreme reading.

As argued previously, one critical way of reading the above argument is that it collapses into relativism and conceptual incommensurability. This led theorists to try to overcome the bugbear of relativism. One strategy has been to search for some kind of thinned down universalism compatible with a constrained contestability. Elements of the above argument were linked with a theoretical construction of a more universal epistemology. This formed the major underpinning for the justice-based arguments. However, the Wittgensteinian argument posits a more far-reaching epistemology. It suggests that there are *no* neutral Archimedean points, *no* final resolutions, and *no* universal manna. There is neither a universal potential for global reasonableness, nor any possibility of a common moral Esperanto to refer to. There are *no* universal human interests or needs, unmediated by forms of life and linguistic conventions. Reason and human knowledge are always particularized. This epistemology denies the possible resolution of the thin universalist argument and configures knowledge, morality, and reason as situated or conventional. It is in this context that the neo-Kantian, Onora O'Neill, for example, takes the philosophical work of the late Wittgenstein as exemplifying, as she puts it, particularity 'with a vengeance'. In Wittgenstein, we therefore learn all our words, concepts, and values in certain *particular* contexts or 'forms of life' (O'Neill 1996: 12). Particularity is thus embedded in language and the whole manner in which we deal with and filter the world. In effect, what we find in Wittgenstein's epistemological thesis is the groundwork for *both* a critique of thin universalism and justice theory, *and* a sketch for an essentialist alternative. Thus a common set of arguments gives rise to *two* different warring perspectives.

The above particularist or conventionalist critique, present in Wittgenstein's later writings, specifically concerning essential contestability, is, in fact, part of a much broader argument, which has multiple repercussions for late twentieth century political theory. These repercussions, in fact, stretch well beyond this present chapter. The concept of 'conventionalism' covers much of the ground here as a linking device to establish overall coherence. The idea has a long prehistory, specifically in terms of what 'kinds' of theories it denotes.

CONVENTIONS

On a simple clarificatory level, the word 'convention' can imply a number of things. It can signify something, which is orthodox or in conformity with pre-established rules. This can simply intimate 'etiquette' or social propriety. Alternatively, in some legal doctrines, convention can imply practices and rules, which are distinct from clear legal rules. Further, a convention can be a meeting, treaty, compact or agreement. Finally, it can denote a continuous or established practice or rule. It is the latter meaning, which will be appropriated for this discussion.[2]

The debate over conventions arose in mainstream philosophy, social science, and political theory in mid-twentieth century debates concerning human action. Conventionalism was one possible broad answer to the question as to how to differentiate action from behaviour. A convention, for many proponents, is an agreed or established manner as to how things are done. Certain kinds of movement—by convention—are considered meaningful. There is, as it were, a 'tacit social agreement' about what it means, socially, to do or say 'x', that is, say, to promise or vote. Bodily movement in terms of a rule—embedded in a convention—makes an action meaningful in a particular social context. The correctness or incorrectness of an action (in specific contexts) confirms that a rule (qua convention) is present. Conventions also act as predictors for future action. Conventions, as such, are not instruments of something else. There is nothing behind or outside conventions. There is no logically-primitive reality underpinning them. Conventions are the shared practices *through* which we think, speak, and act. In this sense, political action is rooted in conventions. They are the ground on which humans think, act, and speak politically. However, it is also important to grasp the point that there is a wide range of 'conventionalisms' in contemporary political theory.

Consequently, the arguments considered in this next section are viewed as examples of conventionalist argument. In this sense, conventionalism entails the very general assertion that, for example, the public culture, nation, state, community, republic or ethos, are the conventional mediums through which rights, freedoms, obligations, and the like, are recognized, articulated, and legitimized. The logic of the conventionalist argument states, on a formal level, that the convention is primary and the right or freedom claim is derivative. The alternative universalist ahistorical scenario is where the right or value is articulated independently of any conventional attachments. For many critics, the conventional character of, for example, rights is a *fait accompli*. It is daydreaming to think otherwise. It is therefore just a mistake to try to find a universal moral theory that could serve as a justification or foundation for, for example, rights.

In the last two decades of the twentieth century a great deal of political theory has moved in a conventionalist direction. Conventionalism, like the thin universalism of 1970s liberal justice theory, premised itself on a rejection of the richer or thicker variants of metaphysical universalism. Thus, the opprobrium directed against traditional metaphysics, begun in the 1930s and 1940s, continued up to the end of the century within conventional normative theories. However, the groundwork for the development of virtually all forms of conventionalism in the 1980s, with some notable exceptions, was formed out of a rejection or scepticism of the thin universalism of liberal justice theory. The first and most well-known of these critiques to develop in the 1980s was communitarianism. However, conventionalism was, as noted, a broad church. It embodied an amalgam of theories. Thus, the last decade of the twentieth century has seen a rash of conventionalisms: such as nationalism, patriotism, neo-Aristotelianism, and republicanism. Rawls' own response to conventionalism was his work on political liberalism.

One major point to stress, concerning these various conventionalisms, is that they were *not* called into being by a rejection of foundationalism *per se*. Most conventionalists argue that the thin universalism of justice theory does not provide a clear enough foundation for reason, politics, and morality. In fact, to pursue this universalist path is effectively to destroy the possibility of sound foundations. Consequently, they suggest that communities, moral systems and human identities are in immanent danger of collapsing, *due* in large part to a specific abstracted rendering of liberal justice and the arguments of thin universalism. Thus, the main conventionalist contention has been that reason and morality needed a firmer, concrete, or more certain, foundation for action and judgment. The task of theory is not to therefore to undermine or reject foundations, but conversely to *shore them up* from a more secure position against the potentially-chaotic forces of modernity.

OAKESHOTT AND CONVENTIONALISM

There are a number of arguments in the early twentieth century, which have upheld more metaphysically rich forms of conventionalism, although they have often tended to be philosophies under pressure, that is rejected by mainstream thought. The present discussion focuses on one representative of this earlier tradition, namely, Michael Oakeshott. Oakeshott was at the end of the powerful tradition of Idealism, which dominated British philosophy up until the 1920s. The roots of this Idealism lay in Scotland and Oxford during the middle of the nineteenth century and rapidly became the dominant philosophy, through the writings and personal influence of such exponents as Fraser Campbell, Edward Caird, T. H. Green, F. H. Bradley, Bernard Bosanquet, Henry Jones, Andrew Seth, D. G. Ritchie, J. S. Mackenzie, William Wallace, W. R. Sorley, J. M. E. McTaggart, and John Watson, until the early twentieth century when its fundamental doctrines were challenged by philosophers such as John Cook Wilson, G. E. Moore, and Bertrand Russell (see Vincent and Plant 1984; Boucher and Vincent 1993 and 2001).[3] However, from the early twentieth century, the march of Idealism was hindered, and by the 1920s it was in slow, if partial, retreat. Yet, the British Idealists still managed through their writings, teaching and personal influence to permeate virtually the whole English speaking world with their doctrines. Even after the death of its leading exponents in the mid 1920s—Bradley, Bosanquet, Jones, and McTaggart—it continued to dominate the professoriate into the 1930s and was able to count in its ranks able young converts such as R. G. Collingwood in Oxford, who published *Speculum Mentis* in 1925, and Michael Oakeshott in Cambridge, who published *Experience and its Modes* in 1933.

In many ways, Michael Oakeshott (1901–90) was the last well-known exponent of the Idealist tradition. However, the impact of both Collingwood and Oakeshott on later twentieth century British philosophy is a testament to the breadth and longer-term impact of the Idealist movement. However, neither of the latter thinkers were part of the heyday of British Idealism. Both worked in a twentieth century environment, which was largely antagonistic to Idealism and where the historical and cultural circumstances had changed significantly. This marks out the character of their work. In this sense, many of the religious, moral, biological, ideological, and economic preoccupations, which underpin thinkers like Green, Bosanquet, Bradley, Jones, and Ritchie do not apply to the twentieth century cultural milieu of Collingwood and Oakeshott. However, it is worth noting that both the latter thinkers began their careers with forceful contributions to the philosophy of religion, a subject that was central to the concerns of their Idealist predecessors. Equally, both clearly rearticulated (in their own terms) the Idealist view of experience, in Collingwood's case viewing the 'totality' of experience as a linked hierarchy of forms, and, in Oakeshott's, as coordinate *modes*, or *arrests*, with philosophy constituting the concrete totality of experience as a whole. Thus, despite their subtle differences from previous Idealism, both Collingwood and Oakeshott played a significant role in keeping the spirit of Idealism alive, not only in social and political philosophy, but also in aesthetics, metaphysics, and the philosophy of history and the social sciences.

The use made of Oakeshott here is simply to indicate that there is a longer standing tradition of sophisticated conventionalism, which predates the debates of the 1980s and 1990s, and which, nonetheless, encompasses many of the central arguments of these latter debates. The only problem in considering Oakeshott—whose last contributions were *On Human Conduct* (1975) and *On History* (1983)—is that he took little, if no time, to debate the arguments within political theory, which were developing in the 1970s and 1980s. Thus, one has to surmise how he would have responded to the likes of Rawls, Habermas, or Skinner. On the other hand, anyone familiar with the deep currents of thought in the first decades of the twentieth century period will recognize many underlying themes and preoccupations in his thought, which stayed with him until his last writings in the 1980s. Thus, for example, his continuing preoccupation with the modern European state in, for example, the last essay of *On Human Conduct*, represents, once again, a form of Idealist orientated philosophical *Staatslehre*. There are indeed some very subtle parallels here with Bernard Bosanquet's *The Philosophical Theory of the State* (1899). In order to grasp Oakeshott's contribution to conventionalism it is necessary to discuss briefly his Idealist philosophical method, which goes back to his first work *Experience and its Modes* (1933). These methods are largely assumed, if modified, within his 1963 book *Rationalism in Politics*, and returned to again, in a slightly different format, in the first essay of his *On Human Conduct*.

Oakeshott's conventionalism can be seen in the premises of his philosophical approach. The central point is that the human agent has no nature. She is what, in conduct, she becomes. Human intelligence creates its own world, but with the ideational material to hand. This ideational material is embodied, for the most part, in what Oakeshott originally called modes (and later conversations and idioms). Oakeshott describes the philosophical impulse as coming to understand, in other terms, what one already understands. The important point here is, though, that we are born into a pre-established intelligible world. This pre-established world of meaning relates to our own contingent historical civilization. We think with and through established conventions, which are characteristic of our own community and civilization. Philosophy, in this sense, is not a search for new knowledge. To be human is to encounter 'what is in some manner understood' (Oakeshott 1975: 1). All facts in the world are mediated through the understood conventions. Facts have no finality in confirming or disconfirming any theory. *All* that we know is experience. Philosophy, in his first and to a less obvious extent in his last works, is the only form of thought, which is sensitive to this *whole* of experience. As he puts it, 'Philosophical experience, then, I take to be experience without presupposition, reservation, arrest or modification' (Oakeshott 1933: 2). In his later work, he describes philosophy as 'an unconditional adventure' (Oakeshott 1975: 11). Philosophy might therefore be described as unconditional experience.

Oakeshott contends, however, that there are multiple modes through which experience takes place. He suggests, though, that there are certain more systematic modes; three such modes are indicated in his first work: practice, science, and history. He later added poetry. Each of these modes is, what he refers to as, an 'arrest in experience' or 'abridgement of meaning', that is, they are abridgements from the totality of experience. Each arrest is a discrete moderately coherent world of ideas. There are direct parallels here between Oakeshott's modes and Wittgenstein's much more diverse conventionalism (in terms of 'forms of life' or 'social practices'). Each mode also has its own sense of the past, its own understanding of truth and its own distinctive postulates. Each, though, is an abstraction from the totality of experience. For Oakeshott, the whole of experience, 'is not made of abstractions, it is implied in them; it is not dependent upon abstraction, because it is logically prior to them' (Oakeshott 1933: 79). The standpoint of totality therefore tolerates no arrest. This view of the totality of experience is equivalent to one reading of the Bradleian or Hegelian absolute. In this sense, philosophy is *not* to be considered a mode. It is undiluted experience.

It is important to realize that the various modes are *not* simply lenses through which we see the real world. They are, literally, all there is. There is nothing outside, external, or beyond these experiences. The mode is the reality. The truth of the mode hangs upon the coherence of its postulates. This implies that the sense we have of the truth of a mode is not something that is to be tested by looking outside it to some purported external reality or some body of fact. Oakeshott also indicates that there cannot be any profitable mixing of modes. History, for example, has nothing to contribute to poetry or practice, and vice versa. Further, in this context, concepts and words will alter both between modes, and also, at points, within modes. Meaning is contextual. One other point which follows from this argument (and is still adhered to in his later works) is that one should not confuse theorizing *about* ethics, history, or politics with the 'knowing how' to subscribe or perform such practices. As Oakeshott comments, 'a theoretical understanding cannot itself be an engagement in the conduct being theorized: to theorize a 'comic' performance (i.e. to understand it in terms of its postulates) is not itself to make a joke' (Oakeshott 1975: 34).

In later work, particularly *On Human Conduct*, Oakeshott indicates that the relation of modes is more fluid and open and can be re-characterized in terms of a conversation in which each voice has a say, but none is dominant. There is also the hint of a more sceptical shift in his thought. Philosophy moves from being experience without arrest to 'the impulse to study the quality and style of each voice, and to reflect upon the relationship of one voice to another' (Oakeshott 1962: 200). This subtle movement of thought continues in *On Human Conduct*, where the voices or modes become idioms of discourse or platforms of understanding. The unconditional engagement with understanding appears now as 'theorizing' (Oakeshott 1975: 1

and 11). Theory belongs to either of two idioms of inquiry, equivalent to the older ideas of *Geisteswissenschaft* and *Naturwissenschaft*. He thus insists on a firm distinction between the 'engagement' with the natural world, as against the intelligible world of human conduct. This distinction has been a mainstay of the humanistic disciplines and interpretative social sciences during the whole twentieth century. Oakeshott is thus insistent that an intelligible belief is and remains a belief and cannot be explained outside itself. Psychology, biology, or sociology are legitimate idioms of inquiry, but they express a profound immaturity when they suggest that all beliefs can be explained through, for example, biological or psychological mechanisms.[4] For Oakeshott, 'psychological mechanisms cannot be the motives of actions or the reason for beliefs' (Oakeshott 1975: 22).

An idiom of inquiry is constituted by a 'system of theorems', which aspires to be a 'science'. It springs from a patient engagement with its postulates. Ethics, jurisprudence, or aesthetics, for example, would be considered intelligible idioms of human inquiry. To theorize within an idiom, for Oakeshott, involves the identification of, what he calls, 'ideal characters', which are, in effect, the essential conditions, or deep 'formal' assumptions, or postulates, of a practice. Theorizing *is* the identification of the postulates of ideal characters. These ideal characters are, in turn, the channels through which we understand the world. Ideal characters can be either crude or sophisticated. However, every form of theoretical understanding is necessarily a creature of an 'ideal character'.

All forms of conduct begin with a 'historic' reflective consciousness (see Oakeshott 1975: 37). As mentioned, intelligible conduct cannot be reduced to anything else outside itself. To understand conduct is not to grasp it causally. For Oakeshott, all human conduct, *per se*, therefore embodies 'ideal characters', embedded within its postulates. Thus, all human conduct is, as Oakeshott puts it, an enactment or disclosure in a performance 'whose imagined and wished-for outcomes are performances of other agents or other performances of himself' (Oakeshott 1975: 36). The postulates of conduct can, however, be used creatively by the agent in different ways. However, conduct, in the final analysis, is what the agent 'enacts for himself in a diurnal engagement, the unceasing articulation of understood responses to endlessly emergent understood situations' (Oakeshott 1975: 41).[5] In sum, all human conduct is essentially a learned conventional activity, which is assimilated by the agents and then used reflectively and creatively, as she matures, for both self-exploration and investigation of her relation with others.

Conventional meanings, roles, obligations, expectations, which are rooted in historic communities and civilizations, form the substance of human conduct. Practices within a community therefore embody meanings. Oakeshott refers to this virtual role-playing aspect of many practices as *personae*. When we participate in a practice we take on *personae*, which, in turn, embody the roles, obligations, and expectations of the practice.[6] For example, the practices of being a neighbour or voting entail *personae*, which are implied in the postulates of neighbourly conduct or the practice of voting. Presumably, for Oakeshott, the *personae* therefore embody the 'ideal characters'. The *personae* do not structurally determine activity, conversely, they embody a language of self-enactment, through which the agent (reflectively) communicates and participates in a practice. The language thus 'permits those who can use it to understand themselves and one another'. It is also, at the same time, a language of self-disclosure. Self-disclosure is used by agents 'in diagnosing their situations and in choosing their response' (see Oakeshott 1975: 63).

All human conduct therefore evolves, initially, as a conventional ritual. Children, for Oakeshott (as for Hegel), are simply a 'helpless subject' of conduct. Conduct is something that has to be learned by being spoken and gradually assimilated from within practices. Like Hegel again, Oakeshott contends that we come into a world 'already illuminated by moral practice' (Oakeshott 1975: 63). The moral and political language is, however, a shifting body of conventions. Oakeshott notes, qua morality, that 'its abstract nouns (right and wrong, proper and improper, obligation, dueness, fairness, respect, justice, etc.), when they appear, are faded metaphors'. Oakeshott adds here, with no doubt a weather eye on many contemporary political theorists, 'it is only the uneducated who insists that each must have a single unequivocal meaning indifferent to context'. Moral language, embodied in conduct, is never fixed or finished. It has no settled meaning. Echoing again a Wittgensteinian theme, he claims that such a language is *only* learned in usage. He comments that moral language '*is* its vicissitudes, and its virtue is to be a living, vulgar language' (Oakeshott 1975: 64). A language of moral conduct 'has rhythms which remain when the words are forgotten'. Thus, there is a sense in which such language is an embedded substrate of actions. Agents will, in fact, often lose any sense of its genesis and 'ideal character', consequently, 'expressions in it harden into clichés and are released again; the ill-educated speak it vulgarly, the purists inflexibly, and each generation invents its own moral slang' (Oakeshott 1975: 65). We might call this argument a strong version of conventionalism.

This strong version can be highlighted more clearly by contrasting it to rule-based theories of morality and politics, which insist on theoretical justification. To focus on 'rules'—as a large number of contemporary moral and political theorists do—is, for Oakeshott, to engage in a total distortion of moral and political conduct. Rules are just 'abridgements', passing contingent snapshots of fluid and restless phenomena. Rules suggest a rigid and abstracted expression of such conduct. Thus, rules are *not* the reality of morality and politics. Further, to place excessive attention on the *justification* of rules is also utterly misplaced, since it again cuts into the living flesh of a moral and political language.[7] Moral and political rules 'are not criteria of good conduct, nor are they primarily instruments of judgement; they are prevailing winds which agents should take account of in sailing their several courses' (Oakeshott 1975: 70). Thus, morality cannot be just about observed rules or obeying injunctions. It is also not concerned with justification. It is a much more complex contingent process used for both exploring one's own self and also one's interaction with other agents. Rules can be elicited as representations of a moment, but morality is emphatically not the same as that 'one moment', nor it is the creation of moralists or grammarians (as Oakeshott phrases it). It is made in and through ordinary conventional usage.

It is worth noting here that this 'usage' theme links up with his thoughts about tradition and practical reason explored in *Rationalism in Politics* in the 1950s.

Tradition, in this latter work, is not something to be taught or put across either in injunctive rationalist texts or moral or political manuals. Practical knowledge is distinct from technical knowledge. Moral and political practices are rooted in a traditional manner of doing things. However, tradition is not a static body of rules. It is, conversely, a contingent, moving and multi-voiced creature—a mixture of conventional aversions, preferences, anxieties, and fears. It consequently provides no unambiguous norms or rules. It has no fixed point or purpose. It therefore cannot be summarized in a firm doctrine. It is diffused between past, present, and future. Consequently, it is a 'tricky thing to get to know'. As Oakeshott remarks, 'Although it moves, it is steady, it is tranquil though never at rest.' He thus describes it as a 'flow of sympathy'. Knowing what to do next, for a traditionalist, is a matter of intimations, not rational rules. The demeanour of the traditionalist has some parallels with the philosophical demeanour outlined in his early work (Oakeshott 1962: 128).

The question arises here as to what bearing does the above analysis of conventional usage have on Oakeshott's conception of political association? There are two possible conventionalist responses here. One argues that all theory can do is observe what 'is' the case in any community—that is, painting its grey upon grey. This conventionalism allows no normative or positive interjections. The second response is more nuanced and has a number of possible subtle variants, some of which will be explored in later sections of this chapter. In Oakeshott's case, he uses the theme of 'ideal character' to suggest that there are, in fact, forms of association. Ideal characters are neither universal, nor do they bear any precise relation to specific historical examples. Thus, although they are conventional and are generated from within the idioms of a particular European 'civilization', nonetheless they do possess a form of partial transcendence. Oakeshott appears to be offering here a form of realistic phenomenology of associations. Political or civil relationships are one amongst many types of human relationship. Oakeshott suggests, in *On Human Conduct*, that there are two forms of association—which he calls *civil* and *enterprise* associations—understood as ideal characters. Humans, reflectively, utilize these ideal characters to both enact and disclose themselves. Any such articulations are, again, not to be seen as deterministic or mechanistic. It is the agent that utilizes them in the understanding, conforming to the *personae* of each form of association (see Oakeshott 1975: 112).

Enterprise associations involve 'joint pursuit of some imagined and wished-for satisfaction'. Relationships are conducted 'in terms of the pursuit of some common purpose, some substantive condition of things to be jointly procured, or some common interests to be continuously satisfied' (Oakeshott 1975: 113 and 114). The association exists in terms of the common pursuit of a substantive purpose, willed by the membership. *Civil* association (which Oakeshott considers preferable) is a relationship 'in respect of common recognition of considerations such as uses or rules intelligently subscribed to in self-chosen performances'. This is a formal, not a substantial relationship, 'that is, association in respect of a common language and not in respect of having the same beliefs, purposes, interests, etc., in making the same utterances'. Citizens (*cives*), in civil association, are not partners in a common enterprise, since there is *no* common purpose (Oakeshott 1975: 121 and 122). Civil association, *per se*, has no substantive purpose. It is not reliant upon will, affection, or a common good. It is rather a system of rules, implying a rule of law. As he states, in his last work, the rule of law (*lex*), 'stands for a mode of moral association exclusively in terms of the recognition of the authority of known, non-instrumental rules (that is, laws), which impose obligations to subscribe to adverbial conditions in which the perform- ance of self-chosen actions of all who fall within their jurisdiction' (Oakeshott 1983: 136). The rule of law is again understood as a vernacular language through which citizens understand themselves and their mutual relations. The rule of law forms the basis of what Oakeshott calls a *respublica*. This does not embody any purpose or any will of the ruler, the authority of *respublica* is the authority of the postulates of civil association itself. It has no moral purpose. Political engagement is a concern with the conditions that both *respublica* and civil association prescribe. Thus, in sum, the 'civil condition is an ideal character glimpsed here or there in the features of human goings-on, intimated in some choices and dispositions to choose . . . but it nowhere constitutes a premeditated design for human conduct'. For Oakeshott, it can in fact be glimpsed in the writings of Cicero, Hobbes, Hegel, and Montesquieu (Oakeshott 1975: 180–1).

In the final part of *On Human Conduct* Oakeshott focuses on the idea of the modern European state. In characterizing forms of state, he utilizes Roman law terms to indicate again two forms of state which parallel—to some degree—the earlier 'civil' and 'enterprise' associations. The terms he uses are '*societas*' and '*universitas*'. Both terms (like civil and enterprise association) are, once again, 'ideal characters', which can, in fact, be found together as 'sweet enemies' within most actual developed states (Oakeshott 1975: 326).[8] Both, however, should only be understood as 'aids to reflection' in thinking about the European state; they are *not* indicating actual or empirical states.

The *societas* state (nomocracy) is essentially a legal state where citizens are linked by non-instrumental rules. This is intimated in the writings of Bodin, Hobbes, Kant, Fichte, Hegel, Hume, J. S. Mill, and Locke (Oakeshott 1975: 252).[9] A *societas* is conventionally a pact or agreement to acknowledge certain conditions of acting (as in civil association). The *universitas* state is a partnership or relationship or persons 'who recognize themselves to be engaged upon the joint enterprise of seeking the satisfaction of some common substantive want; a many become one on account of their common engagement'. It is thus a teleocratic association involving the 'man- agement of a purposive concern' (Oakeshott 1975: 205–6). Oakeshott's discussion of the *universitas* (enterprise-based) form of state becomes much fiercer and more intemperate in the closing stages of *On Human Conduct*. For example, he describes the *universitas* state, at a later point, as a 'corrupted discourse', which has comprom- ised civil law and undermined civil discourse (Oakeshott 1975: 312). This kind of judgement is reminiscent of his earlier critical discussion of rationalism (Oakeshott 1962 and 1991). The *universitas* mentality—paralleling the enterprise association— is a managerial, bureaucratized, corporate state vision, which Oakeshott associates not only with Enlightenment thinking, Cameralism and Baconian utopian ideas, but later sees as caricatured in both early twentieth century British Fabianism, and in the stylized collectivized vision of a British war-based post-1945 polity and economy (see Oakeshott 1975: 269, n.1, 273, 287).[10] This whole argument has strong parallels with Friedrich Hayek's critical distinction between *teleocratic* and *catallactic* orders (Hayek 1976).

The civil association-based *societas* state is also intimately linked, in Oakeshott's mind, with the earlier theme of human conduct, that is, the particular 'ideal character' of exploring, enacting, and disclosing the self. It is also connected to a concept of individualism, not the individualism of nineteenth century liberalism, but an older idea found in the writings of Montaigne, Cervantes, and Pascal. This is an individual life considered as a personal adventure of self-enactment and disclosure, with *no* outside or external moral or political foundations. The *societas* state entails that such individuals are associated, but not joined in any common substantive purpose. The connective between individuals in this civil *societas* is therefore what Oakeshott refers to as a 'watery fidelity'. It is not concerned with affection or mutual concern, rather, it is a recognition of the authority of a system of laws 'composed of conditions to be subscribed to in self-chosen conduct, conditions indifferent to the satisfactions sought in the actions and utterances they qualify' (Oakeshott 1975: 263).

Oakeshott's own political stance is more clearly seen in his earlier *Rationalism in Politics*, although it underpins his debate on *societas*. In a phrase, it is a philosophical conservatism.[11] As Oakeshott states, 'politics is not the science of setting up a permanently impregnable society, it is the art of knowing where to go next in the explanation of an already existing traditional kind of society' (Oakeshott 1962: 58). This is neither a romantic nostalgia, nor a forward-looking optimism. If anything, the argument has affinities with Edmund Burke, although in Oakeshott it is a totally secularized claim and does not sanctify any existing constitution. Oakeshott neither idolizes the past, nor seeks to prevent all change. Traditional politics is rather the 'disposition' of one who has a mature grasp of the character of both human understanding and experience.

The crucial distinction, which underpins this dispositional conservatism is between traditional or practical reason, as against theoretical reason. This distinction, made by Oakeshott, arises in the context of his subtle discussion of rationalism and traditionalism. Political activity, for Oakeshott, is not something that arises from instantaneous desires or principles. The roots of practice are neither simple motivating desires, nor a worked out rational belief. Rather, practice is rooted in an existing tradition of behaviour. A tradition, as mentioned, is a mixture of preferences and aversions, approvals and disapprovals, anxieties, fears, and beliefs. This does not constitute a creed or rationally self-consistent doctrine. For Oakeshott: 'Practical discourse is the process in which (among other things) we elicit from this "tradition" decisions about what to do and justifications of acts or proposals to act' (Oakeshott 1965: 90). Thus, practical knowledge, whether in riding a bike or legislating, is assimilated gradually in the 'doing' within a tradition. It is not something that can be formulated in precise rules. It can only be learnt by participating in a tradition. For Oakeshott, this practical or traditional knowledge is distinct from rationalist theory, ideology, and technical knowledge. The rationalist technician 'insists upon getting a straight answer' (Oakeshott 1965: 90). She selects, abridges, and abstracts to make a self-consistent creed, composed of maxims, rules, and precise concepts. A manual on how to ride a bicycle, or how to cook, is thus equivalent to Lenin's *What is to be Done?*, Rawls' *Theory of Justice*, Brian Barry's *Justice as Impartiality*, or Hayek's *Constitution of Liberty*. The latter are all technical political 'cookbooks', rationalist manuals, which comprised abstract highly-selective rules. The rationalist cannot abide the ambiguity of tradition. It is worth noting here that, for Oakeshott, many 'apparent' conservatives appear in this rationalist category.[12]

One of the many problems with this line of argument is its intrinsic reflexivity. It is clear that both practical reason and knowledge are conceptually structured. They are drawn rationally distinct from theoretical reason. Practical reason provides a coherent principle of interpretation and a prescription for action. Therefore, is Oakeshott's view on tradition and practice an abridgement of tradition? We find Oakeshott speaking in clear intelligible terms about something (tradition), which is supposed to be rationally inchoate. It seems that Oakeshott himself poses the reflexive problem by acclaiming his own position as virtually an Archimedean standpoint on the nature of theory and philosophy. What, for example, is the nature of Oakeshott's linked distinctions between technical and practical knowledge, rationalism and tradition, the conservative disposition and ideological thought? Are these distinctions 'traditionally situated' or 'abridgements of tradition'? In other words, is Oakeshott just a covert conservative ideologist artfully trading on philosophy?

Leaving this criticism to the side, one important argument that Oakeshott uses here is, also, in fact, deeply modernist. His idiosyncratic response to the question of the sources and nature of morality and politics, resonates with aspects of late twentieth century moral and political theory. For Oakeshott, as noted, morality and politics are not and never can be universals. There are *no* external metaphysical or moral foundations. All that exist are 'ideal characters', which relate, in turn, to specific historical civilizations. In fact, for Oakeshott, history is possibly one of the most effective ways of studying human conduct. Religion is also read by Oakeshott as a valuable human resource for both self-enactment and self-disclosure, but, one which, again, *only* reflects a conventional culture, or, one element of the culture of a civilized community of believers (see Oakeshott 1975: 83–5). Every religion is therefore a part of a tradition and traditions are tricky, particularist, and multi-voiced creatures. In consequence of this conventional account of meaning, all universalist claims are regarded with deep scepticism. Neither reason nor justice stand *outside* human conduct. Nothing provides agents with any universal standards, or a 'view form nowhere'. Oakeshott acknowledges, unashamedly, and without any apparent anxiety, that both morality and politics can be and frequently are deeply corrupt, misused, and imperfect, and, that there are potentially many versions of morality and politics. Moral and political pluralism are therefore inevitable. All human conduct is rooted in the diverse conventions (and the ideal characters) of civilized communities.

What actually constrains moral or political conduct is the postulates that intelligent reflective agents utilize for exploring both their own selves and their relation with others. These postulates are all contingent—although at the same time we are *not* determined by them. No universal, whether deontological or consequential, will overcome this contingency. In this sense, Oakeshott implicitly rejects all the liberal 'justice-based' arguments focused on thin universalism. Thus, John Rawls and Brian Barry's arguments are all implicitly excluded. There may well be similarities and overlaps between moral and political languages. Oakeshott is prepared to acknowledge this. He remarks, for example, that 'there should be many such languages in the world, some perhaps with familial likenesses in terms of which there may be profitable exchange of expressions, is intrinsic to their character'. However, he continues, 'This plurality cannot be resolved by being understood as so many contingent and regrettable divergences from a fancied perfect and universal language of moral intercourse (a law of God, a utilitarian "critical" morality, or a so-called "rational morality")'. He adds, quite presciently for the last three decades of the twentieth-century normative political theory, that it is hardly surprising 'that such a resolution should have been attempted: human beings are apt to be disconcerted unless they feel themselves to be upheld by something more substantial than the emanations of their own contingent imaginations. This unresolved plurality teases the monistic yearnings of the muddled theorist, it vexes a morality with ecumenical leanings, and it may disconcert an unfortunate who, having "lost" his morality (as others have been known to "lose" their faith), must set about constructing one for himself and is looking for uncontaminated "rational" principles out of which to make it' (Oakeshott 1975: 80–1). This is a quite apt description for the Rawlsian and post-Rawlsian generation of Kantians and utilitarians.

In the above sense, human nature can never be a given datum of experience. As Oakeshott observes, there are multiple theorems about human nature throughout the history of thought. This is of interest, but Oakeshott denies any possibility of determinism or genetic explanation on the basis of a theory of human nature. Each conception of human nature is a belief, which relates to the conventions of particular societies. What is primary though is our *understanding*. As stated earlier, the human agent, as such, has no ultimate nature. She is what in conduct she becomes. Human intelligence creates its own world, but with the ideational materials and postulates of conduct to hand. Convention, the intelligent use and assimilation of postulates and imagination characterize human conduct.

COMMUNITARIANISM

Most political theorists, in considering conventionalist argument, have generally not tended to consider Oakeshott's thought, although, in reality, it is a deeply sophisticated philosophical rendition of the conventionalist position. Most theorists, who have been attracted by conventionalist argument, over the last two to three decades, have focused their attention on the more general communitarian perspective. This latter perspective has had a relatively brief, if loud, exposure during the 1980s and 1990s. In many ways, it has now become somewhat more dissipated and hackneyed in the early 2000s. However, communitarianism is still useful, in that it focuses attention, quite precisely, on some of the bare bones of current conventionalist arguments.

In this sense, communitarianism lays down a loose template for considering other recent expressions of conventionalist argument. In this context, the discussion of communitarianism will be fairly condensed, since it will appear in tandem with other conventionalist claims.[13]

There are several initial ambiguities, which need reviewing on the term 'communitarianism'. First, it is not altogether clear which theorists are being addressed under the rubric of communitarianism. *Prima facie,* the answer does seem obvious: the standard account is that a movement, commonly called communitarian and focused primarily on the writings of a number of political philosophers, blossomed during the 1980s, partly as a reaction to thin proceduralist versions of liberalism and justice. The political philosophers most closely associated with this movement are Michael Sandel, Charles Taylor, Michael Walzer, and Alisdair MacIntyre. Thus, when communitarian theories are mentioned, in any political theory context, it is usually the latter theorists that are in the spotlight. Despite the fact that this is very widely accepted in the literature, the strangeness of this point is that *none* of the above thinkers accept the term to describe or summarize their work. In fact some, such as MacIntyre, go out of their way to reject it.[14] Amitai Etzioni, a principal figure in the current communitarian movement in North America, consequently accepts MacIntyre's rejection of communitarianism and describes his work as an articulation of a sophisticated moderate social conservatism (Etzioni 1997: 15). In fact, Etzioni continues, that all the above political thinkers have 'been uncomfortable with the label "communitarian" ' (Etzioni 1997: 40). Taylor also, partly because of his quite evident disquiet with nationalism, and also, partly because of his interest in a more multicultural position (in the Canadian context), has also raised profound doubts about the term 'communitarian'. It seems to indicate, for Taylor, too much of a consensual idea of community and does not take enough account of 'deep diversity' (see Taylor in Tully (ed.) 1994: 250 and 256).[15] Further, Sandel, quite simply, does not refer to it at all in his last book, *Democracy's Discontents* (1996). He seems much happier with the denotation republican. The only one of the four theorists to actually give the term 'communitarianism' some intellectual space is Walzer. He notes that he is moderately happy to see his work described as— what he calls—a 'periodic communitarian correction' to some mainstream work in political theory (see Walzer 1990). One could hardly though call this a full-blooded commitment.

Thus, in considering the extensive political theory debates over communitarianism, in the last two decades of the twentieth century, it is curious to note that none of the apparent key philosophical protagonists accept the description. Only one is ready to, very diffidently, accept the label. The others are just antagonistic or uninterested. It is still quite possible to argue that this is all irrelevant and that all do (underneath the denials) subscribe to certain basic assumptions and modes of analysis, which can be called communitarian. There is some truth to this and it is undoubtedly more convenient for critical admirers or antagonists to have this 'apparent consistency' in the communitarian position. It is more difficult, after all, to hit a moving or diffused target, so why not force it to sit still. However, the above consideration should at least make us wary.

After the philosophical flurries of the 1980s, however, communitarianism has changed quite distinctly in character. In many ways, this change also coincided with a subtle slowing of interest in the academic debates during the later 1990s. Communitarianism moved from the forum of academic contestation and took on many of the trappings of a proselytizing political movement—particularly in North America, conversion and commitment are now preferred to being philosophically persuaded. Communitarianism thus began to shift its focus to the domain of public policy-making. This has led to the setting up of organizations such as the Communitarian Network and Centre for Communitarian Policy Studies. The most important organizing figure here in North America is Etzioni. It is in this context that communitarianism has attained some loose advisory links within 'third way' forms of politics, in both Europe and North America. Communitarian activists now have their own websites, think tanks, and journals. All are devoted to recovering this apparently lost sense of community. Etzioni has also contributed a number of more popular polemical texts, such as *The Spirit of Community* and *The New Golden Rule*. The aim is fundamentally more zealous, rather than philosophical. Whether this would be better described now as a 'communitarian ideology' is open to debate. The *Habits of the Heart* book embodies many of the more practical aims of the movement, which is focused on a range of issues concerned with the everyday problems for any community, namely, education, crime, policing, health, and so forth. There is also a strong sense, pervading throughout the whole text of the latter book, that something has gone fundamentally wrong in most American communities, which needs to be addressed on the most basic level. As the book states, 'most Americans agree that things are seriously amiss in our society—that we are not, as the poll questions often put it, "headed in the right direction" ' (Bellah et al. 1996: vii and xxii).

Another issue here concerns what is meant, implied, or required by the concept of community. One problem with more recent communitarianism is that it has tended to be short on history and long on normativity. There is some historical awareness amongst the philosophers, however, it is still a somewhat selective history. The idea and value of coherent consensual community has a long complex history in particularly European thinking. However, the value of community has been a particular interest of thinkers in Europe over the last two centuries. It has inhabited, for example, a wide range of political ideologies during this period, including socialism, anarchism, conservativism, feminism, and environmentalism. In most thinkers, from the eighteenth century, discussions of community were usually punctuated by fixed binary group contrasts, in order to reveal something fundamental about the notion of community. Community usually indicated something that was more organic, natural, or involuntary and this was contrasted to other types of social group which were artificial, constructed, and voluntarist. Thus, G. W. F. Hegel contrasted the idea of an ethical communal state to the rootlessness and fragmentation of civil society. Edmund Burke distinguished a hierarchical, organic, traditional, and stable community from an anomic and individualistically orientated conception promulgated by theories of consent-based politics. Samuel Taylor Coleridge held similar views to Burke, that is, a division between a commercially orientated individualistic society and traditional organic pastoral communities. This was also reflected again in the twentieth century political writings of T. S. Eliot, Charles Maurras, and Christopher Dawson. At the close of the nineteenth and beginning of the twentieth century, the most famous rendition of the distinction was Ferdinand Tönnies' contrast between community and association—*Gemeinschaft* and *Gesellschaft*—also echoed in R. M. MacIver's distinction between communal and associated groups, Otto Gierke's *Genossenschaft* and *Herrschaft* groups and Emile Durkheim's mechanical and organic solidarity. Similar types of contrasts have gone on reappearing in twentieth century theories, and in most, the idea of community usually, though not always, appears as more natural, consensual, and organic.

The above is, by no means, an attempt to give a potted history of the idea of community, rather it is designed to make one point, namely, that the claims of community do mutate between many differing political sentiments. One would be as likely to find community-based language in continental liberalism, utopian socialism, fascism, national socialism, or corporatist authoritarianism. It is a forlorn hope to expect to see communitarian appeals in just one sector of human political experience. However, on a more superficial level, communitarianism does indirectly share much of the mid-twentieth century opprobrium heaped upon nationalism. This is understandable, in so far as 1980s communitarianism never clarified its relationship with nationalism. The conceptual connection of communitarianism to suspect romantic, conservative, fascist, reactionary, nationalist, or just illiberal ideas has been noted many times by commentators during the twentieth century (see Plant 1976: 33–4). This partly explains the zeal of, for example, Stephen Holmes' denunciation of communitarianism, where even soft-hearted political thinkers such as MacIntyre are lumped with ultramontanist conservatives, such as Joseph de Maistre, and national socialists *manqué*, such as Carl Schmitt (see Holmes 1993). However, even the fiercest critiques of liberalism by Taylor, Sandel, or Walzer really do look very meek and mild comparative to, say, Maistre's political jeremiads.

As to exactly why communitarianism developed at such a fast pace during the 1980s is puzzling, although its rapid decline in the late 1990s is equally intriguing. My own suspicion is that its rise is bound up with the deeply-negative feeling generated by the temporary, but stormy, dominance of the 'new right' (in academic as well as policy-related areas) during the same period. An alternative language was being sought, by certain groups, which rejected (what was seen to be) the libertarian and classical liberal theoretical and practice excesses. This language was also one which had to take account of the deep decline of interest in Marxism, particularly after 1989. The language of communitarianism, which had been present within eighteenth century theories of consensual, ethical communities (qua Hegel or Herder), was ideal to fill that gap. The latter language also carried a heavy weight of philosophical gravitas. In addition, globalizing pressures, the unpredictable and random effects of market-based liberal policies, fears over rising levels of immigration and unemployment, the development of an anomic industrial underclass, the growing anomie of atomized conceptions of individualism, fast technological change, and the like, led to a sense of profound loss of communal cohesion. In the terms which have now become more significant—these forces were radically undermining and diminishing 'social capital'. It was therefore seen as undermining those networks of norms, which facilitated cooperation and mutual benefit. In this context, as the *Habits of the Heart* communitarian group noted despondently, 'we have moved from the local life of the nineteenth century—in which economic and social relationships were visible and, however imperfectly, morally interpreted as parts of a larger common life—to a society vastly more interrelated and integrated economically, technically, and functionally. Yet this is a society in which the individual can only rarely and with difficulty understand himself and his activities as interrelated in morally meaningful ways' (Bellah et al. 1996: 50). This sense of social and moral anxiety translated, in turn, into an attraction and longing for a mysterious language of predictable, warm, inertial, safe, consensual community, top-dressed with lashings of social capital. This language promised much—a growth of mutual awareness, active concerned citizenship, healthy caring neighbourhoods, and heightened civic awareness. In some ways part of this language has subtly mutated into the more recent concerns of deliberative democracy.[16]

The problem with this language, despite its seductive appeal, is that it also relies upon a remarkably vague and indeterminate concept, namely, 'community'. Primarily, the naturalness of community implies, on one level, a simple anthropological or sociological statement of fact, that is, humans, as a biological species, have tended to live in groups, for various survival-based reasons. Although important on an empirical level, this fact carries no obvious normative implications. One should not confuse the value of community with the fact that we do live in groups. Further, quite obviously, not all groups are communities. Much of what we might impute to community is not natural, but is rather a normative and artificial addition to an anthropological detail. Community has been claimed (as indicated) by virtually every nineteenth and twentieth century ideology. Its ideological complexion remains therefore kaleidoscopic. Some communitarians have even made a virtue of the openness of the communitarian perspective to all manner of understandings. However, there is something evasive in such ideas. As a matter of basic fact, modern communitarians are *not* open to all understandings of community. They would be psychologically unbalanced if they were. Further, as suggested, there is little, if nothing, that could be described as actually organic or natural in most communities. The terms 'organic' or 'natural' carry many exciting valorizing expectations, but they are all suspect, unless one holds a very catholic understanding of nature.

In addition, because of the sheer range of ideological claims to community, it is clear, minimally, that there are different senses of community. On a fairly simple level there are strong, richer, or thicker senses of community and much weaker, thinner senses. The thicker and stronger senses envisage deep-rooted consensual cultural, moral, or religious values characterizing community. The human self blends and merges into the whole community. For its critics, this idea is impossible to maintain in an advanced industrialized society, with rapid economic change and social mobility (Lesser et al. 1980: 243). The stronger sense of community would therefore be accused of an unnecessary reactionary nostalgia. The weaker sense of community—which in fact characterizes the bulk of 1980s communitarianism—makes much more tentative liberal-minded claims. In point, it might be seen, more straightforwardly, as 'liberal communitarianism'. In this sense, it is theoretically very close to all the modern statements of civic republicanism, neo-Aristotelianism, and liberal nationalism. The exponents of the weaker vision usually limit their arguments to claims about encouraging active citizenship and more generalized commitments to a common culture of decency.

In summary, as regards 1980s communitarianism, it is puzzling as to whom we associate it with. Further, the term community remains radically indeterminate and contested. There are clearly many claimants to community. Minimally, there are weaker and stronger variants. Despite all these conceptual and historical reservations, if we focus on the late twentieth century variants of communitarianism, there are a number of quite recognizable patterns to the arguments. The present account unpacks five formal themes, which characterize the communitarian position, particularly qua conventionalism: first, the embeddedness of human nature; second, a deep background anxiety about a particular species of liberalism; third, a thesis concerning the role of pre-understandings in human judgement; fourth, the demand to respect communities as valuable entities in themselves; and, fifth, a hostility to universalist ethics or, at least, a stress on the situatedness of morality.

First, the structural embeddedness theme asserts that humans are intrinsically social beings. These social beings find their distinctive roles, values, and beliefs from within the conventional structures of communities. Communities are thus the most fundamental ontological units. The conventions of communities form the substance of the self. The outcomes of such social agency might be very diverse, since different communities will give rise to different value systems, but the conditions within which humans establish their differences are nonetheless common to the species. Humans are—to use the favoured terminology—'constituted' by communities. For modern communitarians, it is therefore a core thesis that the self is embedded in the community. In Michael Sandel's phraseology, there are no 'unencumbered selves' standing outside a community frame. There is no sense, therefore, that one could speak of human nature outside of a community and its conventions. This parallels Oakeshott's argument. Thus, for Sandel, we cannot adopt the stance of the early Rawlsian original position, because it makes the gratuitous assumption of the unencumbered self. There is no Archimedean point.[17] If we cannot accept this unanchored insubstantial Rawlsian self, then it follows that we have no ground for accepting the two principles of justice. Thus, in the Sandelian view, Rawls presupposes an implausible account of the moral subject, which is the logical prerequisite for the impartiality of justice. Life in the state and citizenship precede any sense we might have of our unique human individuality. Liberal politics, in the Rawlsian mode (or even more so in the Nozickian mode), lacks any coherent communal underpinning. This argument is also echoed in Alisdair MacIntyre's narrative conception of the self, a self which is constituted, in part, from the history and telos of the community (MacIntyre 1981).[18]

A second communitarian theme is a general concern about liberalism, although we should qualify this immediately and speak of a particular species of liberalism. It is not usually liberalism, *per se*, which is condemned.[19] In fact, the bulk of modern communitarianism has distinctively liberal aspects—although it is a different species of liberalism. In the case of the work of MacIntyre, Sandel, Taylor, or Walzer, the liberalism criticized is, what Taylor has referred to, as a version of 'procedural' liberalism (Taylor in Gutman (ed.) 1994: 60). Others have called this classical or atomistic liberalism. The point that communitarians want to make here is that this latter species of liberalism places far too much emphasis on the individual as a isolated and 'unencumbered' agent. This conception has the effect of divorcing the individual from the community. Such a liberalism is therefore seen to offer a preposterous view of the self, which both ignores and undermines local and cultural communities. For some, this procedural liberalism is regarded as ethnocentric (in an unwitting manner) and also makes erroneous claims about both neutrality and rights. Thus, the idea that rights are transcendent or universal principles is often fostered by procedural liberals. Communitarians lay stress on the contingent and conventional basis of rights. Some communitarians have even suggested moving away from an emphasis on individualistic rights discourse altogether, partly because it can undermine both public reason and communal consensus.

A third communitarian theme focuses on 'pre-understandings'. Communitarians take for granted the idea of shared conventional moral and political resources, which are not always open to critical examination. Such resources rather form a backdrop to discussion. Again, this is something emphasized by Oakeshott, in a more nuanced and sophisticated format. In the communitarian reading, communities are constituted by such 'pre-understandings'—which form a body of internal conventional standards. Thus, the particularity of historical communities is set against the empty claims of deontic and consequentialist ahistorical universality. The community forms the basis for practical reason, value, and political judgement. In this sense, communitarians are sceptical about aspects of Enlightenment thought—and are thus also indirectly or directly sympathetic to the romantic and expressivist movements of the late eighteenth and early nineteenth century—concerning the ability for abstract universal reasoning to stand apart from social and moral traditions. Reason is substantive and situated within communities. The community forms the basis of identity, an identity in large measure inherited from the communal traditions. This body of shared attitudes, habits, and rituals are essential for any community. Such a belief system is not conjured out of thin air. It is always a deeply rooted pre-understanding.

A fourth theme is an implicit egalitarianism in contemporary communitarianism—particularly in the weaker variants. Each community is to be recognized as having a unique identity, which should be respected. There is a pattern of argument here, focusing on the complex linkage between 'recognition' and 'identity', which Charles Taylor has called the 'politics of recognition'. The basic idea is that identity is something which needs to be recognized in order to maintain itself. Isolated individuality does not exist, it rather develops through recognition. Denying recognition is thus a form of oppression, since it denies basic identity. We might recognize this immediately in terms of the rights of the human individual. However, in eighteenth century writers such as Herder, the notion of identity was also linked with the *Volk* (or more loosely public culture). Being true to oneself meant being true to one's originality, which, in turn, was both a uniquely personal *and* cultural phenomenon. Herder is thus often linked to the origins of both nationalist and communitarian thought. It follows that denying recognition to cultures is also oppression of identity. One difficulty with this theme (which will not be dealt with here) is that it gives rise to the conception of community or group rights, which stand in a complex and tense relation with individual rights.

Fifth, there is a strong thesis concerning the ethics of communitarianism. It advocates a conventionalist ethics, which is counterposed to ethical universalism. Thus, communitarians argue that political and moral goods cannot be determined by abstract reasoning. Moral and political goods arise from within particular historical communities. There are no absolute external rational or neutral foundations for ethics or the good life. There is no theory that stands apart from a social context. In this scenario, the notion of neutrality (often dear to procedural liberals) looks suspect. Communities tend to favour their own values and try to promote them. It is thus well nigh impossible, in this context, to foster a neutral conception of the good. Most commmunitarians would add to this the point that a procedural liberal society unwittingly promotes certain conceptions of the good.

For communitarianism, morality is neither invented nor discovered, but interpreted as already existent. Again, this directly parallels Oakeshott's analysis. Michael Walzer comments, therefore, that 'what we do when we argue is to give an account of the actual existing morality' (Walzer 1987: 21). As connected critics we read off an existing tradition of discourse. The community becomes the locus of the good and source of values. Notions of the good are already embodied in 'forms of life' or 'ideal characters'. These form the basis to practical reasoning and political judgement. We do not need external theoretical foundations for a practical life, rather we draw upon the interpretations of a tradition or form of life. For Walzer, therefore, 'We cannot totally step back to assess communities, morality or justice with a view from nowhere, although we can criticize them from within using internal standards of rationality' (Walzer 1987: 6–7). A communal culture does not have to be monolithic. It is rather a set of understandings about how a group of people is to conduct its life together. Our obligations are always deeply coloured by a local ethos. Ethics can still, though, be shaped by rational debate. In the best case scenario, communal identity flows from this rational reflection. However, it is still our prior obligations and loyalties, which give substance to citizenship and justice concerns.

Of course, the above outline does not mean that all communitarian thinkers are indifferent or critical of all forms of universalism. For example, Michael Walzer has argued for a thin version of universal morality, embodying, for example, expectations not to be deceived, treated with gross cruelty, or murdered. These might be thought of as 'limit conditions'— concerning conditions of birth, death, child rearing, and the like—which every human culture must engage with. These limit conditions would constitute the cross cultural requirements of justice. They would hold for all human beings, by the very fact that they *are* human. They would also constitute basic universal norms acknowledged by all. They would thus hold for widely different states. Walzer argues that the 'thicker' morality, embedded in all societies and social practices, which he calls maximal morality, precedes universal minimal morality. In fact, the minimal is abstracted from the maximal (Walzer 1994b: 13). Overall, the thin universalism is regarded as reiterative. However, it still acknowledges that, subject to minimal universal constraints, there are many different and equally valuable ways of life that have an equivalent right to flourish within their respective locations (see Walzer in McMurrin (ed.) 1988: 22). Walzer thus essentially wishes to hold onto the communitarian claim of cultural or communal difference, while at the same time, adhering to a thin universalism. Walzer has to walk a fine path here. His earlier conception of the role of the political theorist does make a clear distinction between the theorist who purports to climb a mountain, moving outside society, as against the theorist as, what he calls, the 'connected critic', who interprets the lives of fellow citizens from within a community. For Walzer, in this latter piece, the connected critic appears to be the only way forward. We cannot simply walk out of a way of life and try to find a universal foundation (see Walzer 1983: xv). We need to look within our own community and culture to find our most secure foundation. Yet, for Walzer, this culture does still contain the trace of thin universals.

POLITICAL LIBERALISM

One effect of this broad communitarian critique has been considerable heart searching in the camp of procedural liberalism. Whether one regards the communitarian critique as cogent or not, it certainly caused a subtle shift in Rawls' own work. How large or how significant that shift is open to debate. On one level, Rawls' political liberalism is a response to the arguments raised by communitarianism. However, at the same time, it is also a somewhat fatalistic recognition of the problem of pluralism.

In the later work of Rawls, it is noticeable that the whole tone becomes altogether more pessimistic. The early confident use of justice theory—even more confident in Rawls' acolytes such as Barry—gives place to something more gloomy and constrained. Rawls main problem is no longer morality, freedom, or even justice, *per se*, but rather *containment* of the effects of pluralism. The pluralism, which Rawls focuses on is one where *reasonable* citizens, accepting the basic conventional structures of a liberal democratic constitutional state, nonetheless diverge on questions of the good. Rawls thinks this divergence inevitable. Reason does not unify. He succinctly states his problem, 'How is it possible that there may exist over time a stable and just society of free and equal citizens profoundly divided by reasonable though incompatible religious, philosophical and moral doctrines?' (Rawls 1993: xviii). Rawls rough answer to the problem of reasonable pluralism is that in 'practical political matter no general moral conception can provide a publicly recognized basis for a conception of justice in modern democratic state' (Rawls, in Strong (ed.) 1992: 96). Instead of a *metaphysical* liberalism Rawls suggests a *political* liberalism.

Political liberalism takes reasonable pluralism for granted. Its task is to work out a conception of justice for a constitutional democratic regime embodying reasonable pluralism. Rawls does not seek a new metaphysical foundation. Rather, the 'aim of political liberalism is to uncover the conditions of the possibility of a reasonable public basis of justification on fundamental political questions' (Rawls 1993: xix). The argument is recognizably transcendental. The need is to set forth the content of these 'conditions of possibility' for a liberal society. This is a constrained view of theory, which 'indicates that the principles and ideals of the political conception are based on principles of practical reason in union with conceptions of society and persons, themselves conceptions of practical reason. These conceptions specify the framework within which principles of practical reason are applied' (Rawls 1993: xx). The principles of political justice are, thus, the result of political constructivism, in which rational persons, subject to reasonable conditions, adopt principles to regulate the basic structure of society. Thus, 'when citizens share a reasonable political conception of justice, they have a basis on which public discussion of fundamental political questions can proceed and be reasonably decided' (Rawls 1993: xix). Within liberal democratic societies we assume citizens are free and equal. We also assume that they have capacities for reason and morality. The idea of citizens, conceived in this way, is an intuitive idea embedded in liberal public culture (Rawls in Strong (ed.) 1992: 104).

Why does Rawls adopt this more pessimistic fearful reading of liberalism? The answer to this lies in his account of the origin of pluralism. Rawls offers a brief historical outline of the problem. Essentially, he thinks that early Greek societies did not have our predicament of pluralism (a predicament which actually generates political philosophy for Rawls). Greek religions were civic and collective. There was no sense to individualized salvation or interests. Even within later Greek thought, when philosophy became the exercise of free disciplined reason, reasoning took place largely within the civic domain of the polis (Rawls 1993: xxi–xxii). For Rawls, Christianity, on the other hand, unlike the older civic religion, tended to be authoritarian and politically absolutist. It was often focused, in a potentially uncivic manner, on personal or individual salvation. It was not directly concerned with unity in the community. It was doctrinal and premised on the idea that people must believe the creedal structure. Priests played a key role as authoritative mediators with God. Finally, Christianity was an intrinsically expansionist religion, recognizing no territorial limits.

For Rawls, the Reformation added a crucial dimension to the monistic vision of late medieval Christianity. The authoritarian, doctrinal, expansionist aspects of Christianity fragmented. Each Reformation sect now *knew* the truth. Believers were not in any doubt about the highest good, but they were divided. Persecution was one obvious path to pursue. However, in many situations this was not practical, especially for religious minorities. For Rawls, this basic pluralism of belief created the need for political liberalism. Although many Christians were in despair over such an idea, Rawls adds that, 'to see reasonable pluralism as a disaster is to see the exercise of reason under condition of freedom itself as a disaster. Indeed, the sources of liberal constitutionalism came as a discovery of a new social possibility: the possibility of a reasonably harmonious and stable pluralist society' (Rawls 1993: xxiv–xxv). Thus, Rawls remarks unequivocally, 'the historical origin of political liberalism . . . is the Reformation and its aftermath' (Larmore 1990: 339; Rawls 1993: xxiv). Political liberalism, qua Shklar, is a response to the fears generated by wars of religion, following the Reformation (see Shklar 1984). For Rawls, religious wars 'profoundly affect the requirements of a workable conception of political justice: such a conception must allow for a diversity of doctrines and the plurality of conflicting, and indeed incommensurable, conceptions of the good affirmed by members of existing democratic societies' (Rawls in Strong (ed.) 1992: 96). Religious civil war therefore created the need for tolerance and tolerance created the ground for political liberalism, where citizens are treated in abstraction from their substantive notions of the good. For Rawls, therefore 'the public conception of justice should be so far as possible, independent of controversial philosophical and religious doctrines . . . the public conception of justice is to be political, not metaphysical' (Rawls in Strong (ed.) 1992: 95).

In summary, Rawls' argument is that political liberalism came about as a result of religious and metaphysical conflict generated by events such as the Reformation. Political liberalism is addressed, almost as a council of despair. The problem of liberalism, for Rawls, is reasonable pluralism. Citizens will disagree about metaphysical and moral issues. However, we can draw upon the 'conditions of possibility'—that is the implicit conventions or 'ideal characters' to Oakeshott—of interaction within liberal democratic cultures. These provide a minimal structure of principles of practical reason, which supply a regulative political groundwork for cooperation, in effect, an overlapping consensus. Rawls' vision of liberal citizenship is thus minimalist, constrained, protective, and negative. Like Richard Rorty and Judith Shklar, he also envisions his own version of liberalism as one arising out of 'fear'. The politically liberal citizen, for Rawls, is thus a fearful being, aware that any substantive moral beliefs she may have will not be carried into the public sphere, and thus seeking minimal conditions for cooperation.

The fact that Rawls' work is so deeply rooted in neo-Kantian thought, is certainly not unrelated to his judgement about the nature and role of comprehensive metaphysics and theology and thus the problem of pluralism. Rawls is, in his own terms, a neo-Kantian constructivist, although it is a much transformed Kantianism. It embodies a political constructivism, rather than a moral constructivism (Rawls 1993: 99 *ff*.). Rawls works with a considerably subdued, thinned down, view of reason. Rawls' own constructivism therefore lacks the will or ability to defend the overarching substantive significance and coherence of reason. Yet, despite Rawls' difference from Kant, he still nonetheless works in the same generic Kantian philosophical framework. He largely accepts the background Kantian assumptions concerning the limits to reason. Kantians, in effect, have all tended to be deeply uneasy with metaphysics. Rawls is but one in a long philosophical tradition. Faith and reason are always rigorously separated. Metaphysical conflict is not something to be resolved. It is always caught in antinomies. Forms of scientific reason come to the fore as the epitome of knowledge. Kantianism has thus become, for many, phenomenalism—a doctrine about the critical limitations of knowledge to sense perception and the natural sciences.

For Hegelian-orientated writers, however, these dualisms of reason and value or fact and value, have always been regarded with deep suspicion. Such dualisms tried to salvage religion from the encroachments of natural science, but they did so at a cost—for example,—relegating reason from the religious and metaphysics sphere. In this context, Rawls' judgements about metaphysical, theological, moral, or general comprehensive doctrines become more understandable. He is even that bit more pessimistic than Kantians earlier in the twentieth century about metaphysics. Furthermore, his response to the Reformation fits into a broader philosophical debate. We should not be misled by the idea that Rawls' response to metaphysics is simply a way of coping with modern pluralism or multiculturalism. Rawls views multi-culturalism, and the like, in the same manner as he views Reformation sectarianism, both exhibit a diversity of metaphysical positions (and one might add, conventional structures), which are *unresolvable* by Kantian reason. Multicultural pluralism is a living body of antinomies. Given Rawls' neo-Kantianism, it is not surprising that he should express disquiet with any metaphysical conception of justice. For Rawls, there is a metaphysical tradition, including Plato, Aristotle, Augustine, Aquinas and, more recently, embracing J. S. Mill, and even Ronald Dworkin and Joseph Raz. This tradition is committed to a rational foundational good. Such theories also tend to be teleological. Institutions are thus just in so far as they promote this good. Rawls sees this as the dominant tradition in moral philosophy. In response, he adopts a form of modified Kantian constructivism, trying to avoid the question of metaphysical truth in order to accommodate pluralism.

Political values, like justice, are thus premised upon 'intuitive ideas that are embedded in the political institutions of a constitutional democratic regime'. The conventional loyalties, which citizens regard as central to their identity, are part of what Rawls calls our 'non-public identity'. They may shape our lives, but humans can convert. The non-public identity then changes, but the public (or political) identity remains. Citizens in democratic societies think of themselves in a particu-lar way. It is a *condition* of their activity. They regard themselves as being able to take responsibility for their lives. These ideas are all embedded in political liberalism. One can accept these notions without necessarily being committed to any compre-hensive metaphysical or foundational liberalism. Thus, the core of Rawls' argument is that comprehensive foundational metaphysics is not a good ground for unifying society—'philosophy as the search for truth about an independent metaphysical and moral order cannot, I believe, provide a workable and shared basis for a political conception of justice' (Rawls in Strong (ed.) 1992: 109–11).

Rawls does though have a problem here. The distinction between politics and metaphysics is central. Yet, he openly admits that there is no commonly accepted understanding of metaphysics. He also agrees that one could unwittingly presuppose a metaphysics. He comments that 'it is not enough simply to disavow reliance upon metaphysical doctrines, for despite one's intent they may still be involved'. He con-tinues that, 'To rebut claims of this nature requires discussing them in detail and showing that they have no foothold.' This is a fairly significant charge, but Rawls concludes, 'I cannot do that here' (Rawls 1993: 29). Despite this avowal, Rawls does attempt an answer of sorts. He is prepared to admit that there may be latent metaphysical belief in his views of liberalism and citizenship. For example, to try to categorically do without a metaphysical doctrine may be to presuppose one. Rawls also suggests that the conception of persons, as the basic units of deliberation and responsibility, may presuppose certain metaphysical ideas. Rawls remarks, 'I should not want to deny these claims'. Nonetheless, he still insists that, as regards political liberalism, 'no particular metaphysical doctrines about the nature of persons, distinctive and opposed to other metaphysical doctrines, appears among its premises or seems required by its argument'. He continues, 'If metaphysical presuppositions are involved, perhaps they are so general that they would not distinguish between the metaphysical views—Cartesian, Leibnizian, or Kantian; realist, idealist or materialist—with which philosophy has traditionally been concerned. In this case they would not appear to be relevant for the structure and content of a political conception of justice one way or the other' (Rawls 1993: 29, n.31).

There is something rather disingenuous in Rawls' position. First, Rawls admits that there is no common understanding of metaphysics. It is also not at all clear what Rawls himself means by it, although it looks like a more general Kantian mistrust. The term 'metaphysics' seems, in fact, gradually less in evidence as Rawls has developed his ideas on political liberalism, maybe this is not wholly fortuitous. Second, Rawls does hint at some meanings to the term. It can imply any fundamental assumption we make, almost in the Collingwoodian sense of an absolute presupposition. Absolute presupposition arises where no conception of truth or falsity is involved, rather, they are absolutely presupposed and no prior questions arise concerning them. Thus, to deny metaphysics absolutely is, paradoxically, to affirm metaphysics.[20] Third, Rawls suggests that conceptions of the 'rational person' might be considered metaphysical in character. This is a more substantive presupposition. Rawls oddly does not deny the possibility of the second and third ideas. Yet, he also contends that his theory does not consciously pursue any metaphysical thesis. Further, if there are metaphysical themes in his work (which he admits is possible), they are so general as to be irrelevant to his theory. How one reconciles these points is left open.

Rawls' answers here are clearly unsatisfactory. Because foundational metaphysical ideas are not fully articulated by a thinker does not lessen the significant point that there are foundational metaphysical premises. This 'inner citadel' of the argument is often its most significant aspect. In fact, Rawls, unexpectedly, admits that there *is* such a metaphysical premise to his political liberalism, but it remains unarticulated. Rawls suggests it is irrelevant. But why does deep-rooted and unarticulated entail irrelevance? Rawls assures his readers that the political notion of the rational person (and citizen), and the assumptions we make about the moral powers of that person, are already deeply embedded in the public reason and public culture of liberal democratic societies. This might be seen as the implicit communitarian thesis in Rawls' argument. Yet, the fact that he assumes persons are like this *and* that he assumes such ideas are embedded, we are to believe, has nothing to do with metaphysics. His contention appears to be that he is offering an empirical account of what is the case. Yet, clearly, there is nothing remotely empirical about such claims. Rather, we might redescribe Rawls' ideas as plausible metaphysical assumptions about human beings and their relation to society. Metaphysics is not about blind prejudice, it rather refers to the most deep-rooted, yet often quite reasonable presuppositions we make about the character of our reality.

Rawls' difficulties with metaphysics (particularly any notion that a liberal society or liberal citizenship could be based upon metaphysics) are not only due to his incipient Kantianism. As part of a powerful generation of post-1945 American intellectuals, Rawls was subject, directly and indirectly, to a range of intellectual pressures. In political science the hegemonic theories during this period were behaviouralism, elite theories, and pluralism, forms of Marxism, rational choice and economistic accounts, all tended to treat politics in an instrumental empirical manner. Metaphysics and moral argument were viewed with deep scepticism, if not outright hostility. Empirical facts had to be kept rigidly apart from 'woolly metaphysical speculation'. Further, in mainstream philosophy in the twentieth century the incipient Kantian mistrust of metaphysics was unwittingly supported, not only by the early twentieth century waves of denunciation in empiricism, naturalism, and realism, but closer to the 1950s, in the strictures of logical positivism, linguistic philosophy, and analytic philosophy in general. Rawls (and many of his acolytes), coming from the hybrid stable of politics and philosophy, could not help but reflect this general intellectual disquiet with metaphysics. Perhaps, the fact that he assumes that many of his readership reflect that same unease, that he, almost symbolically, distances 'political' from 'metaphysical' liberalism and believes that he does not have to explain what he means by metaphysics. Metaphysics is simply wrong-headed. Yet, viewing metaphysics in a longer-term philosophical framework, it is clear that there is nothing intrinsically that rules it out of court, accept an over zealous and uncritical adherence to a particular, if dominant, intellectual tradition.

CONCLUSION

What is the essence of political liberalism? In essence, it allows liberals to both coopt and deflect communitarian criticism. It retains liberal scepticism over communitarian attempts to provide an alternative to liberal practices. On the other hand, it takes on board the communitarian worries over the nature of morality and political values. One crucial point here—which is, in fact, an issue raised by all forms of conventionalism—concerns how we can be *both* deeply attached and situated, yet still retain our independent critical faculties and the freedom to use them. If we are, to a large degree, immersed within communal conventions, how can we retain our ability to critically scrutinize communal conventions? Both Oakeshott and communitarians have their own responses to this issue. Political liberalism provides another answer. The gist of the political liberal case is that the basic conventional practices of liberal democracy presuppose certain values, which are correct and right for us. Yet, these values transcend particular communities. Thus, notions such as rational dialogue, public reasoning, equal basic respect (and ideas of neutrality often engendered by such concepts) are relatively commonplace over a number of states and juridical systems. There is, as it were, a background expectation of the validity of these concepts across many apparent 'communities' or particular political orders. As Charles Larmore puts it, such norms have been 'a part of Western moral thought for centuries' (Larmore 1990: 354). Political liberalism is not just concerned with a *modus vivendi*. In many communities, the values of liberalism are considered to be right or correct. They are not simply the result of living in the West, they rather follow from *believing* in oneself in a particular way—as free and equal. Thus, we do not draw them from our culture, but, conversely, we assume them immanently by *engaging* in practices, such as rational dialogue and equal respect. Norms of equal respect and rational dialogue are central to Western culture, therefore we have to take on board the values implicit within them.

For Larmore, however, Rawls, in one reading, appears to have partly retreated from this universal connectedness. In one sense, as Rawls intimates, even in his earlier work, his theory does not argue for, or assume, any universal claim. Thus the original position, for example, can just be considered a 'device of representation'. However, Larmore is, at the same time, not convinced that Rawls wants to suggest a total loss of universal truth. If Rawls says such values are not universally true, he does not mean, for Larmore, that he does not believe them to be correct. Rather, Rawls wants to dissociate his argument from metaphysics—as outlined above. The notion of *truth* he resists is thus a very particular one, namely, 'implying the existence of an independent order of moral facts'. For Larmore, Rawls appears to employ this weaker notion of truth. It is basically equivalent to rational acceptability (Larmore 1990: 355). The fine line walked by political liberalism here (which is exactly the same precarious line walked by all weaker variants of communitarianism), concerns the question: how do we relate and compare the purportedly 'correct' conventions of liberal democratic societies with the conventions of other societies, specifically where members of those other societies do not believe in 'our' conventions? Larmore quite candidly admits here that he has 'no ready answer'. The key danger though is 'making liberalism yet another controversial and partisan vision of the good life' (Larmore 1990: 357). In place of being a latent resolution, political liberalism turns into part of the dilemma. This is not an unknown conundrum in conventionalist argument.

One other issue, which will be taken up in later chapters, is the point that communitarianism (as a characteristic expression of late twentieth century conventionalism) remains theoretically weak on a range of conceptual issues. It does not have the theoretical sophistication or subtlety of Oakeshott's thought. There is, for example, very little clear thinking about the nature or character of community itself. It is also not clear whether communities coincide, overlap, or internally conflict within juridical states. The relation between the state and community remains profoundly under-theorized. Further, communities themselves can be internally and quite fiercely divided. What is the relation between the human self and the diversity of groupings through which it subsists? The communitarian picture on such issues is hesitant and often muddled. Communitarians—despite the central role played by groups—often seem oblivious to the complexity, hazards, and awkward character of group or associational life. Apart from Walzer's work on complex communities and complex equality, communitarians appear unperturbed about the whole issue of groups. Yet, embed-dedness is far more perplexing than many communitarians seem to be aware. Part of the reason for this is that communitarianism does not really offer a clear account as to what community means. It rests its laurels on an assumed favourable normat-ive harmony—either on a national or local level. It does not explain how the self is constituted by often diverse, overlapping, and conflicting groups, loyalties and associ-ations. Further, the precise relation between the appropriate conventional context and the intelligibility of concepts, is, by the same argument, rendered deeply problematic.

Notes

1. In many ways the new hyper-concept or key 'issue concept' for the 2000s appears to be democracy, specifically deliberative democracy.
2. The explicit focus on 'conventionalism' in twentieth century thought did not initially arise (except indirectly) within the social sciences or political theory. The philosopher of science Henri Poincaré used the term, in 1902, to describe his particular understanding of science. Scientific objectivity, in his view, derived from the general agreement over conventions adopted within the scientific community. Scientific laws were all therefore disguised conventions. Thus, motion in mechanics could not be considered an *a priori* truth. Aristotelian mechanics was markedly different from the Newtonian conception, and so forth. Thus, self-evident truths were ruled out. Further, motion could not be considered an experimental fact. As Poincaré noted, 'experiment may serve as a basis for the principle of mechanics, and yet will never invalidate them', see Poincaré (1902: 105). Thus, conventions were regarded as distinct from both experimental and *a priori* truth.
3. Although having been initially incubated in the Scottish universities and Oxford, and to a lesser extent at Cambridge, it is also worth noting that it was rapidly exported throughout the English speaking world during the same period.
4. Oakeshott asserts here the autonomy and significance of the *Geisteswissenschaften*.
5. Oakeshott recognizes something here that does not appear in the earlier works, that delib-erative reflection is involved with practical action and doing in the world and that persuasive argument can be designed to recommend or prompt choices, Oakeshott (1975: 48).
6. 'An action . . . is an identity in which substantive performance and procedural consideration may be distinguished but are inseparably joined, and which the character of agent and that of practitioner are merged in a single self-recognition', Oakeshott (1975: 57).
7. To justify an action '(that is, to invoke rules and rule-like principles as reasons for having chosen actions) is to embark upon a casuistical enterprise of distinctions, exceptions, and obliquities related to rules in which the vitality of a spoken language of moral intercourse is impaired and its integrity compromised. A calculated observance of specified rules has taken the place of the singleness and spontaneity of morally educated conduct', Oakeshott (1975: 70).
8. 'A state may perhaps be understood as an unresolved tension between the two irreconcilable dispositions represented by the words *societas* and *universitas*', Oakeshott (1975: 200–1).
9. Much of the terminology of both forms of state are seen to be inherited from the tradition and language of the realms and principalities of medieval Europe.
10. In fact he directly associates Fabianism with Cameralism, Oakeshott (1975: 311).

11. There is an elitist element to his writing and deep dislike for all socialist or social democratic experimentation.
12. The problem with citing Oakeshott as a conservative is that he is no ordinary conservative. His conservatism is premised on philosophical grounds. Oakeshott claimed that this is *not*, by definition, a rationalist ideology. The idea implicitly fostered here is that philosophy is distinct from rationalist ideology and furthermore that conservatism, as a traditionalist disposition, is in fact akin to the philosophical demeanour. There are distinct similarities here to other thinkers, on this same point. W. H. Greenleaf, for example, has tried to draw parallels between Oakeshott's conception of philosophy and Wittgenstein's philosophy of language, see Greenleaf (1968). W. H. Walsh, some years ago, also drew a strong parallel between Wittgenstein and Burke on similar grounds, see Walsh (1966: 122 *ff*., also see Covell 1986).
13. This section synthesizes elements from my article Vincent (1997*b*) and the chapter on communitarianism in Vincent (2002).
14. Amitai Etzioni quotes a correspondence from MacIntyre to the communitarian journal *Responsive Community*, indicating this, see Etzioni (1997: 261, n.20). See also MacIntyre (1995: 35).
15. This point will be explored in more detail in Chapter Seven.
16. More recently, deliberative democracy is a rediscovery and rearticulation (in a more veiled format) of the heavily community orientated utopian language of participatory democracy.
17. 'For justice to be the first virtue, certain things must be true of us. We must be creatures of a certain kind, related to human circumstances in a certain way. We must stand at a certain distance from our circumstances, whether as transcendental subject in the case of Kant, or as essentially unencumbered subject of possession in the case of Rawls. Either way, we must regard ourselves as independent; independent from the interests and attachments we may have at any moment', see Sandel (1982: 175).
18. In *After Virtue* MacIntyre looks to a modernized Aristotle for diagnoses of the sickness in liberal society. For him, virtue rests on character and character rests on shared embedded understandings of a community.
19. Although, it is worth noting that in stronger versions of conservative and fascist communitarianism, it is liberalism, in general, which is condemned.
20. This is what I referred to in Chapter One as the logical view of foundationalism.

6

New Conventions for Old

This chapter continues the examination of forms of conventionalism. It focuses on nationalism, neo-Aristotelianism, and republicanism. Each of these doctrines tries self-consciously to recover and reconstitute an older foundationalist conventionalist language. The most recent of these has been republicanism, which has only begun to make headway in the last decade, but now has a growing following within the discipline of theory. Republicanism has though a problematic relationship with both communitarianism and neo-Aristotelianism. Both the latter doctrines, for example, can be seen as extensions or mutations of the republican arguments. Yet this is again hotly contested by many contemporary republicans. However, one of the starkest and most troubling of these conventionalist vocabularies is nationalism. In many ways, although like republicanism and neo-Aristotelianism, an older vocabulary of nineteenth and early twentieth century politics, it nonetheless generates much stronger feelings and reactions than most other doctrines. In fact, both the latter doctrines are uniformly violently opposed to nationalism in much of their recent output. Nationalism has had, in fact, an immensely complex and tangled relationship with twentieth century politics and still appears as a crucial, if ambiguous, driving force in twenty-first century politics. It has also had a problematic relation with political theory in general over the same period, although it now has a number of enthusiastic liberal devotees. Unlike other conventionalist theories, though, nationalism contains a more ambivalent and unwieldy body of ideas. It has also had a more direct relation to ideological theory and political practice than any other form of conventionalist argument. This alone has made many political theorists deeply uncomfortable. This chapter will sketch the conventionalist arguments employed by recent nationalist, neo-Aristotelians, and republicans over the last decade.

NATIONALISM

Basically, there have been two broad approaches to nationalism within the twentieth century political theory. The first has opposed any linkage with nationalism. The sense of deep disquiet with nationalism, in many theorists, was profoundly influenced—on theoretical and practical levels—by the events surrounding the Second World War. The ideological practices of national socialism and fascism marked out nationalism for especial odium. Many academic commentators, from the post-1945 period up to 1989, consequently saw nationalism as tribalist, potentially totalitarian, and an inherently irrationalist doctrine. Both liberal and democratic socialist theories, particularly, self-consciously developed more internationalist stances. The second approach dates originally from the early nineteenth century. This sees a positive value to nationalism. In nineteenth century writers, such as Mazzini, Renan, Herder, and J. S. Mill, amongst others, there was a strong sense of liberation attached to nationalism. Nationalism implied the emancipation of cultures. Yet, the later nineteenth century and early twentieth century also saw the growth of authoritarian, conservative, and later fascist forms of nationalism. This latter development, in many ways, delivered a body blow to the 'liberal' patina of nationalist ideas. Liberation and self-determination were still embedded in the argument, but the focus had shifted to something more ominous.

However, two additional factors in recent years have highlighted the profile of nationalism. Paradoxically, most current positive arguments for nationalism now acknowledge that it embodies a heterogeneous cluster of perspectives. In this sense, it is accepted that there are vicious and unpleasant variants of nationalism, as well as sympathetic liberal forms.[1] This was not envisaged by the early nineteenth century nationalist writers. Thus, nationalism appears as a much more varied pattern of thought than previously imagined. Second, many have also seen a conceptual link between forms of nationalism and liberal values such as freedom, democracy, and popular sovereignty. Consequently, since the collapse of the Berlin wall in 1989, and the changing political landscape of international and domestic politics, there has been once again a surge of theoretical and practical interest in nationalism. Not only are vast amounts being written about it by the academy, from both empirical and normative perspectives, but also it has once again become an important player in world politics.

Post-1945 liberal theory (up to 1989) tended to take a dim view of nationalism, fortuitously a view shared with Marxist internationalism. The only exceptions to this were the socially acceptable liberationist and secessionist anti-colonial nationalisms. For liberals, like Hayek, collectivities such as states, which can be juridically rationalized, are problematic enough, but collectivities such as nations, which often appear to play upon irrationalism, are beyond the pale. The most that classical liberal writers have usually been prepared to admit is that collectivities, such as nations, are fictional aggregates of individuals which, occasionally, could be said to have some form of wholly artificial identity.

By way of introduction, there are two further issues to mention briefly. One is that academic writing about nationalism is very different from its usage in political practice. It is an oft noted point that nationalism, over the last century, has often been theoretically naïve, but immensely powerful in political practice. Thus, theoretical incoherence is combined with political power.[2] The second, related point (which expands and explains the first) is that the concept of the nation and the doctrine of nationalism may not, in fact, be theorizable. This latter point encompasses issues concerning, for example, the irrationality of nationalism. Both nationalists and scholars of nationalism have contributed to this latter account. The roots of the 'untheorizable' idea lie in nineteenth and early twentieth century romantic, vitalist, and intuitivist philosophies and psychologies. Conservative ideologies still find sustenance in such notions. There are, however, a complex range of issues present in this 'untheoretical' point.

First, the idea that nationalism is basically untheoretical can elicit two distinct responses, one positive and the other negative: the 'positive' response by theorists of nationalism sees its untheoretical character as immensely fruitful.[3] Something, which is not easily theorizable or readily embodied in rational categories, is not necessarily irrational. Clarity is therefore not enough and vagueness may be welcomed. All organizations, especially the state, require some kind of collective identity. Thus, there is a kind of 'ghostly presence' behind much politics. Nations are seen as powerfully present, in fact, conditionally necessary for states, yet often invisible. Nationality, therefore, 'makes possible the kind of community required by liberal democratic theories' (Canovan 1996: 68). Nations are indispensable, if hard to deal with conceptually. In fact, nationalism may be regarded as a stage in the evolution of the nation itself; the conceptual presence of nationalism may even mean the absence of the nation *per se. Prima facie*, this view is surprising given that the untheoretical character of nationalism is taken by others as a serious flaw.

The 'negative' response has two possible dimensions, one external and the other internal to nationalism. The *external* dimension sees nationalism as premised on passions and irrationalism, in contrast to theories such as liberalism (and the social sciences in general), which are premised on reason. Elie Kedourie and Karl Popper, amongst others, subscribed to this view. In other words, nationalism is disapproved of as an irrational tribalism. The *internal* dimension is promulgated by certain nationalist writers themselves who also feel distinctly ill at ease with the 'untheoretical' claim. This view denies the 'untheoretical' claim and asserts the need for rational nationalist theory. Yael Tamir, for example, is quite insistent on this (Tamir in Beiner (ed.) 1999: 67). For her nationalism is theorizable. Thus, a theory of nationalism for Tamir structures itself 'independently of all contingencies. Its basis must be a systematic view of human nature and of the world order, as well as a coherent set of universally applicable values' (Tamir 1993: 82). This latter judgement is not helped by the fact that there are *no* great nationalist theorists. There are honorary figures, such as J. G. Fichte, Gottfried Herder, Ernest Renan, Julien Benda, amongst others, but one might hesitate to call them 'self-conscious nationalist thinkers'. Despite this, Tamir's general position is shared by most contemporary political theorists interested in nationalism.

Before turning to a brief discussion of some of these 'theoretical components', one more point needs to be examined. This focuses on the question: can nationalism offer a general or universal theory? One of the central claims, internal to nationalist argument, is that *all* meaning and value are particular to the nation. This is a crucial assumption for nationalism to work. Thus, logically, how can one offer a universal theory from a baseline, which is by definition wholly particular? If all theory (unless it is the one exception to the nationalist theory of meaning and thus the one metatheoretical truth in the world) is particular, then no theory—even a theory of nationalism—can be logically exempt. In this sense, could nationalists even have a universal perspective? Such a theory could not, by definition, logically exist.

Everything depends here on the concept of 'theory'. Empirically-orientated theories (in political science or sociology) tend to search for the causal conditions for nationalism. In this sense, there can be a universal empirical theory of nationalism—but the operative point here is that it is a theory 'of'. Nationalism is a *social object* to be explained via, say, its economic, political, or social function. Nationalism can be universal, since, regardless of its internal rhetoric, in reality, it performs other universal functional roles. However, others would contend that nationalism is *not* a social object, but is rather a *social subject* (fictional or real); in this case it involves normative and ontological theory, which not only gives a descriptive account of how meanings come about, but also indicates what we 'ought' or 'ought not' to do.

However, in fact, neither empirical theory nor more abstract universalist normative theories (Kantianism and utilitarianism), seem really appropriate for nationalist political theory. The form of theory befitting nationalism appears to be a more situated or conventionally based one. Yet a number of problems arise here. There are many conventional forms of social existence (families, neighbourhoods, associations) within which individuals are situated. Why should the conventional structure of nationalism take any priority? It clearly does not figure very predominantly in most people's lives, except in extreme situations, like war or civil conflict. So what reason can be offered? Clearly one answer, which we have already canvassed, is that its non-existence in our everyday consciousness may be a sign of successful or mature nationhood, namely, it is subliminal. However, it is difficult to see how this could be known or proved.

One further related question is: do theoretical beliefs constitute the nation? If they do, then shared characteristics cannot be embedded. In this case, a populace would be reliant upon theorists and politicians to create and feed them their nationalist ideas. Nationalism itself would be pure artifice, *even* when claiming to be natural. Nationalism, in this reading, is an abstract theory, exactly like Kantianism, but embedded within its abstractions is a false claim about the importance of natural embedded particulars. In this sense, it is an elaborate charade. Alternatively, national beliefs could be said to be embedded in the community, in which case an appeal to a political theory called nationalism would be totally superfluous. This is indeed one strong argument underpinning the separation (made by some theorists) between *nation* and *nationalism*, as well as one of the forceful contentions concerning the purported *untheoretical* character of the nation. The problem with this embedded interpretative view is precisely the problem of particularity. How can an untheorizable embedded particular become a universalist theory? Nationalist theorists never actually get round this conundrum. This would particularly be the case with liberal nationalism.

However, given that we accept that some normative case can be made for nationalism, three major arguments usually figure in the liberal nationalist position. First, there is the communitarian argument that we are socially contextual or embedded beings. We are constituted through the community and its values. We cannot be prior to society in any way. Many recent nationalist writers thus advocate a social, embedded, or contextual individualism, as against an atomistic individualism. One can therefore be a normative individualist whilst rejecting methodological individualism. In fact, many proponents contend that the procedural liberal idea of the individual is just deeply implausible (see MacCormick in Twining (ed.) 1991: 13). Thus, Neil MacCormick states, 'The truth about human beings is that they can only become individuals—acquire a sense of their own individuality—as a result of their social experiences within human communities' (MacCormick 1982: 247). Families, local communities, nations, education, jobs, etc. have a formative effect on the individual. However, he adds that 'individuality goes beyond all that—but not in any way that renders all that superfluous or meaningless; human individuality presupposes social existence' (MacCormick 1982: 251). For MacCormick, though, despite the social constitution argument, 'I continue to affirm that the good society is one in which individuals—each individual—are taken seriously' (MacCormick 1982: 247). Membership of groups, like nations, lets individuals transcend the constraints of time and place; it also provides a conceptual framework, which permits them to 'comprehend [their] own existence as belonging within a continuity in time and a community in space'. Human beings take pride in tradition; it allows them to transcend their 'earthly existence'.[4]

David Miller also accepts the communitarian contextual individual claim in terms of his own moderate nationalist conventionalism. For Miller, national communities exist through belief, not race or language. Like Tamir, Miller also partly accepts the artificial dimension of nationalist thought. Yet, there have to be some shared substantive beliefs or 'attitudes, ritual observances and so forth' for nationalism to exist (Miller 1989: 244). It is not, however, a belief system which can be totally conjured out of thin air. There is a prepolitical element to it which forms a precondition to politics. It is an active identity, which embodies historical continuity (see Miller 1989: 238). Yet Miller also suggests that this national identity can be fostered through education. This also leads to a critical unease with multiculturalism. It is an overarching nationhood, which is *the* valid source of human identity.

In addition, like MacCormick and Tamir, Miller thinks that the distinction between the universalism and particularism of nationalism can be overdone. Local loyalties can be linked with universalist claims. The nation is a valid form of ethical community. For Miller, a 'strengthening of commitment to a smaller group is likely to increase our commitment to wider constituencies', the point being, for Miller, that 'if we start out with selves already laden with particularist commitments . . . we may be able to rationalize those commitments from a universalist perspective' (Miller 1988: 661–2; Miller 1995). In general terms, for Miller, a state is more governable if it is a national community. A state—especially a welfare state with programmes of distributive justice—needs trust and voluntary cooperation to achieve its goals. It is thus, apparently, 'self-evident that ties of community are an important source of trust between individuals who are not personally known to one another' (Miller 1994: 142; see also Miller 1995). Social justice and redistributive policies will be considerably facilitated if people see themselves as conationals.

The second component of the liberal nationalist argument—respect for nations— is more strongly emphasized by some theorists than others. For MacCormick, for example, nations make up a part of our identity. Identity is deserving of respect. The principle of respect obliges us to respect that 'which in others constitutes any part of their sense of their own identity'. Thus, MacCormick concludes, 'I assert it as a principle that there ought to be respect for national differences, and that there ought to be an adoption of forms of government appropriate to such differences' (MacCormick 1982: 261–2). Autonomy does not necessarily conflict with national context—'Autonomy is . . . a fundamental good, and thus it is a great social value to uphold societies which facilitate it'. A free society and free nation can be linked. If autonomous individuals require a context of freedom-enabling, 'then the collective autonomy of society itself seems a part of the necessary context' (MacCormick 1991: 14–15). In other words, self-determination by the nations is linked to the self-determining individuals within them (see MacCormick 1990: 16).

The third component of liberal nationalist argument, which follows closely upon the previous points, entails specific recommendations for political arrangements. Nationalism can underpin liberal individuality and democracy, although MacCormick and Tamir add that nations are not necessarily coincidental with states. National communities should have the 'political conditions hospitable to their continuance and free development . . . the whole idea of the desirability of creating the conditions for autonomous self-determination both of individuals—contextual individuals—and of the groups and collectivities constitutive of them leads back to the claim of self-determination as quite properly a claim on behalf of each nation on similar terms to any and every other' (MacCormick 1991: 17).[5] MacCormick suggests that 'any tendency toward a greater democratization of government, a greater re-inclusion of the nation in the state, would surely be welcome, and that on simply democratic grounds' (MacCormick 1991: 11).[6] However, he does express distaste for the concept of sovereignty. Sovereignty and statehood are part of what MacCormick calls the 'inept model' of nationalism derived from 1789. Yet, he still thinks that 'The mode of consciousness which constitutes a national identity includes a consciousness of the need for a form of common governance which recognizes and allows for the continued flourishing of the cultural and historical community in question' (MacCormick 1982: 262). MacCormick sees more hopeful signs in the European community, subsidiarity, and the development of regionalism rather than in statehood or sovereignty.

For Miller, though, state boundaries should as far as possible coincide with national boundaries (Miller 1994: 143). National self-determination is valuable because it corresponds to the idea of nations as active communities. Self-determination follows from the identity argument. If people share substantive beliefs, which are reflected in their acting representatives, then the nation can be said to act and determine itself. Miller also suggests that nationalism and democracy might be linked (Miller 1994: 144). The particular notion that he has of democracy is deliberative. Citizens actively participate, shaping society through public discussion. For Miller, the state is 'likely to be better able to achieve its goals where its subjects form an encompassing community and conversely national communities are better able to preserve their culture and fulfil their aspirations where they have control of the political machinery in the relevant area' (Miller 1994: 145).[7]

Another element of Miller's case is concerned with the questions: does nationalism require state sovereignty, and are there any obligations holding between nation states? Miller takes it for granted that 'each nation in asserting its claim for self-determination must respect the equal claims of others who may be affected by its actions' (Miller 1994: 145). This is essentially the universalist element in particularism. He suggests that complete sovereignty does not follow from nation statehood, trade-offs are possible. Sovereignty should therefore not become a fetish for nationalists. Yet, nation states still, for Miller, retain a right to decide what to secede. There may be good reasons for transferring powers to a confederal body, but the most crucial elements are still rescindable. Miller is thus not interested in applying (like Charles Beitz) the Rawlsian difference principle internationally. Yet international justice can, and frequently does, limit national sovereignty (Miller 1994: 150–2). Miller is perfectly content with this. There can be justice across boundaries if nations choose to act reasonably.

All three central arguments of recent liberal nationalism are unpersuasive. The complex character of the social or embedded constitution of the individual is assumed as unproblematic. In fact, the idea of 'being embedded in conventions' is far more complex and variegated than stressed by most nationalist writers. This will be explored more in the next chapter. Further, the arguments for transferring respect from human individuals to nations also appear woefully inadequate and unsatisfactory. The analogy of individual respect with respect for nations simply does not work and requires further explanation. In addition, self-determination is a profoundly difficult and elusive notion, particularly if carried over onto nations and states. It is certainly not impossible to deploy the term and it may of course be used in a trivial sense by international relations theories, indicating that states appear to act in a unitary manner—however, liberal nationalists want the idea to work harder for them. This 'harder' application is unconvincing. Further, self-determination, by individuals or states, does not lead to or guarantee any particular institutional arrangements. Autocracy or liberalism is an equally possible outcome.

NEO-ARISTOTELIANISM

Unlike nationalism (and aspects of communitarian theory), neo-Aristotelianism has remained a largely academic political theory debate. However, like these other conventionalist doctrines, it shares disquiet with the thin universalism of some liberal justice theories.[8] Equally, although critical, again, it does not seek to overcome the idea of foundationalism. It rather identifies the problem of foundationalism as something that can only be systematically addressed through a qualified form of conventionalism. Thus, like nationalism and communitarianism, it is concerned to 'shore up' the foundations of theory from a qualified conventionalist perspective. There are though variations on a theme here.

Comparative to communitarianism and nationalism, neo-Aristotelianism is more of a minority taste, which only developed in the last two decades of the twentieth century. It does not have a large academic following in comparison to nationalism. However, this latter point might be somewhat misleading for two reasons. First, its pedagogical separation from themes such as communitarianism or republicanism is somewhat artificial. This is a very grey area in contemporary political theory, where groups, individuals, or movements will often be openly associated with certain categories, which are vigorously contested by others, all with startling finality. Many communitarians, for example, have been described as neo-Aristotelians, civic republicans, and even nationalists. Each of these labels generates differing responses, according to affiliations. Thus, no category should be taken as absolute or impermeable. Each of the terms are fluid and contested. The second reason is that Aristotelianism has permeated many other intellectual positions during the twentieth century. Thus, Hannah Arendt's work during the 1950s and 1960s has been seen as articulating a form of neo-Aristotelian theory, although much tempered by both Kant and Heidegger. Similarly, Hans Georg Gadamer's hermeneutics contains elements of Aristotelian thought—also tempered by Heidegger. However, neither of the latter theorists openly proclaimed themselves as systematic neo-Aristotelians. The present section deals largely with those theorists who more openly avow an Aristotelian commitment.

Neo-Aristotelianism is, however, still a broad canvas. The first task is to provide a brief thumbnail sketch of neo-Aristotelianism, as a form of conventionalist theory, then to indicate a common range of Aristotelian criticisms offered of liberalism, communitarianism, and nationalism. The discussion will then distinguish two strands of neo-Aristotelian political theory—positive and negative renderings. The positive sees a definite ideal or good in Aristotle, which can act as a form of foundation—but which also takes on board imperfection and difference. The more negative reading (broadly) emphasizes the contingency of conventions over any notion of an intrinsic universal good.

The first point concerns the basic idea of neo-Aristotelianism. There are three broad dimensions to the attraction of neo-Aristotelianism, which can be given different weightings. The first highlights Aristotelian immanentism. In this context, theory is not seen as a construction or justification of a new way of life. It is rather a reflection on concrete practices, traditions, or pre-existing ways of life. The term '*ethos*' is often used as synonymous for a 'way of life'. An ethos cannot be invented or constructed. It already exists. A moral ethos is not justified or recommended. It is rather observed in certain types of human character and conduct. Certain kinds of conduct arise from a particular type of human character. This character also arises from specific kinds of social milieu. The good can be observed as a reflection on actual practice. Morality is therefore immanent in certain types of character and conduct. Consequently, neo-Aristotelianism has a descriptive, virtually sociological, component to it. Second, the observance of ways of life requires empirical observation of concrete communities and ways of life. Community is used here in generic sense. There is nothing immediately 'ideal' or 'perfectionist' about the term 'community'. A community is just an existing way of life. This gives rise to Aristotle's reputation for both realism and empiricism. It also connects up with Aristotle's awareness (for his defenders) of the inevitability of diverse imperfect ways of life or communities. Third, although there is recognition of contingency, diversity and imperfection, nonetheless, Aristotle also suggests that there are forms of character, conduct, and social existence, which are more conducive to or congruent with human flourishing. For Martha Nussbaum, for example, Aristotelianism is therefore committed to 'the realization of a good human life', yet the manner in which this realization can be achieved is subject to luck. The good is fragile and can easily be undermined or destroyed by circumstances (see Nussbaum 1986: 3).

The second main theme of this section concerns the critique of liberalism, communitarianism, and nationalism. Much of the initial critique of liberalism is shared with both communitarianism and nationalism. Primarily liberalism is seen as too focused on the individual, at the expense of community. One implication of the liberal individualist perspective is that individuals are seen to be autonomously forming their own ways of life, that is, liberals regularly daydream about individuals constituting themselves. For neo-Aristotelians, most individuals are, in fact, *pre-socialized* into given functional social, moral, and political roles. Choice does not usually come into the equation for the majority of human beings. Further, reason (qua liberalism) cannot simply construct a way of life at will. Practical reason is rather a knowing where to go next, within an already existing tradition. Any search for a wholly external or independent reasonable foundation is, for neo-Aristotelianism, bound to be misconceived. Community is prior to the individual. Liberalism, without its tacit and unspoken philosophical anthropology, would be inert in relation to practical dilemmas. For neo-Aristotelians, liberalism also appears unable to function with the idea of its own inevitable historical and sociological contingency. Further, the liberal perspective is seen to foster the idea that individuals confer values on the world. Neo-Aristotelians deny this, seeing reality as something, which is prior to and recognized by individuals. The community is already a potential repository of values. Another implication of the liberal position is the obsessive focus on individual rights, which often encourages an overly adversarial and self-assertive way of life, which undermines communities. Rights, in the neo-Aristotelian perspective, are rooted in a community and are viewed largely as conditions of flourishing. However, for most contemporary neo-Aristotelians the above criticisms do not entail a complete rejection of liberalism. Most—but definitely not all—believe that a neo-Aristotelian ethos can be blended with a reformed or adjusted understanding of liberalism (see Beiner 1992: 9; Salkever 1990; Yack 1993; Nussbaum 1990).

However, one should not jump to the conclusion from the above analysis, that neo-Aristotelianism is simply a variant on communitarianism. Far from it. For neo-Aristotelians, whereas liberalism is committed to an implausible and abstract individualism, communitarians, in general, are seen to be overly committed to an implausible and abstracted conception of the community. Although communitarians focus correctly on the key role of community, it is still a too abstracted, thin, romanticized, and evaluative conception. Neo-Aristotelians tend to use the term community in a more generic descriptive, almost sociological, sense. Communitarians thus often conflate community and communitarianism, that is an evaluative, consensual, and idealized idea with a more contingent, generic, potentially internally divisive, and realist conception. In other words, for neo-Aristotelians, individuals are constituted, shaped, or socialized by communities. However, they do not necessarily idealize or valorize community *per se*. Community is *not* about intense belonging or moral rectitude (see Yack 1993: 26). All kinds of community are therefore of interest to neo-Aristotelianism, the majority of which are contingent, imperfect, and lacking in social harmony. Communitarians, although seeing community as a good, fail to identify and analyse the political and social processes of communities in practice. The problem, for neo-Aristotelians, is that modern communitarianism is largely a contingent reaction to the individualism of liberal justice theory and contractarianism. In trying, polemically, to adjust political theory away from individualism, it fails to probe the alternative—community. It is also worth noting here that most neo-Aristotelians are also critical of both the civic republican and nationalist alternative on similar grounds. That is republicans tend to idealize the 'republic' and nationalists the 'national community'. It is therefore contended that neo-Aristotelianism should be kept distinct from communitarianism, republicanism, and nationalism (see Salkever 1990: 81; Beiner 1992: 123; Yack 1993: 62).

The third main issue of this section concerns the different strands of neo-Aristotelian argument. Up to now the continuity of neo-Aristotelianism has been emphasized. However, it is clear from even the most cursory reading of their writings, that there are marked internal divisions, particularly over issues such as teleology, the metaphysical biology underpinning Aristotle's thought, the nature of the ideal community and the linkage with communitarianism. Two strands of twentieth century neo-Aristotelianism stand out. These can be seen as negative and positive readings. Both forms stress the acceptance of contingency and imperfection. However, the positive reading lays more stress on an achievable ideal form of social existence, which is grounded on practical reason and sound character. This view identifies a definite doctrinal component to Aristotelianism. The negative reading stresses that neo-Aristotelianism has no universally applicable ideal and thus plays upon realism and contingency.

The positive reading of neo-Aristotelianism sees a definite, if qualified, notion of the good. One of the most explicit developments of this positive argument can be found in Martha Nussbaum's writings. She suggests that the nearest approximation to neo-Aristotelian moral and political ideals is, quite literally, twentieth century social democracy. In articulating her view, she tries to steer a course between, on the one hand, a thick perfectionist and paternalistic notion of the good, which liberal pluralists abhor, and, on the other hand, a thin liberal foundational good, which does little or no justice to the particular material, conventional, and empirical realities underpinning human functioning. In other words, she tries to forge a middle path (or third way) between pluralism and monism, universalism and particularism, and between the stability of values and the fact of social contingency. This vision of neo-Aristotelianism acknowledges a difference in values, but still contends that we have a *shared* moral quest—that is to 'live well' and 'flourish'. Her solution to the dilemma of uniting the universal and particular is the idea of a 'thick vague' conception of both human beings and the good. She sees this as doing justice to both liberal anxieties concerning paternalism and a rich sense of communal particularism. The good is thick and 'intercultural', but it is also vague, consequently allowing plurality and difference. There is, therefore, for Nussbaum, an illusory tension between liberal freedom and the perfectionist value of human well being (see Nussbaum 1990: 238–9). Like most mid to late twentieth-century political theorists, neo-Aristotelians, such as Nussbaum, want a firm or thick foundation—something which is shared by humanity—which nonetheless avoids any taint of metaphysics.

The thick vague good is embodied in the claim that all humans wish to live well or flourish. Nussbaum spells out this good in terms of a common sensitivity to the needs of the body, shared sensations of pleasure and pain, the desire for understanding, the use of practical reason, the needs for affiliation with other human beings, a common awareness of infant development and humour. To flourish, in these dimensions, constitutes basic human happiness, but such happiness is not necessarily focused on the acceptance of one uniform belief system. However, one can still describe happiness as integral to the teleology of human nature. The ground for human flourishing is broad (covering humanity in general), but also deep, insofar as it addresses very basic requirements of human functioning; or, as Nussbaum puts it, it focuses on the 'totality of the functionings that constitute the good human life' (Nussbaum 1990: 209). For Nussbaum, 'there is just human life as it is lived. But in life as it is lived, we do find a family of experiences, clustering around certain focuses, which can provide reasonable starting points for cross-cultural reflection' (Nussbaum 1993: 265). For Nussbaum, therefore, despite the awareness and sensitivity to local conventional belief, there is still 'a single objective account of the human good, or human flourishing' which is not justified by an appeal to local or communal traditions (Nussbaum 1993: 243).

For Nussbaum there is no contradiction in the above claim. The aims of local conventional awareness and transcultural justification are compatible. The basic argument here is that a 'sphere of experience' or 'grounding experience'—relating to one's bodily needs, death, the development of children or practical reason, and the like—is universal. However, the particular nature of the choices one makes within that 'grounding experience' relate to differing conventional beliefs. Ethical theory is committed to searching for the best approximation of value to that 'grounding experience' (Nussbaum 1993: 247). A virtue, in any human being, is something which contributes to human flourishing and thus happiness. Virtues are, in this vague sense, unified. Various conventional cultures will give competing answers to the issue of the grounding experience. To exercise virtues requires judgement and prudence. This constitutes the basis to character. Character implies prudence and good judgement in practical situations. Nussbaum suggests that certain responses, types of character, or judgements might approximate more closely to the 'grounding experiences' and thus enhance human happiness.[9]

Politics, in this positive neo-Aristotelian scenario, is concerned primarily with meeting the basic conditions for human flourishing, outlined above. The implication is that neo-Aristotelianism implies some form of ideal social democratic welfare state, equivalent to those found in late twentieth century Scandinavia. This is not, for

Nussbaum, a residual or minimalist welfarism, it is rather 'a comprehensive support scheme for the functioning of all citizens over a complete life' (Nussbaum 1990: 228). The 'thick vague' idea (which is universal) underpins the comprehensive welfare vision. This vision entails a detailed sensitivity to the material, educational, and institutional conditions of human flourishing. In this context, employment conditions, property, rights, land allocation, education, and political participation support human functioning and flourishing and need to be addressed. There is, as Nussbaum puts it, a 'rich neediness' in humans, which has to be taken on board. Thus, neo-Aristotelianism, in cultivating virtue and the variety of human excellences, must also focus on the complex material, social, and educational conditions, which underpin the flourishing of human beings.

However, there is also a more negative perspective on Aristotle. This basically takes two forms. Both express discomfort with any notion of teleology. Both feel uneasy with the attempt to derive a universal or thick conception of the good; such an idea is seen to be impossible in the present modern era. The emphasis on Aristotle thus falls on his realism, conventionalism, and difference. The first form stresses what might loosely be called a hermeneutic dimension. In this reading neo-Aristotelianism is not something, which offers any substantive or thick good. It is not foundational in the sense of other forms of political theory. Rather, it is a way of thinking about and interpreting existing values and assessing their role and function. The second view does, however, settle upon neo-Aristotelianism as providing a rich good. But, it is *not* a universal good, conversely, it is a highly heterogeneous particularist alternative. The stress therefore falls away from Nussbaum's universal 'grounding experiences' towards conventional contingencies. The latter view links neo-Aristotelianism with a version of communitarianism.

The first more hermeneutic view emphasizes Aristotle's realistic awareness of contingency, variety, and difference. The good life in Aristotle is not about rich or thick ideals. Moral and political life is always both extremely fragile and internally diverse. Aristotle is notable, in this reading, for having drawn attention to the tense and imperfect social structures and contingencies within which we try to exercise moral and political beliefs. Bernard Yack, for example, suggests that the bulk of Aristotle's moral and political reflections are tied to his explanation of the ordinary and everyday lives and struggles of humanity. It is a mistaken interpretation of his work to try to discover some kind of universal foundational or universal good in his work. Yack comments, 'Unlike most of Aristotle's contemporary admirers, I do not turn to his work in the hope of finding the objective foundation for our moral and political commitments . . . I fully accept that most of us will continue to seek beyond Aristotelian ideas in order to identify and justify our moral and political commitments' (Yack 1993: 283). In this view, too much attention is given to the notion of an ideal form of social existence. Thus, Yack does not want to see Aristotle as a 'teleological moralist' promoting some kind of definite moral ideal. Politics is rather a 'means through which we identify the changing and often conflicting standards' (Yack 1993: 132). For Yack, Nussbaum's reading of Aristotle—that is identifying the nature of the good for human beings—is a misinterpretation. He contends that it is wrong to suggest that Aristotle considers justice or politics 'as something that can be determined by disinterested analysis of human nature and particular socio-political conditions rather than as something that emerges from political argument and competition.' (Yack 1993: 167). Yack also mentions both Alasdair MacIntyre and Hannah Arendt as distorting Aristotle on this issue.

For Yack, therefore, the idea that there is some kind of putative rich universal good in Aristotle is simply mistaken. Politics rather grows out of the diverse material and empirical needs of human beings. No political communities are well ordered or harmonious. Consequently, not many regimes are praised by Aristotle. All political regimes provide some of the goods necessary for human functioning. All regimes will also contain offensive and unhelpful laws. Further, in Yack's interpretation, politics itself is a comparatively rare activity. It occurs when relatively free and equal citizens can engage in regular public discussion about laws and policies (Yack 1993: 7). This is not a common occurrence, particularly in Aristotle's period. Rather than fostering ideals, the neo-Aristotelian perspective, for Yack, basically helps us to take imperfections and the heterogeneity of values and beliefs more seriously. He helps us to read and understand our flawed social existence. Yack's Aristotle sees the notion of community without any moralistic glow whatsoever. We need therefore to disentangle Aristotle from all the modern debates concerning communitarianism, republicanism, and liberal individualism. Humans might, through politics, be able to achieve some form of excellence. But politics, in itself, can never be the perfection we seek.

The upshot of this reading of neo-Aristotelianism is more interpretive or hermeneutical. It also contends that we should not seek for ideals and moral foundations in neo-Aristotelianism. Conversely, it is a framework of analysis and interpretation, within which we can assess all types of regime or ideals. In a perspective, which bears comparison to Yack's, Richard Salkever also suggests that neo-Aristotelianism can provide a supportive philosophical rapprochement with contemporary liberalism. As he comments, in a quasi-hermeneutic mode, reading Aristotle 'is not a source of solutions to modern problems' (Salkever 1990: 5). For neo Aristotelians, political life is neither a tragic pluralist paradox, nor a perfectly soluble ideal. Rather, for Salkever, neo-Aristotelianism avoids both dogmatism and relativism, both liberal individualism and communitarianism. It proposes a practical way out of these dilemmas. In consequence, it proffers a 'third way' (Salkever 1990: 7–8). In one sense, it is also empty of content. However, in this context, although neo-Aristotelianism does not provide any definitive political ideals, it can, nonetheless 'be a starting point for discussing those problems in new ways, ways that avoid familiar dead ends, such as the opposition between liberal individualism and republican communitarianism, between the politics of the right and the politics of the virtues' (Salkever 1990: 5). Salkever therefore contends that we should neither view neo-Aristotelianism as invoking tragic agonism and paradox, nor offering some perfectible form of life and rich ideal. Humans, for Salkever's Aristotle, 'are neither predictable machines nor self-creating deities'. Neo-Aristotelianism's third way can allow us to analyse, discuss, and defend liberal politics. But, it is quite definitely, for Salkever, not an alternative to liberalism (Salkever 1990: 7–8).

Thus, for Salkever, and others, the neo-Aristotelian perspective is not a premodern alternative to liberalism, but is rather 'a source of education' for liberals about our current way of life or ethos, within modernity. It is not offering us any comprehensive foundationalism. Human affairs (or the *ethos*) are usually resistant to theory. At most, theory can offer a kind of practical wisdom concerning deliberation about the ethos. Practical wisdom is though uncodifiable. Politics is concerned with the conditions for the flourishing of humans. It is not the 'end' of human aspiration for Aristotle. There is little precision and no absolutes in politics. How to act reasonably tends to vary from political and moral context to context. There are no natural laws. Theory can explain complexity and provide rules of thumb, but it cannot provide infallible imperatives. Neo-Aristotelian political theory can therefore improve the quality of analysis and debate, but it does not offer resolutions.

The second negative reading affirms Aristotle's realism. It is also suspicious of any teleology. Yet, it retains, contrary to the hermeneutical view, the idea of a rich 'ideal good'. However, contrary to Nussbaum's view, this good is highly particularist. In this context, neo-Aristotelianism becomes closely identified with communitarianism. This is the view of Alasdair MacIntyre. MacIntyre's neo-Aristotelianism position is part of a more general post-Wittgensteinian critique of extralinguistic thin or thick foundations. The argument is rooted in a commitment to the concrete, particular, and conventional over the abstract and universal.[10]

MacIntyre's main 'disquieting suggestion' (which is rooted in a neo-Aristotelian judgement) is that morality subsists within traditions or particular conventions and that we—in modernity—have lost the context for meaningful moral choices. We are literally 'after virtue', we are no longer sure which rationality, or which justice, to choose and we have no secure standard for adjudication between rival traditions. What we do possess though are a series of fragments of moral and conceptual schemes from past traditions, which all lack context. We have, what MacIntyre calls, 'simulacra of morals' (MacIntyre 1981: 2). Moral argument in the twentieth century is therefore subject to continuous conceptual incommensurability and interminable debate. There is a heterogeneity of philosophical mentors and a whole body of spurious rationalist moral yardsticks, including neo-Kantianism and utilitarianism. MacIntyre sees this whole twentieth century dilemma summed up in emotivism, namely, the belief that morality can be seen as the expression of individual emotion. The emotivist self, for MacIntyre, is not though just an abstract philosophical device. Conversely, it belongs to a particular type of social order in crisis. It is a modern pathology. Emotivism is the result of the breakdown of a culture.

For MacIntyre, the prior culture, identified with classical Aristotelianism and Christianity, had a more unified, personal, and coherent dimension to it. As Stephen Holmes mischieviously puts it, MacIntyre 'continues to use the Greek polis as a large paddle for spanking modern man' (Holmes 1993: 112). Morality, in the classical Aristotelian sense, provides a rich good, but it is always tied to the local and particular. A more accurate way of putting this is that it invokes 'rich goods'. There is no way to act with virtue, except as part of the tradition of shared understanding, which we inherit and inhabit. Practising virtue in the Aristotelian format is a process of character formation and moral habituation within particular communities and traditions. Action presupposes some deliberate choice, which is, in turn, embedded in and nurtured by a way of life or ethos. In this premodern mode of thought, MacIntyre sees the core of the virtues. A virtue is 'an acquired human quality the possession and exercise of which tends to enable us to achieve those goods which are internal to practices and the lack of which effectively prevents us from achieving any such goods' (MacIntyre 1981: 178). Virtue enables us to attain ends internal to practices. But virtues cannot be delineated apart from human relationships. Thus Homeric, Athenian, and Christian virtues become coherent in particular historical and communal settings.

For MacIntyre, the classical Aristotelian tradition was gradually undermined between the fifteenth to the seventeenth century. He offers a genealogy of this process. The final denouement of the tradition was underpinned by arguments from what MacIntyre clumsily calls the 'Enlightenment project' (see Schmidt 2000). It separated reason and value from tradition and community. He takes one of the main preoccupations of the Enlightenment project to discover new secular foundations for morality, outside of Aristotelianism and Christianity. Kant is often seen as the greatest expositor of this trend. However, for MacIntyre, the whole modern enterprise has failed. The really significant figure of modernity is not Kant, but Nietzsche. Nietzsche embodies the key expression of the modern era, representing the collapse into nihilism and emotivism (MacIntyre 1981: 111). In Nietzsche, there is nothing to morality but the expression of my will and what my will creates. Nietzsche's unwitting spawn are taken to be Sartrean existentialism and analytically based emotivism. Thus, the Enlightenment, liberal individualism, Nietzsche, atheistic existentialism, the emotivist self, are all subtly linked in MacIntyre's mind. The Nietzschean scheme, *per se*, is not a critical alternative to liberalism and the Enlightenment; it is part of it.

Hardly surprisingly, the pivotal chapter of MacIntyre's book *After Virtue* (1981) is significantly titled 'Nietzsche or Aristotle'. For MacIntyre, the choice is stark: either one adheres to the 'Enlightenment project' and modern liberalism and ends up with Nietzsche and emotivism, or, one regards the Enlightenment project as misconceived. If we regard it as misconceived, we turn against the modern age and must revindicate Aristotelianism. For MacIntyre, there is no 'third way'—as suggested by Salkever. There are no other alternatives. It is between Nietzsche and Aristotle (MacIntyre 1981: 112). MacIntyre's own sympathies lie with revindicating Aristotelianism. He places this choice before us in deeply apocalyptic almost Straussian terms, suggesting that our civilization has reached a turning point. For MacIntyre, 'we ought also to conclude that for some time now we too have reached the turning point. What matters at this stage is the construction of local forms of community within which civility and the intellectual and moral life can be sustained through the dark ages which are already upon us . . . We are waiting not for a Godot, but another— doubtless very different— St Benedict' (MacIntyre 1981: 263). Thus, monastic rule and neo-Aristotelianism beckon to us.

Neo-Aristotelianism is thus revindicated by MacIntyre in three senses. First, it is needed to restore intelligibility and rationality to morality. This point has resonances with the previous hermeneutic argument. We need to *read* morality and politics correctly. MacIntyre looks to a modernized Aristotelianism to understand our modern sickness. Our sickness is that we have lost any sense of community, defined via common purposes. Virtue has become empty role playing. Morality is just feuding. Although there is no neutral non-perspectival view of morality or rationality, and many moral schemes are literally untranslatable, nonetheless, Aristotelianism can enable us (in an intelligent setting) to engage in a constrained dialogue. Second, neo-Aristotelianism provides a workable particularist alternative. We need local communal particularities to function. This is MacIntyre's contextualism and communitarianism—although it also has resonances with Wittgenstein, Heidegger, and Rorty. This is the only alternative to Nietzscheanism. Third, it is not simply any community that MacIntyre avers to. Political community is also something that 'grounds civility' as well as moral and intellectual life. Precisely what this means remains ambivalent and exactly how it gels with the second particularist argument remains unclear. However, the precise moral content *still* remains particularist. Our 'future' moral content in Western societies waits upon another St Benedict.

MacIntyre nonetheless departs from Aristotle in three respects. First, he totally rejects the metaphysical biology—although this is not uncommon in contemporary neo-Aristotelians. Aristotle's basic teleology is seen to presuppose this biology. For MacIntyre, humans are far more than their biology. Consequently, in rejecting the metaphysical biology, he also discards the teleology, which presupposes identifiable needs and a universal good.[11] Thus, Nussbaum's idea of 'grounding experiences' does not fare well here. Second, he sees a lack of clear historical awareness in Aristotle. Despite his realism and acceptance of communal difference, he still seemed to think that Greeks, slaves and barbarians had fixed natures. This is false to MacIntyre. Third, he disagrees with Aristotle's idea of the unity of the virtues. For MacIntyre, Aristotle believes in 'a cosmic order which dictates the place of each virtue in a total harmonious scheme of human life. Truth, in the moral sphere, consists in the conformity of moral judgment to the order of this scheme' (MacIntyre 1981: 133). MacIntyre, although denying that he is a relativist, still drifts inexorably via his communitarian particularism into a pluralism and relativism of the virtues. Consequent upon this particularism and relativism, the self becomes unanchored. MacIntyre's account of the self moves away from Aristotle. Humans, in MacIntyre, are story-telling animals. Selfhood becomes a narrative construct. However, each narrative is part of an interlocking series of narratives within a community. Human beings thus define themselves by the stories they tell. The self is therefore never settled in MacIntyre, it remains little more than a continuous quest. Despite these differences, MacIntyre still offers us the neo-Aristotelian perspective as the only path for sorting out the disorder of contemporary morality and politics. We still have fragments of the Aristotelian tradition, which can be picked up and utilized. Without it we inevitably collapse into the Nietzschean nihilism.

The ambivalence of the neo-Aristotelian position hangs on the equivocal issue of the conventional particular and universal relation. The stress laid on the realism and recognition of imperfection and contingency implies that there are *no* really clear universal answers to moral issues. Relativism, strict conventionalism, and particularism appear to be the only possible outcome. At most, like MacIntyre, the argument does suggest there can be rich foundations, but these are highly particularist ones. One response to this criticism is that neo-Aristotelianism is itself a fine balancing act between generality and particularity. One can retain both objectivity and contextual responsiveness. Context can change and moral rules can also be adjusted. Perceptions, for example, of acceptable forms of sexuality have changed. However, this, in itself, is not an argument against the grounding experience of sexuality and that it is morally significant. However, if, like Nussbaum, it is maintained that there are universal 'grounding experiences', then the question still arises (from within the neo-Aristotelian framework itself), as to whether any of these experiences can be apprehended, free of particular cultural or conventional mediation. The critic can still argue that there are no primitive human experiences. There is consequently nothing behind or underneath culture or ethos. One answer that certain neo-Aristotelians put forward is that even if judgement is always mediated through culture or ethos, this does not imply that 'anything' is possible. In the area of grounding experience, Nussbaum, for one, suggests that certain experiences (death, child rearing, or sexuality) have a form of commonality. No group is focused—especially in the twentieth century—wholly on itself. Cross-cultural communication is ever-present. In this context, neo-Aristotelianism claims to offer a via media, not unlike forms of weaker communitarianism, Walzer's reiterative universalism, liberal nationalism, and some versions of liberal thin universalism.

REPUBLICANISM

Republicanism is one of the latest of the hopeful candidates of the 1990s to leap into the foundational breach, usually pulling patriotism behind it. It also appears to have generated some heavyweight academic support, which has given it an initially strong impetus. Republicanism itself—like neo-Aristotelianism—has again been purportedly recovered from a historical perception of an older discourse, originating in Roman legal and political thought. The difficulties begin immediately here, since some see the idea originating in Hellenic Aristotelianism. Thus, neo-Aristotelianism can, in some renderings, become an expression of republicanism. This has though been bitterly resisted by other theorists. One way round this issue, which does not appear in many recent republican writings, is to draw a distinction between neo-Athenian republicanism (which can incorporate the neo-Aristotelian perspective) and neo-Roman republicanism. John Maynor, for example, has argued that the neo-Roman variant is far better suited, as philosophical defence of modern republicanism, than the neo-Athenian variant (see Maynor 2003: 6).

The term 'republic' itself is an anglicized form of *res publica* (public thing), as opposed to *res privata* (private thing). The *res publica* of Roman thought was the remote, but attractive, legal abstraction of republican Rome. It retained this attraction even for later Roman Imperial emperors, who tried to continue the republican terminology for several hundred years after it was no longer politically effective. *Res publica* refers, more generally, to the common weal, common wealth or *civitas*. In this generic sense, the term 'republic' (the public thing) is not a particularly helpful term, since it could refer literally to *any* form of political regime with an identifiable public realm. The more specific normative concept of republicanism, which derived from a somewhat rosy reading of Republican Rome, implied that the people (*populus*), or more specifically the citizens, had a decisive role in the organization of the public realm, although we should not mistake this in any way for democracy. The republican citizen, in this scenario, exhibits virtue and rational self-control within the public realm.

In late medieval, renaissance, sixteenth- and seventeenth-century versions of republicanism, this also clearly implied a belief in Christian truths, as well as martial and other such virtues. It was only eighteenth-century republicanism, which became linked with more secular themes. Further, the citizen was viewed as an independent agent in the public arena, but such independence also implied basic property ownership. Property ownership implied that one had a 'stake' in political order and a consequent sense of social responsibility. The language of republicanism is also one of the right to resilient individual liberty, intimately tied to the correlative duty of active service for the community. Each citizen has to be formally willing to renounce private concerns for the common good, order, and flourishing of the community. There was, in addition, a continual fear, in earlier republican thought, of potential degeneracy, institutional decay, loss of public virtue, and corruption. This often led to a pervasive conservative and pessimistic demeanour within republicanism, which originally favoured political stasis.

Whether or not republicanism submerged in the medieval period and re-emerged in renaissance city states is a subject of scholarly debate. The standard view among recent neo-republican writers is that the theory passed through the fifteenth-century Italian renaissance city-states (like Florence), with Machiavelli as a founding figure, to the seventeenth-century English civil war period, emerging also in the Dutch Provinces in their struggle against Spanish Monarchy. It was seen to be revived by writers such as Henry Neville and Algernon Sidney in the 1680s, given an opportunistic rendering in Lord Bolingbroke in the 1720s and restored again by Richard Price and others to defend the American colonists in the 1770s (Skinner 1998: 10–13). The fruits of classical republicanism can be found in doctrines such as the mixed or balanced constitution and American Constitutional separation of powers of the next century. The French Revolution is, however, standardly seen to transform republicanism into a debate about forms of radical democracy.

Most scholars of republican thought thus, conventionally, see it fading into the background in the nineteenth and twentieth centuries, in the face of the rise of ideologies such as liberalism, conservatism, and socialism. However, from the 1960s, some commentators, critical of the idea that American politics was founded in Lockean individualism, identified the alternative real roots of American politics in a civic republican tradition. The culmination of this interpretation was J. G. A. Pocock's magisterial work *The Machiavellian Moment* (1975). Pocock interpreted many important strands of Anglo-American political culture, of the early modern period, as part of a civic humanist or civic republican tradition, derived from Renaissance Italy. Similar themes were developed in the work of Hans Baron, Adrian Oldfield, and Quentin Skinner (Baron 1966; Oldfield 1990; Skinner 1991, 1998; Pettit 1997; Brugger 1999; Maynor 2003). Skinner, and more recent writers such as Philip Pettit, have moved away from the historical commentary into direct normative claims concerning the contemporary relevance of republicanism as an alternative to liberalism (Pettit 1993*a*, 1997). Skinner is slightly more opaque here. But he certainly uses republicanism to question 'liberal hegemony' in political theory.[12] In other words, republicanism provides an intellectual resource for contemporary political theory and practice to counter the hegemony of liberal theory. Republicanism is purported to embody the third, apparently lost, concept of liberty—in addition to negative and positive liberty. This is liberty as non-domination.

If we hone in on recent republican writings a little more closely, there are certain background assumptions, which require further explication. Primarily, there is the mundane assumption of a community made up of rational independent-minded citizens. Even contemporary neo-Roman republicans assume that modern pluralist society will be largely peopled by such agents. Further, there is a supposition of some form of minimal rational public culture—usually focused on a particular and quite idiosyncratic reading of liberty, distinct from notions of negative and positive liberty. Republican laws in this reading, enable citizens. Law socializes and controls natural selfishness. Liberty is seen to be most likely to be preserved under republican institutions and laws, which facilitate individual self-rule. Strengthening individual liberty therefore means strengthening republican institutions. Consequently, republicans emphasize the need for laws to ensure that people act with virtue and within the same generic framework of values. The rational virtues espoused by the republic are now secular in character. Modern republicans are though keen to foster homogenization through civic education and institutional design (see also Maynor 2003, ch. 7).[13]

As mentioned, the only caveat to enter here, on the question of republicanism, is a distinction occasionally drawn between the older stronger as against the more recent weaker manifestations of republicanism, or, alternatively, neo-Athenian and neo-Roman republicanism. The older stronger format emphasizes the civic participation and duty over the mere assertion of civil rights, whereas the weaker seeks the converse. The stronger civic variant thus entails more cultural and moral uniformity. It places a powerful emphasis on virtuous active citizens and an integrating and unifying public good, which should take priority over private goods. The weaker conception, which prevails in most recent expositions, entails therefore a much more restricted pragmatic conception of impartiality. It does not demand that individuals share values, but only that they are prepared to debate their views rationally in a public setting. This distinction can be found in both proponents of and recent commentators on republican political theory. Thus, Brugger, for example, focuses on the difference between Benjamin Barber's tougher republicanism in *Strong Democracy*, as against Pettit's much weaker form. Pettit, in point, refers to his own version as 'gas and water' republicanism—echoing the mild reformist socialism of the British Fabians. Maynor also draws a similar distinction between the communitarian (more neo-Athenian) republicanism of Michael Sandel and the neo-Roman variant of Pettit and Skinner (Barber 1984; Pettit 1997: 239; Brugger 1999: 13–14; Maynor 2003: 31).[14]

Although the Barber and Pettit contrast does not quite work, nonetheless the above argument does lead to a more general distinction in the literature between weaker and stronger forms of republicanism. However, the issue is surely more complex than a distinction between weaker and stronger variants, or even neo-Athenian and neo-Roman variants. There are as many differences between the republicans of the seventeenth and late twentieth century as there are between Roman republicans and seventeenth-century variants. It would be true that the modern variants no longer have a primary focus of independent property ownership in the citizen body. Further, seventeenth-century republicanism strongly emphasises a suffocating civic virtue, strict conditions for military service, good military arms, an underlying deeply conservative, inertial and pessimistic demeanour, belief in universal Christian truths and obsessive fear of institutional decay, instability, and degeneration. These do not sit comfortably at all with modern, dare one say, more liberal republicans' preoccupations. Thus, initially, it is difficult to speak of *the* one singular republican perspective. In point there are four generic contenders for the republican heartland: first, classical republicans (possibly Aristotle, Cicero, Livy, and Machiavelli—unless one separates out the Hellenic Greek, Roman, and Renaissance versions); second, the complex seventeenth- and eighteenth-century variants (Henry Neville, Algernon Sidney, Richard Price); third, neo-classical republicanism in the twentieth century (Viroli, Skinner, Pettit), and, finally, late twentieth century (more neo-Athenian) communitarian republicanism (Charles Taylor). In this more complex scenario, Viroli's or Pettit's attempts to dismiss, for example, recent communitarianism completely from republican ranks is not convincing.

Are there any central themes within republican political theory, which allow us to see a more coherent picture? Many contemporary neo-classical republicans, such as Pettit, seem more directly focused on a distinctive concept of 'resilient negative liberty' (liberty as anti-power or non-dominatory liberty), as the decisive component of republican argument. Another central theme in republican thought is the idea of the *res publica* itself, that is, the 'public thing'. It may seem strange, on a general level, to link republicanism and nationalism under the same broad rubric of conventionalism. After all, as many contemporary republicans would argue, republicanism is apparently utterly opposed to nationalism.[15] This would certainly be the case with Pettit, Viroli, and Skinner, amongst others. However, there are two points to note here. First, no contemporary republicans would deny an intellectual and practical discomfiture with procedural liberalism, a discomfiture they share with *all* conventionalist writers. Thus, there is some shared ground with nationalism and communitarianism. Second, if one focuses on what is distinctive about the opposition to nationalism or communitarianism, then, it is clearly premised on a republican separation between the state and the nation or community. The nation, for example, is seen to 'pervert' state discourse. The object, which is worthy of value and even deep respect is not the nation, but something within the state—namely—the 'public thing' (*res publica*).

The heart of republicanism is this conception of the 'public thing'. The 'public thing' is valuable in terms of what it either embodies or facilitates. This idea of the 'public thing' is neither opposed to nationalism, because of its 'particularist' ontology, nor because of its conventionalist emphasis, but, rather, because the nation is *not* a conventional structure worthy of moral respect. Republicanism therefore remains firmly conventionalist in ontological texture, but it objects to the value structure and character of nationalism in practice. It is worth underscoring another important point here. The 'public thing' is primarily related to the particular state. This is not just any state, but, conversely the conventional, somewhat rare and fragile structure of a republican state. The only way a more universal republican order could prevail is from the 'bottom up', that is, where states become republican. In this sense, republicanism, in itself, is yet another conventionalist alternative to liberal universalism. Just how conventionalist republicanism is, is a matter of how one reads the substantive values of the 'public thing'.

What, in this context, is the 'public thing' and what precisely is valuable within it? It is difficult to generalize here, however, it is possible to gain the gist of what drives contemporary republicans by considering what moral and political values are promoted within, or by, this 'public thing'. The important point, for both Skinner and Pettit, is that the 'public thing' embodies a particular conception of the relationship between law and liberty.[16] This argument is also a way of differentiating procedural liberalism from republicanism. Basically liberals are seen to mistakenly view law as a permanent (if necessary) affront to all liberty. Some commentators have consequently referred to the liberal conception of law and liberty as quantitative, that is, the more law entails the less liberty.[17] In republican theory a more qualitative conception is adopted, such that law is not necessarily a restraint on liberty, conversely it protects it. Thus, for Skinner and others, the republican tradition, stemming from Machiavelli, sees law *preserving* liberty. If citizens are to enjoy any kind of freedom, to pursue their own ends they must live in a state, which embodies a free way of life—a *vivere libero*. A state is free, if and only if, it is self-governing, that is not under the control of others than the citizens. Thus, liberty can only be fully assured 'within a self-governing form of republican community' (see Skinner in Rorty et al. (eds.) 1991: 206–7). For Pettit, particularly, this republican notion of liberty is distinct from both negative and positive liberty. It is not about freedom from interference. It is rather focused on the notion of non-domination—although it might also be seen as a significant modification of negative liberty, namely, 'resilient negative liberty'. However, Pettit insists that there is a marked difference between freedom as non-interference and freedom as non-domination. Freedom as non-domination invokes the notion, not just of interference, but of *arbitrary* interference. An arbitrary act is chosen or not chosen at the agent's pleasure. It is also interference with others, which is chosen or rejected without reference to the interests, or the opinions, of those affected. Freedom or liberty therefore implies institutional and legal protections against arbitrary interference. Thus, it is the *nature*, or qualitative appraisal, of the interference, which is crucial for republicans such as Pettit and Skinner. Republican freedom is not opposed to law, but rather to slavery and arbitrariness. Thus, although liberals and republicans are both committed to a neutral rule of law concept, their understanding (for Pettit) of the relationship between law and liberty is markedly different. Pettit admits that this is a more communally-orientated understanding of freedom, although it is still opposed to communitarianism.[18]

In this context, Pettit is confident about the role of the 'public thing'. Its role is providing the legal and institutional framework for protection against 'arbitrary interference', which, in turn, has a number of wide-ranging policy implications. Non-domination or protection against arbitrary power is either embedded or facilitated by the *res publica* state. Thus, for example, Pettit describes the central thesis of his book *Republicanism* as showing 'how institutions can be designed—specifically designed in a republican pattern—so that people's enjoyment of non-domination is more or less smoothly maximized' (Pettit 1997: 92 *ff.*, see also Pettit in Vincent (ed.) 1997). It would be true to say here that Pettit is much more overtly committed to this ideal of resilient liberty and non-domination than Skinner (see Skinner 1998: 22; Maynor 2003, ch. 2).

Yet, it is never clear, in this republican analysis, where Kant's or Rousseau's self-evident republicanism fits, unless one adopted the strategy of distinguishing complex forms of republicanism, which the majority of contemporary theorists do not do.[19] It is also not clear where social liberal theorists, like T. H. Green, Guido de Ruggiero, or L. T. Hobhouse, slot into the Skinner, Viroli, Pettit scheme. This question becomes more urgent in terms of twentieth-century theorists, such as Hannah Arendt, who clearly saw herself as republican. As Margaret Canovan noted, 'if any label at all were to be pinned on her [Arendt], it could only be "Republican"—not in the sense of the American party, but in the old, eighteenth century sense of a partisan of public freedom, a companion of men like de Tocqueville, Jefferson and Machiavelli' (Canovan 1974: 15). Pettit, however, remarks that *genuine* republicans, like himself, Skinner, John Braithwaite, and Cass Sunstein, are very different creatures from Arendt. The tradition behind Arendt he describes as 'populist', namely, one 'that hails the democratic participation of the people as one of the highest forms of good and often waxes lyrical, in communitarian vein, about the desirability of the close, homogenous society that popular participation is often taken to presuppose' (Pettit 1997: 8). Republicanism, to Pettit, is not populist, like communitarianism. Republican liberty is compatible with pluralism, whereas communitarianism is discomforted by it. Further, although republicanism is interested in democracy, 'it does not treat it as a bedrock value'. Participation is only valuable insofar as it contributes to liberty as non-domination.

Pettit thinks that the mistaken communitarian and populist 'image' of republicanism is largely due to Arendt. The people, in this vision, become a collective 'master' and the state the 'servant'. Representatives, and the like, should not though be relied upon, conversely, direct democratic participation (through plebiscite or an assembly) is favoured. Alternatively, for Pettit, the republican position sees the people as 'trustor' and the state as 'trustee'. The people trust the state to ensure non-arbitrary rule. Direct democracy, in this context, may in fact be the ultimate form of arbitrariness—the tyranny of the majority. Thus, as Pettit concludes, 'so much for the populist alternative to republicanism' (Pettit 1997: 8).

There are a number of points here. It is not clear that populism, conceptually and historically, does directly imply participatory democracy (participatory democracy itself is also an internally complex entity). Favouring the opinions of ordinary people, or focusing on the interests and tradition of the mass of small property owners (Poujadism or Peronism)—both possible readings of populism—do not necessarily entail, in any way, participatory democracy. Dictatorship is, for example, compatible with populism. Further, populism—whatever it means—does not have *any* necessary conceptual links with communitarianism.[20] Communitarianism also has *no* necessary conceptual links with democracy in general, let alone direct democracy in particular. Many contemporary Asian states, for example Singapore, who have made a lot of assertive and loud communitarian noises in the last decade, have nonetheless been deeply sceptical about all but the most constrained democratic practices. We now have terms like 'illiberal democracy' being used appraisively in South East Asia. Finally, to associate Arendt with an open avowal of communitarianism, populism, and explicit (unqualified) direct democracy, is not just misplaced, but just very odd. Pettit is though correct on Arendt's interest in direct democracy. As one commentator has noted, Arendt had an evident preference 'for small-scale republican forms like the revolutionary councils and town-hall meetings over large scale, impersonal . . . representative and bureaucratic institutions' (Hansen 1993: 220). It is worth grasping here, though, exactly why Arendt favoured this idea, since it will also provide an understanding of her conception of republicanism in terms of the value she undoubtedly saw in the 'public thing'.

One of the standard criticisms of Arendt relates to her interest in the ancient form of polis and republic, and the constraining effect that it has on her thought. It is important to take note here of the fact that this kind of accusation is *also* directed at many forms of republicanism.[21] In the case of Arendt, she uses the ancient polis as more of a paradigm or 'ideal type' of a certain kind of political relationship. She was thus more interested in the manner in which they organized their public and private worlds. This should not be taken as overt 'Graecomania' (see Villa (ed.) 2000: 9; see also Euben and Taminaux essays in Villa (ed.) 2000: 161, 176). It is impossible, within the short space available here, to offer anything but the most brief overview of Arendt's diverse and complex work. Indeed, the identity and character of her work, are still a subject of intense scholarly debate. However, it is important here to consider her as a sophisticated exponent of a form of twentieth century republicanism. The theme explored here relates to her idea that Greek and Roman conceptions of the state contained a powerful and overt conception of a 'public realm', whereas, gradually, states in the nineteenth and twentieth centuries have become increasingly fascinated with the social (something considered an extension of the hierarchical order of the family, that is, *oikos* with *dominium*).[22] In effect, the social (and economic) are seen to potentially diminish the public space and the freedom involved with this space. The invasion of the public world by the social world can, for example, be seen in the development of the twentieth-century welfare state (see Brunkhorst in Villa (ed.) 2000, 189 *ff.*).

One important motif that underpins this fascination with the loss of the political to the social is totalitarianism. Both *On the Origins of Totalitarianism* (1958) and her *Eichman in Jerusalem* (1965) were, in part, responses to events in her own time, but, they also contain an idiosyncratic philosophical reading of those events. Both books chart, in one sense, the disintegration of citizenship and a corresponding sense of what it is to be human. Nazism, Stalinism, racism, mass society, and imperialism are all linked in the same destructive matrix as totalitarianism. One might therefore read these as a series of deeply-damaging pathologies (see Villa (ed.) 2000: 3). The totalitarian 'mentality' or pathology is something that could, in fact, reoccur for Arendt in certain configurations of circumstances. It represents the conquest of nature and determinism over human freedom and responsibility. Marx, she considered, unwittingly, facilitated this process. Arendt's book the *Human Condition* (1958) was written against the backdrop of the latter two works. Its primary focus was on the conditions for authentic politics.[23] Totalitarianism implies, as such, the end of politics. It is anti-political. Politics implies another condition of existence. As Margaret Canovan notes, 'just as totalitarian terror ... strips human beings of their plurality and spontaneity in order to reduce them to an animal species, so [Arendt] argues in the *Human Condition* that as labouring values have risen to prominence, something very similar has been happening painlessly in all modern societies' (Canovan 1994: 103; see also Villa (ed.) 2000: 6). It is the public world of politics that guards humanity from both the impetus to totalitarianism and the dominance of nature. The 'public thing' thus takes on a profound significance for Arendt. It is the bastion of both civilization and politics.

Arendt's republicanism is premised on a historical and philosophical response to the role and effect of the totalitarian mentality. Political freedom is not bestowed by nature or history. It is the result of intelligent effort. Further, it is a way of coping with inevitable human diversity. She adopts a similar view of equality here, which is not read in either natural or social terms. Equality is part of the public thing. It is a *result* of human action and is, in fact, contrary to nature. As Canovan comments, Arendt's political thought is thus 'conceived as an attempt to salvage and articulate ancient republican experiences by rethinking the traditional concepts in a way that takes account of human plurality and recognizes the political as something that happens in the spaces *between* plural men' (Canovan 1994: 207). Politics in the modern republic is therefore immensely subtle. It is envisaged as a public space 'between' citizens, and yet, at the same time, belonging to all citizens. Ruling entails utilizing the common support of all citizens. Citizens (as Pettit and Skinner also emphasize) cannot be free if subjected to a master—even a benign master. Political freedom is therefore a public thing, embedded in republican order, and possessed by all citizens of the republic. As such, it is fundamentally important, corresponds with our 'humanity' (against nature), acts as a bastion of civilization, and is an implicit defence against totalitarianism. This concept of freedom (which is again neither negative nor positive) is read partly as the 'capacity to begin', think, and create within this public space, guarded by constitutional arrangements and upheld by the public commitments of all citizens.

Politics, in the republic, therefore requires a level of intelligence and psychological maturity—which Arendt refers to as an 'enlarged mentality'. In other words, politics and the *public thing* requires a level of seasoned thoughtfulness. Republican citizenship is more than just a legal or moral status. It implies a special form of human dignity and a certain range of duties. The public thing does not absorb or muffle individual citizens in some form of common good or overarching unanimity, it rather celebrates their activity and debate in the public forum. Arendt envisages the public forum or public thing as a space for open discussion against the background of constitutional arrangements. This is not the realm of citizen soldier, of earlier Machiavellian republicanism, conversely it is a realm of participation in judgement, debate, and authority. This space allows the development of the capacity for judgement. Debate and deliberation, in this sphere, is between constitutionally equal citizens. It endows human life with significance.

The 'public thing' is therefore not about power, force, or violence, but rather about a sharing of argument and judgement. A challenge to this mentality is embedded in the social and economic spheres. These latter themes are essentially, for Arendt, the non-political ideas, which can undermine the 'public thing'. One unexpected implication of her argument here is her interest in small-scale participatory councils. This is not an antiquarian or utopian interest in small-scale participatory democracy, although she was fascinated, for example, with Jefferson's idea of the 'ward system' of local councils. This is also not a crass populism. In fact, it is rather a way of trying to encourage, or 'make possible', some active citizen participation in the 'public thing' (which was crucial for the maintenance of civilized human existence and human freedom). Interestingly, Canovan (contra Pettit) reads Arendt here as *totally* distinct from communitarianism (see Canovan 1994: 248; Beiner in Villa (ed.) 2000: 44). Arendt was trying, in effect, to bring plurality and the public world within an institutional framework. This is no bland utopia, rather, 'Arendt was always finely balanced between pessimism about the capacity of human beings to establish "lasting institutions", and optimism at the thought that each new member of the human race is, after all, capable of joining with others to make a new beginning amid the ruins of the old' (Canovan 1994: 249).

In summary Arendt is a sophisticated republican. Her argument for the 'public thing' is focused on the values of public equality and non-resilient liberty, which it contains. The 'public thing' is the essence of civilized and rational politics, which, at the same time, is not a bland unanimity, but rather contains diversity and pluralism. On one level, the republican state *is* politics to Arendt. Her interest in participatory mechanisms is simply indicative of her concern to involve citizens in the agora of public debate, deliberation, and authority. It facilitates the development of human thought and judgement. The only point to note here, which no doubt is a source for critical commentary, is that her project is not systematically presented, that is, there is no one definitive work that contains her political theory. She herself was self-consciously unsystematic. Further, it is also a project which remains, in many essentials, unfinished, particularly in the area of republican political theory.[24]

The idea of republicanism, in the way it has been developed by a number of recent writers, has often tried to incorporate a specific understanding of patriotism. In fact, it usually claims some form of quite exclusive and specific insight into patriotism, as distinct from other political doctrines. This republican argument usually entails a fairly vigorous repudiation of the idea of nationalism. There are a number of basic claims within this perspective. Republicanism is seen as a rational doctrine, which is freely adopted, whereas nationalism is something the agent is thrown into through the accidents of ethnicity or birth. The republican patriotic mentality is seen to be more civilized and premised on values such as liberty, whereas nationalism is considered more exclusive, narrow, and basically indifferent to liberty. The concerns of nationalism are seen to be largely parochial, inward-looking and aggressive, whereas republican patriotism is seen as universalistic, outward-looking, if defensive of the values of the regime. Consequent upon these general considerations, patriotism is usually kept rigidly distinct from nationalism.

One of the more eloquent recent defenders of this thesis is Maurizio Viroli, although it is worth noting that Arendt also vigorously opposed nationalism in her various republican writings. For Viroli, the language of patriotism 'has been used over the centuries to strengthen or invoke love of the political institutions and the way of life that sustains the common liberty of a people, that is love of the republic, [whereas] the language of nationalism was forged in late eighteenth century Europe to defend or reinforce the cultural, linguistic and ethnic oneness and homogeneity of a people' (Viroli 1995: 1). Patriotism is intrinsically antagonistic to tyranny, despotism, and oppression. It focuses on the issue of liberty under law. For Viroli, both nationalism and patriotism have fluctuating meanings, nonetheless, he still contends that 'the language of modern nationalism came about as a transformation or adaptation of the language of patriotism, by which words like "country" and expressions like "love of country" were given new meanings, while a number of themes like cultural or ethnic unity and purity that republican patriots did not address at all or treated as minor compared to the main question of common liberty, assumed a central role'. He therefore contends that 'to understand nationalism, we must then begin with patriotism and think in terms of two languages, not a single language unfolding and changing over centuries' (Viroli 1995: 8). Nationalism implies excessive interest in consensus, which tends, in turn, to suffocate a community, in effect, promoting narrow-mindedness (Viroli 1995: 13). Consequently, he is insistent that we should not confound patriotism and nationalism. Yet, like Pettit, Skinner, and other recent republicans, Viroli thinks that republican patriotism had been pushed to the margin of political theory during the nineteenth and twentieth centuries, usually by doctrines such as liberalism and socialism (Viroli 1995: 161). However, it is questionable as to whether patriotism was actually lost in this period. It was rather employed quite widely, although not in a republican format.

As indicated the distinctive signature for republican writers of genuine patriotism is the spirited defence of political liberty and love of country. To love a country is not necessarily to love its culture or ethnicity, it is rather to be deeply focused on the idea and practice of civic or political liberty. Having no specific cultural tie, such liberty can therefore expand 'beyond national boundaries' (Viroli 1995: 12). In this context, the conventional republican norms are salvaged for the 'universal'. This is a common strategy within conventionalist argument during the late twentieth century. It can, for example, be found in liberal nationalism, neo-Aristotelianism, and liberal communitarianism. It aims to link conventions with some form of universal immanent foundation.[25] In consequence, republican patriotism can, on one level, counter the conventional structures of both nationalistic and communitarian argument, as well as conservative claims to patriotism. Communitarianism is repudiated particularly because of its purported focus on positive liberty. This, in some republican writers, also leads to a suspicion of the 'apparent' republicanism of Rousseau and Kant. Communitarianism is also seen to concentrate excessively, in a non-neutral manner, on communal consensus. The early communitarian writings of Charles Taylor are often singled out by recent republicans, such as Viroli, Pettit, and Skinner, particularly on the theme of positive liberty—although John Maynor's recent work provides a partial resolution to this problem (Maynor 2003). Taylor's conception of liberty is seen to concentrate, like Rousseau, on the positive theme of participatory self-rule, which is considered alien to republicanism. Communitarians are also seen to lay too much stress on the conventional character of morality, over-emphasizing local solidarities. One additional annoyance here for republican writers is that Taylor (amongst other communitarians such as Michael Sandel) has configured his own position, occasionally, as a form of communitarian republicanism. He also tends to separate out communitarian republican patriotism from nationalism in a very similar way to republican writers such as Viroli.

One problem here is that it is not that obvious who has a genuine entitlement to be considered republican. It is clear that Pettit, Viroli, Skinner, and others, would clearly like to exclude the likes of Taylor, Arendt, Rousseau, and possibly even Kant, from republican ranks. However, it is far from clear that their own claim to the republican heartland is in any way clearly established. The republican views, for example, of Pettit and Viroli are markedly different to earlier seventeenth and eighteenth-century forms, let alone early Roman or medieval forms. There is no one continuous pristine tradition here, rather multiple strands.

Another more significant criticism though of republicanism comes from critics of conventionalist argument. In the same way that republicans are critical of nationalists and communitarians for over-playing the conventionalist card, so republicans themselves have also been chided for their over-emphasis on communal consensus. This is despite the fierce and repetitive claims of recent republicans to be able to deal both with modern pluralism and conventionalist arguments. Habermas, for example, in a postconventional mode, has expressed deep unease with the more furtive consensual communal demands of recent republicans. Somewhat incongruously, he argues that the republican standpoint is, to all intents and purposes, more or less identical with communitarianism, in laying emphasis on the point that the 'citizen must identify himself "patriotically" with his particular form of life'. The communitarian and republican conceptions therefore imply some form of 'shared consciousness' about liberty within an ethical community. Habermas sees a conceptual link here between republicanism, communitarianism, and nationalism. For Habermas, the 'classic republican idea of the self-conscious political integration of community of free and equal persons is evidently too . . . simple a notion to remain applicable to modern conditions'. Republicans, for Habermas, are thus similar to communitarians and nationalists in regarding the citizen as 'fully integrated' within a communal identity, centred on certain values.[26] One of the primary values appealed to by republicans is a particular conception of liberty, understood via non-domination. This is by no means a weak, neutral or empty value. For Habermas, it is surreptitiously perfectionist, invasive, and clearly non-neutral. This point would figure even more strongly for premodern republicanism that was far more openly conventionalist and had very firm thick consensual conceptions of liberty, amongst other values. This firm sense of ethical probity in many ways still silently underpins modern republicanism.

Republicans, such as Viroli (although Pettit one suspect would have some reservations here), have responded to Habermas on this issue. The response is utterly predictable, for example, if you do not feel comfortable arguing with someone, then absorb them. Thus, Taylor remains outside republicanism and Habermas becomes an unwitting republican by default. The response, again, is premised on the contestable assumption of a consensus on what a pristine republicanism actually looks like. It is focused on a somewhat idiosyncratic late-twentieth century version, which, miraculously, has become the very acme of an unbroken tradition going back to the Roman republic. It may have been partly submerged, historically, a few times, but it has been rediscovered and revived again in the 1990s. In this view, the focus on non-dominatory political liberty is *not* the same as demanding a communal consensus. As emphasized above, Taylor cannot be a republican, for Viroli, because he places the concept of liberty within the context of this communal consensus. Positive liberty becomes participatory self-rule. However, citizenship is not concerned with self-rule in the context of an ethical community, conversely, it is the 'enjoyment and exercise of civil and political rights as a member' of a *respublica* (Viroli 1995: 171, note 23). Love of country is a love of genuine political liberty. Republican liberty and democracy do not require ethnocultural supports. They need, conversely, educated and rational citizens. Viroli suggests that Habermas sees this well enough, and with some minor adjustments to his notion of 'constitutional patriotism', Habermas could be absorbed into the republican fold. Consequently, the conventional republican community-based liberty integrates the universal.[27]

One deeply ambiguous assumption here is that republicanism—as focused on the rule of law and liberty as non-domination—does not presuppose any necessary cultural homogeneity. Leaving aside the question as to whether culture can be so easily bypassed in a state, despite the above avowals, it is clear that there is still a strong demand for some form of homogenous understanding of liberty amongst citizens. In addition, those who understand liberty in contrary ways, would not be acceptable within republican states. Law is *not* seen as neutral, conversely, it ought to embody the means for individuals to exercise genuine political freedom. To accept basic homogenous claims about liberty and law is the background assumption, which enables citizens to *actually* engage in the practices of citizenship, ethics, and political discourse within a republic. The uniformity, or communal agreement, on the perspective of non-dominatory liberty (which would be embodied and enforced through a republican legal system) is crucial. This premise appears to be *precisely* the source of Habermas's disquiet. The republican community will demand an ethical and political conformity to non-dominatory liberty. Despite the apparent allegiance of republicans to modernity, there is still a lingering sense and admiration for the ancient republic, which, in fact, underpins their emphasis on non-dominatory political liberty. Republicans, wittingly or unwittingly, smuggle in the aspects of this ancient model into their current preconceptions. In fact, the ethical and political adequacy of modern states is gauged against the implicit assumptions underpinning the idealized ancient republican model. Unsurprisingly, the real legal, political, and ethical structures of modern states often fall far short. The older republican idea of almost airtight polities, embodying stalwart independent rational citizens who love a particular conception of liberty, retaining powers for limpid judgement, open policy-making, and reasonable institutional design, seem distant and wholly out of kilter with what we actually know of most modern states and their citizens. Although admirable on a theoretical level, republicanism is, at the same time, fanciful.

Second, as regards liberty, republicans stand in a negative relation with any really troublesome pluralism. There is a degree of tolerance of harmless forms of pluralism. However, more vigorous assertions of pluralism are considered with deep suspicion. In being focused on social virtue and the legal coercion of individual action, republicanism implies a far greater conventional homogenization and a much more constrained sense of pluralism, certainly than found in liberalism, or even in some recent versions of communitarianism. Of course, the earlier premodern versions of republicanism would have found all sense of pluralism or multiculturalism as utterly repellent. Recent republicans usually try to contain pluralism (what ever that means to them) through open public dialogue and the insistence on a deep respect for non-dominatory liberty. However, as indicated above, the latter values—particularly the focus on a substantive reading, respect for (and love) of liberty—do imply a much greater degree of homogeneity than might initially be expected. Many republicans have also been keen to promulgate these deep values through civic educational curricula. There is nothing intrinsically wrong with this drift of argument, but it does not rest very easily with republican criticism of other conventionalist doctrines, such as communitarianism and nationalism. The underlying conventional virtues of the older republic are really only just below the surface of the modern claimants.[28] One suspects that this issue is closely connected to Habermas' perturbation with modern republicanism. In this sense, despite their best intentions, there is a moral chauvinism lurking within many contemporary republican arguments. A commitment to non-dominatory liberty does not necessarily avoid intolerance. Republican non dominatory liberty actually demands certain kinds of behaviour from citizens, it is also prepared to enforce it with a republican legal system. This is not a neutral structure of liberty, law, or human action. Republicanism is potentially an intrusive idea. In this sense, it has close parallels with other conventionalist doctrines such as liberal nationalism, liberal communitarianism, and liberal patriotism.

Finally, how seriously can we take the differences between liberalism and republicanism? One problem is that contemporary republicans take little account of the complex history of twentieth-century liberalism. Thus, if a counter example is thrown up within, what has usually been taken to be, liberal thought, which does not correspond with the republican caricature of liberalism, then, it is immediately subsumed into the 'unwitting republican' category. Thus, a collection of theorists during the nineteenth and twentieth century, who, for example, styled themselves as 'social liberals' or 'liberal-minded socialists', suddenly become—with the shake of a republican wand—unconscious or unwitting republicans. All this is rather unsatisfactory.

In fact, the republican reading of history can be regarded as unduly speculative and teleological on this ground. However, if, for the sake of argument, one accepts the republican caricature of liberalism, then even here there are lacunae. Thus, it is difficult to make out a case that, say, a procedural liberal such as Hayek, for example, always opposes law to liberty, which is one of the planks of Pettit's argument. Liberty clearly only exists *under* the rule of law for Hayek. Further, for Hayek, law should be seen as largely independent of the state, reflecting rather a form of pre-established moral or customary and spontaneous order. Hayek's later writings even try to give this some form of slightly weird evolutionary gloss. The state, for Hayek, should therefore be considered an instrument *of* the rule of law. Republicanism, in this sense, for procedural liberals such as Hayek, places too much emphasis on the state and government designing or constructing law. Government *under* the law is different from government operating *through* law. Thus, republicanism is seen to have an inadequate conception of law and liberty. Liberty, in this critical liberal reading, is too closely defined by and linked to the 'public thing'; it implies too much homogenization, which touches again upon points made above. Conversely, it is citizens confident in their personal liberty, under the law, who are the most effective guarantors of liberty. Republicanism, in its pursuit of the values of the 'public thing', is more than likely to ride roughshod over pluralism, specifically the rights of minority interests—a point against republicanism which, ironically, is shared by both Habermas and Hayek.

CONCLUSION

Minimally, the thin universalism of 1970s liberal justice theory—connected to a form of procedural liberalism—tended to overlook the conventional situatedness of individuals. Consequently, for critics, it was seen to contain an implausible account of the person or self. Further, thin universalism also tended to overlook cultural difference and conventional theories of action and meaning, for the sake of a more abstract universal reasonableness. However, without stronger metaphysical agreement, this 'abstract universalism' looked deeply suspect. The foundations were too thin to bear the weight put upon them. Liberal universalism seemed to be skating on very thin ice. The theoretical dissatisfaction with procedural liberalism and thin universalism led to a general search for a political alternative, which combined both the demands for some form of 'rational universalism', with the recognition of the inevitable conventionalism of human thought and value. This elusive compound, as suggested earlier, was already intimately part of the Idealist theoretical framework, being ably rendered by, for example, Michael Oakeshott, or earlier in the twentieth century by Bernard Bosanquet. In communitarianism, this generic search, for various reasons, reached a much wider audience, generating an unexpected cheering chorus in more recent postcolonial theory and Asian values arguments.[29] Communitarianism provided a ready-made answer to the doubts and anxieties concerning thin universalism. It also provided an unwitting answer to the anxieties that many had concerning the 'loss of community'. Communitarianism was, though, not a simple-minded critique. It was a deeper-rooted philosophical and ontological challenge. This made conventionalism (in general) a more acceptable political option and gave a broad philosophical credibility to the challenge to procedural liberalism in the last two decades of the century.

One problem with communitarianism (as noted earlier) was that it did not adequately clarify its own conception of community. Further, one important implication of the communitarian critique of liberalism was that it unwittingly facilitated a more widespread conventionalist drift in political theory. One ramification of this drift was the unanticipated recovery of nationalist political theory in the 1990s. In many ways, nationalism was a reconstitution of an older vocabulary of conventionalism, which had fallen on thinner times in mid-twentieth century thought—although it was *never* absent from political practice. However, the fears of liberals, particularly concerning the bellicose and politically unpredictable character of nationalism, were magically accommodated, during the 1990s, with an ungainly tumble of political theorists trying to synthesize nationalism and liberalism under the political neologism 'liberal nationalism'. However, communitarianism never adequately resolved its relation with liberal nationalism. Many theorist still looked with trepidation on the state of political theory in the 1990s. They were equally dissatisfied, on the one hand, with procedural liberalism and thin universalism, and, on the other hand, with the potentially suffocating consensual identity-based conventionalist politics of both communitarianism and nationalism. The upshot of this dissatisfaction was again a renewed search for 'past' theories, which could incorporate the conventionalist insights *with* some form of 'stretched' or chastened universalism. This was the ethos that characterized many (although not all) of the arguments of both neo-Aristotelianism and civic republicanism. The prevailing assumption was that older expressions of universalism—that is, the richer universalism of older metaphysically inclined theories, and the thinner universalism of procedural liberalism—were both inadequate. The conventionalist premise was accepted, insofar as the idea of universal, external, extra-social, or transhistorical metaphysical foundations, were no longer seen as plausible. However, a chastened vague notion of universal good was still assimilated within the conventional structures of republicanism and neo-Aristotelianism. In this sense, foundations for theory had not been abandoned, but rather modified and 'shored up' in more secure, immanent, and conventional settings.

Notes

1. Contemporary theoretical writings on nationalism are usually premised upon a twofold classification—insular bellicose and liberal variants. John Plamenatz's work is particularly apposite here as one of the unwitting prime movers of liberal nationalism, although he merely reflects Hans Kohn's earlier classification, see Kohn (1945), Plamenatz (1976, 23 *ff.*). This section on nationalism has been synthesized from a number of my writings, that is, Vincent (1995, 1997*a,b,* 2001*b,* 2002).
2. There is possibly a scholarly conceit lurking here, namely, that only sound theoretical positions can have political effect. The reverse might well be the case.
3. The only caveat to enter here is that untheoretical does not necessarily mean irrational, in the same sense that the non-rational may not be irrational.
4. For MacCormick, churches, trade unions, political parties, schools, universities, and even supranational groups 'can have a like significance to human beings in just the same way as can nations', MacCormick (1982: 251–2). MacCormick confesses that he is very much against the notion of ranking such loyalties. It is but a step from ranking nationalism against other loyalties to ranking nations themselves, which he finds intolerable.
5. MacCormick also thinks that 'liberty in a free country requires schemes of redistribution, welfare provision and educational support', see MacCormick (1990: 15; see also Tamir 1993: 16–17).
6. He remarks elsewhere that 'some form of democratic self-determination has to be considered both justifiable and valuable . . . Some form of collective self-constitution, some kind of active participation in shaping and sustaining the institutions of social or communal government whose aim is to advance liberty and autonomy, seems to be a necessary part of the whole ensemble of conditions in which the autonomy of the contextual individual could be genuinely constituted and upheld', see MacCormick (1990: 15).
7. Where nation and state do not coincide, Miller distinguishes ethnicity and nationalism. One can thus have a nation with multiple ethnic groups within it. For Miller, we are thus saved from the problem of giving every ethnic group a state, see Miller (1994: 156).
8. Although the final upshot of its theoretical approach is, in a way, still benignly liberal.
9. As Salkever puts it 'The theory of human good aids practice by serving as a basis for drawing out and criticising presuppositions about human needs that are implicit in particular political institutions and policies. These presuppositions are open to critical evaluation because of the objectivity and commensurability of human goods', Salkever (1990: 7).
10. With my own proviso again that this is not abandoning foundationalism, but rather 'shoring it up' from within immanent conventionalist foundations.
11. Salkever disagrees with MacIntyre here. He sees Aristotle as putting forward a non-determinist non-metaphysical biology, see Salkever (1990: 73).
12. Namely, 'by attempting to re-enter the intellectual world we have lost'; Skinner continues that 'With the rise of classical utilitarianism in the eighteenth century, and with the use of utilitarian principles to underpin so much of the liberal state in the century following, the theory of free states fell increasingly into disrepute, and eventually slipped almost wholly out of sight', Skinner (1998: x and 96).

13. A process that has been deeply familiar to the French Republican tradition.

14. He adds that weak republicans have occasionally denounced Barber's position as virtually communitarian, which Brugger considers deeply misleading, 'since Barber refused to regard community as antecedent to politics', Brugger (1999: 14).

15. This is not always the case, for example, in David Miller's work.

16. I am not concerned here whether the public thing is instrumental to this conception or whether it is embedded in the republican state.

17. 'Liberalism goes for a quantity-centred conception of liberty, a conception to which restraint is the antonym, and sees the law as instrumentally serving the cause of such liberty: law is itself a form of restraint but overall it does more good in this regard than harm. Republicanism prefers a security-centred or quality-centred conception, a conception opposed to servitude . . . the rule of law helps to confer on citizens that secure status in which their liberty consists', Pettit (1993: 179).

18. 'Communitarians deny the possibility of the neutral state or constitution, the state that is justified without reference to any particular conception of the good life. This line is that such a state will end up satisfying no one or will surreptitiously favour one conception of the good life above others. The ultimate communitarian lesson is hard to gauge, and the defenders of the approach are often shy about pointing practical lessons, but the apparent upshot is there can be no satisfactory mapping between pluralist society and a single state or constitution. That lesson is bleak indeed', Pettit (1993: 182).

19. Kant, for example, gets one passing reference in Pettit's 300 page *Republicanism* book, and that is in a list of thinkers associated with positive liberty, which is, to say the least, slightly bizarre.

20. It hardly needs to be pointed out that communitarianism is not a simple entity.

21. Pettit could have associated Arendt with a 'neo-Athenian' republican model. This would have allowed him to get round part of the Arendt issue.

22. ' "the political" (from *polis*) was classically the stage for the individual action among peers, Arendt defines "the social" . . . as the extension, in hierarchical order, of the patriarchal family (oikos) and the realm of collective housekeeping', Springborg (1989: 9–10).

23. As such it is not a work specifying or arguing for an ideal. Thus, in itself, it should not be taken as Arendt's key work in theory.

24. Her lasting legacy is 'her incomplete (and often inconsistent) attempt to combine this egalitarian idea of the human capacity for initiatory action with the older civic republican idea of freedom as self-government', Brunkhorst in Villa (ed.) (2000: 196).

25. Thus, the patriotic republic 'does not fly the field of particular loyalties on which nationalism flourishes, but works on it to make citizenship grow' (Viroli 1995: 14–15).

26. Habermas' own way out of this dilemma is 'constitutional patriotism'. Like Arendt, oddly, Habermas sees the United States as an example of a state in which the political culture 'sharpens an awareness of multiplicity', Habermas (1992: 6, 7, 11).

27. For Viroli, whereas Habermas stresses political and legal factors, communitarians, such as MacIntyre and Taylor, stress the need for particular communal moral values. For Viroli, MacIntyre's notion of patriotism is thus 'really nationalism'—hardly a startling supposition—and the crucial issue is that political liberty disappears in this nationalist setting, see MacIntyre (1984).

28. Despite the more secularized vision of republicanism, presented by late twentieth century exponents, others have drawn attention to its deep traditional Christian roots. This explains partly some of the moral uniformity presupposed within the republican perspective overall.

For Anthony Black, for example, the Christian perspective of republicanism—which dates to the medieval period—did not simply disappear with the Reformation, the scientific revolutions, and the other such harbingers of modernity. It rather penetrated deep into the psyche of all republican thought. Although there are many marked differences between modern republicanism and earlier forms, it is still clear to Black that Christianity (being a deeply malleable political doctrine), helped shape the substance of republican thought, see Black (1997, 1998).

29. These will be examined in Part Four.

PART FOUR

7

Segmented Foundations and Pluralism

Part Three focused on the issue of conventionalism. In my own usage, conventions are deeply-held bodies of shared social practices, rules, and norms. Conventionalism, therefore, entails the very general assertion that bodies of norms, rules, and practices form the linguistic, social, and practical context for action, thought, and speech. In this sense, conventions constitute forms of life. This is the manner in which proponents of conventionalism would like to see themselves.[1] In Chapters Five and Six, the conventional mediums examined were those of the historical-based state, the community, political liberalism, the nation, the Aristotelian ethos, and the civic republic. These were viewed as the rule-governed conventional mediums through which the gamut of concepts such as rights, state, freedoms, obligations, and the like were recognized, articulated, and legitimized. All these conventional mediums embodied forms of both immanent and comprehensive foundationalism, filling the vacuum left by the loss or decline of thin universal foundations.

Two points need drawing out from the above: first, each conventional form of life sees itself as the crucial foundational medium through which concepts, speech, and actions become politically and morally meaningful and legitimate. In other words, each conventional medium provides an answer to both thin universalist critics, and more recent postmodern critics of foundationalism. Once, for example, one knows that one cannot be a disconnected critic or citizen (taking a view from nowhere), and that all our concepts (and sense of what is valuable) derive from our nation, community, particular republic, or communal ethos—a somewhere— then we are no longer morally, politically, or ontologically adrift. We can anchor ourselves unashamedly, nationally, culturally, ethnically, or communally. We have an ethos. These conventionalist arguments therefore provide a response both to critics of foundationalism, as well as an alternative to the thin spectral universalism and egalitarianism of certain recent neo-Kantian and utilitarian theories. In other words, these conventionalist arguments 'shore up' foundations. However, a second critical, and more damaging issue, follows from this latter argument. A review of the different forms of conventionalism should alert us to the point that there are high levels of internal disagreement both within and between conventionalisms. In other words, there are serious conflicts over what actually constitutes the deep conventional substrate. In addition, one of the logical entailments of *all* conventionalist arguments (often criticized by thin universalists) is that if conventions are the source of legitimacy, meaning, thought and action, it follows, for the majority of conventionalists, that these concepts will differ or vary according to distinct nations, communities, and cultures. Thus, the internal logic of conventional argument—even apart from disagreements about the nature of fundamental conventions—generates a growing conceptual diversity of meanings. It is the logic of this latter position that I now wish to examine.

Consequently the aim of this chapter is to pursue the logic of the conventionalist argument several steps beyond Part Three. The basic argument made in this chapter is that conventionalism does not stop at the level of the nation, ethnos, or community. The point here is that every such traditional community, nation, or ethnos is constituted by multiple sub-communities, sub-ethnie, and sub-cultures. Thus, the argument about conventions and meanings is pushed several steps backwards. This point simply follows logically from the emphasis on conventionalism. In other words, the original conventionalisms, which shored up the argument for foundationalism by nationhood, ethos, or community, are *all* flawed foundations. To concentrate on the conventional medium is always to invite further subdivisions, since it is an empirical fact that most societies do actually contain multiple subgroup conventions. Therefore, the basic thesis of this chapter will be that in using conventionalism, as the *modus operandi* for establishing certain foundational goods, those very foundations become, in turn, further segmentalized. This segmentation process does overlap with earlier debates—however, in the present account, they are viewed through the themes of liberal pluralism, multiculturalism, and difference theory. Each of these contains further complex subdivisions.

One key assumption underpinning this chapter is that there is a resonance between the concepts of liberal pluralism, multiculturalism, and difference. Each of these terms has figured prominently in relatively discrete bodies of literature over the last few decades. Further, each concept also has a distinct history, however, they all deal with a similar range of problems. The root problem behind them all is the idea that virtually all societies contain internal diversity—in terms of values and cultures—and that such diversity has to be dealt with, or coped with, in some manner. In fact, virtually all societies have experienced some internal diversity from the early Greek polis to the present day (see Grillo 1998). Social, moral, political, and cultural diversities have not just been invented. However, the idea of such internal diversity took on a much higher intellectual profile during the last two decades of the twentieth century. What is relatively novel is the intensity of the intellectual focus in recent political theory.

Why has the recent interest in pluralism and diversity arisen? Briefly, the immediate background reasons for this lie in the last two decades of the twentieth century, namely, the end of the cold war, the opening up of markets and societies, considerable growth of international population migration, continuous refugee crises, acceleration of trade, vastly-expanded news media, communication, and capital flows across the globe. This complex process has created high levels of political and economic awareness, as well as deep anxiety and sense of social and personal instability and dislocation. One way to both explain and cope with this anxiety has been to re-emphasize older forms of local idiosyncratic attachment, thus the focus on national, cultural, ethnic, or religious affiliations. The fortuitous combination of globalizing forces, the accelerated mixing of populations, together with the renewed interest in ethnicity and culture, has underpinned an interest not only in nations and community, but also in forms of difference, pluralism, and multiculturalism. There is, by globalization, increasing travel, mass media, the Internet, education, and so forth, greater information about and more awareness of the local, indigenous, and different. Diversity has admittedly not been something that has been so evident in more homogenous societies, such as Japan or Iceland—although these societies are not immune from the same disturbing forces. Diversity is more closely linked to large heterogeneous societies with sizeable immigrant populations.

Paradoxically, another underlying reason for the focus on diversity has been the continuing popularity of the idea of the 'nation state'. This compound invokes a vision—in tandem with other concepts such as sovereignty, self-determination, and citizenship—of a consensual cohesive community. However, as already noted, each nation contains sub-ethnicities and sub-national groups. Diversity and difference are the norm. In the same way that nationalism in political theory configures the world as fragmented into distinct communal units, each with their own historical continuity, language, and destiny; so each sub-nationality can claim that each nationality needs to be further fragmented to satisfy the yearning for cultural autonomy, independence, and self-determination. Fragmentation is written into the very fabric of nationalist and communitarian argument. The central point is that nationalism emphasizes the fundamental moral, political, and ontological priority of self-determination for distinct national or ethnic groups. Yet, 'nation states' also contain an internal diversity of sub-national groups. By the same 'self-determination logic', which nationalism applies against other nations, so internal sub-national diversity also demands to be heard. This is the root to most secession claims. Thus, ironically, nationalism both undermines internal diversity through its emphasis on national consensus, and, at the same time, ironically, facilitates this very diversity by throwing its moral and political emphasis on the self-determining right of national groups. Therefore, one key reason for the growing segmentation of foundations has been the internal logic of communities and nations themselves. While nationalism flourishes, so will internal segmentation. Once again, though, foundations are not lost, but rather diversified more radically. The discussion briefly focuses on the concept of pluralism, then turns to a more detailed overview of the three significant forms in which diversity has been employed in the twentieth century—liberal pluralism, multiculturalism, and difference theory. Each of these further segments the whole debate over foundations.

A WORD ABOUT PLURALISM

One common way to approach pluralism is to limit it to liberalism. Multiculturalism and difference are then considered different categories. Although pluralism has had close associations with liberalism, in the two decades of the twentieth century, this is still historically fortuitous. It misses the point that pluralism is a much richer and more varied concept in twentieth-century thought. There is therefore *no* necessary conceptual link between pluralism and liberalism, any more than there are necessary conceptual ties between pluralism and relativism, or difference and multiculturalism. In my own usage, pluralism is taken as the key background, if multi-dimensional, concept. In this sense, there can be liberal pluralism, multicultural pluralism, and difference-based pluralism. Before moving to the central discussion it is important, however, to say a few initial words about this generic concept of pluralism.

One difficulty here is that each of the above concepts—pluralism, liberalism, multiculturalism, and difference—carry their own idiosyncratic baggage. In the case of pluralism, for example, when mentioned in political settings, it still conjures up visions of massed ranks of bright-eyed and bushy-tailed, usually North American, political scientists ready to do battle over interest groups. If one mentioned pluralism to most political theorists, before the 1980s, they would probably have looked slightly blank, or mentioned, tentatively, Isaiah Berlin, or more sophisticated North American pluralists, such as Robert Dahl, or, if they were longer in the tooth, English pluralists such as John Neville Figgis or G. D. H. Cole. To philosophers of ethics and epistemology, pluralism conjures up debates over moral or conceptual relativism, or again, if they were longer in the tooth, it would raise the spectre of philosophical pragmatism.

This present discussion distinguishes briefly philosophical, socio-cultural, political, and ethical dimensions of pluralism. In the final analysis, there are overlaps between all of these categories. The distinctions drawn here are simply pedagogical devices to focus discussion. Philosophical pluralism refers to long-standing philosophical traditions concerned with multiple worlds, realities, and truths. This implies that both our 'being in the world' and our 'knowledge of it' are irretrievably fragmented. This, implicitly or explicitly, underpins most serious pluralist arguments of any form. As mentioned, one earlier articulation of philosophical pluralism can be found in the twentieth century pragmatist school of William James, John Dewey, C. S. Peirce and later Richard Rorty and Hilary Putnam. In this scenario, pluralism was not equivalent to relativism. For pragmatists, the focus was on the application of ideas, deliberation being a concern with ways of acting. Ideas were plans of action. Pragmatists argued that knowledge was not fixed, but open to continuous critical change. This implied that there were no absolute or monistic solutions to human problems. All beliefs were open to experiential test and criticism. We could therefore be said not to live in a universe, but a multiverse. This was the thesis developed by William James in his book *The Pluralistic Universe* (1909). It was not a relativist standpoint. It rather postulated the idea of a pragmatic community of rational enquiry.

Socio-cultural pluralism implies that humans are subject to diverse social and cultural conditions. Plural societies are those that contain a number of ethnic, cultural, or sub-national groups. Socio-cultural pluralism can mean, either, the empirical recognition of diverse social practices, or, the normative claim that such separate cultures are in some way intrinsically or consequentially valuable. The empirical assertion of anthropological difference is not a normative claim. It also has no necessary logical bearing on the question as to whether different communities or cultures ought or ought not to abide by certain universal moral imperatives. Socio-cultural pluralism is therefore still potentially compatible with an objectivist ethics. A cognate area is ethical pluralism, which is concerned with a diversity of ethical norms, rules, and ends. It embodies the general thesis that there are many different (often incommensurable) goods required for human flourishing. Moral values are therefore both plural and internally complex. Nineteenth and twentieth-century variants of ethical pluralism have usually drawn upon anthropological and sociological evidence of moral diversity to bolster their perspectives. The majority of contemporary liberal theorists now tend to acknowledge some form of ethical pluralism as a basis for reflection. Yet, again, this does not imply any necessary relativism. Universal reason and a minimal universal ethical code can be maintained with ethical pluralism. The more radical relativist, opposed to this latter view, would have to show—for liberal thinkers at least—that reason is not universal. Logically, this is a very tricky thing to do, partly because the relativist critic has to assume the universality of reason in order to convince us that it is not universal.

Finally, political pluralism focuses on the institutional recognition, accommodation, or representation of social or cultural differences. There have been many forms of political pluralism in the twentieth century. Liberalism is but one of a list. The more obvious representatives of this perspective would be the English, French, and German political and juridical pluralist writers, for example, Figgis, Cole, Herbert Laski, Leon Duguit, and Otto von Gierke, further, guild socialists and the amazingly diverse forms of anarchism and anarcho-syndicalism (see Vincent 1987: ch. 6 or Vincent 1989). In terms of mid-twentieth century political pluralism, empirical political science dominated much debate. This latter idea moved away from normative argument for groups towards the empirical study of interest groups; although in writers such as Dahl it still retained a normative dimension. This conception of empirical political pluralism still figures in the specialist political science literature. From the 1980s another normatively orientated language of political pluralism began to develop, which became closely associated with contemporary liberalism.

LIBERAL PLURALISM

The majority of post-1980s liberal theorists, when speaking about diversity, usually feel more comfortable with the concept of pluralism. Further, liberal exponents think that liberalism has always addressed itself to something like pluralism. Finally, most contemporary liberals, nonetheless, set their faces against the idea of relativism.[2] They are adamant that liberal pluralism does not entail relativism. The fear or anxiety about relativism has, though, been part of the more general grammar of political theory, as a discipline, certainly since the 1950s. Liberal pluralists are therefore not alone in this repudiation of relativism. Anxiety about relativism stretches across a broad range of quite different theorists, including Leo Strauss, Jürgen Habermas, Theodore Adorno, Max Horkheimer, or Roger Scruton. Ironically, whereas conservative and certain socialist theorists blame relativism on liberalism, liberals frequently associate it with conservative historicism and multiculturalism.

Under the broad rubric of post-1980s liberal pluralism, a number of subtle variants have arisen, which essentially try to examine liberalism as accommodating both pluralism and a core of immanent universal (if often very thin) values. There are though two dimensions to the liberal perception of diversity. First, liberalism usually invokes pluralism, as a value, by its concept of the individual. The human 'individual' is accorded a fundamental moral or ontological status. This is also the groundwork for liberal interest in both substantive and formal equality. Each individual is considered wholly unique. In many ways, this is a very *positive* perspective, which celebrates the conditions for individual autonomy. Individuals ought to have the basic conditions and opportunities to be able to construct their own plans of life. One upshot of this is a society constituted by a diversity of individual goals and plans of life. This point concerning individuality is worth underscoring, since much of the more recent debate about pluralism, has ironically often been focused on groups or cultures, rather than individuals.

The second dimension of the liberal pluralism has been the awareness of the need for some form of constitutional arrangement to cope with the *negative* dimensions of plurality. Liberal conceptions of pluralism do not always contain a celebration of individuality. Much liberal thought has been given, conversely, to a pragmatic or prudential response to the potential conflictual pressures of diversity. This is the idea of liberalism, which arose, for many liberal commentators, unwittingly, from the constitutional settlements arising out of protracted vicious religious civil wars during the sixteenth and seventeenth centuries. In other words, liberal pluralism is a practical response to dealing with the negative side of diversity. Its main suggestion is that if individuals (and groups) wish to live in peace, they will have to agree upon certain general conditions (or publicly reasonable grounds), whereby it becomes possible to live together. This involves putting their religious, cultural, or moral views aside in the public sphere.

In the present account, the more general liberal responses to pluralism are reviewed. The first three will be examined in the present section, the fourth opens up another distinct sphere of pluralism and is considered in the next section. The initial three responses focus on individuals as the key 'particles of difference'. They also take a very wary and critical view of the role of groups and cultures in political argument.

The first conception of liberal pluralism is underpinned by a forceful rendition of the moral superiority and universality of reasoned liberal arguments. Liberalism is seen as neutral between competing goods. Oddly, though, it is only in comparatively recent mid to late twentieth-century literature on liberalism that the term 'neutrality' has come to the fore. The nub of the argument is that liberal reason is regarded as something universal and applicable to all human beings regardless of state, culture, or ethnicity. Because reason is universal and impartial it therefore embodies a basic neutrality over the good. This might be called the *neutral universalist* position. Reason is essentially concerned with abstract conclusions drawn from premises that everyone accepts. One key example of this process of argument (which has already been examined) is Rawls' earlier book *A Theory of Justice* (1971). The discussion focused on intellectual devices such as the 'veil of ignorance', which are essentially ways to try to ensure fairness and neutrality. There is also no doubt here about the universal role of reason and justice. Reason has *no* history or cultural linkage.[3] The universality of reason is insisted upon, to a greater or lesser degree, by thinkers as diverse as Martin Hollis, Steven Lukes, Onora O'Neill, Alan Gewirth, or Jürgen Habermas. The basic point is that unless we presume a transconventional or universal conception of reason, there could be no human understanding. Reason remains the constant neutral universal, which mediates between the various claims made by individuals. The idea of neutrality ties in closely with individualism. Where there are a diversity of competing rich moral or cultural goods of individuals, then the liberal state should remain neutral. Equal concern, consideration, and respect should broadly be shown to all individuals, as long as they are not harming others. Liberalism, in this sense, also claims to be anti-perfectionist. There is no way of rationally assessing different preferential ways of life.[4]

There is one slight exception—in appearance only—to the above neutralist argument, in contemporary liberal theory. On the surface it trades upon recent debates about groups and cultures, however, it is still very much rooted in an older conception of liberalism. This is the work of Chandran Kukathas, which adopts what might be termed a 'positive indifference' model, which begins and ends with individual rights and neutral indifference. In this scenario, classical liberalism does not actually have to change its spots in dealing with a plurality of groups or cultures. Groups and cultures are considered, methodologically, as just aggregations of individuals. Kukathas's tone is atomistically individualist, formally egalitarian, and universalist. The rights envisaged are non-discriminatory, universal, and negative, implying correlative duties of forbearance. Despite the talk of cultures, individuals are really ontologically primary. Groups *per se* are not special, but liberal institutions should, as far as possible, be neutral and uphold the rights of individual agents to participate actively in groups, even illiberal groups. No cultural group should therefore be singled out for specific cultural rights or privileges. This is not because cultures are valueless, but rather that the value that they may have is just immaterial to the liberal public sphere. In fact, Kukathas emphasizes the consequential dangers of any public recognition of cultures. The public realm rather upholds the general conditions of peace and order (rule of law), where cultures are neither supported nor penalized, but rather allowed to exist by negative liberty. Kukathas thus remarks 'liberalism puts concern for minorities at the forefront. Its very emphasis on *individual* rights or *individual* liberty bespeaks not hostility to the interests of communities but wariness of the power of the majority over the minorities' (see Kukathas in Kymlicka (ed.) 1995: 230). Thus, groups have no distinctive rights (or real existence) in themselves and have no claim on the support of society, but they have the negative freedom to exist. Behind the fashionable hype of a 1990s debate with Kymlicka, Kukathas offers nothing new, just a warmed up Hayekian classical liberalism with a cultural top-dressing.[5] Kukathas's 'indifference perspective' is predictably what one would expect from an unreconstructed Hayekian liberal. Hayek would no doubt have approved, although he would probably have been uneasy about giving groups and cultures so much intellectual space in the first place.[6]

The second broad position of liberal pluralism still insists upon the universal applicability of liberal reason and liberal goods. However, unlike the neutralist position, it insists upon the open and unashamed promotion of liberal goods and liberal reason. Thus, William Galston, for example, claiming to be a committed universalist liberal, goes out of his way to deny the neutrality claim, asserting that liberals should rather, unashamedly, affirm a liberal universalist perfectionism (see Galston 1991). Galston bewails (what he considers) Rawls' abandonment of comprehensive metaphysical resources and accuses him of still being caught in a dangerously one-sided view of the liberal tradition. Adopting the thick and thin metaphor, favoured in contemporary political theory, if Rawls thickened out slightly with his later 'political liberalism', then Galston becomes happily obese (although with a very different perspective to political liberalism). The root of Galston's substantive good(s) is what he disarmingly calls, 'a native element of American culture' (see Galston 1991: 8, 17).[7] Liberalism miraculously embodies these 'native' components. Consequently, Galston repudiates the idea of neutrality for the sake of a thickened up, perfectionist, ethical liberalism, asserted forcefully through the educational curriculum and state action. This might therefore be entitled a *universal perfectionist* liberalism. In other words, liberal goods are seen to be morally preferable. Galston in fact identifies various generic elements, which are seen as definitely constitutive of the good life of all human beings. In many ways, this conception of liberalism is also characteristic of some earlier expressions of nineteenth century liberalism in, for example, J. S. Mill or T. H. Green. The room for pluralism in this framework is curtailed, except that a number of groups and individuals will be allowed to flourish, *as long as* they do not undermine general liberal purposes. Liberalism therefore circumscribes diversity through perfectionism. But, for Galston, liberals should not be worried about this, since its own aims are clearly the most worthwhile and universal.

The third liberal perspective emphasizes rights, justice, and neutrality, again, but in a more hesitant negative format. In the mind of its proponents, the origins of this argument go back to the complex sixteenth and seventeenth century constitutional arguments on how to deal with religious civil war. The later John Rawls—of political liberalism—adopts a variant of this reading (as discussed in Part Three). Rawls' main problem, therefore, is not freedom, *per se*, but the containment and management of pluralism. Rawls' reasonable pluralism is one where citizens, accepting the basic structures of a liberal democratic constitutional state, nonetheless diverge on substantive questions of the good. Rawls thinks this divergence inevitable but also deeply worrying. Reason does not unify in any substantive way. Rawls' later vision of liberalism (qua diverse cultures) is more minimalist and constrained, certainly in comparison to Brian Barry's position. Political liberalism takes the pluralism of groups for granted, but regarded as unavoidable problems. The task of political liberalism is then to work out a conception of justice for a constitutional democratic regime embodying, if possible, a reasonable pluralism. The neutrality of public reason is maintained. However, Rawls *neither* seeks a perfectionist foundation, *nor* any overt universalist claims. Universality is sidelined, and in its place is a tacit admittal of a conventionalist particularist framework. For Rawls the 'aim of political liberalism is to uncover the conditions of the possibility of a reasonable public basis of justification on fundamental political questions' (Rawls 1993: xix). The whole liberal enterprise, *vis-à-vis* pluralism, can thus be seen as a form of *particularist neutrality*. The problematic element of pluralism is largely groups (taken in a broad sense), not individuals. However, one suspects that no political liberals would accept the methodological collectivism of certain group-based arguments. In this sense, although the individual fades in political liberalism, the 'group concept' never attains any clear shape either.

Another variation on the 'particularist neutrality' thesis is more self-consciously concerned with the immediate personal and public tragedy which faces us with cultural diversity. This is the counter-Enlightenment liberalism of Isaiah Berlin, which, consciously or not, contrasts itself to the more effusive confidence of Enlightenment liberalism. As Berlin stated, 'if, as I believe, the ends of men are many, and not all of them are in principles compatible with each other, then the possibility of conflict— and of tragedy—can never wholly be eliminated from human life, either personal or social' (Berlin 1997, 239). Society is punctuated by numerous opposing values and cultures, which cannot be amicably combined in an individual life or society. There is thus no uniquely right solution. As Berlin put it, 'forms of life differ. Ends, moral principles, are many' (Berlin quoted in Ignatieff 1998: 285). Thinkers such as Stuart Hampshire and Bernard Williams link up with this perspective, arguing that there are, in effect, no single truths in morality. No ultimate commensurability is ever possible. This conception of liberal value pluralism thus emphasizes the tragic incompatibility and contingency of values.

Berlin is though a more difficult figure to place. He was undoubtedly sympathetic to the legal and political ideas underpinning the first two accounts of liberal pluralism. In fact, many have wanted to place him quite squarely in this position. His basic views appear more in tune with an orthodox liberal individualism. In this sense, the pluralism referred to in Berlin's writings is a plurality of individuals. However, Berlin's intrinsic difficulty here is his deep underlying admiration for the likes of Gottfried Herder, and the more general 'culturalist', counter-Enlightenment, group-based standpoint in politics. This makes him a more sympathetic, if indecisive, observer of cultural pluralism, whilst at the same time being painfully aware of the tragic problems this gives rise to in practice. In consequence of this latter view, some have even categorized Berlin as a 'cultural difference' theorist manqué.

MULTICULTURAL PLURALISM

The fourth perspective on liberal pluralism moves the argument into a different sphere.[8] Although there are fairly innocuous formulations of multiculturalism within the first three formulations of liberal pluralism, the stronger statements on multiculturalism begin with the fourth dimension. One definite intellectual shift to be found in multicultural pluralism, as distinct from the bulk of earlier liberal pluralism, is that the prefix 'multi' conventionally applies largely to groups, not individuals. Because of the emphasis on groups, as opposed to individuals, multicultural pluralism often finds itself in direct conflict with certain liberal pluralists. In broad overview, there-fore, multicultural pluralism views society as composed of groups, each constituted by their own culture. Culture refers very loosely to the beliefs, symbols, and values of the group. However, what a group is and whether it qualifies for a culture, and, in addition, what a culture is, remain as open and unresolved questions.

Multiculturalism, *per se*, is seen as a relatively novel phenomenon by most com-mentators, although it has obvious antecedents in older political organizations, such as empires.[9] Yet, the serious political theory focus on multiculturalism developed comparatively recently, initially in Australia, Canada, and New Zealand from the 1970s, and then migrated to the United States and European politics in the sub-sequent two decades.[10] In each case, the idea of multiculturalism usually figures as a more accidental response to circumstances of, for example, increasing immigration or cultural assertiveness. In most states it is still a seriously contested idea in the public policy forum.

Before discussing liberal multiculturalism, it is important to note that there are dif-ferent forms of multiculturalism. A common distinction is between thinner and more robust forms (Miller 1995: 133; Shachar 2000: 67–8, Baumeister 2000; Parekh 2001; Shachar 2002). The thinner form is essentially developed in liberal multiculturalism. The significant change to more traditional liberal pluralist argument is that the vital 'particle of difference' becomes the group (or the individual considered primarily in relation to the group). For example, Shachar considers Kymlicka as an exponent of this thinner liberal multiculturalism.[11] The present discussion considers two arguments: liberal multicultural pluralism and communitarian multicultural pluralism. The real difference between these latter two can be gauged in terms of just how seriously they take the ontology of groups.

Liberal multicultural pluralism can be regarded as the fourth variant on liberal pluralism. It tries to forge a middle path between the liberal individualism (of the earlier formulations of liberal pluralism) and a form of value collectivism (focused on ontology cultural groups). It is therefore still premised on the moral importance of the individual, but, it also suggests that individuals can only realize themselves and exercise their autonomy fully in the context of groups. Thus, the collective goods of cultures become crucial for individuals. It follows that a theory of differentiated groups rights—with the ontological status of groups being bracketed—is required for a genuine liberal individualism. Thus, the positive sense of individuality and human autonomy is retained, but this is viewed through the lens of diverse groups and cultures. The diversity of groups, in this sense, is viewed in a very much more emphatic light. The argument is neither advocating a neutral constitutional settlement, non-neutral perfectionism, nor a fearful recognition of groups. It is rather a celebration of cultural primary goods as valuable *for* individual autonomy.[12]

This fourth liberal response (liberal multicultural pluralism) moves the argument, by degrees, into a slightly different ontological setting. In summary, the first liberal pluralists' setting emphasizes tolerance, neutrality, and non-discriminatory universal individual rights; the second abandons neutrality in favour of a liberal perfection-ism, which is still of universal significance; the third view emphasizes, less positively and more fearfully (or tragically in Berlin's case), a political liberalism which is still premised on rights and justice, which nonetheless recognizes their particularity and local character. However, the fourth category *embraces* groups and cultures. It openly identifies the pluralism to be dealt with as group and culture-based, rather than premised on distinct individuals. The point here would be that although the groups and cultures are linked conceptually to individuals, nonetheless, the individuals can only be individuals in the context of groups and cultures, thus the ontology subtly shifts from the other conceptions of liberal pluralism.

Kymlicka's own commitment to liberal multiculturalism—which might also be called cultural liberalism—is focused on the theme of collective cultural goods. In this argument, culture, for Kymlicka, implies national or ethnic attachments. Liberal multiculturalism is critical of the previous forms of liberal pluralism for becoming overly concerned about an abstracted individualism and individual rights claims. The important point for Kymlicka is to try to link individual rights and autonomy— prized within liberal pluralism—with the right-based claims of cultures. Cultural groups and individual rights are not necessarily therefore at odds. The baseline for the whole argument is that individual agency is established through cultural heritage. Culture is the normative precondition for the exercise of effective individual choice. Thus, 'the primary good being recognized is the cultural community as a context of choice' (Kymlicka 1991: 165 and 172). In short, individual agency involves culture. The flourishing of culture is not just about protecting minorities under a rule of law, or allowing individuals the right to choose a private cultural form, but is rather focused on the actual core beliefs of a liberal society. Liberal societies should therefore safeguard minorities, not simply because they form a legitimate community, but rather because cultures are the prerequisite for liberal autonomy. Cultures provide us with our conceptual maps to navigate the social and political world.

However, one should not mistake the above argument for undiluted communitarianism. Kymlicka considers communitarian theory as far too prepared to absorb the individual. There is a subtle but important ontological difference here to communitarianism. He is also insistent that all human agents can critically abstract themselves from their cultures or communities. This is crucial to his whole case. We can therefore partly disencumber ourselves. In other words, there is a universal core lurking within a culturally particular identity. Liberal societies have a duty to support minority cultures, because they provide a context for the universal themes of choice. Liberal multiculturalism is consequently viewed as is the key exemplar for any contemporary, open, and plural societies. This does not mean we abandon rights, however, we should have a more flexible differentiated response to them. There is though still a perfectionist and universalist element to this argument, although in Kymlicka's case it is concentrated and realized within particular cultural groups.

A similar pattern of argument can be found in Joseph Raz's writings. The core perfectionist value of western liberalism, for Raz, is autonomy, and any modern liberal polity should uphold it (Raz 1986: 369). Liberalism is thus seen as the political form necessary to nourish a particular conception of well-being. However, autonomy implies (as in Kymlicka) cultural contexts. Cultural membership provides agents with meaningful choices and determines the boundaries of the imaginable. Culture, trains and channels human desires and choices (see Raz 1986: 375 *ff*.). Autonomy is therefore empty without culture. Membership of a culture is considered crucial for a person's autonomy, well-being and self-respect—with the proviso again that there is a right of exit. This also means that the flourishing and prosperity of the culture is important for the well-being of its members. It is important that such identity is respected and not subject to ridicule or discrimination. As both Raz and Margalit argue, people's 'membership of encompassing groups is an important aspect of their personality', and, 'expression of membership' includes 'manifestation of membership in the open, public life of the community' (Margalit and Raz in Kymlicka (ed.) 1995: 90). Respecting autonomy entails respecting a cultural membership in political terms. For Raz, it is inevitable that within any society there will be differing cultural forms, entailing value pluralism, thus, a form of 'multiculturalism' is considered inevitable in most developed Western societies.[13] The perfectionist ideal is autonomy, however, autonomy entails unimpeded membership of cultures. If autonomy entails cultural membership and this, in turn, entails diversity, then, the liberal state or public realm ought to uphold and support positively cultural communities.

A second version of multicultural pluralism arises under the rubric of communitarianism—although it is a peculiar and unresolved formulation. Communitarianism (as discussed in Part Three) is focused on the survival and flourishing of communal cultures. In this context, communities require protection, in some shape, because they provide the basis for human identity. However, identity is not something we invent as individuals. We cannot simply step out of that identity at will. Identity is absorbed from within a culture. There is an ontological difference here to Kymlicka's account—something that contemporary republicans are keen to point out. Individuals are not so likely to try to step outside their community. This does not imply though that all cultures are equally worthy.[14] However, there is still a tacit logic within the communitarian argument, which is conditioned to endorse any collective identity. Individual rights and individual identity become far less significant. Further, most communitarians have also tended to focus on an inclusive consensual culture for the 'whole' of society. As a consequence of the implicit logic of their position—despite the focus on a consensual community—it is almost inevitable that communitarians will stray into multicultural territory. The logic of the identitarian arguments leads them inexorably to a recognition of plurality *within* a community.

This does generate an inherent tension within communitarian theory. In this context, Charles Taylor has articulated a more general discomfiture with terms such as communitarianism and nationalism (Taylor in Tully (ed.) 1994: 206). This is, partly, because he is so closely linked with recent debates about multiculturalism and deep diversity in Canada. In this sense, the idea of a national unity in Canada is viewed as a somewhat crass misnomer. Further, Taylor sees communitarian and nationalist ideas as profoundly monocultural in temper.[15] Communitarianism, therefore, as suggested, contains a tacit logic which leads to potentially-contradictory outcomes. Overtly, it appears committed to the ideal of a unified consensual community of values. However, unwittingly, because of its attachment to identitarian criteria, it also responds to the expressed needs of diverse or plural cultural groups to develop their own moral, political, or even legal frameworks. In this sense, communitarianism is trapped in a contradiction. Although logically predisposed to be amenable to diverse cultures, the occurrence of polyethnicity and multiculturalism also engenders some apprehension amongst communitarians.[16]

DIFFERENCE PLURALISM

This is a convenient point to move the discussion to the final and most recent form of pluralism, the difference theory. In certain respects, if liberal multiculturalism embodies a thinner form of multiculturalism, then difference theory incorporates a more robust and occasionally illiberal form of multiculturalism. The genealogy of the term difference embodies forms of postmodernism, post-positivism, post-Marxism and feminism, amongst other elements. One should not necessarily expect much coherence here. In addition, some understand difference as just an instrument of investigation, others see it as a specific political doctrine (see Benhabib, introduction to Benhabib (ed.) 1996: 12; Vincent 2003).

In reviewing this area, various species of difference are drawn distinct, that is, ethnographic, postcolonial, gendered, postmodern, agonistic, and total difference. The one proviso to add here is that, once again, not only have some communitarians, such as Walzer, been associated with difference, but also, more surprisingly, certain liberals. Thus, Berlin and Kymlicka have been categorized as 'difference theorists'. Walzer has indeed categorized his own theory in this manner. Difference has even been used as a basic synonym for 'liberal pluralism' (see Baumeister 2000). Usually the argument maintains, first, that more radical difference theorists misunderstand the deep internal complexity and resilience of liberalism and have neither taken on board the counter-enlightenment, nor the community-sensitive liberal variants, which are much more attuned to real difference. Second, in a broader vein, liberalism has been, historically, well able to cope with all forms of difference. In fact, liberalism, as a political doctrine, was founded on the problem of difference.

The present discussion neither seeks to defend nor prosecute so promiscuous a concept as 'difference', but rather to trace its genealogy. The broadest assumption to make about it is that it lays an inordinate stress upon uniqueness and incommensurability. However, there are some mistaken assumptions concerning difference theory to note immediately: first, that difference is solely associated with either liberal pluralism or multiculturalism, and second, that it has intimate associations with postmodern theory. It is undoubtedly true that a version of difference theory does underpin radical multicultural arguments, but *only* one version. It has also been used to describe liberal pluralism. However, difference, in itself, does not necessarily imply either multiculturalism or liberal pluralism. Second, although postmodern theory does quite definitely cultivate a difference perspective, nonetheless, this alone does not suffice to explain difference. The more complete difference perspective is altogether more nuanced, messy, and confused. In fact, it is a somewhat nightmarish mixture of normative, critical, and empirical claims.

First, during the twentieth century, a number of sociological and anthropological theories have, wittingly or not, articulated the theme of social and cultural difference. Despite the fact that this was part of the staple diet of such disciplines, by the end of the 1970s and 1980s, the acknowledgement of difference had mutated into a much more reflexive debate. Two points arose here in this debate: first, the empirical data of, particularly, cultural anthropology did give rise to a sense of a broad diversity of cultural meanings. This, in turn, appeared to generate a strong sense of social and cognitive pluralism, or relativism for some. All the agitated debates concerning rationality and relativism, during the 1970s, arose largely from reflections on the extensive amounts of empirical data from anthropology and ethnography. The standard debates circled around the issue of whether a universal understanding of rationality could be retained in tandem with the acknowledgement of cultural difference (e.g. see, Lukes and Hollis (eds.) 1982; Hollis in Joppke and Lukes (eds.) 1999). However, during the 1980s, a second more invasive question arose, namely, is social science (and anthropology in particular) itself the expression of a particular culture? Thus, the anthropologist may well be able to observe other cultures, or 'primitive' societies, and study them with the objective analytical tools of social science. However, what happens when the anthropological investigator, and the disciplinary structure of social science, are themselves viewed as particular cultural practices? Anthropology, ethnography, and sociology are, in this perspective, as much in need of serious investigation and explanation as any other social practices. The central question is therefore: are the social sciences universal and objective modes of rational discourse, or, alternatively, are they just surreptitious imposed forms of Western cultural parochialism? In this context, the purported universalism of the social sciences teeters on the edge of an idiosyncratic localism, which, in turn, raises the spectre of difference.

In summary, the general point was that classical anthropology (for its difference-based critics), reinforced the idea of the inferiority and subjugation of the 'studied groups'—the colonized or postcolonial peoples. The growth of the discipline itself, during the late nineteenth and early twentieth century, corresponded with the expansion of European states and empires. There were also strong implications in such early anthropology of national and racial difference, and in many cases, superiority. From the mid-twentieth century this latter aspect diminished. However, the contrast between the 'social scientific researcher' and the 'studied society' retained some aspects of this subtle hierarchical difference. By the last few decades of the twentieth century, anthropologists had become much more aware of the delicacy of these questions. The critical movement away from the hierarchical mentality was precipitated by poststructural theory, which stressed the fabricated character of academic discourse.[17] Postcolonial thought, in the language of postmodernism, is therefore seen as articulating forms of marginalized knowledge. Narratives, such as liberal universalism, are seen to try to suppress local cultural difference. In consequence, a more reflexive postpositivist anthropology grew in response to these criticisms (e.g. see, Clifford and Marcus (eds.) 1986; Marcus and Fischer 1986; Clifford 1988; Geertz

1988). Difference, in this context, not only was enshrined in the external subject of anthropological investigation, but also, reflexively, within the internal structure of the discipline itself.

The discussion of anthropology may appear, *prima facie*, unrelated to political theory. However, this anthropological debate impacted strongly on *all* forms of cultural study during the last few decades of the twentieth century. In fact, it is largely the anthropological use of the term 'culture', which underpins much of the recent debates about multiculturalism, group rights, and cultural nationalism in contemporary political theory. Admittedly, there are some liberal political theorists who would not consider any of these latter conceptions as genuine political theory, however, this kind of dogmatic judgement could arise from literally every dimension of contemporary theory and will thus be ignored as fatuous.

The second broad dimension of difference argument is postcolonial theory, which has been defined as a 'theoretical resistance to the mystifying amnesia of the colonial aftermath . . . a disciplinary project devoted to the academic task of revisiting, remembering and, crucially, interrogating the colonial past' (Gandhi 1998: 4). The key issue here is that the bulk of the nineteenth and twentieth-century history of empires, colonies and the like, has been largely composed from within the imperial and colonial university centres. Such history will—according to its critics—inevitably, if surreptitiously, represent the dominant perceptions of the colonial regimes. Those who write the history are the dominant participants; the silent subjects (the other) they write about are the postcolonial peoples. Postcolonial theory is thus concerned with the idea that formal history (or anthropology) embodies power. This thesis is embedded, for example, in Edward Said's well-known discussion of 'orientalism'—or more precisely the discursive Western construction of the orient. Colonialism represents not just a political, economic or military invasion, but also a textual onslaught. The general impetus of postcolonial theory is thus a critique of this literary onslaught. Although the actual overt military and political dominance has largely dissipated in the process of decolonization, nonetheless, a much more indirect form of power is exercised through academic discourses. Even apparently fair-minded discourses, such as European or North American liberalism, are tarred with the same brush. Thus, in the words of one critic, postcolonial theory wishes to 'undo the Eurocentrism produced by the institution of the West's trajectory, its appropriation of the other as History' (Prakash in Haynes and Prakash (eds.) 1992: 8). Liberalism, and consequently liberal pluralism, are often taken as exemplars of this subtle colonial discourse, masquerading as universal theory. More recently the term 'postcolonial liberalism' has been coined to try to cope with and assess this new development (see Ivison in Vincent (ed.) 1997c; Ivison 2002).

There are though three areas that can be identified under the broad rubric of postcolonial theory. One key area, from which postcolonial argument initially developed, is subaltern studies.[18] The term 'subaltern' has both a military and a Marxist origin. It implies one in a lower rank or subjugated position. The Italian Marxist Antonio Gramsci, for example, used the term within his writings. In postcolonial theory, this sense of the subjugated groups can be taken very broadly to include ethnicity, culture, gender, or class. Subaltern studies therefore involves the investigation of the perceptions and experience of these subjugated groups. It also attempts to recapture the experiences of those who had been silenced by colonial rule. As indicated, Western colonial history is seen to distort or mystify what actually took place under colonial rule (Gandhi 1998: vii). The second aspect on postcolonial writing is (as mentioned) Edward Said's work, particularly his work *Orientalism* (Said 1978). The latter book focuses, like subaltern studies, on colonial ideology, which is seen to embody power (in the largely Foucaultian sense), particularly in writing about the orient. The discursively constructed Orient implies, for Said, power over and within knowledge. This fabricated 'Orient' configures the attitudes and perceptions of particularly the subjugated peoples. Said uses the writings of both Gramsci and Foucault here.[19] Foucault is crucial to the view of the power of orientalism as an impersonal force underpinning knowledge. Gramsci is used to root the arguments in a more materialist and emancipatory analysis.

The third postcolonial argument concerns the comparatively recent Asian values debates.[20] The core of the, by now familiar, argument is that all forms of universalism (e.g. human rights discourse) are, once again, seen as part of a localized parochial Western narrative. As one recent exponent argues, 'Because cultural context is integral to the formulation and implementation of all state polices, including those that have clear human rights consequences, [thus] detailed and credible knowledge of local cultures is essential for the effective promotion and protection of human rights in any society' (Abdullah A. An-Na'im in Bauer and Bell (eds.) 1999: 147). Liberal universalism, and the like, are seen therefore as intrinsically expressions of Western cultures. Most liberal commentators however fail to see this basic point and blithely assume the rational superiority of their own perspective. As Charles Taylor comments, on this latter standpoint, 'An obstacle in the path to . . . mutual understanding comes from the inability of many Westerners to see their culture as one amongst many' (see Taylor in Bauer and Bell (eds.) 1999: 143). For such Asian values proponents, it is important that Western commentators should be aware that Asian (and other societies) have not gone through the same historical trajectory as the West.[21] There may well be therefore very different sets of values concerning morality, legality, religion, and politics, which we neglect at our peril.[22]

There is a relatively clear pattern of argument in all the above views. Anthropology, ethnography, postcolonial theory (as a broad category), all privilege alterity, difference, and the local indigenous narrative over the universal or global. They see their task to 'provincialize' Europe and North America. Difference, in this context, embodies both a critical challenge to universalism (of all types)—the recurrent criticism being that such universalism is a shield for another localized national narrative— and a more suppressed claim concerning emancipation. The latter involves a more obscure point—that recognized and respected difference equates with emancipation. However, this leaves open the following question: if the basic acknowledgement of difference actually constitutes some kind of advance or liberation, what precisely does this mean? What meaning should we attribute to liberty here? If it is a localized meaning it is irrelevant (since it would have no universal sense), yet if it is universal it undermines the substance of the difference argument. This point, although important for difference theorists, remains undertheorized and inchoate.

One further point to underscore here is that the difference theory (as outlined above) does *not* necessarily equate with multiculturalism. It certainly prioritizes and valorizes difference, but not necessarily *within* any regimes or communities. This is the point made earlier in the discussion—that 'difference' does not necessarily entail internal multicultural difference. In fact, it might well be antagonistic to this form of segmentation, in the sense that it might well be antagonistic to even further fragmentation within a locality or culture. In this sense, difference theory (qua post-colonialism) might well, in the final analysis, have far more in common with some formulations of cultural nationalism. An account of difference, within the postcolonial mode, is still crucial to the argument, but, it usually refers to external difference of cultures, for example, oriental versus occidental, subaltern versus hegemonic, or Asian Confucianism set against Western liberalism.

The third major category of difference theory is gender based. This is a highly self-conscious and polemical expression of difference, although its internal theoretical articulation has been very complex (see Vincent 1995: ch. 7; Squires 1999). The first of these polemical arguments arose from feminist interest in difference during the 1960s and 1970s. However, this was quite definitely not the same notion of difference as that articulated in the 1990s. It should also be noted that many liberal and socialist feminist arguments have always been deeply impatient with difference-based claims, partly because they (particularly liberal feminists) have seen equality and justice as crucial universal values to foster and promote. The views of liberal feminists, such as Susan Moller Okin discussed in Chapter Four, are clearly deeply antagonistic to the claim that justice and equality are intrinsically gendered. Difference, for Okin or Nussbaum, is *not* a valid ground for feminist argument (see Okin 1989; Nussbaum and Glover (eds.) 1995). To defend difference, for Nussbaum for example, is tantamount to defending oppressive practices *against* women in different cultures (see also Cohen, Howard, and Nussbaum (eds.) 1999). There may be biological, social, or sexual differences between men and women, but these are morally and politically irrelevant. The really important issue is about attacking the gendered distortion of equal treatment, social justice, and fairness. Thus, for liberal feminists, apart from irrelevant biological differences, the only differences worth tackling are negative 'social' and 'artificial' ones. It is in this context that Okin has argued for the extension of Rawlsian arguments, about justice and impartiality, into the family (Okin 1989). The artificial gender-based readings of equality and justice are intrinsically irrational. They are imposed by patriarchy and need to be forcefully addressed and ultimately eradicated from the language of rationality, equality, and justice. Similarly, for Marxist and socialist feminists, difference is something which is related to certain types of highly contingent economic arrangements (capitalism and liberal free markets) and should be systematically overcome with economic and political reform.

Yet outside the liberal and socialist feminists' concerns, a large number of feminists have become very exercised by the concept of difference. The earlier grounds for difference are though quite diverse and the history of its development since the 1960s has been conceptually tangled. The roots of early 1970s feminist arguments on difference were primarily social, biological, and psychological. The original critical interests in difference go back to theorists, such as Kate Millet, who saw the masculine/feminine distinction as part of a deep structure of patriarchal psychological exploitation. The differences were viewed, initially, as social or psychological artefacts, constructed within patriarchy, to keep women oppressively within certain roles. This idea was also developed by certain radical feminist writers. The emphasis was then thrown onto the ideal of androgyny. The central argument for androgyny effectively aimed to destroy any political use for difference.

The androgyny thesis was then, in turn, subject to vigorous criticism. It was seen to obscure the whole process of the struggle against patriarchy.[23] Difference therefore reappeared positively, and with particular vehemence, in what is often referred to as the second phase or wave of radical feminism. Initially, in certain radical feminist writers, difference encompassed notions of female supremicism, the value of sisterhood, political lesbianism, and separatism from men. Political lesbianism denoted 'one who has withdrawn herself from the conventional definitions of femininity' (Eisenstein 1984: 51). It was contended that women naturally had a very different attitude to their bodies, nature, and human relationships. Motherhood was also seen in positive light by certain writers, although not all shared the perspective of the radicals (see Dinnerstein 1976; Ruddick 1980; Elshtain 1981). The capacity to physically bear children gave women highly positive life-affirming attitudes, whereas the male was more easily caught up in negative life-denying aggression, competitiveness, ambition, and social destructiveness. Andrea Dworkin, from a quite definitely radical perspective, consequently characterized the male attitude to life as summed up in rape and pornography (see Dworkin 1974, 1987). This particular theme was also taken up again by some eco-feminists who linked environmental crises with destructive patriarchal values.

In summary, this initial phase of difference theory often focused on what is loosely termed 'woman centred analysis', emphasizing the biological and psychological difference between men and women. Thus, a frequent accusation made by radicals (and 'maternal thinking' feminists) against socialist and liberal feminist theories is that they are 'difference blind'. The primary aspect of this critical process is an emphasis on the point that difference is a crucial mode of feminist emancipation. This form of argument is also linked to some feminist writers' assertions that there may be such a thing as totally separate forms of feminine logic, epistemology, ontology, philosophy, or even basic natural science. Thus, for example, it is possible to consider the whole process of institutional, rational, and scientific discourse as inherently masculinist. Feminist difference-based argument also took on a highly emblematic existence in the psychologically- and morally-orientated work of Carol Gilligan, particularly in her book *In a Different Voice* (1982), which basically argued that men and women respond psychologically in very different ways in the field of ethics. Men function in terms of a colder and more impersonal ethic of justice-based rules and women function through an ethic of care and nurturance. The ethic of care, set against the ethic of justice, marked out a great deal of feminist discussion in the closing two decades of the twentieth century.[24] In this sense, it can be understood as another, if subtly distinct, manifestation of the broader debate between universalist and conventionalist arguments in political theory.

The third phase of feminist difference had no biological or psychological trappings. Its roots were in postmodern theory. This perspective developed initially from French feminists, such as Julia Kristeva, Hélène Cixous, and Luce Irigaray—although it has much broader following in North America and Britain.[25] They were suspicious of notions of formal equality, and even of the title feminism. Although influenced by deconstructive and genealogical methods and suspicious of the biological conceptions of difference, they nonetheless repudiated the masculine 'phallocentric' domination of language and called for a unique recoding of language away from masculinity—an *écriture feminine*. Language was thus seen as a primary mode of male domination. In this argument, difference settled upon the theme of language and the manner in which identity is constructed. Postmodern theory, in general terms, has been standardly critical of theories of identity and language. The beginnings of this critical unease can be found in 'critical theorists', such as Adorno and Horkheimer, who focused critically on the 'logic of identity' present in Enlightenment thought and consequently, what they referred to, as the 'terrorizing unity' implicit in such identity. Unified identity is revealed through what it excludes. Identity, qua Enlightened reason, is thus indifferent or hostile to difference. This latter focus also clearly resonates with the early work of both Jacques Derrida and Michel Foucault. For Iris Marion Young— following this line—rationality, impartiality, and neutrality, within current mainly neo-Kantian inspired justice and rights-based theory, 'expresses a logic of identity that seeks to reduce differences to unity'. Identity abstracts from particularity in order to generate the universal. The reduction to a single unified substance represses difference denying the uniqueness or character of the 'different'. For Young, 'difference . . . names both the play of concrete events and the shifting differentiation on which signification depends'. She continues that 'reason . . . is always inserted in a plural, heterogeneous world that outruns totalizing comprehension'. In summary, for Young, 'the logic of identity flees sensuous particularity' (Young, 1990: 97–9). It is worth noting here that Young's work on difference is a blend of radical feminism, critical theory and poststructural theory. The problem for postmodern difference-based theory though is where feminism is to go next.[26] Once one has acknowledged the heterogeneous public and 'revisioned' or 're-sited' the political, where do we go next (see Coole 2000: 350)? As has recently been observed, the strategy of postmodern displacement 'largely adopts a critical perspective . . . but has few of the theoretical tools necessary to assert a practical alternative' (see Squires 1999: 224).

The fourth major form of difference is embodied in poststructural and postmodern theory—although as indicated, it also underpins a great deal of contemporary feminism, anthropology, and some postcolonial theory.[27] The rational human agent is seen by, for example Foucault, as an accidental phenomenon, which takes little or no account of the contingencies of human nature. Whereas neo-Kantians and utilitarians, to the present day, think of rationality as universal and transcending contingency, Foucault considers it a highly specific social and historically contingent notion requiring genealogical investigation.[28] This view of reason defines humans in certain ways, namely, according to their possession of this conception of practical reason. For the proponents of this postmodern argument, this process gives rise to the concept of the 'inhuman'—namely those aspects that do not conform to this specific vision of reason. In effect, the practical reason argument rules out other ways of being human. For postmodern writers, this in turn leads to other cultures, minorities, women, or the colonized being viewed as immature, uneducated, or childish, simply because they do not conform to acceptable definitions of humanity. Thus, the establishment of what it is to be human—in postmodern terminology—always carries its 'other' or the 'inhuman' with it.

This postmodern perspective on difference impacts upon a wide range of recent writers. Thus, Bonnie Honig, for example, sees difference present in all claims to identity. This implies, for her, 'agentic fragmentation' (Honig in Benhabib (ed.) 1996: 258 and 260). Difference not only exists externally within and between societies, it is also embedded within all individual and group identities. Difference, in this context, is far more than just liberal pluralism, which she considers a purely external domesticated form of diversity. Difference is not therefore just an *adjective* of identity, it is the *substance* of every claim to identity. Honig views difference, therefore, as a form of 'agonism'. On a broader political level, she sees certain positive dimensions to this recognition of agonism. Thus, agonism is seen to enable 'more coalitional variants of social-democratic organization' (Honig in Benhabib (ed.) 1996, 260, 270–1). Honig's account also parallels the work of William Connolly, who also fulsomely embraces the agonism thesis.[29] Both, in consequence, advocate, what they call, an 'agonistic democracy'. Consequently, the problems we experience in plural or diverse societies are not the result of difference, *per se*, but rather of the attempt to find or impose an identity. One small step beyond this is radical difference, which is one other possible further reading of postmodern argument. Such radical difference focuses on total fragmentation of society, conceiving each culture to be uniquely particular. It implies complete 'incommensurability' of perspectives. Critics of this position (which would include figures such as Honig and Connolly) maintain that it is flawed since it tries, in effect, to 'essentialize' extreme differences of identity. There are, as such, fewer example than one think of this position. One possible exemplar of this position (although he does not really fit with the critics' view of radical difference) is Jean Francois Lyotard. For Lyotard, genres of discourse are not only plural, but also utterly heterogeneous and irreducible to any common vocabulary. This is what he calls the *differend*—namely, an irresolvable conflict.[30]

CONCLUSION

Briefly summarizing the discussion: many political theorists, in the closing two decades of the twentieth century, moved away from the thin universalist account of liberal justice and formal equality-based arguments. These latter arguments came under sustained critical assault from a range of conventionalist theories. However, the critique by conventionalist theories was not simply a negative assessment of thin universalist liberalism. It was also, oddly, partly a defence of liberalism and liberal values. In this sense, many of the conventionalist arguments (examined in Part Three) tried to defend liberal values by showing them as deeply embedded *within* certain communities. Consequently, a number of unexpected compounds developed during the 1980s and 1990s, such as liberal nationalism or liberal communitarianism, which exemplify this embedding process. Although partly abandoning thin universalist themes, an attempt was still made to 'shore up' the foundations of theory by focusing on the values within particular communities, nations, or republics.

One important implication of this argument has been that communities and nations have been seen as relatively self-sufficient and self-determining entities. The concept of self-determination is important here. Each nation, community, ethnie, or republic is seen as requiring the right to freely determine its own destiny. The analogy of the group with the human individual is strong here. As the free human individual must be able to determine his or her own action, so a free community, ethnie, or nation (especially one which embodies liberal values), must analogously also be able to determine its own actions. However, as suggested, this conventionalist argument carries a subversive internal logic—a logic mapped out in this chapter—which creates the potential for further social segmentation. Consequently, prioritizing the autonomy, right, and self-determination of the particular group, has given rise, in turn, to a subversive cultural or group rights logic.[31]

Within late twentieth-century political theory, the major disagreements between liberal pluralism, liberal multicultural, and difference theories, were largely over the significant 'particles of difference'. For most liberal pluralists, the key particle of difference was the human individual.[32] For multicultural pluralists, the particle of difference became the individual *as shaped by the group culture*. In stronger forms of multiculturalism, the shift was made to cultures and groups as the key organic particles. In 1990s difference theory, the incommensurability thesis accelerated even further. Each fragmented group was seen as distinctive and wholly different. The background for this latter concept of difference focuses on complex developments in anthropology, feminist theory, postmodern, postcolonial, and agonistic arguments. Particles of difference shifted between cultural, ethnographic, gendered, linguistic, historical, and psychological factors.[33]

In conclusion, the basic argument made in this chapter can be put quite simply: it is that the logic of conventionalism does not cease at the level of the nation, ethnos, republic, or community. Every community, nation, or ethnos is constituted by multiple sub-communities, sub-ethnie, and sub-cultures. Thus, the argument about conventions (and social and moral meanings) is pushed several steps backwards, ultimately into the potential incoherence of difference theory. If the logic of the argument is that each group is significant and potentially self-determining (to a degree), then pluralism, multicultural pluralism, and difference theory further fragment the foundational concerns of political theory, in some cases to the point of incoherence.

Brian Barry states the logic of this point rather well:

Suppose . . . that we were to imagine the principles laid down in the Peace of Augsburg applied not between states but within states. We would then indeed get an approximation to a policy of promoting group diversity by state action. To the principles that 'Where there is one ruler, there should only be one religion' would correspond the maxim 'Where there is one group, there should be only one set of beliefs and norms'. (Barry 2001: 127)

Such a logic is clearly in the end practically unsustainable.

Notes

1. As Stanley Cavell views them, conventions are 'those forms of life which are normal to any group of creatures we call human, any group about which we will say, for example, they *have* a past to which they respond', Cavell (1979: 111).
2. For more contemporary liberal pluralists, pluralism is broadly seen as a meta-ethical idea which suggests that there is no singular source of moral authority. Pluralism is thus often viewed as an objective claim about the real nature of morality and other forms of value. As indicated earlier though, it is a crucial aspect of pluralism, for many of its liberal proponents, that there are still universal values, which draw it distinct from all forms of relativism. The assertion of pluralism thus implies universal normative criteria for choice 'among competing values'. Two important claims are therefore made here, namely, that pluralism 'is not simply a matter of maximizing quantities of value, but also involves seeking coherence among values. Diversity thus involves a balance between "multiplicity" and "coherence" in the promotion of plural goods', and second, that the 'pluralist balance between multiplicity and coherence is best achieved by the liberal combination of freedom and order' (see Crowder 2002: 135–6). For George Crowder, for example, choice among plural values is hard, in the sense that choices must be made without the direction of monistic rules. On the other hand, from the pluralist perspective, 'reasons to choose' emerge not only from attention to the context for choice, but from attention to the formal components of value pluralism. In other words, pluralism presupposes universal values, plurality, incommensurability, *and* conflict, see Crowder (2002: 44 *ff.*).
3. For Barry's broadside on the culture-based arguments, see Barry (2001). For a culturalist critique of Barry see Daniel Bell (1998). Parekh, from the culturalist standpoint, describes Barry's position as one which is 'incoherent, rests on circular reasoning, and has been a source of much violence and moral arrogance', see Parekh (2001: 111).
4. Many commentators, however, do distinguish between different types of neutrality: for example, neutrality of aim (where the state does not promote any conception of the good life), neutrality of procedure (where policy is decided without recourse to the superiority of any one conception of the good—characteristic of the work of Ackerman and Dworkin), neutrality of outcomes or consequences (where social and political institutions will not favour any one outcome over another), and finally neutrality of grounds (such that all persons will be treated with equal respect). This debate will be left to one side, see Bellamy (1992: 219 *ff.*).
5. It is odd, in this sense, that his work should have been taken that seriously, apart from contingent fashions.
6. However, it is important to remind ourselves here that culture and groups *per se* have no substantive place in the public realm of Kukathas's Hayekian liberalism.

7. I am sure he cannot mean 'the' native element in American culture.

8. The underlying template of this argument has been drawn from my chapter on multiculturalism in Vincent (2002).

9. For example, the Hapsburg Empire, which was one classic attempt to deal with multiculturalism.

10. Nathan Glazer, for example, suggests that multiculturalism is, characteristically, a North American concept (linked to a strong rights-based tradition with deep immigrant and racial divisions in society) and consequently has no real connection with European politics, see Glazer in Joppke and Lukes (eds.) (1999: 183–4).

11. Lukes and Joppke offer a different typology distinguishing between 'hodgepodge' and 'mosaic' forms. The former implies intermingling and fusion. The latter idea—whose foremost spokesman they see as Kymlicka—implies that individuals are linked to the larger society through the prior membership of cultural groups, see Joppke and Lukes (ed.) (1999: 9–11). They express their own qualified sympathy for the 'hodgepodge' idea, on the basis that 'cultures are not windowless boxes', consequently there is considerable interchange and overlap between cultures.

12. In contemporary political theorists this complexity of response to both pluralism and diversity is partially recognized in distinctions commonly made between, usually, two varieties of liberalism, for example, autonomy and tolerance-based liberalisms (Kymlicka), enlightenment and reformation liberalisms (Galston), comprehensive and political liberalisms (Rawls), procedural and non-procedural liberalisms (Taylor), or autonomist and integrationist liberalisms (Walzer).

13. Raz does not appear that confident, however, in dealing with illiberal or nonliberal cultures. In his book, the *Morality of Freedom*, he advocates toleration if such cultures are harmless.

14. Ideally, for communitarians, democracy should only recognize those cultures that respect diversity or pluralism.

15. Consequently, he notes that 'the insistent demand for common traits, goals, or purposes—not in itself, because plainly these have their importance, but as the only basis for Canadian unity—has the effect of delegitimating, and hence further weakening what is in fact an essential element of this unity', Taylor in Tully (ed.) (1994: 255).

16. The same implicit logic allows another apparently 'communitarian' theorist, Michael Walzer, to even describe his own work as 'difference orientated', see Walzer in Benhabib (ed.) 1996. He is also sympathetically considered by recent difference theorists, particularly in terms of his conceptions of complex equality and spheres of justice. Iris Young (a more overt difference theorist) comments that 'Walzer's analysis . . . has resonance with my concern to focus primarily on the social structures and processes that produce distributions'. However, she continues that he still addresses us in a reified liberal language which assumes an impartial conception of reason and a unitary public realm, which disconnects us from diversity (Young 1990: 18). She describes this 'neutral reason' as a 'normative gaze' which 'expresses a logic of identity that seeks to reduce differences to unity', Young (1990: 11 and 97).

17. Poststructural theory will be examined in greater detail in Chapter Eight. However, it is important to note here that the postmodern and poststructural category interweaves with the ethnographic, subaltern, and gendered perspectives.

18. Particularly the work of Partha Chatterjee and Ranajit Guha, see Guha (1982: vol.1).

19. For Foucault, the categories of universalist liberal thought can no longer be taken for granted, insofar as they have been deployed in the dubious projects aimed at 'civilizing' subjugated peoples and encouraging their 'development'.

20. Asian values-argument would not necessarily directly associate their idea with postcolonial theorizing (qua subaltern studies) but there are enough close parallels to discuss them under this rubric.

21. Consequently, Taylor continues, 'Only if we in the West can recapture a more adequate view of our own history, can we learn to understand better the spiritual ideas that have been interwoven in our development and hence be prepared to understand sympathetically the spiritual paths of others', see Taylor in Bauer and Bell (ed.) (1999: 143–4).

22. There are various perspectives on the relation of Asian values to human rights. Some see human rights as just alien. Others see human rights already present within authoritative value traditions or texts, like Confucius's *Analects* or the Islamic *Qur'an*. Thus, human rights can be seen as distinctively Asian. Others see a space for active internal religious and legal reform. In the latter two, the crucial contention is that human rights need to be reconsidered and redrafted through the medium of Asian values. The ASEAN Bangkok declaration of 1997 (which recast universal human rights in the light of Asian values) is characteristic of this general process. Further, priority is given to social and economic rights over political and civil human rights. Some of the enthusiasm of this debate was dampened by the Asian finance crisis (1997–8).

23. As Alison Jaggars comments: 'Even if androgyny were an adequate moral ideal, many radical feminists argue that it would be totally inappropriate as a political objective. Androgyny may be a broad humanistic ideal for both sexes, but it contains no recognition of the fact that, in order to approach that ideal, women and men must start from very different places . . . radical feminists argue that men derive concrete benefits from their oppression of women, and they conclude that feminists must struggle against rather than with men in order to achieve liberation' (Jaggar 1983: 88).

24. Some have more recently wanted to try to link the two perspectives, see Held (1993) or Lister (1997).

25. Judith Squires, for example, in a synoptic text, refers to this as an important current perspective within feminism. She sees it characterized by a strategy of 'displacement' which essentially aims to destabilize or deconstruct previous narratives or discursive regimes. Its method is usually genealogical and Foucaultian, see Squires (1999: 3 *ff*. or 110–11).

26. Feminists now are 'more likely, under the influence of Foucault, in particular, to integrate everything into the discursive on the grounds that it is within discursive fields that structures of power are constituted and that there is no prediscursive reality that acts as an independent referent. In this sense, the validity of postmodernism's representations of more heterogeneous spaces cannot be established simply by appealing to a reality whose truth they might more or less accurately convey' (Coole 2000: 351).

27. This will be examined in detail in Chapter Eight.

28. The idea of universal reason 'is an event, or set of events and complex historical processes, that is located at a certain point in the development of European societies' (Foucault in Rabinow (ed.) 1984).

29. Connolly suggests, for example, that the liberal and communitarian visions are all located in the same exclusionary Enlightenment frame, see Connolly (1991: 29). Connolly will be discussed in Chapter Eight.

30. Lyotard's ideas will be discussed in Chapter Eight. However, radical difference undermines itself in the same way that thorough-going scepticism undermines itself, as soon as it makes any claim about the truth of scepticism. The thesis of radical incommensurability is basically incoherent. If cultures are so distinct we would, by definition, have no common lexicon to even circumscribe them as cultures.

31. The preliminary grounds for this argument had already been sketched within the philosophical perambulations of post-1960s liberals around the theme of pluralism. Mostly these arguments were made in ignorance of the tangled conceptual history of pluralism and group theory in the early twentieth century.

32. It is, however, worth noting that pluralism, *per se*, even when focused on an individualist ontology, is not *necessarily* linked with liberalism, although much of the writing about it has been. The work of political theorists like Jon Kekes and John Gray has shown pluralism decoupled from liberalism. In the case of Kekes, pluralism has been developed in the context of conservatism and in Gray within (most recently) an anti-liberal pragmatism.

33. Admittedly, even some recent difference theorists have found this whole idea intolerable, partly because it still tends to essentialize groups—whether they are cultural, gendered, or postcolonial. In this context, Iris Young, for example, has denied all 'essentialism' in groups and speaks rather of 'relational involuntary affinity groups'. Theorists, such as Homi Bhabha, have also spoken of hybridity and mixing of groups. James Tully also sees all cultures as continually 'contested, imagined and re-imagined, transformed and negotiated . . . The identity, and so the meaning, of any culture is thus aspectival', Tully (1995: 11). He suggests that societies should be considered as 'intercultural' rather than 'multicultural'. It is not quite clear where this latter argument takes difference theory.

8

Standing Problems

Chapter Seven dwelt on the idea that conventionalist argument was pushed back from nationalist and communitarian arguments by various forms of multiculturalism, pluralism, and difference-based theories. The basic logic of the case is that every community, nation, or ethnos can also be seen as being constituted by multiple, conventionally-based, sub-communities, sub-ethnie, and sub-cultures. Consequently, conventionalism does not stop at the level of the nation, ethnos, republic, or community; it potentially implodes into a labyrinth of sub-conventions and sub-cultures. In this sense, foundationalism becomes a permanently receding option. One of the important strands of argument, encountered in Chapter Seven, which has been frequently employed to support the latter arguments, is the loose conglomerate of postmodern and poststructural theorizing. This conglomerate (particularly postmodernism) is a potentially unwieldy topic. In raising it within this chapter, I wish to pursue one important theme—that postmodern theory pushes the logic of conventionalism (in political theory) several steps beyond even difference theory. At least within communitarianism, nationalism, or indeed liberal multiculturalism, there are some foundational grounds on which the individual can justify, legitimate, or premise moral or political action. Although it is difficult to generalize about the postmodern and poststructural conglomerate, it is safe to say that a large part of its case has been based on the idea that there are *no* secure foundations for justification or legitimation in political theory. This claim is premised upon a much more vigorous prosecution of the conventionalist case, particularly in epistemology. Although the difference perspective does embody a fairly strong commitment to postmodern argument, it still does not fully engage with the complete logic of the conventionalist position.

The logic of this conventionalist position leads in unexpected directions. As mentioned, one of these is to undermine the whole idea of any foundations in political theory. However, this *not* a wholly consistent picture. There is still, ironically, a deep yearning, within areas of postmodern and poststructural theory, to recover something more secure, grounded, and meaningful. This yearning appears in the most unlikely areas.

My argument in this chapter, in a nutshell, is that conventionalist argument, if pursued, is profoundly still reductionist, although there are several *degrees* of reductionism. The committed postmodern or poststructural critic aims to track down secure foundational commitments in all the remote and hidden corners of political theory. Morality and politics are all just human conventions or artefacts, pure and simple, with nothing to mediate between multiple incommensurable conventions.

The discussion will begin with a substantive discussion of Nietzsche and Heidegger, both of whom in different ways set the tone of the postmodern debate in the twentieth century. It then turns to a closer critical scrutiny of the development of recent postmodern and poststructural political theories.[1]

NIETZSCHE AND THE TWILIGHT OF THE IDOLS

The roots of postmodern argument lie within Friedrich Nietzsche's thought. In many ways Nietzsche encapsulates the whole postmodern momentum. The specific roots of postmodern political theory in fact lie in Nietzsche's deeply negative appraisal of foundational metaphysics (more precisely, the metaphysics of modernity). Therefore, although Nietzsche is not precisely a twentieth-century writer, he nonetheless encompasses most of the dilemmas and themes of twentieth-century postmodern theory in a very effective manner.

Nietzsche is a deeply paradoxical figure and it is always difficult to get a handle on his thought, partly because he eschewed the whole idea of system. He has also been many things to many people. Numerous artists, poets, and writers have claimed him for their own. His short aphoristically and stylistically pithy books no doubt have contributed to this popularity. However, he also had a profound influence in certain domains of philosophy and political theory. There have thus been many Nietzsches. There is the existentialist Nietzsche (Camus), the fascist Nietzsche (Mussolini), the Nietzsche of moral relativism and moral disintegration (Bloom), the Nietzsche who took the Enlightenment to its moral demise in nihilism (Alisdair MacIntyre), and the feminists' Nietzsche (Kristeva). Nietzsche has been recruited for vegetarianism, Zionism, sexual liberation, socialism, and all manner of causes. The present discussion is more bounded. It tries to show his formative impact on one important dimension of twentieth-century political theory. This impact cannot necessarily be divorced from many of the other views mentioned here, however space is limited, therefore the aim is to set out the broad parameters of his theory and its influence, not to discuss the minutiae of its effects.

In exploring Nietzsche's impact on political theory the discussion begins first with his more negative critique of metaphysics, then turns to his critique of epistemology and his own doctrine of perspectivism. Second, it moves to his critique of morality and religion. Perspectivism also underpins the conception of morality. The critique of morality in turn allows us to see more clearly his critical conception of normative theory. The third section of the discussion is a brief accounting on his 'positive ideas'. This focuses on his conception of individualism, his formulation of the *übermensch* (overman), his notion of the will to power, eternal recurrence, and, finally, the aesthetic conception of life. This will then facilitate insights into his political ideas and their impact.

First, metaphysics, for Nietzsche, is the 'science . . . which deals with the fundamental errors of mankind—as if they were fundamental truths' (Nietzsche 1968: appendix D, 192). Traditional metaphysics is largely a useless phenomenon to Nietzsche. He saw himself, to some extent, as a materialist or extreme empiricist. For Nietzsche, this meant literally the inaccessibility of *any* supramundane reality. All we know or can know are phenomena. There are no noumena. In effect, there is no God, no teleology, no inner purpose, no historical progress, no essences, and no universal reason. His materialism was not however a philosophical support for positivism or science. Positivistic science was as flawed in its own way as traditional metaphysics—this point is brought out better in the discussion of perspectivism.[2] There are in other words no changeless empirical facts in the world. It was the material world, as the continuously mutating physical condition of our concrete empirical lives, which really interested Nietzsche. There is no static form or sense of being outside of this physical existence, an existence which is itself a ceaseless becoming or flux of sensation. This idea is reflected in one of Nietzsche's favourite Greek philosophers, Heraclitus, who, contrary to Plato or Parmenides, posited a world stripped of any stability or predictability, a world of continuous becoming.

In his book *The Twilight of the Idols*, in the section entitled 'How the "Real World" at last Became as Myth', Nietzsche gives an inordinately compressed but intellectually dazzling account of the manner in which humanity has viewed foundational reality. The whole history is cast in the form of a continuous and compounded chain of errors. In the first stage, the real world is only attainable by the wise, the thinker is the embodiment of the truth. Nietzsche associates this with Plato. In the second stage, reality becomes unattainable, although it is then promised to the wise, virtuous, or pious. This is the first indication of Christian metaphysics. In the third stage, the real world becomes unattainable and 'cannot be promised'. This is the Kantian metaphysics of the *ding an sich*. In the fourth stage the real world is utterly unattainable and unknown. There is therefore 'no consolation, no redemption, no duty: how could we have a duty towards something unknown?'. This is the world of late nineteenth- and early twentieth-century positivist metaphysics. In the fifth stage the idea of a real world is completely abolished. This is the world of 'free spirits'. This appears to be Nietzsche's own transitional moment, elucidated fully in the final, seventh stage, when it is fully recognized that the real world has been abolished—there is no god, no reason, no telos, and they are no longer sought. With this stage, says Nietzsche, we realize that 'with the real world we have also abolished the apparent world!' This is the moment for mankind as Zarathustras (Nietzsche 1968: 40–1). We become the creators of our own reality—'overmen'.

The reaction to metaphysics can be further elucidated in what many take to be the central theme of his philosophy—his epistemological thesis on perspectivism. The central questions underpinning this thesis are: What is the relation between the 'chaotic becoming' of the world and the intellectual structures that we bring to bear upon them? Further, do our intellectual structures actually give us any insight into the 'reality' of this becoming or flux? In addition, does this 'becoming' have any meaning that can be unscrambled through our intellectual structures? These are important questions for early twentieth-century thought in general. The first assumption to note, underpinning Nietzsche's responses to these questions, is his perspectivism. In his *Genealogy of Morals* Nietzsche summarizes the doctrine concisely. He notes that we always need to be on our guard against the philosopher's idea of a 'pure, will-less, painless, timeless knower', pure reason and absolute knowledge 'presuppose an eye . . . no living being can imagine'. This is the core of his rejection of classical metaphysics. Conversely, for Nietzsche 'all seeing is essentially perspective, and so is all knowing' (Nietzsche 1956: 255). Perspective is the fundamental condition of all human existence. There are no facts, only interpretative perspectives. As such the world *per se* gives no pointers or directives. There is *no* objective standpoint, no *deus ex machina*, and no god's eye view.

As a consequence Nietzsche had little patience with orthodox epistemology and theories of truth. His perspectivism led him to reject correspondence theories of truth and representational accounts of knowledge. Truths are not discovered, represented, or found for Nietzsche, conversely, they are created. Knowledge is not about an increasingly adequate grasp of reality, it is rather about greater mastery and the will to power by the subject. Logic, equally, is not about careful methodical thought processes, rather it is again a *perspective* reflecting the self-constitutive will to power. Truth and falsity do not exist as absolutes anywhere. We should, however, be interested in how far any idea cultivates strength and the will to power. Truth, logic, and knowledge are thus highly overrated ideas for Nietzsche—they are nothing but conventional fictions invented by the human subjects to exercise power. In one sense, Nietzsche's arguments here are very close to a form of solipsism. As Nietzsche comments, 'No matter how far a man may extend himself with his knowledge, no matter how objectively he may come to view himself, in the end it can yield him nothing but his own biography' (Nietzsche 1986: 182). We fabricate our own realities and then dress them up in the clothes of knowledge and truth and claim that they mirror some external reality. Academic knowledge is one of the worst offenders here. In fact, art is much more important for Nietzsche than academic truth or knowledge. Art allows us the possibility of coping and living joyfully in the world that we create. The bulk of academic knowledge, however, is not only false, encouraging us to live inauthentically and slavishly, but it is also utterly without any efficacy for human life.[3]

Perspectivism is the essence of what I have termed the 'radical use' of conventionalism. In effect, our truths are nothing but conventions. To briefly repeat the questions outlined earlier: What is the relation between the 'chaotic becoming' of the world and the intellectual structures that we bring to bear upon them? Further, do our intellectual structures actually give us any insight into the 'reality' of this becoming or flux? In addition, does this becoming have any meaning that can be unscrambled through our intellectual structure? Nietzsche's answer to the first question is not an isolated response. In effect, for Nietzsche our conceptual structures (our knowledge, truths, sciences, and the like) are a subjective grid placed over the flux and chaos of sensation. These grids help us to organize the chaos (subjectively), however such structures are *purely* instrumental and conventional in character. The conventions are *our* fictions.

It is worth noting in passing that Nietzsche was not alone in this account of human knowledge. In one sense, the seeds are present in Kant's distinction between the phenomenal and noumenal worlds. We can thus never have knowledge of reality or the noumenal 'thing in itself'. However, in Nietzsche's own time, Henri Bergson also premised his whole philosophical system on a resonant distinction between the vital process of the 'élan vital of life' or 'real duration' (which could never be grasped by intellectual manifolds or endeavours) and the mechanistic processes of thought and the surface consciousness of everyday existence (which distort reality). Thought, in this context, always fails to grasp the becoming and flux of real life. The same theme also appears in Williams James's writings in his distinction between the 'stream of consciousness' (James was the first to coin this latter term) and the pragmatic uses of concepts that actually guide us through the daily routines of life. A similar distinction also occurs in the idealist philosopher F. H. Bradley, whose metaphysics is again premised upon a fundamental distinction between 'immediate experience' (which incorporates absolute reality), as against the often feeble and highly partial intellectual attempts to grasp that reality. This is the core of Bradley's distinction between 'appearance' and 'reality'. A similar idea can also be found in psychoanalysis (in fact some see a close relation between Freud's basic ideas and Nietzsche's), in the distinction between the 'unconscious' (an idea that was being used long before Freud) and the impotent distortions of our conscious intellectual faculties.[4] Closer into the twentieth century, a parallel distinction can be seen in structuralist arguments in linguistics and anthropology, in writers such as Saussure and Levi-Strauss, on the basis that the surface of speech (*parole*) is distinct from the deep reality structure of language (*langue*). A parallel idea is also present in Heidegger (who will be returned to), in his fundamental distinction between on the one hand 'Being', and on the other hand 'Being in thought' or the '*what* of Being'; the latter is an idea dominating Western metaphysics from the Greeks onwards, which in essence distorts the reality of Being. In many ways, Heidegger's *oeuvres* are premised on this simple but influential distinction. Reality again continuously eludes our often instrumental intellectual grasp.[5]

Moving to the second question: do our intellectual structures actually give us any insight into the 'reality' of this becoming or flux? Nietzsche again is not alone here in thinking that our intellectual endeavours in fact do *not* provide any fundamental insight. Why should they? If all we know is what we intellectually construct and constitute, then, asking if our views are true or false is pointless. To think otherwise is to be in thrall to an older foundational metaphysics that identifies reality as *other* than ourselves, that is, some standard or template to match up with outside or 'deep inside' ourselves. The answer of other late nineteenth- and early twentieth-century thinkers mentioned earlier varies, although most are in accord with Nietzsche's answer—that the deeper sense of life and reality always eludes our intellectual grasp. This would certainly be the case for Bergson, Bradley, Freud, Heidegger, or James.

The difference between Nietzsche and the latter thinkers is revealed in answering the last question: does this deeper elusive reality—call it élan vital, stream of consciousness, deep cultural or linguistic structure, immediate experience or becoming—have any meaning that can be unscrambled through our intellectual endeavours? Nietzsche's answer here does reveal a quite idiosyncratic position. For the majority of the other thinkers, including Heidegger, we *do* have some pathway to reality. We can unscramble the deep structure. The unscrambling may not be by conventional paths, but they are still pathways to reality. Thus, in Bergson it is via 'intuition', in Freud it is through the analysis of dreams, in Levi-Strauss it is a deep structural analysis, and in Heidegger it is a meditative waiting on Being to disclose itself in art, and the like. For Nietzsche, however, the flux of sensation, or the unconscious, *has* absolutely no meaning, other than that *we* imbue it with an artifice of conventional meaning. As he states, 'The habits of our senses have woven us into lies and deception of sensation: these again are the basis of all our judgments and "knowledge"—there is absolutely no escape, no backway or bypath into the *real world*! We sit within our net, we spiders, and whatever we catch in it, we can catch nothing at all except that which allows itself to be caught in precisely *our* net' (Nietzsche 1982: 73). Thus, the obscure flux of the world has no inner sense of meaning. There is nothing to be discovered, no inner telos, no god, no core of reasonableness, no metaphysical Esperanto. Literally, all we have are our conventions. There is *no* reality above or beyond our conventions and perspectives. We float, as it were, in a sea of these conventions.

The perspectivist thesis underpins Nietzsche's account of morality. There are two aspects to morality. The first is his negative critique, the second concerns his more positive ideas on morals, which focus on notions like the will to power and *übermensch*. For Nietzsche the important point in considering issues of morality (or religion) is that since all morality is just conventional perspective, and there is no inner, true, or correct perspective in knowledge of any kind (moral or otherwise), it makes no sense to ask about true or false moralities or even whether something is moral or immoral. In morals, all values are just our *own* values imposed on the flux of the world. As Nietzsche put it, 'value judgments concerning life, . . . can in the last resort never be true: they possess value only as symptoms, they come into considerations only as symptoms—in themselves such judgments are stupidities' (Nietzsche 1968: section 2, 30; see Hollingdale 1999: 134 *ff.*). There are no hard and fast moral rules. Morality is simply what is conventional or customary. Given that we *create* morality, it might therefore be more apt to think of morality via aesthetics. Morality is about the creative will and the power of the individual imposing a particular rule or code upon themselves and the world.

The more negative critical dimension of morals can be summed up in one word—genealogy. Genealogy is a historical tracing of words to grasp the metaphoric process through which these words take on moral meanings. The task that Nietzsche set himself moves against the standard conceptions of moral philosophy. He is not interested in normative persuasion or reasoned judgement. He conceives of his task as primarily based upon a historical and psychological method—although there is no sense of any teleological history. In effect, he suspends all direct normative and teleological concerns. The genealogical method undermines the universalist enterprise and humanist affectations of morality. For Nietzsche, man is by nature neither a political nor moral animal. He has been trained and cultivated in certain ways. There is no universal morality, conversely there are a series of moralities both within and between individuals and cultures. Genealogy traces out the minute and complex ways through which humans absorb and take on moral terms and then construct a vision of the human self, as if all this were natural to us. In this sense, genealogy initiates a form of detailed self-examination of how the self is formed historically. The genealogy of morals is indeed at the same time the genealogy of the modern self, via customary moralities. Genealogy thus has the effect of subverting the deep assumptions of both morality and selfhood. It also provides an arbitrary chart of the formation of the self and the way it both constructs and disciplines itself. Genealogy also shows how we become our own prison wardens. We entrap ourselves in moral webs of our own making and feel guilt, twinges of conscience, and anxiety. Each morality has its own core of technicians and rule-structures who administer the processes—thus psycho-therapists, priests, confessions, and the like. Even the idea of an 'interior self' is a perspective created, not discovered. Self-discovery of this interior self is another more refined form of self-entrapment.

Nietzsche's idea that morality and the self (as mentioned earlier) are the creation of power, leads to a more positive conception of the future of morality. However, it is important to realize that Nietzsche's concept of power is not that of an overt physical force. There is no Hobbesian sovereign forcing actions on us through legal penalties. It is a more psychological process of immense subtlety. The crucial point is that morality can either be taken inauthentically, or it can be understood genealogically for what it actually is. To understand it for what it is *is* to realize that morality is neither a true nor false idea. These are inappropriate adjectives. Morality is rather a manifestation of the will to power. It is a created and self-sustained *perspective* or convention. It has no meaning above or beyond that perspective. It is neither universal, reasonable, teleologically appropriate, nor natural to us. To adopt morality *as if* it had some kind of inner or outer purpose is to treat it inauthentically. It is to allow one's self to be 'vivisected' through notions such as conscience or guilt. It is to adopt the slave or herd position. The inauthentic slave mind (typical of Christianity or liberalism to Nietzsche) sees morals as external imperatives or rules validated by a god, reason, the inner self, or society. However, to grasp morality as the product of a will to power—an individual or group imposing their will upon the chaotic flux of the world through some custom or convention—is to move (usually via some form of genealogical scrutiny) beyond the realm of morality. When one grasps the source of morals as being the will to power, one has already begun to overcome one's self or the perception formed of oneself as a moral being. Nietzsche quite explicitly calls this 'self-overcoming'. It is also a realization of one's own 'will to power', and at the same time is a revaluation of all values.

This grasp of the constitutive aesthetic character of the self as a will to power means that the individual subject no longer abides by 'others' moralities'. Slave morality no longer has any hold. The subject has gone beyond good and evil in the usual sense. Individuals can now 'be themselves'. This is the essence of Nietzsche's call to 'live dangerously'. It is an affirmation of life as one's own creation. One has overcome oneself. This again is the core of Nietzsche's concept of the overman (*übermensch*) and an important aspect of his doctrine of aristocratic radicalism.[6] It is essentially a psychological thesis concerned with rising above the external and internal restrictions placed upon us by traditional metaphysics, religion, and morality and grasping the practical and ontological core of perspectivism. This is the noble human agent who says 'yes' to a dedivinized reality. This is the agent who grasps with joy their own will to power and regards nihilism as a positive and open opportunity. It is also an acceptance of the primary role of the aesthetic creative dimension of human existence over the ethical or religious. In essence it is a form of joyful nihilism.

The upshot of Nietzsche's theory here is to undermine the entire structure of Western metaphysics, morality, religion, and politics through the systematic and extreme use of conventionalist argument. For in political theory there is *nothing* to found any judgement on, except a recognition of the will to power. Political theory, as much as anything else, is subject to the extremes of perspectivism and nihilism. Some might find this world of 'free spirits' a terrifying or depressing vision. For Nietzsche it was liberating. Such Nietzschean freedom has neither telos nor purpose. The difficulty for Nietzsche (as for later postmodern writers) is what exactly is one liberated for *or* to do. For many contemporary political theorists, to be without any telos or substantive aim is to risk apathy, irresponsibility, or just insanity. In one sense, it would not be an exaggeration to say that coming to terms with Nietzsche *is* coming to terms with both modernism and postmodernism.

HEIDEGGER AND HUMANISM

Before discussing the wider impact of Nietzsche's philosophy on postmodern theories, it is worth mentioning briefly the role of Heidegger. Nietzsche was viewed by Heidegger in a specific way. He saw Nietzsche's extreme perspectivism and conventionalism, particularly his focus on the constitutive role of the will to power, as not so much destroying Western metaphysics as ironically contributing another (and final) strand to it. Although thinking through nihilism, Nietzsche, for Heidegger, was still the victim of classical metaphysics. Nietzsche may have replaced the secure foundationalism of Western metaphysics with the Heraclitean world of flux, becoming, and indeterminacy. However, for Heidegger, metaphysics had not disappeared here, it had rather arisen again from the flames of perspectivism as an extreme subjectivist and nihilist metaphysics. In this sense, Nietzsche's extreme subjectivism was seen to be in the same mould as Descartes—but in this case a Cartesianism without God. As Heidegger commented, 'No matter how sharply Nietzsche pits himself time and again against Descartes, whose philosophy grounds modern metaphysics, he turns against Descartes only because the latter *still* does *not* posit man as *subiectum* in a way that is complete and decisive enough' (Heidegger 1982: 30).

The critique of metaphysics is crucial to understanding Heidegger's oblique contribution to postmodern argument. My main sounding board in analysing metaphysics is Heidegger's 'Letter on Humanism' (which Arendt referred to as Heidegger's *Prachtstück*—splendid effort). A series of distinctions runs through Heidegger's essay. The most crucial is that of thinking in and outside structured channels or disciplines. A second distinction is between humanism and the inhuman—a distinction that Heidegger himself admits can be markedly misinterpreted. Finally, there is a distinction between Being (Dasein) and what might be called 'representations of being'. The latter might be described as a move from metaphysics to ontology. Each of these distinctions overlaps. First, for Heidegger logic, physics, ethics, and other disciplinary structures developed in the Greek schools of Plato and Aristotle. They arose in the form of distinct sciences or disciplines concerning knowledge (epistemes). With the arrival of universities in Europe they become institutionalized academicized pursuits, like philosophy. However, Heidegger suggests that prior to the schools of Plato and European universities, individuals knew no formal ideas of logic, ethics, metaphysics, and the like, yet we should not imagine that their thinking was either illogical or unethical. One does not need these particular disciplinary structures to think.

Thought, which takes place within disciplinary confines, often becomes rigid and stultified. To teach philosophy (and the like) means to make it into an educational technique. As Heidegger put it, 'philosophy becomes a technique (*techne*) for explaining from highest causes'. He continues that, in this context, 'one no longer thinks; one occupies oneself with "philosophy". In competition with one another, such occupations publicly offer themselves as "isms" ' (Heidegger 1993: 221). Institutions in the public realm—presumably autocratic university departments—decide in advance what is to count as 'intelligible'. Individuals can be very cultivated and sophisticated exponents of philosophy, but merely being cultivated, intelligent, or sophisticated is not enough. In this, what Heidegger ironically calls, 'dictatorship of the public realm', the great issues of humanity become intelligent 'chatter'.[7] Here Heidegger makes a subtle dig at the private realm of the individual—presumably directed at Weimar liberalism. The private is just another product of the public realm. It is an illusion that one can think freely or autonomously in a private sphere.

Outside these formal structures, thinking still takes place. In fact, for Heidegger, it is crucial that it does. Thought, within these academic structures, denies its essence. As Heidegger cryptically puts it, 'thinking is "the thinking of being" ' (Heidegger 1993: 220). This introduces the central motif of Heidegger's thought, that is, there is something which is addressed in all thinking—uniquely by humans—and that is *Being*. Humans are the only beings who have the possibility of an 'understanding relation' to Being. Philosophical thinking in formalized institutional settings keeps trying to address Being, but affixes it to abstracted names or metaphysical concepts like *actus* or *potentia*. Heidegger comments that 'if man is to find his way once again into the nearness of Being he must first learn to exist in the nameless. In the same way he must recognize the seductions of the public realm as well as the impotence of the private. Before he speaks man must first let himself be claimed by Being again, taking the risk that under this claim he will seldom have much to say' (Heidegger 1993: 223). Not something unfortunately that ever afflicted Heidegger.

This leads to the second distinction—humanism and the inhuman. Philosophers have endlessly debated about the fundamentals of human nature. Heidegger explicitly mentions different perspectives: the Roman republican, Christian, and Marxist perspectives. The central problem for Heidegger is that these debates involve formalized conceptual structures. For Heidegger all of these humanisms agree that humanity 'is determined with regard to an already established interpretation of nature, history, world, and the ground of the world, that is, of beings as a whole'. Thus, he continues, significantly, 'Every humanism is either grounded in a metaphysics or is itself made to be the ground of one. Every determination of the essence of man that already presupposes an interpretation of beings without asking about the truth of Being' (Heidegger 1993: 225–6). The deep metaphysical questions about human nature are institutionalized in humanism and avoid the real issues about Being.

There are three sub-issues here. First, for Heidegger, 'every humanism remains metaphysical'. In remaining metaphysical, it does not ask about the relation of Being to the essence of man—'because of its metaphysical origin humanism even impedes the question by neither recognizing nor understanding it' (Heidegger 1993: 226).[8] Thus, humanism embodied in metaphysics impedes the grasp of Being. Humanism is *not* about genuine thinking. Second, the institutionalization of metaphysical questions about humanity stops genuine thinking. Thinking if inflexible can disrupt 'the flow of life' and Being. Thus, it is an implicit threat to humanity—humanity whose essence is thinking. Third, the lurking distinction behind this is the human and inhuman. Given Heidegger's Nazi reputation in the 1930s in Freiburg, the 'inhuman' is a difficult concept to deal with. Basically, what Heidegger (like Nietzsche, Foucault, and others who employ the same idea) meant is that if humanism impedes and distorts thinking then the 'inhuman' denotes new vistas or some form of emancipation, minimally, for Heidegger, the possibility of thinking about Being. The inhuman is not the barbaric (Heidegger 1993: 249). For Heidegger, the highest essence of humanism does not reach man's highest dignity. Man, as he puts it, is the 'shepherd of Being'. Thus, if metaphysics equates with humanism then, as Heidegger declares, his major book *Being and Time* is against all forms of humanism (Heidegger 1993: 233–4).

This leads to the third distinction between 'Being' and 'representations of being'. The major point that Heidegger wants to make here is that metaphysics is the prime candidate for offering us 'representations of Being'. Representations of Being, however, close our minds to Being. Thus, the history of metaphysics is the forgetting of Being. Humanity is therefore more than metaphysics tells us. Being is already lost in Plato and Aristotle.[9] As Heidegger puts it: 'Metaphysics does not ask about the truth of Being itself. Nor does it therefore ask in what way the essence of man belongs to the truth of Being. Metaphysics has not only failed up to now to ask this question, the question is inaccessible to metaphysics as such' (Heidegger 1993: 226–7). For Heidegger, it is only when one radically posits the question—'what is metaphysics?'— that the possibility of the awareness of Being arises. For Heidegger, metaphysics always 'closes itself to the simple essential fact that man essentially occurs only in his essence, where he is claimed by Being. Only from that claim "has" he found that wherein his essence dwells' (Heidegger 1993: 227–8). Thus, the question—what is man?—cannot be answered by referring to an unchanging essence (qua a Christian soul), or existence preceding essence (qua Sartre). All this is metaphysics. Metaphysical systems offer us mere representations. Both *essentia* and *existentia* denote 'forgetfulness of being'. Man is always homeless outside Being. Heidegger rather suggests that man 'ek-sists'. Ek-sistence means 'standing out into the truth of Being' (Heidegger 1993: 232 and 230).[10] To ek-sist is not to exist. Ek-sisting means dwelling and caring in Being.

There are many questions to ask here—not least what on earth is Being?[11] The separation between Being or 'ek-sistence' from actual human life remains unexplained. Surely, Being looks like another metaphysical abstraction? This chapter is not an analysis of Heidegger *per se* so I put aside these and other questions. Basically, Heidegger's response to metaphysics is negative. It is not wholly negative insofar as metaphysics deals with Being as outward appearance. All metaphysics thus belong to the 'history of the truth of Being', but metaphysics *per se* nonetheless distorts and misleads us and obscures authentic Being.

In conclusion there are two alternatives here with regard to metaphysics, which lead in radically different directions. The first is to be found in Nietzsche—that the upshot of his perspectivism is simply a homeless nomadic self and an infinite 'oblivion of being'. Heidegger regards this perspective as still nonetheless rooted in the metaphysical impulse. It is still a reading firmly grounded on the metaphysics of modernity, premised in Nietzsche's case on the isolated ego or subject. This is one important reading of the postmodern condition (which it should be noted Heidegger is critical of), and it is a path adopted by many postmodern writers (although they would vigorously deny the role of metaphysics). For Heidegger, the purported attack on metaphysics has simply produced more metaphysics—a metaphysics that has cast humans that much more adrift. The second alternative is to acknowledge (once again) something deeper than conventional philosophy and thinking, which roots humanity in the world. For Heidegger this does not call for a metaphysics but rather a *listening* and *waiting* upon Being, as the real dwelling place of humanity. Heidegger is insistent that this is not a new form of transcendental metaphysics. This latter path both touches upon postmodern themes and also moves outside them. The stress on Being particularly is deeply unpostmodern. In this sense, Heidegger's contribution to postmodernism lies ambiguously in *two* points. The first concerns his critical pursuit of Nietzsche, in essence accusing him of still propounding a 'metaphysics of subjectivism'. In this sense, Heidegger pushes once again at foundational arguments at an even deeper level than Nietzsche. Heidegger in this sense can be seen as more radical and postmodern than Nietzsche in attacking foundational claims even more systematically. Second, the root of Heidegger's critique of Nietzsche is his own view of the history of Western metaphysics as one long series of errors and myths. This has been pursued several steps again by writers such as Derrida. Both these arguments therefore correspond closely to what has happened subsequently in postmodern theory—particularly in writers like Derrida, Foucault, Rorty, and Lyotard. Where Heidegger does diverge from postmodern theory and paradoxically returns to an older non-postmodern argument, is in his own fundamental idea of Being.

DERRIDA AND FOUCAULT

Moving from Heidegger and Nietzsche into more recent postmodern argument, there is one very important implication of Heidegger's argument that needs to be underscored. Metaphysics, for Heidegger, distorts and merely represents Being. Metaphysics remains caught in a humanism that centres on man or humanity as the core of what is real. Heidegger's alternative is the inhuman in the shape of *Being*, thus displacing the centrality of the human. However, what happens if one takes Heidegger's *Being* out of the philosophical equation? The upshot is no logos, no presence, no foundation nor ground and God is—of course—dead. Thus all we have are a number of fictional systems addressing Being or 'presence' (which are also *in absentia*). In some ways we are back with one important perception of Nietzsche.

It is interesting here that the thinker Jacques Derrida who is seen as a key impetus to postmodern theory, is and has been an obsessive critical interpreter of Heidegger. Derrida's reading of Heidegger can be utilized as another dimension of an introduction to the themes that have obsessed postmodernism. These themes can be drawn out from Derrida's relatively early, but incisive, essay, 'The Ends of Man' (1968). Derrida essentially traces the manner in which the terms 'man' and 'humanism' have been used. He approves of Heidegger's account of the early origins of humanism and its links with metaphysics. He comments that 'any questioning of humanism that does not first catch up with the archaeological radicalness of the questions sketched by Heidegger, and does not make use of the information he provides concerning the genesis of the concept and the value of man (the rendition of the Greek *paideia* in Roman culture, the Christianizing of the Latin *humanitas*, the rebirth of Hellenism in the fourteenth and eighteenth centuries, etc), any metahumanist position that does not place itself within the opening of these questions remains historically regional . . . and peripheral' (Derrida 1993: 144–5). With the decline of what Derrida refers to as a spiritual humanism in the late nineteenth and early twentieth century in thinkers such as Bergson and Alain, an irreducible anthropologism begins to dominate in terms of Christian and atheistic existentialism, personalism, and Marxism—some also associate this anthropologism with Hegel and Husserl.[12] The irreducible horizon is a human reality and, like Heidegger Derrida regards it as still unremittingly metaphysical and ontotheological—in some cases a form of transcendental humanism.

The case of Heidegger is most interesting here. Although the overt aim of Heidegger's work is an attack on Sartre and metaphysics and an attempt to displace humanism, Derrida maintains that the upshot of Heidegger's *Essay on Humanism* is yet *another* humanism and metaphysics. In Derrida's estimation, in Heidegger 'we already conduct our affairs in some understanding of Being' and there is a clear 'self-presence' of being in the human interrogator (Derrida 1993: 140). The point is a difficult one, but essentially what Derrida is saying is that Being is present in all humans in their understanding; it constitutes their essence for Heidegger. Derrida thus comments 'Just as Dasein—the being that *we ourselves are*—serves as an exemplary text, a good "lesson" for making explicit the meaning of Being, so the name of man remains the link or . . . guiding thread that ties the analytic of Dasein to the totality of the metaphysics of traditional discourse'. Dasein, although not man, is 'nothing other than man' (Derrida 1993: 143). Thus, in this essence of man we find, says Derrida, a return to both metaphysics and humanism. Essentially, what is at issue here in Heidegger, says Derrida, is a 'revalorization of the essence and dignity of man. What is threatened in the extension of metaphysics and technology . . . is the essence

of man'. Thus, in this analysis Derrida claims that Heidegger takes us back to humanism and the 'essence of man' in metaphysics (Derrida 1993: 145). Restoration of this
essence means the restoration of man's and Being's dignity. Traditional humanism is
opposed by Heidegger, according to Derrida, because it does 'not set the *humanitas*
of man high enough' (Derrida 1993: 147). Man is the proper place of Being—there is
a 'co-propriety' of humanity and Being.

What we find here is that Derrida accuses Heidegger of exactly the same collapse
into metaphysics as Heidegger had accused Nietzsche (see Derrida 1976: 19). Thus,
Derrida pushes once again against the whole idea of foundations. Metaphysics could
only be routed if the idiom of philosophy was 'deconstructed'. Language was viewed by
the philosophical tradition as a transparent medium of thought, where the signified
(objects in the world or mind) could be caught in the web of our language and words
(signs). This point touches upon the better-known dimensions of Derrida. However
it approaches the same thought on metaphysics (outlined earlier) from a different
direction.

The other side of his critique, which I will only briefly summarize, is Derrida's critique of structuralism.[13] Derrida basically criticizes structuralism immanently—that
is, from within (which is characteristic of deconstruction in general). For Derrida,
neither structuralists nor Heidegger pushed their arguments hard enough. Both
are seen to be on the cusp of an antihumanism. Structuralism opposed the diachronic analysis of language—that is, focusing on the history of words. Conversely,
it argued for a synchronic form of explanation, which implied that meaning depends
on relations between an existing system of signs. A linguistic sign was viewed as a
deep structural relation between a word (signifier) and concept (signified). Meaning
was thus dependent on the *relations* between signs—many of which functioned in
terms of basic binary contrasts. One important upshot of structuralism was that it
undermined the idea of any linguistic presentation as being mere presence. It also
destabilized humanity by placing it within a complex web of linguistic relations.
However, for structuralists there was also a stable centre that could be studied (by
structural linguistics or structural anthropology). Derrida fundamentally disagreed
here. Pushing hard at Saussure's and Levi-Strauss' arguments, Derrida argues that
the sign in language and the signified (the object) actually *never* come together. *All*
we have are signs. Words are necessary but always inadequate. They never capture a
reality. Meaning remains the elusive property of signs and corresponds with nothing
outside them—except other texts or signs. Derrida describes this latter idea as 'intertextuality'. Copying Heidegger here—who found the word 'Being' simply inadequate
and therefore crossed it out within his texts—Derrida also widens the net to a more
consistently applied 'writing under erasure'. Each sign is inexhaustible and there is
no way to resolve differences of meaning. This is the core of Derrida's neologism
différance. It implies that—in the final analysis—meaning has always to be deferred.
It also underscores the permanent mutation and becoming of language. We can never
master language and we can never discover any true meaning. Representation can
never indicate a 'presence', since it must always involve the recognition of permanent *différance* implicit in the signs we use, which implies in turn endless deferral or

infinite signification. It is worth remarking here—as is emphasized by most post-modern writers—that literature and poetry is obviously better able to accommodate this thesis than philosophy or technical 'science' orientated disciplines.

Those metaphysicians—structuralist and Heideggerians included—who believe that there is a metaphysical core, foundation, or stable centre, are dubbed logo-centrists. The term *logos* derives from the Greek word for word, reason, or language. Logocentrists assume that a core metaphysical presence *precedes* any signification. Presence, for Derrida, however is always mediated to us in linguistic signs. Nothing precedes signs. The intelligible is thus always woven with the sign. There is nothing outside of the sign. A more adequate account of language here—even technical lan-guage in science and philosophy—would be one focusing on metaphor. Metaphor accommodates the 'rhetorical character' of philosophical discourse. In fact, the his-tory of metaphysics and philosophy might be redescribed as a history of metaphors. Further, against the tradition that focuses on speech as primary—as the medium of thought (Derrida dubs this false focus on speech as phonocentrism)—Derrida pri-oritizes writing. The core of his argument here is that phonocentrism (focusing on speech) is a duplicitous way of making the self-presence of consciousness a primary reality that can be signified (another manifestation of logocentrism in this case aimed at Husserlian phenomenology). However, for Derrida speech is not aware of the gap between the 'word as sound' and the 'infinity of possible meaning'. Speech in effect is a second-hand form of writing. Writing however makes us aware that mean-ing incorporates and generates endless difference. Further, for Derrida the written text—because of *différance*—necessarily becomes disengaged from the intentions of the writer. Intentionality and authorship in general are dismissed. Derrida rather celebrates readers who construct their own meaning. This theory about writing over speech is the core of his early works such as *Of Grammatology*, *Speech and Phenomena*, and *Writing and Difference*.

For Derrida, the origin of phonocentrism and logocentrism can be found in the history of Western thought from Plato. The deconstructive method is basically the exposing of this process—usually from within the thinkers own terms and vocabulary. For Derrida it is often the casual metaphors, footnotes, or margins of the text that are most revealing of these underlying assumptions. It is thus that we have his work *Margins of Philosophy*. The main aim of deconstruction is thus to expose metaphysics and logocentrism. It shows us the unfamiliar at the heart of the familiar.

In summary, for Derrida all foundations are dead. Our conceptual ordering of the world does not reveal anything about the nature of the world. There is no nature to reveal. There is no reason able to grasp the world. There are no ontological or metaphysical 'centred structures', although the bulk of Western metaphysics (qua Heidegger), in fact the history of the West, has been in his words 'a series of substi-tution of centre for centre... This history of metaphysics... is the history of these metaphors' (Derrida 1978: 227–8). Western metaphysics has always sought reas-surance and certitude by naming this centre, time and time again, from Plato and Aristotle up to Heidegger. It is the source of a very deep human arrogance. The centre contains a 'presence' (such as Being, God, spirit, reason, or the Form of the Good).

It is not surprising in this context that Derrida accuses Heidegger of posing as the 'personal secretary of Being' (quoted in Wood 1990: 40). Deconstruction calls into question the whole idea of presence. There is no transcendental signified that matches the transcendental signifiers of metaphysics. Metaphysical foundations also embody 'ontotheological' hierarchies containing repressions, violence, and subordinations. Each centre therefore has its *other*, which it wishes to exclude or suppress. In this context, Derrida cites the entire range of unspoken binaries that underpin the most rational thinking—notions of mind and body, masculine and feminine, reason and emotion, sameness and difference, and so forth. The binaries create paradoxes that entrap the unwary participant in the discourse. Deconstruction exposes these unrationalized paradoxes. Every centre will be premised on these binaries. What is needed is a 'decentering' of the tacit hierarchies buried in our language, hierarchies that locate speech above writing, the author above the reader, or the signified above the signifier. The decentering having been done by deconstruction, we can then float free in a sea of signs with no anchorage and no references.

The crucial question arising here is: what happens next? Fine words butter no parsnips. If, as Derrida portends, all metaphysics, humanism, logocentrism, and phonocentrism have to be rooted out, where does humanity go from here? Derrida suggests *two* alternatives, which he sees as two central 'motifs' of deconstruction. The first is Heideggerian and emphasizes an immanent critique—a 'deconstruction without changing terrain, by repeating what is implicit in the founding concepts and the original problematic, by using against the edifice the instrument or stones available in the house'. The danger here, for Derrida, is that the 'continuous process of making explicit, moving toward an opening, risks sinking into the autism of the closure'. In other words, it risks being taken over by metaphysics and humanism again—as Derrida claims Heidegger's own work was. The second alternative is to change the terrain in 'irruptive fashion', that is, by placing oneself brutally outside and by affirming an absolute break and difference (Derrida 1993: 151). What is left is the radical arbitrariness of the sign. Derrida sees this as more characteristic of the post-1960s French poststructuralists and postmodernists. Derrida suggests that ideally it would be best to weave the two together, however, he confesses that ultimately metaphysical language *per se* can never be completely evaded. What he does claim though is that deconstruction implies a continual vigilance. The philosophical point is not to stress what is said, rather to hold open the action of saying. Every position therefore becomes provisional. In this sense, deconstruction is envisaged as not so much a position as a method of exposing and encouraging difference and alterity, which, it is hoped, will have salutary effects. Derrida thinks it is necessary to speak in many styles and languages and to be prepared to both vacate and move between plural positions.

Presciently, the last paragraph of his essay is devoted to Nietzsche and the *übermensch*. This is something that Derrida pursues further in his book *Spurs: Nietzsche's Styles* (1979). Nietzsche appears to come closest, for Derrida, to the alternative to metaphysics, although what that would be remains somewhat puzzling. He disagrees with Heidegger's reading of Nietzsche, suggesting that Nietzsche's notion of the will to power and eternal recurrence should not be viewed as metaphysical categories or essences. For Derrida, Nietzsche was suspicious of all totalizing metaphysical categories. He seems to be the epitome of the attempt to become postmetaphysical. However, in both Derrida and Nietzsche we still seem to be permanently strung out between metaphysics and the postmetaphysical world.

Mentioning Nietzsche marks a convenient point to turn to Foucault's work. Foucault is one of the most consistent and preeminent Nietzschean thinkers in the twentieth century. He commented, 'I am simply Nietzschean, and I try to see, on a number of points, and to the extent that it is possible, with the aid of Nietzsche's texts' (Foucault 1988: 250–1). He claimed to have been converted by reading Nietzsche's *Untimely Meditations* in the late 1950s, although his actual direct commentaries upon Nietzsche are rare. However, in substance all his writing bears witness to the influence and many have regarded his work on asylums, prisons, hospitals, and the like, as an extension of Nietzsche's *Genealogy of Morals*. Foucault in effect tried to look at society through the eyes of a Nietzschean genealogist. Like Derrida, he also resisted the humanistic perspective, however, he was more historically and—and in terms of Derrida's earlier work—more politically focused than Derrida.

One essay Foucault devoted to Nietzsche is characteristically focused on genealogy. He sees the source of genealogy in Nietzsche. Genealogy unpacks the fundamental ideas through which humanity constitutes itself. It also aims to make us critical of our present discourses. In other words, it destabilizes the present as much as the past. It is not the same as orthodox history. It does not discover any sequence or chronology. It is not a search for origins.[14] In fact, genealogy teaches us to laugh at the solemnities of historical origins, great individuals, and great events. It 'rejects the metahistorical deployment of ideal significations and indefinite teleologies'. Genealogy does not capture the essence or teleology of anything, because nothing has an essence, telos, chronology, or underlying sequence. Essences assume immobility and secure identities. What one finds, for Foucault, as regards human thought and action in general is 'the secret that they have no essence or that their essence was fabricated in a piecemeal fashion'. There is no inviolable identity to events, only disparity. In rending the veil of the past we do not then encounter any universal truth about humanity or history. For Foucault, 'the very question of truth, the right it appropriates to refute error and oppose itself to appearance, the manner in which it developed (initially made available to the wise, then withdrawn by men of piety to an unattainable world, where it was given the double role of consolation and imperative, finally rejected as a useless notion, superfluous and contradicted on all sides)—does this not form a history, the history of an error we call truth?' (Foucault 1986a: 76–80). This quote, which Foucault uses as a motif for his own thought, is a direct exegesis of Nietzsche's one-and-half-page history of Western metaphysics (referred to earlier in the Nietzsche section) from the *Twilight of the Idols*. In substance, it is an exemplification of Nietzsche's doctrine of 'perspectivism'.[15] One of his earlier and most brilliantly executed books *Les Mots et Les Choses* (1966)—translated as *The Order of Things*—is in some ways a book-length expansion of the same Nietzsche passage. This is a passage that Derrida amongst others also refers to with admiration. Essentially it is a critique of the way Western discourses (from the Renaissance to the present) have ordered knowledge under different perspectives (or epistemes). The central paradox (which Foucault explores with great insight) is the emergence of the human being in modernity as the measure of all things. The paradox is that the human being is *both* the subject *and* object of her own investigations.

What we are looking at here in Foucault is an attack on metaphysics, in terms of its association with humanism. Like Nietzsche, Heidegger, and Derrida, Foucault thinks that traditional metaphysics seeks the underlying end, purpose, or meaning of history—in the modern era it seeks it in an anthropomorphic essential human self. In exactly the same context as Nietzsche and Derrida, he is convinced that humanity invents itself and that the history of foundational metaphysics is a history of an error. Ethics in this scenario is also directly equivalent to Nietzsche's will to power. Ethics is an invention and a process of self-constitution, which is better grasped as a form of aesthetics. This issue is explored in some of Foucault's last writings, particularly the *Care of the Self* (1990). There is therefore neither essence, end, nor centre to human beings, only discontinuity, randomness, and chance. This point is portrayed out well in his essay 'What is an Author?' Foucault sees deep-rooted transcendental barriers to doing away with authors as intentional human subjects. He notes that many ancient societies did not have this obsession in their literature. The key genealogical question that should be asked in relation to both the author and human subject in modernity is 'How, under what conditions and in what forms can something like a subject appear in the order of discourse? What place can it occupy in each type of discourse?' For Foucault, the crux of the matter is 'depriving the subject . . . of its role as originator, and of analyzing the subject as a variable and complex function of discourse' (Foucault 1986b: 118). In Foucault, therefore, the author as subject 'is a certain functional principle by which, in our culture, one limits, excludes, and chooses; in short, by which one impedes the free circulation, the free manipulation, the free composition, decomposition, and recomposition of fiction' (Foucault 1986b: 119).[16] The whole tenor of the argument is deeply Nietzschean.

There are certain crucial points being made in the quoted passage: the self is an *invention* and an *effect* of power. There is nothing inevitable about the self and the way it is formed. What we call the subject (from Descartes to Husserl) is the result of an anthropomorphic metaphysics (qua Nietzsche, Heidegger, and Derrida). The subject (like the author) is just a function of certain discourses. The human self is a 'disciplinary project' formed within specific cultures and metaphysical assumptions. Further, like Nietzsche and Derrida he suggests that there is nothing 'underneath', no 'noumenal', no 'centre', or 'interior life' of any human individuals. There is in effect no self prior to descriptions of the self in discourse. The way in which this self forms needs to be understood through genealogy. Genealogy 'does not pretend to go back in time to restore an unbroken continuity that operates beyond the dispersion of forgotten things'. In this sense, for Foucault Kantian questions such as 'What is man?' are regarded as simply a waste of time and fraudulent. We need to relinquish all this striving for truth and objectivity.

The issue of power is crucial here. Power is not overt Hobbesian physical or intentional force or threat. It is *not* about sovereignty, explicit intentional political action, authority, or law. Law is as much about normalizing behaviour. Government, law, and punishment in the modern era are thus regarded as but one modality of the exercise of power. Power is *not* housed in any one singular place. Although earlier forms of power were juridical in character, the more significant power that Foucault sees developing in the modern era bears upon what might conventionally be called free actions. Both the wielder and the subject of juridical power are imbricated in this Foucaultian power. Power is seen as constitutive not just prohibitive. It is also impersonal and flows through or insinuates itself into language, knowledge (in humanities and natural science), and institutional practices. Just using language is a way of exercising power. There can be no neutral language—every discourse involves a perspective. It follows (for both Nietzsche and Foucault) that there can be no truth outside power (see Foucault 1986c). Knowledge and power cannot be separated— Foucault in fact preferred the terminology power/knowledge (see Foucault 1980). There are no standards, such as logic, rationality, clinical excellence, or justice that are external to conventional perspectives. Nothing stands above power relations, thus these purported standards are manifestations of or part of power—a power that regularizes and normalizes behaviour.

A great deal of Foucault's substantive research work was consequently taken up with practices—in prisons, hospitals, psychiatry—as manifestations of this impersonal power. Scientific classification itself is also regarded as a mode of manipulation and normalization. This forms the substance of books such as *Madness and Civilization*, *The Birth of the Clinic*, and *Discipline and Punish*. Thus, in terms of either external reason of government, or the purported humanitarian reason of hospitals, clinics, asylums, and the like, Foucault sees power at work. It is power via routine regimentation of thought and action. It is not exercised by a subject, it is 'unowned' and works at the micro-level. Power might thus be described as a net of normalization, forging what Foucault referred to as a 'docile body'. This power extends into our own purported 'self-regulation', for example, of our own dress, eating habits, or sexuality. What we call sexuality is in fact for Foucault very much the modern invention of certain discourses. His last work on the *History of Sexuality* was therefore an attempt to trace genealogically the emergence of a series of discourses and practices surrounding sexuality that are involved in making the human subject docile and 'self-responsible'. Even the human body is moulded by many discourse regimes. Foucault referred to this as 'bio-power', that is, where the health and welfare of the body are manipulated by subtle technologies and disciplinary practices.[17]

Genealogy therefore plays a crucial role in Foucault's work. Its central motif is to 'show' the dimensions and extent of such micro-power—the 'hazardous play of dominations'. Genealogy in fact charts the emergence of all the diverse disciplines of power (see Foucault 1986a: 81–3). Genealogy is not interested in politics at a grand level, that is, in states, sovereigns and the like. It is more interested in the way power functions effectively at a micro-level—'governmentality' as *opposed* to 'government'. It is in this context that Foucault commented that political theory in general 'has never ceased to be obsessed with the person of the sovereign'. He continues that 'Such theories still continue today to busy themselves with the problem of sovereignty. What we need, however, is a political philosophy that isn't erected around the problem of sovereignty... We need to cut off the King's head: in political theory that has still to be done' (Foucault 1980: 121). Thus, political theory becomes a more localized genealogical enterprise.

The other point to note here is that Foucault tries to disabuse us of any sense of progress in our understanding towards, for example, democracy or liberalism. He comments, 'humanity does not gradually progress from combat to combat until it arrives at universal reciprocity, where the rule of law finally replaces warfare; humanity installs each of its violences in a system of rules and thus proceeds from domination to domination'. Success in history is seizing rules in terms of one's own pattern of domination. There is no sequence here, no progress, no improvement, only 'substitutions, displacements, disguised conquest' (Foucault 1986a: 85–6). For Foucault it is traditional humanistic metaphysics that wants to see a unified sequence however, genealogy 'easily disintegrates this unity'. History for Foucault is always 'haphazard conflicts' and 'randomness' (Foucault 1986a: 87–8). What we see in all societies, individuals, and cultures is therefore nothing factual, universal, or objective but rather a range of interpretations. The role of genealogy is to record these interpretations and their effects.

RORTY AND CONNOLLY

The impact of the aforementioned thinkers has been profound in late-twentieth-century thought. In my reading they (particularly Nietzsche) constitute the substance to postmodern political theory. One can find innumerable instances of their influence. However, I examine briefly just two examples—Richard Rorty and William Connolly.[18] Connolly's own movement to a postmodern position can be seen developing gradually through the 1980s in the various additions to the editions of his book *The Terms of Political Discourse*, particularly in terms of his growing admiration for Foucault and Nietzsche. Intellectual parallels between Wittgenstein and certain postmodern arguments also arise in Connolly's arguments. In other words, for Connolly there are grounds for seeing the essential contestability thesis as a precursor to deconstruction and genealogy (see Connolly 2nd edition 1983: 321 ff.). Connolly's *Political Theory and Modernity* (1988) ends presciently with a very positive chapter on Nietzsche. The Nietzsche chapter is interesting since it suggests that Nietzsche's perspectivism and genealogy allow us to see the illusions and myths that have pervaded the entire political theory project in the twentieth century. The project of modernity and political theory are seen as a depoliticized world where things that escape our control (or will to power) are designated as 'chaos' or 'mad'. The key Nietzschean/Foucaultian contribution is seen to be the link between power and knowledge. Political theory should no longer be focused on issues such as sovereignty and statehood. The key issue is micro-power constituting and normalizing subjects and their desires. These themes are developed in books such as *Identity/Difference* (1991) and the *Ethos of Pluralization* (1995). Rorty's contribution to postmodern thinking has been controversial and he has been unhappy with the title 'postmodern'. His own contribution to postmodern thinking also owes a lot to his unique use of pragmatism (and late Wittgensteinianism). However, it is still quite legitimate to consider his *Contingency Irony and Solidarity* (1989) as making a significant neo-Nietzschean contribution to political theory debate. The difference between Nietzsche and Rorty is that the latter is altogether more optimistic. Rorty sees no need to agonize over culture, decadence, and contemporary politics. In fact for both Connolly and Rorty, Nietzschean aristocratic radicalism needs to be considerably softened if not bypassed; postmodern radicalized liberal democracy is reconciled in itself to the private world of self-creation as distinct from the public world.

In the *Identity/Difference* book, the main thesis is that all identity entails difference and exclusion—difference is built into all identity. Connolly predictably takes the Enlightenment conceptions of reason as a vehicle of closure and fixed identity excluding difference. Connolly suggests, for example, that the liberal individualist, collectivist, and communitarian visions are all located in the same exclusionary Enlightenment frame, that is, 'a matrix, in which the categories across the horizontal axis are mastery and attunement and on the vertical axis are the individual and the collectivity' (Connolly 1991: 29). For Connolly, a postmodern position embraces difference and otherness and rejects closure.[19] Critics of postmodernism who accuse it of making surreptitious truth claims are brushed aside by Connolly. He contends that postmodernists are more interested in the way that accusation is framed. The accusation in fact presupposes an 'either/or' mentality and therefore seeks closure and exclusion of postmodernism as 'other'. As Connolly observes, the postmodernist is thus more interested in the 'subterranean rhetorical configuration' behind the accusation (Connolly 1991: 59–61). Such critics are afraid of what Connolly calls, the 'infinite openness' of postmodernism. The critic is thus always trying to convert the 'code of paradox' back into the 'code of coherence'. This is a clear use by Connolly of both Nietzschean genealogy and perspectivism. Rorty's answer to this 'truth criticism' is more subtle than Connolly's, however the Nietzschean influence remains strong. Rorty contends, 'To say we should drop the idea of truth as out there waiting to be discovered is not say that we discovered that, out there, there is no truth' (Rorty 1989: 8). This would be claiming to know what has already been claimed cannot be known. Language for Rorty is non-representational. There is nothing intrinsic about it. Thus, the task of the theorists for both Connolly and Rorty is to counterpose genealogical and perspectivist irony against all forms of transcendental piety (Connolly 1991: 61). This leads to an acceptance of radical contingency.

Contingency forms Rorty's main theme in his book *Contingency Irony and Solidarity*. The idea of contingency rests on the Nietzschean argument that truth is *made* and not *discovered*. This also echoes the themes of his earlier book *Philosophy as the Mirror of Nature*.[20] Theory never represents or mirrors the real. There is only the text and nothing outside it. Connolly, who also takes this position—employing Heideggerian terminology—describes such attempts at mirroring, representation, and closure, as collectively 'ontotheology'.[21] John Rawls, for example, becomes in Connolly's terminology an overt 'ontotheologist' trying to escape into some form of liberal hermeneutic in his later work (Connolly 1991: 73). Thus, for both Connolly and Rorty *all* we have are interpretations or perspectives (or viewed from another perspective, metaphors). They are essential to life, however, such interpretations often congeal and masquerade as a foundational reality and need to be deconstructed or genealogically exposed. Both Connolly and Rorty therefore seek a political theory that recognizes its own contingency. Rorty, for example, notes favourably Kierkegaard's remark that if Hegel had prefaced his great *Science of Logic* by remarking that this was just another thought experiment he would have been the greatest philosopher ever (Rorty 1989: 104).

Rorty's account of truth is again deeply Nietzschean, although with a much lighter and wittier touch. Providing his own genealogy, Rorty suggests that made truth has a comparatively recent history, part of which is reliant on the idea of the nineteenth-century romantic poets' notion of self-creation. In philosophy, the German Idealists were the first to grasp the self-constitution or self-creation nettle. However, the Idealists, although seeing much of the construction of the world as tied to the mind, still insisted that mind or spirit had an essential underlying nature and teleology (Rorty 1989: 4).[22] For Rorty, however, nothing has an essential nature or teleology. He therefore distinguishes the claims that 'the world is out there' from 'the truth is out there'. To say that truth is not out there is 'simply to say that where there are no sentences there is no truth, that sentences are elements of human language, and that human languages are human creations' (Rorty 1989: 5). There are, in other words, no sentence-shaped chunks in the world. The idea that truth is 'out there' waiting to be discovered or mirrored, for example, in the natural sciences, is for Rorty a legacy of the contention that God (or Being) is out there waiting to be discovered. If we change our views, it is not forced upon us by the world, rather we get out of the habit of using certain words and we adopt others. Nothing actually 'fits' the world. There is no real self, no essential nature to the world, and no essence to politics. Nothing is essential to the self any more than sensitive genitals are essential to the body (Rorty 1989: 188). There are only different vocabularies (or conventional perspectives) that make claims to finality. As Rorty contends, 'if we could ever become reconciled to the idea that most of reality is indifferent to our descriptions of it . . . then we should at last have assimilated what was true in the Romantic idea that truth is made rather than found' (Rorty 1989: 7). Vocabularies are not representational jigsaws that fit over the world, rather they are pragmatic tools made by human beings.[23] Truth, as Nietzsche emphasized, is metaphor—or more precisely what are called truths are worn-out metaphors. Scientific revolutions are metaphoric redescriptions.[24] Human history is a succession of grand metaphors. To see the world this way is to dedivinize it. In short, viewed as a sequence: love of God was replaced by love of truth; love of truth by love of science; love of science was replaced by love of self (in the romantics); and now love of self has been replaced by love of nothing (or whatever comes along for private self-creation). In future, according to Rorty we should aim for 'tingles' rather than 'truths' (Rorty 1989: 152).

This leads to another Nietzschean theme: if we *make* rather than *discover* truth, then imagination, aesthetics, and creativity take on a crucial role in cognition. In Rorty's terms (as for Nietzsche) the poet and aesthete take priority. The self if created is essentially an imaginative construction.[25] The self becomes a work of art or self-creation. Given that the self and its vocabulary construct the world, there is *nothing* intrinsic, foundational, or fundamental to represent.[26] Values (ethical and otherwise) are not found but created. The heroization of the isolated artist as shaman in the nineteenth and twentieth century (indeed some argue that art has begun to replace religion as a key system of values and worship) is symptomatic of the same movement—except that there has been a democratization of such themes. In this case, each human being is potentially a playful Zarathustra, as long as they do not hide in some bogus foundational world focused on reason, a god, or the like.

Self-creation, rather than representation, has come to the fore for most post-modern practitioners. However, self-creation still remains vaguely rooted if there is 'something' for the self to create with, that is, if there is something *beyond* the self and its creativity. In Rorty and Connolly, the self appears to self-create from within a particular liberal cultural ethos—we engage, work within, ironize about, and play with the complex pre-understandings of 'rich lucky liberal states'. However, this ethos of pre-understandings has *no* ontopolitical or ontotheological status; it just happens—in Rorty's and Connolly's cases and much of their readerships' cases—to be liberal and democratic. The arguments of Rorty and Connolly are thus addressed to the potential (updated) Zarathustras of modern Western liberal culture. Such free radical liberal spirits should be 'strong ironic poets', unafraid of the loss of metaphysical and ontological foundations. Rorty, for example, takes figures such as Proust, Nietzsche, and Derrida as exemplars of this mentality. Rorty comments: 'To see one's language, one's conscience, one's morality, and one's highest hopes as contingent products, as . . . metaphors, is to adopt a self-identity which suits one for citizenship in such an ideally liberal state' (Rorty 1989: 61). Oddly, this seems to stop short from a full recognition of the ambiguity of self-creation, that is, where there is a recognition of *no* horizon, *no* order beyond the self.

In summary, in Rorty and Connolly, the following Nietzschean themes are crucial: truth is 'made up' metaphors and not discovered in the world; poetic creativity (and *poeisis*) is set over representation or correspondence; aesthetics is prioritized over ethics (ethics is in fact created by aesthetics); irony and gaming are set over knowledge; foundational moral or political beliefs are rejected out of hand in favour of perspectives and interpretation. There is also an acceptance of difference, set against all claims for strict identity. Finally, the self-referential or self-reflexive agent is also set against ontological claims to communal or historical rootedness.

LYOTARD AND THE DIFFEREND

There are postmodern theorists who do actually take on the full logic of self-creation, although they are rarer than one might think. This is self-creation without any apparent horizon, foundation, or pre-understanding. It is, though, a deeply problematic and disturbing vision that is in permanent danger of collapsing into a nihilistic melancholy. One case in point is the work of Jean-François Lyotard, particularly his theory of the 'differend'. Lyotard sees his own work on the differend in the context of a more widespread decline of universalism, the attack on humanism and metaphysics, the turn to language in philosophy, and more general weariness with theory.

Lyotard's book *The Differend* is less well known although more philosophically sophisticated than the earlier *The Postmodern Condition*. However, the latter contains the most widely used definition of postmodernism as 'incredulity toward metanarratives' (Lyotard 1991*a*: xxiv; see also Lyotard 1997).[27] *The Postmodern Condition*, largely, utilizes Wittgenstein's theory of language games to elucidate the postmodern mentality (see Lyotard 1991*a*: 9 *ff*.). There is no world as such, only a multiplicity of language games. In *The Differend* the term 'phrase' replaces 'language game'. Yet, the two thinkers Lyotard considers as most overtly influential on his perspective are Kant (particularly of the 3rd *Critique*) and Wittgenstein (qua the *Philosophical Investigations*). Yet, again, he sees both as transitional thinkers or as he puts it, 'epilogues to modernity and prologues to an honourable postmodernity'. In effect, they 'draw up the affidavit ascertaining the decline of universalist doctrines' (Lyotard 1999: xiii). Unsurprisingly, Descartes is seen (with Husserl) as the ultimate philosophical expression of modernity. In the case of Kant and Wittgenstein, however, something unique happens. In Kant, the 'free examination of phrases leads to the (critical) dissociation of their regimens (the separation of the faculties and their conflict . . .)'. In Wittgenstein, there is a 'disentanglement of language games'. Together both thinkers 'lay the ground for the thought of dispersion which, . . . shapes our context'. The problem with both thinkers, which Lyotard wishes to slough off, is what he calls the 'cumbersome debt to anthropomorphism (the notion of "use" in both, an anthropomorphism that is transcendental in Kant, empirical in Wittgenstein)' (Lyotard 1999: xiii). In other words, both thinkers are still too taken up with the vestiges of foundational metaphysics and humanism.

Lyotard's own theory of the differend can be stated quite briefly. He lays it out with admirable clarity in the opening section of *The Differend*. Essentially, a differend is 'a case of conflict, between (at least) two parties, that cannot be equitably resolved for lack of a rule of judgment applicable to both arguments. One side's legitimacy does not imply the other's lack of legitimacy . . . applying a single rule of judgment to both in order to settle their differend as though it were a litigation would wrong (at least) one of them'. The key issue is that a 'universal rule of judgment between heterogeneous genres is lacking' (Lyotard 1999: xi). The core of the book is contained in these few sentences, although its ramifications are considerable.

The key term 'phrase', which replaces the anthropomorphism of 'language games', is employed somewhat abstractly, although it can still be viewed as a socio-linguistic conventional practice (as in a language game). Phrases are constituted by sets of rules that Lyotard calls 'regimens'. There are a number of 'phrase regimens', for example, knowing, describing, recounting, and so forth. Phrase regimens are linked together by various (what Lyotard calls) 'genres of discourse'. Genres 'supply rules for linking together heterogeneous phrases, rules that are proper for attaining certain goals: to know, to teach'. However, Lyotard insists that 'there is no "language" in general, except as the object of an Idea'. In other words, there is no overarching or metalanguage that covers all genres and regimens.[28] A genre of discourse provides a range of possible phrases; however, for Lyotard it is crucial to acknowledge that there is no way at all to resolve differences between phrase regimens. As he puts it, there is no 'non-phrase . . . There is no last phrase'. For Lyotard, therefore, there are two key assumptions underpinning his theory: '1) the impossibility of avoiding conflicts (the impossibility of indifference) and 2) the absence of a universal genre of discourse to regulate them' (Lyotard 1999: xii).

If we translate the argument here: Lyotard is suggesting that *all* we have are phrases. There is nothing underneath, behind, developing within or as references for, phrases. The term 'phrase' here functions in the same way as Nietzsche's 'interpretative perspective' or Foucault's 'episteme'. There is no pre-understanding prior to phrases. Reality and truth are embedded in phrases. In breaking from the anthropomorphism of Wittgenstein and Kant, Lyotard is also asserting the importance of the inhuman (in the same spirit as Nietzsche, Heidegger, Derrida, and Foucault). He also thinks that traditional metaphysics is committed to the error of the 'Idea' of the human. As Lyotard comments, the inhuman means 'incompatible with an Idea of humanity' (Lyotard 1999: 18; see also Lyotard 1991b). Lyotard predictably repudiates such a metaphysical use. What we loosely call reality is in fact 'a swarm of senses', which directly parallels Nietzsche's 'flux of sensation'. There is no meaning to this 'flux' or 'swarm' unless we apply a phrase to it, or as Lyotard puts it, unless part of this flux is 'pinpointed by a world' (Lyotard 1999: 50). For Lyotard, phrases belong 'to heterogeneous families', and all proper names are situated in these different 'families' (Lyotard 1999: 49). There are, for Lyotard, as many families as there are phrases. In terms of the multiplicity attached to any proper name, Lyotard, with an ironic eye on his own Marxist past, gives the example: '*That's Stalin, here he is*. We acknowledge it. But as for what *Stalin* means? Phrases come to be attached to this name, which not only describe different senses for it (this can still be debated in dialogue), and not only place the name on different instances, but which also obey heterogeneous regimens and/or genres. This heterogeneity, for lack of a common idiom, makes consensus impossible. The assignment of a definition to Stalin necessarily does wrong to the nondefinitional phrases relating to Stalin, which this definition, for a while at least, disregards or betrays' (Lyotard 1999: 55–6). It is worth underscoring this point that is, phrases just *cannot* be translated into one another.

Some philosophers, for Lyotard, have seen this baffling sense of what is real or what underlies our conceptual schemes as implying something mystical. He accuses both Kant and Wittgenstein of this credulity. In his own reading, however, 'We see no reason to grant a "mystical" profundity to the abyss that separates cognitives and prescriptives'. Incommensurability is not mysterious, the 'heterogeneity of phrase regimens and of the impossibility of subjecting them to a single law (except by neutralizing them), also marks the relation between either cognitives or prescriptives and interrogatives, performatives, exclamatives . . . For each of these regimens, there corresponds a mode of presenting a universe, and one mode is not translatable into another' (Lyotard 1999: 128). Phrase regimens coincide with nothing.

In articulating his theory of the differend, Lyotard does though introduce a uniquely idiosyncratic idea—derived from Kant's *Critique of Judgement*—which enables a profounder grasp of the differend (Lyotard 1994). When Kant focused on aesthetics something unusual took place. Aesthetic judgement was encapsulated in a free play of imagination and understanding. Contemplating aesthetic beauty involved both imagination and understanding, in other words a form of subjective universality—it was a conceptualism that remained rooted in subjective feeling.[29] In his 'Analytic of the Sublime' Kant also distinguished the sublime from the beautiful. The concept of the 'sublime' basically defied any sense of aesthetic proportion. In the sublime the imagination and understanding were both engaged (as in the beautiful), but unlike the beautiful in art the sublime *remained* incomprehensible. Beauty was also limited by form, but the sublime was regarded as limitless. Further, whereas the beautiful could and often was represented, the sublime by contrast exceeded representation and often did violence to human sensibilities and imagination. The sublime therefore was not necessarily pleasurable for Kant, in fact it could be painful because it was so indeterminate. Our imaginations were engaged and awestruck, but neither our imaginations nor our understanding could actually grapple with it. Whereas the aesthetically beautiful could educate and civilize humans, the sublime could have the effect of isolating humans by revealing the incomprehensible and indeterminate nature of things.

Kant does go on to distinguish types of sublimity, however I leave this aside, suffice it to say that Lyotard finds a direct analogy in Kant's concept of the aesthetic (and more particularly his concept of the sublime) for his own perspectivist epistemology of the differend. The aesthetic is a struggle to bring together (in a subjective manner) our imagination and understanding. There is, in other words, a separation, or even chasm, between our faculties; any resolution remains subjective. Further, there is nothing objective or external founded in aesthetic judgement. It remains in the sphere of subjective taste. In the sublime, however, a chasm opens up and remains open. The differend is such an epistemological chasm. The sublime is thus directly analogous, for Lyotard, to the unbridgeable difference between phrase regimens. They disclose the unrepresentable and unpresentable. There is no 'metanarrative' or 'metalanguage' that can surmount this. A postmodern incredulity towards metanarratives—where no metalanguage or metaphrase exists—is thus seen as equivalent to Kant's feeling of the sublime.

The effect of this conclusion is twofold. First, Lyotard suggests that *whenever* we make judgements (using phrases) we are in exactly the same position as Kant's agent experiencing beauty. We have no universals or pre-understanding to go on. Our rationalizations are always completely removed from the world and incommensurable with other rationalizations. In fact, the 'world' *per se* makes no sense, we only have phrases. There are no foundations to appeal to settle the matter, unless we simply force the other to adopt our 'phrase'. Lyotard repudiates any idea of a '*sensus communis*'. Every consensus is just another imposed 'phrase regimen'. He completely rejects, for example, Habermas's idea of a possible communicative consensus. In consequence, we remain entrapped forever in phrases. This can generate a sense of incomprehensibility. Whatever one encounters and tries to formulate, remains in excess and outside of that which can be comprehended. Second, on a more positive note this situation can generate experimentation. Lyotard associates this claim with Aristotle. He observes 'we judge without criteria. We are in the position of Aristotle's prudent individual, who makes judgements about the just and the unjust without the least criterion'. Thus, judging justice, for example, is always a matter of striving out of nothing, with no fixed rules (see Lyotard 1985: 14).[30] He calls this a 'pagan' standpoint, since it judges outside of all the older metanarratives. Truths are singular, local, particular, and multiple. The same point would apply to even apparently serious moral wrongs.

In many ways this idea of judging beyond rules, making decisions without an established criterion, and being premised on a particular phrase regimen, with no possibility of overcoming the differend, is once again Nietzsche's argument concerning the end of metaphysics, the birth of the *übermensch* and Zarathustra, and the movement beyond good and evil. In Nietzschean terms, morality, law, politics, and culture are underpinned by the will to power. In this scenario there will be inevitable differences—a multiplicity of incommensurable differences. But at least the agent is free to constitute itself as a free spirit. In Rorty and Connolly there are limits—relating to our own ethos and society. In this sense, self-creation and self-constitution do have boundaries. In Lyotard—as one senses in many but not all of Nietzsche's writings— something more disturbing is taking place. We are simply creatures of conventional phrases. We float in a sea of these phrases, with no anchor, no land, and no sense of direction. We are also invited to jump ship to other vessels, to experiment. However, we should never expect to make any sense, since there is nothing to makes sense of, except a multiplicity of phrase regimens. We can create and go on creating ourselves endlessly. We are back here with Nietzschean nihilism and the radical arbitrariness of signs, although exactly what this means politically remains much more obscure.

CONCLUSION

In discussing the aforementioned thinkers several themes emerge, which appear regularly in postmodern theory. I summarize them briefly since the more substantive detail has already been covered in the body of this discussion. The most obvious critical point to come out of postmodernism is a rejection of both humanism and traditional metaphysics. Metaphysics and humanism are seen as two sides of the same coin. The human subject (and author) is in effect decentered. The 'idea' of the human self does not predate language, interpretation, or perspective. The self is a random and arbitrary product of language. To grasp this point requires deconstruction and/or genealogy. Genealogy and deconstruction are historically-inclined methods that 'show us' the course of an idea, but not in any narrative, coherent, or chronological sequence. History has no logic or purpose.[31] The human self is thus understood as a creative or self-constituted phenomenon. The metaphysics of modernity and the bulk of modern epistemology (the Cartesian cogito, Kantian transcendental ego, Husserlian transcendental subjectivity, or the empirical concept of mind) are seen to be premised on this false conception of an essential self prior in some manner to language.

Further, traditional metaphysics and epistemology assume (falsely) that there is something outside language and linguistic signification that can be represented or spoken about sensibly. This is dubbed logocentrism or the metaphysics of presence by Derrida, or ontotheology by Heidegger. For Nietzsche, also, this traditional perspective indicates a deep error that has permeated Western thinking since Plato. In Lyotard we find the most well-known formulation of this notion, where postmodernism is defined as an 'incredulity towards metanarrative'—metanarrative being roughly equivalent to the use of terms such as foundation, objective truth, classical metaphysics, regime of truth, or presence. What remains is heterogeneity, difference, and fragmentation and at most particularized or localized knowledge. There is therefore nothing for language to correspond to or represent. Human vocabularies are, as Rorty thinks of them, conventional pragmatic tools to navigate the world.

In addition, philosophy is not some specialized metalanguage, it is just another type of writing, the bulk of which is in error. In rejecting metaphysics, traditional epistemology, and humanism, postmodernism tends to be radically anti-foundational. Language does not refer to anything outside itself, or as Lyotard would have put it phrases just refer to other phrases. Meaning is inexhaustible because words have no essences. It just depends on our ability to experiment. We should therefore relinquish the idea that language gives us unique access into the reality of the world. What we call truth is in fact not discovered or proved to be the case; conversely it is created. What this reveals is that all discussion of knowledge is simply a discussion of particular interpretative perspectives. All human knowing *is* perspective. All else is academic pretension. This is the core of Nietzsche's doctrine of perspectivism. The abandonment of foundations and objective truth also entails the abandonment of all secular universals such as reason. Reason is always particular never universal. More importantly reason is also embedded—as in all human endeavours including natural science and morality—in what Nietzsche referred to as the will to power and Foucault as power/knowledge. The linkage of power and knowing leads to a more sceptical view of the boundaries between disciplines. Disciplinary boundaries are conventional artifices underpinned by a will to power. Overall, this is the core of what I have taken as a radical use of conventionalist argument characterizing postmodernism.

However, the question arises as to the effects all these have on political theory and politics in general. More pertinently, where does politics go from here? As I stated in the opening section of the chapter, there is still a yearning for some form of grounding in postmodern theory, even if it is a dedivinized and fragmented ground. There are therefore degrees of enthusiasm through which the conventionalist logic is pursued. Another way of putting this would be that there are degrees of postmodern scepticism. The underpinning for this lies in a point noted by a number of commentators on postmodernism, that is, that there are various schools, types, or forms of postmodern argument. Common distinctions are made in the literature, for example, between sceptical and affirmative, conservative and radical, positive and negative, or hard and soft sceptical postmodernisms.[32] There is some truth to this issue concerning types of postmodern theory. My own view is to also distinguish two basic responses that tend to overlap. One way of thinking about these responses is to associate them with more specific political considerations.

The first response involves a vigorous prosecution of the conventionalist argument, and Nietzsche is undoubtedly the key influence. However, in many ways it also provides a thin (unwitting) foundation for some postmodern argument—that Nietzsche's individual subject, exercising a will to power, provides for admirers and critics alike a new veiled form of metaphysical foundation. In this sense, many postmodern readers of Nietzsche have (despite appearances) read some positive political and ethical components into his arguments. This, to a large extent, forms the somewhat loose subtext to difference and some recent multicultural theories use of postmodern argument, that is, where the conventionalist critique is seen inevitably to terminate in either fragmented postmodern individuals, cultures, or new social movements. In other words, there is still *some* basis on which humans can make moral and political judgements. The difference between more orthodox exponents of liberal or libertarian individualism, culture, social movements (encountered in previous chapters), and postmodern and difference-based renditions is on the one hand that the former attach some 'truth status' and 'ontological character' to their commitments. The postmodern exponents of this position have on the other hand usually abandoned any such commitments. The convention becomes a more ephemeral, strategic, if still important, dimension of argument.

The second response (which also bears upon a reading of Nietzsche) takes the conventionalist claim a step further, that is, it suggest *nothing* exists unless we constitute it—our whole notion of reality becomes a game between conventions, none of which has any ontological primacy or status. This position tries to overcome every taint of humanism, metaphysics, and ontology. It is a position most closely akin to the popular image of nihilism, although it is important to be circumspect here in relation to the Nietzschean reading of nihilism. Nietzsche unlike Schopenhauer was not pessimistic about the role of the will. He describes the experience of the will to power as one of both risk but also joy. This position does not envisage any possibility of consensus or foundation. It rather suggests a radical form of 'gaming' between irreconcilable differences. It involves a 'total acceptance of the emphemerality, fragmentation, discontinuity, and the chaotic' (Harvey 1989: 44). It swims in the chaotic. This is a position that I have associated with the later work of Lyotard, although Jean Baudrillard would be another possible example.

The key issues with regards to politics (and political theory) can be viewed through the aforementioned two lenses. In the case of Connolly and Rorty the political stance presents no immediate problems. Both theorists are moderately clear on their beliefs and fit easily within the first category. However, it is not so straightforward in the case of Nietzsche, Heidegger, Derrida, and Foucault. Even Lyotard has some altruistic souls who wish to democratize him. In the case of Nietzsche, for example, Connolly sees a need for a Nietzschean political theory lending support to a radical reconstituted liberalism and democracy, sensitive to difference. He admits that Nietzsche does not quite present what people would normally expect as a 'normal political theory'.[33] However, given that Nietzsche treats modernity as something alien, he can make us reflect on our present beliefs and our frequent 'self-deceits'. This is envisaged as an opening up of new political possibilities. Nietzsche's work also enables us to come to terms with difference in a new way. It allows us, in Connolly's terms, to adopt an ethic of 'letting be'. It also enables the self to begin to 'craft' or 'form itself' without any transcendental or ontological supports.

In summary, for Connolly 'a democratic politics provides the best way to incorporate the experience of contingency into public life. This would still leave much to be thought about the relations between the contingent subject and the forms of otherness it engenders' (Connolly 1988: 159–60). Similarly, there are viable notions of both justice and equality that can be integrated within a postmodern Nietzschean society. Connolly thus notes, 'Perhaps a reconstituted, radicalized liberalism is needed today; one which reaches into the subject itself rather than taking it as a starting point for reflection; one which challenges the hegemony of economic expansion rather than making it a precondition of liberty; one which treats nature as a locus of difference and resistances essential to life as well as a shelter and set of resources for human use' (see Connolly 1988: 171–2). Essentially Connolly wants to rewrite the nihilistic aristocratic radical Nietzsche as a democratic postmodern liberal sensitive to a multicultural or difference-based society. The operative faith is that 'an ethical orientation to life does not depend upon the demand to lock all reverence for life into some universal theistic faith, rational consensus, secular contract, transcendental argument, or interior attunement to a deep attunement' (Connolly 1995: 27). Most of our problems come not from fragmentation and heterogeneity *per se* but the attempt to give that particularity some kind of moral foundation. Connolly thus has the same basic view as Foucault.[34]

A Nietzschean and Foucaultian dedivinized radical liberalism also forms the main text to Connolly's own work. Connolly's vision of society is an 'agonistic democracy', containing decentralization and local democracy. Where neutralist or procedural liberals try to shield society from strong identities, Connolly wants a future liberal society to encompass them. The crisis of society is not fragmentation but rather the attempt to fix and close identities. Connolly, following Nietzsche and Foucault, favours a 'cultivation ethics' over a 'command ethics'; the former celebrates difference, exposes paradox rather than suppressing it, and accepts self-creation. There are no 'either/or's in agonistic democracy. Connolly makes ethical hay here while the deconstruction sun shines. Derrida's *différance*, Heidegger's 'destruction', and Nietzsche's perspectivism become supports for a cultivation 'ethic of care' (Connolly 1991: 50; see also White 1991: 96 *ff.*). Connolly takes the refusal of closure as a prime mark of postmodernism.[35]

Rorty's political vision is less overtly Nietzschean than Connolly's, although the intellectual influences are still quite obvious. However, the final upshot is not that different from Connolly. Rorty values a liberalism without foundation and without any Enlightenment moral baggage. It is non-universalist, non-rationalist, and accepts the claim that 'there is no standpoint outside the particular historically conditioned and temporary vocabulary we are presently using'.[36] It is a liberalism that affirms the need for a private narcissism of self-creativity together with a public solidarity and loathing for cruelty. Rorty claims that this does justice to both self-creationists and certain community rationalists (Rorty 1989: xiv). Rorty thus defends Isaiah Berlin's arguments on negative freedom and the incommensurability of values against Michael Sandel's accusations of moral relativism, by claiming that Sandel himself has preclosed the whole debate by using Enlightenment language, which assumes itself to be a 'final vocabulary' (see also Gray 1993: 289). Rorty's (like Connolly's) interest is therefore to resist closure before one gets to the argument about relativism. Criticisms of postmodernism as relativist are therefore dissolved rather than solved.

For Rorty, liberalism does not need a new ontological or metaphysical foundation, conversely it needs to be poeticized (Rorty 1989: 53). Liberalism *cannot* be justified. Yet, Rorty also wishes self-creation to be privatized. He considers liberalism to be about the avoidance or diminishment of cruelty. This potential solidarity is another major component of his argument along with irony and contingency. However, the language of liberalism is firmly tied to place, circumstance, history, and ethos. We must accept this contingency, but we can *still* loathe cruelty. Even if our language is detheologized and there is no metalanguage to justify it, we can still affirm solidarity with our fellow human beings. Even if we have 'made' the solidarity we can still die for it—although this seems an amazingly tenuous notion of solidarity.[37] We have here though a precise formulation of—what I would call—a *contingent political liberalism*, which is essentially the same as Connolly's dedivinized *agonistic liberalism*.[38]

Nietzsche however is not alone in this redemptive democratizing effort. Leslie Thiele, in a comprehensive study of Heidegger, attempts to reassert Heidegger's democratic potential. He remarks, for example, that 'the affirmation of human plurality that sits at the core of democratic politics must be retrieved from Heidegger in spite of his withholdings'. He links this with Heidegger's attack on humanism and metaphysics and his focus on Being, remarking, 'Heidegger's philosophical dissolution of metaphysics has its counterpart in a democracy infused with a disclosive freedom that celebrates relations of self and other in their contingency' (Thiele 1995: 163 and 167–8).

Lyotard has also been subject to the same redemptive exercise. In a passage, for example, in *The Differend*, Lyotard comments that in 'the deliberative politics of modern democracies, the differend is exposed'. In other words, democracies are more likely to disclose heterogeneity. A few pages later he continues in the same spirit that 'the deliberative is more "fragile" than the narrative . . . it lets the abyss be perceived that separate genres of discourse from each other and even phrase regimens from each other, the abysses that threaten "the social bond". It presupposes and registers a profound dislocation of narrated worlds' (Lyotard 1999: 147 and 150). There are those who consequently see a deep postmodern participatory democratic message in Lyotard (see Keane 1992; Young 2002). However, Lyotard does add a rider to his comment about deliberative democracy, which is worth reflecting on. He notes that democracy contains the 'transcendental appearance of single finality that would bring resolution'; this appearance then 'persists in helping forget the differend, in making it bearable'. Lyotard detests any form of 'essentialism'—democratic, socialist, liberal, or feminist. Democracy is not prioritized. Rather, as a matter of fact, it tends to reveal differences quicker than other doctrines. The danger is that many think of it as a form of normative finality. In itself, democracy—or feminism for that matter—has *no* normative significance (see Lyotard 1999: 147; also Browning 2000: 16).

A similar reasoning holds for Nietzsche, Heidegger, and Foucault. In the latter two the case is starkly obvious. Nietzsche, as even the most cursory reader will be aware, held democracy, liberalism, socialism, anarchism, nationalism, and the like in withering contempt. They were in fact his key targets (as the secular spawn of Christianity)—as exemplars of an inauthentic cringing slave morality that denied the will to power. Socialism is corrupt to the core, egalitarianism of all types is a sign of deep weakness, and liberalism denotes a flimsy and undisciplined notion of freedom and an empty-headed relativism. He sees nothing of any significance in these doctrines. The will to power requires a sense of high culture and a pyramidal society with elites and various castes. This is Nietzsche's doctrine of aristocratic radicalism. As one Nietzschean scholar remarks, 'There is something risible about the attempt to enlist Nietzsche's political thinking to the cause of postmodern liberalism. Is Nietzsche not the great decodifier who resists all attempts to rigidify life and so prevent the flow of self-overcoming, whether through Christian ethics or bourgeois politics' (Ansell-Pearson 1994: 178). A similar criticism could be made of the democratic Heidegger. Heidegger had a deep sympathy and enthusiastic direct involvement in National Socialism during the 1930s, further he refused till the end of his life to condemn or show any remorse for the actions of Nazis (*particularly* of the holocaust). In addition, Heidegger viewed liberal democracy as not so much a solution, but rather as a symptom of a calamity and crisis in Western thought (particularly over technology). Foucault also, like Lyotard, was only interested in liberalism and democracy insofar as it revealed more directly incommensurable differences. Many have strained to bring Foucault into the radical democratic liberal fold, and nearer the end of his life there are signs that Foucault was aware of the problem, but it is hard to see any support for it in his primary texts.

A final poignant example of this is Derrida. His deconstruction method has been in many ways at the very core of the postmodern attack on normativism, foundationalism, and universalism. As I mentioned earlier, the core of Derrida's theory is that our conceptual ordering of the world does not reveal anything about the nature of the world, since there is no nature to reveal. We float in a sea of signs with no anchorage and no references. This is certainly the Derrida of the 1960s and 1970s.[39] He resolutely denied, initially at least, that any political programme could be read into his deconstruction method. He appeared to be at most, as Terry Eagleton once described him, a libertarian pessimist. However, in the last eight years there has been a flurry of short books from Derrida, for example, *The Other Heading: Reflections on Today's Europe*, *Specters of Marx: The State of the Debt, the Work of Mourning, and the New International*, *Politics of Friendship*, and *On Cosmopolitanism and Forgiveness*, which seem to yearn mournfully for something more universal and normative. Derrida's major problem is that in attacking logocentrism so dynamically and in declaiming his method as unsettling *all* the self-confidence of Western normative thinking, the question arises as to where to go next and how would one know where to go next? Clearly Derrida became increasingly disturbed during the 1980s and 1990s by issues such as human rights, justice, racism, hospitality, friendship, immigration, asylum-seeking, globalization, cosmopolitanism, and forgiveness, amongst other issues. The central question is, given what he has already done with deconstruction, how does he account for this new mood of responsibility? Further, how would he justify it, would he even want to justify it? Some have seen Derrida's struggles here as tied up with his rediscovery of the ethical writing of his old teacher Emmanuel Levinas.[40]

If everything is a conventional linguistic sign (and nothing else), surely all existing normative or ideologically orientated theories succumb to the same logic. Miraculously, in some way, Derrida believes that there is an idea of justice, in fact he even equates deconstruction with justice, since deconstructing the rationale of justice enables the *presence* of justice to arise in some way (see Beardsworth 1996: 132–3). Similarly, Derrida suggests in his book *On Cosmopolitanism and Forgiveness* (2002) that in thinking about refugees, we should try to recover something he calls 'an original concept of hospitality, of the duty of hospitality', which he considers as constituting a 'new cosmopolitics'. This, in turn, involves 'dreaming of another concept, of another set of rights' that transcend international law. This new ethic of hospitality is not one ethic amongst others, rather 'ethics is hospitality'. Ethics is 'co-extensive with the experience of hospitality'. Apparently, 'being at home with oneself (. . . the other within oneself) supposes a reception or inclusion'. The debate about cosmopolitanism and how to deal with the rights of refugees 'is a question of knowing how to transform and improve the law, and of knowing if this improvement is possible within a historical space that takes place *between* the Law of an unconditional hospitality . . . and the conditional laws of a right to hospitality, without which *The* unconditional Law of hospitality would be in danger of remaining a pious and irresponsible desire' (Derrida 2002: 5, 8, 17, 22–3). Cosmopolitan hospitality calls forth, it appears, a 'just' response.

The cosmopolitan essay is followed by another equally baffling essay on themes of forgiveness. The overriding thought arises here that if a new 'young' Derrida (mark 2) encountered the above writings, he would surely set about gleefully deconstructing all their hidden presences, normativism, and teleology. The 'ends of man' have crept back here within Derrida's anfractuous prose. These later works seem to be the work of frustrated melancholy. He obviously does 'feel' concerned about refugees, racism, and the like, he also has valid thoughts about a Europe that could be more tolerant and open to difference, but in a sense he is at the same time hoisted by his own youthful petard. His last gasp here is to think of ethics and justice as actually embodied in deconstruction. If deconstruction functions successfully on the humanistic rationalism of the West, then it will create a space for something else—but what? Derrida intimates that it will be something really just and ethical, but there is absolutely *no* reason why that should be the case, unless Derrida wants to incorporate some benign rationalist teleology. The outcome could just as well turn into rampant racism or xenophobia.

Derrida is not alone in this problem. The milder sceptics of course have their own way out of this postmodern normative dilemma. They utilize rigorous conventional argumentation up to a point, then stop and appeal to a culture or ethos. The argument does not claim any ontological status, but simply views itself as a *fait accompli*, that is, *this* is where we are. The strong scepticism and rigorous perspectivism of Nietzsche, the younger Foucault and Derrida, and older Lyotard, do not have the luxury of appealing to any dedivinized or desacralized ethos, culture, or teleology. They disrupt everything. Nothing holds us. Nothing actually matters. We swim in a chaotic sea of conventional signs, acknowledging irresolvable difference. Milder-mannered, more optimistic American postmodernism finds this all too much. Rorty, for example, views this latter idea as 'a reductio ad absurdum of the philosophy of subjectivity' (Rorty 1989: 62).[41] In Rorty, postmodernism almost becomes a benign modern epicureanism. Strongly sceptical postmoderns, however, carry the deconstructive effort against foundationalism to the point of perpetually deconstructing themselves and *permanently* postponing any meaning. The total critique still, however, leaves something present—a spectral presence—but with no content, no world to confer standards, no ontotheology, no logocentrism, only the total ever-present possibility to create or will their own standards—a will to power. This is pristine absolute self-creation. The upshot of this for political theory is to undermine any foundations. Minimally that means subsisting strategically and ironically with an ethos or culture, maximally it entails unending critique.

Notes

1. Poststructuralism and postmodernism are not identical. Poststructuralism has a more overt methodological and philosophical focus. Postmodernism and postmodernity are more inclusive (one might say promiscuous) terms, involving much broader cultural critiques and range of referents. However, there is still a definite overlap and community of concerns between these terms. In this chapter postmodernism is taken as the core idea, of which poststructuralism is a methodological component. Postmodernism is viewed as a critical reaction to both structuralism and to the very broad phenomenon of modernity and an attempt at dissolution of the forms that are associated with modernity. It is a movement that crystallized in the early 1970s. It developed initially in the area of literary criticism, partly because of the deep emphasis on language in much postmodern thinking. By the 1980s, debates became more deeply involved in Derrida's deconstruction ideas and Foucault genealogical critiques. However, a large grouping of theorists including Frederick Jameson, Jean Baudrillard, and Jean Francois Lyotard, amongst many others, have also developed postmodern ideas in their own distinctive ways.

2. 'One ought not to make "cause" and "effect" *into material things*, as natural scientists do (and those who, like them, naturalize in their thinking), in accordance with the prevailing mechanistic stupidity which has the cause press and push until it "produces an effect"; one ought to employ "cause" and "effect" only as pure *concepts*, that is to say as conventional fictions for the purpose of designation, mutual understanding, *not* explanation. In the end, "in itself" there is nothing of "causal connection", of "necessity", of "psychological unfreedom"; there "the effect" *does not* "follow the cause", there is no "law" rules. It is *we*

alone who have fabricated causes, succession, reciprocity, relativity, compulsion, number, law, freedom, motive, purpose', Nietzsche (1974: section 21).

3. '*From a doctorate exam*—"What is the task of all higher education?"—To turn a man into a machine.—"By what means?"—He has to learn how to feel bored.—"How is that achieved?"—Through the concept of duty.—"Who is his model?"—The philologist: he teaches how to *grind*.—"Who is the perfect man?"—the civil servant.—"Which philosophy provides the best formula for the civil servant?"—Kant's: the civil servant as thing in itself set as judge over the civil servant as appearance', Nietzsche (1968: section 29, 84).

4. Some have suggested, for example, that Freud's *Civilization and its Discontents* is a conscious reworking of Nietzsche's *Genealogy of Morals*.

5. In Heidegger the distinction appears in a contrast between 'types' of thinking: meditative and calculative. The latter is what most humans engage in and for Heidegger it reveals little about 'Being'.

6. I want to return to this doctrine later in the discussion of what postmodern politics looks like.

6. Ironic given Heidegger's political affiliations.

7. 'Philosophy, even when it becomes "critical" through Descartes and Kant, always follows the course of metaphysical representation', see Heidegger (1993: 234).

8. For Heidegger, Marx and Hegel recognized this homelessness of modern man and 'This homelessness is specifically evoked from the destiny of Being in the form of metaphysics, and through metaphysics is simultaneously entrenched and covered up as such', Heidegger (1993: 243).

9. In ek-sisting man 'sustains *Da-sein* in that he takes the *Da*, the clearing of Being, into "care"', see Heidegger (1993: 231).

10. Heidegger's answer (if it qualifies as an answer) to this is Being is 'It Itself'. It is neither God, nor a cosmic ground. rather 'Being is farther than all beings and yet is nearer to man than every being'; further, 'Being is the nearest. Yet the near remains farthest from man', see Heidegger (1993: 234).

11. Derrida thinks it is actually a mistake to associate Hegel and Husserl with anthropologism, see Derrida (1993: 138).

12. The term 'structuralism' has a comparatively recent history, dating from the early to mid-twentieth century. Its most well-known rendition was as a social scientific (mainly anthropological and sociological) method for studying differences between cultures, in the hope of one day achieving a more genuinely universal understanding. The initial idea was derived from Ferdinand Saussure's structural linguistics. The central issue was that language embodies our sense of reality. Saussure saw speech as a collection of signs, underpinned by language. Language was understood as a formal system of underlying deep structural conventions. Thus *langue* (language) and *parole* (speech) were seen, on one level, as distinct. Speech was a collection of signs that were, in turn, underpinned by the deep structural conventions of language. Speech was therefore made possible by language. Meaning was not therefore about an individual's intention in speech. Meaning was not attributable to individual speakers. Meaning existed in the relation between the elements of language. The laws of language formed a deep structure to speech; these underlying structures could be studied under the aegis of a scientific linguistics. This claim is important since it reinforces the implicit anti-humanist aspect of structuralism. In this sense, structuralism was opposed to the diachronic analysis of language—that is focusing on the history of words, qua classical philology. Conversely, it argued for a synchronic form of explanation, which implied that meaning depends on facts and

relations between an existing system of signs. A linguistic sign was viewed as a structural relation between a word (signifier) and concept (signified). Meaning was thus (as emphasized) dependent on the *relations* between signs—many of which functioned in terms of basic binary contrasts. It followed that different languages entailed different relations of signs and different conceptual distinctions. The structuralist idea was deeply influential on a number of anthropologically inclined theorists such as Claude Levi-Strauss and Roland Barthes during the 1950s and 1960s. The common theme was that underlying structures had to be uncovered to reveal meanings. Since linguistic signs do not work on their own, but only in the context of a network of contrasts, oppositions, or differences (which constitute a language), these need to be unpicked for a real anthropological grasp of that culture. Thus, kinship structures and myths could be treated as the deep level structures of that society. They form a kind of genetic code for that society.

13. 'The genealogist needs history to dispel the chimeras of origin', Foucault (1986a: 80).
14. Another thing that separates historians from genealogists, is that the latter have acknowledged their own implicit perspectivism. Foucault comments 'Historians take unusual pains to erase the element in their work which reveals their grounding in a particular time and place, their preferences in a controversy—the unavoidable obstacles of passion', Foucault (1986a: 90).
15. In a similar way words to Foucault do not correspond with things, rather words are aspects of a network of texts, a network that involves practices which constitute the object.
16. As Foucault puts it 'The body is the inscribed surface of events (traced by language and dissolved by ideas), the locus of a dissociated self (adopted in the illusion of a substantial unity) . . . Genealogy, as an analysis of descent, is thus situated within the articulation of the body and history. Its task is to expose a body totally imprinted by history and the process of history's destruction of the body', see Foucault (1986a: 83).
17. This is not an attempt to do justice to their considerable range and output.
18. Or, as Rorty maintains, a postmodern open-mindedness undermines liberal foundationalism, see Rorty (1989: 52).
19. The earlier book, although ground breaking, ended more on a hermeneutic than a postmodern position.
20. Connolly, however, has no sympathies (like Derrida) with Heidegger's arguments about Being.
21. See also 'Nineteenth Century Idealism and Twentieth Century Textualism', see Rorty 1982.
22. 'Truth is a property of sentences, since sentences are dependent upon vocabularies, and since vocabularies are made by human beings, so are truths', Rorty (1989: 21).
23. This might be another—more radical way—of expressing Thomas Kuhn's thesis about science and paradigms.
24. One point of origin for this idea lay in the Kantian focus on the self-legislating self, which so affected the Romantics.
25. The most interesting and resonant chapter in Connolly's book, *The Ethos of Pluralization*, is entitled 'Nothing is Fundamental', chapter 1, (Connolly 1995).
26. Lyotard's later books, such as *The Differend*, tend to be critical of the earlier work.
27. In one sense, Lyotard is immediately open to the charge here of a performative contradiction, that is he appears to be doing (providing an overarching account of language) what he claims is impossible.

28. For Kant, there is first an aesthetic pleasure that accompanies the perception of an object, but the pleasure tells us nothing about the *content* of the object. We thus apprehend the *form* not the *content*. The aesthetic pleasure remains, crucially, a *subjective* feeling, yet, it is, at the same time, judged as necessarily connected with the perception of the object. It is almost a noumenal *ding an sich* of the object. Kant is insistent that one cannot logically move from the conception of the form *to* its pleasantness. We can only know the *formal* properties. Nothing is therefore known of the *content*, judged as beautiful; but, importantly, it is still asserted that, *a priori*, there is a feeling of pleasure connected with it in the subjective consciousness. Kant identifies this aesthetic subjective feeling as nonetheless based on the 'finality' that the representation of the object possesses for our faculty of knowledge.

29. Most judges, Lyotard thinks, do this most of the time anyway.

30. As one commentator notes, 'postmodernism abandons all sense of historical continuity and memory, while simultaneously developing an incredible ability to plunder history and absorb whatever it finds', Harvey (1989: 54).

31. See, for example, Rosenau (1992: 14 and 16, n.11); Harvey (1989: vii); Rengger (1992: 564).

32. 'A political theory delineates the parameters of a way of life, defending the limits it must accept in light of the possibilities it realizes. It provides answers against which we can test ourselves while rethinking assumptions and demands . . . In this respect Nietzsche is a disappointment. But perhaps this deficiency is also an advantage in some respects. For it stimulates thought about the presumptions within which contemporary political discourse takes place without requiring the thinker to commit oneself in advance to a single theory of politics', Connolly (1988: 168).

33. In fact he sees similar logic at work in Judith Butler, Jacques Derrida, Gilles Deleuze, Luce Irigaray, Ernesto Laclau, and Chantal Mouffe, see Connolly (1995: 25).

34. The 'either/or' mentality is taken, in fact, by Connolly as 'masculinist', Connolly (1991: 53)—whatever that means.

35. Rorty remarks that a 'critical vocabulary which revolves around notions like "rational", "criteria", "argument" and "absolute" is badly suited to describe the relation between the old and the new', Rorty (1989: 49). There are some parallels here with some of the work of John Gray, see Gray (1993: 259 *ff.*).

36. There are undoubtedly individuals who would die for such ideas, but they are rare. Not many of us, I think, have the capacity to say 'this principle is something I made up and it has no universality whatsoever, but I will still sacrifice my life for it'. In Rorty solidarity sounds more like a plea.

37. It is not surprising here that Rorty expressed some satisfaction at Rawls's move to political liberalism, although he would obviously have liked him to go a few steps further, see Rorty (1989: 78 *ff.*).

38. Although the writings of Christopher Norris have continuously and quite touchingly carried on believing in Derrida's real Enlightenment and philosophical qualifications, against all comers, see, for example, Norris (1987: ch. 6).

39. 'There is clearly a story within a story in this transition or shift from the Derrida of 1966 to the Derrida of 1986, which would seem to have much to do with his move from a confrontation with structuralism to his discovery or rediscovery of Emmanuel Levinas. The grammar of responsibility, which guides Derrida's response . . . has a heavy Levinasian tone', Schrag (1997: 14, n. 3).

40. It is worth noting that Rorty does think that Foucault can be assimilated into a genuine postmodern liberal perspective.

PART FIVE

9

Dialogic Foundations

The upshot of Chapter Eight is that political theory, in its postmodern mode, takes the conventionalist form of argument to a negative and self-destructive denouement. The argument is that conventionalism, if pursued, is unremittingly reductionist. The committed postmodern or poststructural critic aims to destabilize foundational commitments in all the hidden corners of political theory. Morality and politics are regarded as wholly contingent human conventions or artefacts, pure and simple, with nothing to mediate between them. One immediate upshot of this position is that postmodernism appears to lack any normative resources. However, as suggested, this 'destabilizing' critique has been pursued with degrees of rigour. The underpinning for this judgement lies in a point that there are various *forms* of postmodern argument.

My own view is to distinguish between two broad, if overlapping, postmodern responses. The milder form, in writers such as Rorty or Connolly, utilizes conventionalist argumentation up to a point, then stops and appeals (often with sentiment rather than reason) to an existing (multi)culture or ethos. The argument does not claim any ontological status for the ethos or culture, but simply views it as a *fait accompli*. The stronger perspectivism of Nietzsche, the younger Foucault and Derrida, and the differend of the older Lyotard, tends to destabilize even this minimal *fait accompli*. Thus, in this latter case, nothing holds. We float without purpose in a sea of conventional signs. The upshot of this for political theory is to undermine all foundations and emphasize its apparent pointlessness. However, as argued, not all postmodernists stay with this radical critique. Even the more hard-bitten postmoderns, such as Derrida, have tried to find a way out of this conundrum. Thus, the older Derrida's tentative association of 'justice' with 'deconstruction' (which has some of the hallmarks of Mikhail Bakunin's famous anarchist slogan—the destructive urge is a creative urge) is the final, somewhat poignant if ironic, epitaph to this faltering perspective.

There is, though, an important alternative to this postmodern movement, which appeared in the mid-twentieth century and developed in parallel with it to the end of the century, that is, late forms of critical theory and hermeneutics. Both encompass a wide range of thinkers, however, for the sake of brevity, the focus of this and Chapter Ten will be on the work of Jürgen Habermas and Hans-Georg Gadamer. The choice of these two thinkers is not fortuitous. They represent, in many ways, the apogee of these philosophical movements in the twentieth century. In my own rendering, the central theme for these thinkers is a postconventional concept of dialogue. In one reading, this theme could be seen as a new form of foundation. However, it is important to clarify this point immediately. The foundationalism articulated by Habermas and Gadamer is not the same as the older forms. It is definitely a new form that accommodates itself to many of the central postmodern criticisms of foundationalist argument. It also plays between universalism and conventionalism. In this sense, the views of Habermas and Gadamer (particularly Gadamer) can appear, on another reading, as anti-foundational. However, it is no surprise, at another level, that Habermas and Gadamer are deeply critical of postmodern and poststructural ideas. Part of the reason for the vigour of, particularly Habermas's rebuttal of postmodernism, is that they are also painfully aware of issues of historical contingency, questions of cultural difference and problems within Enlightenment thought. Equally, both Gadamer and Habermas resist a philosophy based on the subject and consciousness, one of the targets for postmodern critics.

In short, there are some strong intellectual resonances between critical theory, hermeneutics, and postmodernism. However, it is also important to emphasize that neither Habermas nor Gadamer follow the postmodern or poststructural path. Yet at the same time, it is this very intellectual nearness, which generates the negative passion against postmodernism. In fact, they both present viable alternatives to postmodernism or poststructuralism. Another key reason for discussing these two thinkers is that, not only are they profoundly perceptive concerning the dilemma of late-twentieth century political and moral theory, presenting a clear and critical alternative to postmodernism (whilst also absorbing many of the deep concerns of postmodern theory), but they are also, interestingly, at loggerheads themselves over certain crucial philosophical issues. The Habermas–Gadamer debate is in many ways a very deep-rooted philosophical conflict that reveals many intellectual fissures, which characterize the present problematic position of political theory at the beginning of the new century.

This chapter will first provide a brief overview of the context underpinning the work of Habermas and Gadamer. It will then review Habermas's central ideas with specific regard to political theory. The critique of Habermas will be delayed to the next chapter, which initially examines Gadamer's contribution and then the central themes underpinning the Habermas–Gadamer debate. The linking element underpinning these discussions is the focus on language and dialogue, as the central facets of political theory. Although both thinkers, in my view, successfully utilize the notion of language and dialogue to develop a new perspective on theory, it is Gadamer's hermeneutic theory, which with some reservations, engages with the problems facing theory in this next century. In my reading, it is Gadamer's development of the 'hermeneutic circle', which embodies his solid achievement.

THE PHILOSOPHICAL CONTEXT

The first point to note about the later manifestations of critical theory and hermeneutics is that both doctrines are marked by a strong emphasis on language, communication, and dialogue. In saying that language, communication, and dialogue are central to the ideas of both Habermas and Gadamer, it should also be emphasized that language particularly (as has already been noted throughout this book) has been the more general growth area of twentieth-century humanistic and social thought. As the idea of a deep-rooted metaphysical foundation for moral and political beliefs has become, over the twentieth century, more questionable, thinkers, such as Habermas and Gadamer, have focused more intensely on language and dialogue as supplying a more defensible ground on which to articulate and defend certain social and political practices. However, language is no longer considered to be a translucent medium through which we account for, defend, or represent an external objective order or world. This is neither to say that the latter 'representative' idea is not compatible with a focus on language, nor that language has a centrality for all twentieth-century thinkers. Karl Popper, for example, although having deep critical reservation over 'representational accounts of knowledge', was nonetheless adamant in opposing the language emphasis of philosophy. For Popper, there were real philosophical problems, which were not linguistic. His antipathy, particularly to Wittgenstein and linguistic philosophy, is legendary (see Popper 1976). However, there has, nonetheless, been a quite marked shift of focus in twentieth-century thought towards the issue of language.

Gadamer, Wittgenstein, Habermas, and Derrida all take the 'linguistic turn' in their own distinctive ways, although their differences are as striking as their similarities. The language focus has appeared quite differently within distinct intellectual traditions. Thus, in Anglo-American thought, from the 1930s up to the 1980s, the impact of Wittgenstein's late *Philosophical Investigations* (already examined in Part Two), the writings of J. L. Austin, the views of John Searle on speech act theory, and many similar thinkers, were largely hegemonic. The long tail of this form of philosophical theory still wags, somewhat more disconsolately now, at the opening of the twenty-first century. The aim of philosophy, in this perspective, was to clarify a predominantly 'public', analytically-orientated conception of language. In France, a linguistic perspective also came to the fore, initially in the structural linguistics of Saussure and Mauss's semiotics, and then to a strange fruition of sorts in Derrida's *Grammatology* and Foucault's *Order of Things* (examined in Part Four). In Germany—where the emphasis largely falls in this chapter—the linguistic emphasis came through strongly in developments within critical theory (particularly in the later writing of Habermas) and in hermeneutics.[1] Although there are deep differences between all of these linguistically-orientated philosophies, they still all focus on language as the key to comprehending reality.

Second, in the light of the critical theory and hermeneutic focus on language as a key for the comprehension of social reality, there was a wide-ranging scepticism concerning Cartesianism and the role played by individual human consciousness in apprehending the world. Intersubjectivity and dialogue—or the total loss of the human subject in some cases—became the primary medium for understanding. More significantly, in any discussion of human knowledge, there was a rejection of a 'human subject-centred' paradigm of epistemology, that is, bringing the world under the reflective control of individual reason, cognition, and will. This was a philosophical theme, which dominated European thought from Descartes to Husserl. Modern critics were also dubious about, or hostile to, the idea of any private language and subjective notions of 'interiority'. Further, all denied the idea that language simply pictured, corresponded with, or represented an external world. A great deal of what we call reality subsisted in language. Both Habermas and Gadamer, in fact, tended to emphasize what might be termed the rhetorical and pragmatic dimensions of language.

Third, this scepticism concerning the idea of an external empirically apprehended reality, led to an unease with the role of 'positivism', empirical knowledge, technical knowledge, and the importation of natural science modes of explanation into the humanities. There was nothing to stop natural science being considered as another body of signs or linguistic conventions. Nevertheless, the claim to superiority of this form of knowledge, over all others, was treated with critical anxiety and deep scepticism. One of the earlier critical theory texts, by Adorno and Horkheimer, *The Dialectic of the Enlightenment*, encapsulated this anxiety. The unease of language-based thought with natural science and positivistic assumptions did not mean that all such movements simply abandoned the idea of 'empirical knowing'. Far from it; three strategies were adopted. The first ruled out science-based accounts from linguistic analysis. Natural science was regarded as a special case of knowledge not subject to linguistic problems. In many ways, this was the easiest response. The second claimed to situate empirical and natural science based explanations, as a 'sphere of language', which worked through a particular and unique method of analysis. However, it did not proceed beyond this position. In many ways, this is part of Gadamer's central argument in his *magnum opus Truth and Method*. The third strategy was more daring, if problematic. It was one, which could be found earlier in the century within Idealist philosophy. Essentially, this strategy differentiated 'knowledge spheres'.[2] The different knowledge spheres needed to be held in tandem. Natural science became one of these legitimate spheres. However, it was important that any particular knowledge sphere should try not to colonize the whole ground of human knowledge. This is the strategy taken initially by Habermas. It was also part of his own strategy for dealing with the claims of Gadamerian hermeneutics, Wittgensteinian theory, and the more 'positivistic' claims of both Marxism and empirical social science.

A fourth feature underpinning critical theory and hermeneutics was the opposition to classical foundational metaphysics. Metaphysics was seen as caught in a traditional humanism, which centred on humanity as the core of what is real. Heidegger (as we have seen) had already heavily criticized this perspective. His alternative was the 'inhuman' in the shape of *Being*, thus displacing the centrality of the human. Neither Gadamer (who had been Heidegger's student), nor Habermas (who studied Heidegger closely, but violently rejected him), followed this conception of Being. However, both, like Heidegger, reject the older search for foundational metaphysical premises. Not unexpectedly, this rejection is something shared with postmodernists, such as Foucault and Derrida (amongst others). In consequence, their opposition to metaphysics is still, in part, an opposition to traditional humanism (in Heidegger's sense). Thus, both Habermas and Gadamer consider themselves, with some qualifications, to be 'post-metaphysical thinkers'. In this sense, both have critical reservations about overt claims to both foundationalism and universalism. It would however also be true (as I will argue) that both do, at the same time, configure their arguments under the rubric of a qualified conception of universalism and a more immanent foundationalism. Finally, one of the additional claims that characterize both theorists—particularly Gadamer—is a stress on historical change and contingency. In subtle, but quite definite ways, although we are not determined by our historical situation or indigenous traditions, our language and our political lives are still deeply affected and shaped by historical change and contingency.

CRITICAL THEORY

In terms of the influences on his first systematic work *Knowledge and Human Interests*, Habermas brings into play elements of Marxism and neo-Marxism (specifically through the critical theory school), classical German Idealism (Kant, Fichte, Schelling, and Hegel), hermeneutics (Dilthey and Gadamer), American pragmatism (G. H. Mead and C. S. Peirce) and Anglo-American analytic/linguistic philosophy (Wittgenstein, Searle, and Austin), as well as a wide range of social scientific and psychological theories. Given this eclectic approach, it might seem inappropriate, on one reading, to characterize him as a critical theorist. Habermas does, in fact, view his later work as more explicitly neo-Kantian in inspiration. However, neo-Kantianism and critical (Marxian-inspired) theory are *not* necessarily opposed. In fact, there is a powerful twentieth-century tradition, particularly in Austria and Germany, which linked these theoretical perspectives.[3] In addition, the critical theory project marks out the beginning of Habermas' work, particularly in his early critical reaction to figures such as Marx and Heidegger. The initial Marxian inspired 'emancipatory aim' of critical theory has remained an underlying motif in all Habermas's work, even if, by 2000, it acquired a much more 'liberal' edge and had become predominantly focused on working out the complex ramifications of communicative ethics.

One of the most important aspects of Habermas' perspective derives from his initial contact with the critical theorists. Habermas became associated with the critical theory project largely through his contact with Institute for Social Research in the post-1945 period. Critical theory itself, initially, developed in terms of Marxist disappointment over the absence of revolution in the West, the growth of Stalinism, and the fascist successes in Germany and elsewhere. Like most of the work of the critical theory group, Habermas is also deeply sensitive to the specifically German context of debates about reason. National socialism, and its historical impact, not only condition his response to Heidegger, Nietzsche, and German conservatism, but also form side constraints to his theorizing in general. In point, his response to the whole postmodern tradition is coloured by this underlying theme. As Habermas remarks, with hindsight, for critical theory writers it appeared that 'the last sparks of reason were being extinguished' during the 1930s and 1940s (see Habermas 1998: 117). Marxism is no longer seen as in any way immanent. This is particularly the case in terms of the growth of post-1945 affluent societies in the West. Such societies appear in fact to contradict the logic of Marxist historicism. Critical theory therefore aims to free itself from more classical historical materialism and revolutionary communism. In fact, the critical theory group went back self-consciously to Hegelianism for certain intellectual resources. It also showed little direct systematic interest in political economy.

However, one of the strong prevailing themes underpinning critical theory work was the view that the compound of instrumental reason, positivism, and natural science-based explanatory theory had begun to dominate all areas of human cognition. In effect, this natural science-based conceptual compound, which had been used painstakingly for the examination of the inanimate world, had been turned (quite illegitimately for critical theorists) to the analysis of human action in the social, political, and economic spheres. For the critical theorist, Max Horkheimer,

the manipulation of physical nature and of specific economic and social mechanisms demand alike the amassing of a body of knowledge such as is supplied in an ordered set of hypotheses. On the other hand, it made facts fruitful for the kind of scientific knowledge that would have practical application in the circumstances, and, on the other, it made possible the application of knowledge already possessed. (Horkheimer 1972: 194)

The origins of this conceptual compound were seen in the very beginnings of modern philosophy, especially Cartesianism and aspects of Kantianism. Critical theory, in general terms, set its face against this compound. This critical stance underpinned the protracted 'positivism debates' of the mid-twentieth century. The analysis of this compound—in critical theory—also owed a great deal to the work of Max Weber and his rich sociological account of the rationalization of society. For Weber, in modernity, both capitalism and bureaucracy embodied this one-sided instrumental positivist sense of rationality—a rationality that contained no normative or substantive ends. Rationalization, for Weber, was seen in terms of an 'iron cage', constricting substantive human reasoning.

In sum, critical theorists rejected this domination by positivist-inspired 'instrumental reason'. They also saw the potential for this intellectual dominance as imminent in the whole enterprise of the European Enlightenment. More significantly, in this context, instrumental reason was seen to gradually undermine itself. As Habermas noted, summarizing what he took to be Adorno's and Horkheimer's central position, Enlightenment reason 'destroys the humanity it first made possible', consequently, from its outset 'the process of enlightenment is the result of a drive to self-preservation that mutilates reason, because it lays claim to it only in the form of a purposive-rational mastery of nature' (Habermas 1998: 110–14); or, as Horkheimer put it, 'progress has a tendency to destroy the very ideas it is supposed to realize and unfold' (Horkheimer 1996: 359). Reason had thus become overly focused on an instrumental format, and this, in turn, was seen to suffer from a deep affliction. Such a concept of reason provided increased technical expertise and control, however, this control moved in tandem with 'deepening impotence against the concentrated power of the society'. The technological advances of bourgeois thought and practice were inseparably connected to this function, in the pursuit of science and instrumental reason. Consequently, 'a technical civilization has emerged from precisely that undaunted Reason which it now is liquidating' (Horkheimer 1996: 360). Humans had become shallower and more uni-dimensional, and societies more subtly oppressive. A more populist analysis of the theme was also contained in Herbert Marcuse's book *One Dimensional Man* (1964). In summary, 'the dwindling away of the philosophical substance, as it were, of all the decisive ideas in the face of the seemingly victorious Enlightenment, is one of the instances of the self-destructive trends of Reason' (Horkheimer 1996: 363).

The real problem with this pessimistic and deeply critical analysis of Enlightenment reason is—parallel to the postmodern critique—where to go next in political theory? Critical theory, with its Marxist root, did contain the seeds of a practical and positive intent, trying, in effect, to foster future human emancipation—although revolution seemed primarily to be in the realm of consciousness rather than in political action.[4] Thus, Horkheimer thought that critical theory could play an authentic role in facilitating human self-awareness of its situation and could be constitutive of socially-transformative activities. However, the critique of traditional social and political theories (qua ideology critique), and the advocacy of a positively worked-out alternative, were never fully developed by critical theorists, certainly not before Habermas. There were admittedly strong intimations—in early critical theory—that art or psychoanalysis might provide some way out of this exploitative situation.[5] Yet the more overwhelming sense was negative and pessimistic, as indeed Horkheimer commented: 'if neither the revival of old nor the invention of new mythologies can check the course of Enlightenment, are we not thrown into a pessimistic attitude, a state of despair and nihilism?'. Horkheimer goes on to remark, somewhat cynically, on the 'mortgage' on our current thinking, namely what he calls 'a self-imposed obligation to arrive at a cheerful conclusion'. He continues, 'The compulsive effort to meet this obligation is one of the reasons why a positive conclusion is impossible. To free Reason from the fear of being called nihilistic might be one of the steps in its recovery', thus, 'One might define the self-destructive tendency of Reason in its own conceptual realm as the positivistic dissolution of metaphysical concepts up to the concept of Reason itself.' Consequently, rather than paper over these deeply pessimistic cracks, Horkheimer exhorts his readers to accept the deeply paradoxical negative consequences (Horkheimer 1996: 366–7). We live, for Horkheimer, within a contradictory condition. Reason seems to be permanently against itself—a constant performative contradiction. Despite appearances, some recent commentators have seen a quite positive agonistic vision arising from this sense of deep negativity and contradictoriness (e.g. see, Coles in White (ed.) 1995: 34–8).

Adorno reflected on this more pessimistic contradictory theme, much more systematically than Horkheimer. The 'negative dimension' was considered dialectically in his book *Negative Dialectics* (1966). For Habermas, however, Adorno's *Negative Dialectics* 'reads like a continuing explanation of why we have to circle about within this *performative contradiction* and indeed even remain there' (Habermas 1998: 119). Thinking, as totalizing critique, remained a strong theme throughout Adorno's work. In one sense, Habermas's criticism of Adorno embodied earlier pre-1939 emancipatory themes from the critical group, Adorno's negative dialectics being seen as a failure of critical nerve. For Habermas, Adorno remained trapped in a modern paradigm of subjectivity—a paradigm that gave rise to the whole problem of negative self-destructive reason.[6] In consequence, for Habermas, Adorno's and Horkheimer's *Dialectic of Enlightenment* 'holds out scarcely any prospect for an escape from the myth of purposive rationality' (see Habermas 1998: 110–14). He traces the origin of doubts about this notion of reason to *ideology critique*, namely, where the reason underpinning ideology critique becomes itself ideologically suspect (see Habermas 1998: 116). Consequently, suspicion of ideology becomes more or less total, which, in turn, undermines the whole concept of reason. For Habermas, both Adorno and Horkheimer, therefore, 'surrendered themselves to an uninhibited scepticism regarding reason' (Habermas 1998: 129). This reflexive movement of 'reason against itself' (the performative contradiction), is something that Habermas traces to the impact of Nietzschean ideas. In fact, he sees Nietzschean 'destructive' and 'self-reflexive' ideas at work, surreptitiously, within Adorno's and Horkheimer's own theories. However, he continues that, 'Horkheimer and Adorno find themselves in the same embarrassment as Nietzsche: If they want to renounce the effect of a final unmaking and still want to *continue with critique*, they will have to leave at least one rational criterion intact for their explanation of the corruption of *all* rational criteria' (Habermas 1998: 127). The answer to this philosophical conundrum can be found in the groundwork of Habermas's own theory.

CRITICAL THEORY FULFILLED

One important hiatus therefore within critical theory, specifically in the work of Adorno, Marcuse, and Horkheimer, was that they did not offer any sustained argument or worked-out alternative to the inadequacies of traditional theory and subject-based instrumental reason. In this sense, Habermas stands out from the critical theory grouping, insofar as this is precisely what he has tried to do. Habermas developed a deeply worked-out project, premised on a critical interpretation of occidental thinking from Aristotle to the present era—although with particular reference to philosophical writing from the eighteenth century to the present. In reconstructing this tradition, he advances a comprehensive theory of communicative competence and a consensus theory of truth, which contains powerful implications for both philosophy and the social sciences.

Yet, debate about Habermas is at an odd stage, at the present moment. There is already, like Rawls, a mountain of literature concerning his work, and he is still actively writing and developing his ideas. He also has multiple interpreters, sympathizers, and critics. It is difficult to get a clear handle on such a technically sophisticated thinker as Habermas, without some distance in time, certainly to pick up the subtle transitions and mutations in his ideas. For example, Habermas has clearly gone through certain intellectual transitions—although the precise relations of these transitions to any consistent themes in his work remains unclear. Originally, in the 1960s, and early 1970s, his ideas were more obviously connected to the neo-Marxist aspirations of the critical theory school (tempered by a more eclectic philosophical stance). Although not Marxist in any orthodox sense, his project for a more rational legitimated society was informed initially by the emancipatory aims of socialism. At this point, he also flirted with Freudian psychoanalytic theories and ideology critique. In addition, he also critically addressed the Heideggerian critique of technology, assembling, in effect, a 'left' substitute to Heidegger's ideas in his *Technology and Science as Ideology* (1968). However, by the 1990s and 2000s, many of these preoccupations had quietly dropped into the background and were replaced by the political and philosophical framework of neo-Kantianism and a republican-inclined social liberalism.

Second, Habermas' overall project in the 1960s was focused on the critical theory motif of resisting the reduction of knowledge and human reason to instrumental–technical or strategic calculations (of an essentially individual subject). This latter theme was summarized in his well-known inaugural lecture in 1965, as well as his *Knowledge and Human Interest* (1968). This critique of instrumental–technical reason formed the backdrop to his ideas on emancipation, within a rational society, in books such as *Towards a Rational Society* (1971) and *The Legitimation Crisis* (1973). This critique also led Habermas to the ideas of Gadamer. However, his focus shifted again in the two volume book, *The Theory of Communicative Actions* (1981), and carried through systematically in later books, such as *The Philosophical Discourse of Modernity* (1985), and *Between Facts and Norms* (1992). This latter phase enunciated a dynamic move to communication and language. The language issue is of crucial importance. There are, though, the seeds of a possible future debate here, namely, are there two or more Habermasian theories, or just the one singular set of arguments? For some commentators, there are many consistent themes at work throughout all his writings (e.g. see, introduction in White (ed.) 1995: 5). Thus, the central theme of his *Structural Transformation of the Public Sphere* (1962), although more sociologically configured, is still embedded in the significance of an active, rational, critical, intersubjective public sphere of discussion (in salons, coffee houses, clubs and a free press, during the eighteenth century). This theme reappears, in slightly different formats, in other works during the 1970s. For some, this also foreshadows the later focus on communicative action and universal pragmatics in the 1980s and 1990s.[7]

However, Habermas is in many ways a paradoxical thinker. On the one count, he can, and does appear (especially in his later work) as someone who is self-consciously post-metaphysical. He sees himself moving beyond old traditions and paradigms of philosophy and social theory, concerned with the human subject and philosophy of consciousness. As mentioned earlier, he has consequently taken on some of the external accoutrements of the 'postmodern'; yet, at the same time, he sees both the Enlightenment and modernity as wholly unfinished projects. Habermas, indeed, sees himself as fulfilling the inner purposes of these latter projects in his own work. This places him in direct opposition to the postmodern. In many ways, though, like Gadamer, Habermas presents a *via media* between, on the one hand, the more extravagant, optimistic, and universalist foundationalist claims of political theory, as against the more negative, pessimistic, anti-foundationalism of the postmodern stance. He thus negotiates his way between both universalism and conventionalism and difference and identity. However, although obviously admiring the impetus of

Enlightenment stance, his conception of both philosophy and political theory is something which is, at the same time, born out of certain fundamental doubts over modernity, a critique of reason, serious misgivings over the emphasis on the human subject and 'philosophy of consciousness', and major doubts over the inevitability of human progress solely through scientific reason.

Another aspect of Habermas' theory, which accounts partly for his idiosyncratic approach, is his theoretical need to reconstruct thought. In Hegelian terms, he takes up the passion of the logic of a long period of occidental thinking. In one sense, he sees his task as reconstructing the deep underlying patterns of reason present in the history of occidental philosophical thought. This gives his theory a depth and thoroughness, however, it also evinces, at times, a programmatic technical abstractness and somewhat artificial quality, which is deeply off-putting. One aspect of this reconstructive process is his attempt to incorporate apparently widely different theoretical perspectives and to show their inner communicative logic, and, where necessary, to show where they have gone wrong. This requires him to make sense of both recent postmodernism and classical metaphysics. His most systematic study of this former debate is contained in his *Philosophical Discourses of Modernity*. His work, in consequence, is undoubtedly one of the most bold and innovative philosophical projects at the end of the twentieth century.

His overall aim—which will be returned to—is to provide a comprehensive and thorough reconstruction of the occidental tradition, showing the profound, diverse, and expansive roles of human reason. Initially, his idea was to argue that one particular conception of reason should not dominate. By the 1980s and 1990s, his arguments on reason became more complex and nuanced, and a singular notion of intersubjective communicative reason began to figure prominently in the work. In addition, initially, he wanted to show the relation of this expansive conception of reason to both human emancipation and to the construction of a rational society. The fundamental intuition underpinning the latter idea (which is a fairly old political theme) is the ideal of particular form of community whose legal and moral norms are both freely and equally accepted and regarded as reasonable by those subject to them. The idea of rational informed public discussion can therefore be taken as a crucial theme running through Habermas' work.

POSITIVISM AND KNOWLEDGE SPHERES

For Habermas, the gist of the problem of positivism and instrumental reason (which he refers to as the 'empirical-analytic' conception) is that this particular conception had begun to dominate all spheres of human cognition and knowledge, particularly in the social sciences. Positivistic reason also viewed itself as free from dogmatic associations and personal interests. If seen as the sole dimension of knowledge and reason, then, for Habermas, such 'objectifying descriptions of society migrate into the lifeworld, [then] we become alienated from ourselves as communicatively acting subjects' (see Habermas in Schmidt (ed.) 1996: 419). Empirical, science-based, reason feeds on many of the traditional understandings of theory, reason, and knowledge, implicit in older classical philosophy. However, it then proceeds to destroy them. As Habermas notes, empirical positivist theory borrows 'two elements from the philosophical heritage: the methodological meaning of the theoretical attitude and the basic ontological assumption of a structure of the world independent of the knower.' However, he continues, it then abandons 'the connection of *theoria* and *Kosmos*, of *mimesis* and *bios theoretikos* that was assumed from Plato through Husserl. What was once supposed to comprise the practical efficacy of theory has now fallen prey to methodological prohibitions. The conception of theory as a process of cultivation of the person has become apocryphal' (Habermas 1971: 304). In other words, this positivistic conception of reason undermines the crucial dimensions of reason, which underpin human understanding and communication. Technical progress, in the human and social sciences, is not the same as providing the conditions for rational human conduct. This point extends earlier arguments that Habermas had made over the question of technocratic ideology. As Thomas McCarthy comments:

The growth of productive forces and administrative efficiency does not itself lead to the replacement of institutions based on force by an organization of social relations bound to communication free from domination. The ideals of the technical master of history and of liberation from the quasi-natural forces of social and political domination, as well as the means for their realization, are fundamentally different. (McCarthy 1978: 36)

In the final analysis, positivism facilitates, unwittingly, the development of negative dialectics and neglects the crucial relation between knowledge and human interests. Yet Habermas neither wants to abandon this positivist conception, nor to despair over its impact. As long as it is correctly grasped, as a sphere of knowledgeable understanding connected to particular human interests, it can have a role in the human and social sciences. In this context, a more balanced, nuanced, and expansive 'interest-based' conception of reason is required.[8]

In his *Knowledge and Human Interest* Habermas therefore separates out various dimensions of knowledge, associating them with differing uses of reason. His basic claim is grounded in a philosophical anthropology, namely that what we call knowledge claims are in fact, rooted in certain human interests, or, more precisely 'knowledge-constitutive interests'. Thus, one cannot single out spheres of knowledge for abstract study—as in epistemology—distinct from material human concerns. Interest means, 'cognitive interest', and cognitive interests are rooted in human (specifically social) activities. Certain kinds of human activity are therefore the grounds for knowledge-constitutive interests. Habermas isolates three non-reducible human interests: technical, practical, and emancipatory. The first is concerned with work, the second with interaction, and the third with power relations. These interests are then seen to correspond to three major-knowledge-based sciences (and in effect understandings of reason), that is, the *empirical–analytic* sciences, focused on technical cognitive interests or technical control of the world; second, the *historical–hermeneutic* sciences embodying practical interests, communication, and symbolic interaction; third, *critical orientated social sciences*, incorporating emancipatory interests (see Habermas 1971: 308). The sciences are thus premised on human cognitive interests, but the interests differ and are equally valid. The empirical–analytic category embodies essentially the claims of positivist reason, controlled observation, predictive knowledge, and technical manipulation. The historical–hermeneutic understanding embodies the claims of literature, aesthetics, history, and textual studies. This is the area where Habermas admires Gadamer's theoretical contribution. The critically orientated social sciences are concerned with cognitive emancipatory interests. Habermas identifies this sphere with the social sciences of economics, political science and sociology.[9] This is also the area, which resonates with Habermas's concern with 'ideological criticism'. He considers both the empirical–analytic and historical–hermeneutic dimensions as incapable of dealing with issues of power, ideology, distortion of ideas, and thus genuine emancipatory concerns.

All the above knowledge dimensions are required for human existence. They are all implicit, as Habermas would put it, in the human lifeworld. In this sense, Habermas's reading of positivism is not to undermine it, or to rest its case on negative dialectics, but rather to suggest that notions of reason and science are more complex and variegated, and that we should rather try to, first, *show* this variegation within the various knowledge-constitutive interests. Science—regardless of how it perceives itself—*is* a social interest and it cannot be grasped outside of this sociality. Second, it is important to situate the more positivistic mentality within a broader cognitive framework. In this sense, much of what has gone on under the rubric of positivism can now be situated under the empirical–analytic (or analytic–instrumental) category. It follows that although positivist reason is now intellectually situated, as a valuable human cognitive interest, it is not a perspective that should be allowed to colonize the whole human lifeworld. Symbolic interaction and communication, for example, are not about technical control. Communicative interaction, in the practical sphere, should not therefore be reduced to the analytic–empirical category. To rationalize and control is neither to communicate effectively nor emancipate humans. Despite dealing with 'transitory things and opinions', the historical–hermeneutic category still embodies 'scientistic' concerns. However, although embodying a 'scientistic consciousness', the hermeneutic category is *not* concerned with general laws. Yet as Habermas comments, the cultural sciences still describe 'a structured reality within the horizon of a theoretical attitude' (see Habermas 1971: 303).

THE CRITIQUE OF FOUNDATIONALISM AND THE SUBJECT

For Habermas the problem of the 'subject' is something that arises in modernity. In point, the human subject is the *key* fact of modernity. The idea of the subject determines the character of modern culture (Habermas 1998: 18). He sees the philosophy of the subject developing in a range of philosophers from Descartes through to Kant and Hegel. In the earlier tradition, it still had an emancipatory dimension. For Habermas, Kant's transcendental arguments on the crucial role of the subject in knowledge, eventuates in Hegel's formal method for directing consciousness dialectically back on itself. Thus, what Hegel calls dialectical 'is the reconstruction of . . . recurrent experience and its assimilation by the subject' (Habermas in Baynes et al. 1993: 300). Most Kantians and Hegelians still hold to subject-based reason as a supremely emancipatory and illuminating device. For Habermas, this sets off neo-Kantians, such as Popper, from the likes of Feyerabend, or Horkheimer and Adorno from Foucault. He notes that Popper, Adorno, and Horkheimer 'still say *something* about the indispensable conditions of claims to the validity of those opinions we hold to be justified, claims that transcend all restrictions of time and place' (Habermas in Baynes et al. 1993: 304). However, with Nietzsche, 'the criticism of modernity dispenses for the first time with its retention of an emancipatory content'. Nietzsche even 'bids farewell' to the dialectic of the Enlightenment. (Habermas 1998: 94).[10] In Nietzsche subjectivity turns totally against itself. In my own reading, this process comes to fruition in thinkers such as Lyotard. For Habermas, after Nietzsche, the philosophy of the subject was taken up, with a vengeance, by postmodernists. The postmodernists focus exclusively on their own subjectivity and its contingency, regardless of any social utility, solidarities, or emancipatory concerns. Politics, for such writers, becomes merely a supplementary concern. Some philosophers have tried to overcome this dilemma. Habermas, for example, sees strong intimations of an alternative in Hegel's early writings on love. However, ultimately, he sees that the later Hegel still 'conceives the overcoming of subjectivity within the boundaries of a philosophy of the subject' (Habermas 1998: 22).[11] For Habermas, in sum, beginning with isolated or atomized subject—mournfully examining its own inwardness—is bogus. In this mode of subject-based thinking—within postmodernists such as Derrida, Bataille, and Foucault—Habermas sees the total exhaustion of the philosophy of the subject.

However, in attacking the philosophy of the subject, Habermas is not falling into the embrace of an older foundationalism. He is convinced that philosophy has lost its authoritative position in the human and social sciences. Neo-Kantian philosophy, for example, particularly, has frequently posed 'as the highest court of appeal *vis-à-vis* the sciences and cultures as a whole' (Habermas in Baynes et al. 1993: 298). For Habermas, it is now clear, though 'that philosophy has no business playing the part of the highest arbiter in matter of science and culture' (Habermas in Baynes et al. 1993: 308–9). More rigorous neo-Kantianism is simply wrong. Yet, Habermas does not accept the contingencies built into the postmodern rejection of rationalist philosophy. It is crucial to realize that a critique of older foundationalist arguments does not entail a total rejection of foundationalism. We can, he thinks, learn from the mistakes of earlier concepts of modernity. In many ways, Habermas can therefore be seen as navigating a middle course between the potential irrationalism of the postmoderns and the naïve universalist foundationalism of many neo-Kantian thinkers. He thinks that philosophical thought can still be—as he calls it—a 'stand in interpreter' and 'guardian of rationality'. Thus, there are universalistic elements to Habermas's thinking (reminiscent of the older foundationalist claims), however, these are then given a more 'fallibilistic' rendering. Reason is historically situated and premised ultimately in everyday processes of communication and understanding. However, for Habermas, as indicated in the 'knowledge spheres'—qua human interests—discussion, there are different 'forms' of reason and therefore differing modes of communication. Philosophy, in this context, takes on a more self-effacing role, interpreting, and arbitrating between types of substantive forms of reason or knowledge spheres, making sure that one particular sphere of knowledge does not dominate. It is important to note here that for Habermas it is not only the danger of positivistic instrumental reasoning dominating the lifeworld.[12] There is also a danger of the historical–hermeneutic perspective becoming dominant for other sectors—as a form of 'positivism' of the cultural sciences.

In his reconstructive enterprise, Habermas sees a fertile development in philosophical doctrines such as pragmatism and hermeneutics. The importance he sees in both doctrines is their move away from the philosophy of the solitary subject and philosophy of consciousness. They rather stress 'an idea of cognition that is mediated by language and linked to action' (Habermas in Baynes et al. 1993: 304). They both underscore the dimension of communication. In other words, as opposed to stressing the epistemologically based philosophy of the subject, they emphasize the intersubjectivity of acting and speaking.[13] Both doctrines epitomize issues of human action and language over the subject-centred self-reflective consciousness. Thus issues, such as those attacked by Richard Rorty, like the 'mirror of nature' in representational epistemology, are seen as irrelevant to the communicative or intersubjective stance. What is of more importance, for Habermas, is that the intersubjective paradigm raises the question of the context of intersubjectivity, namely the preunderstandings. The implicit danger of moving into the realm of ordinary intersubjective communication is that for some this can translate as an 'anti-philosophical stance', or, as Habermas puts it, a 'good riddance to philosophy' perspective. This entails that once one moves away from the tight rationalist paradigm of the epistemology of the subject, by definition, one appears to move away from philosophy. In this sense, for some, the radical attack on the subject means the end of philosophy.

Habermas sees three possible modern variants of the 'end of philosophy' idea: the therapeutic, heroic, and salvaging farewell. The 'therapeutic' refers to Wittgenstein's language games, which have no need of any philosophy to function. Philosophy could thus be seen as utterly parasitic. For Habermas, in this context, anthropology seems most likely to replace philosophy. He describes Rorty as the potential Thucydides of this perspective! The 'heroic' can be found in the destructive moves of Heidegger and Bataille. The bogus role of philosophy is replaced by something deeper, such as Heidegger's mystificatory 'waiting on Being'. Habermas sees the 'salvaging farewell' perspective present in hermeneutics. It focuses on the assimilation of texts 'that were once thought to embody knowledge, treating them instead as sources of illumination and edification' (Habermas in Baynes et al. 1993: 307). All these anti-philosophical views go wrong for Habermas in that 'philosophical conversation cannot but gravitate towards argumentation and justificatory dispute. There is no alternative' (Habermas in Baynes et al. 1993: 309). However, the need is for theories of rationality which are more sensitive to difference and fallibilism, thus avoiding strong foundationalist or absolutist claims.

UNIVERSAL PRAGMATICS AND FALLIBILISM

The question arises as to what this more fallibilistic rationality, rooted in intersubjectivity, would look like for Habermas? The discussion now moves to the centre stage of Habermas's developed thinking. In many ways, Habermas clearly accepts the point that the more traditional foundational moral and political belief systems are now untenable. As argued, he also disputes the postmodern reading. His own alternative, which had been intimated from some of his earlier writings of the 1960s, is to focus on discourse as a basis for social and political legitimacy. As Habermas himself notes, there are strong parallels between his work and that of Karl-Otto Apel (Habermas 1979: 1–2). Apel is concerned with the point that any meaningful action presupposes some form of ideal intersubjective communicative community—a realm of unhindered discourse—within which validity can be assessed. For Apel, all logical argumentation 'already *presupposes* an intersubjectively valid ethics as conditions of its possibility'. The preconditions of any rational argument are therefore reliant upon certain conditions being met. Thus, there is a form of underlying consensual community present in the way that we communicate with one another. For Apel, 'This means. . . that no one can honestly come to terms with himself in his own thought unless he has in principle accepted all the norms of sincere communication predicated on the reciprocal recognition of communication partners' (Apel 1978: 96–7). All human interests and needs, which can be validated, would be open for debate in this sphere of, what Apel calls, 'non-repressive deliberation'. Thus, in summary, every speaker presupposes an ideal speech situation and community. Emancipation, for Apel, will be 'the progressive implementation of the standard of ideal communication and non-repressive deliberation within the real communication community' (Apel 1978: 99).

Habermas basically adopts a more systematically developed form of the above argument. He tries to defend a more universalistic understanding of reason, which is embedded in ordinary human discourse and knowledge claims. The position is fallibilist, and yet at the same time, a modest universalist account of reason. It is essentially concerned with what we presuppose when we speak and try to understand. For Habermas, this perspective allows philosophical reason to work constructively with all the various sciences or knowledge domains. Philosophy therefore embodies a more reticent role, arbitrating between types of substantive reason. As he notes:

Even in the most difficult processes of reaching an understanding, all parties appeal to the common reference point of possible consensus, even if this reference point is projected in each case from within their own contexts. For, although they may be interpreted in various ways and applied according to different criteria, concepts like truth, rationality, or justification play the *same* grammatical role in *every* linguistic community. (Habermas in Schmidt (ed.) 1996: 417)

As opposed to just unravelling the particular domains of substantive reason and knowledge, Habermas indicates the common consensual underpinning rules which function in *any* such discourse and have in turn deeply subtle but definite ethical and political implications. Each sphere of knowledge presupposes concepts which are vital to it. However, for Habermas, these concepts cannot be enunciated *within* the substantive terms of that sphere. The upshot of this is the demand for a form of transcendental pragmatism.

One of the more systematic turning points for this perspective is Habermas's essay 'What is Universal Pragmatics?'. He indicates, in this essay, that 'The task of universal pragmatics is to identify and reconstruct universal conditions of possible understanding. In other contexts one also could speak of "general presuppositions of communication", but I prefer to speak of general presuppositions of communicative action' (Habermas 1979: 1). The gist of this perspective, for Habermas, is that any speech act raises 'universal validity claims . . . that can be vindicated [or redeemed: *einlösen*]. Insofar as he wants to participate in a process of reaching an understanding, he cannot avoid raising the following validity claims' (Habermas 1979: 2). Not all speech acts are aimed at genuine communication, they may be purely strategic, symbolic or just instrumental to further an agent's personal interest. However, if the aim of a speech act is to be understood and really communicate, then, it follows, for Habermas, that validity claims are presupposed implicitly. The *modus operandi* of this argument is the ability to redeem 'validity claims' present in ordinary language. These embody the normative foundation of what ideal speech requires.

The validity claims are: comprehensibility or intelligibility, truthfulness, sincerity, and rightness.[14] The agent in any speech act must want to be understood or must want to try to come to an understanding with another. The speech act therefore must be comprehensible or intelligible intersubjectively, qua a society of speakers. Second, the speaker must 'have the intention of communicating a *true proposition*', namely, he 'must want to express his intention *truthfully*' (Habermas 1979: 2). The condition of the truth of a statement is the potential agreement of speakers and hearers. Third, the speaker will want to express his intentions with sincerity—namely that the speaker is honest and sincere in what he says. Fourth, the speaker 'must choose an utterance that is right so that the hearer can accept the utterance' (Habermas 1979: 3), that is to say what the speaker says is right in the light of existing social norms and values. The goal of speech acts is to come to an understanding, or, to share the knowledge of a speaker. Such validity claims can also be used to challenge particular utterances. If and when claims are challenged, they can only be rescued through further interaction that discloses as to whether the speaker has been genuine.[15] It is important to realize that, for Habermas, any understanding that is in any way forced by an external authority is not valid. It is the force of the argument that should be crucial. Any discourse is gauged by the 'ideal speech situation', which is, by definition, free from power and domination—equivalent to Apel's concept of 'non-repressive deliberation'.[16]

A key theoretical background influence here on Habermas' theory is J. L. Austin's account of the 'illocutionary force' of speech acts.[17] For Habermas, communicative action is linguistic interaction where participants pursue illocutionary aims. The speakers have the direct intention in a speech act of communicating a true propositional content.[18] For Habermas, therefore, 'In all cases in which the illocutionary role expresses not a power claim but a validity claim, the place of the empirically motivating force of sanctions . . . is taken by the rationally motivating force of accepting a speaker's guarantee for securing claims to validity' (Habermas 1984: 302).[19] Thus, in every act of communicative action, 'the system of all validity claims comes into play; they must always be raised simultaneously' (Habermas 1979: 65–6). They are universal and inherent in all speech which genuinely tries to reach an understanding. These validity claims are the taken for granted background to any communicative action, thus, the 'participants presuppose that they know what mutual recognition of reciprocally raised validity claims mean'. As Habermas continues, 'I have proposed the name *universal pragmatics* for the research program aimed at reconstructing the universal validity basis of speech' (Habermas 1979: 5). This is neither, for Habermas, an epistemological enterprise, nor a concern with the human subject, but one rather wholly orientated to intersubjectivity, speech, and dialogue.[20]

Three further implications are worth noting here. Habermas has been accused of fostering, once again, foundational or universalist claims and riding roughshod over diverse cultures and social difference. Clearly Habermas does feel strongly that some cultures (such as the occidental) 'have had more practice than others at distancing themselves from themselves' (Habermas in Schmidt (ed.) 1996: 417). Despite this, Habermas is still convinced, minimally, that 'all languages offer the possibility of distinguishing between what is true and what we hold to be true'. He continues, 'The *supposition* of a common objective world is built into the pragmatics of every single linguistic usage. And the dialogue roles of every speech situation enforce a symmetry in participation perspectives. They open up both the possibility for the ego to adopt the perspective of alter and vice versa, and the exchangeability of the participant's and observer's perspectives' (Habermas in Schmidt (ed.) 1996: 417). To deny these inner validity claims of language is to commit a 'performative contradiction'. This contradiction he sees rife in postmodern writing.[21]

The second point to note here is that this is not an 'extramundane' context free, asocial or ahistorical view of reason. Reason is still situated and, to a degree, contextual, despite being pragmatically transcendent. For Habermas, reason is therefore both immanent *and* transcendent. In Habermas's words, 'the validity claimed for propositions and norms transcends spaces and times, but in each actual case the claim is raised here and now, in a specific context, and accepted or rejected with real implications for social interaction' (Habermas in Schmidt (ed.) 1996: 417). A related point to bear in mind here for Habermas is that we should not separate out universals and particulars, or identity and difference, so rigidly. It is not a question, for him, of considering cultures at the expense of universal reason, or universal reason at the expense of cultures. There is relation between these phenomena, as he puts it, somewhat abstractly, 'Repulsion towards the One and veneration of difference and the Other obscures the dialectical connection between them' (Habermas in Schmidt (ed.) 1996, 418). Third, in offering this reconstruction of reason, which underpins all knowledge spheres and mediates between them, Habermas sees the possibility of a new constellation of knowledge, or new possibilities for understanding. Philosophy will be, as he says, a new 'stand-in interpreter'. This, for Habermas, indicates a more fruitful relation between the various knowledge spheres. For example, the empirical sciences may, in future, provide indirect confirmation of the reconstructive philosophical theory itself.

DISCOURSE ETHICS AND DELIBERATIVE DEMOCRACY

One of the important aspects of Habermas's communicative theory is its strong implications for theories of ethics and politics. Yet discourse, as a basis of political and social legitimacy, does move the argument away from a *substantive* towards a more *procedural* conception of ethical and political theory. Ethics and politics are seen to presuppose a moral community whose norms are fully, freely, and equally acceptable to those subject to them.

In many ways Habermas's conception of ethics is mid-way between Hegel and Kant. As Habermas comments, 'discourse ethics takes up [the] basic intention of Hegel so as to redeem it by Kantian means' (Habermas 1990: 197). Habermas is a deontologist concerned with the procedurally right over the good, however, at the same time, he is also sensitive to contextualist, conventionalist, and historical claims concerning ethics. His position (particularly his position from the 1990s), can be described as a conventionalist-inclined neo-Kantianism. The neo-Kantianism is manifest in his concern for the procedurally right, his formalist defence of a procedure of moral and political argumentation, rather than immediately fostering substantive moral principles, and his concern with procedural universalism. His Hegelian, and quasi-Aristotelian emphasis, is manifest in his implicit conventionalism and historical sensitivity, as well as his focus on intersubjectivity. The crucial ethical question, for Habermas, is not focused on the individual *subject* raising a categorical imperative for itself, it is rather centred on what *intersubjectively* valid norms (and ultimately institutions and institutional processes) would participants, in an ideal speech community, agree to best characterize their common rational concerns. In other words, ethical norms arise *from* established reasonable communication practices *within* conventional society. Habermas, in one sense, is therefore reformulating the Kantian imperative that one ought rationally to will those common intersubjectively valid norms, which are implicit in any ideal socially communicative act. Insofar as one does 'will' these intersubjective norms, one furthers the realization of the ideal communal life—an update on the kingdom of ends.

Habermasian discourse ethics are premised on a moderately cooperative community (an existing lifeworld), who are already engaged in discourse or deliberation. It is premised therefore on human praxis. It maintains that by examining what is presupposed in the existing conventions of reasonable communication, one can ascertain, extract, and reflect on these basic presupposed components, for example, the validity claims discussed earlier. These presupposed components embody (procedurally) the basic structure of an ethics and an account of justice that only those norms, which are actually commonly accepted (and rationally shown) as presupposed within communicative endeavours, will meet with the approval of participants in discourse. There is an implicit egalitarian and non-repressive (or non-dominatory) principle implicitly present here. Valid norms are collectively achieved and embody a common good. For Habermas, such basic ethical structures can be given a rational justification. In essence, Habermas builds and justifies an ethics by examining and bringing to light the norms which are implicit in all ideal communicative situations. Such norms, for Habermas, embody both equality, universality, and impartiality. Norms cannot be valid except when they are rationally agreed to by *all* participants in discourse. The validity of norms is not premised solely on social conventions, but, conversely, on whether they could be justified in practical discourse. This is the central 'trick' of the Habermasian scheme. Valid norms are *not* determined by conventions, but, at the same time, they are claimed to be the essential component *of* ordinary conventions. This combines both Kant and Hegel.

Habermas wants to make clear here the point that norms are derived from examining what is implicit in intersubjective dialogue. However, any discussion and evaluation of these norms would *also* have to proceed within the terms of rational intersubjective dialogue, or, an open process of discussion. It could not be derived from the monologic reflections of an isolated or solitary human subject. Real dialogue must, in turn, logically presuppose the validity of those very norms, which are themselves under discussion. In other words, as soon as one enters upon any attempt to openly and rationally communicate, or engage in rational dialogue, one immediately presupposes, invokes and confirms the 'ethics of discourse' or 'valid ethical norms', which are implicit in dialogue. To try to communicate openly is to immediately confirm the point. In other words, ethics is implicit in terms of the transcendental conditions for any attempt at rational communication.

The above theory also accounts for Habermas' distinctive theory of democracy. Within recent political theory three basic models of democracy stand out: liberal, republican, and deliberative. The liberal model envisages government as an apparatus of public administration and society as a series of market-orientated contractual interactions among private persons or interest groups. Liberal democratic politics is seen to aggregate private preferences. Democracy then transmits the atomistic preferences of civil society to the political apparatus. Individuals, in the liberal model, never leave the domain of their private interests. Democracy is an instrumental process of expressing preferences and registering them through a vote. The goal is to decide what leaders or policies will best serve the greatest aggregate of individuals. Communitarians and republican theories are antagonistic to this model. One reason for the upsurge of the communitarian movement in the 1980s was in fact a rejection of the individualistic, aggregative conception of social life, implicit within this liberal conception.

Under the civic republican view, individuals consociate under law. Politics is the articulation of the common good of all citizens. Republicanism thus embodies a more substantive consensual ethical vision of the good life. Democracy is not the mere coordination of interests within civil society. It is rather concerned with directly promoting a solidarity, integration, and common good amongst its citizens. Democratic rights embody the right to participate, to perform duties and deliberate over public issues. The republican trust in public discussion stands in marked contrast to some liberal scepticism about public reason. Theorists, such as Taylor and Sandel, at one point, explicitly linked republicanism with communitarianism. For such theorists, freedom is a crucial value. Taylor's 'civic freedom' is not though negative freedom, but rather 'democratic participatory self-rule', which he links with positive freedom. Positive freedom, for Taylor, is central to establishing a conscientious citizenship, public morality, and common good. As we have seen, many current republican theorists reject this. For example, both Pettit and Viroli see a transformed notion of 'negative liberty' (non-dominatory liberty) as crucial to the republican perspective. They therefore deny the conceptual link between communitarianism and republican democracy.

Like communitarian republican theories, Habermas's deliberative theory is critical of the individualized (subjective and instrumental) understanding of interests within liberal democracy. Deliberative democracy is a model for organizing the public exercise of power, in the major institutions of a society, on the basis of the principle that decisions touching the well-being of a collectivity are perceived to be the outcome of a *procedure of free deliberation* (as outlined earlier). Democracy is therefore a process of communication and discourse that helps form a public. It does not, however, allow the citizen to reason from the standpoint of a private subjective consumer. Democracy is the institutionalization of intersubjective public reason, jointly exercised by autonomous rational citizens. The public sphere of deliberation (premised on validity claims) about matters of mutual concern, is essential to the legitimacy of democratic institutions. Some communitarian writers have been attracted to this conception of democracy. However, Habermas views both republicanism and communitarianism as committing the same basic error. Both rest on an overly homogenizing consensual model of community identity. For Habermas, this homogenizing vision overburdens the democratic process by forcing politics into an artificial collective identity. He thus separates out deliberative democracy from communitarianism and most exponents of republicanism. Habermas has also used the communicative theory to analyse comprehensively conceptions of law and human rights, particularly in his book *Between Facts and Norms* (1992).

CONCLUSION

It should be emphasized that Habermas does not engage in any systematic construction of a vision of a rational, democratic, or just society (see Habermas 1990: 211). He rather takes one step back from this and suggests that participants in public dialogue within a society can construct that vision for themselves by grasping and understanding what is implicit in their everyday communicative (not instrumental or strategic) endeavours. They simply do not need a neo-Kantian, republican, or utilitarian political philosopher, as a *deus ex machina*, or authoritative figure, to declare the principles of the just society. Dialogue will embody valid norms and when these are made explicit, then a community of speakers will rationally premise their substantive ethics, justice, legal, and democratic institutions upon them. For Habermas, this argument immediately addresses the issue of any plurality of goods in society. He is content to indicate that as long as the basic processes of open communication are followed, he is satisfied. Different cultures and historical societies will construct their own substantive structures, but the procedural conditions in which they do actually construct, will universalize (not contextualize) the content. Rules implicit within communication and argumentation will act as procedural constraints on all such discourse. However, Habermas believes that these rules do not violate historical communities or cultures.

The above argument also accounts for his general response to John Rawls' work. He envisages his own communicative theory in relation to Rawls as a 'familial' dispute within the broad church of neo-Kantianism—although in his own case a neo-Kantianism modified by Hegelianism. Both want to 'preserve the intuition underlying the Kantian universalization principle' (Habermas 1995: 117). He sees Rawls as committed, correctly, to rejecting radical conventionalism, value scepticism, and moral systems such as utilitarianism. Rawls is also committed to an implicitly intersubjective perspective. Habermas therefore comments that he 'admires' Rawls's basic project, 'shares its intentions' and regards 'its essential results as correct' (Habermas 1995, 110). Both theorists are responding, in their own ways, to the problems of pluralism, contextualism, and universalism. The difference between Habermas and Rawls hangs upon the way the procedural impartiality and universalization are achieved. In Rawls, contextualism and pluralism are defined out through artificial devices such as the 'veil of ignorance'. However, Habermas sees impartiality arising from the 'inner workings' of communication and discourse. As he comments, 'Rawls imposes a common perspective on the parties in the original position through information constraints and thereby neutralizes the multiplicity of particular interpretive perspectives from the outset. Discourse ethics, by contrast, views the moral point of view as embodied in an intersubjective practice of argumentation which enjoins those involved to an idealizing *enlargement* of their interpretive perspectives' (Habermas 1995: 117). Participants in such a discourse can critically assess and reassess, for themselves, their moral intuitions. He notes, therefore:

In my view, the moral point of view is already implicit in the socio-ontological constitution of the public practice of argumentation, comprising the complex relations of mutual recognition that participants in rational discourse 'must' accept (in the sense of weak transcendental necessity). Rawls believes that a theory of justice developed in such exclusively procedural terms could not be 'sufficiently structured'. (Habermas 1995: 127)[22]

One additional feature of Habermas' communicative theory here—which blends with his belief that a new knowledge-based constellation may well be arising—is that he clearly believes that his own theory may well be part of (what he refers to as) an empirically-based social evolutionary process. There is strong hint of philosophical hubris here. He further contends that there may well be some empirical evidence to support his philosophically-based arguments. He thus enlists, for example, the work of Kohlberg on moral development to underpin his view of universal pragmatics and discourse ethics (see Habermas 1979: 69–94). Communicative competence is something, for Habermas, that clearly has to be and *can be* acquired. It can there-fore be part of a process of cognitive and moral learning. To develop morally, for Habermas, is to learn empirically how to competently interact. This has enormous moral implications for the whole process of education and national curricula.[23] The latter empirical, psychological, and evolutionary aspect of Habermas' work is prob-ably the most thin and philosophically suspect. Chapter Ten will critically review Habermas' project in the context of Gadamer's hermeneutics.

Notes

1. The other major hermeneutic philosopher is Paul Ricoeur, however the constraints of space does not allow a consideration of his work.
2. Not though in terms of any scale of forms. The idea of different knowledge spheres can also be found in the work of F. H. Bradley, Michael Oakeshott, Benedetto Croce, and R. G. Collingwood.
3. The diverse links between neo-Marxism, Hegelian-Marxism, and forms of Kantianism were particularly strong and fruitful in the twentieth century.
4. For Horkheimer 'By criticism, we mean that intellectual, and eventually practical effort which is not satisfied to accept the prevailing ideas, actions, and social conditions unthink-ingly and from mere habit; effort which aims to coordinate the individual sides of social life with each other and with the general ideas and aims of the epoch', Horkheimer (1972: 270).
5. Or, in Marcuse's case, famously, student revolt.
6. Habermas's own 'intersubjective paradigm', which moves around this dilemma, will be explored later in the chapter.
7. Indeed, in one of his 1970s works, Habermas explicitly argues for a 'participatory remodel-ling of administrative structures' on grounds very similar to the later ideal speech situation of communicative action, Habermas (1975: 58).
8. As McCarthy comments, 'For this reason it is of decisive importance for a critical theory of society that the different dimensions of social practice be made explicit; only then can we comprehend their inter-dependence', McCarthy (1978: 36).
9. For Habermas this latter category has the same goal 'as do the empirical–analytic sciences, of producing nomological knowledge', Habermas (1971: 310). However, they also advance in a different domain to the empirical–analytic in considering ideological understanding.
10. Nietzsche is in many ways the main agenda permeating the whole of Habermas's seminal work *The Philosophical Discourse of Modernity*.
11. 'In the end, this gives rise to a dilemma: Hegel has ultimately to deny to the self-understanding of modernity the possibility of a critique of modernity. The critique of a subjectivity puffed up into an absolute power ironically turns into a reproach of the philosopher against the limitations of subjects who have not yet understood either him or the course of history', Habermas (1998: 22).
12. Equally, the paradigm of the philosophy of the subject—an isolated atomized being—underpinned this domination.
13. In terms of form of life, practices, linguistically mediated interaction, language games, conventions, and tradition.

14. Speech acts would be 'based on recognition of the corresponding validity claims of comprehensibility, truth, truthfulness and rightness', Habermas (1979: 3). Occasionally Habermas indicates three such claims and sometimes four.
15. 'In context of communicative action, we call someone rational not only if he is able to put forward an assertion and, when criticized, to provide grounds for it by pointing to appropriate evidence, but also if he is following an established norm and is able, when criticized, to justify his action by explicating the given situation in the light of legitimate expectations', Habermas (1984: vol. 1, 15).
16. 'What Habermas seeks to establish in his theory of communicative competence. . . parallels what Marx sought to accomplish in his own critique of political economy. Marx argues that, implicit in the concrete historical forms of alienation and exploitation that now exist, are the real dynamic potentialities for radically transforming this existing historical situation', Bernstein (1978: 209).
17. In Austin locutionary acts refer to a propositional content, perlocutionary refers to the effect on speakers and illocutionary refers to the act performed in saying something.
18. As a result of the 'appeal to universal validity claims, the speech-act-typical commitments take on the character of obligations to provide grounds or to prove trustworthy, the hearer can be rationally motivated by the speaker's signalled engagement to accept the latter's offer', Habermas (1979: 63).
19. Or, as he states more fully elsewhere, 'The analysis of what Austin called the illocutionary force of an utterance has led us back to the validity basis of speech. Institutional unbound speech acts owe their illocutionary force to a cluster of validity claims that speakers and hearers have to raise and recognize as justified if grammatical (and thus comprehensible) sentences are to be employed in such a way as to result in successful communication', (Habermas 1979: 65–6).
20. We need a concept of reason 'that attends to the phenomenon of the lifeworld and permits the outmoded concept of the "consciousness of society as a whole" (which comes from the philosophy of the subject . . .) to be reformulated on the basis of a theory of intersubjectivity', Habermas in Schmidt (ed.) (1996: 419).
21. He sees Derrida, for example, as even denying the validity of everyday communication.
22. Discourse ethics rests on the intuition that the application of the principle of universalization, properly understood, calls for a joint process of 'ideal role taking'. It interprets this idea of G. H. Mead in terms of a pragmatic theory of argumentation. Under the pragmatic presuppositions of an inclusive and noncoercive rational discourse among free and equal participants, everyone is required to take the perspective of everyone else, and thus project herself into the understandings of self and world of all others; from this interlocking of perspectives there emerges an ideally extended we-perspective from which all can test in common whether they wish to make a controversial norm the basis of their shared practice; and this should include mutual criticism of the appropriateness of the languages in terms of which situations and needs are interpreted, Habermas (1995: 117).
23. As far as I have been able to ascertain though Habermas has not addressed himself to the reform of national educational curricula in Germany or elsewhere

10

Circular Foundations

The second broad dimension of dialogue to be dealt with is hermeneutics and particularly the work of Hans-Georg Gadamer. It is important briefly to situate and explain the term hermeneutics. The term 'hermeneutics' derives from the name Hermes—the divine messenger of the gods to humanity. At its simplest, hermeneutics denotes an art, science, or skill of interpretation. Traditionally, it has been associated with the effort to interpret and understand the unfamiliar text, work of art, historical event, or possibly even conversation. It is therefore concerned with bridging the gap between the familiar and unfamiliar through interpretation.

Its roots, as an approach, lie, first, in seventeenth century German reformation biblical studies. Martin Luther's writings are cited, for example, by Wilhelm Dilthey as hermeneutical in character—although some also see the hermeneutic perspective as implicit in much earlier theological writers such as St Augustine. There is an extensive amount of Biblical scholarship in this area. The second major development of hermeneutics is found in the philologically orientated work of the German theologian Friedrich Schleiermacher. His focus is, again, primarily religious, yet, he considered thought as a whole as both linguistically based and interpretive. Schleiermacher tries, in effect, to formulate a consistent and universal 'method' or 'rule' of interpretation. The hermeneutic interpreter must, for example, aim, in trying to grasp a text, to master the generic and grammatical character of the language, which underpins the text, as well as its more idiosyncratic employment by the individual author. Schleiermacher also calls for a more psychologically orientated understanding of the author. For Schleiermacher, therefore, no text is straightforward. It has to be reconstructed by disciplined methods, which will address the historical and linguistic context from which the text emanated. Schleiermacher's emphasis therefore falls on the interpretive efforts of placing the author and text in a linguistic and historically constituted universe, in order to comprehend its meanings.

Schleiermacher's most famous biographer, Wilhelm Dilthey, forms the third key figure of the hermeneutic tradition. In Dilthey, there is a continuation of some of Schleiermacher's ideas. Human action is meaningful activity. Part of the aim of the observer is also to try to grasp the intentions of the author. Dilthey accepted, and is a theorist closely associated with, the distinction between human or moral sciences (*Geisteswissenshaften*) and natural sciences (*Naturwissenschaften*). This became a central theme in later nineteenth century German historical scholarship. The natural sciences deal with matter and natural causation. In the human or moral sciences we deal with human beings, who reflect and try to embody meanings into their activity.

This is another way of speaking of the distinction between understanding and explanation. Activity can be elucidated through expressions revealing mental intentions. For Dilthey, the comprehension of meaning, that is of the 'mental' expression, is the 'understanding'. The understanding is based primarily on recovering the psychology and intentionality of the author. This theme of recovering intentions, within a historical and social context, has remained an important element in some hermeneutic writings to the present, for example, in the work of Emilio Betti, E. D. Hirsch and, to some extent, Quentin Skinner.

For Dilthey, to bring together a number of acts of 'understanding', in order to grasp a more complex expression, involves 'interpretation'. The method, which deals with interpretation is hermeneutics. Because, for Dilthey, the human sciences in general—by which he meant disciplines such as sociology, philosophy, politics, jurisprudence, literary studies, and literary criticism—are constituted or constructed by these complexes of expressions, it follows that hermeneutics is central to the study of human sciences. Hermeneutics is involved therefore with the science of interpretation of texts, events, and discourse.[1] However, it is important to grasp that this is an understanding of the 'knowing subject' of Cartesianism, a theme which is still present very much in Dilthey's position. Dilthey tended also to associate the meaning of a text with the subjective intention of the author. However, the knowing subject is still tied to her physical body, a body which exists within a particular social and historical situation.[2]

The fourth stage in the development of hermeneutics takes us firmly into the twentieth century and the work of Gadamer. Before discussing Gadamer's hermeneutics in detail, there are certain general points concerning twentieth century hermeneutics, which should be underscored. First, hermeneutics has now come to be seen as far more than a method for historical or social study (qua Dilthey). In fact, some twentieth century hermeneutics is totally opposed to viewing it this way. Second, a much richer hermeneutical theory has been developed, which proposes a sophisticated ontology and a social and political theory, premised on dialogue and communication. Parallel to Habermas's work, twentieth century hermeneutics is post-conventional in texture and tries to mediate between conventionalism and universalism. Third, this conception of hermeneutics is very much a product of intellectual debates concerning both conventionalism and postmodernism. It is therefore set against the backdrop of perspectivism (as examined in Part Four), although it reads this perspectivism in a very different and unique manner. Fourth, hermeneutics tends to view our perspectives as pragmatic historical interventions. Our judgements and perceptions are not therefore representations or reflections of the world, but rather constitutive interpretations.

Finally, it is clear from this brief discussion that hermeneutics is *not* one thing. An initial distinction can be drawn between, first, hermeneutics as a method and, second, hermeneutics as an ontology. The 'method' conception is one that is still present in the twentieth century in writers such as Betti, Hirsch, or Skinner. It shows little interest in anything but the methodological concerns.[3] In Gadamerian hermeneutics, this method-based perspective is rejected in favour of an ontological theory. However, this second type of ontological hermeneutics can be further subdivided again between what Paul Ricoeur has conveniently referred to as a hermeneutics of recollection of primal meanings and a hermeneutics of suspicion (see Ricoeur 1970: 26 *ff.*). The first, more positive, reading of recovering primal (possibly universal) meanings, sees the world of language positively, as full of meanings, which can be regained and interpreted. Although this latter view does not precisely map onto Gadamer, I would associate his work with the more positive rendering of the ontological conception. In the second, Ricoeur associates the hermeneutics of suspicion perspective with a mistrust of the surface of language and the need to look underneath the overt statements, or forms of life, to grasp the real ontology. Ricoeur draws his net fairly widely on the suspicion category. He traces it to figures such as Nietzsche, Freud, and even Marx. In some ways, many postmodern writings could equally be recategorized as extreme examples of the hermeneutics of suspicion—although in their case, despite holding to the idea of genealogically decoding and deconstructing, they have, nonetheless, given up on any ontology of discoverable meaning. They have, in other words, given themselves over totally to radical conventionalism.

THE HERMENEUTIC CONTEXT

One key background point here is that Gadamer was a student of Heidegger. Although by the 1930s—and Heidegger's direct involvement with national socialism—Gadamer had many deep reservations, he nonetheless derived a deep stimulus for his own work on hermeneutics from Heidegger's early interests in the 1920s, particularly from early lectures and importantly from *Being and Time*.[4] As we saw in Part Four, Heidegger moves away from epistemology towards ontology. He also takes a rigorous anti-subjectivist and anti-humanist line. Thus, the rationalist tradition of philosophy, beginning with Descartes, is largely abandoned. Language is also seen to be the 'house of our being'. The world we inhabit is saturated with language. Further, language is not, for Heidegger, just a technical instrument; rather we are encompassed *by* language. It is prior to any subject, and, in one sense, speaks through us and to us. This gives rise to Heidegger's idiosyncratic use of hermeneutics. He also discards Dilthey's use of hermeneutics as method; hermeneutics is rather about intensifying our sense of Being (*Dasein*). Instead of being lost in various conceptual schemes and interpretations, which alienate us and separate us from Being, Heidegger is concerned, at this stage, to reawaken the primordial sense of *Dasein* through hermeneutics. In avoiding setting up his own new system of concepts as a new scholasticism, he develops a distinction (which is also crucial for Gadamer), between philosophical propositions, which are 'formally indicative' and 'language which invites one to self-reflection and self-interpretation', namely, something which enables one to pierce through the veil of misleading concepts to the Being underlying them.[5] Thus, propositional forms are distinct from the 'world-disclosing language' of hermeneutics.

One significant Heideggerian assumption here (which partly remains with Gadamer) is that there is a primitive, pre-predicative or primordial dimension to human experience. It is partly equivalent to what Habermas and Dilthey call the lifeworld. In Heidegger, it is the 'fore-structure', which is grounded in our existential situation.[6] This fore-structure 'is intended to be a hermeneutics of everything that is at work behind statements. It is an interpretation of Dasein's care structure, which expresses itself before and behind every judgment' (see Grondin 1991: 93). This kind of pre-given ability with knowing is something that, for Heidegger, remains underneath the whole process of scientific understanding through formal propositions. We should not assume though that all efforts at scientific understanding are simply dealing with determinate (what Heidegger calls) 'present-to-hand' objects. Such an assumption often leads to conceptual misunderstanding, that is, if it only focuses on the formal propositions. In one sense, for Heidegger, the history of Western philosophy has been a long litany of conceptual misrepresentations of 'Being'. There is therefore a crucial distinction in Heidegger between 'Being' and the diverse 'representations of being'. Actual Being is distinct from 'Being in thought' or (as Heidegger puts it) the '*what* of Being'. It is the latter idea, which has dominated Western philosophy from the Greeks onwards and which distorts the reality of Being.

One additional facet of the idea of a fore-structure is that we do not create or constitute it, we are rather 'thrown' into it (see Gadamer 1977: 49). It is here—at least in the initial stages of Heidegger's thought—that hermeneutic interpretation is seen as the subtle elucidation of this fore-structure. Interpretation is about enabling the fore-structured understanding to acquire translucence. Thus, in every valid interpretation, the aim is to become reflectively aware of the fore-structure of understanding. For Heidegger, the elucidation is not concerned with conceptually grasping a state of affairs, but rather with unfolding the possibilities of Being, or allowing Being to disclose itself. In Gadamer, this idea of fore-structure becomes transmuted into the concepts of prejudice and tradition. However, understanding, for Gadamer, is not a rigorous conceptual analysis by an autonomous subject, it is rather about a participating in a historical tradition of language and dialogue. The other issue which arises here in the fore-structure—and within Gadamer's notion of tradition and prejudice—is the hermeneutic circle (which will be returned to). Essentially, the circle implies that the interpretation moves back continuously to the fore-structured understanding. This circular motion of interpretation and the understanding is not an epistemological trap for Heidegger, it is rather ontological. It is of the fundamental nature of all human understanding and interpretation. Every act of understanding is conditioned by underlying prejudices or fore-structure. It is irremediably *how* and *who* we are. It therefore is not a logically vicious circle.

LANGUAGE, HISTORY, AND PREJUDICE

Hermeneutics therefore is not seen by Gadamer as just another method for the human or social sciences. His central theme is the 'linguisticality' and 'dialogic' character of all human experience.[7] Gadamer, in rejecting Dilthey's hermeneutics, moves the discussion away from the method-based study of the 'cultural sciences' and the psychology of the reflective subject. Like Habermas, he rejects the idea of the subject in favour of intersubjectivity, as manifest in language. In fact, Gadamer suggests that 'translation' is the most apt term to describe what happens in virtually all human communication and dialogue. Dialogue and linguisticality, *per se*, are regarded as the dominant aspect of human experience. In this sense, the emphasis shifts in Gadamer away from the epistemology of the subject (and epistemology in general) towards ontology. Our being is within our language; as Gadamer remarks, 'being that can be understood is language' (Gadamer 1977: 103). The manner in which this ontological linguisticality is best dealt with is through hermeneutics, for 'hermeneutics reaches into all the contexts that determine and condition the linguisticality of the human experience of the world' (Gadamer 1977: 19). Gadamer's hermeneutics is essentially a move away from method, a deeper focus on language and dialogue, a concentration of practical philosophy and a sharper observation of historical consciousness.

In effect, for Gadamer, language (and dialogue) have now replaced thought in philosophy. As he notes, 'Language is the fundamental mode of operation of our being-in-the-world and the all embracing form of the constitution of the world' (Gadamer 1977: 3). This point is linked to his more well-known comment quoted above—which gives rise to many misunderstandings—namely that being that can be understood is language. For Gadamer, this is 'not a metaphysical assertion. Instead, it describes, from the medium of understanding, the unrestricted scope possessed by the hermeneutical perspective' (Gadamer 1977: 103). Language, as a *modus operandi*, requires hermeneutics. However, this is not an abstracted method of hermeneutics. Writers, such as Humboldt and Herder, had already focused on the crucial role of language. However, the problem arises, for Gadamer, when one tries to view language objectively, scientifically, or methodically. Such a science implies a distancing from the object of study. The real problem with this perspective for Gadamer is that 'all thinking about language is already drawn back into language. We can only think in language, and just this residing of our thinking in a language is a profound enigma that language presents to thought'. Language is not just a tool or instrument at our disposal. In Gadamer, language is ontological and not an epistemological issue. It is only in language that we understand and are at home in the world. Language is, in effect, all we have. It is not something that mirrors or represents the world, conversely, 'it is the living out of what is with us—not only in the concrete interrelationships of world and politics but in all the other relationships and dependencies that comprise our world' (see Gadamer 1977: 32).[8] It is neither an anonymous practice, which can be studied by science, nor something at the mercy of historical processes. Language is the *whole* process itself. Understanding language is not simply an activity of consciousness, it is 'itself a mode of the event of being' (Gadamer 1977: 50).

There are a number of constraints on language in the above context. Gadamer argues, first, that our language is embedded in history, and second, that this 'sense of history' is embedded in tradition and prejudice. Our historical situatedness is not something to be bypassed for Gadamer. In fact, it is *the* major issue of twentieth century thought. Taking up Heidegger's point, Gadamer sees humans as 'thrown' in historical and linguistic terms. In effect, we are all temporal, finite, historically situated creatures and our language inevitably reflects these factors. There are, therefore, no timeless metaphysical absolutes, no ultimate universal foundations and no way of stepping outside our historical finitude. The problem of history, therefore, in a nutshell, is that we are irremediably historical beings and our language reflects this; thus, 'the consciousness that is effected by history has its fulfilment in what is linguistic' (Gadamer 1977: 13). Our language, and consequently our very being, are rooted in history. However, a great deal of historical work is premised on the false assumption that it possesses some kind of suprahistorical truth, universal norm, or knowledgeable authority, that is, that it stands outside time, commenting upon passing events. The problem of history is therefore seen as external to the discipline itself, to be dealt with by some form of rigorous academic method. The historian would therefore see her task as transcending the prejudices of her own finite historical situation. Conversely, for Gadamer, history is at work in all human language and consciousness. We cannot avoid, or step outside, our prejudices or our traditions.

However, the inevitable historical character of both language and knowing, is not a harmful restriction. Philosophical hermeneutics rests on its own finiteness and historicity. Historical awareness is no inhibition, rather it is central to the practice of hermeneutics and the hermeneutic circle. The past, in such a scenario, becomes, as such, an *infinite* range of probabilities. Gadamer's own sense of what it is to be historically 'thrown' is revealed in a number of central concepts. As indicated, his own version of Heidegger's fore-structure is implicit within his concepts of prejudice, tradition, and authority. Basically, every interpretation draws on the anticipations of the understanding. For Gadamer, these anticipations are part of what he calls our prejudices. For Gadamer, it is therefore 'our prejudices that constitute our being'. He admits that this could sound 'a provocative formulation'. However, he contends that he is restoring prejudice to 'its rightful place as a positive concept'. He suggests that this positive idea of prejudice 'was driven out of our linguistic usage by the French and the English Enlightenment'. For Gadamer, however, 'Prejudices are not necessarily unjustified and erroneous', they do not necessarily 'distort the truth'. In fact, for Gadamer, 'the historicity of our existence entails that prejudices, in the literal sense of the word, constitute the initial directedness of our whole ability to experience. Prejudices are biases of our openness to the world. They are simply conditions whereby we experience something' (see Gadamer 1977: 9). Prejudices are therefore the pre-judgements, anticipations, or fore-structures, which give actual substance to human experience. They also constitute what we regard as authoritative. Gadamer is insistent here that all human organizations contain some form of authority. But to be an authority also requires recognition. Authority is not therefore the same as coercion or force. Tradition and authority are not simply to be considered as dogmatically opposed to reason. Reason and traditional authority are not necessarily at odds. As he comments, 'I cannot accept the assertion that reason and authority are abstract antitheses, as the emancipatory Enlightenment did. Rather, I assert that they stand in a basically ambivalent relation' (Gadamer 1977: 34). In fact, the antithesis of reason and prejudice, embraced by the Enlightenment, 'is a mistake fraught with ominous consequences. In it, reflection is granted a false power' (Gadamer 1977: 33).[9]

Prejudice therefore constitutes the substance of a tradition. To be outside a tradition and prejudice is to be outside human understanding. It is simply a myth of Enlightenment conceptions of reason to believe that one could stand outside prejudice. Importantly, though, for Gadamer, despite the fact that we cannot shuffle off our prejudices, we can recognize them and work with them critically and interpretatively. There is, in other words, an implicit distinction between critical and uncritical prejudices or traditions. As Gadamer comments, 'A person who comes of age need not . . . take possession of what he has obediently followed. Tradition is no proof and validation of something, in any case not where validation is demanded by reflection . . . The real question is whether one sees the function of reflection as bringing something to awareness in order to confront what is in fact accepted with other possibilities—so that one can either throw it out or reject the other possibilities and accept what the tradition *de facto* is presenting—or whether bringing something to awareness *always dissolves what one has previously accepted*' (Gadamer 1977: 34) What this implies for Gadamer is that 'there is no societal reality, with all its concrete forces, that does not bring itself to representation in a consciousness that is linguistically articulated'. Gadamer is insistent, in a resonant phrase, that 'Reality does not happen "behind the back" of language', conversely, 'it happens rather behind the backs of those who live in the subjective opinion that they have understood "the world" . . . . Reality happens precisely *within* language' (Gadamer 1977: 35; see also 38). Thus, critics of prejudice (qua those who conjure with abstract reason) are not offering an alternative to prejudice, conversely they are offering their prejudice as crucial. Humans in dialogue simply trade their prejudices (see Gadamer 1977: 32–3).

Prejudice, for Gadamer, draws attention to our limits, our temporality, and finiteness (see Gadamer 1977: 37). Our language—in which our very being is rooted—is temporal, finite, and historically mutable. Language embodies our understanding, therefore our understanding is mutable. What hermeneutics does is to encourage us to recognize this finiteness, mutability, and temporality of our understanding, and through careful interpretation, to bring our prejudices into the full daylight. This entails, for Gadamer, that we are never necessarily tied to one conception of the world. The possibilities for interpretation are infinite. As Gadamer notes, 'I affirm the hermeneutical fact that the world is the medium of human understanding, but it does not lead to the conclusion that cultural tradition should be absolutized and fixed . . . The principle of hermeneutics simply means that we should try to understand everything that can be understood' (see Gadamer 1977: 31). Hermeneutics loosens the inevitable hold of prejudices. It prevents language becoming ossified. In this context, prejudice, as Gadamer notes, does not function 'behind my back', or, behind the back of language. This reflective consciousness itself is constituted through prejudice. We have, for example, a prejudice *for* reason. As he comments 'the prejudgements that lead my preunderstanding are also constantly at stake, right up to the moment of their surrender' (Gadamer 1977: 38). The recognition of this point facilitates our awareness of the way all interpretation circles back to its own embodied prejudices, preunderstandings, traditions, and historical finiteness. The surrender of a prejudice, though, is, at the same time, a form of self-transformation, which implies a 'dialectical' growth in the person. Gadamer uses the term *Bildung* to describe this growth (see Gadamer 1979: 10*ff*, Grondin 1991: 109).[10] At the same time as being a self-transformation, it is also envisaged by Gadamer as a quite definite form of human emancipation.

Thus, those who say that we are constrained by our historical condition and prejudices into a hazardous linguistic relativism do not really grasp Gadamer's point. He comments, 'there is absolutely no captivity within language—not even within our native language'. The reason for this is that any language 'in which we live is infinite . . . , and it is completely mistaken to infer that reason is fragmented because there are various languages . . . Precisely through our finitude, the particularity of our being, which is evident even in the variety of languages, the infinite dialogue is opened in the direction of the truth that we are' (Gadamer 1977: 16).

In summary, Gadamer focuses our attention on the relation between every act of knowing or theorizing and its historical situation. Further, all knowing is linguistic. Language is not, though, just an instrument or tool, it is our actual being in the world. It is therefore ontological. We understand ourselves and others in and through language. Language and understanding are rooted in prejudice and tradition. We always think and act within a traditional horizon. When dealing with human knowing we cannot coldly or impersonally consider ourselves as epistemologists, dealing at a distance with various knowledge claims. Conversely, we are examining, first, the way humans actually exist in the world. Second, we are evaluating and reflecting on them *through* our own prejudices. There is no prejudice-free thought. Hermeneutics facilitates us in bringing these prejudices to the foreground. This thinking within prejudice is not though a negative limit. For Gadamer, importantly, it is the productive basis of all human understanding. There are indeed many ways of interpreting our prejudices. We are formed by historical prejudices in an infinity of ways—all of which are potentially open to examination. This is not, for Gadamer, a theory, but the human condition.

ENLIGHTENMENT AND POSITIVISM

The concept of prejudice is also useful for unpacking Gadamer's view of Enlightenment reason, positivism, and natural science. He shares with Habermas a deep unease that these latter views have begun to dominate the way in which we think in all spheres. One way to introduce this discussion is to invoke a standard criticism of Gadamer: how could one distinguish between true and false or right or wrong prejudices? For Gadamer, there are a strong vestiges of positivism in this question. The assumption behind the criticism is that there is a vital distinction to be made between reason (as the Enlightenment developed it) and prejudice (which opposes reason). Reason is therefore seen as open, self-critical, and universal and is the very opposite of prejudice. It is this 'distancing' impartiality of reason (drawing our attention away from our unreasoned beliefs, customs, mores, prejudices, and the like), which is crucial for being able to formulate scientific 'methods' for the study of natural or social phenomena.

One dimension of Gadamer's initial responses to this criticism is to suggest that false or wrong prejudices, in fact, give rise to misunderstandings of the world. However, the positivist criticism bites again in suggesting that it is still not clear what would actually determine a misunderstanding, except another prejudice. Gadamer takes the edge off this criticism by indicating that a better substitute for true and false prejudices would be fruitful and unfruitful, or, appropriate and inappropriate prejudices. Decisive truth or falsity is not something that can be attained in such matters—especially in the human sciences. Gadamer also suggests that some temporal distance from a prejudice allows us to make safer judgment about its fruitfulness or appropriateness. However, the positivist-based critic could still come back, again, with the question: what determines the fruitfulness or appropriateness of a prejudice? Surely, Gadamer seems to be desperately struggling not to talk about the difference between something, which is preeminently reasonable, as against something which is prejudiced or unreasonable?

Gadamer's response to this latter query is connected to a much more far-reaching thesis, which is central to his magnum opus, *Truth and Method*. One target of the book is 'method', or, 'natural scientific method'.[11] Admittedly, his criticism is largely directed at late nineteenth and early twentieth-century views of natural science. In this sense, it is disappointing that there is little or no cognizance in Gadamer of the diverse work of postpositivist theories of the sciences, in writers such as Kuhn, Feyerabend, Hesse, or Lakatos. However, in sum, Gadamer basically wants to counter the association of universal truth with method. His focus is on empirical science-based method, which he (like Habermas) associates with the rise of Cartesianism and the philosophy of the subject—a philosophy, which separates mind from matter and subject-based reason from the objective world. As in Heidegger, Husserl, and Habermas, Descartes is seen as one of the key foundations of twentieth century Western thought on philosophy and science. He also sees Kant's *Critique of Pure Reason* developing the deeply subtle and far-reaching epistemological defence of this method-based perspective.

One key reason he adduces for the dominance of this 'method' perspective relates to another of Kant's works, namely, the *Critique of Judgment*. One initially low-key (but none the less deeply prescient) question of this latter work is: where does the aesthetic stand in relation to reason?[12] Kant's notion of reason implies unity and system (which links in closely with the idea of the ordering of our sense impression and our understanding of the physical world); second, it implies self-criticism and self-determination (which implies controlling our practical actions under rules). These two main functions of reason constitute 'theoretical' and 'practical' spheres. This scenario places aesthetic feeling and judgment in a peculiarly complex situation. It is neither an element of reason, nor a simple causal phenomenon related to nature. Yet, Kant—although no great aesthete—was nonetheless aware of the important role art played in all human activity and obviously felt an impulsion to systematize it. For Gadamer, Kant's response indelibly, if unwittingly, marked out the position of knowledge within the natural and human sciences. Basically, in trying to situate aesthetic judgement, Kant subjectivized it in notions such as 'taste'. Thus, the aesthetic is denied any *real* cognitive value. In consequence, the methodically orientated sciences are viewed as the premise of objective cognitive knowledge and all else is subjective (non-cognitive). Kant thus unwittingly facilitates (via his judgement of aesthetics) the exclusion of the human sciences (in general) from the realm of genuine cognitive knowledge, unless, of course, they take on the truth-bearing properties of the natural sciences. The history of the human and social sciences in the twentieth century is then the sad tale of a desperate attempt to adopt method-based reason. This is, for Gadamer, bound to fail, and thus the equation of method with truth is the root to the decline in the human and social sciences.

The gist of the book *Truth and Method*, therefore, is not concerned with introducing a new or better method. It is rather focused on a deep rooted critique of the whole association of 'truth' with 'scientific' or 'empirically-based method'. Science-based method is neither the truth, nor is it appropriate for the human sciences. The central argument that Gadamer makes here is that the scientific method-based view, and indeed the Enlightenment itself, *are*, in fact, unselfconscious deep-rooted prejudices. To reiterate the point made earlier, in rehabilitating prejudice and reminding the method-based sciences that they are also based on prejudice, Gadamer is not asking us to be uncritical. He is, in fact, asking for a more thorough-going criticism, and it is hermeneutics, which invokes this demand. The hermeneutical experience, as he puts it, is 'prior to all methodical alienation because it is the matrix out of which arise the questions that it then directs to science' (Gadamer 1977: 26).

Gadamer has no overt foundational claims to make concerning politics or ethics. He is rather—in his own terms—describing human understanding. One important consequence of this argument is that method-based reason and science, which is premised on the rigid separation of prejudice and reason, logically implodes (see Gadamer 1977: 10).[13] Gadamer therefore resists the idea that we can wend our way around or repudiate our prejudices by using science-based method or universal reason. This is a delusion, which the whole argument of *Truth and Method* is designed to counter. However, Gadamer is also insistent that hermeneutics is not designed to undermine the natural or social sciences.[14] Conversely, hermeneutics can act as a handmaid, reminding science of what it can and cannot claim for itself. The paramount task of hermeneutics is to encourage us to critically and rigorously reflect on our own prejudices (Gadamer 1977: 93). If the hermeneutic task is fulfilled, then it becomes clear that natural science method is not the highest authority in knowledge. It is a valid form of knowledge, but it is one amongst many forms. Thus, hermeneutical reflection tries 'to preserve us from naïve surrender to the experts of social technology' (Gadamer 1977: 40).

DIALOGUE AND FUSION

What role does hermeneutics have in relation to ethics and politics? One of the assumptions concerning hermeneutics is that it is just a way of interpreting and reading texts. Undoubtedly, Gadamer incorporates an account concerning how we read texts, however, as already stressed, his, like Heidegger's sense of hermeneutics, is far more than this. He does not conceive hermeneutics as a method. It is an ontological view. The discussion now turns to the question of how Gadamer's theory might be widened into a more general, ethical, and political theory. The crucial concepts to explore here are those of conversation or dialogue and the notion of understanding as a fusion of horizons.

For Gadamer, the ideas of conversation and dialogue are fundamental to understanding. We converse with ourselves, others, and texts in order to develop our understanding. Any attempt to understand therefore involves some form of dialogue or conversation. For Gadamer (unlike Heidegger), dialogue involves a dialectical growth or *Bildung* of the person. In trying to grasp, for example, a text or a point of view, we enter into a dialogue, which implies a process of give and take. There is no sense here in Gadamer that understanding or interpreting is a 'waiting upon being'. Further, Gadamer makes a point of associating himself with Hegel's negative idea of the 'bad infinite'—implying something, which is quantitatively endless, an *ad infinitum*. All dialogue, and most forms of interpretation, are therefore viewed as open-ended and infinite. Complete knowledge is impossible. In fact, he describes all real human experience, in *Truth and Method*, as intrinsically negative (see Gadamer 1979: 354). To really experience something (and to try to understand it) is often to have one's previous knowledge undone. Genuine experience refutes what we thought we knew. Our finiteness, life-situation, and temporality accounts for much of this. Since we are contingent upon our historical use of language and our finite cultural situation, it is inevitable that our perspective will always be open to disconfirmation.[15] There is, for Gadamer, nothing above or below our prejudices, tradition, and culture. We cannot step outside these with a 'view from nowhere'. There is no ultimate knowledge of our situation. Further, there is no implicit end point to any dialogue or conversation. If dialogue ends it is *not* because it cannot continue. As Gadamer comments, 'every dialogue also has an inner infinity and no end. One breaks it off, either because it seems that enough has been said or because there is no more to say. But every such break has an intrinsic relation to the resumption of the dialogue' (Gadamer 1977: 67).

Further, for Gadamer, understanding, particularly in the human sciences, is a two or more-sided event. We depend, to a large degree, on other interlocutors. The point of dialogue is that interlocutors can and do answer back. In addition, for dialogue to work, one has to listen. Yet, as stated above, this implies that one becomes open to alternative interpretations and experiences. Dialogue is not about forcing one's view on the other, winning the game, or dominating their perspective. There is therefore a negativity (as in any real experience), built into all dialogue. Understanding is not about producing a facsimile of established knowledge. The hermeneutic problem usually materializes either when there is no tradition able to contain one's own view, or, when encountering an unfamiliar or unknown tradition (see Gadamer 1977: 46).

The other dimension to conversation and dialogue is the question of what happens in conversation such as to facilitate understanding. For Gadamer, importantly, experience is, as mentioned, negative; further, conversation and interpretations are infinite and open-ended; yet, he also suggests that this endless 'give and take' is the manner in which we grow and develop (*Bildung*) as human beings. One aspect of this is his view of understanding as a 'fusion of horizons'.[16] A horizon provides a traditional vista, but it also denotes a restriction—an area within which we can see. A horizon is thus a 'standpoint that limits the possibility of vision' (Gadamer 1979: 269). To fuse a horizon *is* therefore, by definition, to expand one's field of vision.[17] This is the way in which we grow and deepen our selves. In effect, we critically appropriate other prejudices, and traditions through dialogue. When I experience and understand another person or text, I bring my horizon (my finite traditions, prejudices, and interpretations), and I fuse them with another horizon (of finite traditions, prejudices and interpretations). The other point to bear in mind here is that no horizon is fixed, all change and mutate. The outcome of any fusion is therefore unpredictable. Interlocutors, of course, need, to some degree, to be aware of their historical situation and must be willing to engage in dialogue. Gadamer links this with the idea of 'effective historical consciousness', for example, the awareness of the inevitability of some fusion, of one's own historical finiteness and of the inevitable dynamics of hermeneutical experience. Further, what one understands has an immediate effect on what one does in the world. Understanding is thus linked immediately to practical action.

In accounting for conversation and dialogue, Gadamer uses the analogy of play or games. If understanding, experience, and the fusion of horizons imply that our present sense of our own self is unstable and mutable, then we appear to be in danger of a loss of self, within the play of dialogue (see Gadamer 1977: 51). Changing our understanding is altering our self, our actions, and our being in the world. In a dialogue between human beings, this process affects all parties. Genuine dialogue, understood as play, takes on its own subtle identity, an identity which transcends the participants. In other words, there is a form of self-forgetfulness, or 'I-lessness', in the play of dialogue. Thus 'the more language is a living operation, the less we are aware of it. Thus it follows from this self-forgetfulness of language that its real being consists in what is said in it' (Gadamer 1977: 65). The analogy he uses to explain this forgetfulness is *play*, thus 'the back and forth movement that takes place within a given field of play does not derive from . . . playing as a subjective attitude. Quite the contrary, even for human subjectivity the real experience of the game consists in the fact that something that obeys its own set of laws gains ascendancy in the game . . . The back and forth movement of the game has a peculiar freedom and buoyancy that determines the consciousness of the player. It goes on automatically—a condition of weightless balance'. The play of dialogue is not an altercation between two subjects. It is rather 'the formation of the movement as such'. To be absorbed in the play is for Gadamer 'an ecstatic self-forgetting that is experienced not as a *loss* of self-possession, but as the free buoyancy of an elevation above oneself' (Gadamer 1977: 53–5, 92). Being, as linguistic understanding in dialogue, is therefore a kind of playing. In a sense, to use, but extend, Wittgensteinian terminology, all human understanding (and activity) takes place in language games. Being, in a sense, is serious play, that is, the 'life of language consists in the constant playing further of the game that we began when we learned to speak'.[18]

Something slightly different, but parallel, happens with reading of texts. We also engage, for Gadamer, in the play of dialogue when reading a text. It obviously does not answer back, however, as we read we bring our prejudices and interpretations to bear. Each reading, as a fusion of horizons, can potentially bring new answers from the text—as filtered through our prejudices. For Gadamer, the results are again unpredictable. Consequently, he is insistent that there is no text with one meaning.[19] In an analogous way, Gadamer uses the serious play point to speak of works of art. As he puts it, 'the work of art has its true being in the fact that it becomes an experience changing the person experiencing it. The 'subject' of the experience of art, that which remains and endures, is not the subjectivity of the person who experiences it, but the work itself. This is the point at which the mode of being of play becomes significant. For play has its own essence, independent of the consciousness of those who play'. It is important to note here that play (or the game) is Gadamer's particular reading of the motif of intersubjectivity. Play does not require a subject. Like intersubjectivity, it is itself a 'going on', which absorbs the individuals into itself (Gadamer 1977: 92–3).

ETHICS AND POLITICS

Gadamer is often taken to be a conservative writer with little direct interest in politics. There is some truth to the claim that he appears to take little overt interest in political events in his main writings. There is also a sense that his own historical approach and focus on dialogue inhibits him. The critic could quite justifiably say that if a substantive political or ethical theory were forthcoming from Gadamer, then it could be interpreted either as offering another 'method' as 'truth', or, alternatively, rendering his own prejudices with universal import. Gadamer would, no doubt, find both these conclusions unpalatable.

However, what is interesting about Gadamer's hermeneutic theory is still the possibility of another way of viewing ethical, and political theory. However it is, like Habermas, a way which does not directly involve recommending substantive foundational claims. What is distinctive about both his (and Habermas's) vision is that he sees language and dialogue as crucial. Language has replaced thought and the philosophy of the self-conscious subject. Communication and discourse are the universal medium through which we deal with social, ethical, and political life. This leads both thinkers to emphasize the intersubjective character of human existence. Like Habermas, again, Gadamer stresses the historical and mutable character of language. Furthermore, the manner in which we deal with conflict or difference is through practical dialogue and communication, which can be misleading, or might indeed have little effect. However, in the final analysis, there is no other way to address such problems.[20] What both Habermas and Gadamer do, in focusing on language and dialogue, is, on the one hand, to stress the contextual or conventional character of our moral and political values. This emphasizes the potential differences between, for example, cultures. However, they also focus, on the other hand, on the universal medium of language and dialogue, through which we discuss our differences. Like Habermas, Gadamer's theory uses dialogue as a way to negotiate his way between both universalism and conventionalism. The norms and processes, implicit in dialogue, absorb the subjectivities of the participants. The dialogue itself is not *premised* on the thick social conventions, but, conversely, on whether there is a genuine fusion of horizons. This is the central 'trick'—referred to earlier in the Habermas discussion— of both the Habermasian and Gadamerian schemes. It is not determined by social conventions (contra strong contextualism), but, at the same time, it is still claimed to be the essential element of ordinary conventions (contra universalism). It is clear, on one level, that Gadamer does not exactly go out of his way to acknowledge any universalist themes in his work. In fact, his overt reputation is more historically relativist.

However, the most productive domain for considering these universalist themes is through a consideration of his use of a number of arguments: first, the hermeneutic circle, second, the coming to an understanding in terms of a fusion of horizons, third, the concept of intersubjective play, fourth, the negative reading of human experience and finally, the infinite character of interpretation. The final upshot of this understanding of Gadamer is that there is an implicit, pragmatically orientated, political, and ethical theory present in his work. He is neither claiming to establish any overt normative foundations, nor is he advocating a fragmented conventionalist thesis. It would thus be a travesty to think of his work as relativist, Nietzschean or postmodern.

First, the hermeneutic circle has a number of possible senses. The most significant are the methodological, epistemological, and ontological. The first two will not detain us. The methodological reading can be found specifically in some of the earlier hermeneutic writings. It essentially focuses on the circular interrelation between a reader and the text. Another early formulation is the relation between the part and whole. For example, a particular text may need to be grasped through the whole of a language, but the whole only makes sense in relation to the particular texts. In the epistemological reading, the methodological point is sharpened, insofar as the circle declaims that one always assumes what one is trying to prove, which is a classic logical conundrum. In essence, in the methodological and epistemological readings of the circle it sounds like a vicious logical fallacy, which one should try to avoid.

However, in Gadamer's ontological reading of the hermeneutic circle, something new is proposed. The circle is tied *universally* to the very nature of human language, thought, and practice. In this sense, the circle is rooted in our very being-in-the-world and consequently it is seen as ontological. For Gadamer, it is neither a vicious logical circle, nor something to be avoided. It is rather to be embraced. The essence of the ontological character of the circle is that every interpretation inevitably draws on our anticipations, prejudices, and unspoken traditions. There is a continuous reflexivity, or circling back, which is characteristic of the whole human species. Reflexivity is an ontological universal. There are no substantive normative vantage points, and no presuppositionless knowing. This is the sense in which Gadamer denies that 'method', qua natural science, can be true in any absolute manner. We cannot put aside our prejudices or tradition, since to speak, to analyse, to converse, to inter-pret is to invoke them immediately. In one sense, prejudices and traditions are the transcendental conditions of any dialogue. The major issue here is whether we actu-ally recognize our situation and work self-critically and openly with our prejudices. We need, therefore, to make our own fore-structure clear to ourselves and others. This 'making clear' to others, in dialogue, situates us in an already interpreted world of traditions. It is also a process of dialectic and *Bildung* (growth and maturity of the individual).

Further, the process of dialogue and conversation is understood as a 'fusion of horizons', which implies that in dialogue our own prejudices mutate and potentially fuse with other prejudices. In this sense, the circle is productive and creative for indi-viduals, it continuously reminds us not only of our fallibility, finitude, temporal, and historical character, but, it also offers us the possibility of change and creative growth. For Gadamer, genuine dialogue (as mentioned earlier) not only means the poten-tial for fusing traditions and prejudices, developing new perspectives and growing (*Bildung*), but it also gives rise to a form of momentary 'loss of self' or 'I-lessness'. Thus, he describes conversation as a form of buoyant play, where the play itself over-takes and absorbs the players into itself. A fourth feature is the negative character of human experience. To genuinely experience for Gadamer is negative. It means to have one's prejudices overturned or altered. Genuine experience therefore does not confirm an established truth, but challenges it. Finally, to grasp the radical aspect of language and experience is to be aware of the infinity of interpretations. Every word we use, as Gadamer puts it, is surrounded by a 'circle of the unexpressed'. It should be stressed here immediately that, for Gadamer, these philosophical (phenomenolo-gical) 'devices' of the hermeneutic circle, fusing horizons, intersubjective play (as loss of self), negative experience and infinite possibilities for interpretation are *universal* aspects of being human.

In my own reading, all of these claims in Gadamer have powerful ethical and political implications. Ethics and politics, for Gadamer, cannot be simply reduced to techniques or methods (travestied in the modern preoccupation with rational choice). No universal principles can be deduced from foundational principles to show us where to go. However, it is clear, on one level, that individuals do have a range of possible substantive norms and practice available, via their own rich traditions and prejudices. We can only reflect on what we *already* know as ethics or politics.[21] Gadamer clearly wants to emphasize this. However, he adds a twist to this apparently conservative and relativist appearance. Gadamer's own theory works at a more subtle, pragmatic, and complex level than simply the practice of existing moral or political prejudices. His theory contends that it is the *nature* of all human practice that judgements and interpretations continuously circle back to our fore-understandings. Once we are aware of this ontological circle, it makes us alert to our own fallibility and finiteness, particularly in our 'knowing' within politics and ethics. It creates a predisposition not to universalize combatively our moral or political prejudices. We are aware of our own and all others' fallibility.

Second, in fusing our horizons in genuine dialogue, we are prepared to listen to another, to vacate, or to mutate our own assumptions, and thus to detach ourselves, in play, from our own interests. In the third sense, Gadamer's notion of conversation as a buoyant play, which detaches the players from their selves, achieves something very similar to Rawls's procedural veil of ignorance, or Habermas's ideal speech situation. However, Gadamer is closer to Habermas on this point, in suggesting that the normative constraints on rationality are implicit in the process of genuine dialogue and conversation. Fourth, if all ethical and political experience, by definition, is negative for Gadamer, then it prevents *any* moral or political absolutes or dogmas being cultivated. Political and ethical dialogue becomes a creative, open-ended series of challenges. Ethical and political norms—almost in a Popperian sense of falsification—become permanently open to critical challenge and dialogue. Ethical and political experience, then becomes something (by definition), which raises doubts in us about the validity of existing norms. This sense of the rational open-ended fallibility, built into the integuments of dialogue both about, and within ethics and politics, is reinforced by Gadamer's sense of the infinite possibilities of interpretation. This opens up the whole sphere of practical judgement and reason (*phronesis*). Whereas in postmodernism the spaces, which open up here, in the signifiers, remain unresolved, in Gadamer differences can be dynamically and creatively fused. There is a dialectic of growth, change, and psychological maturity in individuals.

In the above sense, ethical theory, and indeed political theory, can be viewed as a form of pragmatics (see Warnke in Dostal (ed.) 2002: 82 *ff.*). Gadamer is not offering us a deductive, universalist, or objective perspective, conversely, it is one based upon what is implicit in substantive actual human dialogue—*once* we grasp that being in the world is within language and dialogue, and that no language actually represents the world, but rather circles back continuously into its own fallible and finite fore-understanding and traditions. As Warnke observes, 'At work is a dialogue of ethical cultures and understandings in which each addresses and is addressed by the claims of the other and in which each provides for the other the check of ethical knowledge ... We possess this check not through recourse to thin moralities, however, but through an openness to thick ethical cultures' (Warnke in Dostal (ed.) 2002: 94).

Ethical and political theory, in the above sense, both observes and creates the communicative disposition to act in certain ways which can be described, *ex post facto*, as virtuous. Thus, the arguments and claims deployed by Gadamer do not substantively describe an ethical or political disposition, but, they rather create the pragmatic conditions for an ethical demeanour and for certain forms of politics to be realized and practised. We reflect and conjecture how to act in a dialogic, finite, and fallible setting.[22] It is clear that the arguments discussed about, for example, the hermeneutic circle, the play of dialogue, and the intrinsic negativity of experience, would not be conducive to many more rigid ideological perspectives on politics, deployed during the twentieth century. It would, though, be conducive to a view of politics which was, for example, non-absolutist, profoundly self-critical, open-ended, open to alternative understandings, procedurally fair and egalitarian, and one which facilitated and encouraged wide-ranging open discussion. The democratic and pluralistic implications of this position are obvious.

A DIALOGIC CONFLICT

As stressed already, there are clearly a number of important areas of agreement between Habermas and Gadamer. Both see communication and dialogue as replacing philosophies of thought and consciousness—or, at least, *language* to Gadamer and *discourse* to the later Habermas. Language is, thus, a 'pragmatic universal' for both. They both also reject the philosophy of the subject. Their focus on language is on intersubjectivity, which constitutes the bulk of human existence and activity in the world. Given this intersubjectivity, language, texts, and the like, always exceed speakers and authors. Meaning is rooted in sedimented intersubjective traditions. Thus, texts, language and discourse are open to manifold interpretations. There is a rejection in both thinkers of the more classical claims of foundational metaphysics. Further, they are both agreed that our awareness of the historicity of language and our sociality is crucial. In addition, they concur that dialogue or discourse are the means for the resolution of ethical and political questions. The grounds for this resolution are seen as internal to language or discourse. They are philosophically retrievable and justifiable. Both thinkers are also critical of the hegemony of the positivistic account in the social sciences. They therefore object to the takeover or 'colonization' of the lifeworld by the methods of the natural sciences, or any other form of 'objectivism'. Every interpreter is already situated within a particular cultural, social, and historical context. In this sense, both Habermas and Gadamer oppose, to a degree, truth to method. History and the mutability of language and discourse are incompatible with the absolutist and foundational claims of natural science methods. Habermas does, though, have his own strong reservations to make on this point. Further, both thinkers agree that to partake fully in a language and discourse is to have a full self-understanding and awareness of 'what' one is doing or saying. In this sense, a basic hermeneutic sense is crucial for any communication.

In the above senses, it can be seen that there is a great deal of common ground between both thinkers. Thus, in his *On the Logic of the Social Sciences*, Habermas enrols Gadamer as a definite intellectual collaborator. There is also one further area of agreement here worth remarking on. Both share a critical view of Wittgenstein. They agree with Wittgenstein on the importance of language and that it is learned experientially. However, Habermas and Gadamer are concerned, unlike Wittgenstein, to stress the point that we have the means to transcend particular languages—in terms of a unity of reason. With Wittgenstein, however, we are lost to particular language games or conventions. There is no arch-game. Games are isolated—the only linkage being the vaguery of 'family resemblances'. In this sense, one can see clearly why so many postmodernists, such as Lyotard, Connolly, or Rorty, deeply appreciate the work of the late Wittgenstein. Yet, for Habermas and Gadamer, we *can* translate between language games or discourses; we can fuse the horizons of distinct games.

Further, for both the latter theorists, there is a self-reflectivity within language use and an ability to examine (through the hermeneutic circle and the play of dialogue in Gadamer), one's own preconditions and assumptions. Both are also agreed in seeing Wittgenstein caught in a far more deterministic, quasi-positivistic format, where competent speakers simply master and reproduce the rules and techniques of discourse (see Habermas 1996b: 144–5).[23] Wittgenstein therefore fails to question the structures and preconceptions of language use itself. As Habermas comments, 'In grammatical rules Gadamer sees not only institutionalized forms of life but also delimitation of horizons. Horizons are open, and they shift; we wander into them and they in turn move with us . . . The lifeworlds established by the grammar of language games are not closed life forms, as Wittgenstein's monadological conception suggests' (Habermas 1996b: 147). Speaking a language adequately therefore is not the same as the hermeneutic reflexivity of language.[24] The latter involves a deep reflexivity concerning one's language use and preconceptions. Further, learning a language, for Habermas and Gadamer, is not just a matter of being passively socialized or assimilated into a practice or form of life. It is more an active dialogic, reflective, dynamic process of continuously translating and trading preconceptions or prejudices within a dialogic frame. For Gadamer, particularly, unlike Wittgenstein, prejudices also play a crucial role in human understanding. There are though no original or completely correct meanings of words, however, multiple meanings remain possible for us. All can potentially be fused with.

Habermas therefore sees ontological hermeneutics as a definite philosophical improvement on Wittgensteinian theory. First, it deals with the pluralism of perspectives by avoiding the path of linguistic description and determinism. As Habermas comments, hermeneutics 'does not preserve the unity of reason in the pluralism of languages by means of a metatheory of ordinary language grammars, as the program of general linguistics claims to do'. Conversely, for Habermas, it exploits the self-transcendent power, which is already implicit in all language use, thus, 'only by destroying the particularities of *language*, which are the only way in which it is embodied, does reason live in *language*' (Habermas 1996b: 144). There is no problem therefore with an external or objective context.[25] The interpreter already belongs to the objective context in terms of tradition. Second, hermeneutics is premised on the idea that conversing entails participants interpreting one another. The simple technical application of a rule misses this point. Third, all language spheres are porous and historical. They are subject to change and mutation through dialogue and interpretation of traditions (Habermas 1996b: 149). There is no perfect world of rules within ordinary language. Fourth, hermeneutics is premised on the circular character of interpretation, it moves back upon itself continuously. Wittgensteinian theory does not do this, consequently, it cannot even explain its *own* language game. It has no grasp of the hermeneutic circle (Habermas 1996b: 152–3). Hermeneutics demonstrates that 'understanding is necessarily related, on the transcendental level, to the articulation of an action-orientating self-understanding' (Habermas 1996b: 162).

However, Habermas, despite his sympathy with Gadamer's hermeneutics, does have a number of fundamental objections. To understand the basic points that

Habermas wants to make here, one needs to reiterate and underscore the basic thesis of his early book and inaugural lecture *Knowledge and Human Interest*. Habermas basically views knowledge in a more comprehensive all-inclusive manner than Gadamer. There are, in other words, a number of legitimate knowledge spheres. Although it is clear, first, that no knowledge sphere should be allowed to 'colonize' the whole lifeworld of human thought—which is the core to both Gadamer's and Habermas's critique of positivism—nonetheless, each knowledge sphere, for Habermas, still has a crucial role. The 'historical-hermeneutic' perspective has a place in practical knowledge, but it should not, for Habermas, become the 'positivism of the human sciences'. In this sense, Habermas suggests that Gadamer has made too rigid a distinction between 'truth' and 'method' and has given too much credence to the hermeneutic sphere over that of the empirical–analytic and method-based sphere. In consequence, he thinks that Gadamer has given up any aims to achieve more objective knowledge. Gadamer's appeals to conversation, play, and practical philosophy are too lightweight and idealized to deal seriously and comprehensively with the serious pathologies of modern society, legal systems, and constitutional structures. For Habermas, what Gadamer calls method, is in fact an intimate part of human knowledge and understanding. He sees Gadamer, therefore, as altogether too restrictive on the issue of knowledge. The comprehensive knowledge of human action requires the empirical–analytic, as well as the hermeneutic sciences.

Second, Habermas sees Gadamer as muddying the whole issue of human emancipation. His focus is seen to be anti-Enlightenment, overly concentrated on passive readings of tradition, prejudice, and authority, and thus caught in a deeply conservative social and political stance. The fundamental failure here in Gadamer is to deny the full capacity for human reason. As Habermas comments, 'Gadamer is motivated by the conservatism of the first generation, by the impulse of a Burke not yet directed against the rationalism of the eighteenth century. True authority, according to Gadamer, distinguishes itself from false authority through being acknowledged' (see Habermas 1996*b*: 169). What is needed, for Habermas, is a rigorous critique of tradition, prejudice, and authority, on the basis of open reasoned reflection. Tradition and authority, for Habermas, are thus in conflict with the comprehensive 'power of reflection' (Habermas 1996*b*: 170).[26] What unfettered reflection will reveal is what Gadamer cannot see, for example, the *power* and *domination* implicit within much language use. What needs to be guarded against is manipulated or pseudo-communication. In his early work, Habermas suggests, therefore, that there is a need for additional forms of social and psychological analysis—that is actual psychoanalysis and a critique of ideology. Once these are fully engaged with there is at least a possibility of a distortion free dialogue.[27] Whereas Gadamer is accused of seeing language as an unfettered pristine system of exchange; Habermas suggests that language can be, as much, a system of power, deception and domination, and consequently it needs a deeper ideological critique.

On one reading, Habermas offers an ideal solution to the question of different spheres of human knowledge. However, it is never clear, what the precise relation is *between* the instrumental reason of the positive empirical sciences and Habermas's own notion of communicative reason. Sometimes they appear to be very similar, or, ideally, using the same basic notion of reason, at other times Habermas seems keen to stress their difference. A broader, but related question, is what is the precise relation between these knowledge spheres delineated by Habermas in *Knowledge and Human Interest*? In separating out spheres in this manner, it allows one to integrate and broaden the range of knowledge, but, at the same time it does not solve issues of tensions between spheres, between for example, truth and method; it rather postpones debate about such issues. For Gadamer, Habermas has, in fact, solved nothing with his comprehensive theory of knowledge spheres, except that he has succumbed, almost unwittingly, to the worst of the Enlightenment utopian illusions—the idea of a comprehensive overarching critical social science of humanity. For Gadamer, however, reason, although 'potentially' emancipatory, cannot be a separated out as an objective cognitive concern. Reason is always intrinsic and situated in hermeneutic understanding. Basically, therefore, Habermas wants to stress, on one count, the hermeneutic linguistic or dialogic circle, and, then, he wants, at the same time, to be able to remove himself (and empirical–analytic method) at will. This latter utopian 'opt-out' allows him to engage in a 'critique of ideology' and show the power and domination present in language. For Gadamer, Habermas' 'opt-out' is a sleight of hand.

Gadamer's response also addresses Habermas's second criticism. The idea that reason can, at will, just step outside tradition and become somehow a completely pristine self-critical mode of abstract reflection is just rather silly. Reason *is* a prejudice and, in Habermas, part of an obvious occidental linguistic tradition, thus, to state that reason can step outside all tradition is, by definition, just another language-based prejudice. For Gadamer, to be outside prejudice and tradition is to be outside language and human understanding. The hermeneutical fact is 'that the world is the medium of human understanding', however, this by no means entails that 'cultural tradition should be absolutized and fixed' (Gadamer 1977: 31). Hermeneutical reflection is not premised upon a perfect ideal of dialogue. The idea that ideology critique can reveal something extra, or more fundamental, here about language is deeply problematic. Gadamer suggests that the question we must ask ourselves here is 'whether such a conception does justice to the actual reach of hermeneutical reflection: does hermeneutics really take its bearing from a limiting concept of perfect interaction between understood motives and consciously performed action'. In Gadamer's estimation, however, 'the hermeneutical problem is universal and basic for all interhuman experience, both of history and of the present moment, precisely because meaning can be experienced even where it is not actually intended'. Consequently, he continues, 'The universality of the hermeneutical dimension is narrowed down . . . when one area of understood meaning (for instance, the "cultural tradition") is held in separation from the other recognizable determinants of social reality that are undertaken as the "real" factors' (Gadamer 1977: 30–1). Habermas clearly does think that certain concrete issues—work, labour, and human domination—need to be studied empirically. However, as Gadamer asks, 'Who says that these concrete factors are outside the realm of hermeneutics? From the hermeneutical standpoint, rightly understood, it is absolutely absurd to regard the concrete factors of work and politics as outside the scope of hermeneutics' (Gadamer 1977: 31).

Whereas Habermas views authority and prejudice as opposed to Enlightenment reason, Gadamer contends that this abstract distinction 'is a mistake fraught with ominous consequences. In it, reflection is granted a false power, and the true dependencies involved are misjudged on the basis of a fallacious idealism' (Gadamer 1977: 33). He admits that there are tensions and ambivalences in the relation between emancipatory reason and authoritative traditions, but he is also clear, in his own mind, that the distinction should not be casually accepted.[28] Gadamer's basic point, mentioned earlier about tradition and authority, is that one should minimally make a distinction between critical recognized authority, as against uncritical unrecognized forms. Authority functions seriously, for Gadamer, when it is actually fully and freely recognized. Authority is not the same as dogmatic force. Further, does reason, when it engages and reflects upon the world of traditions and authorities, undermine or destroy prejudice. Gadamer suggests that reason might well be present within the traditions and authorities.[29] The important issue, which gives more substance to Gadamer's point here, is his insistence on the ontology of language. Reality—even empirical–analytic, work-based, dominatory or ideological forms—does not happen 'behind the back' of language. Nothing happens outside of language. There is no conceptual clarity, empirical reference or logical self-consistency, which magically exceeds language. This is *not* saying that language determines reality; that would be a different argument from Gadamer's. However, everything is, nonetheless, internal to language and interpretation. Nothing exceeds it. One may merge with a different horizon, which will radically change the description or explanation of the world, one may even have the impression that one has stepped outside language. The Freudian, Marxist, and Frankfurt school 'ideology critique' give this impression. However it is an illusion. To be open to present or past traditions is not to cave in to mindless dogma, it is to freely recognize other horizons.

Once one has grasped the logic and presence of the hermeneutic circle, it is difficult not to see Habermas himself as struggling, but failing, to jump out of it. Even the Habermasian 'ideal speech situation' and 'discourse ethic' can be seen as yet another surreptitious classical metaphysical attempt to stop time, history, and human mutability and attain a 'still point of unchanging foundational calm'. Habermas does, in fact, have a small range of justificatory strategies here. There is, first, a much more overtly Kantian transcendental claim for the ideal speech situation, which appeals to transcendental conditions for any speech situation. However, in the Kantian mode, this appears to invoke a strongly subject-orientated reason, which, of course, Habermas himself has repudiated, *vis-à-vis* his emphasis on intersubjectivity. He is also particularly critical of Kant's philosophy, for example, when it posed 'as the highest court of appeal *vis-à-vis* the sciences and cultures as a whole' (Habermas in Baynes et al. 1993: 298). For Habermas, it is clear 'that philosophy has no business playing the part of the highest arbiter' (Habermas in Baynes et al. 1993: 308–9). Thus, a *strong* transcendental argument does not seem to work for Habermas. In consequence, there is another transcendental strategy, which is commoner amongst Habermasians, to appeal to the logically performative contradiction of those who reasonably, but sceptically, attack universal reason. Although initially successful in countering the sceptic, such an argument is clearly not tough enough to make the stronger case for reason (qua the ideal speech situation) as transcending differences, prejudices, and traditions. Habermas also tries to utilize some empirical, psychological, and evolutionary theories to make his case about a more universal abstracted reason. However, the evolutionary and psychological arguments are *very* thinly sketched and provide little really concrete evidence for his over-ambitious claims. Further, it is not at all clear how Habermas conceives of the relation between the knowledge sphere embodying 'evolutionary determinism', and the 'free use' of practical reason within other knowledge spheres. This remains a continuing problem in his whole philosophy. Further, any attempt he does make to rationally construct an evolutionary or psychological development presupposes that we accept this contestable body of assumptions (horizons), concerning evolution or psychology. In other words, Habermas, unwittingly, reinvokes the hermeneutic circle again.

Habermas's response to Gadamer raises certain fundamental issues. He sees Gadamer's use of the ontology and historicity of language (which is correct to a degree for certain facets of human knowledge) as avoiding the issue of the conditions in which language is constituted. Thus, Gadamer 'does not see that in the process of tradition he must consider as already mediated what in terms of its ontological difference is not capable of mediation: linguistic structures and the empirical condition under which they change historically'. Gadamer's argument abstracts certain properties from language and gives them an empirical externalized imprimatur. Habermas continues that 'only because of this can Gadamer also conceal from himself the fact that the practical connection between understanding and the initial hermeneutic situation of the interpreter requires a hypothetical anticipation of a philosophy of history with practical intent' (Habermas 1996: 174–5). For Gadamer, though, Habermas' argument reinvokes, once again, the idea of separate knowledge spheres, some of which can be abstracted from the hermeneutic circle. It thus avoids (by metaphysical stipulation rather than argument) the fundamental ontology of language and the hermeneutic circle.

CONCLUSION

In many ways, Gadamer and Habermas, although rejecting older forms of foundationalism, both still mediate between radical conventionalism and an overt universalism. Both are acutely focused on intersubjectivity and language as the *modus operandi* for any future ethical or political theory. Nonetheless, they represent very different approaches to human dialogue. They also embody different response to hermeneutics. In Habermas, it is a hermeneutics of radical suspicion (resonant of some more traditional critical theory), which demands that language and practice need a much more thorough-going analysis, from the standpoint of much broader or more comprehensive grasp of human knowledge. For Habermas, it is the empirical, psychological, economic, social, and evolutionary *conditions* in which language develops and is used, that need rigorous attention and painstaking analysis from various knowledge positions. Only this comprehensive rigour will ensure that the potential, deeply subtle, distortions, and forms of domination can come to light and potentially be eliminated. This, in turn, supports the more philosophically orientated vocation to formulate the logical, pragmatic, and practical conditions for universal, distortion-free open speech. This also forms the basis for theories of discourses ethics, deliberative democracy, human rights, and law. Philosophy can articulate, then, what Habermas calls the 'general presuppositions of communicative action' (Habermas 1979: 1). In this sense, philosophy supports other dimensions of social, psychological, and evolutionary theory. Gadamer, however, represents another form of hermeneutics, which is more intensely self-critically philosophical and sees all the dimensions of knowledge *through* the ontology of language and the hermeneutic circle. Nothing can escape this. This, I have suggested, has deep and subtle repercussions on the way we perceive ethical and political practice. In itself, though, it is not a normative political theory. Gadamer does not deny other spheres of knowledge. He is neither anti-science nor anti-enlightenment, however, he does view these as ways or modes of understanding, which are all, at root, linguistic. Further, they all presuppose prejudices and traditions. Gadamer does not provide any (what might be regarded as) rigorous resources for analyzing the pathologies of human social and political life, but, he does remind us philosophically of the finitude, historical mediation, and temporal nature of all our knowledge claims. Thus, as suggested, many of Gadamer's central arguments concerning human finitude, fallibilism, and dialogic play contain indirect, subtle, and complex implications for ethical and political theory, which are often missed by critics of hermeneutics.

Notes

1. In fact, he posited that hermeneutics is about interpretation in general. Phenomena, which happen to us on a day by day basis need to be interpreted. Thus, hermeneutics can be read, on the broadest level, as the paradigm of systematic cognition.
2. 'The whole context of the mind-constructed world emerges in the subject; it is the mind's effort to determine the meaningful pattern of that world which links the individual, logical processes involved. On the one hand, the knowing subject creates this mind-constructed world and, on the other, strives to know it objectively. How, then, does the mental construction of the mind-constructed world make knowledge of mind-constructed reality possible? This is the problem of what I have called a Critique of Historical Reason', Dilthey (1976: 207).
3. This would not be true though of Dilthey.
4. Sections 31–33, particularly, in Heidegger's *Being and Time*.
5. 'A critical hermeneutics of facticity that calls Dasein back to itself and its possible freedom thus has the purpose of dismantling or deconstructing these traditional explications of Dasein which have become self-evident and resistant to criticism', Grondin (1991: 99).
6. In Habermas this lifeworld, as far as one can ascertain, has a deeply rational content.

7. As Gadamer notes, linguisticality is deeply embedded in the whole 'sociality of human existence', Gadamer (1977: 20).
8. Learning to speak 'means acquiring a familiarity and acquaintance with the world itself and how it confronts us', Gadamer (1977: 63).
9. 'If we seek to illuminate this history we may be able to make ourselves conscious of it and overcome some of the prejudices which have determined us', Gadamer in Hahn (ed.) (1997: 95).
10. The basic idea of *Bildung* for Gadamer is that 'Every single individual that raises himself out of his natural being to the spiritual finds in the language, customs and institutions of his people a pre-given body of material which, as in learning to speak, he has made his own'. Thus, every individual, wittingly or unwittingly, is engaged in a *Bildung* process in getting beyond naturalness, Gadamer (1979: 15).
11. Like Heidegger (and Habermas to a limited degree) he is critical of important aspects of the occidental philosophical tradition as it developed from the seventeenth century.
12. A similar theme was explored and used by Lyotard, see Part Four, Chapter Eight.
13. As mentioned earlier, Gadamer's argument would be far less effective here against post-positivist theories of science.
14. 'My only concern . . . was to secure a theoretical basis that would enable us to deal with the basic factor of contemporary culture, namely, science and its industrial, technological utilization', Gadamer (1977: 11).
15. The manner that Gadamer speaks of this is almost equivalent to a continuous Popperian falsification, each experience falsifies what we thought we knew.
16. He took the term 'fusion of horizons' from Edmund Husserl.
17. Gadamer admits that this idea of an horizon is, to a degree, illusory. In practice, there are no hard and fast lines between horizons. Past horizons, prejudices, and traditions are inevitably implicit within our present horizons, see Gadamer (1979: 271). However, the notion of an horizon does nonetheless serve an heuristic function.
18. In dialogue we repeatedly move into the 'thought worlds' of others; the play of dialogue is not a total loss of self, conversely, it is a dialectical 'enrichment', see Gadamer (1977: 56–7). Gadamer refers to play, at one point, as 'sacredly serious', see Gadamer (1977: 92).
19. 'The real event of understanding goes beyond what we can bring to the understanding of the other person's words through methodical effort and critical self-control. Indeed, it goes far beyond what we ourselves can become aware of. Through every dialogue something different comes to be', Gadamer (1977: 57–8).
20. Other than of course the usual human resort to violence.
21. We acknowledge our embeddedness in thick cultures 'and if we want nonetheless to monitor the ethical trajectory on which they seem to place us, then we must assume that other thick cultures and other understandings of our own trajectory can speak to us and teach us about ourselves. We assume that our ethical knowledge is prejudiced, his- torically conditioned, and incomplete and that the ethical knowledge of others is at least potentially capable of expanding our ethical understanding. We monitor and check on the adequacy of our ethical knowledge and culture not by thinning either into a procedure for validating norms that can hold for anyone but rather by comparing the norms and values that hold for us against other thick possibilities of what we might believe and be', Warnke in Dostal (ed.) (2002: 95).
22. As Gadamer comments 'I affirm the hermeneutical fact that the world is the medium of human understanding, but it does not lead to the conclusion that cultural tradition should

be absolutized and fixed . . . . The principle of hermeneutics simply means that we should try to understand everything that can be understood', Gadamer (1977: 31).

23. Wittgenstein 'remained positivistic enough to think of this training process as the reproduction of fixed pattern, as though socialized individuals were wholly subsumed under their language and activities. The language game congeals in his hands into an opaque oneness', Habermas (1996*b*: 148–9).

24. 'Hermeneutic self-reflection goes beyond the sociolinguistic level of linguistic analysis marked out by the later Wittgenstein', Habermas (1996*b*: 148).

25. 'Because hermeneutics understanding itself belongs to the objective context that is reflected in it, its overcoming of temporal distance should not be thought of as a construction of the knowing subject. The continuity of tradition has in fact already bridged the interpreter's distance from his object', Habermas (1996*b*: 153).

26. 'Reflection does not wear itself out on the facticity of traditional norms without leaving a trace', Habermas (1996*b*: 170).

27. In his later writings in the 1990s the psychoanalytic component quietly drops out. Ideology stays, but is less emphasized.

28. 'I cannot accept the assertion that reason and authority are abstract antitheses, as the emancipatory Enlightenment did. Rather, I assert that they stand in a basically ambivalent relation which I think should be explored rather than casually accepting the antithesis', Gadamer (1977: 33).

29. What is in dispute with Habermas is 'whether reflection always dissolves substantial relationships or is capable of taking them up into consciousness', Gadamer (1977: 34).

Conclusion

The central theme of this book has been an examination of the nature of political theory. This nature has been viewed as intrinsically polyvocal. In order to find a way through this diversity of approaches, the concept of foundationalism has been employed to bring coherence and clarity to an internally complex practice. The book consequently has focused on the various foundations, both repudiated and sought for, by the diverse schools of political theory. Political theory has been understood, in this text, as a specialized *self-conscious disciplinary practice (or set of practices)*, which is largely the product of a twentieth century academicized profession.

During the twentieth century, the idea of foundations has been subject to a chequered and intricate usage. First, foundationalism can imply an overarching comprehensive view, often involving a perfectionist strategy and a concept of transcendence. As suggested, this use of foundationalism was an important feature of political theory in the early 1900s, up to the 1930s. Foundational metaphysical arguments were openly discussed and assessed as part of the subject matter of political theory. In many of these earlier political theory arguments, the relations between the individual and the state or human nature and politics, were therefore quite standardly assessed in terms of rich foundational metaphysical claims. Thus, books with titles such as the philosophical or metaphysical theory of the state figured prominently in political theory discussion (see Bosanquet 1899; Hobhouse 1918). There was, in other words, an open acceptance of the importance of foundations (first principles or metaphysics). However, this comprehensive foundationalism was reacted to, with deep negativity and an excoriating scepticism in the 1930s and 1940s, within a variety of movements, such as empirical political theory, pragmatism, logical positivist thought, and various forms of linguistic philosophy. There was also an explicit and vigorous denial that it was the task of political philosophers to discover such comprehensive foundational principles.

This essentially negative moment constituted the second foundationalist phase. Much mainstream political philosophy, in this phase, looked like a descriptive, usually linguistic, phenomenology of social life. The traces of this approach are still present today. Foundational beliefs were (as I suggested) not abandoned in this second phase. They were rather replaced by different sets of—often partly hidden—foundational beliefs or presuppositions concerning the nature of empirical knowledge. This was not usually something that they wished to be discussed too openly.

Third, in the late 1970s, foundationalism was prosecuted more openly again, but this time in a more *immanent* manner. Avoiding open avowals concerning human nature, and the like, there was an attempt to resurrect aspects of a more immanent foundationalist discussion. Although the older comprehensive foundational metaphysical ideas were still decisively rejected, nonetheless, there was a strong sense that a thinned down, bleached, self-denying, and more minimalist foundationalism was still profoundly relevant. Those influenced by neo-Kantian, contractarian, rational choice, or utilitarian preconceptions, therefore tended to focus on foundational ideas, such as universal human interests, wants, preferences, universal reason, instrumental rationality, or contractualism, as immanent foundational starting points for theorizing. This immanent foundationalism fuelled, for example, much of the Rawlsian (and various anti-Rawlsian) and contractualist industries of the 1970s and 1980s.

The fourth phase, which developed initially in the 1980s, was a negative reaction to the 'rational universalism', implicitly or explicitly affirmed in the immanent foundationalism or minimalist metaphysics of the Rawlsians, utilitarians, libertarian, and contractarian writers. The basic critical theme which developed here was not a wholesale denunciation of foundationalism, *per se*, far from it, but rather a rejection of its universalist aspirations. The central argument, of this phase, was premised on the idea of a far more realistic, rooted foundation to be found in the *conventions* of communities, nations, cultures, patria, ethnos, republics, and the like. Nonetheless, most conventionalist theories still try to link their ideas with some form of universalist understanding. This conventionalist standpoint has formed a dominant motif of much political theory debate until the present day.

However, the original conventionalist position has one central difficulty. There is no agreement as to what *is* the significant foundational convention—and there have been a number of contenders. The debates, which developed between these various conventionalist factions during the 1990s and early 2000s, have, though, all been premised upon an internally destructive logic. Not only is there an *external* debate as to what is a viable conventional foundation between, for example, republican, communitarian, or nationalist contenders, but, there is also an *internal* debate within communities, nations, and republics themselves, manifest in arguments about secession, multiculturalism and cultural difference. This is usually embedded in the term 'pluralism'. This also has large implications for issues of immigration and citizenship. Consequently, if the realistic, immanent foundation is identified with the conventional structures of 'internally-divergent cultures', then the debate moves inexorably away from nations or republics into the spheres of fragmented micro-conventions and micro-foundations. This forms the groundwork for multicultural and difference-based debates.

In the 1980s, and particularly the 1990s, a fifth phase developed, which overlapped with the previous two phases of minimal universalism and the diverse forms of conventionalist foundationalism. This postmodernist phase evinces a deep scepticism concerning the whole foundationalist enterprise. It can also be reconceptualized as an *extremely radical* use of conventionalist argument, taking conventionalism to its abstracted final denouement in perspectivism. It is though, at the same time, avowedly and self-consciously anti-foundationalist and anti-metaphysical. It dismisses the whole foundational enterprise. The roots of this movement can be traced to the late nineteenth century and the early twentieth century. The background figures, who are of key significance, are Friedrich Nietzsche and Martin Heidegger. It is the anti-foundationalist writings of both these thinkers which are crucial for grasping this latter phase. This anti-foundational perspective promotes the view that political theorists have a vital, but overwhelmingly negative, role to play. However, there are a number of important ambiguities in the way that the postmodern argument has been deployed. There are also considerable doubts as to whether they actually escape foundational claims. In summary, a great deal of the attention of anti-foundational theorists has been directed to genealogically exposing, unmasking, or deconstructing the unrationalized, arbitrary, and contingent elements which have figured in much humanistic and social discourse.

The final phase is premised upon a rejection of both the radical conventionalist and positive universalist arguments. It is, in fact, self-consciously post-foundationalist. It envisages itself as part of new constellation of ideas which have outgrown, dialectically, both conventionalist and universalist foundationalism. Its focus is largely on language and dialogue. In this context, political theories can be derived from fundamental considerations presupposed within the nature of all language, rational discourse, and communication. This is a general theme which was developed, initially in the mid to late twentieth century, and has subsisted contemporaneously with the other phases outlined. It is focused, in this study, on developments in both critical theory and hermeneutics and has been explored in the writings of both Jürgen Habermas and Hans-Georg Gadamer. In my own reading, though, despite rejecting comprehensive views of metaphysical foundations, both theorists still find an immanent and logically prior foundation for political theory within 'dialogue'. In this sense, it is a qualified, occasionally circumspect, yet still bold attempt, to reconstitute political theory on the basis of the implications of dialogue.

The above phases are not considered progressively. Although there are some vestiges of a chronology here, it is not meant to be teleologically significant. All of these phases outlined coexist, to a degree, at the present moment. Some of the phases have been given greater, or much less, emphasis at certain points during the twentieth century. In summary, this book has examined a number of variations on the theme of foundationalism. The above discussion is only a spare outline summary, not a definitive categorization.

THE HERMENEUTIC CIRCLE AGAIN

There is one further critical supposition underpinning this book which needs to be briefly articulated. This is the idea of the hermeneutic circle, developed in thinkers such as Gadamer. In this sense, it is not fortuitous that the present study ends with an account of Gadamer on dialogue. The hermeneutic circle, qua Gadamer, as indicated in Chapter Ten, is understood as intrinsic to the human condition, and is consequently considered ontologically, rather than epistemologically. The circle is a universal facet of human existence. It is not a logically-vicious circle. It is not something to be just avoided. The core of the ontological nature of the circle is that all interpretation, inescapably, brings into play our prejudices and traditions. There is an incessant reflexivity, or 'circling back' to our prejudices. The prejudices and fore-structures are considered, in this book, to be the *foundations* on which we premise our judgements. Reflexivity is therefore configured as an ontological aspect of all human thought, that is, the folding back of reasoning upon its own foundations is part of our nature, and therefore inevitably part of the nature of political theory. There is *no* presuppositionless political knowing. We cannot disregard our prejudices or tradition, since to converse, to examine, to analyse, or to theorize is to summon them (wittingly or unwittingly). Prejudices and traditions are the conditions of all dialogue. The key point is to acknowledge this state of affairs and operate self-critically and candidly with and through our prejudices. We therefore have to make our own fore-structure as transparent as possible both to ourselves and others. This process can be achieved in the play of dialogue. Despite its central place in human thought, this hermeneutic task is infrequently practised, even within universities. Students are not actually given the space, time, or encouragement to think in this critical humanizing manner. The positivistic and empiricist mentality is intrinsically always impatient with the utility of such hermeneutic study. There is a peculiar myopia concerning this mentality in much recent academic work. This can be as true of philosophy as any other discipline.[1]

Open critical dialogue situates us in an already interpreted world of traditions. For Gadamer, as suggested, this is a process of dialectic and *Bildung*—closely linked to the psychological and moral growth and maturity of the individual. Being attuned to the ontological nature of the circle, makes us heedful of our own fallibility and finiteness, particularly in terms of our knowing within politics and ethics. It creates an inclination to not exaggerate or to assert the superiority of our own moral or political prejudices. In my reading of Gadamer it also has close conceptual links with the idea of coming to an understanding, in terms of a fusion of horizons, the idea of dialogue as intersubjective play, and the essentially negative reading of human experience (genuine experience being understood as a continuous challenge to our existing suppositions). As argued in Chapter Ten, the final upshot of these ideas is an implicit, pragmatically orientated, political and ethical theory, which is neither claiming to establish any overt normative foundations, nor is it advocating a fragmented conventionalist thesis.

One way of reformulating the above point is that political theory needs to shift back towards and reflect upon the prejudices and traditions which constitute human lives. This would entail a shift towards the 'rhetoric of ordinariness', that is to say, political theory needs to acknowledge the primacy of ordinary human practice and the prejudices and traditions which constitute it. Further, we need, once again, to value reasonable uncertainties, ambiguity, hesitancy, and vacillation in human affairs, over and against the demands for absolute rational certainty, fixity of purpose, and decisive proof. We should not be so concerned to place a template of universalistic rationality over the world, which it has to measure up to. The world will always disappoint the universalist and rationalist. Conversely it is the fore-structure of our prejudices which constitute our practice. There is nothing outside them. Practical knowledge is embedded knowledge; it provides answers to certain questions. But, it also recognizes that certain questions might well be unanswerable, or imply multiple answers. This draws our attention to the point that our reasonable moral, political, religious, and aesthetic judgements (which constitute all that is of value in our lives), are all finite, contingent, and fallible. There are no timeless truths, but rather timed and particular historically situated truths. This is not a collapse into relativism, but, conversely, is a philosophical acknowledgement of our finiteness, the crucial role of language in constituting our lives, the important character of the rhetoric of the ordinary, the often local character of our knowing, that our roots are always embodied in contingent traditions and that we are all fallible. To think of political theory in this manner is *not* to move from a universal, ordered and objectively rational world to a particular, anarchic and irrational world. Conversely, it is simply to be fully aware of the local, timed, contingent, and concrete nature of our existence. When we reflect and speak, we circle back continuously to our foundational prejudices. In this sense, our norms are *not* determined by social conventions, but, at the same time, they are seen to be the essential component *of* ordinary conventions.

What the above outline gives rise to is a different conception of political theory, understood as a more rhetorically based discipline, more attuned to practice, history, and ordinariness. This alone would enable a more sympathetic judgement to be made of ideology as a mode of thought more directly adjusted to human practice, that is, human 'thought behaviour' embodied in ordinary spoken and written language and used to navigate the political world. Overall, this approach implies a distinction between a political theory which embodies an awareness of the hermeneutic circle, which is self-critical, ecumenical, sceptical, fallibilistic, and orientated to the rhetoric of ordinariness, as against a conception of political theory which is unreflexive, rationalistic, abstract, obsessed with its own universality, orientated to impose its order upon others, is combative, scornful of the local and concrete, and favours rigorous exact logic over rhetoric. In the latter doctrine of theory, the foundational metaphysics are usually self-consciously obscured, whereas in the former the foundational metaphysics becomes, through the hermeneutic circle, a dynamic aspect of theory itself, productive of a particular disposition to the world.

In the unreflexive rationalistic conception of theory there is a casuistical certainty and dogmatic quality to the foundational metaphysics.[2] Consequently, in the final analysis, a veiled conversion is usually required from the listener within the hyper-rationalist view. The speaker is frequently engaged in monologic preaching—usually hidden under the guise of 'seeking adequate or reasonable justifications'. Theory becomes a form of subtle argumentative coercion. Discussion is focused on winning or losing arguments, *not* understanding. The aim of such theory is always to narrow the debate down to the pre-chosen assumption (in fact prejudice). In the fallibilistic conception, the style of theory is more open, inquisitive, and investigative. The debates are not foreclosed. The hermeneutic circle necessarily undermines the potential hubris of universalism. In sum, the rationalistic and universalist conception of theory embodies an implicit demand for a theoretical *Gleichshaltung*.[3] Such rationalist theories usually automatically assume their own epistemological correctness—in fact they also assume that epistemology exists. They will therefore insist that it is pointless to mull over the nature of theory. The point is to 'do theory', not to think about the nature of theory. In the fallibilistic investigatory conception of theory, there is continuous circling back to theoretical foundations and an incessant curiosity about, and openness to, the untidy theoretical disorder of the world.

The latter fallibilistic and investigatory view of theory is one which I would link directly with the conception of the hermeneutical circle. What is particularly attractive with this view is that, on one level, it is not *directly* advocating a particular way of being in the world. It is not advocating any first order liberal *Gleichschaltung*. Conversely, by continuously raising the hermeneutic circle, it reminds us of our finitude and temporality. This, as argued, contains an indirect ethics, which is not preached or forced, but is rather actualized in thinking and judging. It is the process of continually moving back to the awareness of our finitude, which creates a certain type of character, demeanour, or disposition of critical reflexivity and implicit moral awareness. Further, this reflexivity is most often engaged in dialogue. Dialogue can be serious play. As in any serious play, the dialogue can absorb the players within it—unless of course one member wants to engage in a coercive monologue, then we swing back to the *Gleichschaltung* mentality of political theory. The latter is the reality of the sophisticated or unsophisticated dogmatist who wants, in essence, to preach a sermon about her rationalist prejudices. The only possible outcome of such a discussion is your agreement with the terms of the sermonizer, or, alternatively, being swept into heterodox darkness.

The study of the various finite forms of human understanding can be an immensely fulfilling enterprise, if practised with the reflexive humility of the hermeneutic circle. Hermeneutics permits one, in fact encourages one, to participate or enter into the passion of the logic of diverse standpoints. Thus, one can with some sensitivity and effort begin (in dialogue) to explore the world through diverse ontologies. However, the trick of the hermeneutic circle, is that this is always done with the continuous proviso that these ontologies are always considered finite temporal prejudices. The study of these various forms of understanding is integral to what I would call a political metaphysics. The hermeneutic circle is viewed as a productive and necessary component to the practice of political metaphysics.

SUMMARY

One key assumption of the book is therefore that what we have actually been examining in the various phases of the discussion of political theory has been various forms of political foundationalism. In fact, this form of study might justifiably be considered a new dimension of political theory. Yet, ironically, time and again, it has been one of the standard arguments, throughout the bulk of twentieth-century political theory, to oppose or resist such foundationalist study—from various theoretical standpoints. Ironically, this has been a common theme in utilitarianism, rational choice, neo-Kantianism, logical positivism, linguistic philosophy, Heideggerians, pragmatists, Habermasians, and postmodernists, throughout the twentieth century. The standard criticism is that foundational concerns foreclose, falsify or constrain discourse, language, or reason. They also invoke a knowledge beyond experience and focus on overly-monistic answers to the problems of morality and politics.

However, there is no need for systematic foundationalist study to be conceived in this manner. The study of foundations, in the context of the hermeneutic circle, is both an exercise in political and moral theorizing. Such a study entails a recognition of our finiteness and our inability to attain objective knowledge. As C. S. Peirce reminds us, we can never attain 'absolute certainty, absolute exactitude, [or] absolute universality' (Peirce 1940: 54–6). This loss of certainty, however, does not, in itself, undermine the examination of foundationalism, *per se*. It may, however, conflict with *one* perception of foundationalism, namely one which demands singular, objective, comprehensive, and universal answers to political or moral questions. The 'loss of exactitude' can be interpreted positively therefore as a call for a political philosophy which has given up monomyths—whether they are about discourse, gender, rights, utility, or rationality. This entails a focus on foundations which are considered more ordinary and multiversal, rather than extraordinary and universal. Such foundational issues are fundamentally important to us, on an ordinary and everyday basis. We cannot help thinking foundationally. But, such issues—as the nature of politics or morality—even though deeply important are never fully resolvable. This is because foundational arguments are intrinsically unresolvable. Yet, the impulse to keep asking foundational questions still reoccurs. As Peirce put it, 'our knowledge is never absolute but always swims, as it were, in a continuum of uncertainty and of indeterminacy' (Peirce 1940: 356). Another way of stating this point is, that it is in the nature of foundational problems to be both ordinary and to be unfinished. To have multiple foundational problems and answers, which are not finished, is deeply irritating for some, but is quite normal and ordinary for humanity, and should become normal and ordinary within political theory.

In this sense, the question concerning the nature of political theory inevitably has a number of possible foundational answers. These can be studied systematically. Foundational non-agreement is though inevitable and possibly valuable, as long as we think and let others think. We may not be able to identify absolutes, but neither can we avoid foundationalism. This non-absolute conception of humanity is therefore involved with a defence of the multiple ordinary ways in which we account for our political and moral existence. Perfectionist foundationalism or absolute claims for one particular comprehensive foundation distort the ordinary. Human freedom, in this sense, is dependent on a separation of foundational powers. This argument therefore uses multiple foundational arguments *against* any absolute expectations in political theory.

In sum, my argument in this book is that it is the nature of human beings to try to understand. The understanding we seek *is* the nature of our being. In political theory we try to understand the nature of our political being. We do this with the foundational symbols to hand. Foundational questions, although continuously asked, are never resolved. Yet, we still feel compelled to ask them. A concern with these multiple foundational readings can be re-described as a concern with political metaphysics. In this reading, political theorists who are concerned with political metaphysics, can be defined as those who have never finished with problems, and political metaphysics itself can be defined as the 'science of the unfinished problems of political ordinariness'. This is the real value of political metaphysics. It asks systematically about what is most familiar and yet unresolved and keeps encouraging us to try to explain it. In this sense, it is the most indelibly human of all our thoughtful occupations. Consequently, a key assumption of this present book has been a foundational pluralism underpinning political theory. Political theory is intrinsically a plural discipline—a mixed mode or polyvocal form of study. Further, it assumes that there are no overarching authoritative exemplars, methods, or absolutely key foundational concepts within the discipline. The book has, therefore, been about the diverse foundational approaches *within* political theory. To adopt one particular univocal approach (or focus on one particular concept) undermines this aim. This does not mean that there are no theorists, texts, ideas, or theories which claim to be authoritative or hegemonic. The history of the twentieth century has been, in fact, punctuated by such claims. However, my assumption is always to remain sceptical of authorities or schools of thought on metaphysical and hermeneutic grounds.

NOTES

1. There is no more philosophical activity, even if it is bound to scandalize any normally constituted 'philosophical mind', than analysis of the specific logic of the philosophical field and of the dispositions and beliefs socially recognized at a given moment as 'philosophical' which are generated and flourish there, thanks to philosopher's blindness to their own scholastic blindness. The immediate harmony between the logic of a field and the dispositions it induces and presupposes means that all its arbitrary content tends to be disguised as timeless, universal self-evidence. The philosophical field is no exception to this rule. (Bourdieu 2000: 29).
2. As Collingwood stated 'any positivist stands logically committed to the principle that metaphysics is impossible. But at the same time he is quite at liberty to indulge both in metaphysics and in pseudo-metaphysics to his heart's content, so long as he protests that what he is doing is just ordinary scientific thinking... that is, so long as he finds himself disposed for what I call the "heads I win" attitude of pretending that a given absolute presupposition is a generalization from observed fact'. (Collingwood 1969: 149).
3. *Gleichshaltung*—a demand for conformity in moving together, or being forced into line.

Bibliography

Ackerman, B. (1992). *The Future of Liberal Revolution* (New Haven and London: Yale University Press).

Ansell-Pearson, Keith (1994). *An Introduction to Nietzsche as a Political Thinker: A Perfect Nihilist* (Cambridge: Cambridge University Press).

Apel, Karl-Otto (1978). 'The Conflict of our Time and the Problem of Political Ethics', in Fred R. Dallmayr (ed.), *From Contract to Community* (New York and Basel: Marcel Dekker Inc.).

Arendt, H. (1958*a*). *The Human Condition* (Chicago: Chicago University Press).

——(1958*b*). *The Origins of Totalitarianism* (New York: World Publishing Co., Meridian Books).

——(1965). *Eichmann in Jeruasalem: A Report on the Banality of Evil* (New York: Viking Press).

Aristotle (1966). [Translated by Ross, W. D.] *The Nichomachean Ethics* (Oxford: Oxford University Press).

Armitage, David (1999). 'Answering the Call: The History of Political and Social Concepts in English', Symposium on *The History of Political and Social Concepts: A Critical Introduction* by Melvin Richter in *History of European Ideas*, 25: 1–2.

Arrow, K. (1951). *Social Choice and Individual Values* (New Haven: Yale University Press).

Ashcraft, R. (1975). 'On the Problem of Methodology and the Nature of Political Theory', *Political Theory*, 3: 1.

——(1980). 'Political Theory and the Problem of Ideology', *The Journal of Politics*, 42.

Austin, J. L. (1962). *How to Do Things with Words* (Oxford: Clarendon Press).

——(1971). *Philosophical Papers* (Oxford: Clarendon Press).

Ayer, A. J. (1952). *Language Truth and Logic* (New York: Dover Press).

Ball, T. (1987). *Idioms of Inquiry: Critique and Renewal in Political Science* (New York: State University of New York Press).

——(1988). *Transforming Political Discourse: Political Theory and Critical Conceptual History* (Oxford: Blackwell).

—— Farr, J., and Hanson, R. L. (1989). *Political Innovation and Conceptual Change* (Cambridge: Cambridge University Press).

Barber, B. (1984). *Strong Democracy: Participatory Politics for New Age* (Berkeley: University of California Press).

——(1988). *The Conquest of Politics: Liberal Political Philosophy in Democratic Times* (Princeton, NJ: Princeton University Press).

Barker, Ernest (1978). 'The Study of the Science of Politics', in P. King (ed.), *The Study of Politics* (New York and London: Frank Cass).

Baron, Has (1966). *The crisis of the Early Italian Renaissance: Civic Humanism and Republican Liberty in an Age of Classicism and Tyranny* (Princeton, NJ: Princeton University Press).

Barry, Brian (1983). 'Self-Government Revisited', in D. Miller and L. Seidentop (eds.), *Nature of Political Theory* (Oxford: Clarendon Press).

——(1989). *Theories of Justice* (Hemel Hempstead: Harvester Wheatsheaf).

——(1990). *Political Argument: A Reissue* (Hemel Hempstead: Harvester Wheatsheaf).

——(1991). 'The Strange Death of Political Philosophy', in B. Barry (ed.), *Democracy and Power: Essays in Political Theory*, Vol. 1 (Oxford: Clarendon Press).

Barry, Brian (1995*a*). 'Spherical Justice and Global Justice', in D. Miller and M. Walzer (eds.), *Pluralism, Justice and Equality* (Oxford: Oxford University Press).

—— (1995*b*). *Justice as Impartiality* (Oxford: Clarendon Press).

—— (2001). *Culture and Equality* (Cambridge: Polity).

Barry, N. P. (1989). *An Introduction to Modern Political Theory*, 2nd edn (London: Macmillan).

Bateson, G. (1973). *Steps to an Ecology of Mind* (London: Paladin).

Bauer, J. R. and Bell, Daniel (eds.) (1999). *The East Asian Challenge for Human Rights* (Cambridge: Cambridge University Press).

Bauman, Zygmunt (1993). *Postmodern Ethics* (Oxford: Blackwell).

Baumeister, A. (2000). *Liberalism and 'the Politics of Difference'* (Edinburgh: Edinburgh University Press).

Baynes, K., Bohman, J., and McCarthy, T. (eds.) (1993). *Philosophy: End or Transformation* (Cambridge, MA: MIT Press).

Beardsworth, R. (1996). *Derrida and the Political* (London and New York: Routledge).

Beiner, R. (1992). *What's the Matter with Liberalism?* (Berkeley: University of California Press).

—— (ed.) (1999). *Theorizing Nationalism* (New York: State University of New York Press).

Beitz, C. (1979). *Political Theory and International Relations* (Princeton, NJ: Princeton University Press).

Bell, D. (1965). *The End of Ideology: On the Exhaustion of Political Ideas in the 1950s* (New York: Free Press).

Bell, Daniel (1993). *Liberalism and Communitarianism* (Oxford: Clarendon Press).

—— (1998). 'The Limits of Liberal Justice' *Political Theory*, 26: 4.

Bellah, Robert, et al. (1996). *Habits of the Heart: Individualism and Commitment in American Life*, updated edn (Berkeley, CA: University of California Press).

Bellamy, R. (1992). *Liberalism and Modern Society* (Oxford: Polity).

—— (1999). *Liberalism and Pluralism: Towards a Politics of Compromise* (London: Routledge).

Benhabib, S. (ed.) (1996). *Difference and Democracy: Contesting the Boundaries of the Political* (Princeton: Princeton University Press).

Bennett, David (ed.) (1998). *Multicultural State: Rethinking Difference and Identity* (London: Routledge).

Berger, S., Donovan, M. and Passmore, K. (eds.) (1999). *Writing National Histories* (London: Routledge).

Berlin, I. (1962). 'Does Political Theory Still Exist?', in P. Laslett and W. G. Runciman (eds.), *Politics, Philosophy and Society* (Oxford: Blackwell).

—— (1997). *The Proper Study of Mankind* (London: Chatto and Windus).

Bernstein, R. J. (1983). *Beyond Objectivism and Relativism* (Oxford: Blackwell).

—— (1991). *The New Constellation: the Ethical-Political Horizons of Modernity/Postmodernity* (Cambridge: Polity Press).

Bevir, M. (1999). *The Logic of the History of Ideas* (Cambridge: Cambridge University Press).

—— (1994). 'Are there Perennial Problems in Political Theory', *Political Studies*, XLII.

Black, A. (1997). 'Christianity and Republicanism: From St. Cyprian to Rousseau', *American Political Science Review*, 91.

—— (1998). 'Christianity and Republicanism: A Response to Nederman', *American Political Science Review*, 92.

Blackstone, W. (1973). *Political Philosophy: An Introduction* (New York: Thomas Y. Crowell Company).

Blakey, R. (1855). *A History of Political Literature from the Earliest Times* (London: Richard Bently).

Bloom, Allan (1980). 'The Study of Texts', in M. Richter (ed.), *Political Theory and Politcal Education* (Princeton, NJ: Princeton University Press).

—— (1987). *The Closing of the American Mind* (New York: Simon and Schuster).

Bluntschli, J. C. (1895). *The Theory of the State* (Oxford: Oxford University Press).

Boling, P. (1991). 'The Democratic Potential of Mothering', *Political Theory*, 19: 4.

Bosanquet, Bernard (1899). *The Philosophical Theory of the State* (London: Macmillan).

Boucher, D. (1984). 'The Denial of Perennnial Problems', *Interpretation*, 12: 2, 3.

—— (1985). *Texts in Context: Revisionist Methods for Studying the History of Ideas* (Hague: Martinus Nijhoff).

—— (1989*a*). *The Social and Political Thought of R.G. Collingwood* (Cambridge: Cambridge University Press).

—— (1989*b*). 'Philosophy, History and Practical Life: The Emergence of the History of Political Thought in England', *Australian Journal of Politics and History*, 35.

—— (1991). 'Ambiguity and Originality in the Context of Discursive Relations', in W. J. Van der Dussen and Lionel Rubinoff (eds.), *Objectivity, Method and Point of View: Essays in the Philosophy of History* (Hague: E. J. Brill).

—— (1997). 'Political Theory, International Theory, and the Political Theory of International Relations', in A. Vincent (ed.), *Political Theory: Tradition and Diversity* (Cambridge: Cambridge University Press).

—— (1998). *Political Theories of International Relations* (Oxford: Clarendon Press).

Boucher, David and Vincent, Andrew (1993). *A Radical Hegelian: The Political and Social Philosophy of the Henry Jones* (Cardiff and New York: University of Wales Press and St. Martin's Press).

—— and —— (2001). *British Idealism and Political Theory* (Edinburgh: Edinburgh University Press).

Bourdieu, Pierre (2000). [Translated by R. Nice] *Pascalian Meditations* (Cambridge: Polity).

Bowle, John (1947). *Western Political Thought* (London: Jonathan Cape).

Bradley, F. H. (1935). 'Mr. Sidgwick's Hedonism', in F. H. Bradley (ed.), *Collected Essays*, Vol. 1 (Oxford: Clarendon Press).

—— (1962). *Ethical Studies* (Oxford: Clarendon Press).

—— (1969). *Appearance and Reality: A Metaphysical Essay* (Oxford: Oxford University Press).

Brecht, A. (1959). *Political Theory: The Foundation of the Twentieth Century* (Princeton, NJ: Princeton University Press).

Brennan, G. (1997). 'Rational Choice Political Theory', in A. Vincent (ed.), *Political Theory: Tradition and Diversity* (Cambridge: Cambridge University Press).

Browning, Gary (2000). *Lyotard and the End of Grand Narratives* (Cardiff: University of Wales Press).

Brugger, Bill (1999). *Republican Theory in Political Thought: Virtuous or Virtual?* (London: Macmillan).

Brunkhorst, H. (2000). 'Equality and Elitism in Arendt', in D. Villa (ed.), *Cambridge Companion to Hannah Arendt* (Cambridge: Cambridge University Press).

Buchanan, J. (1975). *The Limits of Liberty: Between Anarchy and Leviathan* (Chicago: University of Chicago Press).

Buchanan, James, M., and Tullock, G. (1962). *The Calculus of Consent* (Ann Arbor: University of Michigan Press).

Campbell, Tom (1988). *Justice* (London: Macmillan).

Canovan, M. (1974). *The Political Thought of Hannah Arendt* (London: J. M. Dent).

—— (1994). *Hannah Arendt: A Reinterpretation of her Political Thought* (Cambridge: Cambridge University Press).

—— (1996). *Nationalism and Political Theory* (Cheltenham: Edward Elgar).

—— (1999*a*). 'Is There an Arendtian Case for the Nation State?', in *Contemporary Politics*, 5: 2.

—— (1999*b*). 'The Skeleton in the Cupboard: Nationhood, Patriotism and Limited Loyalties', in Beiner, R. (ed.), *Theorizing Nationalism* (New York: State University of New York Press).

Carver, T. and Thomas, P. (eds.) (1995). *Rational Choice Marxism* (London: Macmillan).

Castiglione, D. and Hampsher-Monk, I. (eds.) (2001). *The History of Political Thought in National Context* (Cambridge: Cambridge University Press).

Cavell, S. (1979). *The Claims of Reason* (Oxford: Oxford University Press).

Chodorow, Nancy (1978). *Mothering: Psychoanalysis and the Sociology of Gender* (Berkeley: University of California Press).

Clifford, James (1988). *The Predicament of Culture* (Cambridge, MA: Harvard University Press).

—— and Marcus, G. E. (eds.) (1986). *Writing Culture: The Poetics and Politics of Ethnography* (Berkeley: University of California Press).

Cohen, J., Howard, M., and Nussbuam, M. (eds.) (1999). *Is Multiculturalism Bad for Women?* (Princeton, NJ: Princeton University Press).

Coles, Romand (1995). 'Identity and Difference in the Ethical positions of Adorno and Habermas', in S. K. White (ed.), *Cambridge Companion to Habermas* (Cambridge: Cambridge University Press).

Collingwood, R. G. (1969). *An Essay on Metaphysics* (Oxford: Clarendon Press).

—— (1993). [Revised by Jan van der Dussen] *The Idea of History* (Oxford: Clarendon Press).

Collini, S., Winch, D., and Burrow, J. (1983). *That Noble Science of Politics* (Cambridge: Cambridge University Press).

Condren, C. (1985). *The Status and Appraisal of Classic Texts* (Princeton, NJ: Princeton University Press).

Connolly, W. E. (1983). *The Terms of Political Discourse*, first published in 1974 (Oxford: Martin Robertson).

—— (1988). *Political Theory and Modernity* (Oxford: Blackwell).

—— (1991). *Identity/Difference: Democratic Negotiations of Political Paradox* (Ithaca: Cornell University Press).

—— (1995). *The Ethos of Pluralization* (Minneapolis: University of Minnesota Press).

Coole, D. (2000). 'Cartographic Convulsions: Public and Private Reconsidered', *Political Theory*, 28: 3.

Copleston, F. C. (1972). 'The Function of Metaphysics', in F. Copleston, *Contemporary Philosophy* (London: Search Press).

—— (1983). 'Philosophy and Ideology', in A. Parel (ed.), *Ideology, Philosophy and Politics* (Waterloo, Ontario: Wilfrid Laurier University Press).

Corbett, P. (1965). *Ideologies* (London: Hutchinson).

Covell, C. (1986). *The Redefinition of Conservatism: Politics and Doctrine* (London: Macmillan).

Crospey, J. and Strauss, Leo (eds.) (1987). *History of Political Philosophy* (Chicago: Chicago University Press).

Crowder, G. (2002). *Liberalism and Value Pluralism* (London and New York: Continuum Press).

Dallmayr, Fred R. (ed.) (1978). *From Contract to Community: Political Theory at the Crossroads* (New York and Basel: Marcel Dekker Inc).

Davidson, D. (1973–4). 'On the Very Idea of a Conceptual Scheme', *Proceedings and Addresses of the American Philosophical Association*, 47.

Delueze, Gilles (1983). *Nietzsche and Philosophy* (New York: Columbia University Press).

Derrida, J. (1976). [Translated by G. C. Spivak] *Of Grammatology* (London and Baltimore: Johns Hopkins University Press).

—— (1978). [Translated by Alan Bass] *Writing and Difference* (Chicago: Chicago University Press).

—— (1979). *Spurs: Nietzsche's Styles* (Chicago: Chicago University Press).

—— (1993). 'The Ends of Man', in Baynes et al. (eds.), *Philosophy: End or Transformation* (Cambridge, MA: MIT Press).

—— (2002). [Translated by Mark Dooley and M. Hughes] *Cosmopolitanism and Forgiveness* (London: Routledge).

Dicey, A. V. (1927). *An Introduction to the Law of the Constitution* (London: Macmillan).

Dilthey, W. (1976). [Translated by H. P. Rickman] *W. Dilthey: Selected Writings* (Cambridge: Cambridge University Press).

Dinnerstein, D. (1976). *The Mermaid and the Minotaur: Sexual Arrangements and Human Malaise* (New York: Harper Colophon).

Dostal, R. J. (ed.) (2002). *The Cambridge Companion to Gadamer* (Cambridge: Cambridge University Press).

Downs, A. (1957). *An Economic Theory of Democracy* (New York: Harper and Row).

Doyle, Phyllis (1949). *A History of Political Thought* (London: Jonathan Cape).

Dunn, John (1995). *The History of Political Theory* (Cambridge: Cambridge University Press).

Dunning, William Archibald (1902). *A History of Political Theories Ancient and Modern* (London: Macmillan).

Dworkin, Andrea (1974). *Women Hating* (New York: Dutton).

—— (1987). *Intercourse* (London: Arrow Books).

Dworkin, R. (1980). 'Liberalism', in S. Hampshire (ed.), *Public and Private Morality* (Cambridge, MA: MIT Press).

Dyson, K. H. F. (1979). *The State Tradition in Western Europe: A Study of an Idea and Institution* (Oxford: Martin Robertson).

Easton, David (1951). 'The Decline of Political Theory', *Journal of Politics*, 13.

—— (1953). *The Political System: An Inquiry into the State of Political Science*, 2nd edn in 1971 with a new epilogue (New York: Alfred A. Knopf).

—— (1997). 'The Future of the Postbehavioural Phase in Political Science', in K. R. Monroe (ed.), *Contemporary Empirical Political Theory* (Berkeley: University of California Press).

Eckstein, H. and Apter, D. (eds.) (1963). *Comparative Politics: A Reader* (New York: Free Press).

Eisenstein, H. (1984). *Contemporary Feminist Thought* (London: Unwin Hyman).

Eisenstein, Z. (1981). *The Radical Future of Liberal Feminism* (New York and London: Longman).

Elshtain, Jean Beth (1981). *Public Man, Private Woman* (Princeton, NJ: Princeton University Press).

Etzioni, A. (1997). *The New Golden Rule: Community and Morality in a Democratic Society* (London: Profile Books).

Euben, P. (2000). 'Arendt's Hellenism', in Villa, D. (ed.), *Cambridge Companion to Hannah Arendt* (Cambridge: Cambridge University Press).

Eulau, H. (1962). *The Behavioural Persuasion in Politics* (New York: Random House).

Evans, P. B., Rueschemeyer, D., and Skocpol, T. (eds.) (1985). *Bringing the State Back In* (Cambridge: Cambridge University Press).

Farr, James, and Seidelman, Raymond (eds.) (1993). *Discipline and History: Political Science in the United States* (Ann Arbor: University of Michigan Press).

——Dryzek, John S., and Leonard, S. (ed.) (1995). *Political Science in History* (Cambridge: Cambridge University Press).

Flathman, R. (1989). *Towards a Liberalism* (Ithaca: Cornell University Press).

Foucault, Michel (1977). [Translated by Alan Sheridan] *Discipline and Punish: The Birth of the Prison* (Middlesex: Penguin).

——(1980). In Colin Gordon (ed.) *Power/Knowledge: Selected Interviews and Other Writings* (Hemel Hempstead: Harvester Wheatsheaf).

——(1986*a*). 'Nietzsche, Geneaology, History', in Paul Rabinow (ed.), *Foucault Reader* (Middlesex: Penguin).

——(1986*b*). 'What is an Author?', in Paul Rabinow (ed.), *Foucault Reader* (Middlesex: Penguin).

——(1986*c*). 'Truth and Power', in Paul Rabinow (ed.), *Foucault Reader* (Middlesex: Penguin).

——(1988). 'The Return of Morality', in L. Kritzman (ed.), *Michel Foucault: Politics, Philosophy, Culture* (London and New York: Routledge).

——(1990). [Translated by R. Hurley] *The Care of the Self: The History of Sexuality*, Vol. 3 (Middlesex: Penguin).

——(1996). [Translated by K. P. Geiman] 'What is Critique?', in Schmidt (ed.), *What is Enlightenment?*

Frazer, Elizabeth, and Lacey, Nicola (1993). *The Politics of Community: A Feminists Critique of the Liberal Communitarian Debate* (Hemel Hempstead, Harvester Wheatsheaf).

Freeden, M. (1978). *The New Liberalism: An Ideology of Social Reform* (Oxford: Clarendon Press).

——(1996). *Ideologies and Political Theory* (Oxford: Clarendon Press).

——(1997). 'Ideologies and Conceptual History', *Journal of Political Ideologies*, 2: 1.

Freeman, M. and Robertson, D. (eds.) (1980). *The Frontiers of Political Theory: Essays in a Revitalised Discipline* (Brighton: Harvester).

Fukuyama, F. (1992). *The End of History* (London: Hamish Hamilton).

Gadamer, Hans-Georg (1977). [Translated by D. E. Linge] *Philosophical Hermeneutics* (Berkeley and London: University of California Press).

——(1979). [Translated by W. Glen-Doepel] *Truth and Method* (London: Sheed and Ward).

Gallie, W. B. (1955–6). 'Essentially Contested Concepts', *Proceedings of the Aristotelian Society* LVI (London: Harrison and Sons).

Galston, W. (1991). *Liberal Purposes: Goods, Virtues and Diversity in the Liberal State* (Cambridge: Cambridge University Press).

Gandhi, Leela (1998). *Postcolonial Theory: A Critical Introduction* (Edinburgh: Edinburgh University Press).

Gaus, J. (2000). *Political Concepts and Political Theories* (Boulder, CO: Westview Press).

Gauthier, D. (1986). *Morals by Agreement* (Oxford: Clarendon Press).

——(1988). 'Morality, Rational Choice, and Semantic Representation: A Reply to My Critics' in E. F. Paul et al. (eds.), *The New Social Contract: Essays on Gauthier* (Oxford: Blackwell).

Geertz, Clifford (1988). *Works and Lives* (Stanford: Stanford University Press).

—— (1993). *The Interpretation of Cultures* (London: Harper Collins).

Germino, D. (1967). *Beyond Ideology: The Revival of Political Theory* (Chicago: Chicago University Press).

Gewirth, A. (1965). *Political Philosophy* (New York and London: Macmillan Collier).

—— (1978). *Reason and Morality* (Chicago: Chicago University Press).

Gilligan, Carol (1982). *In a Different Voice* (Cambridge, MA: Harvard University Press).

Ginsberg, Morris (1956). *On the Diversity of Morals* (London: Mercury Books).

Glazer, N. (1997). *We are All Multiculturalists Now* (Cambridge, MA: Harvard University Press).

Goodin, R. E. (1995). *Utilitarianism as a Public Philosophy* (Cambridge: Cambridge University Press).

—— (1997). 'Utilitarianism as a Public Philosophy', in A. Vincent (ed.), *Political Theory: Tradition and Diversity* (Cambridge: Cambridge University Press).

—— (ed.) (1998). *The Theory of Institutional Design* (Cambridge: Cambridge University Press).

—— and Pettit, P. (eds.) (1993). *Companion to Contemporary Political Philosophy* (Oxford: Blackwell).

Gordon, Daniel (1999). 'Modernity and its Discontents: Some Critical Thoughts on Conceptual History', Symposium on *The History of Political and Social Concepts: A Critical Introduction* by Melvin Richter in *History of European Ideas*, 25: 1–2.

Gray, J. (1977). 'On the Contestability of Social and Political Concepts', *Political Theory*, 5: 2.

—— (1978). 'On Liberty, Liberalism and Essential Contestability', *British Journal of Political Science*, 8.

—— (1993). *Post-Liberalism: Studies in Political Thought* (London and New York: Routledge).

—— (1995). *Enlightenment's Wake: Politics and Culture at the Close of the Modern Age* (London: Routledge).

Green, D. P. and Schapiro, Ian (1994). *Pathologies of Rational Choice Theory: A Critique of Applications in Political Science* (New Haven: Yale University Press).

Greenleaf, W. H. (1964). *Order, Empirical Politics* (Oxford: Oxford University Press for the University of Hull).

—— (1966). *Oakeshott's Philosophical Politics* (London: Longmans).

—— (1968). 'Idealism, Modern Philosophy and Politics', in Preston King and B. Parekh (eds.), *Politics and Experience: Essays Presented to Michael Oakeshott on the Occasion of his Retirement* (Cambridge: Cambridge University Press).

Grillo, R. (1998). *Pluralism and the Politics of Difference: State, Culture, and Ethnicity in Comparative Perspective* (Oxford: Clarendon Press).

Grondin, Jean (1991). [Translated by J. Weinsheimer] *Introduction to Philosophical Hermeneutics* (New Haven: Yale University Press).

Guha, R. (1982). Subaltern Studies Vol 1 (Delhi: Oxford University Press).

Gunnell, J. (1986). *Between Philosophy and Politics: The Alienation of Political Theory* (Amhurst: University of Massachusetts Press).

—— (1987). *Political Theory: Tradition and Interpretation* (New York: University Press of America).

—— (1993a). 'American Political Science, Liberalism and the Invention of Political Theory' in J. Farr and R. Seidelman (eds.), *Discipline and History* (Ann Arbor: University of Michigan Press).

Gunnell, J. (1993*b*). *The Descent of Political Theory: The Genealogy of an American Vocation* (Chicago: Chicago University Press).

—— (1998). *The Orders of Discourse: Philosophy, Social Science and Politics* (New York and Oxford: Rowman and Littlefield).

Gutman, Amy (ed.) (1994). *Multiculturalism: Examining the Politics of Recognition* (Princeton, NJ: Princeton University Press).

Haakonssen, Knud (1995). *Natural Law and Moral Philosophy: From Grotius to the Scottish Enlightenment* (Cambridge: Cambridge University Press).

Habermas, J. (1971). *Knowledge and Human Interests* (Boston: Beacon).

—— (1975). [Translated by T. McCarthy] *Legitimation Crisis* (Boston: Beacon Press).

—— (1979). [Translated by T. McCarthy] *Communication and the Evolution of Society* (London: Heinemann).

—— (1984). [Translated by T. McCarthy] *The Theory of Communicative Action: Rationality and Rationalization*, Vol. 1 (Boston: Beacon Press).

—— (1987). 'Modernity—An Incomplete Project', in Paul Rabinow and William Sullivan (eds.), *Interpretive Social Science: A Second Look* (Berkeley: University of California Press).

—— (1990). [Translated by C. Lehnhardt and S. Weber] *Moral Consciousness and Communicative Action* (Cambridge, MA: MIT Press).

—— (1992). 'Citizenship and National Identity: Some Reflections on the Future of Europe', *Praxis International*, 12: 1.

—— (1993). 'Philosophy as Stand-in Interpreter', in K. Baynes, J. Bohman, and T. McCarthy (eds.), *Philosophy: End or Transformation* (Cambridge, MA: MIT Press).

—— (1995). 'Reconciliation Through the Public Use of Reason: Remarks on John Rawls's *Political Liberalism*', *Journal of Philosophy*, XCII: 3.

—— (1996*a*). 'The Unity of Reason in the Diversity of Voices', in J. Schmidt (ed.), *What is Enlightenment?* (Berkeley: University of California Press).

—— (1996*b*). [Translated by Shierry Weber Nicholsen and Jerry A Stark] *On the Logic of the Social Sciences* (Cambridge, MA: MIT Press).

—— (1998). [Translated by F. Lawrence] *The Philosophical Discourse of Modernity* (Cambridge: Polity).

Hacker, Andrew (1961). *Political Theory: Philosophy, Ideology, Science* (New York: Macmillan).

Haddock, Bruce and Sutch, Peter (eds.) (2003). *Multiculturalism, Identity and Rights* (London: Routledge).

Hadot, Pierre (1995). *Philosophy as a Way of Life* (Oxford: Blackwell).

Hahn, L. E. (ed.) (1997). *The Philosophy of Hans-Georg Gadamer*, The Library of Living Philosophers, Vol. XXI, (Chicago and LaSalle: Open Court).

Hampshire, S. (ed.) (1980). *Public and Private Morality* (Cambridge: Cambridge University Press).

Hampton, Jean (1998). *Political Philosophy* (Boulder, CO: Westview Press).

Hansen, P. (1993). *Hannah Arendt: Politics, History and Citizenship* (Cambridge: Polity).

Hart, H. L. A. (1961). *The Concept of Law* (Oxford: Clarendon Press).

Harvey, David (1989). *The Condition of Postmodernity* (Oxford: Blackwell).

Hayek, F. A. (1944). *The Road to Surfdom* (London: Routledge and Sons).

—— (1976). *Law Legislation and Liberty* (London: Routledge).

—— (1978). *New Studies in Philosophy, Politics, Economics and the History of Ideas* (London: Routledge and Kegan Paul).

Haynes, D. and Prakash, G. (eds.) (1992). *Contesting Power* (Berkeley: University of California Press).

Heelas, P., Lash, Scott, and Morris, P. (eds.) (1996). *Detraditionalization* (Oxford: Blackwell).

Heidegger, M. (1982). [Translated by F. Capuzzi] *Nietzsche*, Vol. 4 (New York: Harper and Row).

—— (1993). 'Letter on Humanism', in D. F. Krell (ed.), *Basic Writings* (London: Routledge).

Held, D. (ed.) (1991). *Political Theory Today* (Stanford: Stanford University Press).

Held, Virginia (1993). *Feminist Morality: Transforming Culture, Society and Politics* (Chicago: Chicago University Press).

Hesse, Mary (1981). *Revolutions and Reconstructions in the Philosophy of Science* (Brighton: Harvester Wheatsheaf).

Hobhouse, L. T. (1918). *The Metaphysical Theory of the State* (London: George Allen and Unwin).

Hollingdale, R. J. (1999). *Nietzsche: The Man and His Philosophy* (Cambridge: Cambridge University Press).

Hollis, Martin (1982). 'The Social Destruction of Reality', in M. Hollis and S. Lukes (ed.), *Rationality and Relativism* (Oxford: Blackwell).

—— and Lukes, Steven (eds.) (1982). *Rationality and Relativism* (Oxford: Blackwell).

Holmes, Stephen (1993). *The Anatomy of Anti-Liberalism* (Cambridge, MA: Harvard University Press).

Homans, G. (1967). *The Nature of Social Science* (New York: Harcourt Brace and World Inc).

Honig, Bonnie (1993). *Political Theory and the Displacement of Politics* (Ithaca: Cornell University Press).

Horkheimer, Max (1972). *Critical Theory* (New York: Seabury Press).

—— (1996). 'Reason Against Itself: Some Remarks on Enlightenment', in J. Schmidt (ed.), *What is Enlightenment?* (Berkeley: University of California Press).

Hume, David (1975). *Enquiry Concerning Human Understanding and Concerning the Principles of Morals* L. A. Selby-Bigge (ed.); revised by R. H. Nidditch (Oxford: Clarendon Press).

—— (1981). *A Treatise of Human Nature* L. A. Selby-Bigge and R. H. Nidditch (eds.) (Oxford: Clarendon Press).

Ignatieff, Michael (1998). *Isaiah Berlin: A Life* (London and New York: Metropolitan Books).

Ivison, D. (1997). 'Postcolonialism and Political Theory' in A. Vincent (ed.), *Political Theory: Tradition and Diversity* (Cambridge: Cambridge University Press).

—— (2002). *Postcolonial Liberalism* (Cambridge: Cambridge Univesity Press).

Jacobson, Norman (1978). *Pride and Solace: The Functions and Limits of Political Theory* (London: Methuen).

Jaggar, A. (1983). *Feminist Politics and Human Nature* (Brighton: Harvester Wheatsheaf).

James, William (1909). *The Pluralistic Universe* (Cambridge Mass: Harvard University Press).

Jensen, Richard (1969). 'History and the Political Scientist', in S. M. Lipset (ed.), *Politics and the Social Sciences.*

Joppke, Christian and Lukes, Steven (eds.) (1999). *Multicultural Questions* (Oxford: Oxford University Press).

Jordan, Grant (1990). 'Policy Community Realism versus "New" Institutionalist Ambiguity', *Political Studies*, XXXVII.

Kant, I. (1965). [Translated by John Ladd] *The Metaphysical Elements of Justice* (New York: Bobbs-Merrill Company Inc).

Kateb, G. (1968). *Political Theory: Its Nature and Uses* (New York: St. Martin's Press).

Keane, J. (1992). 'The Modern Democratic Revolution: Reflections on Lyotard's *The Postmodern Condition*', in A. Benjamin (ed.), *Judging Lyotard* (London and New York: Routledge).

Kekes, J. (1993). *The Morality of Pluralism* (Princeton, NJ: Princeton University Press).

King, Preston (ed.) (1978). *The Study of Politics* (New York and London: Frank Cass).

Kohn, Hans (1945). *The Idea of Nationalism: A Study in its Origins and Background* (New York: Macmillan).

Konwitz, M. R. and Murphy, A. E. (eds.) (1948). *Essays in Political Theory Presented to George H. Sabine* (Ithaca: Cornell University Press).

Kosellek, R. (1985). [Translated by Keith Tribe] *Futures Past: On the Semantics of Historical Time* (Cambridge, MA: MIT).

—— (1996). 'A Response to Comments on the *Geschichtliche Grundbegriff*', in H. Lehmann and M. Richter (eds.), *The Meaning of Historical Terms and Concepts: New Studies on the Begriffsgeschichte* (Washington, DC: German Historical Institute).

Krasner, S. (1978). *Defending the National Interest* (Princeton, NJ: Princeton University Press).

Kuhn, Thomas (1962). *The Structure of Scientific Revolutions* (Chicago: Phoenix Books, Chicago University Press).

Kukathas, C. (1995). 'Are there any Cultural Rights?', in Will Kymlicka (ed.), *The Rights of Minority Cultures* (Oxford: Clarendon Press).

Kymlicka, Will (1990). *Contemporary Political Philosophy: An Introduction* (Oxford: Clarendon Press).

—— (1991). *Liberalism, Community and Culture* (Oxford: Clarendon Press).

—— (ed.) (1995). *The Rights of Minority Cultures* (Oxford: Clarendon Press).

Larmore, Charles (1990). 'Political Liberalism', *Political Theory*, 18: 3.

Laski, H. J. (1978). 'On the Study of Politics', in P. King (ed.), *Study of Politics* (New York and London: Frank Cass).

Laslett, Peter (ed.) (1956). *Philosophy, Politics and Society*, 1st Series (Oxford: Basil Blackwell).

—— and Runciman, W. G. (eds.) (1962). *Philosophy, Politics and Society*, 2nd Series (Oxford: Basil Blackwell).

Lawson, Hilary (1985). *Reflexivity* (London: Unwin Hyman).

Leslie, M. (1970). 'In Defence of Anachronism', *Political Studies*, XVIII: 4.

Lesser, H., Plant, R., and Taylor-Gooby, P. (1980). *Political Philosophy and Social Welfare* (London: Routledge and Kegan Paul).

Lipset, S. M. (1969a). *Political Man* (London: Heinemann).

—— (ed.) (1969b). *Politics and the Social Sciences* (New York: Oxford University Press).

Lister, Ruth (1997). *Citizenship: Feminist Perspectives* (London: Macmillan).

Lukes, S. (1975). *Power: A Radical View* (Atlantic Highlands, NJ: Humanities Press).

—— (1982). 'Relativism in its Place', in M. Hollis and S. Lukes (eds.), *Rationality and Relativism* (Oxford: Blackwell).

Lyotard, Jean-François (1985). [Translated by W. Godzich] *Just Gaming* (Manchester: Manchester University Press).

—— (1991a). [Translated by G. Bennington and Brian Massumi] *The Postmodern Condition: A Report on Knowledge* (Manchester: Manchester University Press).

—— (1991b). [Translated by G. Bennington and R. Bowlby] *The Inhuman: Reflections on Time* (Cambridge: Polity Press).

—— (1994). [Translated by E. Rottenberg] *Lessons on the Analytic of the Sublime* (Stanford, CA: Stanford University Press).

—— (1997). [Translated by G. van Den Abbeele] *Postmodern Fables* (Minneapolis: University of Minnesota Press).

—— (1999). [Translated by G. van Den Abbeele] *The Differend: Phrases in Dispute* (Minneapolis: University of Minnesota Press).

MacCallum, G. C. (1987). *Political Philosophy* (N.J. Prentice Hall: Englewood Cliffs).

MacCormick, N. (1982). *Legal Rights and Social Democracy: Essays in Legal and Political Philosophy* (Oxford: Clarendon Press).

—— (1990). 'Of Self-Determination and other Things', *Bulletin of the Australian Society of Legal Philosophy*, 15.

—— (1991). 'Is Nationalism Philosophically Credible?', in W. Twining (ed.), *Issues in Self Determination* (Aberdeen: Aberdeen University Press).

MacIntyre, A. (1981). *After Virtue* (London: Duckworth).

—— (1984). *Is Patriotism a Virtue?* (Kansas: University of Kansas Press).

—— (1990). *Three Rival Versions of Moral Enquiry* (London: Duckworth).

—— (1995). 'The Spectre of Communitarianism', *Radical Philosophy*, 70 (March/April).

Macpherson, C. B. (1962). *The Political Theory of Possessive Individualism* (Oxford: Oxford University Press).

Magee, B. (1978). *Men of Ideas* (New York: Vintage Books).

Mannheim, Karl (1966). *Ideology and Utopia: An Introduction to the Sociology of Knowledge* (London: Routledge and Kegan Paul).

March, J. and Olson, J. P. (1984). 'The New Institutionalism', *American Political Science Review*, 78.

Marcus, George and Fischer, M. M. J. (1986). *Anthropology as Cultural Critique* (Chicago: Chicago University Press).

Marcuse, Herbert (1968). *One Dimensional Man* (London: Sphere Books).

Margalit, G. and Raz, J. (1995). 'National Self-Determination', in W. Kymlicka (ed.), *The Rights of Minority Cultures* (Oxford: Clarendon Press).

Marx, K. and Engels, F. (1968). *Selected Works* (London: Lawrence and Wishart).

Maynor, J. (2003). *Republicanism in the Modern World* (Cambridge: Polity).

McCarney, J. (1980). *The Real World of Ideology* (Brighton: Harvester Wheatsheaf).

McCarthy, T. (1978). *The Critical Theory of Jürgen Habermas* (Cambridge, MA: MIT Press).

McMurrin, S. M. (ed.) (1988). *The Tanner Lectures on Human Values* vii (Salt Lake City: University of Utah Press).

Miller, David (1979). *Social Justice* (Oxford: Clarendon).

—— (1988). 'The Ethical Significance of Nationalism', *Ethics*, 98.

—— (1989). *Market State and Community: Theoretical Foundations of Market Socialism* (Oxford: Clarendon Press).

—— (1994). 'The Nation-State: A Modest Defence', in Chris Brown (ed.), *Political Restructuring in Europe: Ethical Perspectives* (London: Routledge).

—— (1995). *On Nationality* (Oxford, Clarendon).

—— (1999). *Principles of Social Justice* (Cambridge, MA: Harvard University Press).

—— and Seidentop, Larry (eds.) (1983). *The Nature of Political Theory* (Oxford: Clarendon Press).

—— and Walzer, Michael (eds.) (1995). *Pluralism, Justice and Equality* (Oxford: Oxford University Press).

—— et al. (1987). *The Blackwell Encyclopaedia of Political Thought* (Oxford: Blackwell).

Minogue, K. (1985). *Alien Powers: The Pure Theory of Ideology* (London: Weidenfeld and Nicholson).

Mitchell, William C. (1969). 'The Shape of Political Theory to Come: From Political Sociology to Political Economy', in S. M. Lipset (ed.), *Politics and the Social Sciences* (New York: Oxford University Press).

Monroe, Kristen Renwick (ed.) (1997). *Contemporary Empirical Political Theory* (Berkeley: University of California Press).

Mouffe, C. (1993). *The Return of the Political* (London: Verso).

Mueller, D. C. (1989). *Public Choice* (Cambridge: Cambridge University Press).

Mulhall, Stephen and Swift, Adam (1996). *Liberals and Communitarians*, 2nd edn (Oxford: Blackwell).

Muller, J. Z. (1999). 'Begriffsgeschichte: Origins and Prospects', Symposium on *The History of Political and Social Concepts: A Critical Introduction* by Melvin Richter in *History of European Ideas*, 25: 1–2.

Nagel, E. (1961). *The Structure of Science* (London: Routledge and Kegan Paul).

Nietzsche, F. (1956). [Translated by F. Golffing] *The Birth of Tragedy and the Genealogy of Morals* (New York: Doubleday Anchor).

—— (1967). [Translated by Walter Kaufmann and R. J. Hollingdale] in Walter Kaufmann (ed.), *The Will to Power* (New York: Vintage Books).

—— (1968). [Translated by R. J. Hollingdale] *Twilight of the Idols and The Anti-Christ*, (Middlesex: Penguin Classics).

—— (1974). [Translated by R. J. Hollingdale] *Beyond Good and Evil* (Middlesex: Penguin Books).

—— (1982). [Translated by R. J. Hollingdale] *Daybreak: Thoughts on the Prejudices of Morality* (Cambridge: Cambridge University Press).

—— (1986). [Translated by R. J. Hollingdale] *Human, All Too Human: A Book for Free Spirits* (Cambridge: Cambridge University Press).

Nordlinger, E. (1981). *On the Autonomy of the Democratic State* (Cambridge, MA: Harvard University Press).

Norris, C. (1987). *Derrida* (London: Fontana Collins).

Nozick, Robert (1974). *Anarchy State and Utopia* (Oxford: Blackwell).

Nussbaum, M. (1986). *The Fragility of Goodness: Luck and Ethics in Greek Tragedy and Philosophy* (Cambridge: Cambridge University Press).

—— (1993). 'Non-Relative Virtues: An Aristotelian Approach', in M. Nussbaum and A. Sen (eds.), *The Quality of Life* (Oxford: Clarendon Press).

—— and Sen, A. (1993). The Quality of Life (Oxford: Clarendon Press).

—— (1990). 'Aristotelian Social Democracy', in R. B. Douglass, G. Mara, and H. Richardson (eds.), *Liberalism and the Good* (New York and London: Routledge).

—— (1992). 'Human Functioning and Social Justice: In Defence of Aristotelian Essentialism', *Political Theory*, 2.

—— and Glover, J. (eds.) (1995). *Women Culture and Development* (Oxford: Clarendon).

—— and Sen, A. (eds.) (1993). *The Quality of Life* (Oxford: Clarendon Press).

O'Neill, Onora (1996). *Towards Justice and Virtue: A Constructive Account of Practical Reasoning* (Cambridge: Cambridge University Press).

Oakeshott, Michael (1933). *Experience and its Modes* (Cambridge: Cambridge University Press).

—— (1962). *Rationalism in Politics* (London: Methuen).

—— (1965). 'Rationalism in Politics: A Reply to Professor Raphael', *Political Studies*, XIII: 1.

—— (1975). *On Human Conduct* (Oxford: Clarendon Press).

—— (1983). *On History* (Oxford: Blackwell).

—— (1991). *Rationalism in Politics and other Essays* (Indianapolis: Liberty Press).

—— (1993). *Morality and Politics in Modern Europe: the Harvard Lectures* (New Haven and London: Yale University Press).

Okin, S. M. (1979). *Women in Western Political Thought* (Princeton, NJ: Princeton University Press).

—— (1981). 'Women and the Making of the Sentimental Family', *Philosophy and Public Affairs*, 11: 1.

—— (1987). 'Justice and Gender', *Philosophy and Public Affairs*, 16: 1.

—— (1989). *Justice, Gender and the Family* (New York: Basic Books).

Olsen, J. P. (1991). 'Political Science and Organization Theory: Parallel Agendas but Mutual Disregard', in R. M. Czada and A. Windhoff-Heritier (eds.), *Political Choice: Institutions, Rules, and the Limits of Rationality* (Frankfurt: Campus Verlag).

Olson, M. (1965). *The Logic of Collective Action* (Cambridge, MA: Harvard University Press).

Oppenheim, F. (1981). *Political Concepts: A Reconstruction* (Oxford: Blackwell).

Pagden, A. (ed.) (1987). *Languages of Political Theory in Early Modern Europe* (Cambridge: Cambridge University Press).

Parekh, B. (2001). *Rethinking Multiculturalism: Cultural Diversity and Political Theory* (London: Palgrave).

Pateman, C. (1988). *The Sexual Contract* (Cambridge: Polity).

Peirce, C. S. (1940). *Philosophical Writings*, J. Buchler (ed.) (New York: Dover Publications).

Perelman, C. (1963). *The Idea of Justice and the Problem of Argument* (London: Routledge and Kegan Paul).

Pettit, Philip (1993*a*). 'Liberalism and Republicanism', *Australian Journal of Political Science*, 28.

—— (1993*b*). *The Common Mind: An Essay on Psychology, Society and Politics* (Oxford: Oxford Univesity Press).

—— (1997). *Republicanism: A Theory of Freedom and Government* (Oxford: Clarendon Press).

Phillips, Anne (1996). 'Dealing with Difference: A Politics of Ideas, or a Politics of Presence?', in S. Benhabib (ed.), *Democracy and Difference* (Princeton, NJ: Princeton University Press).

Pitkin, H. (1972). *Wittgenstein and Jusitce: On the Significance of Ludwig Wittgenstein for Social and Political Thought* (Berkeley: University of California Press).

Plamenatz, J. (1960). 'The Use of Political Theory', *Political Studies*, VIII.

—— (1963). *Man and Society* in two volumes (New York: McGraw Hill).

—— (1968). *Consent Freedom and Obligation* (Oxford: Oxford University Press).

—— (1976). 'Two Types of Nationalism', in E. Kamenka (ed.), *Nationalism: The Evolution of an Idea* (London: Edward Arnold).

Plant, Raymond (1976). *Community and Ideology: An Essay in Applied Social Philosophy* (London: Routledge).

—— (1991). *Modern Political Thought* (Oxford: Blackwell).

Plato (1948). *The Republic* (London: J. M. Dent).

Pocock, J. G. A. (1972). *Politics Language and Time* (London: Methuen).

—— (1980). 'Political Ideas as Historical Events: Political Philosophers as Historical Actors', in Melvin Richter (ed.), *Political Theory and Political Education* (Princeton, NJ: Princeton University Press).

Pocock, J. G. A. (1987). 'The Concept of a Language and the Métier d'Historien: Some Considerations on Practice', in A. Pagden (ed.), *Languages of Political Theory* (Cambridge: Cambridge University Press).

Poincaré, H. (1902). *Science and Hypothesis* (New York: Dover).

Pollock, F. (1890). *An Introduction to the History of the Science of Politics* (London: Macmillan).

Popper, Karl (1976). *Unended Quest: An Intellectual Autobiography* (London: Fontana).

Prakash, Gyan (1990). *Bounded Histories: Geneaologies of Labor Servitude in Colonial India* (Cambridge: Cambridge University Press).

Quinton, A. (ed.) (1967). *Political Philosophy* (Oxford: Oxford University Press).

—— (1978). *The Politics of Imperfection* (London: Faber and Faber).

Raphael, D. D. (1976). *Problems of Political Philosophy* (London: Macmillan).

Rawls, John (1971). *A Theory of Justice* (Oxford: Oxford University Press).

—— (1992). 'Justice as Fairness: Political not Metaphysical', in Tracy B. Strong (ed.), *The Self and the Political Order* (Oxford: Blackwell).

—— (1993). *Political Liberalism* (New York: Columbia University Press).

Raz, Joseph (1986). *The Morality of Freedom* (Oxford: Clarendon).

Rengger, N. (1992). 'No Time like the Present? Postmodernism and Political Theory', *Political Studies*, XL.

—— (1995). *Political Theory, Modernity and Postmodernity* (Oxford: Blackwell).

Ricci, D. M. (1984). *The Tragedy of Political Science* (New Haven and London: Yale University Press).

Richter, M. (1995). *The History of Political and Social Concepts* (Oxford: Oxford University Press).

—— (1999). 'Reply to Comments' Symposium on *The History of Political and Social Concepts: A Critical Introduction* by Melvin Richter in *History of European Ideas*, 25(1–2): 31–38.

Ricoeur, Paul (1970). [Translated by D. Savage] *Freud and Philosophy: An Essay on Interpretation* (New Haven: Yale University Press).

Riker, William T. (1990). 'Political Science and Rational Choice', in J. E. Alt and K. A. Shepsle (eds.), *Perspectives on Positive Political Economy* (Cambridge: Cambridge University Press).

Roemer, J. (1986). 'Rational Choice Marxism: Some Issues of Methods and Substance', in Roemer (ed.) *Analytical Marxism* (Cambridge: Cambridge University Press).

Rorty, R. (1980). *Philosophy as the Mirror of Nature* (Oxford: Blackwell).

—— (1982). *Consequences of Pragmatism* (Hemel Hempstead: Harvester Wheatsheaf).

—— (1983). 'Postmodernist Bourgeois Liberalism' *Journal of Philosophy*, XXX: 10.

—— (1989). *Contingency, Irony and Solidarity* (Cambridge: Cambridge University Press).

—— et al. (eds.) (1991). *Philosophy in History* (Cambridge: Cambridge University Press).

Rosenau, P. M. (1992). *Postmodernism and the Social Sciences: Insights, Inroad and Intrusions* (Princeton, NJ: Princeton University Press).

Rosenblum, N. L. (ed.) (1989). *Liberalism and the Moral Life* (Cambridge, MA: Harvard University Press).

Rubinstein, N. (1987). 'The History of the Word *Politicus* in Early Modern Europe', in A. Pagden (ed.), *The Languages of Political Theory* (Cambridge: Cambridge University Press).

Ruddick, S. (1980). 'Maternal Thinking', *Feminist Studies*, 6: 2.

Sadurski, W. (1985). *Giving Desert its Due* (Dordrecht: D. Reidel).

Said, Edward (1978). *Orientalism* (London: Routledge and Kegan Paul).

Salkever, Stephen G. (1990). *Finding the Mean: Theory and Practice in Aristotelian Political Philosophy* (Princeton, NJ: Princeton University Press).

Sandel, M. (1982). *Liberalism and the Limits of Justice* (Cambridge: Cambridge University Press).

—— (1996). *Democracy's Discontents: America in Search of Public Philosophy* (Cambridge, MA: Belknap Press of Harvard University Press).

Schapiro, Ian (2002). 'Problem, Method, and Theories in the Study of Politics, or What's Wrong with Political Science and What to do About it', *Political Theory*, 30: 4.

Schmidt, James (ed.) (1996). *What is Enlightenment? Eighteenth Century Answers and Twentieth Century Questions* (Berkeley and London: University of California Press).

—— (1999). 'How Historical is *Begriffsgeschichte?*', Symposium on Melvin Richter's *The History of Political and Social Concepts: A Critical Introduction* in *History of European Ideas*, 25: 1–2.

—— (2000). 'What Enlightenment Project?', *Political Theory*, 28: 6.

Schrag, Calvin O. (1997). *The Self after Postmodernity* (New Haven and London: Yale University Press).

Scruton, Roger (1990). 'In Defence of the Nation', in R. Scruton (ed.), *The Philosopher on Dover Beach* (London: Carcanet Press).

Self, Peter (1993). *Government by the Market: The Politics of Public Choice* (London: Macmillan).

—— (2000). *Rolling Back the Market: Economic Dogma and Political Choice* (London: Macmillan).

Shachar, Ayelet (2000). 'On Citizenship and Multicultural Vulnerability', *Political Theory*, 28: 1.

—— (2002). *Multicultural Jurisdictions* (Cambridge: Cambridge University Press).

Sher, G. (1987). *Desert* (Princeton, NJ: Princeton University Press).

Shils, Edward (1968). 'The Concept and Function of Ideology', *International Encyclopaedia of the Social Sciences*, Vol. VII.

Shklar, Judith (1984). *Ordinary Vices* (Cambridge, MA and London: Belknap Press of the Harvard University Press).

Sidgwick, Henry (1907). *Methods of Ethics* (London: Macmillan).

Silverman, Hugh, J. (ed.) (1991). *Gadamer and Hermeneutics* (London: Routledge).

Simhony, A. and Weinstein, D. (eds.) (2001). *The New Liberalism* (Cambridge: Cambridge University Press).

Simon, H. (1952). 'The Development of the theory of Democratic Administration: Replies and Comments', *American Political Science Review*, 46.

Simons, Jon (1995). 'The Exile of Political Theory: The Last Homeland of Legitimation', *Political Studies*, XLIII.

Skinner, Q. (1965). 'History and Ideology in the English Revolution', *Historical Journal*, VIII.

—— (1966). 'The Ideological Context of Hobbes' Political Thought', *Historical Journal*, IX.

—— (1969). 'Meaning and Understanding in the History of Ideas', *History and Theory*, 8.

—— (1978). *The Foundations of Modern Political Thought*, Vols. 1 and 2 (Cambridge: Cambridge University Press).

—— (1991). 'The Idea of Negative Liberty: Philosophical and Historical Perspectives', in Richard Rorty et al. (eds.), *Philosophy in History* (Cambridge: Cambridge University Press).

—— (1998). *Liberty before Liberalism* (Cambridge, MA: Cambridge University Press).

Skocpol, T. (1979). *State and Revolutions* (Cambridge: Cambridge University Press).

Smith, Adam (1979). *An Enquiry into the Nature and Causes of the Wealth of Nations* (Oxford: Clarendon Press).

Soffer, Reba (1994). *Discipline and Power: The University and the Making of an English Elite 1870–1930* (Stanford: Stanford University Press).

Spragens, T. (1973). *The Dilemma of Contemporary Political Theory: Towards a Post-Behavioural Science of Politics* (New York: Dunellen Publishing Co).

Springborg, P. (1989). 'Hannah Arendt and the Classical Republican Tradition', in G. T. Kaplan and C. S. Kessler (eds.), *Hannah Arendt: Thinking, Judging, Freedom* (London and Syndey: Allen and Unwin).

Squires, Judith (1999). *Gender in Political Theory* (Cambridge: Polity).

Storing, H. J. (ed.) (1962). *Essays on the Scientific Study of Politics* (New York: Holt, Rinehart and Winston).

Strauss, Leo (1959). *What is Political Philosophy* (Illinois: The Free Press).

—— (1977). *City of Man* (Chicago: Chicago University Press).

Strawson, P. F. (1974). *Individuals: An Essay in Descriptive Metaphysics* (London: Methuen).

Strong, T. B. (ed.) (1992). *The Self and the Political Order* (Oxford: Blackwell).

Strong, Tracy (1990). *The Idea of Political Theory: Reflections on the Self in Political Time and Space* (Notre Dame: Notre Dame University Press).

Tam, H. (1998). *Communitarianism: A New Agenda for Politics and Citizenship* (London: Macmillan).

Taminiaux, J. (2000). 'Athens and Rome', in D. Villa (ed.), *Cambridge Companion to Hannah Arendt* (Cambridge: Cambridge University Press).

Tamir, Y. (1993). *Liberal Nationalism* (Princeton, NJ: Princeton University Press).

—— (1999). 'Theoretical Difficulties in the Study of Nationalism', in R. Beiner (ed.), *Theorizing Nationalism* (New York: State University of New York Press).

Taylor, C. (1989). *Sources of the Self: The Making of Modern Identity* (Cambridge: Cambridge University Press).

—— (1992). *The Ethics of Authenticity* (Cambridge, MA: Harvard University Press).

Taylor, M. W. (1992). *Men Versus the State: Herbert Spencer and Late Victorian Individualism* (Oxford: Clarendon Press).

—— (1994). 'Reply and Re-articulation', in J. Tully (ed.), *Philosophy in an Age of Pluralism* (Cambridge: Cambridge University Press).

Thiele, Leslie Paul (1995). *Timely Meditations: Martin Heidegger and Postmodern Politics* (Princeton, NJ: Princeton University Press).

Tuck, Richard (1993). *Philosophy and Goverment 1572–1651* (Cambridge: Cambridge University Press).

—— (1993). 'The Contribution of History', in R. E. Goodin and P. Pettit (eds.), *A Companion to Contemporary Political Philosophy* (Oxford: Blackwell).

Tully, James (ed.) (1988). *Meaning and Context: Quentin Skinner and his Critics* (Cambridge: Polity Press).

—— (ed.) (1994). *Philosophy in an Age of Pluralism* (Cambridge: Cambridge University Press).

—— (1995). *Strange Multiplicity: Constitutionalism in a Age of Diversity* (Cambridge: Cambridge University Press).

Twining, W. (ed.) (1991). *Issues in Self Determination* (Aberdeen: Aberdeen University Press).

Villa, Dana (ed.) (2000). *The Cambridge Companion to Hannah Arendt* (Cambridge: Cambridge University Press).

Vincent, Andrew (1984). 'The Poor Law Reports of 1909 and the Social Theory of the Charity Organization Society', *Victorian Studies*, 27.

—— (1987) *Theories of the State* (Oxford: Blackwell).

—— (1989). 'Can Groups be Persons?', *Review of Metaphysics*, 42.

—— (1990). 'The New Liberalism in Britain 1880–1914', *The Australian Journal of Politics and History*, 36: 3.

—— (1995). *Modern Political Ideologies*, 2nd edn (Oxford: Blackwell).

—— (1997*a*). 'Liberal Nationalism: An Irresponsible Compound?' *Political Studies*, 45: 2.

—— (1997*b*). 'Liberal Nationalism and Communitarianism: An Ambiguous Association', *The Australian Journal of Politics and History*, 3: 1.

—— (ed.) (1997*c*). *Political Theory: Tradition and Diversity* (Cambridge: Cambridge University Press).

—— (1998). 'Marx and Ethics', in Ruth Chadwick (ed.), *Encyclopaedia of Applied Ethics*, (New York and London: Academic Press of America).

—— (2001*a*). 'Citizenship and the New Liberalism', in A. Simhony and D. Weinstein (eds.), *The New Liberalism* (Cambridge: Cambridge University Press).

—— (2001*b*). 'Power and Vacuity: Nationalist Ideology in the Twentieth Century', in Michael Freeden (ed.), *Reassessing Political Ideologies: The Durability of Dissent* (London: Routledge).

—— (2002). *Nationalism and Particularity* (Cambridge: Cambridge University Press).

—— (2003). 'What is so Different About Difference?', in B. Haddock and P. Sutch (eds.), *Multiculturalism, Identity and Rights* (London: Routledge).

—— and Plant, Raymond (1984). *Philosophy Politics and Citizenship: The Life and Times of the British Idealists* (Oxford: Blackwell).

Viroli, M. (1995). *For Love of Country* (Oxford: Clarendon Press).

Walsh, W. H. (1966). *Metaphysics* (London: Hutchinson University Library).

Walzer, Michael (1983). *Spheres of Justice: A Defence of Pluralism and Equality* (Oxford: Martin Robertson).

—— (1987). *Interpretation and Social Criticism* (MA: Harvard University Press).

—— (1988). 'Interpretation and Social Criticism', in S. M. McMurrin (ed.), *The Tanner Lectures on Human Values*, vii. (Salt Lake City: University of Utah Press).

—— (1990). 'The Communitarian Critique of Liberalism', *Political Theory*, 18: 1.

—— (1994*a*). 'Comment', in A. Gutman (ed.), *Multiculturalism* (Princeton NJ: Princeton University Press).

—— (1994*b*). *Thick and Thin: Moral Argument at Home and Abroad* (Notre Dame and London: Notre Dame University Press).

Warnock, G. J. (1969). *English Philosophy Since 1900* (Oxford: Oxford University Press).

Weldon, T. D. (1953). *The Vocabulary of Politics* (Harmondsworth: Penguin).

—— (1956). 'Political Principles', in P. Laslett (ed.), *Politics Philosophy and Society* (Oxford: Blackwell).

Wertheimer, A. (1976). 'Is Ordinary Language Analysis Conservative?', *Political Theory*, 4: 4.

White, S. K. (ed.) (1989). *Life-World and Politics: Betweeen Modernity and Postmodernity: Essays in Honor of Fred R. Dallmayr* (Indiana: University of Notre Dame Press).

—— (1991). *Political Theory and Postmodernism* (Cambridge: Cambridge University Press).

—— (ed.) (1995). *The Cambridge Companion to Habermas* (Cambridge: Cambridge University Press).

Winch, Peter (1958). *The Idea of Social Science* (London: Routledge and Kegan Paul).

Wittgenstein, L. (1963). [Translated by G. E. M. Anscombe] *The Philosophical Investigations*, first English edn in 1953 (Oxford: Basil Blackwell).

—— (1972). [Translated by D. F. Pears and B. F. McGuinness] *Tractatus-Logico Philosophicus*, first English edn in 1922 (London: Routledge and Kegan Paul).

Wolin, Sheldon (1960). *Politics and Vision: Continuity and Innovation in Western Political Thought* (Toronto: Little, Brown and Co).

Wood, David (1990). *Philosophy at the Limit* (London: Unwin Hyman).

Wootton David (1993). Edition and introduction *John Locke: Political Writings* (Middlesex: Penguin).

Yack, Bernard (1993). *The Problems of a Political Animal: Community, Justice, and Conflict in Aristotelian Political Thought* (Berkeley: University of California Press).

Young, Iris Marion (1990). *Justice and the Politics of Difference* (Princeton, NJ: Princeton University Press).

—— (2002). *Inclusion and Democracy* (Oxford: Clarendon).

Index

absolute presuppositions 6–7, 166
Ackerman, Bruce 132, 134
Adorno, T. 78, 94, 11, 225, 274, 276–8, 283
Almond, G. 54
American Political Science Association 29
analytic philosophy 9, 50, 70–1, 84, 85, 87, 95, 96, 108–9
anarcho-syndicalism 94
androgyny 230
Apel, Karl-Otto 285–6
Arendt, H. 24, 41, 50, 54, 64, 70, 78, 93, 192–6, 197
Aristotelianism 9, 13, 22, 111–12, 177–87, 207
Aristotle 4, 8, 26, 53, 110, 111, 136, 165, 170, 177–87, 190, 202, 240, 245, 257, 278
Arrow, K. 61
Ashcraft, R. 68, 77
Asian values 201, 230
Augustine, St. 4, 26
Austin, J. L. 43, 44, 88, 89, 90, 96, 97, 106, 273, 286, 293
autonomy 217–18
Ayer, A. 86, 106

Bakunin, M. 271
Barber, B. 189–90, 202
Barker, Ernest 39, 53, 59
Barry, Brian 59, 92–3, 126–7, 111, 130, 131, 133, 134, 137, 153, 228, 288
Barthes, R. 266
behaviouralism 54–5, 58, 78, 88
behaviourism 54–5
Beitz, C. 137
Benda, J. 173
Benn, S. 104–5
Bentham, J. 27
Bergson, H. 235–6
Berlin, I. 95, 215
Betti, E. 295
Bhabha, H. 231
Birch, A. H. 76
Blackstone, W. 25
Blakey, Robert 40
Bloom, Allan 42, 43, 233
Bluntschli, J. C. 31, 75

Bodin, J. 9, 151
Bolingbroke, Lord 188
Bosanquet, B. 29, 91, 93, 145–6
Boucher, D. 77
Bourdieu, P. 26
Bradley, F. H. 145, 236, 292
Braithwaite, J. 192
Brecht, A. 56, 78
Brennan, G. 80
British idealism 30, 84, 145–6
Brugger, B. 189
Bryce, James 30
Buchanan, J. 61, 112, 124, 133, 137
Burgess, J. 30
Burke, E. 9, 26, 31, 156
Butler, J. 267

Caird, Edward 30
Campbell, Fraser 145
Canovan, M. 192, 194, 195
Carnap, R. 56, 86, 106
Cartesianism 8, 9, 273, 295
catallactic order 152
Cavell, S. 228
Chicago University 54
Chinese Revolution 94
Chodorow, N. 130
Christianity 22
Cicero 190
citizenship 94
civil rights movement 59, 95
Cixous, H. 225
classical normative political theory 19–28, 53, 59, 64, 76, 106, 109
Cole, G. D. H. 93, 210
Coleridge, S. T. 156
Collingwood, R. G. 6–7, 39, 41, 43, 93, 145, 166, 292, 326
communitarianism 127, 154–62, 166, 167, 168, 170, 171, 177, 179, 180, 184, 201, 217, 229, 290
    connected critic and 161
    forms of liberalism and 160
    ideology of 158
    morality thick and thin 161

communitarianism (*cont.*)
  problems with 201
  recognition and identity 160–1
  unencumbered self and 159
  weak and strong forms 158–9
Comte, A. 27
Condren, C. 95, 107
Confucianism 230
Connolly, W. E. 106, 226, 230, 250–3, 257, 259, 260, 266, 267, 271, 310
contractarianism 23, 96, 113, 116, 119–20, 124–7, 131, 320
conventionalism 13–14, 44, 143–5, 207–9, 227–8, 232, 320
  communitarianism and 154–62, 290
  difference theory and 210, 219–26, 227–8, 232, 320
  multiculturalism 215–9
  nationalism and 159, 171–7, 179, 180, 197, 201
  neo-Aristotelianism and 159, 171, 177–87, 197, 201
  Oakeshott and 145–54,
  perspectivism and 13, 233–4, 237, 238
  political liberalism 162–8
  post-conventionalism 14
  republicanism and 159, 171, 180, 187–200
  thin universalism and 144, 201
  Wittgenstein and 143
conventions 13, 143–5
Cook Wilson, J. 145
counter culture 95
Counter Enlightenment 215
critical theory 14, 272–8
  and Habermas 278ff (*see* Habermas)
Croce, B. 25, 39, 93, 292
Cropsey, J. 75
Crowder, G. 228

Dahl, R. 56, 210
Davidson, D. 79
Dawson, C. 157
death of political theory 24, 28, 56, 59, 91–5
decolonization 94
Deleuze, G. 267
deliberative democracy 136, 170, 288–9
depth grammar 97
Derrida, J. 85, 88, 225, 242–7, 248, 259, 260, 262–3, 264, 267, 271, 273, 293
  cosmopolitanism 263
  deconstruction 244, 246
  différance 244–5, 245

forgiveness 263
foundationalism and 245
Heidegger and 242–3, 244, 245, 246
humanism and inhuman 243
intertextuality 244
logocentrism and 245
metaphysics 242–4, 245, 246
Nietzsche and 243, 244, 246–7
ontotheology 246
phonocentrism 245
presence 245
structuralism 244
writing under erasure 244
Descartes, R. 302
Desert and non-desert arguments 112–13, 115–18
Deutsch, K. 56
Dewey, John 93, 260
dialogic foundations 14, 271–92
Dicey, A. V. 30
difference theory 210, 219–26, 227–8, 232, 320
  anthropology 220–1
  Asian values 222
  difference blindness 224
  emancipatory project of 222–3
  feminism and 223–6
  forms of 220–6
  illiberalism and 219
  liberalism and 219, 227
  orientalism 222
  particles of 212
  pluralism and 210, 219–26
  postcolonial theory 221–2, 220
  postmodern 225–6
  subaltern studies and 222, 281
Dilthey, W. 39, 41, 43, 294–5, 296, 297
discourse ethics 288–90
Downs, A. 61
Duguit, L. 23, 29, 93, 211
Dunn, J. 47
Dunning, W. A. 30
Durkheim, E. 23, 29, 66
Dworkin, A. 224
Dworkin, R. 132, 134, 165

Easton, D. 54–5, 56, 58, 59, 92
École Libre des Sciences Politiques de France 32
Eliot, T. S. 157
Elshtain, Jean Beth 130
empirical political theory 51–64
  behaviouralism 54–5, 58, 61, 64
  behaviourism 54–5, 58, 61, 64
  colonization of politics and 64–5, 108

Comte and 57, 58
economic analysis and 59
end of ideology and 27–8, 55–6 (*see* ideology)
Enlightenment and 52–3
epistemology of 60–1
explanation and understanding 60
facts and values 57–8
historical theory and 64
hypothetico-deductive method and 60
informal politics and 60
institutional theory and 51, 64
Kant and 57, 58
logical positivism and 60, 108
ontology and 60–1
political economy 52, 53
political science 52–4
positivism 56–8, 108
post-behaviouralism 52, 59–60, 79
post-empiricism 60–1, 64, 78
public choice 62
rational choice 61–5
Staatslehre 53–4
end of ideology 27–8, 55–6, 92
Enlightenment 52–3, 65, 185, 225
environmentalism 76
essential contestability 98–104, 108–9, 133, 141–3
as linguistic idealism 96
as metaphysical position 100
Begriffsgeschichte and 101–2
Connolly 100–1, 250
critique of 100–4
essences 98
Gallie and 98–100
John Gray and 100, 103–4
justice theory and 109, 132–5, 141–2
language games and 97
Lyotard and 101
negative views 102–4
positive views 100–2
reconstruction theory and 102–3
Rorty and 101
Sattelzeit and 102
value cognitivism and 103
ethic of care and justice 130
ethical pluralism 94
Etzioni, A. 155, 156, 170
Eulau, H. 56
evolutionary theory 94

Fabianism 32, 169
Farr, J. 66, 77
fascism 94

Feigl, Herbert 86
feminism 94, 127–30, 223–6
Ferguson, A. 52
Feyerabend, P. 60, 283, 302
Fichte, J. G. 27
Figgis, J. N. 210, 211
Flathman, R. 107
Foucault, M. 27, 69, 85, 225–6, 229, 230, 247–50,
    255, 266, 271, 273
  biopower 249
  body and 249
  Enlightenment and 250
  genealogy 100, 247, 248, 249, 250
  governance 249
  history 248, 250
  Kant and 248
  knowledge 249, 250
  language 249
  metaphysics 247, 248, 250
  Nietzsche and 247–8
  on the author 248
  perspectivism 247
  power 248, 249–50
  progress 250
  self 248, 249
  sexuality 249
  sovereignty 249–50
Foundationalism 3–7, 11–12, 319–21, 324–6
  anti-foundationalism 4, 12–13, 14, 321
  bleached 14, 108–38, 319–20
  circular foundations 14, 321–4
  comprehensive 3, 4, 319–20
  conventionalism 13–14, 44, 143–5, 207–9,
    227–8, 232, 320
  critique of metaphysics and 86
  degrees of truth and reality 4
  dialogic and 14, 217–318, 320–1
  immanent 3, 4, 12, 13, 319–20
  logical 3, 6, 170, 319
  metaphysics and 3, 4, 6–7, 86
  perfectionist 4
  perspectivism and 233–4, 237, 238, 320
  post-metaphysics and 4, 12–13, 14, 320–1
  postmodernism and 232–68
  segmented 207–31
  thick and thin 19
  transcendental 4
Fourier, C. 27
Frege, G. 86
Freud, S. 236
Fukuyama, F. 80

Gadamer, Hans Georg 14, 92, 178, 317, 318, 321,
    322, 271–2, 294–316
  central theme 307
  conflict with Habermas 310–15
  dialogue 14, 303–6, 320
  Enlightenment 299, 301–3
  experience 305
  fallibilism 308, 323–5
  fusion of horizons 304–6, 308, 317, 322
  hermeneutic circle 14, 307–8, 321–4
  ideology 312, 313–14
  Kant's aesthetic 302–3
  method and 303
  natural science and 303
  on ethics 306–10
  play of dialogue 305, 308
  politics and 306–10
  positivism and 301–3
  tradition 314
  Wittgenstein 312–13
Galston, W. 214
Gauthier, D. 79, 112, 118–20, 124, 127, 131–2,
    135, 137
Geist 4
Geisteswissenschaft 30, 148, 294
Gentile, G. 93
Gerber, Carl von 75
Germino, D. 22, 70, 93
Geschichtliche Grundbegriff 49
Gewirth, A. 5–6, 135
Gierke, Otto von 75, 157, 211
Gilligan, C. 130, 224–5
Gramsci, A. 68, 221
Grand École tradition 32
Gray, J. 94, 100, 103–4, 231
Greek political theory 8
Green, T. H. 26, 145, 192
Greenleaf, W. H. 22, 75, 76, 170
Grice, H. P. 43
Gunnell, J. 32, 38, 56, 75, 78, 92

Habermas, J. 4–5, 14, 92, 197–8, 199, 211, 271–92,
    293, 316, 318
  ambiguity of reason 312–13
  Apel and 285–6
  central theme 289
  communicative action 4, 293
  communitarianism 290
  critical theory and 275–80
  critique of Gadamer 272, 310–15
  deliberative democracy 288–90
  development of work 278–80

discourse ethics 288–90, 293
empirical-analytic sciences 281
end of philosophy 284
Enlightenment 277
fallibilism 4, 284, 285–8
foundationalism 279, 282–4, 287–8
hermeneutics 272, 284
historical-hermeneutic sciences 281
ideal speech 285, 293, 314
ideology critique 278, 282, 312
knowledge spheres and 274, 280–2, 292, 313–14
metaphysics 4–5, 274
negative dialectics 277
Nietzsche 275
overall aims 280
philosophical premises 272–5
positivism 274, 280–2
post-metaphysics 279–80
postmodern critique 279–80
pragmatism 284
Rawls and 278, 291
republicanism 289–90
social strategic action 4
speech acts 286–7, 293
the subject 282–4
universal pragmatics 284–8
Hacker, A. 24
Hadot, Pierre 14
Hampton, J. 25
Hart, H. L. A. 111
Hayek, F. 24, 47, 94, 112, 152, 153, 172, 200, 213
Hegel, G. W. F. 3, 26, 37, 39, 75, 85, 149, 156, 157,
    252, 304
Hegelianism 9, 98, 147
Heidegger, M. 21, 41, 88, 178, 186, 236, 239–42,
    255, 258, 274, 279, 317, 321
Herder, G. 26, 157, 160, 172, 173, 215
hermeneutic circle 14, 307–8, 321–4
hermeneutics 14, 294–318
  Bildung 301, 304, 305, 308, 317, 320
  circle 14, 307–8, 321–4
  critique of positivism and 301–3
  dialogue 297–301
  Dilthey and 294–5, 297, 316
  Enlightenment 299, 301–3
  fore-structures 296–7
  forms of 294–6
  Heidegger and 296–7
  history 297–301
  language 297–301
  origin 294–5

prejudice 297–301
primal meanings 296
reflexivity 307–8
Schleiermacher 294
suspicion and 296
temporality and finiteness 300–1
tradition 300
Hesse, Mary 60, 302
Hirsch, E. D. 295
historical comparative method 30
historical political theory 37–50, 93, 147
    authorial intentions 44
    Begriffsgeschichte 49, 77
    concept of 37–8
    contextualism 44–6
    education and 40
    empirical theory and 64–5
    external appeal 39
    historicism 42
    history of thought and 39
    ideological context 45–6
    impurists 47–8
    internal appeal 38
    langue and *parole* 44
    liberal education and 40
    nationalism and 40, 76–7
    normative theory and 39
    Pocock and 43–4
    political science and 38, 39, 50
    role of 40
    Skinner and 43–9
    Staatslehre and 50
    Strauss and 42–3
    teleology and 39
    two waves and 41–9
    undergraduate texts and 24–5, 40–1
history 37, 147
Hobbes, Thomas 22, 50, 65, 93, 124, 127–8, 151, 238
Hobhouse, L. T. 29, 75, 93, 192
Hollis, M. 213
Holmes, S. 157, 184
Homans, G. 58
Honig, B. 226
Horkheimer, M. 52, 53, 211, 225, 274, 276–8, 292
human nature 20–1
human rights 22, 25
Hume, David 26, 85, 151, 176
Husserl, Edmund 254, 281, 302

Ideal types 22
Idealism 3, 30, 39, 50, 84, 145–6

Ideological political theory 8, 10–11, 27–8, 45, 65–72
    Ashcraft and 68
    behaviouralism and 66–7
    classical normative theory 66–7
    communitarianism 67–8
    conceptual morphology and 71–3
    ecumenical political theory and 74
    empirical theory and 65
    epistemes and 69
    false consciousness 66
    Foucault and 69
    Freeden and 71–3
    Gramsci and 68
    language and 68–9
    Marxism and 66
    negative integration thesis 65–7
    negative segregation thesis 70–1, 72–3
    Oakeshott and 70
    origins 65
    positive integration thesis 67
    positive segregation thesis 71–3, 74
    Quentin Skinner on 67
    representation theory and 69
    Rorty and 69–70
    second wave theory and 67
    Strauss and 70
informal politics 36
institutional political theory 12, 19, 28–37, 38, 74
    (*see* state theory)
    Staatslehre 28–30, 34, 34–6, 48, 50, 53–4
    state and 29ff
Irigary, L. 225
issue orthodoxy 1, 85, 104–5, 133

Jaggars, A. 230
James, William 210, 236
Jameson, F. 264
Jellinek, G. 75
Jones, Henry 30, 145
Jouvenal, Bertrand de 24
justice 12, 13, 108–32
    anti-metaphysical theory 135
    Aristotle and 110
    assumptions of 112
    bleached foundations 135
    Brian Barry and 111, 112, 126–7, 130, 132, 133, 134
    character and justice 116–17
    commutative 111, 112
    concept of 109–11
    conceptions of justice 111–13, 133

justice (*cont.*)
    constructivism and 135
    contemporary root 132
    contractarian 113
    corrective 111
    David Miller and 132, 133, 136, 137
    desert and non-desert 112–13, 115–18, 124–5
    deserving and undeserving 116–17
    diachronic analysis and 133
    distributive theory 112, 136
    empiricism and 113, 117
    end-state principles 114–15
    entitlement theory of 112, 114–15
    equality and 110, 111, 112
    essential contestability and 109, 132–5, 141–2
    feminism and 127–30, 137
    formal logic and 110–11
    Gauthier 112, 118–20, 124, 127, 131–2,
        135, 137
    Hart and 111
    Hayek and 112, 113, 114, 129
    ideology and 133–5
    impartiality and 111, 113, 124–7
    issue orthodoxy approach 133, 136
    lexical ordering and 126
    liberalism and 133–5, 138
    maximin principle 126
    mutual advantage 113, 118–20
    need and 113, 117–18
    Nozick and 114–15
    ordinary language theory and 132, 141–3
    original position 125–6
    patterned and unpatterned distribution 115
    Perelman and 110
    Plato and 110
    procedural theory 113–15, 133, 136, 138
    rational choice 118–20, 123
    rationalist theory 113, 117
    Rawls 124–7 (*see* Rawls and justice)
    reason and 110, 111, 132–3
    rights and 115
    sexual 127–30
    social minimum and 117–18
    spheres of 113, 130–2
    Staatslehre and 109–10
    utility and 120–4
    veil of ignorance 125–6
    Walzer and 130–4
justificatory reasoning 72–4, 109, 133, 322–4

Kant, I. 26, 50, 125, 134, 151, 178, 185, 192, 203,
    235, 254, 255, 256–7, 267, 275, 277, 283,
    302–3, 314
Kantianism 4, 9, 57, 58, 122, 124, 132–3, 134, 135,
    143, 154, 166, 167, 174, 184, 207, 225, 249,
    288, 290
Kateb, G. 25
Kedourie, E. 173
Kekes, J. 231
Kelsen, H. 93
Key, V. O. 54
Kohn, H. 202, 302
Koselleck, R. 49
Kraft, V. 86
Kristeva, J. 225, 233
Kuhn, T. 25, 43
Kukathas, C. 213, 228
Kymlicka, W. 25, 217–19

Laband, P. 75
Laclau, E. 267
language and political theory 86–9, 95–105, 106,
    273–4
Larmore, C. 168
Laski, H. J. 38, 211
Laslett, P. 91, 92, 93
Lasswell, H. 54
Le Bon, G. 35
legal pluralism 94
Lenin, V. I. 153
Leninism 94
Levi-Strauss, C. 236, 244, 266
Levinas, E. 263
liberal pluralism 211–15
liberalism 50, 133–5, 160, 200–1, 211–15, 227, 229
Lieber, F. 30
lifeworld 288–9, 296–7
Lipset, S. M. 55
Locke, J. 47, 65, 85, 125, 128, 157
logical foundationalism 6
logical positivism 60, 83–88, 89, 92, 105, 108
    analytic and empirical propositions 87
    emotivism 87, 90
    empirical theory and 86, 88
    facts and values 91
    logic 87
    meaning and 87
    metaphysics 86ff
    verification and 86
    Vienna group 87
    Wittgenstein and 87

London School of Economics and Political
Science 32
Lowi, T. 31–2
Lukacs, G. 94
Lukes S. 106, 213
Lyotard, J. F. 226, 230, 253–7, 258, 259, 261–2,
264, 266, 271, 317

Machiavelli, N. 9, 21, 50, 65, 190, 195
MacIntyre, A. 96, 155, 157, 170, 184–7, 233
MacIver, R. M. 29, 157
Mackenzie, J. S. 145
Macpherson, C. B. 43, 51, 77
Magee, B. 106
Maine, Henry 30
Maistre, Joseph de 157
Maitland, F. W. 30
Mannheim, K. 27–8
Marcuse, H. 78, 94, 277
Maritain, J. 94
Marx, K. 23, 37, 65–6, 194, 293
Marxism 9, 157, 167, 172, 240, 275
maternal thinking 130
Maurras, C. 157
Maynor, J. 187, 189–90, 197
Mazzini, G. 172
McCarthy, T. 281, 292
McCarthyism 56
McCormick, N. 175–6, 202
McTaggart, J. M. E. 145
Merriam, C. 30, 54, 75, 78
Mill, J. S. 26, 121, 130, 151, 172
Miller, David 25, 132, 175, 176, 177, 202, 203
modernity 21–2
Moore, G. E. 145
moral philosophy 8
Mouffe, C. 14, 267
multiculturalism 165, 208–9, 211, 215–19, 223,
227, 229, 232

Nagel, E. 78
nation-state language 31
nationalism 13, 94, 171–7
central arguments of 174–7
democracy and 176
empirical theory of 174
identity and 175–6
justice and 175
liberal theory of 172
origin 171–2
secession 172
self-determination and 176–7
sovereignty 177

Naturwissenschaft 148, 294
negative dialectics 277
neo-Aristotelianism 171, 177–87
attraction of 178–9
communitarianism and 179–80
critique of liberalism 178–9
ethos and 178
grounding experiences and 182, 186
key arguments 178–80
social democracy and 181–2
strands of 180–1
thick vague goods 181, 182
third way and 183
Neurath, Otto von 86,
Neville, H. 188, 190
New Deal 30
new institutionalism 36
New Labour 75
Nietzsche, F. 21, 57, 185–6, 233–9, 248, 250–3,
255, 258, 259, 260, 262
aristocratic radicalism 238
conventionalism and 235, 237, 238,
259, 263–4
epistemology 235
genealogy 237–8
morality 233, 237–8
on metaphysics 233–4, 239
overman doctrine 233, 237, 238–9, 257
perspectivism 233–4, 237, 238
Plato and 234
self 238
truth and 235
will to power 238, 258
nihilism 21, 233, 257
normative theory 12–13, 19–28, 108–132
classical 19–28, 53, 59, 64, 76, 106, 109
classifications of 21–5
communitarianism 154–62
essential contestability theory 109, 132–3
justice theory and 108–38
multiculturalism 215–19
nationalism 171–7
neo-Aristotelianism 177–87
Oakeshott and 145–54
political liberalism 162–8
republicanism 187–200
Norris, C. 267
North American Social Science Research
Council 78
Nozick, R. 47, 112, 113, 114–15
Nussbaum, Martha 137, 180–2, 184, 186,
187, 223

O'Neill, O. 213
Oakeshott, Michael 13, 24, 37, 41, 70, 94, 98,
    145–54, 159, 160, 169, 201, 292
  civil association 151–2
  conservatism 152–3
  contemporary political theory and 154
  enterprise association 150–1
  ideal characters 148, 150, 152, 153
  ideology and 70
  idioms 147, 148, 150
  modes of experience 146–8
  personae 148–9
  practical knowledge 150
  rationalism 151–2
  republicanism 151
  rule of law and 151
  societas 151–2
  tradition and 149–50, 152–3
  universitas 151
Okin, S. M. 127–39, 225
Oldfield, A. 189
Olsen, M. 61
Oppenheim, F. 61
ordinary language philosophy 70, 88–91, 97
  Austin 89, 90, 96, 97, 106
  conceptual inflation 107
  conservativism and 106
  facts and values 91
  logical positivism and 88–9
  metaphysics 89–90
  normative political theory 90–1
  speech act theory 89
  Weldon and 88, 90
  word essences 90

paradigms 25
Parekh, B. 228
partiarchy 128, 224
Pateman, Carole 128
Peirce, C. S. 6, 14, 210, 325
Perelman, C. 110
Peters, R. 104–5
Pettit, P. 25, 93, 94, 189, 190–1, 192–3, 198,
    200, 290
Plamenatz, J. 24, 43, 77, 202
Plato 4, 8, 9, 22, 111, 165, 234, 240
pluralism 207–31
  anthropology 220–1
  Asian values 222
  communitarian 217–19
  concept of 209–11
  conventionalism and 207ff

difference and 210, 219–26
  ethical 210–11
  feminism and 223–6
  forms of 211
  illiberalism and 219
  liberal 210, 211–15, 215–19, 229
  multiculturalism and 215–19
  nation state and 209
  neutral universalist 212–13
  particularist neutrality 215
  postcolonial theory and 221–2
  postmodern 225–6
  relativism and 211
  subaltern theory 222
  universal perfectionism 214
Pocock, J. G. A. 43, 188–9
Poincaré, H. 169
Polanyi, M. 60
policy communities 36
Polis 20
political economy 52–3, 78
political liberalism 162–8
political science 33–4, 50, 52–4
political theory
  and its object 9–10
  and its past 12, 19–20, 25–7
  canon of 26
  classical normative 19–28
  communitarianism 154–62
  concept of 8–9
  conventionlist 13–14, 44, 143–5, 207–8, 227–8,
    232, 320
  dialogue and 321–4
  difference theory 219–26
  eclectic subject 1–3
  ecumenical 74
  empirical 12, 19, 25, 51–74
  foundations 3–7, 11–12, 319–21, 324–6
  Gadamer and 294–316
  Habermas and 271–92
  hermeneutic circle 14, 307–8, 321–4
  historical 37–51
  human nature and 20–1
  ideological 65–72
  institutional 28–37
  issue orthodoxy and 1, 85, 104–5, 133
  linguistic phenomenology 108, 319
  multiculturalism 215–19
  nationalism and 13, 94, 171–7
  neo-Aristotelian 177–87
  Oakeshott and 45–54
  perennial concerns of 20

pluralism and 207–31
political metaphysics 321–4
political philosophy and 7
politics and 1–2, 27, 21–2
practical discipline 1–2, 31–2
presentism 25
self-conscious discipline 1, 10, 26–7, 39–40,
   133, 319
sociology of 27–8
Staatslehre 28–30, 34–6, 48, 50, 53–4
term 8
textbooks and 24, 104–5, 108
Popper, Karl 106, 173, 273, 283
positivism 9, 7–10, 56–8
postcolonial theory 101, 201, 221–2
postmodern political theory 9, 13, 14, 232–64,
   264, 271
   conventionalism and 232–3, 237, 259, 262–4
   democracy and 260–2
   liberalism and 260–2
   metaphysics and humanism 257–8
   perspectivism 233–4, 237, 238–9
poststructuralism (*see* postmodernism) 9, 13, 14,
   232–3, 264
pragmatism 9, 210
Price, R. 188, 190
private language argument 96–7
Proudhon, P. J. 27
public choice 62
Putnam, H. 210

Quesnay, F. 78
Quine, W. O. 38

Ramsey, F. P. 87
Raphael, D. D. 24, 105
rational choice 61–5, 167 (*see* Gauthier)
Rawls, J. 12, 13, 14, 64, 71, 83, 96, 109, 111,
   113, 124–7, 129–30, 132, 134, 137, 144, 153,
   159, 162–8, 214–15, 252 (*see* justice theory)
Rawlsians 8, 96, 129–32, 135, 165, 320
Raz, J. 165, 217–18, 229
Relativism 61
Renan, E. 172, 173
Republicanism 13, 77, 171, 187–200, 290
   Arendt 192–6
   Christianity and 203–4
   citizenship 194–5, 198–9
   communitarianism 190, 192, 193, 195, 197–8,
   201, 203
   democracy and 192, 193, 195
   education 189

   forms of 187, 189–90
   French 202
   Habermas on 289
   ideology of 188
   liberalism and 182, 191–2, 199–200
   liberty and 188, 189, 190, 191–2, 194, 198–200
   nationalism 190, 196–7, 201
   neo-Athenian and neo-Roman 189
   origin 187–8
   patriotism 196–7, 203
   populism 192–3
   public thing 190–1, 194, 195
   state 191, 192–3
   universal and particular 197–8, 201
return of grand theory 23–4, 39, 109
Ricci, D. 78
Ricoeur, P. 292, 296
Riker, W. 62
Ritchie, D. G. 30, 145
Rorty, R. 186, 250–3, 259, 260–1, 264, 267, 271,
   284, 310
Rousseau, J. J. 21, 125, 192, 197
Ruddick, S. 130
Ruggiero, G. de 192
Russell, B. 86, 91, 93, 106
Russian Revolution 94
Ryle, G. 88, 91

Sabine, G. H. 41, 77
Salkever, R. 183–4, 202
Sandel, M. 138, 155, 157, 160, 169, 190, 290
Sartre, J. P. 93
Saussure, F. 244, 265, 273
Scanlon, T. 112, 133, 135
Schachar, A. 216
Schleiermacher, F. 294
Schlick, M. 86
Schmitt, C. 93
Scruton, R. 211
Searle, J. 43, 97, 273
Sellars, W. 79
Seth, A. 145
Shils, E. 66
Shklar, J. 164
Sidgwick, H. 30
Sidney, Algernon 188, 190
Simon, H. 54, 59
Simon, Y. 24
Skinner, Q. 43–9, 64, 67, 77, 189, 190, 191,
   192, 194, 196, 202, 295 (*see* historical political
   theory)
Smith, Adam 26, 47, 52

Soffer, R. 76–7
Sorel, G. 35
Sorley, W. R. 145
Spencer, H. 8, 94, 123
Squires, J. 230
Staatslehre 28–30, 34, 35, 36, 48, 50, 53–4
State theory 20, 28–37 (*see* institutional
     political theory)
  Aristotle 34
  bringing state back in 36
  citizenship education 32
  civics 32
  classical political theory and 33–4
  comparative politics 35
  constitutional studies 35
  contest of the faculties 33
  creative 33
  decline of 34
  empirical method and 34
  Greek and Roman 33
  is and ought dimensions 34–5
  new institutionalism and 36
  philosophy of 35
  political pluralism and 34
  political science and 32–3 (*see* empirical
     theory)
  political sociology and 35
  scepticism of 34
  science of 34
  Second World War and 34
  sovereignty 33
  Staatslehre 28–30, 34, 35, 36, 48, 50, 53–4
  state-making 31
  strategic 33
Stein, Lorenz von 75
Strauss, L. 21–2, 24, 41, 42–3, 56, 64, 70, 75, 77,
     92, 93
Straussians 22, 43, 50
Strawson, P. F. 89–90
structuralism 265–6
Stubbs, W. 30
Sunstein, C. 192

Tamir, Yael, 173
Taylor, C. 95, 97, 134, 138, 155, 157, 160, 190, 197,
     218–19, 222, 230, 290
Teleocratic order 152
Theoria 8
theory 7–10, 15
Tocqueville, Alexis de 27
Tönnies, F. 23, 29, 157

Truman, D. 54
Tuck, R. 47, 93, 94
Tullock, G. 61
Tully, J. 47, 67, 101, 231
Turgot, A. R. J. 52, 78

utilitarianism 63, 120–4, 184, 207, 320

Verstehen 98
Vietnam war 59, 96
Viroli, M. 190, 192, 196–8, 203, 290
Voegelin, E. 23, 41, 54, 70, 78, 94

Waismann, F. 86
Wallace, W. 145
Wallas, G. 35
Walzer, M. 113, 130–2, 155, 157, 161, 162,
     168, 229
Warnock, G. J. 106
Watson, J. B. 55
Watson, John 145
Webb, Sidney 32
Weber, Max 23, 57–8
Weil, S. 3, 24
Weldon, T. D. 80, 90–1, 94–5, 97, 105, 106
Whitehead, Alfred North 86, 106
Willoughby, W. W. 30
Wilson, Woodrow 30
Winch, P. 60, 96, 97
Wittgenstein, L. 12, 70, 83–4, 87–8, 90–1, 95–105,
     141–3, 170, 186, 254, 273, 274, 284, 312–13
Wittgensteinianism 84, 95–100, 143
  depth grammar 97
  essential contestability 98–100
  forms of life 97
  Gallie 98–100
  Hegelianism and 98
  human action 97
  language games 97
  linguistic idealism and 96
  normativism 98
  Oakeshott and 98
  private language argument 96–7
  Verstehen and 98
Wollstonecraft, M. 130
Woosley, T. D. 30
Wootton, D. 77

Yack, B. 182–3
Young, Iris Marion 225, 231